ISBN 978-0-428-51734-2
PIBN 11303158

1 MONTH OF
FREE
READING

at

www.ForgottenBooks.com

By purchasing this book you are eligible for one month membership to ForgottenBooks.com, giving you unlimited access to our entire collection of over 1,000,000 titles via our web site and mobile apps.

To claim your free month visit:

www.forgottenbooks.com/free1303158

English
Français
Deutsche
Italiano
Español
Português

www.forgottenbooks.com

Mythology Photography **Fiction** Fishing Christianity **Art** Cooking Essays Buddhism Freemasonry Medicine **Biology** Music **Ancient Egypt** Evolution Carpentry Physics Dance Geology **Mathematics** Fitness Shakespeare **Folklore** Yoga Marketing **Confidence** Immortality Biographies Poetry **Psychology** Witchcraft Electronics Chemistry History **Law** Accounting **Philosophy** Anthropology Alchemy Drama Quantum Mechanics Atheism Sexual Health **Ancient History** **Entrepreneurship** Languages Sport Paleontology Needlework Islam **Metaphysics** Investment Archaeology Parenting Statistics Criminology **Motivational**

OFFICIAL PROCEEDINGS

OF

The Railway Club of Pittsburgh

Organized October 18, 1901

Published monthly, except June, July and August, by the Railway Club of
Pittsburgh. J. D. Conway, Secretary, 515 Grandview Ave., Pittsburgh, Pa..

Entered as Second Class Matter February 6, 1915, at the Postoffice at Pittsburgh,
under the Act of March 3, 1879.

Vol. No. IXXXV	Pittsburgh, Pa., Nov. 21, 1935	$1.00 Per Year 25c Per Copy

Central - Adult

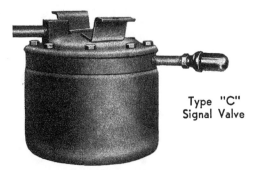

INDEX—ADVERTISERS.

The Railway Club of Pittsburgh:

....19.........

Gentlemen:

Will you kindly consider my Application for Membership in your Club at the next meeting:

Name...

Title..

Company...

My Address...

....

Recommended by.......... .. ..

OFFICIAL PROCEEDINGS

OF

The Railway Club of Pittsburgh

Organized October 18, 1901

Vol. No. IXXXV	Pittsburgh, Pa., Nov. 21, 1935	$1.00 Per Year 25c Per Copy

OFFICERS FOR 1935-1936

President

R. P. FORSBERG,

Chief Engineer, P. & L. E. R. R. Co., Pittsburgh, Pa.

First Vice President

E. A. RAUSCHART,

Mechanical Supt , Montour Railroad,
Coraopolis, Pa.

Secretary

J. D. CONWAY,

Railway Supply Manufacturers' Association,
Pittsburgh, Pa.

Second Vice President

G. M. SIXSMITH,

Supt., Pennsylvania Railroad,
Pittsburgh, Pa.

Treasurer

E. J. SEARLES,

Manager, Schaefer Equipment Co.,
Pittsburgh, Pa.

EXECUTIVE COMMITTEE:

FRANK J. LANAHAN, Chairman, President, Fort Pitt Malleable Iron Co., Pittsburgh, Pa.
A. STUCKI, Engineer, A. Stucki Company, Pittsburgh, Pa.
SAMUEL LYNN, Supt. Rolling Stock, P. & L. E. R. R., McKees Rocks, Pa.
D. F. CRAWFORD, Consulting Engineer, Pittsburgh, Pa.
G. W. WILDIN, Consulting Engineer, Westinghouse Air Brake Company, Pittsburgh, Pa.
W. S. McABEE, Vice Pres. & General Supt., Union Railroad Co., East Pittsburgh, Pa.
E. W. SMITH, Vice President, Pennsylvania Railroad, Pittsburgh, Pa.
LOUIS E. ENDSLEY, Consulting Engineer, 516 East End Avenue, Pittsburgh, Pa.
F. I. SNYDER, Vice President & General Manager, B. & L. E. R. R. Co., Pittsburgh, Pa.
C. O. DAMBACH, General Manager, P. & W. Va. Ry. Co., Pittsburgh, Pa.
R. H. FLINN, General Superintendent, Pennsylvania Railroad, Pittsburgh, Pa.

SUBJECT COMMITTEE:

D. W. McGEORGE, Chairman, Secretary, Edgewater Steel Company, Pittsburgh, Pa.
JOHN B. WRIGHT, Asst. Vice President, Westinghouse Air Brake Co., Wilmerding, Pa.
M. R. REED, General Supt. Motive Power, Pennsylvania Railroad, Pittsburgh, Pa.

ADVERTISING COMMITTEE:

E. A. FOARD, Chairman, Supt. Stations & Transfers, Pennsylvania R. R., Pittsburgh, Pa.
KARL BERG, Superintendent Motive Power, P. & L. E. R. R. Co., McKees Rocks, Pa.
H. E. PASSMORE, Representative, .The American Hammered Piston Ring Co., Pgh., Pa.

RECEPTION AND ATTENDANCE COMMITTEE:

J. D. BELTZ, Chairman, Superintendent, B. & O. R. R. Co., Pittsburgh, Pa.
·W. C. BUREL, Vice Chairman, Master Mechanic, Western Allegheny Railroad, Kaylor, Pa.
J. B. BAKER, Chief Engr. Maintenance of Way, Pennsylvania Railroad, Pittsburgh, Pa.
WALTER C. SANDERS, Gen. Mgr., Railway Div., Timken Roller Bearing Co., Canton, O.
G. A. BLACKMORE, President & Gen. Mgr., Union Switch & Signal Co., Swissvale, Pa.
J. S. LANAHAN, Vice President, Fort Pitt Malleable Iron Company, Pittsburgh, Pa.
J. A. WARFEL, Special Representative, Air Reduction Sales Co., Pittsburgh, Pa.
J. C. SHINGLEDECKER, Supervisor of Service Stations, The Pennzoil Co., Pittsburgh, Pa.
J. C. DILWORTH, Mgr. of Railroad Sales, Carnegie-Illinois Steel Corp., Pittsburgh, Pa.
G. H. BURNETTE, Assistant Chief Engineer, P. & L. E. R. R. Co., Pittsburgh, Pa.
W. R. TRIEM, Superintendent, Pennsylvania Railroad, Pittsburgh, Pa.
J. W. HOOVER, Asst. Chief of Transpn., Subsidiary Cos. U. S. Steel Corp., Pittsburgh, Pa.
J. W. JOHNSON, Superintendent, Railway Express Agency, Pittsburgh, Pa.
A. A. READ, Duquesne Slag Products Company, Pittsburgh, Pa.
C. P. SCHRECONGOST, Traffic Manager, Hillman Coal & Coke Company, Pittsburgh, Pa.

ENTERTAINMENT COMMITTEE:

J. PORTER GILLESPIE, Chairman, Asst. Gen. Supt., Lockhart Iron & Steel Co., Pgh., Pa.
FRANK E. WEIS, Vice Chairman, Transportation Clerk, Penna. R. R., Pittsburgh, Pa.
E. H. HOLMES, Sales Department, Fort Pitt Malleable Iron Co., Pittsburgh, Pa.
C. C. CLARK, Sales Manager Central District, Pressed Steel Car Co., McKees Rocks, Pa.
A. L. KESSLER, Clearance Clerk, Pennsylvania Railroad, Pittsburgh, Pa.
T. F. SHERIDAN, Asst. to S.M.P. and S.R.S., P. & L. E. R. R. Co., McKees Rocks, Pa.
JAMES NAGEL, Superintendent Transportation, Montour Railroad, Coraopolis, Pa.

FINANCE COMMITTEE:

J. L. O'TOOLE, Chairman, Asst. to Gen. Manager, P. & L. E. R. R. Co., Pittsburgh, Pa.
G. W. HONSBERGER, Transpn. Mgr., Westinghouse Electric & Mfg. Co., Pittsburgh, Pa.
F. J. RYAN, District Representative, Detroit, Toledo & Ironton Railroad, Pittsburgh, Pa.
C. E. CATT, Division Accountant, B. & O. R. R. Co., Pittsburgh, Pa.
J. W. BOYD, Superintendent, Monongahela Railway Company, Brownsville, Pa.

MEMBERSHIP COMMITTEE:

WILLIAM R. GELLATLY, Chairman, Pres., Superior Railway Products Corp., Pgh., Pa.
T. E. BRITT, Vice Chairman, Division Storekeeper, B. & O. R. R. Co., Pittsburgh, Pa.
A. B. SEVERN, General Manager, A. Stucki Company, Pittsburgh, Pa.
W. P. BUFFINGTON, Traffic Manager, Pittsburgh Coal Company, Pittsburgh, Pa.
R. S. BULL, Supt. Power & Inclines, Pittsburgh Railways Co., N. S., Pittsburgh, Pa.
A. F. COULTER, Master Car Builder, Union Railroad Co., East Pittsburgh, Pa.
T. R. DICKINSON, Purchasing Agent, B. & L. E. R. R. Co., Pittsburgh, Pa.
D. K. ORR, Road Master, Monongahela Railway Co., Brownsville, Pa.
C. M. WHEELER, Sales Engineer, Union Switch & Signal Company, Swissvale, Pa.
A. C. POLLOCK, District Sales Manager, Jones & Laughlin Steel Corp., Pittsburgh, Pa.
W. F. AMBROSE, Master Mechanic, Aliquippa & Southern Railroad, Aliquippa, Pa.
JOHN I. MULVEY, Traffic Manager, Hubbard & Company. Pittsburgh, Pa.
THOMAS R. FITZPATRICK, Freight Traffic Mgr., P. & L. E. R. R. Co., Pittsburgh, Pa.
P. W. HEPBURN, Sales Engineer, Gulf Refining Company, Pittsburgh, Pa.
W. B. MOIR, Chief Car Inspector, Pennsylvania Railroad, Pittsburgh, Pa.
C. W. TRUST, Assistant Traffic Manager, Carnegie-Illinois Steel Corp., Pittsburgh, Pa.

PAST PRESIDENTS:

*J. H. McCONNELL	October,	1901, to October, 1903
*L. H. TURNER	November,	1903, to October, 1905
*F. H. STARK	November,	1905, to October, 1907
*H. W. WATTS	November,	1907, to April, 1908
*D. J. REDDING	November,	1908, to October, 1910
*F. R. McFEATTERS	November,	1910, to October, 1912
*A. G. MITCHELL	November,	1912, to October, 1914
*F. M. McNULTY	November,	1914, to October, 1916
*J. G. CODE	November,	1916, to October, 1917
*D. M. HOWE	November,	1917, to October, 1918
*J. A. SPIELMAN	November,	1918, to October, 1919
H. H. MAXFIELD	November,	1919, to October, 1920
FRANK J. LANAHAN	November,	1920, to October, 1921
SAMUEL LYNN	November,	1921, to October, 1922
D. F. CRAWFORD	November,	1922, to October, 1923
GEO. D. OGDEN	November,	1923, to October, 1924
A. STUCKI	November,	1924, to October, 1925
F. G. MINNICK	November,	1925, to October, 1926
G. W. WILDIN	November,	1926, to October, 1927
E. J. DEVANS	November,	1927, to October, 1928
W. S. McABEE	November,	1928, to October, 1929
E. W. SMITH	November,	1929, to October, 1930
LOUIS E. ENDSLEY	November,	1930, to October, 1931
*JOHN E. HUGHES	November,	1931, to October, 1932
F. I. SNYDER	November,	1932, to October, 1933
C. O. DAMBACH	November,	1933, to October, 1934
R. H. FLINN	November,	1934, to October, 1935

*—Deceased.

Meetings held fourth Thursday of each month except June, July and August.

PROCEEDINGS OF MEETING
NOVEMBER 21, 1935

The meeting was called to order in the English Room of the Fort Pitt Hotel at 8 o'clock P. M., with President R. P. Forsberg in the chair.

Registered attendance, 295, as follows:

MEMBERS

Adams, Frank W.
Allen, Earl M.
Ambrose, W. F.
Ament, F. Chalmer
Aulbach, A. J.
Baker, William E.
Balzer, C. E.
Bancroft, A. G.
Barr, H. C.
Barr, S. T.
Bauer, F. C.
Baughman, G. W.
Baumann, E. G.
Beam, E. J.
Beatty, Raymond N.
Beeson, H. L.
Beltz, J. D.
Berg, Karl
Berghane, A. L.
Bergman, C. R.
Best, D. A.
Beswick, R. M.
Bradley, J. P.
Brennan, J. T.
Britt, T. E.
Buffington, W. P.
Burnette, G. H.
Burriss, Walter E.
Callahan, D. E.
Campbell, F. R.
Campbell, W. T.
Carey, C. D.
Catt, C. E.
Chaffin, H. B.
Chilcoat, H. E.
Christy, F. X.
Christy, G. J.
Clowes, W. K.
Cochran, H. A.
Conway, J. D.

Courtney, Harry
Crawford, A. B.
Crawford, Burt H.
Cree, W. M.
Cruikshank, J. C.
Cunningham, R. I.
Dalrymple, R. W.
Dalzell, W. E.
Dambach, C. O.
Darrah, C. B.
Davis, Charles S.
Day, T. R.
Dean, E. E.
Dickinson, B. F.
Dierker, R. H.
Diven, J. B.
Down, S. G.
Durell, W. A.
Durnell, William E.
Eaton, Frederick H.
Egly, M. J.
Ellis, C. B.
Emery, E.
Endsley, Prof. Louis E.
Evans, Charles S.
Fair, J. M.
Falkner, A. J.
Farlow, G. B.
Ferguson, George
Fitzsimmons, E. J.
Flinn, R. H.
Foard, E. A.
Forsberg, R. P.
Frauenheim, A. M.
Frauenheim, Pierce H.
Freshwater, F. H.
Fults, J. H.
Galloway, W. R., Jr.
Gilg, Henry F.
Glaser, J. P.

Glenn, J. H.
Goble, A. S.
Goldstrom, G. E.
Gray, M. L.
Gray, T. H.
Greek, Joseph
Gross, John
Groves, W. C.
Grunden, B. C.
Haller, Nelson M.
Harper, G. C.
Hassler, E. S.
Hayward, C.
Heed, H. L.
Hemma, Charles H.
Higginbottom, S. B.
Hofmann, E. L.
Holmes, E. H.
Hoopes, R. E.
Hoover, J. W.
Hopper, George
Horne, J. S.
Hornefius, S. R.
Huff, A. B.
Hughes, I. Lamont
Huston, F. T.
Johnson, Ira S.
Johnson, J. W.
Johnson, Le Vere H.
Kapp, A. C.
Keck, L. M.
Kellenberger, K. E.
Kentlein, John
Kessler, A. L.
King, E. C.
Kirk, W. B.
Krause, H. A.
Kulp, J. G.
Kusick, Harry F.
Lanahan, Frank J.
Lanahan, J. S.
Larsén, W. E.
Lee, L. A.
Loder, C. C.
Long, R. M.
Lowry, William F., Jr.
Lynn, Samuel
Mahaney, A. R.
Mann, Henry S.
Marble, A. E.
Masterman, T. W.
Mayer, L. I.

Metzger, C. L.
Mills, O. B.
Mitchell, W. S.
Moir, W. B.
Morgan, A. L.
Morton, Robert A.
Mowry, John W.
Musgrove, W. W.
Mussey, D. S.
Myers, Arnold
McCandless, William A.
McDowell, C. G.
McGaughey, J. V.
McGeorge, D. W.
McIntyre, R. C.
McKenzie, Edward F.
McKinley, A. J.
McLaughlin, H. B.
McLean, J. L.
McOsker, C. T.
McPherson, A. R.
McQuiston, C. A.
Nagel, James
Nieman, C. J.
Norris, J. L.
Orbin, Joseph N.
Osborne, Raymond S.
O'Sullivan, John J.
O'Toole, J. L.
Overholt, B. C.
Paisley, F. R.
Pehrson, A. K.
Poe, C. F.
Porter, H. N.
Posteraro, S. F.
Prichard, H. R.
Pringle, H. C.
Prinkey, C. M.
Purchard, Paul
Ralston, J. A.
Rauschart, E. A.
Read, A. A.
Reed, E. S.
Renshaw, W. B.
Reymer, C. H.
Rizzo, C. M.
Roberts, E. L.
Robinson, L. L.
Rowles, H. N.
Rudd, W. B.
Rupp, Edwin S.
Rushneck, G. C.

2

Rutter, H. E.
Sample, W. E.
Schadt, A. D.
Schrecongost, C. P.
Searles, E. J.
Sekera, C. J.
Severn, A. B.
Shellenbarger, H. M.
Shuster, W. W.
Sixsmith, G. M.
Slater, A. H.
Smith, Robert B.
Steiner, P. E.
Stewart, C. D.
Stewart, J. C.
Stoffregen, Louis E.
Strople, George H.
Stucki, A.
Sutherland, Lloyd
Swope, B. M.
Thomas, H. N.
Thomas, T.
Thompson, H. C.
Thornton, A. W.
Tipton, G. M.

Tomasic, N. M., Jr.
Tracey, J. B. A.
Trax, L. R.
Triem, W. R.
Troxell, H. K.
Tryon, I. D.
Tucker, John L.
Unger, Dr. John S.
Van Blarcom, W. C.
Van Woert, F. E.
Van Wormer, G. M.
Vowinkel, Fred F.
Waxler, Brice
Webster, R. L.
Weis, Frank
West, Troy
Wheeler, C. M.
Wikander, Oscar R.
Wildin, G. M.
Wilson, W. S.
Wilson, W. Stuart, Jr.
Wright, John B.
Wuerthele, H. A.
Wyke, J. W.
Yarnall, Jesse

Yohe, J. K., Jr.

VISITORS

Anderson, Ross
Anderson, R. E.
Aulbach, Ralph
Boyd, John R.
Boyer, W. W.
Boyle, C. O.
Byham, D. E.
Cunningham, Howard L.
Derrenbacher, Andrew
Eisenbauer, George E.
Finney, G. C.
Follett, W. F.
Funk, M. S.
Gardner, G. A.
George, W. J.
Harshberger, R. W.
Henderson, Reed R.
Hildenbrand, L. R.
Huber, George
Hutchinson, P.
Kulesz, W. G.
Lewis, S. B.
Lichtenfels, Percy V.

Lichtenfels, Mrs. P. V.
McCloy, R. B.
McKee, D. L.
McKim, Hollis
McKim, James
Neff, Charles
Oyen, Finn
Pagett, V.
Patterson, W. J.
Pickels, H. D.
Pilliod, August P.
Post, W. M.
Quinn, John J.
Ramsey, Dennis W.
Robinson, H. J.
Ruffini, M.
Scheuerle, Andrew, Jr.
Seidell, D. W.
Sherron, John P.
Smith, Sion B.
Stroble, Clarence W.
Stephens, E. C.
Stevenson, L. N.

Stright, A. J.
Telly, George B.
Tomkin, Robert
Tomlinson, Charles H.
Travis, C. R.
Tress, George A.
Vandivort, R. E.

Von Pier, A. N.
Wible, Paul A.
Wiechelt, W. L.
Wiland, O. M.
Winton, C. A.
Workman, J. C.
Young, Charles R.

The business meeting was preceded by a delightful musical program given by the Allegro Mandolin Sextette and assisting artists.

PRESIDENT FORSBERG: Gentlemen: You have just listened to a very delightful entertainment by the Allegro Mandolin Sextette and assisting artists: Percy Lichtenfels, Director, assisted by Lloyd E. Longacre, five string banjo soloist, son of a retired Pennsylvania Railroad engineer (we will not hold that against him); Don Byham, baritone, Assistant Store Keeper, Pennsylvania Railroad; Andrew Scheuerle, xylophone and traps, Welder, Pennsylvania Railroad; and Flora K. Lichtenfels, piano. This is one of the pioneer radio orchestras in Pittsburgh and was the first to be heard in overseas broadcasts. Our Club is very grateful to them for the splendid entertainment they have given us this evening. It is a matter of general regret that they have to cut short their program in order to keep their usual broadcast engagement.

We will now proceed with the regular order of business, and the first thing is the calling of the roll. Inasmuch as each one of you has placed his name on the registration card and deposited it with the gentlemen at the door, we have a record of that and we will forego the roll call.

Next is the reading of the minutes of the last meeting. The minutes will appear in print in the next issue of the Proceedings and the Secretary informs me that he expects to have the Proceedings mailed to us by the middle of next week. So with your permission we will not have the reading of the minutes of the last meeting at this time.

Next in order of business is the reading of proposals for membership. I told you at the last meeting of our Club that Rufus Flinn and his Membership Committee had corralled every available member in Western Pennsylvania and the only hope of our new Membership Committee was to get those who had attained their majority since the last meeting of our Club. Our Membership Committee finds there have been a few that have come to years of discretion since that time and we have promptly herded them in. We have the Committee out for those who are coming of age before the next meeting.

I am going to make a slight change in the method of bringing new members into our fold. I am sure you will agree with me that it is very necessary when a member joins this Club for us to see his face as well as hear his name and be able to connect the two. I am, therefore, going to ask the Secretary to read the list of names of those who are presented for membership tonight, and when he has completed the reading of these names I am going to ask those who are present if they will kindly stand and then in turn I will ask you to state your name so we may know just who you are. The Secretary will now read the list of proposals for membership.

SECRETARY: We have the following proposals for membership:

Barnett, George, Salesman, W. W. Lawrence & Company, West Carson Street, Pittsburgh, Pa. Recommended by E. A. Rauschart.

Campbell, F. R., Shop Foreman, Donora Southern Railroad Co., 664 Thompson Avenue, Donora, Pa. Recommended by F. E. Van Woert.

Clarke, A. C., Assistant Chief Engineer, B. & O. R. R. Co., Maloney Building, Pittsburgh, Pa. Recommended by R. P. Forsberg.

Coakley, John A., Jr., Secretary, Lincoln Electric Railway Sales Company, Marshall Building, Cleveland, Ohio. Recommended by E. A. Rauschart.

Day, Tom R., Chief Draftsman, Pennsylvania Railroad, 179 Steuben Street, Crafton, Pittsburgh, Pa. Recommended by C. M. Wheeler.

Dillon, H. W., Sales Engineer, Paxton-Mitchell Company, 312 Main Street, South Amboy, N. J. Recommended by E. A. Rauschart.

Follett, W. F., Assistant Superintendent, Aliquippa & Southern Railroad Company, 652 Highland Avenue, Aliquippa, Pa. Recommended by W. F. Ambrose.

George, W. J., Assistant Sales Manager, Edgewater Steel Company, P. O. Box 478, Pittsburgh, Pa. Recommended by R. J. Matthews.

Green, M. E., Assistant Chief Clerk to Vice President, P. & L. E. R. R. Co., P&LE Terminal Building, Pittsburgh, Pa. Recommended by R. P. Forsberg.

Harper, James W., Jr., Locomotive Engineer, Montour Railroad Co., 1610 Vance Avenue, Coraopolis, Pa. Recommended by E. A. Rauschart.

Higginbottom, S. B., Supervisor Telegraph & Signals, Pennsylvania Railroad, Pennsylvania Station, Pittsburgh, Pa. Recommended by C. M. Wheeler.

Luce, W. A., Master Mechanic, Pittsburgh, Lisbon & Western Railroad Co., Darlington, Pa. Recommended by E. A. Rauschart.

Miller, S. H., Secretary and Treasurer, Fort Pitt Chemical Company, 26th & Smallman Streets, Pittsburgh, Pa. Recommended by Daniel H. Kirby.

Mulligan, Michael, Engine House Foreman, Monongahela Railway Company, 315 Water Street, South Brownsville, Pa. Recommended by H. L. Beeson.

McKim, Hollis, Office Manager, Edgewater Steel Company, P. O. Box 478, Pittsburgh, Pa. Recommended by R. J. Matthews.

Neff, Charles, Yard Master, Pennsylvania Railroad, 2909 Jenny Lind Avenue, McKeesport, Pa. Recommended by H. N. Rowles.

Rambo, M. H., Station Inspector, Pennsylvania Railroad, Pennsylvania Station, Pittsburgh, Pa. Recommended by E. A. Foard.

Seitz, Warren W., Circuit Engineer Telegraph & Signal Department, Pennsylvania Railroad, 1559 Montier Street, Wilkinsburg, Pa. Recommended by C. M. Wheeler.

Showalter, Joseph, Boiler Maker Foreman, Aliquippa & Southern Railroad, 116 Carrol Street, Aliquippa, Pa. Recommended by W. F. Ambrose.

Stone, E. C., Assistant to President, Philadelphia Company, 435 Sixth Avenue, Pittsburgh, Pa. Recommended by T. Fitzgerald.

Westerman, M. A., Sales Department, Edgewater Steel Company, P. O. Box 478, Pittsburgh, Pa. Recommended by R. J. Matthews.

Wilkins, Harry, Acting Chief Train Clerk, Office Superintendent Passenger Transportation, Pennsylvania Railroad, 203 Allegheny Avenue, Emsworth, Pa. Recommended by W. B. Moir.

Yohe, J. K., Jr., Supervisors' Field Man, P. & L. E. R. R. Co., 2215 Hawthorne Street, Pittsburgh (18), Pa. Recommended by G. H. Burnette.

After the reading of the list the new members present rose in their places, at the request of the President, and gave their names.

PRESIDENT: We will next have communications. Mr. Secretary do we have any?

SECRETARY: Since our last meeting we have received information of the death of Daniel F. Downes, Division Operator, Pennsylvania Railroad, which occurred October 31, 1935.

PRESIDENT: A suitable memorial will appear in the next issue of the Proceedings.

We are signally fortunate tonight in having with us the Director of the Bureau of Safety of the Interstate Commerce Commission, who has his headquarters at Washington, D. C. This gentleman makes an investigation and a report upon every train accident that occurs in the United States in which a fatality results. He does not make an investigation of every derailment or collision; but of every one that results in a fatality. These investigations are exhaustive and complete and copies of them are sent to all steam railroads. And I can say very candidly that of all the reports that come to my desk I do not think there are any that I read with more interest than I do the reports of the Director of the Bureau of Safety of the Interstate Commerce Commission. They are very thorough and he always states his own conclusion relative to the cause of the accident. Knowing that great minds run in the same channel, I often form my own conclusion before reading his, and to my great satisfaction sometimes we are in agreement.

The gentleman who will present the paper this evening is Mr. William J. Patterson and his title is Director of the Bureau of Safety, Interstate Commerce Commission, Washington, D. C. His subject is, "Some Improvements in Design and Maintenance of Railroad Equipment."

Some Improvements In Design And Maintenance Of Railroad Equipment

By W. J. PATTERSON, Director, Bureau of Safety,
Interstate Commerce Commission, Washington, D. C.

Mr. Chairman, Members of the Railway Club of Pittsburgh, and Guests:

The importance of Pittsburgh as a railroad center, and the large volume of railroad equipment and supplies manufactured in this district make it appropriate to bring before this club for consideration and discussion the subject of improvement in the design of new equipment, improved maintenance of equipment, and the conversion of equipment already in service to conform to higher standards. A great deal of time and effort has been devoted to the development of lightweight, stream lined, high speed trains for passenger service, light weight freight cars, and the application of diesel engines to meet varied railroad operating requirements. These developments have attracted widespread attention in railroad circles as well as by the general public. There are other developments now in progress, in connection with conventional or standard equipment, which are far-reaching from the standpoints of both safety and efficiency of operation.

I will confine my remarks this evening to a brief discussion of the development and current situation concerning air brakes, trucks and draft gears for freight cars, since these three items appear to me to be of primary importance just at this time.

AB BRAKES FOR FREIGHT CARS

The development of the AB type of brake equipment for freight cars was the result of a long period of investigation and test. In 1922 the Interstate Commerce Commission entered upon a proceeding of inquiry and investigation, the stated purpose of which was

"to determine whether, and to what extent power brakes and appliances for operating power brake systems, now generally in use upon the locomotives and cars of carriers by railroad subject to the interstate commerce act, are adequate and in accordance with requirements of safety, what improved appliances or devices are available for use, and what improvements in power brakes and appliances may or should be made, to the end that increased safety in train operation may be obtained."

A report was issued in 1924 which pointed to the need, first, for better maintenance of existing air brake equipment to effect an immediate improvement in the operation of power brakes, and, secondly, for improvements in power brake appliances.

Following conferences between representatives of the Bureau of Safety and the American Railway Association, the A. R. A. rules for maintenance of power brake equipment were revised, effective in January, 1926, the higher standards which were set up by these revised rules have resulted in substantial improvement in the condition of power brake equipment in general service.

With respect to improvement in the fundamental design of freight brake equipment, tentative specifications which proposed additional functions, were issued by the Commission in November, 1924, following which extensive tests were made, both on test racks and in road service, of devices which had been developed by air brake manufacturers and which were designed to meet, in whole or in part, the tentative specifications of the Commission. Rack tests were made at Purdue University from November, 1925, to January, 1929. Road tests were made on the line of the Southern Pacific Company in Oregon and California from August, 1929, to March, 1931.

These tests demonstrated the need for improvement in freight brake equipment, the inadequacy of standard K equipment safely to control long trains, inability to secure necessary functioning of this apparatus under certain conditions frequently encountered in practical service, and susceptibility to undesired emergency operations which often result in severe slack action causing damage to equipment and lading as well as personal injuries to employes.

The principal limitations of the type "K" equipment include the following:

1. Failure of all brakes to apply promptly in long trains with light brake pipe reductions, particularly in cases where minimum brake pipe leakage exists.

2. Failure to obtain uniform initial brake cylinder pressure on all cars under tapered train line conditions.

3. Inflexibility of the equipment for control of trains on grades.

4. Failure of all brakes to release promptly in long trains and properly to control the readjustment of train slack during the release.

5. Variation in performance between long and short trains.

6. Attainment of emergency applications when only service applications are intended.

7. Inability to bring about an emergency application following even a relatively light service application.

8. Damaging shock attendant upon emergency applications with long trains at critical speeds.

9. Erratic functioning of the equipment under less than intensive maintenance and supervision when used in long freight trains or trains of even modern length.

10. Comparatively slow emergency propagation rate.

11. Liability of heavy shocks due to the lack of properly controlled emergency brake cylinder pressure development.

The tests also demonstrated that material improvements in power brake equipment for freight cars were feasible. While some of the equipment of new types employed in these tests was experimental in form, improved functions which the tests had demonstrated were practical and desirable were afterwards incorporated in commercial apparatus known as the AB type of freight brake equipment.

Extensive tests of AB equipment were made, rack tests were conducted, the equipment was applied experimentally to a considerable numbers of cars, road tests were conducted, and the operation of this equipment in actual service, and when intermingled with cars having standard K equipment, was observed. Subsequently the Mechanical Division of the American Railway Association revised its specifications for brake equipment for freight cars, effective September 1, 1933, and applicable to all cars built or rebuilt after that date, establishing the AB type equipment as standard.

As compared with the type K equipment now generally in service on freight cars, the type AB equipment constitutes a material improvement in freight brake equipment. It provides greater reliability and safety in the control particularly of long trains, and in a measure the functioning of K-type equipments is improved by association with a number of AB-type equipments.

Advantages and savings resulting from application of AB brake equipment are brought about by:

1. Greater reliability and flexibility in the control of trains.

2. Possibilities of reduction in damage to lading.

o

3. Reduction in time in starting after service stops due to prompt and certain release of all AB brakes.

4. Decrease in time in starting after an emergency stop.

The improved functions and operation of AB freight brake equipment have fully established its practicability and desirability and · have warranted measures to bring about more rapid introduction into general use of this type of equipment. Accordingly, upon recommendation of the Federal Coordinator of Transportation and his Mechanical Advisory Committee, A. A. R. interchange rules have been revised to require existing equipment to be converted, so as to conform to the new standard, progressively on an annual basis, this program to be completed in a ten-year period. The following was added to Paragraph 4, Section (a), Interchange Rule 3:

> "On and after January 1, 1945, all freight cars in interchange service must be equipped with air brakes meeting the requirements of the A. R. A. specifications for Air Brakes adopted in 1933. Each car owner shall make a report quarterly to the American Railway Association, showing by months the number of freight cars acquired and the number of freight cars on which brake equipment is converted, which information will be filed quarterly with the Interstate Commerce Commission and the Coordinator."

The progress report as to September 30, 1935, which has been compiled from returns filed in accordance with this rule, shows the following:

| Car Owners Reporting | Number | Interchange Freight Cars | | |
		Number Owned	Number Equipped with AB Brakes	Per cent
Railroads	205	2,040,056	33,295	1.63
Private Car Lines	217	289,965	2,625	0.91
Total	422	2,330,021	35,920	1.54

I have thus reviewed somewhat in detail the principal developments in connection with the present standards for freight brake equipment in order that you may have a correct picture of the present situation. Some articles and references which appeared in the press shortly after the action taken last year by the Association of American Railroads, to require the more rapid, progressive introduction of the new standard and the general use of this standard equipment by 1945, stressed the amount of expenditures by the carriers which would be required and at least conveyed the inference that the proposed change was an arbitrary and burdensome requirement which was not warranted. On the contrary, a review of the facts in the case shows clearly that an extended and comprehenhive investigation was made, the need for improvement was definitely established, and material advantages of equipment conforming to the revised standards were thoroughly demonstrated, which has since been confirmed by service results. The adoption of this new standard brake equipment on all freight cars in interchange service will make it possible to secure to a greater extent the operating improvements obtainable from long trains, heavy tonnage trains and increased freight train speed. While the type AB brake equipment does not fulfill all of the tentative specifications which were issued by the Commission in 1924, continued experience with this equipment in practical service may demonstrate that it adequately meets the need for improvement in power brakes and appliances for freight trains which prompted the initiation of this investigation in 1922.

CAR TRUCKS

The extensive changes which have been witnessed in freight car construction have been accompanied by equally important and extensive developments in the design and construction of car trucks. Many of the earlier designs have long since become obsolete and entirely eliminated from service. Unfortunately, however, some other trucks which have also become obsolete have not thus far been eliminated from service. I refer specifically to freight car trucks of the arch-bar type which were introduced into service approximately 70 years ago; experience has demonstrated that trucks of this design cannot now be relied upon to withstand stresses which have resulted from increased axle loads and train speeds of present-day service. There are approximately 735,000 cars so equipped still in service.

The failures, weaknesses and hazards of arch-bar trucks are referred to in the proceedings of the American Railway Association over a long period of years prior to the date of any action by that organization to actually curtail their use. As early as 1921 the question of eliminating arch-bar trucks was considered by the committee on Car Construction and advocated by some members of the committee and also in discussions by other members of the association. No definite

11

action was taken at that time, however, as the committee on Car Construction was engaged in designing a standard cast-steel side frame, with due consideration for previous developments which had been made by the manufacturers, the Master Car Builders' Association, and the designs which had been put into use by the United States Railroad Administration. It is to be noted that cast-steel truck side frames were used on approximately 100,000 new freight cars built under the United States Railroad Administration and also that cast-steel side frames were specified for all necessary renewals on existing equipment. The activities of the American Railway Association culminated in 1923 in the adoption of the cast-steel side frame as recommended practice. The design was revised in 1925, and in 1927 a rule was passed making it mandatory that cast-steel truck side frames, conforming to American Railway Association specifications, be applied to all interchange freight cars built on or after July 1, 1928.

At various times attempts have been made to improve and strengthen arch-bar truck design, but with the increased load capacities and increased train speeds this type of truck continued to fail, and proved to be such a hazard in operation that additional mandatory rules were promulgated by the American Railway Association to eliminate it entirely from interchange service. In 1928 a rule was adopted by the American Railway Association, effective January 1, 1929, to the effect that new trucks would be equipped with cast-steel side frames when applied to new or rebuilt cars on or after October 1, 1929. In 1929 a rule was adopted, effective January 1, 1930, requiring that new trucks applied to any car on or after March 1, 1930, and second-hand trucks applied to new or rebuilt car bodies on or after January 1, 1930, would be equipped with cast-steel side frames; and a rule effective January 1, 1931, provided that trucks with arch-bars would be prohibited in interchange effective January 1, 1936; this effective date, however, has since been extended to January 1, 1938.

The number of accidents investigated by the Bureau of Safety in which the failure of arch-bar trucks has been involved has increased considerably during the past year. During the 5-year period ended June 30, 1935, investigations were made of 14 accidents involving arch-bar trucks, these 14 accidents resulting in the death of 23 persons, the injury of 24 persons, and a cost of damage to track and equipment and clearing wreckage amounting to approximately $275,000. Seven of these 14 accidents occurred during the year ended June 30, 1935, and in the reports covering several of these accidents attention has been called to the necessity for eliminating arch-bar trucks from service.

The use of arch-bar trucks is not confined to freight equipment; in fact, figures obtained in connection with the investigation of several recent accidents show that on some roads a large percentage of locomotive tenders are equipped with arch-bar trucks. Attention is further directed to the fact that tank cars have been involved in many accidents caused by the failure of arch-bar trucks and it frequently happens that fire breaks out in the wreckage, adding to the destructive results of the accident, because such tank cars are loaded with gasoline or other dangerous or inflammable liquids.

The figures previously given, indicating for only 14 accidents an expense of approximately $275,000, not including damage to lading, represent only a very small percentage of the total expense to the railroads of the country as a whole as a result of the use of arch-bar trucks. Several railroads do not keep records which enable them to determine what expense they are incurring for repairs to arch-bar trucks, but in some cases where such records are kept the expense so incurred is very large; on the Missouri Pacific, for example, where several accidents due to arch-bar truck failures have been investigated it was found that in one year the cost of repairs and the cost of accidents involving arch-bar trucks amounted to $183,817, this amount being divided about equally between cost of repairs and expense of accidents. Undoubtedly it is a conservative statement that arch-bar trucks are costing the railroads of the country millions every year for accidents and repairs. Some railroads are taking the only effective step which can be taken to combat this situation; they are eliminating, and in some cases already have eliminated, such trucks from service. On the other hand, however, little if any progress is being made by many railroads and private-car lines, and in view of the accumulated record of failures surrounding the use of these trucks it is apparent that more concerted efforts and more effective measures must be taken to avoid the continual hazards incident to the use of arch-bar trucks.

As a result of the investigation of several accidents due

13

to this cause the Bureau of Safety has made the following recommendations:

1. That arch-bar trucks be removed from service at the earliest practicable date.

2. That until arch-bar trucks can be eliminated from service, a reduction sufficient to guarantee safety of operation should be made in the permissible load limit on cars equipped with such trucks.

3. That inflammables, explosives or other dangerous articles should not be transported in cars which are equipped with arch-bar trucks.

4. That provision be made in interchange rules whereby a receiving line may refuse to accept from a connecting line any car equipped with arch-bar trucks.

The adoption of these recommendations would surround the continued operation of cars having arch-bar trucks with a measure of increased safety; and if the continued operation of this equipment were permitted only under the recommended restrictions of reduced load limits and of certain limitations as to the lading of such cars, any carrier having removed arch-bar trucks from its own cars would be in position consistently to refuse to receive from connecting lines any cars still equipped with this obsolete and inherently dangerous type of car truck. Thus these recommended penalties to accompany continued operation would exercise a potent influence in hastening the day when equipment of this character will be entirely eliminated from service.

FREIGHT CAR DRAFT GEARS

The subject of draft gears and attachments in freight cars has long been one of major importance in railroad operation.

The first friction draft gears appeared in service about 1896 and by about 1908 friction type draft gears had gained quite general acceptance by the railroads as being superior to the spring type of gears. The first comprehensive tests, for the purpose of establishing comparative ratings, were made under the United States Railroad Administration in 1919, in connection with the extensive car construction program then under way, valuable data and improvement resulting from this series of tests.

In 1927 the American Railway Association began a series of tests at Purdue University which culminated in the adoption in 1931 of specifications for approved draft gears for freight service. In these specifications a schedule of tests has been provided; these tests are conducted at the Association of American Railroads' draft gear testing laboratory at Purdue University, and gears which meet the prescribed tests are given certificates of approval by the Association of American Railroads. At the present time, nine draft gears have been thus approved and the Association of American Railroads has adopted rules which provide that only such certified approved draft gears shall be applied to new freight cars built on or after January 1, 1934. The rules further provide that new draft gears applied to any car after January 1, 1935, shall comply with the approved specifications if the pocket dimensions permit. Approximately 84,000 cars have been equipped with Association of American Railroads' certified draft gears.

These specifications for standard approved draft gears are predicated upon extensive practical experience as to their functioning requirements and upon extensive research and tests to determine their capacity, action, reliability and general ruggedness and they therefore represent the accumulated knowledge and experience of chosen, practical men and committees in that particular art.

Freight car draft gears serve to cushion impacts when cars are coupled, protect the car structure against damage, protect the lading against damage and act as a restraint against recoil from impacts and also against slack action in trains. All of these features are well known to those who have been charged with the important duty of setting up standard functioning qualities for present-day service conditions and the present approved standard specifications are calculated to bring about a progressive improvement in the condition of draft gears in use on freight cars in this country.

The disturbing action set up by a high percentage of recoil is an important feature which requires further attention. The fact that the friction type gear provides a means of restraining such action is an important feature of superiority over spring gears, which contributed to its general adoption. While the Association of American Railroads' specifications for approved draft gears have not as yet set up a maximum permissible recoil, the addition of this provision to the specification has been strongly advocated. Aggressive action to thus improve and perfect the specifications and advance the progress toward standardization of draft gears is worthy of earnest consideration.

15

Approximately 2,000,000 freight cars in interchange service are not equipped with modern Association of American Railroads' draft gears. Of this number it is estimated that 750,000 are equipped with spring draft gears and it is reasonable to expect that the greater portion of these cars with spring gears will not be equipped with approved draft gears but will be retired from service in the next few years. In round numbers there are one and one-quarter million cars with friction draft gears other than standard Association of American Railroads' gears that are subject to maintenance and replacement. The gears in these cars consist of many kinds and classes with such material differences in important functioning qualities, that smooth, uniform action in long trains and in high speed trains is practically impossible of attainment.

Following the adoption, in 1931, of specifications for approved draft gears, an effort was made to expedite weeding out and eliminating some of the most inefficient draft gears from freight cars by designating a considerable number of gears as "obsolete", as shown in Section III of Rule 101 of the 1935 code of interchange rules; only a scrap value charge for such obsolete gears is permitted if applied either complete or in part.

Further recognition of the growing need for improvement in draft gear conditions is evidenced by the adoption of Recommended Practice rules covering "Inspection and Maintenance of Draft Gears and Attachments by Car Owners", which became effective March 1, 1935, which provide as follows:

"1· When cars are on repair tracks for periodic air brake attention, examine and renew defective parts of draft gears, couplers and their attachments and supports. This will not require removal of draft gear for this examination, except where found defective or where total slack from coupler horn to striking casting exceeds 1½ in.; slack to be the difference in distance between coupler striking horn and striking casting when coupler is pulled out with a bar and sledged back solid.

"2· When cars are undergoing general repairs, draft gears will be dropped for examination, and couplers, their attachments and supports will be in-

16

spected and necessary repairs and replacements made.

"3· In renewing defective draft gears. certified gears should be applied if spacing permits, or serviceable second-hand gears of other types not considered inefficient or obsolete as per list shown in A.A.R. Interchange Rule 101, may be applied. Certified gears must be renewed with certified gears."

In order to further stress the need for action, an Association of American Railroads' circular dated January 7, 1935, was also sent to all carriers, quoting the above recommended practice rules, with the following paragraph added:

"Car owners are requested to see that these rules are strictly enforced on their own cars, in order to improve the conditions of the couplers and draft gears by the elimination of the slack in the gears as far as possible."

In the report of this committee in 1935, in the discussion of the reduction of unresisted slack in train service, it is stated:

"The 1½" limit was established because of the high percentage of cars that will require attention even under this limit."

Further in their report it is stated that:

"Appreciable and effective reduction in unresisted slack will be realized through the application of certified draft gears and the reduction of unresisted slack through compliance with the draft gear maintenance program that was established the first of this year."

Inspections which I have had carried out on this subject disclose that on some roads prompt action was taken in response to adoption of the recommended practice rules on draft gears and that the prescribed practice is being followed. On some important railroads, however, no general instructions corresponding to the Association of American Railroads' recommended practice rules have as yet been issued, and foremen in direct supervision of car repairs at many points are not advised of such action; the old method of using their own judgment as to when and why couplers shall be dropped to repair draft gears or eliminate free slack is still being followed.

The Bureau of Safety recently investigated a disastrous derailment in which a severe run-in of slack in the train, without any application of brakes, was considered by train employees, as well as operating and mechanical officials an important factor in the cause. It was found that 72% of cars in the train were foreign and private line cars. It was also found that the railroad on which the accident occurred had promptly issued general instructions in response to Association of American Railroads' recommended practices on draft gears and that they were being reasonably well followed out.

This leads to the question as to what should be done to protect the railroad which complies with the rules against the inaction or neglect of the car owners who do not make a proper effort to conform to the higher standards.

The recommended practice as formulated by the Association of American Railroads has linked the draft gear question with periodical air brake attention, so that in the natural course of events all freight cars (excepting those with AB type brakes) will have been on repair tracks within about 15 months from March 1, 1935, and if the rule on draft gear maintenance as set up by the Association of American Railroads is properly observed during this time, slack in excess of 1½" will be eliminated and a great improvement thereby effected.

The Association of American Railroads has officially recognized the need of corrective action, has set up a reasonable, uniform method for relieving the situation and has made special request on all car owners to comply strictly with the prescribed rules. The thing that now remains to be done is to observe and enforce the rule.

The penalty for failure of any car owner to respond to the urgent need for improvement in the draft gear situation should properly revert back directly to such owner and it is therefore my belief that a provision should be written into the rules at earliest possible date to the effect that couplers with free slack, (longitudinal travel unresisted by draft gear compression) exceeding 1½" will be prohibited on all cars, effective July 1, 1936, from owners. Thus 16 months after the date the draft gear maintenance rule became effective the car owner who has not concerned himself about complying with the rule will be faced with an appropriate penalty for his inaction.

Excessive free slack in draft gears is a hazard to train operation and appropriate means for a strict enforcement of the existing rules to improve this condition are strongly urged.

CONCLUSIONS

Improvement in railroad operation is accompanied by, and in large measure results from the development of railroad equipment, and in the very nature of the case such equipment is in a state of constant evolution. A modification in any portion of freight car equipment when applied to all cars in the country is a vast undertaking, and naturally should be made only after the necessity for the change has been fully determined, or the advantages to be derived therefrom have been demonstrated to be worth while. However, once the decision has been made measures to effect the necessary changes should be vigorously pressed, in order that the railroads and the public may within a reasonable period obtain the advantages which will result from these improvements.

PRESIDENT: We have just listened to a most masterful presentation of a most interesting subject. Mr. Patterson has very kindly consented to, as he says, attempt to answer any questions that may be asked relative to the paper he has presented. I think you will all agree that one of the best parts of a meeting is the discussion we have after the presentation of the paper and the questions that bring out certain points in the paper. I will ask that you volunteer to say something relative to the paper, for I want to go on record with you that I will not call on any person to speak in connection with the paper unless it is absolutely necessary. I know some of our members do not want to be called on, and I have heard indirectly of some men who have actually stayed away from the meetings for fear they might be asked to speak. I promise you I will never embarrass any one in that manner. But I will expect you to reciprocate by volunteering to say something about the paper or ask some question concerning it. The subject is now in your hands for such purpose.

MR. J. H. GLENN: I would like to ask Mr. Patterson if he has a record showing just what the slack condition actually is at the present time in the equipment that you have had opportunity to observe.

MR. PATTERSON: Frankly I have observed very little, but the reports that our field men make indicate that it is not uncommon to find 4".

MR. GLENN: That would be 2½" more than the recommendation of your Department as the allowable limit?

MR. PATTERSON: On particular cars, yes sir.

MR. H. E. CHILCOAT: I would like to ask Mr. Patterson a question. He stated that there were 14 arch bar accidents in a certain period of time. How many cast steel side frame accidents occurred during that same period?

MR. PATTERSON: I am not able to answer that question except to say that we investigated no accidents due to a side frame failure during that period.

MR. CHILCOAT: You do have records of all failures, do you not, or only a record of failures resulting in fatalities?

MR. PATTERSON: The Interstate Commerce Commission have such a record as the railroads furnish, which includes accidents resulting in deaths, personal injuries or property damage of $150.00 or more. In the Bureau of which I am Director there is no record of accidents except certain ones that result in fatalities.

MR. M. R. REED: I do not know that I have any questions to ask Mr. Patterson. Our superior officers on the railroad frequently ask me questions about things that happen to freight cars and other equipment and the cause of failures, many of which are of the very nature that Mr. Patterson has talked about tonight. I know you have all enjoyed this paper, as he has touched upon many matters that have been the cause of serious trouble on everybody's railroad, particularly draft gears, trucks and air brakes. He has done us all a distinct favor in covering some of the conditions resulting in such failures of equipment, and I sincerely hope that his paper has been of as much interest to everyone here as it has been to me. Every mechanical man, as well as operating men, should be very much benefited by the excellent material Mr. Patterson has brought to us.

While he has touched principally on draft gears, air brakes and truck sides of freight cars, there are many other things, of course, on passenger train cars, locomotives, etc., that have a very distinct bearing on safety and economy of operation, all of which needs our careful attention.

I am very grateful myself to Mr. Patterson for his visit here and the interesting and instructive paper he has given us. I hope everybody has been benefited by it as much as I have.

MR. C. O. DAMBACH: Since I believe we will have the arch bar truck with us for considerable time, I was wondering whether from Mr. Patterson's investigation regarding arch bar failures, he could tell us the principal contributing factor in order that we may make the necessary repairs with a view to reducing accidents to a minimum while these trucks are still in service.

MR. PATTERSON: I do not know that I can exactly agree with your premises because I am not in agreement that we are going to have them with us for a long time.

MR. DAMBACH: I can remember when we were facing the same problem in connection with old link and pin coupler and it was a very long time before we got them all off. I imagine it will be some time before all the arch bar trucks are done away with. If they have a definite place in your experience as an occasion of failures we might get some assistance as to additional safety.

MR. PATTERSON: I may say that because of the time it took to eliminate the link and pin couplers we gained some experience ourselves and we have improved our procedure since that time.

MR. S. G. DOWN: Mr. Patterson said some very kind words about Air Brakes so it is perhaps in order for me to say some kind words about Mr. Patterson. It is always a pleasure to listen to him because when he talks he has something to say. I think it is fortunate that the Bureau of Safety of the Interstate Commerce Commission has a man at its head having the experience and knowledge of Mr. Patterson.

When he talks of safety appliances, he knows what he is talking about. He got his early experience on railways in the Middle West where he frequently had occasion to screw up the old style hand-brakes and climb up the side of box cars in the days when grasp irons were not securely fastened and sometimes fell off, when automatic couplers were not of the best type and properly maintained, and many other appliances were not designed and maintained in the best interest of safety.

Mr. Patterson and his organization are great exponents of the "Safety First" movement and direct their attention to installation and proper maintenance and operation of the so-called safety appliances to the end that our transportation operations may be on a safe basis.

I remember a number of years ago, we used to look upon the Bureau of Safety as the "Big, Bad Wolf." Today, I am sure we look upon it as a great blessing because with the general interchange of equipment on the roads in our forty-eight states, cars are scattered over all the country and become "Orphan Annies" on foreign lines. In other words, human nature being as it is, such foreign cars do not perhaps receive the same kindly consideration and treatment as is true of the home car.

It has been suggested that technically a railroad owns all of the cars they have purchased and paid for, whereas, practically under our interchange operation, they only own such cars as are on their line on any particular day, and their own cars scattered throughout the country are obviously subject to such treatment as the foreign line will give them. If the car is in good condition, the foreign line may endeavor to obtain all the service possible from it with the least expenditure of money for upkeep.

The Association of American Railroads, in the interest of better maintenance, have established a checking organization somewhat supplementary to Mr. Patterson's so that with both organizations functioning properly, it goes without saying that we may expect a continued improvement in the maintenance of safety appliances.

I understand from railway officers that Mr. Patterson is very tolerant in administrating the Safety Appliance Act. This perhaps is largely due to the fact that his broad railway experience has given him an understanding of the difficulties confronting the operating managements of our railways.

I am sure you will agree with me when I say we are grateful and honored in having Mr. Patterson with us tonight to deliver his message on safety appliances.

MR. SAMUEL LYNN: Mr. President, members and guests of the Railway Club, I am going to let you in on a little secret. Two weeks ago tonight in Chicago I had a visit with our good friend Mr. Patterson, and during our visit he informed me that he expected to be in Pittsburgh in a couple of weeks and present a paper before the Railway Club and wanted me there for that meeting to render my assistance in case there was a general discussion of his suggestions and recommendations.

A day or two ago our President asked me to call at his office where he showed me the card notice of this meeting and informed me that he wanted me to take part in the discussion. I asked him what Mr. Patterson was going to talk about and he said his subject would be "Equipment" and I told him that this covered a pretty broad scope. He then said that it was his understanding this would cover rolling stock or car equipment and that I should know all about it.

As you can see, I really had orders from two bosses— Mr. Patterson wanted me on his side of the question and it is apparent that our President wanted me to get up and start something at this meeting. It is therefore plain to railroad mechanical men present that I have been placed "on the spot." If I deviate from what Mr. Patterson has said, all these field men to which he referred would no doubt be on our railroad going over our air brakes, couplers, trucks, etc.; and if I do not say something our President, Mr. Forsberg, would in all probability invite me to his office tomorrow morning.

Seriously speaking, Mr. Patterson has given us a splendid talk on what he considers some of the most important items in railroad transportation—car trucks, slack in couplers and air brake equipment. However, I will not go into details as Mr. Patterson knows that I am a member of the A. A. R. Coupler and Draft Gear Committee, which Committee was responsible for some of the improvements with respect to couplers and draft gears. Mr. Patterson also is aware of the fact that I was a member of the A. A. R. Committee that was appointed to try and bring about an improvement with respect to slack in couplers and draft gears and before that Committee arrived at any conclusions Mr. Patterson was consulted by the members of this special committee and in conference with him on the subject he informed the members of the Committee that he wanted the slack reduced to 1". After considerable discussion it was finally agreed that we would formulate rules and set the maximum allowance of slack at 1¼", and as Mr. Patterson realized that the railroad mechanical men had a real job to perform he willingly agreed to go along with the 1¼" for a start but informed us that we would have to do better than that in a very short time.

Now, gentlemen, taking into consideration the facts that I have stated, it is evident that Mr. Patterson is very well informed as to my activities on these Committees. However, I want to say that he has given us a splendid paper and we mechanical men who are responsible for the maintenance of equipment know that the different topics on which he has touched tonight are very important in safety to the employes on the railroad and in the prevention of damage to equipment. I consider it a privilege to have been acquainted with Mr. Patterson for a number of years and to have had an opportunity to confer with him quite frequently on the subjects that he has presented to us tonight. During the years that I have known him he has always found time to let me have an audience, and has given me very valuable information, therefore, it is a pleasure to be here tonight and hear him present his paper. It is also a privilege for me to have this opportunity to express publicly my personal appreciation of Mr. Patterson's kindness to me when I have conferred with him on A. A. R. subjects.

Therefore, Mr. President, I would like to make a motion that this Club extend to Mr. Patterson a rising vote of thanks for the splendid paper presented this evening.

MR. PATTERSON: If I may be permitted, I just want to observe that if it were convenient or possible for me to put forty men on his railroad I am sure he would be delighted to have them for I am sure it would show the equipment on his line in excellent condition.

The MOTION for a rising vote of thanks was adopted by unanimous vote.

There being no further business, ON MOTION Adjourned.

J. D. CONWAY, Secretary.

In Memoriam

DANIEL F. DOWNES,
Joined Club December 18, 1930
Died October 31, 1935

MORE MILES - - SAFER
WITH NEW PENNZOIL!

OFFICIAL PROCEEDINGS

RAILWAY CLUB OF PITTSBURGH

$1.00 Per Year   25¢ Per Copy

Vol. XXXV.   DECEMBER 19, 1935.   No. 2.

INCOME AND ECONOMIC PROGRESS

By J. STEELE GOW, Director,

The Maurice and Laura Falk Foundation, Pittsburgh, Pa.

The proof of your interest

in the Club can be

enhanced

by securing a

NEW MEMBER.

Application form is available

in this magazine. Look

it up and

"ACT NOW."

OFFICIAL PROCEEDINGS

OF

The Railway Club of Pittsburgh

Organized October 18, 1901

Published monthly, except June, July and August, by the Railway Club of
Pittsburgh, J. D. Conway, Secretary, 515 Grandview Ave., Pittsburgh, Pa..

Entered as Second Class Matter February 6, 1915, at the Postoffice at Pittsburgh,
under the Act of March 3, 1879.

Vol. XXXV No. 2	Pittsburgh, Pa., Dec. 19, 1935	$1.00 Per Year 25c Per Copy

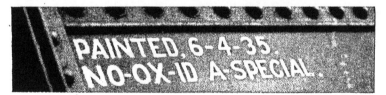

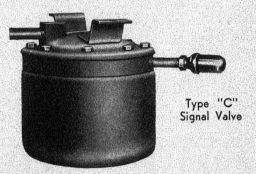

EQUIPMENT FOR RAILROADS

INDEX—ADVERTISERS.

NOTE—This form to be filled out in full by typewriter or printed and mailed to J. D. Conway, Secretary, 1941 Oliver Building, Pittsburgh, Pa. Membership fee, including dues, is $3.00 for each fiscal year or part thereof, except those proposed in September or October. Those proposed in these months will be credited upon payment for the following fiscal year. Dues are payable in advance.

The fiscal year ends with the month of October.

The Railway Club of Pittsburgh:

....19..........

Gentlemen:

Will you kindly consider my Application for Membership in your Club at the next meeting:

Name...

Title...

Company...

My Address...

....

Recommended by...

OFFICIAL PROCEEDINGS
OF

The Railway Club of Pittsburgh

Organized October 18, 1901

Vol. XXXV No. 2	Pittsburgh, Pa., Dec. 19, 1935	$1.00 Per Year 25c Per Copy

OFFICERS FOR 1935-1936

President
R. P. FORSBERG,
Chief Engineer, P. & L. E. R. R. Co., Pittsburgh, Pa.

First Vice President
E. A. RAUSCHART,
Mechanical Supt., Montour Railroad,
Coraopolis, Pa.

Secretary
J. D. CONWAY,
Railway Supply Manufacturers' Association,
Pittsburgh, Pa.

Second Vice President
G. M. SIXSMITH,
Supt., Pennsylvania Railroad,
Pittsburgh, Pa.

Treasurer
E. J. SEARLES,
Manager, Schaefer Equipment Co.,
Pittsburgh, Pa.

EXECUTIVE COMMITTEE:

FRANK J. LANAHAN, Chairman, President, Fort Pitt Malleable Iron Co., Pittsburgh, Pa.
A. STUCKI, Engineer, A. Stucki Company, Pittsburgh, Pa.
SAMUEL LYNN, Supt. Rolling Stock, P. & L. E. R. R., McKees Rocks, Pa.
D. F. CRAWFORD, Consulting Engineer, Pittsburgh, Pa.
G. W. WILDIN, Consulting Engineer, Westinghouse Air Brake Company, Pittsburgh, Pa.
W. S. McABEE, Vice Pres. & General Supt., Union Railroad Co., East Pittsburgh, Pa.
E. W. SMITH, Vice President, Pennsylvania Railroad, Pittsburgh, Pa.
LOUIS E. ENDSLEY, Consulting Engineer, 516 East End Avenue, Pittsburgh, Pa.
F. I. SNYDER, Vice President & General Manager, B. & L. E. R. R. Co., Pittsburgh, Pa.
C. O. DAMBACH, General Manager, P. & W. Va. Ry. Co., Pittsburgh, Pa.
R. H. FLINN, General Superintendent, Pennsylvania Railroad, Pittsburgh, Pa.

SUBJECT COMMITTEE:

D. W. McGEORGE, Chairman, Secretary, Edgewater Steel Company, Pittsburgh, Pa.
JOHN B. WRIGHT, Asst. Vice President, Westinghouse Air Brake Co., Wilmerding, Pa.
M. R. REED, General Supt. Motive Power, Pennsylvania Railroad, Pittsburgh, Pa.

ADVERTISING COMMITTEE:

E. A. FOARD, Chairman, Supt. Stations & Transfers, Pennsylvania R. R., Pittsburgh, Pa.
KARL BERG, Superintendent Motive Power, P. & L. E. R. R. Co., McKees Rocks, Pa.
H. E. PASSMORE, Representative, The American Hammered Piston Ring Co., Pgh., Pa.

RECEPTION AND ATTENDANCE COMMITTEE:

J. D. BELTZ, Chairman, Superintendent, B. & O. R. R. Co., Pittsburgh, Pa.
W. C. BUREL, Vice Chairman, Master Mechanic, Western Allegheny Railroad, Kaylor, Pa.
J. B. BAKER, Chief Engr. Maintenance of Way, Pennsylvania Railroad, Pittsburgh, Pa.
WALTER C. SANDERS, Gen. Mgr., Railway Div., Timken Roller Bearing Co., Canton, O.
G. A. BLACKMORE, President & Gen. Mgr., Union Switch & Signal Co., Swissvale, Pa.
J. S. LANAHAN, Vice President, Fort Pitt Malleable Iron Company, Pittsburgh, Pa.
J. A. WARFEL, Special Representative, Air Reduction Sales Co., Pittsburgh, Pa.
J. C. SHINGLEDECKER, Supervisor of Service Stations, The Pennzoil Co., Pittsburgh, Pa.
J. C. DILWORTH, Mgr. of Railroad Sales, Carnegie-Illinois Steel Corp., Pittsburgh, Pa.
G. H. BURNETTE, Assistant Chief Engineer, P. & L. E. R. R. Co., Pittsburgh, Pa.
W. R. TRIEM, Superintendent, Pennsylvania Railroad, Pittsburgh, Pa.
J. W. HOOVER, Asst. Chief of Transpn., Subsidiary Cos. U. S. Steel Corp., Pittsburgh, Pa.
J. W. JOHNSON, Superintendent, Railway Express Agency, Pittsburgh, Pa.
A. A. READ, Duquesne Slag Products Company, Pittsburgh, Pa.
C. P. SCHRECONGOST, Traffic Manager, Hillman Coal & Coke Company, Pittsburgh, Pa.

ENTERTAINMENT COMMITTEE:

J. PORTER GILLESPIE, Chairman, Asst. Gen. Supt., Lockhart Iron & Steel Co, Pgh., Pa.
FRANK E. WEIS, Vice Chairman, Transportation Clerk, Penna. R. R., Pittsburgh, Pa.
E. H. HOLMES, Sales Department, Fort Pitt Malleable Iron Co., Pittsburgh, Pa.
C. C. CLARK, Sales Manager Central District, Pressed Steel Car Co., McKees Rocks, Pa.
A. L. KESSLER, Clearance Clerk, Pennsylvania Railroad, Pittsburgh, Pa.
T. F. SHERIDAN, Asst. to S.M.P. and S.R.S., P. & L. E. R. R. Co., McKees Rocks, Pa.
JAMES NAGEL, Superintendent Transportation, Montour Railroad, Coraopolis, Pa.

FINANCE COMMITTEE:

J. L. O'TOOLE, Chairman, Asst. to Gen. Manager, P. & L. E. R. R. Co., Pittsburgh, Pa.
G. W. HONSBERGER, Transpn. Mgr., Westinghouse Electric & Mfg. Co., Pittsburgh, Pa.
F. J. RYAN, District Representative, Detroit, Toledo & Ironton Railroad, Pittsburgh, Pa.
C. E. CATT, Division Accountant, B. & O. R. R. Co., Pittsburgh, Pa.
J. W. BOYD, Superintendent, Monongahela Railway Company, Brownsville, Pa.

MEMBERSHIP COMMITTEE:

WILLIAM R. GELLATLY, Chairman, Pres., Superior Railway Products Corp., Pgh., Pa.
T. E. BRITT, Vice Chairman, Division Storekeeper, B. & O. R. R. Co., Pittsburgh, Pa.
A. B. SEVERN, General Manager, A. Stucki Company, Pittsburgh, Pa.
W. P. BUFFINGTON, Traffic Manager, Pittsburgh Coal Company, Pittsburgh, Pa.
R. S. BULL, Supt. Power & Inclines, Pittsburgh Railways Co., N. S., Pittsburgh, Pa.
A. F. COULTER, Master Car Builder, Union Railroad Co., East Pittsburgh, Pa.
T. R. DICKINSON, Purchasing Agent, B. & L. E. R. R. Co., Pittsburgh, Pa.
D. K. ORR, Road Master, Monongahela Railway Co., Brownsville, Pa.
C. M. WHEELER, Sales Engineer, Union Switch & Signal Company, Swissvale, Pa.
A. C. POLLOCK, District Sales Manager, Jones & Laughlin Steel Corp., Pittsburgh, Pa.
W. F. AMBROSE, Master Mechanic, Aliquippa & Southern Railroad, Aliquippa, Pa.
JOHN I. MULVEY, Traffic Manager, Hubbard & Company, Pittsburgh, Pa.
THOMAS R. FITZPATRICK, Freight Traffic Mgr., P. & L. E. R. R. Co., Pittsburgh, Pa.
P. W. HEPBURN, Sales Engineer, Gulf Refining Company, Pittsburgh, Pa.
W. B. MOIR, Chief Car Inspector, Pennsylvania Railroad, Pittsburgh, Pa.
C. W. TRUST, Assistant Traffic Manager, Carnegie-Illinois Steel Corp., Pittsburgh, Pa

PAST PRESIDENTS:

*J. H. McCONNELL	October, 1901, to October, 1903
*L. H. TURNER	November, 1903, to October, 1905
*F. H. STARK	November, 1905, to October, 1907
*H. W. WATTS	November, 1907, to April, 1908
*D. J. REDDING	November, 1908, to October, 1910
*F. R. McFEATTERS	November, 1910, to October, 1912
*A. G. MITCHELL	November, 1912, to October, 1914
*F. M. McNULTY	November, 1914, to October, 1916
*J. G. CODE	November, 1916, to October, 1917
*D. M. HOWE	November, 1917, to October, 1918
*J. A. SPIELMAN	November, 1918, to October, 1919
H. H. MAXFIELD	November, 1919, to October, 1920
FRANK J. LANAHAN	November, 1920, to October, 1921
SAMUEL LYNN	November, 1921, to October, 1922
D. F. CRAWFORD	November, 1922, to October, 1923
GEO. D. OGDEN	November, 1923, to October, 1924
A. STUCKI	November, 1924, to October, 1925
F. G. MINNICK	November, 1925, to October, 1926
G. W. WILDIN	November, 1926, to October, 1927
E. J. DEVANS	November, 1927, to October, 1928
W. S. McABEE	November, 1928, to October, 1929
E. W. SMITH	November, 1929, to October, 1930
LOUIS E. ENDSLEY	November, 1930, to October, 1931
*JOHN E. HUGHES	November, 1931, to October, 1932
F. I. SNYDER	November, 1932, to October, 1933
C. O. DAMBACH	November, 1933, to October, 1934
R. H. FLINN	November, 1934, to October, 1935

*—Deceased.

Meetings held fourth Thursday of each month except June, July and August

PROCEEDINGS OF MEETING
DECEMBER 19, 1935

The meeting was called to order at the Fort Pitt Hotel at 8:00 o'clock P. M., with President R. P. Forsberg in the chair.

Registered attendance, 286, as follows:

MEMBERS

Adams, Frank W.
Aivalotis, John
Allison, John
Ambrose, W. F.
Arnold, J. J.
Aulbach, A. J.
Babcock, F. H.
Baker, J. B.
Batchelar, E. C.
Beam, E. J.
Beattie, J. A.
Beatty, Raymond N.
Beeson, H. L.
Betlz, J. D.
Best, D. A.
Beswick, R. M.
Blair, John R.
Brahm, Donald P.
Britt, T. E.
Buffington, W. P.
Burel, W. C.
Butcher, F. M.
Campbell, F. R.
Carey, C. D.
Carlson, H. E.
Carmody, J. J.
Carroll, D. C.
Carruthers, G. R.
Carter, S. T.
Chaffin, H. B.
Chilcoat, H. E.
Code, C. J.
Conway, J. D.
Crawford, A. B.
Cree, W. M.
Crenner, J. A.
Cunningham, J. D.
Daugherty, W. A.
Davis, Charles S.
Day, T. R.
Dean, W. A.

Dennis, J. G.
Devine, J. C.
Dickinson, B. F.
Dierker, R. H.
Diven, J. B.
Doggett, A. L.
Downing, J. A.
Egbert, J. A.
Emery, E.
Endsley, Prof. Louis E.
Fair, J. M.
Farlow, G. B.
Ferguson, R. G.
Fike, J. W.
Fitzgerald, T.
Flinn, R. H.
Follett, W. F.
Forsberg, R. P.
Fox, M. C.
Fralic, C. F.
Frauenheim, A. M.
Frauenheim, Pierce H.
Freshwater, F. H.
Friend, Edward F.
Fry, L. H.
Furch, George J.
Gardner, George R.
Gauvey, Fred J.
Gellatly, William R.
George, W. J.
Gilg, Henry F.
Gillespie, J. Porter
Glaser, C. J.
Glaser, J. P.
Glenn, J. H.
Goda, P. H.
Goodwin, A. E.
Gray, M. L.
Greek, Joseph
Grieve, Robert E.
Grunden, B. C.

Haller, C. T.
Haller, Nelson M.
Hamsher, W. E.
Hankey, E. B.
Hansen, William C.
Harter, Arnold
Hayward, C.
Hellriegel, W. H.
Higginbottom, S. B.
Hilstrom, A. V.
Hodges, A. H.
Holmes, J. R.
Honsberger, G. W.
Hoover, J. W.
Hopper, George
Hornefius, S. R.
Huber, H. G.
Huff, A. B.
Huston, F. T.
Hutchinson, G. C., Jr.
Hykes, W. H.
Irwin, R. D.
Jennings, A. S.
Johnson, J. W.
Johnson, W. M.
Keck, L. M.
Kentlein, John
Kimling, Karl
Kirk, W. B.
Knable, G. Elkins
Kraus, Raymond E.
Krause, H. A.
Kroske, J. F.
Larson, W. E.
Layng, F. R.
Lee, L. A.
Litty, J. H.
Long, R. M.
Longstreth, W. L.
Mahaney, A. R.
Masterman, T. W.
Mayer, L. I.
Megee, C. R.
Menaglia, V. A.
Misner, George W.
Mitchell, F. K.
Mitchell, W. S.
Moir, W. B.
Morgan, A. L.
Morgan, Homer C.
Moore, D. O.
Morris, W. F., Jr.

Moser, G. B.
Mulligan, Michael
McCormick, E. S.
McGeorge, D. W.
McHail, J. L.
McIntyre, R. C.
McKay, N. H.
McKim, Hollis
McKinley, John T.
McLaughlin, H. B.
McOsker, C. T.
McPherson, A. R.
McQuiston, C. A.
McWilliams, J. B.
Nagel, James
Newman, S. A.
Nichols, Samuel A.
Nies, E. L.
O'Leary, J. J.
O'Toole, J. L.
Palmer, E. A.
Peirce, W. B.
Phillips, Robert A.
Posteraro, S. F.
Pringle, Paul V.
Purchard, Paul
Quinn, W. P.
Rauschart, E. A.
Record, J. F.
Reed, M. R.
Reeve, George J.
Reifsnyder, J. W.
Renshaw, W. B.
Rizzo, C. M.
Roberts, E. L.
Robertson, A. S.
Rodkey, C. C.
Roney, H. E.
Rowles, H. N.
Rutter, H. E.
Schadt, A. D.
Semmer, M. R.
Sersch, J. G.
Servais, Francis W.
Shafer, J. S.
Shellenbarger, H. M.
Sheridan, T. F.
Shingledecker, J. C.
Showalter, Joseph
Shull, George S.
Shumaker, John W.
Sixsmith, G. M.

Snyder, F. I.
Stevenson, H. J.
Stevenson, R. F.
Stoffregen, Louis E.
Strople, George H.
Stucki, A.
Sullivan, P. W.
Sutherland, Lloyd
Swope, B. M.
Taylor, H. D.
Ternent, H. J.
Terry, Edward
Teufel, W. O.
Thornton, A. W.
Tracey, J. B. A.
Trax, L. R.
Tryon, I. D.
Unger, John S.

Van Blarcom, W. C.
Van Nort, C. W.
Van Wormer, G. M.
Vollmer, Karl L.
Walter, E. R.
Walton, W. K.
Warfel, John A.
Weaver, W. Frank
Weis, Frank E.
West, G. S.
West, Troy
Westerman, M. A.
Wilkinson, W. E.
Wilson, J. M.
Wilson, James R.
Wilson, W. Stuart, Jr.
Wyke, J. W.
Yohe, J. K., Jr.

VISITORS

Aulbach, R.
Beck, Robert A.
Bennett, M. E.
Bessinger, H. L.
Bogovek, Joseph
Bouchat, Louis
Brown, R. J.
Buchanan, F. K.
Burd, William J.
Burrel, J. C.
Carson, C. E.
Carter, J. D.
Chapman, W. K.
Chase, D. K.
Connelly, W. G.
Croft, James M.
Dankmyer, F. C.
Davis, I. L.
Dawe, G. E.
Durham, C. W.
Emery, J. E.
Fitzgerald, T., Jr.
Floyd, Alfred
Gaines, Alva.
Hibbert, Charles
Hibner, A. J.
Houston, H. A.
Jungk, H. G.
King, William R.
Kearfott, W. E.
Kouche, N. J.
Latshaw, T. R.

Lewis, S. B.
Lincoln, R. B.
Longstreth, Wendell L.
Mackinsen, R. W.
Maxwell, T.
Montgomery, D. B.
Myers, B. E.
McDonald, Robert H.
McPherson, K. W.
Neubert, J. V.
O'Toole, C. R.
Parsons, W. V.
Pederson, M. A.
Prendergast, A. P.
Quinn, J. J.
Ramsey, Dennis W.
Reymer, R. E.
Richards, J.
Robinson, H. J.
Seidell, D. W.
Sherron, John P.
Shoemaker, P.
Sixsmith, W. L.
Smith, Sion B.
Strable, Clarence W.
Thomas, C. H. !
Turner, Fred F.
Ward, Howard E.
Ward, N. H.
Warner, R. H.
Weis, Mrs. Frank E.
Zell, H. A.

Before the business meeting was taken up a very enthusiastic community sing was led by Mr. Frank E. Weis, with the assistance of Mrs. Weis at the piano. At the conclusion of the sing President Forsberg expressed to Mr. and Mrs. Weis the pleasure and appreciation of the Club for their assistance.

PRESIDENT FORSBERG: Our first order of business is the roll call. If we proceeded to call the roll it would be necessary for Secretary Conway to read 1,157 names. I am sure the Secretary does not want to do this, and I am equally sure you do not want him to do it. You placed your names on the registration cards and deposited them with the Reception Committee at the door when you came in this evening, and your attendance at the meeting, therefore, will be duly recorded. We will, therefore, dispense with the roll call.

Reading of the Minutes of the last meeting is next in order. The printed Proceedings of the November meeting have been mailed to each one of our members, so it will not be necessary to read the Minutes of the last meeting.

The next order of business is the reading of the list of proposals for membership. Following the same form of procedure we employed at the last meeting, I will ask the Secretary to read the names of those proposed for membership in our Club, and when he has completed the reading of the names I will ask all those in the room, whose names have been read, to kindly stand and give their names, so we can correlate the name and the face and be able to call you by name the next time we see you.

SECREARY: We have the following proposals for membership:

Anderegg, G. W., Electrician, P. & L. E. R. R., 814 Freeland Street, Pittsburgh, Pa. Recommended by George Dittman.

Armstrong, J. L., Foreman P. P. & Elec., Pennsylvania Railroad, 2 Grandview Avenue, Crafton, Pittsburgh, Pa. Recommended by W. B. Moir.

Arnold, C. C., Water Service Inspector, P. & L. E. R. R., Room 506 Terminal Building, Pittsburgh, Pa. Recommended by G. H. Burnette.

Boyd, John R., Designing Engineer, P. & L. E. R. R., Room 506 Terminal Building, Pittsburgh, Pa. Recommended by G. H. Burnette.

Burkhart, G. A., Engine House Foreman, Monongahela Railway Company, Box 97, Hiller, Pa. Recommended by H. L. Beeson.

Cable, H. E., District Engineer, National Aluminate Corporation, 150 South Euclid Avenue, Bellevue, Pittsburgh, Pa. Recommended by E. A. Rauschart.

Christy, W. A., Assistant Chief Clerk, P. & L. E. R. R., 299 Fifteenth Street, Monaca, Pa. Recommended by W. E. Davin.

Creighton, D. M., Engineers Field Man, P. & L. E. R. R. Co., Kennedy Place, New Brighton, Pa. Recommended by A. W. Thornton.

Deakins, H. H., Chief Clerk, Superintendent Freight Transportation, Pennsylvania Railroad, Pennsylvania Station, Pittsburgh, Pa. Recommended by W. B. Moir.

Dean, William A., Signal Supervisor, P. & L. E. R. R., 1515 Grandin Avenue, Dormont, Pittsburgh, Pa. Recommended by Harry E. Roney.

Diettrich, John J., President, J. J. Diettrich & Son, 417 Chartiers Avenue, McKees Rocks, Pa. Recommended by H. B. Kelly.

Dillon, Arthur L., Engineer Computer, P. & L. E. R. R., 77 Hawthorne Avenue, Crafton, Pittsburgh, Pa. Recommended by M. Z. Balph.

Dittman, George, General Foreman, P. & L. E. R. R., 100 Roycraft Avenue, Mt. Lebanon, Pittsburgh, Pa. Recommended by R. M. Long.

Donovan, Lawrence T., Car Inspector, Pennsylvania Railroad, 146 Noble Avenue, Crafton, Pittsburgh, Pa. Recommended by W. B. Moir.

Duffley, F. M., Machinery Inspector, P. & L. E. R. R., 902 Liberty Street, McKees Rocks, Pa. Recommended by George Dittman.

Edwards, H. F., Road Foreman of Engines, Monongahela Railway Company, South Brownsville, Pa. Recommended by H. L. Beeson.

Emery, L. F., General Foreman, P. & L. E. R. R., 180 Marion Avenue, Struthers, Ohio Recommended by W. E. Davin.

Forsyth, D. B., Chief Clerk to Engineer Maintenance of Way, P. & L. E. R. R., P&LE Terminal Building, Pittsburgh, Pa. Recommended by W. E. Davin

Galbraith, James R., Fire Marshal, P. & L. E. R. R, 500 Rossmore Avenue, Brookline, Pittsburgh, Pa. Recommended by F. T. Sladden.

Goodwin, A. E, Tool Designer, Westinghouse Electric & Manufacturing Co., 602 Marion Avenue, Forest Hills, Wilkinsburg, Pa. Recommended by A. V. Hilstrom.

Haase, L. R., District Boiler Inspector, B. & O. R. R. Co., 324 Ashton Street, Hazelwood, Pittsburgh, Pa. Recommended by T. E. Britt

Haser, A J., Funeral Director, 512 Chartiers Avenue, McKees Rocks, Pa. Recommended by H. B. Kelly.

Herring, John R, Conductor, P. & L. E. R. R., Moredale Street, South Hills Branch, Pittsburgh, Pa. Recommended by M. Murphy

Irvin, Robert K., Conductor, P. & L. E. R. R, 427 South Main Street, Pittsburgh, Pa. Recommended by M. Murphy.

Johnston, J. T., Clerk, P. & L. E. R. R, 1418 Fourth Street, Beaver Falls, Pa. Recommended by H. R. Richardson.

John, William, Freight Claim Agent, P. & L. E. R. R. Co., 202 Dewey Street, Edgewood, Swissvale P. O., Pa. Recommended by F. T. Sladden.

Kamerer, R. W., General Agent, P. & L. E. R. R Co., Terminal Building, Pittsburgh, Pa. Recommended by F. T. Sladden.

Kleber, P. C., Gang Leader, P. & L. E. R. R. Co., 603 Eighth Street, McKees Rocks, Pa. Recommended by George Dittman

Kroen, Vincent, Supervisor Express Service, Pennsylvania Railroad, Pennsylvania Station, Pittsburgh, Pa. Recommended by W. B. Moir.

Langhurst, R O., Gang Leader, P. & L. E. R. R. Co, 1502 Orchlee Street, N. S., Pittsburgh, Pa Recommended by George Dittman.

Lavine, Ralph D., Chief Rate and Division Clerk, P. & L. E. R. R. Co., 324 Ophelia Street, Pittsburgh, Pa. Recommended by F. J. Kennedy

Lunz, G. J., Chief Clerk, Freight Traffic Department, P. & L. E. R R. Co., Terminal Building, Pittsburgh, Pa. Recommended by F. T. Sladden

Macdonald, George F., Chief Clerk to Chief Engineer, P. & L. E. R. R. Co., Pittsburgh, Pa. Recommended by R. P. Forsberg.

Mayer, George E., Photographer, P. & L. E. R. R. Co., Terminal Annex Building, Pittsburgh, Pa. Recommended by G. H. Burnette.

Moser, G. B., Clerk, Pittsburgh, Chartiers & Youghiogheny Railway Company, P&LE Terminal Annex Building, Pittsburgh, Pa. Recommended by R. P. Forsberg.

Murphy, Martin, General Yard Master, P. & L. E. R R Co., 316 Jucunda Street, Knoxville, Pittsburgh, Pa. Recommended by R. M. Long.

Murray, Thomas A., Stenographer, P. & L E. R. R. Co, Terminal Building, Pittsburgh, Pa. Recommended by W. E. Davin.

McBride, Gordon P., Supervisors Field Man, P. & L. E. R. R. Co, Terminal Building, Pittsburgh, Pa. Recommended by W E. Davin.

McCowin, John, Signal Supervisor, P. & L. E. R. R. Co., 236 Ann Street, McKeesport, Pa. Recommended by I. S. Raymer

Nelson, King R. H, Assistant Director of Exhibits, American Sheet & Tin Plate Company, Morrowfield Apartments, Pittsburgh, Pa. Recommended by Karl Berg

Nies, E. L., Chief Clerk, Railway Express Agency, 926 Penn Avenue, Pittsburgh, Pa Recommended by C. A. McQuiston.

Obley, J. S., File Clerk, P. & L. E. R. R. Co., Terminal Building, Pittsburgh, Pa. Recommended by A. W. Thornton.

Phillips, Robert A., Purchasing Agent, Safety First Supply Company, Glenfield, Pa. Recommended by John S. Shafer.

Phillips, T. H., Boiler Maker, P. & L. E. R. R. Co., 632 Woodward Avenue, McKees Rocks, Pa. Recommended by George Dittman.

Robinson, G. H., Machinery Inspector, P. & L. E. R. R. Co., 531 Chatauqua Street, Pittsburgh, Pa. Recommended by George Dittman.

Robison, Ernest N., District Passenger Agent, P. & L. E. R. R. Co., Terminal Building, Pittsburgh, Pa Recommended by F. T. Sladden.

Rogers, Robert E., Coal Freight Representative, P. & L. E. R. R Co., Terminal Building, Pittsburgh, Pa. Recommended by F. T. Sladden.

Rohyans, A. V., Clerk, Pennsylvania Railroad, 262 Center Avenue, Emsworth, Pittsburgh, Pa. Recommended by W. B. Moir.

Sanner, B. H., Clerk, P. & L. E. R. R. Co., Terminal Building, Pittsburgh, Pa. Recommended by W. E. Davin.

Seidel, John, Jr., Chief Clerk, P. & L. E. R. R. Co., Terminal Building, Pittsburgh, Pa Recommended by G. H. Burnette.

Simpson, Clifford E., Assistant General Freight Agent, P. & L. E R. R. Co., 329 Stratford Avenue, Pittsburgh (6), Pa. Recommended by F. T. Sladden.

Sipe, C. P., Supervisor, Pennsylvania Railroad, Federal Street Station, N. S., Pittsburgh, Pa. Recommended by C. M. Wheeler.

Smith, E. E., General Passenger Agent, P. & L. E. R. R. Co., Terminal Building, Pittsburgh, Pa. Recommended by F. T. Sladden.

Stapleton, H. B., General Agent, P. & L. E. R. R. Co., Brownsville, Pa. Recommended by F. T. Sladden.

Stephens, E. C., Conductor, Pennsylvania Railroad, 1613 Alverado Avenue, Pittsburgh, Pa. Recommended by R. N. Beatty.

Stewart, C. G., Leading Draftsman, P. & L. E. R. R. Co., Wildwood, Pa Recommended by G. H. Burnette.

Taggart, J. G., Transitman, P. & L. E. R. R. Co., 719 Thirty-fifth Street, Beaver Falls, Pa. Recommended by G. H. Burnette.

Terry, Edward, Salesman, Safety First Supply Company, Brady Building, Pittsburgh, Pa. Recommended by A. E. Herrold.

Von Pein, A. N., Assistant Traffic Manager, Oliver Iron & Steel Corporation, 1001 Muriel Street, S. S., Pittsburgh, Pa. Recommended by T. E. Britt.

Ward, Norval H., Air Brake Instructor, P. & L. E. R. R. Co., 3031 Glenmawr Avenue, Pittsburgh, Pa. Recommended by H. B. Kelly.

Weniger, Oscar S., Sales Engineer, Electric Storage Battery Company, Union Trust Building, Pittsburgh, Pa. Recommended by I. S. Raymer.

Williamson, E. F., Movement Director, Superintendent Passenger Transportation, Pennsylvania Railroad, 609 Dick Street, Carnegie, Pa. Recommended by W. B. Moir.

Following the reading of the list, the new members were formally received.

SECRETARY: Since our last meeting we have received information of the death of one of our members; C. A. Croft, Salesman, A. M. Byers Company, Pittsburgh, Pa., died November 25, 1935.

PRESIDENT: In accordance with our customary procedure, an appropriate memorial will appear in the next issue of the Proceedings.

I have been requested to read this notice:

The musical group of the Railway Club expects to organize again this year and would like to have the names of all those members who have any musical ability. This includes those who play musical instruments as well as singers. Will you please give your names to any of the members of the Entertainment Commiteee or to any of the Club officers, so that we can notify you of our meetings.

On Tuesday last, Mr. Gellatly, Chairman, and Mr. Britt, Vice Chairman, held a meeting of the Membership Committee, and discussed from Alpha to Omega the question of securing new members for our Club. The Membership Committee recognizes the fact that the basic or fundamental purpose of the Club is not to build a mammoth membership, but it feels that it is the responsibility of that Committee to secure new members for our organization.

And so, despite the fact that the field has been pretty well canvassed, the Committee set a goal and decided that it would strive to increase the enrollment of our Club to 1,500 members by October 31, 1936. Such an enrollment will make it easier for Mr. Foard to secure desirable advertisers, reduce the cost per number of printing our Proceedings, make it easier for our Subject Committee to secure desirable speakers, and many other real advantages to our Club in which we all take a pardonable pride. Mr. Gellatly is with us and I will ask him to say a few words relative to his plans.

MR. W. R. GELLATLY: I do not know whether you fellows all appreciate just what this 1,500 members will mean to this Club. Fifteen hundred members will put us ahead of several railroad clubs a lot older than we are and that is the goal that this Committee of which I have the honor to be Chairman is striving for. We of the Committee cannot see every person who might be a desirable member of this Club and you could help us a lot if you would give us the names of any persons you think might enjoy being a member. We are quite sure the good they will get out of this Club will be worth the amount of dues they pay, and our job will be a lot easier if each one of you will give the names of persons you think might take an interest and enjoy being here and we will surely enjoy having them. When these names occur to you just jot them down and hand them to us and we will contact them and sell them the Club.

Now about this goal of 1,500, I would like to make that a minimum. Let us go to 1,700 or 1,750. The reading of the list of these new members tonight shows what can be done. Sixty-two is a very fine showing and it will not take long to line up 1,500. If we can have the co-operation of you all we will certainly appreciate it.

PRESIDENT: We know that the attendance at our December meetings is usually very low, probably on account of the nearness of the holiday season. I recall that a year ago it was a stormy night, the weather was about as bad as we have tonight and we did not have the attendance we should

31

have had. Mr. McGeorge, Chairman of the Subject Committee, knowing the kind of program that had been prepared for tonight, the splendid speaker and the interesting subject, did not want a small attendance, so he undertook the Herculean task of writing a letter to every member of The Railway Club of Pittsburgh, a personal letter, 1,157 in all. Perhaps twenty or twenty-five per cent of the people replied to him, and I have had the privilege of reading those replies. I wish I could read some of them to you tonight. The general tenor of them was to thank Mr. McGeorge for bringing to their attention the fact that they had not of late been privileged to enjoy the associations of the Club. They said they would be more regular in attendance in the future and try to sell the Club to those who did not at the present time belong. One thing that attracted my attention was that fifteen or twenty per cent of the replies complimented the Railway Club on the departure from the established plan of discussing only railroad subjects and suggesting that it would be very acceptable to have an occasional discussion of some subject of general interest, not necessarily allied with the railroads.

In this large batch of letters there was one that Mr. McGeorge requested me to read an excerpt from. I am going to put one over on "Mac." and read the entire letter, though it was, of course, not intended that I do so.

"Dear Mr. Forsberg:

"Attached hereto is another consignment of replies to my circular letter of December 12th.

"I will confess that I am holding out on you to the extent that I am not sending one reply, which is the best of all, but there are some uncomplimentary remarks about me which I do not want to let get out. However, I am quoting below one paragraph of this letter and would suggest that you read it at the next meeting.

"'As to the activity of Past President, Mr. Rufus H. Flinn: That is what they tell all retiring Presidents—about the wonderful job they have done. In fact, I imagine that is what they will say about President Roosevelt twenty-five years from now, but at the present time they sure are giving him Hell.'"

I apologive to "Mac." for having read the letter in its entirety.

Gentlemen, I feel that I would stultify myself if I undertook to introduce to a Pittsburgh audience the gentleman who will favor us with an address this evening. The Railway Club has been especially fortunate in securing a man so well qualified to speak upon a subject that is quite apropos at the present time, and I am sure he will have your best interest and attention as he addresses us. We are to have the pleasure of listening to Mr. J. Steele Gow, Director of The Maurice and Laura Falk Foundation of Pittsburgh, who will speak upon the subject, "Income and Economic Progress." Mr. Gow:

INCOME AND ECONOMIC PROGRESS

By J. STEELE GOW, Director,
The Maurice and Laura Falk Foundation, Pittsburgh, Pa.

No intelligent citizen of the United States can have lived through the past six years without having a grave concern for the economic welfare of his country. The depression has been widespread and deep. Scarcely an individual has escaped its ravaging sweep. One would be hard put to it to find an institution that has not been jarred to its foundations by the quake-like tremors that have reached down to the roots of our economic order.

Fortunately, we now seem to be past the worst of it. On all sides there are signs of a recovery that promises to be more enduring than the short upturns that have offered us false encouragement at least twice during the past four years.

Although we recover, will we, it is fair to ask, be on solid ground for the long pull ahead? Will our recovery bring us to a sound basis for sustained progress, not for just a brief year or two but for an indefinite period? Or, is it true that the prosperity which we seem now to be approaching will be less enduring and less ample than it might be if we would but adjust some of our basic economic policies?

. These are fundamental questions. On the intelligence with which we attend to them depends in no small way the economic welfare of the generations which will follow us.

The extent of the public's concern about our national economic welfare has brought its full share of reformers who would radically revise the basic fundamentals of our economic system. Among them are many whose sincerity cannot be questioned, although their competence to advise us is, at the best, doubtful. Of these, none is more vociferous than the amateur economist who abounds in unusually large numbers today as a phenomenon of the current depression. He is ready, on the least provocation, to tell us precisely what is wrong and to provide a nice panacea to correct our economic ills and prevent their recurrence. He is emboldened to draw a master plan for our destiny because he has bothered so little to master a knowledge of the actual conditions under which the world's work is done. He knows so little of the inherent complications of the economic order that he is perfectly serene in offering us some formula which ignores the facts and is always as worthless and usually as dangerous as it is lacking in reality.

The sane commonsense of the American public has repudiated most of the wild plans of the amateur economist, but at the same time the public has often failed to differentiate between the amateur and the trained economist, who has a thorough understanding of our problems and our possibilities. In failing to differentiate between the doctrines of the two, the public has been the loser, for there is a sound body of economic knowledge that is priceless if we but accept its guidance.

Personally, I am most anxious to be exempt from the charge of appearing before you as an amateur economist, and I am equally anxious to make clear that I have no claim as a trained economist whose personal advice is worth your attention. My role is merely to present to you, in as brief compass as I can, a faithful resume of an important economic study, recently completed, whose findings are generally accredited with being sound doctrine for the years ahead. My task is complicated by the fact that I have only thirty minutes or so to give you the essence of this investigation, which required for its completion three years' work by a large staff of the nation's leading economists at the Brookings Institution in Washington, D. C., under a grant of funds from the Maurice and Laura Falk Foundation, of which I am the executive director.

May I make clear at the outset that as the director of the Falk Foundation, which provided the funds for the study, my task has been merely to see to it that the study was completed as expeditiously as the complex and difficult nature of its problem permitted. I neither performed nor directed the research. I, therefore, have no need to defend this study.

My function is merely to report it to you as faithfully as I know how.

Three years ago the Brookings Institution asked the Falk Foundation for an appropriation of $150,000 to study the question: What is the effect on the economic progress of the United States of the way in which the wealth and income of the nation are distributed? Is the distribution a reasonably even one, or is it grossly uneven, and what, in any case, is the effect of this distribution on our progress in the production of goods and services? In other words, is the distribution such as to impede our making full use of our productive capacity and, if so, what method or methods of adjustment promise to be the most helpful in overcoming the difficulty?

That this is a fundamental problem not only in depression times but also in good times is evidenced by industrial history, which shows clearly that even in our most prosperous years business enterprises seldom produce at full capacity. It is natural, then, to ask: Is there not some underlying difficulty in our present economic organization which accounts for this inefficiency in the operation of the system?

Granted that there is some underlying difficulty, public opinion has held divergent points of view as to its nature. One view holds that the center of the economic system is production—that in the long run we produce all that we are physically able to turn out and our consumption is determined simply by the amount of product of which the economic machine is capable. The opposite view contends that since consumers have unsatisfied wants at the same time that producers are suffering from the burden of excess capacity, the trouble must lie in the failure of the system to transmit purchasing power broadly to the masses.

The area marked off by these questions and these points of view are the field of the study. Obviously its scope made it necessary that the investigation be laid out in segments of manageable size and that each segment be substantially completed before the succeeding segment should be undertaken.

Time permits only a cursory description of the various segments into which the diagnostic stage of the study was divided. I wish to reserve the major portion of my time for a discussion of the prescription stage of the investigation.

The first segment was concerned with ascertaining the degree to which, under ordinary circumstances, we use our productive resources. The object was to make a realistic appraisal of our productive capacity in order to see whether or not we are, in the long run, producing all that we can. The results of this segment were published under the title "America's Capacity to Produce." The findings showed that in the most prosperous year we have had—1929—we utilized only about 80 per cent of our productive capacity. Further, the study showed that the margin between our productive capacity and the degree to which we used that capacity changed little, if at all, during the thirty-year period from 1900 to 1930. In short, then, we were not, during the gay twenties, overbuilding America. But, on the other hand, we have not during the past three decades made any substantial progress toward utilizing more fully our capacity to produce.

I should like to emphasize that this measurement of America's capacity to produce was a realistic measurement in the sense that it took into consideration and made allow- ances for such practical items as shutdowns for repair, the usual practices of industry respecting single or double shifts, seasonal fluctuations in the production of certain goods, etc. In other words, it was a measurement, in realistic terms, of the American industrial system as it actually exists, and it was not a Technocrat's estimate of what we might have pro- duced had all the conditions in industry been ideal and had we been able to put into operation without delay all the tech- nological improvements which are in the minds of men.

If, then, we were not producing all that we might have produced, were there any impediments or maladjustments within this productive mechanism itself which prevented our making 100 per cent use of it? The finding of the study was that there were no impediments or maladjustments in the productive mechanism as such. In other words, there was no impediment in the way of a shortage of raw materials, in- dustrial plant or equipment, power or fuel, transportation facilities, money or credit, or labor to act as a bottle-neck to hinder the flow of goods and services from producer to con- sumer.

In logical order, the next point of inquiry was whether there was any maladjustment between productive capacity and consumptive capacity which prevented our making full use of our productive mechanism. Here the findings of the study were that the great mass of the population had incomes which were insufficient for their primary requirements. In 1929, for instance, nearly 6 million families, or more than 21 per cent of all families in the United States, had incomes of less than $1,000; about 12 million families, or more than 42 per cent, had incomes of less than $1,500; nearly 20 million, or 71 per cent, had incomes of less than $2,500. Only a little more than 2 million families, or 8 per cent, had incomes in excess of $5,000, and about 600,000 families, or 2.3 per cent, had incomes in excess of $10,000. If $2,000 may be regarded as sufficient, at 1929 prices, to supply the basic necessities of a family—and this is a lower figure than the United States Government authorities suggest—we find that 16 million families, or about 60 per cent of all families, were below this income level. $2,500 is a closer approach to what the government authorities say is the minimum for the basic necessities of a family. Simple arithmetic shows that if we were to raise to the $2,500 income level all families with incomes below that level—without making any changes above that level—the demands of these families for goods and services would have more than closed up the 20 per cent unutilized margin in our productive capacity. Here, then, was a challenging market for the goods America could have produced. A potential demand existed vastly greater than could have been supplied had we operated our economic system at full power. These facts and conclusion were published under the title of "America's Capacity to Consume."

From this point the study proceeded to an examination of the effect of this unequal distribution of income on the allocation of the total income of the nation as between spending for consumption and saving for investment. It was found that out of the $15,000,000,000 of individual savings in 1929 as much as $13,000,000,000 were made by 10 per cent of the population and, further, that the capacity of people to save increased very rapidly as their income level was raised. The figures showed that inasmuch as the number of people in the higher income groups was increasing throughout the period of the twenties the percentage of the national income which was being diverted into savings available for investment was increasing.

Naturally the next diagnostic step was to examine the question of whether or not the restricted flow of funds into consumption channels—as opposed to savings—resulting from this increasing tendency of the national income to distribute itself unequally served to impede the operation of the economic system. The study showed that the growth of new plant and equipment—which is, of course, our means of increasing our production and therefore of adding to our wealth ––is adjusted not to the volume of savings available for investment purposes but rather to the rate of increase of consumptive demand. In short, it was found that, on the one side, the flow of money into consumption channels was inadequate to call forth the full use of existing plant and equipment and that, on the other side, the flow of funds into savings available for investment was excessive and resulted in a spilling over in investment channels which helped to produce the security market boom whose ultimate collapse in 1929 was probably one of the important factors in precipitating the depression. These conclusions were published under the title of "The Formation of Capital."

Putting together these diagnostic steps as they were developed, stage by stage, in the three publications—"America's Capacity to Produce," "America's Capacity to Consume," and "The Formation of Capital"—we may draw these two basic conclusions:

1. The unbalanced distribution of income and the consequent restricted flow of purchasing power through consumption channels explains our inability to find markets adequate to absorb the full output of our productive establishment.

2. The slow rate of growth of consumptive demand has served to retard the rate at which new capital is constructed and hence the rate of economic progress, because it is only as we make full use of our present capacity and then create a larger and still larger capacity that we shall progress as a wealth-producing nation. In the long run, America's economic progress is to be measured by a more and more complete use of a growing capacity to produce essential goods and services.

If then, this is the diagnosis, what are the possible lines of progress? By what means might the flow of the income stream to the various groups in society be modified so as to expand progressively an effective demand for consumption goods and hence call forth an even greater volume of production than we have yet realized? The answer to this question is attempted in the fourth and final volume of the study published in September under the title of "Income and Economic Progress."

The public's concern about this question and its hunger for a solution has given us in recent days plenty of advocates of the so-called "share-the-wealth" movements. However, the Brookings Institution study showed that a mere redistribution of the income of society would not at all accomplish the desired results. In the most prosperous year we have had, an absolutely equal distribution of the income of the nation would have given each of us about $665. If all the income derived from investments in 1929 and, in addition, all the salaries received by corporation officials had been conscripted and distributed to the masses, the per capita income would have been increased by only about $140. It is obvious that the effect of such redistribution is so small as to be of almost negligible significance.

The important thing—let me emphasize this—is to increase progressively the total amount of income available for distribution. Let me say it again—the important thing is not a redistribution of existing income but the progressive increase of the total amount of income available for distribution. The distribution of income from year to year is of significance not so much for its momentary effects on the wellbeing of the masses as for its possible cumulative effects in promoting a fuller use of our productive capacity and a consequent increase in the aggregate income which is available for division.

If a mere redistribution of existing income is not the way out, where shall we turn? This study showed clearly that there is no easy formula in the way of a quick panacea, but that there are, on the other hand, several ways of gradual progress. Although these ways are of unequal merit, they all have values to commend them.

In general, there are two methods of bringing about a different division of income—the one direct and the other indirect. The direct method involves a modification of the income stream at its source—that is in the disbursing offices of business enterprises. The indirect method involves an unmodified initial distribution and then a subsequent redistribution.

Taxation is a good example of the indirect method and is the method advocated by many people. With respect to taxation, however, the study reached the conclusion that though it has a place in a program for redistributing income, it is not entitled to a place of primary or fundamental importance.

It is true that through the years taxation has played a role in raising the standard of living of the masses through providing free services in the way of education, recreation, public health, etc. But the important point is that many of the types of public expenditures made from tax funds are not of great significance to the masses because they do not increase the output of basic necessities of which the masses are in need primarily. Public expenditures of tax receipts in the form of public works—which is the thing usually proposed by advocates of taxation as a means of distributing income—will not solve the problem so long as widespread underconsumption of basic necessities exists. Furthermore, the burden imposed on the general taxpayer has become very large and is increasing cumulatively as new public enterprises are completed. As a rule, public enterprises pay no taxes and yield no revenues, and as the tax-free public property increases, the tax burden on private industry becomes progressively heavier. If in the future we are to provide public enterprises to reduce unemployment, we must either adopt the policy of constructing only self-liquidating enterprises or face the alternative of steadily increasing the tax burdens on a relatively stationary volume of private business. Of course, it is clear that the financial exigencies arising out of the depression have been of such magnitude that the great problem for the next few years will be to maintain financial equilibrium.

Let me turn now to the direct methods of distributing income. Here there are two principal alternatives. The first is the increase of money wages without proportionate increase of prices. The second is the reduction of prices without a proportionate reduction in wages.

By and large, public interest has been focused chiefly on the wage-increase method. Therefore, let us give it first consideration. The study examined very exhaustively the possibilities of this method and concluded that it is subject to several very definite limitations. In the first place, the wage-method of distributing the benefits of technological progress would extend to not more than 40 per cent of the population. The income of the other 60 per cent is not in the form of wages. In particular, our farm population, whose inadequate purchasing power has been one of the most critical points in our whole problem, would be helped but little by the wage-increase method. In sum, then, though the wage-increase method can help and has over a long period of years had some influence, it cannot reach the bulk of our population and even for those it can reach its process is so slow and gradual that it is scarcely to be depended on as the primary way of bringing about the increase of production which is the measure of our economic progress.

We return now to the other principal alternative, which is price reduction—that is reducing the prices of goods without proportionate reduction of wages. Here, the study's analysis showed, the entire population will benefit. The price-reduction method will not only add to the purchasing power of labor-employee groups but it will also increase the real income of the non-wage urban population and of the farm population as well. Further, since the benefits are distributed throughout the entire economic system, a better balance will be maintained among the different divisions of our economic system. As an added advantage, it is obvious that this method —price reduction—would help us in competition for foreign trade. Again, the price-reduction method would do much to avoid precipitating those labor-capital disputes which usually mark the wage-raising method.

It is of high importance, though, to remember that when price reductions are effected through cutting wages, the benefits are to a large degree nullified. The essential thing is the spread between wages and prices. While this spread might be increased either by raising wages without raising prices or by price reductions without cutting wages, the study's conclusion is that the most beneficial way, from a national point of view, of widening that spread is by the price-reduction method.

It is interesting to note that the general theory underlying the capitalistic system of production and distribution which prevails in this country clearly recognizes the necessity of an ever-expanding mass purchasing power in order to absorb the expanding capacity of the productive establishment. The findings of this study are not so much a new truth, then, as they are a confirmation of the soundness of some of the basic principles on which our capitalistic economy rests. The study's conclusion is, therefore, a chart of economic progress without economic revolution. To make the point clear, let me quote Dr. Moulton's description of the principles on which the capitalistic system rests:

"First, it is pointed out that under a system operated for private profit each business manager naturally seeks to reduce costs by increasing the efficiency of production. He may accomplish this by the construction of a larger and more efficient plant, by the installment of improved equipment, by the introduction of superior internal management, by improved methods of marketing, by integrating various stages in the productive process, or by a combination of various methods.

"Second, having reduced costs of production, he is in a position to increase his profits in one or another of two ways. He may continue to sell at the same price as before, enjoying the advantage of a wider margin between cost and selling prices; or he may expand the volume of his business by means of price concessions. It was reasoned that since the increase in efficiency which is responsible for the reduction in costs commonly involves an expansion of productive capacity, and since the maximum economies can be obtained when operating at full capacity, the greatest profits will result if the output is expanded by means of a reduction in prices. The wise alternative, then, is to expand sales by offering the products at a low price.

"In short, increased efficiency makes possible lower prices, while the profit incentive insures the actual reduction of prices. The greatest profit to the business enterpriser is thus derived through giving to the masses the most for their money. The interest of the profit-maker therefore coincides with the welfare of the community.

"Third, the process naturally involves the continuous elimination of obsolescent or otherwise inefficient, high cost, or marginal establishments. The fit, as gauged by ability to sell at a minimum price, alone survive; moreover, the efficient of today promptly become the inefficient of tomorrow. A particular business man, firm, or corporation may indeed survive over a long period of years, but only if the production methods employed keep always abreast of changing times. Note that this theory of progress requires the maintenance of money wages—for if they are not maintained, the real purchasing power or income of the laboring class will not be expanded. The reduction of prices which is significant is that reduction which results from increased productive efficiency."

Though these principles have stood the test of the most critical judgment of experts, the fact is that in the actual operation of our business system these principles have not always been adhered to. On this point, I should like again to quote Dr. Moulton:

"First, the importance of maintaining the general level of wages as a part of the process has too often been forgotten. The individual business manager is naturally tempted to cut wages as a means of reducing costs, but if all business men cut wages as a means of reducing costs and ˙selling prices, they would not thereby expand the purchasing power of the wage-earning population. Labor is more than a commodity. It is a consumer.

"Second, instead of reducing prices as a means of expanding markets, there has been a growing tendency to maintain prices and let well enough alone."

The growing tendency to retard price reductions has been the result largely of certain developments in our industrial history, notably the growth of the unified monopoly or industrial combination under a single management, the cartel and the trade association. Often the tendency of these organizations is to make prices inflexible and let production be adjusted to a fixed price structure. When this adjustment means the curtailment of production, it is obviously a brake against the creation of additional wealth and an impediment, therefore, to economic progress.

The decade of the twenties gives us a clear picture of the results of inflexible-price policies. This was a period of remarkable technological advancement. Both the amount of capital and the efficiency of its use increased in nearly all lines of production. However, the benefits of this increased efficiency were not automatically passed on to the masses of consumers either through the medium of proportionate wage increases or proportionate price reductions. During the period wholesale prices of manufactured commodities declined a scant 5 per cent, but retail prices did not decline at all. In some lines of industry there were, of course, substantial decreases of prices, but in other lines there were substantial increases, and in still other lines virtually no changes at all.

What did business men do during this period when they found themselves faced with productive capacity in excess of existing consumer demand at the fixed price level they had set? The study points out that, in general, business men pursued one or more of the following policies:

1. They attempted to stimulate consumptive desire through extensive advertising campaigns.

2. They attempted to stimulate consumptive demand by sales on the installment plan.

3. They attempted to stimulate consumption by sales in foreign markets.

Now what was the value of these efforts, so far as their effect on stimulating the increased production of wealth is concerned?

Well, it is clear that competitive advertising could do little to increase the aggregate consumptive demands of the masses, since it did not increase their purchasing power, and we must remember that the volume of their savings which could be diverted to consumption was of negligible significance. In the case of installment selling, we can see that it would give a bulge to immediate purchases, but it is clear that it would not increase the aggregate purchasing power over a period of years. Even a casual analysis of the export device shows that exports can be expanded relatively to imports only so long as foreign credits are extended.

What came largely to be ignored by business men during this period was the remaining alternative—that of expanding the market for all the great necessities and conveniences of life through a reduction of prices. Instead of trying to put additional consumptive power back of new additions to productive power, as the capitalistic theory presupposes, business sought, by and large, to maintain the price structure by stabilizing existing conditions. The result of this policy was not only to curtail economic expansion but also to sow the seeds of economic instability for the future.

Naturally the question will be raised: Is not price stability essential to the welfare of business? Does not price-cutting inevitably tear down the business structure and demoralize the markets and thus do vastly more harm than good? In answering this question, we must distinguish carefully between the conditions which prevail in a period of an acute depression and those which exist in prosperous times. When in a period of depression prices in general are falling sharply, with each new decline intensifying business uncertainty, further price reductions clearly do not constitute a remedy for the existing demoralization. Stabilization at some point has to be achieved before recovery can begin. It is the vivid experience of business men with such destructive price warfare in disorganized periods of general deflation that has made them so fearful of general price reductions.

In a period of prosperity, on the other hand, a reduction of prices made possible by improvement in productive efficiency need have no such demoralizing effects. From the very nature of the case, price reductions under such conditions would be gradual in character and, since they would not be accompanied by either a restriction of output or a decrease in buying power, the stability to which they would contribute would be of an enduring character.

It is an unpleasant but true charge to say that industrial policy which focuses merely on the maintenance of an existing favorable situation is usually a shortsighted policy. The maintenance of the status quo in prices is a barrier to progress. As a general principle, it is safe to say that unless wage increases or other offsetting factors intervene, economic growth is measured by the extent to which prices are reduced.

In the consideration of this doctrine, one matter that will greatly bother business men is the effect of price reductions on profits. The reduction of prices during a period of increasing technological improvements will not destroy profits for businesses which are increasing their efficiency. If the reduction of prices is matched by increases in efficiency, which means a reduction in costs, it is obvious that the margin of profits is not affected adversely. On the contrary, insofar as the reduction of prices expands purchasing power and permits a larger volume of sales, the unit cost of production is reduced and profits increase.

The interrelation of volume of production, unit costs, and profits is of high importance in the consideration of the policy advocated by this study. To assume that the cost of production is something that is definitely fixed by the existing costs of labor, materials, etc., is too broad an assumption. In view of the overhead cost factor, unit costs decline with the increase in volume, even though the direct expenses remain unchanged. Accordingly, there are two ways by which costs may be reduced; first, by increased efficiency in the productive process and, second, by reaping the advantages inherent in capacity operation. It follows that if the latter type of gain is to be realized, the policy of price reductions must be an aggressive and not a lagging one. In other words, price reductions should not be delayed until reductions in cost are clearly established. Industrial history teaches that those enterprises which rapidly install more efficient equipment and aggressively endeavor to expand the volume of business through lower prices need have no fear on the score of profits over the long run of years.

Let me now summarize succinctly the essential conclusions of this far-reaching study:

1. We have never lived beyond our economic means or capacity.

2. We have not been suffering from general overproduction.

3. We have not as yet reached a stage in our economic evolution at which it is possible to provide adequate standards of living for everybody.

4. It would require less than a 25% increase in purchasing power among the masses to absorb our full productive capacity.

5. Production curtailment programs — whatever their merit in meeting temporary maladjustments—can only lead to national impoverishment.

6. Our inability to find markets adequate to absorb the full output of our productive establishments is explained by the unequal distribution of income and consequent restricted flow of purchasing power through consumptive channels.

7. The slow rate of growth of consumptive demand serves to retard the rate at which new capital is constructed and hence the rate of economic progress.

8. The primary need is a rapidly expanding total income, and a broader diffusion of this income among the masses of the people.

9. A broader diffusion of income can best be achieved by reducing prices as rapidly as increasing efficiency will permit. That is to say, the benefits of technological progress, mass production, and low unit costs must be promptly passed on to consumers in the form of lower prices—giving more for each dollar.

10. The successful operation of the economic system requires that back of each new unit of productive power there be placed a corresponding unit of consumer power. The economies of mass production cannot be realized unless we have corresponding mass consumption.

This problem with all its implications—I have touched on only a few of those that are covered in the study—is the problem of the American business man. To those who are most intelligently concerned with our economic future, it seems clear that on the way the American business man meets this issue will depend largely the future of private business initiative in this country. If the private business system fails to provide that broad distribution of purchasing power on which not only the welfare of the masses but also the prosperity of the business system itself depends, then it is almost certain that we shall have increasing efforts on the part of the government to exercise control over the activities of business. If we are to avoid further inroads of government into business and preserve the capitalistic system of economy, then it is up to our business leaders to see that the system in its operation adheres to the principles on which it is based. They must show courage as well as intelligence in the development and application of a price policy which will create and sustain a purchasing power ample to take off the markets the goods we can produce.

Naturally the man of business, who is accustomed to concreteness in all his work, would like to have a detailed program for accomplishing the objectives here outlined. To his probable disappointment, it must be said that there is no single program for all industry except the program of government control. If this way is to be avoided, then business leaders must recognize that the problem is a subject for their immediate study to devise ways and means of applying the doctrine in terms of their varying enterprises. In the course of that study they will no doubt find that the method of application will need to vary from industry to industry, depending on the nature of their individual businesses. One would be blind who would not admit that in many cases there will be difficulties in developing these methods, but the greatest initial difficulty is psychological. So long as the disposition of business is to find all the possible reasons why prices cannot be reduced not much may be expected. The first requirement is a basic change of attitude respecting prices and then a systematic study of possible ways and means whereby all along the line prices may be cumulatively reduced. The word **cumulatively** is important because in an interrelated business structure price reductions at one place facilitate the making of reductions at other stages in the productive process.

Let me pause to emphasize that this study was not a search for a quick cure-all for the depression, but was concerned with a sound and fundamental analysis of the requirements for economic progress through the years. Therefore, its conclusions relate not so much to conditions of the moment as to longer-run possibilities. If we are to retain the capitalistic system of private business, then, in the opinion of many of our leaders, this study has pointed out the crucial spot on which the intelligence of our business leadership must now focus its attention.

Mr. Alfred P. Sloan, President of General Motors Corporation, said publicly after reading these studies:

"The demands of our national economy require that we assure the customer in the form of the lowest economic price the benefit of the highest standard of efficiency in management—this to be superimposed on a foundation of the most advanced technological development."

Mr. Walter C. Teagle, President of the Standard Oil Company of New Jersey, spoke business leaders' approval of the conclusions of this study when he wrote in the November issue of FORTUNE Magazine:

"After six years of depressed business activity and experimenting with new remedies, the economics of industrial problems have become of interest to every household in America.

"This brilliant and informative series of studies by the Brookings Institution is therefore most timely. It emphasizes anew the fact that useful production creates wealth; hence that artificial restrictions and price control only serve to block the approach to a higher standard of living. Free play for competitive forces makes for increased efficiency and lower prices. Thus consumption is stimulated and more production is demanded, giving employment and income to more people."

Walter Lippman paid his tribute in these words:

"The four volumes . . . seem to me to be incomparably the most useful economic study made in America during the depression. They are so important that it may fairly be said that no one is qualified to discuss contemporary American affairs who has not mastered the analysis, the argument, and the conclusion. This is a work from which it is possible to dissent, but not one which it is possible to ignore."

We of the Falk Foundation, which granted the funds for this study, have only one thing to ask—that you and people like you examine the analysis and the conclusions in an impartial spirit and that you let the study stand or fall on its merits, as you find them. We believe that it has presented a great and sound challenge to American business men for a new consideration of their responsibilities to our nation in the years that lie ahead.

PRESIDENT: Since the inception of this Club we have had some worth while papers presented to us by outstanding men. Mr. Gow has this evening made a substantial contribution to our library, and we are very grateful to him. We will look forward with much interest to receiving the printed copy of his address, which will be reproduced in full in the next issue of the Proceedings. He has certainly given us all something to think about.

I read a few days ago in a trade journal a little poem that illustrates some of the conditions he has described, the lines of which, if I can recall them, read as follows:

> Two frogs fell into a deep cream bowl,
> One was an optimistic soul,
> But the other took the gloomy view,
> "We shall drown," he cried, without more ado.
> So with a last despairing cry
> He folded his legs and said, "good bye."
> Quoth the other frog, with a knowing grin,
> "I can't get out, but I won't give in,
> I'll just swim around 'til my strength is spent,
> And then I'll die the more content."
> Bravely he swam, 'til it would seem,
> His efforts began to churn the cream,
> On top of the butter at last he stopped,
> And out of the bowl he gaily hopped,
> What is the moral? 'Tis easily found,
> If you can't get out, keep swimming around.

Now, we all know that Uncle Sam is deep down in the old cream bowl, but like the optimistic frog he is still swimming around, and it is my opinion that if he will put into practice some of the valuable suggestions that Mr. Gow has just outlined, they will prove of valuable help in extricating him from his unfortunate position.

Mr. Gow has kindly consented to make, as he states, an attempt to answer any questions that may be asked relative to the subject he has presented. Following the same order of procedure announced at the last meeting, I will not call on any one to ask any questions or make any comments, unless you make it necessary. So, for the next fifteen minutes, the meeting is in your hands.

MR. T. E. BRITT: May I ask what steps the Falk Foundation is taking to acquaint the masses of the people with the study and its conclusions?

MR. GOW: It is taking several steps. Ordinarily the history of such research projects as this is that when the research is finished it gets attention for a short time from interested scholars, and then the publications resulting from it go into library shelves to gather dust. The general public gives little attention to the studies. The Falk Foundation desired to disseminate the findings of the study widely among the general population. To that end we made a brief digest in simple language of each volume and distributed these digests free of charge.

Hundreds of thousands of copies of the digest of each volume have been distributed this way. Further, we have financed at the Brookings Institution a program whereby the president and officers of the Institution will engage in extensive speaking tours to interpret the study to the general population. As an additional effort, the Brookings Institution plans to develop talking motion pictures of Dr. Moulton lecturing on the study. These pictures will be distributed throughout the schools of the United States.

MR. R. W. MACKINSON: May I ask whether you have completed your studies in this line or whether you contemplate further research?

MR. GOW: We are developing at the Brookings Institution several other studies which will take the findings of the present study and focus them into more concrete terms in relation to particular industries, specific economic situations, etc. This study of the distribution of wealth and income in relation to economic progress becomes therefore a base-study out of which we expect to have develop other studies which will focus this research more and more definitely as the research proceeds. At the moment we contemplate at the Brookings Institution these two studies—(1) a study of corporate fiscal practices as they relate to wage policies, dividend policies, depreciation policies, surpluses, etc., and (2) a study of trade practices whereby analysis will be made of the factors in industry which actually determine price structures.

MR. A. STUCKI: We all know that we can only compete with two items in foreign trade, automobiles and films. We cannot compete in any other thing. And what is the result? Mr. Gow has touched on it. We use foreign products instead of increasing our consumption by using our own produts. We are underbid by foreign countries in spite of the cost of transportation to this country. Take for instance steel. What Mr. Gow says is correct, namely, that our price is not low enough to keep out foreign competition.

The truth of this is even more significant when we read the import report for the year 1935 compiled by the Department of Commerce as follows:

	1935	1934
Meat Products	86,989,050#	45,152,181#
Beef and veal	7,684,637	138,283
Ham, bacon, etc.	2,846,005	626,148
Canned meat	57,533,869	30,450,789
Lard, etc.	13,506,540	308,839
Butter	21,948,458	535,144
Corn (bushels)	34,809,120	816,091
Oats (bushels)	10,092,444	410,175
Wheat (bushels)	13,446,009	3,336,188
Wheat flour	1,277,822	152,821
Raw Cotton	36,353,324	7,328,084

It is astounding that foreign countries send to us grain, meat, and cotton, and it shows that the price raised artificially and by rude methods does not benefit the country as a whole.

So I agree with Mr. Gow that it is the proper thing to reduce prices and increase consumption and the balance will take care of itself.

He has mentioned different things that influence that consumption or the amount of consumption, and he has mentioned trade associations. Could we hear from him more about the effect these associations have on prices and to what extent they are desirable?

MR. GOW: I think not. The study points out that when trade associations have engaged in practices which interfere with the gradual and orderly reduction of prices they are then obstacles to economic progress. However, there are many other respects in which the practices of trade associations have probably promoted economic progress. I think it should be said that if trade associations are strategically enough located to impede the reduction of prices, then they might be used in co-operation with business men as instruments whereby a policy of gradual and orderly price reductions might be affected.

PROFESSOR LOUIS E. ENDSLEY: Would you mind naming some American industry that exemplifies more than any other industry the principles advocated as a result of this study?

MR. GOW: To my mind, the automobile industry is the outstanding example of the application of the principles advocated by this study. Through the years the automobile industry has passed on to the consumer, in the form of lower prices, much of the gain it has made by technological improvements. The result has been that this industry has created for itself additional markets by bringing its product within the reach of lower income groups.

MR. F. I. SNYDER: I have no question to ask Mr Gow but I do want to express my personal appreciation for his relieving me of the task of reading this whole report. I have been ambitious to do that. The summary he has given us will tide me over until such time as I can read it. I think in these difficult depression years we are quite likely to lose our perspective. I find there is a great deal of muddy thinking on this question of capitalism. Just what is a capitalist and what is capital? It might be illustrated by the case of an individual, Tony or Bill or Jack. He comes to his majority and he has nothing but his brawn and his brain. He gets a job in a labor gang at the standard rate of labor wages. As he works along he finds that a fellow in another gang gets 2c an hour more because he owns his pick and shovel. So Tony saves and buys a pick and shovel and gets a job at 2c an hour more. But here is another fellow that he knows who has half a dozen picks and shovels and half a dozen fellows working for him. He thinks that is a good idea so he gets six picks and shovels and gets six men to work for him. He is making money. He sees a contractor over here with a steam shovel. By this time he has a good reputation and can finance the purchase of a steam shovel. Before long he has a string of caterpillar shovels and trucks, and caterpillar shovels and trucks are capital equipment. Tony is now a capitalist. At one time he was a laborer. When did he acquire capital and when did be become a capitalist? I think when he got his first shovel.

I believe the opinion may be growing, fostered by the demagogue and agitator, that capital is the wealth of the country held in the hands of the few. That is not the case in the United States. There is a very general distribution of capital, even in these times. We can not see that quite as clearly as we could a few years ago, but there is a distribution of capital as well as income. To a greater extent than in any other country the American citizen is a capitalist. The question of distribution was mentioned. I am not competent to discuss that, but I do remember something I read some years ago, before the depression, by an economist— Sir Edgar Salks, I believe—who said we would not have reached the saturation of production and distribution until every Hottentot had a bath tub.

MR. RUFUS FLINN: Since the annual meeting I have succeeded in keeping out of the lime light, but after listening to this wonderful talk I am constrained to get on my feet any say a few words. Fundamentally I think the positions are absolutely sound and Mr. Gow has presented them to us in a very understandable way. Most of the people in this country have been considered economic illiterates but we all know that in the last few years the depression has brought on more economic discussion than at any time before in history. We have been thinking over and paying more attention to these economic problems and their proper solution. As Mr. Gow said, there is not any one answer. It is a very complex thing. The fundamental thing is an increase of production and trade, in the final analysis. One of our members asked Mr. Gow the question as to what efforts had been made to distribute the results of these studies, and I would like to ask Mr. Gow if there is any specific place where members of the Railway Club who might want to go farther into the subject could get the full text as well as the digests of the four studies. I think it should be given more general distribution and I recommend to you members that you not only read the Proceedings but talk with other people, because the time is coming when we have got to know more about this and we have got to get the rest of the people in this country to know a great deal more about it. Indeed it might be a good idea if the Falk Foundation would present the full text of these studies to some of these apostles of the New Deal. It might do them some good.

MR. GOW: The President has read all four volumes, if I may interrupt.

MR. FLYNN: I did not intend to make a speech when I got up. I feel so strongly on this subject that I think we all should give some serious attention to it and inform ourselves on this economic problem. And I think this Club owes a very great debt of gratitude and thanks to Mr. Gow for giving us this very intelligent and very comprehensive and understandable talk on a most important subject. And I would therefore move as an expression of that feeling that we give Mr. Gow a rising vote of thanks.

The motion prevailed by unanimous vote.

PRESIDENT: I am advised by the Entertainment Committee that there are 286 present this evening, a splendid attendance for the month of December. The Committee has arranged a little entertainment on the stage at the end of the room to my right and I will ask you to turn your chairs toward the stage. After the entertainment the usual lunch will be served at the opposite end of the room.

J. D. CONWAY, Secretary.

In Memoriam

C. A. CROFT
Joined Club December 20, 1934
Died November 25, 1935

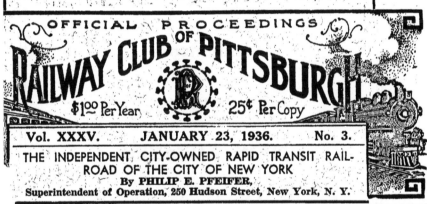

OFFICIAL PROCEEDINGS
RAILWAY CLUB OF PITTSBURGH
$1.00 Per Year   25¢ Per Copy

| Vol. XXXV. | JANUARY 23, 1936. | No. 3. |

THE INDEPENDENT, CITY-OWNED RAPID TRANSIT RAIL-ROAD OF THE CITY OF NEW YORK
By PHILIP E. PFEIFER,
Superintendent of Operation, 250 Hudson Street, New York, N. Y.

The proof of your interest

in the Club can be

enhanced

by securing a

NEW MEMBER.

Application form is available

in this magazine. Look

it up and

"ACT NOW."

OFFICIAL PROCEEDINGS

OF

The Railway Club of Pittsburgh

Organized October 18, 1901

Published monthly, except June, July and August, by the Railway Club of
Pittsburgh, J. D. Conway, Secretary, 515 Grandview Ave., Pittsburgh, Pa..

Entered as Second Class Matter February 6, 1915, at the Postoffice at Pittsburgh,
under the Act of March 3, 1879.

| Vol. XXXV
No. 3. | Pittsburgh, Pa., Jan. 23, 1936. | $1.00 Per Year
25c Per Copy |

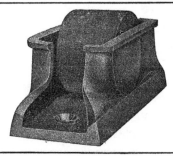

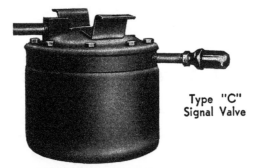

INDEX—ADVERTISERS.

NOTE—This form to be filled out in full by typewriter or printed and mailed to J. D. Conway, Secretary, 1941 Oliver Building, Pittsburgh, Pa. Membership fee, including dues, is $3.00 for each fiscal year or part thereof, except those proposed in September or October. Those proposed in these months will be credited upon payment for the following fiscal year. Dues are payable in advance.

The fiscal year ends with the month of October.

The Railway Club of Pittsburgh:

....19..........

Gentlemen:

Will you kindly consider my Application for Membership in your Club at the next meeting:

Name...

Title...

Company...

My Address..

....

Recommended by...

OFFICIAL PROCEEDINGS

OF

The Railway Club of Pittsburgh

Organized October 18, 1901

Vol. XXXV No. 3.	Pittsburgh, Pa., Jan. 23, 1936.	$1.00 Per Year 25c Per Copy

OFFICERS FOR 1935-1936

President
R. P. FORSBERG,
Chief Engineer, P. & L. E. R. R. Co., Pittsburgh, Pa.

First Vice President
E. A. RAUSCHART,
Mechanical Supt., Montour Railroad,
Coraopolis, Pa.

Secretary
J. D. CONWAY,
Railway Supply Manufacturers' Association,
Pittsburgh, Pa.

Second Vice President
G. M. SIXSMITH,
Supt., Pennsylvania Railroad,
Pittsburgh, Pa.

Treasurer
E. J. SEARLES,
Manager, Schaefer Equipment Co.,
Pittsburgh, Pa.

EXECUTIVE COMMITTEE:

FRANK J. LANAHAN, Chairman, President, Fort Pitt Malleable Iron Co., Pittsburgh, Pa.
A. STUCKI, Engineer, A. Stucki Company, Pittsburgh, Pa.
SAMUEL LYNN, Supt. Rolling Stock, P. & L. E. R. R., McKees Rocks, Pa.
D. F. CRAWFORD, Consulting Engineer, Pittsburgh, Pa.
G. W. WILDIN, Consulting Engineer, Westinghouse Air Brake Company, Pittsburgh, Pa.
W. S. McABEE, Vice Pres. & General Supt., Union Railroad Co., East Pittsburgh, Pa.
E. W. SMITH, Vice President, Pennsylvania Railroad, Pittsburgh, Pa.
LOUIS E. ENDSLEY, Consulting Engineer, 516 East End Avenue, Pittsburgh, Pa.
F. I. SNYDER, Vice President & General Manager, B. & L. E. R. R. Co., Pittsburgh, Pa.
C. O. DAMBACH, General Manager, P. & W. Va. Ry. Co., Pittsburgh, Pa.
R. H. FLINN, General Superintendent, Pennsylvania Railroad, Pittsburgh, Pa.

SUBJECT COMMITTEE:

D. W. McGEORGE, Chairman, Secretary, Edgewater Steel Company, Pittsburgh, Pa.
JOHN B. WRIGHT, Asst. Vice President, Westinghouse Air Brake Co., Wilmerding, Pa.
M. R. REED, General Supt. Motive Power, Pennsylvania Railroad, Pittsburgh, Pa.

ADVERTISING COMMITTEE:

E. A. FOARD, Chairman, Supt. Stations & Transfers, Pennsylvania R. R., Pittsburgh, Pa.
KARL BERG, Superintendent Motive Power, P. & L. E. R. R. Co., McKees Rocks, Pa.
H. E. PASSMORE, Representative, The American Hammered Piston Ring Co., Pgh., Pa.

RECEPTION AND ATTENDANCE COMMITTEE:

J. D. BELTZ, Chairman, Superintendent, B. & O. R. R. Co., Pittsburgh, Pa.
W. C. BUREL, Vice Chairman, Master Mechanic, Western Allegheny Railroad, Kaylor, Pa.
J. B. BAKER, Chief Engr. Maintenance of Way, Pennsylvania Railroad, Pittsburgh, Pa.
WALTER C. SANDERS, Gen. Mgr., Railway Div., Timken Roller Bearing Co., Canton, O.
G. A. BLACKMORE, President & Gen. Mgr., Union Switch & Signal Co., Swissvale, Pa.
J. S. LANAHAN, Vice President, Fort Pitt Malleable Iron Company, Pittsburgh, Pa.
J. A. WARFEL, Special Representative, Air Reduction Sales Co., Pittsburgh, Pa.
J. C. SHINGLEDECKER, Supervisor of Service Stations, The Pennzoil Co., Pittsburgh, Pa.
J. C. DILWORTH, Mgr. of Railroad Sales, Carnegie-Illinois Steel Corp., Pittsburgh, Pa.
G. H. BURNETTE, Assistant Chief Engineer, P. & L. E. R. R. Co., Pittsburgh, Pa.
W. R. TRIEM, Superintendent, Pennsylvania Railroad, Pittsburgh, Pa.
J. W. HOOVER, Asst. Chief of Transpn., Subsidiary Cos. U. S. Steel Corp., Pittsburgh, Pa.
J. W. JOHNSON, Superintendent, Railway Express Agency, Pittsburgh, Pa.
A. A. READ, Duquesne Slag Products Company, Pittsburgh, Pa.
C. P. SCHRECONGOST, Traffic Manager, Hillman Coal & Coke Company, Pittsburgh, Pa.

ENTERTAINMENT COMMITTEE:

J. PORTER GILLESPIE, Chairman, Asst. Gen. Supt., Lockhart Iron & Steel Co., Pgh., Pa.
FRANK E. WEIS, Vice Chairman, Transportation Clerk, Penna. R. R., Pittsburgh, Pa.
E. H. HOLMES, Sales Department, Fort Pitt Malleable Iron Co., Pittsburgh, Pa.
C. C. CLARK, Sales Manager Central District, Pressed Steel Car Co., McKees Rocks, Pa.
A. L. KESSLER, Clearance Clerk, Pennsylvania Railroad, Pittsburgh, Pa.
T. F. SHERIDAN, Asst. to S.M.P. and S.R.S., P. & L. E. R. R. Co., McKees Rocks, Pa.
JAMES NAGEL, Superintendent Transportation, Montour Railroad, Coraopolis, Pa.

FINANCE COMMITTEE:

J. L. O'TOOLE, Chairman, Asst. to Gen. Manager, P. & L. E. R. R. Co., Pittsburgh, Pa.
G. W. HONSBERGER, Transpn. Mgr., Westinghouse Electric & Mfg. Co., Pittsburgh, Pa.
F. J. RYAN, District Representative, Detroit, Toledo & Ironton Railroad, Pittsburgh, Pa.
C. E. CATT, Division Accountant, B. & O. R. R. Co., Pittsburgh, Pa.
J. W. BOYD, Superintendent, Monongahela Railway Company, Brownsville, Pa.

MEMBERSHIP COMMITTEE:

WILLIAM R. GELLATLY, Chairman, Pres., Superior Railway Products Corp., Pgh., Pa.
T. E. BRITT, Vice Chairman, Division Storekeeper, B. & O. R. R. Co., Pittsburgh, Pa.
A. B. SEVERN, General Manager, A. Stucki Company, Pittsburgh, Pa.
W. P. BUFFINGTON, Traffic Manager, Pittsburgh Coal Company, Pittsburgh, Pa.
R. S. BULL, Supt. Power & Inclines, Pittsburgh Railways Co., N. S., Pittsburgh, Pa.
A. F. COULTER, Master Car Builder, Union Railroad Co., East Pittsburgh, Pa.
T. R. DICKINSON, Purchasing Agent, B. & L. E. R. R. Co., Pittsburgh, Pa.
D. K. ORR, Road Master, Monongahela Railway Co., Brownsville, Pa.
C. M. WHEELER, Sales Engineer, Union Switch & Signal Company, Swissvale, Pa.
W. F. AMBROSE, Master Mechanic, Aliquippa & Southern Railroad, Aliquippa, Pa.
JOHN I. MULVEY, Traffic Manager, Hubbard & Company, Pittsburgh, Pa.
THOMAS R. FITZPATRICK, Freight Traffic Mgr., P. & L. E. R. R. Co., Pittsburgh, Pa.
P. W. HEPBURN, Sales Engineer, Gulf Refining Company, Pittsburgh, Pa.
W. B. MOIR, Chief Car Inspector, Pennsylvania Railroad, Pittsburgh, Pa.
C. W. TRUST, Assistant Traffic Manager, Carnegie-Illinois Steel Corp., Pittsburgh, Pa

PAST PRESIDENTS:

*J. H. McCONNELL	October,	1901, to October, 1903
*L. H. TURNER	November,	1903, to October, 1905
*F. H. STARK	November,	1905, to October, 1907
*H. W. WATTS	November,	1907, to April, 1908
*D. J. REDDING	November,	1908, to October, 1910
*F. R. McFEATTERS	November,	1910, to October, 1912
*A. G. MITCHELL	November,	1912, to October, 1914
*F. M. McNULTY	November,	1914, to October, 1916
*J. G. CODE	November,	1916, to October, 1917
*D. M. HOWE	November,	1917, to October, 1918
*J. A. SPIELMAN	November,	1918, to October, 1919
H. H. MAXFIELD	November,	1919, to October, 1920
FRANK J. LANAHAN	November,	1920, to October, 1921
SAMUEL LYNN	November,	1921, to October, 1922
D. F. CRAWFORD	November,	1922, to October, 1923
GEO. D. OGDEN	November,	1923, to October, 1924
A. STUCKI	November,	1924, to October, 1925
F. G. MINNICK	November,	1925, to October, 1926
G. W. WILDIN	November,	1926, to October, 1927
E. J. DEVANS	November,	1927, to October, 1928
W. S. McABEE	November,	1928, to October, 1929
E. W. SMITH	November,	1929, to October, 1930
LOUIS E. ENDSLEY	November,	1930, to October, 1931
*JOHN E. HUGHES	November,	1931, to October, 1932
F. I. SNYDER	November,	1932, to October, 1933
C. O. DAMBACH	November,	1933, to October, 1934
R. H. FLINN	November,	1934, to October, 1935

*—Deceased.

Meetings held fourth Thursday of each month except June, July and August.

PROCEEDINGS OF MEETING
JANUARY 23rd, 1936

The meeting was called to order by President R. P. Forsberg at the Fort Pitt Hotel at 8:00 o'clock, P. M.

Registered attendance, 119, as follows:

MEMBERS

Adams, Frank W.
Anderson, Burt T.
Aulbach, A. J.
Baer, Harry L.
Barr, H. C.
Barth, Herman
Batchelar, E. C.
Beam, E. J.
Beck, C. H.
Bell, R. A.
Berghane, A. L.
Blackmore, G. A.
Bradley, J. P.
Burnette, G. H.
Burriss, W. C.
Carey, C. D.
Chaffin, H. B.
Clardy, W. J.
Coakley, John A., Jr.
Conway, J. D.
Cowen, Harry E.
Crawford, Burt H.
Cree, W. M.
Cunningham, J. Donald
Cunningham, R. I.
Dambach, C. O.
Davies, James
Down, S. G.
Egley, M. J.
Enders, I. O.
Endsley, Prof. Louis E.
Flinn, R. H.
Forsberg, R. P.
Fox, George W.
Frauenheim, Pierce H.
Freshwater, F. H.
Fry, L. H.
Galbraith, James R.
Gellatly, W. R.
George, W. J.
Gillespie, J. Porter

Glaser, J. P.
Harger, M. L.
Haser, A. J.
Hayward, C.
Hepburn, P. W.
Hughes, I. Lamont
Hutchinson, G. C., Jr.
Johnson, J. W.
Keck, L. M.
Kentlein, John
Kessler, A. L.
Kroske, J. F.
Lanahan, Frank J.
Lanahan, J. S.
Lincoln, R. B.
Long, R. M.
Lowry, William F., Jr.
Misner, George W.
Moir, W. B.
Morgan, Homer C.
Mulvey, John I.
Murray, Stewart
McGeorge, D. W.
McHail, J. L.
McKim, Hollis
McKinley, John T.
McLean, J. L.
Palmer, E. A.
Passmore, H. E.
Pfeifer, P. E.
Reed, M. R.
Renshaw, W. B.
Robertson, A. S.
Rutter, H. E.
Sarchet, Roger
Severn, A. B.
Shepherd, W. B.
Sheridan, T. F.
Simpkins, Fred E.
Sixsmith, G. M.
Smith, Folger M.

Smith, R. B.
Stevenson, W. M.
Stoffregen, Louis E.
Sudell, D. W.
Sullivan, R. J.
Sutherland, Lloyd
Triem, W. R.

Troxell, Henry K.
Unger, Dr. J. S.
Van Wormer, George M.
Wheeler, C. M.
Wildin, G. W.
Wilt, Howard H.
Wright, John B.

Yohe, J. K., Jr.

VISITORS

Galloway, William R.
Harnich, Harry K.
Harwig, C. G.
Hutchinson, A. H.
Hutchinson, Mrs. A. H.
Johnson, J., Jr.
Keim, C. C.
Lanken, C. C.
Lentzner, H. H.
Lewis, S. B.
Lindemann, P. A.

Maltman, A. L.
Moore, M. K.
Quinn, John J.
Ruos, H. D.
Shippert, Frank
Smith, Sion B.
Street, C. K.
Thompson, Robert
Tramblie, H. I.
Wickersham, A. P.
Woodburn, Bert W.

Before the regular business meeting a most enjoyable song recital was given by Mr. Alfred H. Hutchinson, of the Pittsburgh & Lake Erie Railroad, who was accompanied at the piano by his wife, who added much to the pleasure of the recital. Mr. Hutchinson sang before the Club two years ago, with so much satisfaction to the members that they urgently demanded his reappearance.

At the close of the songs the President expressed to Mr. and Mrs. Hutchinson the pleasure and the appreciation of the Club for their entertainment.

PRESIDENT FORSBERG: The first order of business is the roll call. We have a record of your attendance on the registration cards made out by you when you came in, so we will dispense with the calling of the roll.

The next is the reading of the minutes of the last meeting. Inasmuch as the printed Proceedings have been mailed to you, it will not be necessary to read the minutes, and unless there is objection the reading of the minutes will be dispensed with.

Next we go to the reception of proposals for membership. I will ask Secretary Conway to kindly read the list of proposals for membership.

SECRETARY: I am sure it will be pleasing to you to know that our Membership Committee has been active and efficient since our last meeting. Due to their activity we have the following list of names proposed for membership at this meeting:

Ater, Byron F., Assistant Secretary, Y. M. C. A., P. & L. E. R. R. Co., Newell, Pa. Recommended by R. M. Long.

Bain, Clarence R., Triple Valve Repairer, P. & L. E. R. R. Co., 532 Russellwood Avenue, McKees Rocks, Pa. Recommended by R. M. Long.

Barkley, Sherwood W., Triple Valve A. B. Tester, P. & L. E. R. R. Co., Box 126, R. D. 1, McKees Rocks, Pa. Recommended by R. M. Long.

Barth, Herman, Triple Valve Repairer, P. & L. E. R. R. Co., 1119 Faust Street, Pittsburgh (4), Pa. Recommended by R. M. Long.

Barton, E. E., Assistant Local Treasurer, P. & L. E. R. R. Co., 1718 Ridge Avenue, Coraopolis, Pa. Recommended by R. S. Hervey.

Bauer, R. B., General Yard Master, P. & L. E. R. R. Co., Dickerson Run, Pa. Recommended by F. M. Brown

Beall, C. R., Assistant Chief Engineer, Union Switch & Signal Company, Braddock Avenue, Swissvale, Pa. Recommended by C. M. Wheeler.

Beck, C. H., General Sales Manager, Westinghouse Air Brake Company, Empire State Building, New York, N. Y. Recommended by P. E. Pfeifer.

Beitsch, George F., Gang Foreman, Pennsylvania Railroad, 1110 Allegheny Street, New Brighton, Pa.

Bell, R. A., Clerk, P. & L. E. R. R. Co, 325 Mathews Avenue, Carrick, Pittsburgh, Pa. Recommended by J. W. McElravy.

Best, Rankin M., Clerk, P. & L. E. R. R. Co., Monaca, Pa. Recommended by F. M. Brown.

Bickett, M. A., Freight Agent, P. & L. E. R. R. Co., 303 Boyles Avenue, New Castle, Pa. Recommended by F. M. Brown.

Biggerstaff, James M., Electrical Foreman, P. & L. E. R. R. Co., P. O. Box 48, Wireton, Pa. Recommended by R. M. Long.

Binyon, Thomas E., Telegraph & Telephone Engineer, Pennsylvania Railroad, Pennsylvania Station, Pittsburgh, Pa. Recommended by Tom R. Day.

Bosley, Norman D., Gang Leader, P. & L. E. R R. Co., R. D. — Poplar Street, McKees Rocks, Pa. Recommended by R. M. Long.

Boyd, Samuel S, Assistant Supervisor, Union Railroad Company, 551 Fourth Street, Pitcairn, Pa Recommended by Troy West.

Brandt, George F., Triple Valve Repairer, P. & L. E. R. R. Co., 799 Thirteenth Street, McKees Rocks, Pa. Recommended by R. M. Long.

Brunnings, George H., District Manager, American-Hawaiian Steamship Company, Gulf Building, Pittsburgh, Pa. Recommended by J. I. Mulvey.

Button, D. G., Yard Master, P. & L. E. R. R. Co., 313 College Avenue, California, Pa. Recommended by F. M. Brown.

Carpenter, J. F., Agent, P. & L. E. R. R. Co., Monaca, Pa. Recommended by F. M. Brown.

Chase, Daniel K., Superintendent, Pennsylvania Railroad, Pennsylvania Station, Pittsburgh, Pa. Recommended by W. B. Moir.

Clemens, E. G, General Foreman's Clerk, B & O. R. R. Co., 140 Parkfield Street, Pittsburgh (10), Pa. Recommended by T. E. Britt.

Copeland, T. A., General Yard Master, P. & L. E. R. R. Co., 677 McKee Avenue, Monessen, Pa. Recommended by F. M. Brown.

Cowen, Harry E., Triple Valve Tester, P. & L. E. R R. Co., 1115 Adon Street, Pittsburgh (4), Pa. Recommended by R. M. Long.

Cox, George P., Supervisor, Monongahela Railway Company, Union Street, Brownsville, Pa. Recommended by D. K. Orr

Dalzell, J. C., Chief Clerk, Assistant Freight Agent, P. & L. E. R. R. Co., 307 Natchez Street, Pittsburgh, Pa. Recommended by R. S. Hervey.

Danielson, W. D., Assistant Supervisor of Track, P. & L. E. R. R. Co., 113 Duquesne Avenue, Dravosburg, Pa. Recommended by F. R. Paisley.

Davies, Benjamin S., General Secretary, Y. M. C. A., P. & L. E. R. R. Co., 2685 Wilson Avenue, Campbell, Ohio. Recommended by R. M. Long.

Davin, John P., W. B. Clerk, B. & O. R. R. Co., 1814 Belleau Street, N. S., Pittsburgh, Pa. Recommended by T. E. Britt.

Deutsch, Albert G., Yard Master, P. & L. E. R. R. Co., 512 Ninth Street, Monessen, Pa. Recommended by F. M. Brown.

Dindinger, Charles C., Agent, P. & L. E. R. R. Co., 487 Duquesne Drive, Mt. Lebanon, Pa. Recommended by F. M. Brown.

Dipper, F. W., Cashier, Pittsburgh-West End, P. & L. E. R. R. Co., Churchview Avenue, Carrick, Pittsburgh, Pa. Recommended by J. W. McElravy.

Dusenberry, S. H., Engine House Foreman, P. & L. E. R. R. Co., P. O. Box 532, Newell, Pa. Recommended by J. J. Donovan.

Easler, E. H., Chief Clerk to Superintendent, Monongahela Railway Company, 11 Third Avenue, Brownsville, Pa. Recommended by D. K. Orr.

Enders, I. O., Superintendent Labor & Wage, Pennsylvania Railroad, Pennsylvania Station, Pittsburgh, Pa. Recommended by Roger Sarchet.

Feeley, J. D., General Agent, M. K. T. R. R. Lines, Clark Building, Pittsburgh, Pa. Recommended by J. I. Mulvey.

Feidt, J. J., Chief Clerk Operating Department, P. & L. E. R. R. Co., 863 Marshall Avenue, N. S., Pittsburgh, Pa. Recommended by F. M. Brown.

Flanigan, A. C., Freight Agent, P. & L. E. R. R. Co., McKees Rocks, Pa. Recommended by F. M. Brown.

Funk, E. J., General Foreman, P. & L. E. R. R. Co., 42 Laclede Street, Pittsburgh, Pa. Recommended by J. W. McElravy.

Gatens, A. J., Assistant Chief Clerk, P. & L. E. R. R. Co., 302 South Pacific Avenue, E. E., Pittsburgh, Pa. Recommended by J. W. McElravy.

Gordon, C. M., Assistant Auditor Disbursements, P. & L. E. R. R. Co., 995 Second Street, Beaver, Pa. Recommended by J. P. Glaser.

Gow, J. Steele, Director, The Falk Foundation, Farmers Bank Building, Pittsburgh, Pa. Recommended by J. D. Conway.

Gregory, Walter H., Machinist, P. & L. E. R. R. Co., 123 Owen Street, McKees Rocks, Pa. Recommended by R. M. Long.

Hague, James R., Clerk, P. & L. E. R. R. Co., 5120 Second Avenue, Pittsburgh, Pa. Recommended by J. W. McElravy.

Hardy, James E., Agent, P. & L. E. R. R. Co., 303 Monongahela Avenue, Otto-McKeesport, Pa. Recommended by F. M. Brown.

Harger, M. L., Foreman, Car Repairs, P. & L. E. R. R. Co., Newell, Pa. Recommended by R. M. Long.

Hartnett, C. J., Supervisor of Tracks, P. & L. E. R. R. Co., 610 Arlington Avenue, McKeesport, Pa. Recommended by F. R. Paisley.

Herpst, R. C., Sales Agent, American Steel Foundries, 29 DeFoe Street, N. S., Pittsburgh, Pa. Recommended by E. A. Rauschart.

Hill, George W., Blacksmith Foreman, B. & O. R. R. Co., 310 Twenty-sixth Street, McKeesport, Pa. Recommended by T. E. Britt.

Hoffman, Charles H., District Manager, Luckenbach Steamship Company, Inc., Oliver Building, Pittsburgh, Pa. Recommended by J. I. Mulvey.

Holtzworth, C. H. Chief Clerk Engineering Department, B. & O. R. R. Co., Maloney Building, Pittsburgh, Pa. Recommended by T. E. Britt.

Hood, A. N., Freight Agent, P. & L. E. R. R. Co., 831 Neely Heights Avenue, Coraopolis, Pa. Recommended by F. M. Brown.

Hoop, J. H., Freight Agent, P. & L. E. R. R. Co., 413 Eleventh Street, Beaver Falls, Pa. Recommended by F. M. Brown.

Huggans, A. V., Agent, P. & L. E. R. R. Co., 1211 Berkshire Avenue, Pittsburgh, Pa Recommended by F. M. Brown.

Jahnke, Karl W., Air Brake Inspector, P. & L. E. R. R. Co., 238 Singer Avenue, McKees Rocks, Pa. Recommended by R. M. Long.

Jennings, John E., Yard Master, P. & L. E. R. R. Co., 44 Aliquippa Street, Monessen, Pa. Recommended by F. M. Brown.

Johnson, Nelson E., Gang Leader, P. & L. E. R. R. Co., 1429 Summit Street, McKees Rocks, Pa. Recommended by R. M. Long.

Johnston, Harvey F., Freight Rate Clerk, P. & L. E. R. R. Co., 3255 Motor Street, Pittsburgh, Pa. Recommended by F. M. Brown.

Jones, Edward W., Correction Clerk, B. & O. R. R. Co., 2410 Glenroy Street, Pittsburgh, Pa. Recommended by T. E. Britt.

Kelly, Eugene V., Yard Master, P. & L. E. R. R. Co., 313 Oneida Street, Duquesne Heights, Pittsburgh, Pa. Recommended by F. M. Brown.

Largent, J. R., Ticket Agent, P. & L. E. R. R. Co., P&LE Station, Pittsburgh, Pa. Recommended by F. M. Brown.

Lauderbaugh, Moss, Freight Agent, P. & L. E. R. R. Co., 16 Fifth Srteet, Ellwood City, Pa. Recommended by F. M. Brown.

Lawrenee, Norman M., Superintendent E. & A. Division, Pennsylvania Railroad, 322 East Lincoln Avenue, New Castle, Pa. Recommended by W. B. Moir.

Leonard, P. J., General Foreman, B. & O. R. R. Co., 5220 Holmes Street, Pittsburgh, Pa. Recommended by T. E. Britt.

Lincoln, R. B., Director of Weld Testing, Pittsburgh Testing Laboratory, Locust and Stevenson Streets, Pittsburgh, Pa. Recommended by J. W. Reifsnyder.

Lloyd, J. A., General Freight Agent, Pittsburgh Railways Company, Exposition Building, Pittsburgh, Pa. Recommended by C. W. Trust.

Lowe, William T., General Freight Agent, American Window Glass Company, Farmers Bank Building, Pittsburgh, Pa. Recommended by R. H. Flinn.

Malone, Creed, General Yard Master, Monongahela Railway Company, Morgantown, W. Va. Recommended by J. W. Boyd.

Marquis, G. E., Chief Train Master, P. & L. E. R. R Co., 702 Sixth Avenue, New Brighton, Pa. Recommended by J. P. Goff.

Mason, W. N., General Yard Master, P. & L. E. R. R. Co., 936 Atlantic Avenue, Monaca, Pa. Recommended by F. M. Brown.

Maxwell, Thomas, Foreman Tool & Equipment Design Department, Westinghouse Air Brake Company, 933 Milton Street, Pittsburgh, Pa. Recommended by R. D. Irwin.

Merk, Joseph S., Statistical Clerk, P. & L. E. R. R. Co., 6417 Marchand Street, Pittsburgh (6), Pa. Recommended by J. P. Glaser.

Mittelstadter, Howard, Foreman, P. & L. E. R. R. Co., 1139 Wisconsin Avenue, Dormont, Pittsburgh, Pa. Recommended by J. W. McElravy.

Moulis, F. J , Cash Clerk, B. & O. R. R. Co., 1412 Alton Street, Beechview, Pittsburgh, Pa. Recommended by T. E. Britt.

Murphy, Edward P., Yard Master, P. & L. E. R. R. Co., 540 Isabella Avenue, Lock No. 4, Monessen, Pa. Recommended by F. M. Brown.

McCarthy, Frank C., Fitter, Mesta Machine Company, 307½ Fiske Street, Pittsburgh, Pa. Recommended by J. I. Mulvey.

McCready, R E., General Foreman, Water Supply, P. & L. E. R. R. Co., 296 Park Street, Beaver, Pa. Recommended by R. M. Long

McKibbin, J. S., Local Treasurer, P. & L. E. R. R Co, Terminal Building, Pittsburgh, Pa. Recommended by F. T. Sladden.

McVicker, Allen, Agent, P. & L. E. R. R. Co., P. O. Box No. 36, West Pittsburgh, Pa Recommended by F. M. Brown.

Parkhill, Ray T., Chief Demurrage Clerk, B & O R. R. Co, 1615 Columbus Avenue, N. S., Pittsburgh, Pa. Recommended by T. E. Britt.

Parry, J. E., Clerk, P. & L. E. R. R. Co., 1821 Plainview Avenue, Pittsburgh, Pa. Recommended by J. W. McElravy.

Pfeifer, P. E., Superintendent of Transportation, Independent City-Owned Rapid Transit Railroad of the City of New York, 250 Hudson Street, New York, N. Y. Recommended by C. H. Beck.

Reardon, M. J , General Yard Master, P. & L. E. R. R. Co., 414 Kendall Street, Coraopolis, Pa. Recommended by F. M Brown.

Robinson, W. H., Chief Delivery Clerk, B & O. R. R. Co., 668 Boggs Avenue, Pittsburgh, Pa. Recommended by T. E. Britt.

Sager, Ray I., Yard Master, P. & L. E. R. R. Co., 419 Green Street, South Brownsville, Pa Recommended by F. M Brown.

Schultz, H. P , General Yard Master, P. & L. E. R. R Co., 2714 Fifth Avenue, Beaver Falls, Pa. Recommended by F. M Brown.

Schweinsberg, C. E., Joint Chief Clerk, P. & L. E.-P. R. R. Warehouse & Terminal Station, 213 West Canal Street, N. S., Pittsburgh, Pa Recommended by J. W. McElravy.

Shira, William A., Yard Master, P. & L. E. R. R. Co., 134 Euclid Avenue, New Castle, Pa. Recommended by F. M. Brown

Simpson, Walter B., Salesman, A. M. Byers Company, Clark Building, Pittsburgh, Pa. Recommended by D. K. Orr.

Smith, Folger M., Traffic Manager, Federal Laboratories, Inc., 185 Forty-first Street, Pittsburgh, Pa. Recommended by J. I. Mulvey.

Stevens, Ernest, Assistant Head Clerk, A. F. A. Department, P. & L. E. R. R. Co., P&LE Terminal Building, Pittsburgh, Pa. Recommended by R. S. Hervey.

Stocker, H. F., President, H. F. Stocker & Company, Clark Building, Pittsburgh, Pa Recommended by C. O. Dambach.

Strahl, Herman, Chief Clerk Auditor Freight Accounts, P. & L. E. R. R. Co., Pittsburgh, Pa. Recommended by R. S. Hervey.

Sudell, Donald W., Lubrication Engineer, Crew-Levick Company, 738 Brookline Boulevard, Pittsburgh, Pa. Recommended by Pierce H. Frauenheim.

Sutton, K. B , Chemist, P. & L. E. R. R. Co., 1056 Hiland Avenue, Coraopolis, Pa. Recommended by G. H. Burnette.

Swank, W. E., Chief Clerk to Freight Agent, B. & O. R. R. Co., 38 Cowan Street, Pittsburgh, Pa. Recommended by T. E. Britt.

Sylvester, H. G., Freight Agent, P. & L. E. R R. Co., Monessen, Pa. Recommended by F. M. Brown.

Teerkes, Charles A., Freight Agent, P. & L. E. R R. Co., Aliquippa, Pa. Recommended by F. M. Brown.

Thiele, Fred, Assistant General Yard Master, P. & L. E. R. R. Co., 543 Woodward Avenue, McKees Rocks, Pa. Recommended by F. M. Brown.

Thunell, Frederick G., Rate Clerk, B. & O. R. R. Co., 301 Marie Avenue, Avalon, Pittsburgh, Pa. Recommended by T. E. Britt.

Todd, A. H., Agent, P. & L. E. R. R. Co., 706 Lincoln Street, Monongahela, Pa. Recommended by F. M. Brown.

Trumpeter, W. C., Chief Clerk, P. & L. E. R. R. Co., 917 Indiana Avenue, Monaca, Pa. Recommended by F. M. Brown.

Villee, R. E., Chief Clerk, P. & L. E. R. R. Co., 344 Kambach Street, Mt. Washington, Pittsburgh, Pa. Recommended by J. W. McElravy.

Wagoner, Karl J., Assistant Engineer, Engineering Department, B. & O. R. R. Co., Maloney Building, Pittsburgh, Pa. Recommended by T. E. Britt.

Weltz, E. E. Assistant Agent, Twenty-third Street Station, P. & L. E. R. R. Co,, 2218 Lutz Avenue, Pittsburgh, Pa. Recommended by J. W. McElravy.

Wenzel, J. Louis, Assistant Manager Tool Department, Hubbard & Company, 6301 Butler Street, Pittsburgh, Pa. Recommended by J. I. Mulvey.

Werner, L. A, Chief Clerk, P. & L. E. R. R. Co,, 3608 Mayfair Street, McKeesport, Pa. Recommended by F. M. Brown.

Whipkey, Daniel L, Relief Yard Master, P. & L. E. R. R. Co., P. O. Box No. 444, Newell, Pa. Recommended by F. M. Brown.

White, A. F., Time Clerk, P. & L. E. R. R. Co., 47 Haberman Avenue, Pittsburgh, Pa. Recommended by J. W. McElravy.

Wilson, J. N, President, Aliquippa & Southern Railroad Co., 311 Ross Street, Pittsburgh, Pa. Recommended by W. F. Ambrose.

Wolf, William M., Chief Clerk A. F. A. Department, P. & L. E. R. R. Co., 358 LaMarido Street, Pittsburgh, Pa. Recommended by R. S. Hervey.

Yohe, J. K., Train Master, Monongahela Railway Company, Brownsville, Pa. Recommended by J. W. Boyd.

PRESIDENT: Following our custom, I will ask those who are present on the list just read to stand up and give your names, so we may associate the name with the face.

Gentlemen, we welcome you into the fellowship of our Club and hope the pleasure of our association will be as pleasant as you have every right to expect it to be.

The next order is the reading of communications. The Secretary informs me there are no communications, so we will proceed at once to the paper of the evening. I know it is a matter of deep regret to you, as it is to me, that we have to have the coldest night on record in Pittsburgh for thirty-seven years for the regular meeting night of our Railway Club. But there are some things that even the New Deal cannot control, and the weather is one of them. It is just too bad that a gentleman has to come from New York and not have a larger audience to talk to than we have with us this evening. Under normal weather conditions this room would have been full to overflowing.

We are honored to have as our speaker tonight Mr. P. E. Pfeifer, of New York City, Superintendent of Operation, Independent Subway System of the City of New York, and he will speak to us on the subject, "The Independent City-Owned Rapid Transit Railroad of the City of New York." Mr. Pfeifer.

THE INDEPENDENT CITY-OWNED RAPID TRANSIT RAILROAD OF THE CITY OF NEW YORK

By PHILIP E. PFEIFER,
Superintendent of Operation, 250 Hudson Street, New York, N. Y.

Mr. Chairman and Members of the Railway Club of Pittsburgh:

A rapid transit line may be defined as an urban railroad

operating on an exclusive right of way for the transportation of passengers only.

The first rapid transit railroad (known as the New York and Yonkers Patent Railway) was authorized by the Legislature of the State of New York in 1866. This first authorization was for a half mile of elevated cable railroad in Greenwich Street, New York, this installation being of an experimental nature with the understanding that if the experiment was successful, the line could be extended northerly to the upper part of the city. In two years the experiment had proved successful, and thereafter other railroads were built, most of which are still operating.

The first subway in this country was completed in Boston in the year 1901. In 1900 the construction of the first subway in New York City was started, extending from Brooklyn Bridge to 145th Street, and was placed in operation in the year 1904. Since that time there has been almost continuous building of subways. Elevated lines have also been built in New York City, Chicago, Boston, Philadelphia, and in the latter city, a subway.

The rapid transit lines in New York City are operated by three organizations, the Interborough Rapid Transit Company, the New York Rapid Transit Corporation, and the City of New York through its Board of Transportation. The last named, (which is called the Independent City-Owned Rapid Transit Railroad of the City of New York) is the latest and most modern subway to be built. It is only about 60% in service now, although the installation of tracks, station finish, and equipment for the remaining 40% is under way and will be completed within the next two years.

(NOTE:—Pictures as described by the speaker were shown on the screen).

(SLIDE No. 1—MAP OF SYSTEM)

This slide shows the Independent Subway System. That part of the line that is now in operation extends from 207th Street, Manhattan, to Church Avenue, Brooklyn; from 145th Street, Manhattan, to 205th Street, in The Bronx; from 50th Street, Manhattan, to Roosevelt Avenue, Queens; from Queens Plaza Station in Queens, to Nassau Avenue in Brooklyn; and from West 4th Street, Manhattan, to Jay Street, Brooklyn.

Work is also progressing rapidly on the Fulton Street Line, extending from Court Street to Rockaway Avenue, and the Brooklyn-Crosstown Line, extending from Nassau Avenue to Hoyt-Schermerhorn Streets. The last link under construction, with the exception of the Sixth Avenue Line, will probably be completed early in 1937, and will extend the present Queens Line from Roosevelt Avenue to 169th Street, Jamaica.

Construction of the subway was started with a breaking of ground at Hancock Square, 123rd Street and St. Nicholas Avenue, on March 14, 1925. When finally completed the System will have cost approximately $750,000,000.

The first link in this new rapid transit railroad, extending from 207th Street to Chambers Street, Manhattan, a distance of 12 miles, was ready for operation in September, 1932. The Board of Transportation had advertised for its operation under a form of contract, but receiving no satisfactory bids, was on June 17, 1932, authorized to operate and maintain the railroad, to be known as the Independent City-Owned Rapid Transit Railroad. The Board immediately directed that there be organized the following subdivisions for its operation:

Transportation, Station, Maintenance of Way, Power, Cars and Shops, Purchasing, Storehouse, Audits, Claims and Medical. This involved the selection, training and distribution of a competent operating force, to open for revenue service on September 10, 1932, the first section, from 207th Street to Chambers Street. As this portion of the railroad was physically complete, there was no reason to delay setting the opening date of revenue operation. This was the signal for action, and what a hot summer that turned out to be.

Examination boards for each division, with the respective division head as chairman, were selected and approved by the Municipal Civil Service Commission. Each Board began the selection of the personnel necessary for the operation of its division, from a voluminous number of applications submitted.

Until January 1, 1935, the status of practically all the personnel of the railroad were non-competitive Civil Service employees, but on January 1, 1935, they were transferred to the competitive class.

The men in the train service and most of the other branches were recruited in the main from former employees of electric and steam railroads in the vicinity of New York City, at a time when a large group of competent railroad men were available because of the reduction in the forces of those carriers. Each applicant was carefully examined as to his ability to perform the duties of the position for which he had applied, it of course being realized that a trained man must be in place for each of the coordinated functions of the system in order to maintain the desired high standard of dependable, efficient, and safe operation. Any attempt to select other than qualified men in one or more links of the inter-dependent chain, such as the operation of trains, interlocking plants, electric power plants, operation and maintenance of the signal system, maintenance of cars, .tracks, structures, and other equipment, in a safe and reliable manner, might possibly have resulted in definite hazards, not only to the patrons and employees of the railroad, but to the safe operation of the system. Therefore, considerable time and thought was given to the selection of experienced employees. Although qualified as experienced railroad men, they were starting on a new railroad and had, in the nature of things, to spend some time in learning the physical characteristics and details of this new railroad before they were competent to safely function independently. Another thing that was considered was the fact that the public judges a railroad by the treatment it receives from the employees, and for that reason those employees who were to come in direct contact with the public were especially selected and trained to be courteous and neat in appearance.

After a satisfactory period of trial operation with each employee in his place, the first branch of the railroad, extending from 207th Street to Chambers Street, Manhattan, was opened for revenue operation at 12:01 A. M. September 10, 1932. This branch extended for a distance of 12 miles, as previously mentioned, and was serviced by 28 stations.

Before a new line is placed in operation it is of course necessary, after the line is released by the Construction Division, for the transportation, maintenance and power divisions to do a general clean-up job, and to test out the signal and power systems; also to operate "break-in" trains for a period. Prior to the time the Brooklyn extension from Bergen Street to Church Avenue was placed in operation a gang of porters, all new recruits, was sent over the line to clean the stations, booths and platforms. They were all congregated at the Canal Street Station waiting for a group leader to assign them. I happened along and saw one of the porters lying on his back on the cement floor. Another porter came up and said, "What's the matter, big boy, is you tired?" The reply was, "No, I'se not tired." "What you lying down there for?" "In case I do get tired."

Express service was provided between 207th Street and Chambers Street, and local service between 168th Street and Hudson Terminal. Prior to the establishment of this service it was of course necessary to prepare rules and regulations governing the employees engaged in operation, which were issued in book form to each employee. It was also necessary to prepare operating train schedules. These schedules were prepared by experienced schedule makers after they had made a study of traffic conditions paralleling the railroad. They synchronized all train service so as to provide even intervals to take care of the traffic, and to insure economical operation. These schedules since the commencement of operation and the addition of new lines had to be changed from time to time. Studies are constantly being made to determine car requirements to meet the constant increase of traffic. The schedules of the Independent Subway have been computed so as to give the public the maximum service permitted by the most modern equipment, as the public measures the distance from its home to its work by transportation time, as exemplified by the slide which will now be shown.

(SLIDE No. 2—TRANSPORTATION TIME)

The growth of rapid transit building and riding has been given a great deal of study by the Board of Transportation and its predecessors and the data derived from these studies has been the basis of many important decisions as to various features of new rapid transit lines.

(SLIDE No. 3—POPULATION CURVES)

This chart shows the rate of increase in population of New York City since 1900 and also the rate of increase in rides per capita per annum on all public transportation services—rapid transit lines, surface cars and busses—during the same period. You will note that while sub-normal business conditions during the depression had a very adverse effect on the riding habits of the people, it had only a very slight effect on the growth in population. It is interesting to note that the riding habits of the people increased faster than the population, there having been 200 riders per capita, per annum, in 1900; 314 in 1910; 412 in 1920 and 450 in 1929, which was just before the beginning of the depression. In 1933, which according to this chart was the low point of the depression, the rides per capita, per annum, had dropped to 380, but fortunately are now on the upgrade.

Last November the Transit Commission released comparative figures in which it was shown that the rapid transit lines operating in New York City carried one billion, 816 million, 900 thousand passengers during the fiscal year ending June 30, 1935, representing an increase of 17 million, 900 thousand, or one per cent, as compared with the year 1934. The Independent System carried a total of 203 million passengers, representing an increase of 41 million, 300 thousand, or twenty-five and six-tenths per cent increase over 1934. The Transit Commission figures also disclose revenue passengers per revenue car mile ending June 30, 1935, as follows:

New York Rapid Transit Corporation........ 6.03
Interborough, Subway Division 4.64
Independent System 5.77

It is gratifying to know that in comparison with the other rapid transit lines the youthful Independent System is more than holding its own.

As ten per cent of the entire population of the United States is located within a circle of fifty miles radius, with the center at City Hall, City of New York, and a large part of that ten per cent has its place of business in New York City, and as seven million, 400 thousand people reside within the three hundred and twenty square miles that comprise the corporate limits of New York City, it was reasonable to expect that a proportionate part of that population would patronize the Independent Subway. This was used as the basis for the first traffic estimates. These first estimates were soon reached and it is a pleasure to report that traffic has increased beyond all expectations.

On the first day of revenue operation 204 thousand passengers were transported, and during the fiscal period of September 10, 1932, to June 30, 1933, 59 million passengers were carried. During the fiscal year ending June 30, 1934, the railroad handled 161 million, seven hundred thousand passengers, or an average of 443 thousand passengers daily, and during the year ending June 30, 1935, there were handled 203 million passengers, or an average of 556 thousand passengers daily.

The greatest number of passengers carried in one day during the fiscal period ending June 30, 1933, was on Friday, April 21, 1933, at which time there were handled 252,610 passengers. The heaviest traffic during the fiscal year ending June 30, 1934, was on Monday, May 28, 1934, at which time there were handled 625,692 passengers. The heaviest traffic during the fiscal year ending June 30, 1935, was on Monday, February 4, at which time there were handled 704,-899 passengers. Since June 30, 1935, a new high was reached on Monday, January 6, 1936, when 784,281 passengers were carried.

This growth in traffic has been due to the very efficient service and the gradual addition of new extensions. During the year 1933, thirty-six additional stations were placed in operation, and four more on January 1, 1936, making sixty-eight stations now in service.

To furnish efficient and frequent train service it is necessary to add trains and cars as the service is built up to accommodate the morning peak hours of traffic, to lay up trains and cars during the non-rush hour period of the day, and to again build up the service for the evening peak hours, and then to once more taper off the service during the night and early morning hours. During the morning peak hours ten car trains are operated on a minute and one-half express interval.

(SLIDE No. 4—HOURLY TRAFFIC)

An interesting chart pertaining to this subject is the distribution of business over the twenty-four hour period. In two peak hours, twenty-two and one-half per cent of the entire twenty-four hour traffic is carried, and in four hours, 7:00 to 9:00 A. M. and 5:00 to 7:00 P. M., about forty per cent.

(SLIDE No. 5—MONTHLY TRAFFIC)

The seasonal traffic is explained in this slide. This of course means that for economical operation it is necessary to cut out cars commensurate with the traffic during the months when the riding is at a minimum, and is done by developing the schedules previously described. The resulting schedules also act as a basis for computing crew assignments, and determining the number of cars in service at any time of the day, the interval or headway between trains, and the interlocking of local and express trains to effect convenient transfers at important express stations.

The layman can hardly appreciate the problems which arise in every day operation, such as providing cars to take care of the service, and the proper crewing of trains, at times made difficult by some of the personnel of the crew failing to report for duty because of sickness, or otherwise.

Considerable comment, and in fact criticism, had been made from time to time as to the magnitude of the stations. The stations of the Independent System average 640 feet in length. In fact, newspaper comments in the early stages of operation called attention to the scarcity of passengers on the stations and in the cars of the trains. You should see them now! Those responsible for the design and construction very wisely looked into the future and provided for the most modern station layout, and signal and power systems, with the result that there have been but few changes made in order to take care of the added traffic. Peak load traffic in the morning, especially on the Washington Heights Line, has about reached its maximum.

The traffic problem is interesting, as one can never fully visualize to what extent traffic will develop. As an illustration: The 175th Street Station on the Washington Heights line was designed by the engineers to have a twenty-four hour control on the southerly end of the station and a part time control on the northerly end of the station. The first few months of operation a part time control, as designed, was in service on the northerly end of the station. At the commencement of operation the average daily number of passengers entering those controls at the northerly end of the station was 5,000 daily. Patrons in New Jersey, however, soon found the advantages of the Eighth Avenue subway by the use of busses across the George Washington Bridge to the 175th Street Station, with the result that patronage at that station has grown from 5,000 to 17,500 daily. This, of course, is one-way traffic, and includes incoming passengers only.

The direct operation of cars and trains in yards and on the road is under the jurisdiction of the Assistant Superintendent of Operation, who directs a force of approximately 1,050 men, including Trainmasters, Motorman-Instructors, Dispatchers, Towermen, Yardmasters, Motormen, Conductors and Platform-men.

Assisting the Assistant Superintendent of Operation is a staff of Trainmasters and Motorman-Instructors. The Trainmaster is in direct contact with all yards, Dispatchers offices and interlocking towers. He controls the pulse of the railroad, makes the quick decisions of importance, and in case of power interruption is the only one with authority to restore the power to the contact rails.

Trainmasters and Motorman-Instructors constantly ride the trains to observe Motormen and Conductors in the performance of duty. With their help the Motormen and Conductors have become highly efficient.

For convenience in operation, the railroad is divided into operating districts under the jurisdiction of train dispatchers, each dispatcher being responsible for the operation of his district, including lay-up yards. There is a loud speaker telephone circuit extending over the entire line, with connections at each Dispatcher's office, interlocking tower, and the Trainmaster's office, so that interruptions in service, reports, or instructions can be communicated simultaneously to those interested.

The Dispatcher or his Assistant inspects each Motorman and Conductor for fitness and neatness before permitting him to go on duty.

It is the Dispatcher's duty, under the supervision of the Trainmaster, to see that trains are started on time, to provide intervals and adequate cars according to the schedule, and in case of breakdowns or unavoidable delays, to reroute trains in order to take care of the traffic. This is all done with but little delay and usually without the public knowing that anything unusual had occurred.

The railroad is completely signaled—that is—all main tracks are equipped with automatic block signals throughout their length and all switches on both main line and yards are interlocked. All signal equipment is of the latest type, embracing the best safety features which have been developed for the conditions prevailing on a Rapid Transit Railroad. The signals are the color light type, both in the subway and outdoors. All main track signals and principal yard signals have automatic stops which so operate that if a train attempts to pass a signal indicating "STOP", the train stop will cause an emergency application of the brakes and bring the train to a stop before reaching any danger point.

(SLIDE No. 6—AUTOMATIC STOP, Etc.)

A speed control system is also used on steep descending grades to prevent excessive speed and also in the approach to stations to permit closing in, thus increasing the possible headway of trains on the Railroad. The signal system was designed to permit operation of 30 11-car trains per hour, with station stops not to exceed one minute, with a margin to take care of operating contingencies. Due to this margin and the train stop being somewhat less than anticipated, it has been found possible to operate trains on a minute and a half headway.

All interlocking is either electric or electric-pneumatic, the entire work having been approximately evenly divided between the General Railway Signal Company of Rochester, which furnishes electric interlocking, and the Union Switch and Signal Company of Swissvale, Penna., which furnishes electro-pneumatic interlocking.

Due to the impossibility of Towermen seeing more than a very little of the Railroad under their control, indicators are used in all signal towers, which gives the Towerman complete information as to the position of all trains within his territory.

The signal system when completed about a year hence will have cost approximately $20,000,000.

(SLIDE No. 7—SIGNAL TOWER—207th STREET)

The railroad is also equipped with a complete telephone, emergency alarm and fire protection system. Telephones are installed in all Signal Towers, Dispatchers' Offices, Change Booths, Maintenance Quarters and Offices, and also at intervals of approximately 500 feet throughout the length of the subways. At each of these line locations there is also an emergency alarm box similar to a fire alarm box, which may be used by anyone in emergency to cut power off the third rail in the zone in which the box is located. The zones extend from Substation to Substation, a distance of approximately a half a mile to two miles. When an emergency alarm box is pulled and power cut off the third rail, the code number of the box pulled, indicating its location, is sounded in the Chief Power Dispatcher's Office and in the Operating Headquarters and is also recorded on a tape. The person operating the emergency alarm immediately uses the telephone to inform headquarters as to the prevailing conditions. A fire extinguisher is also located at each emergency location and in all Towers and Maintenance Quarters.

(SLIDE No. 8—EMERGENCY ALARM)

Primary electrical energy for the power equipment is purchased from the New York Edison Company and is converted by some 212,000 kilowatts of conversion apparatus into direct current for train propulsion.

Conversion is effected in most part by unit underground installations of mercury arc rectifiers placed directly alongside the right-of-way. There are 50 non-attended substations in operation.

(SLIDE No. 9—SUBSTATION)

They are fully automatic and monitored at a central point on the railroad—the Power Dispatcher's Office.

At this point a large control board is manned by two operators per watch who normally record the automatic movements in a log book, but who can intervene and operate any of the remote power or ventilation units.

(SLIDE No. 10—SUPERVISORY LAYOUT)

This is, I think, the largest automatic supervisory system in the world.

All of our tracks except yard tracks, sidings and through special work (frogs and switches), are of the concreted type or as we call it, Type 2 track. In this construction the rails are independently supported on short wooden blocks imbedded in concrete with a trough between the rails for drainage. Blocks are 6 inches by 10 inches creosoted, prime long leaf yellow pine spaced 18 to the 33 foot rail length, imbedded in the concrete approximately for the full 6 inch depth with the concrete sloping toward the center trough. One hundred pound ARA Type B rail on single shoulder tie plates with screw spikes are used throughout Type 2 track.

(SLIDE No. 11—SHOWING TRACKS)

This type of construction was adopted for our railroad after a number of years of satisfactory service in stations and river tunnels and for a considerable length of continuous track in other New York City subways. Some of the tie blocks in this type of track have already been in service for about twenty years with very little indication of deterioration or mechanical wear and it is our expectation that they will last for thirty-five years or more before it will be necessary to renew them.

In our ballasted type of track, owing to the shallow concrete invert in which the tracks are laid, we get only about 7 inches of broken stone underneath the ties. All ties are 6 inches by 8 inches laid with the 6 inch depth and are creosoted, prime long leaf yellow pine. One hundred pound ARA Type B rail, tie plates and cut spikes are used in all ballasted track except for storage tracks in yards, where

.85 pound ASCE rail without tie plates is used. On all curves of more than 2½ degrees a guard rail with 2 inch flange-way is installed on the low side. Curves are super-elevated in accordance with the usual steam road and AREA formula for an approximate 40 to 45 mile express track speed and 25 to 30 local track speed, as predetermined by operating factors, such as station stops, length of run between stops, grades, train schedules, etc. All guarded curves are amply transitioned. All switches are housed and all frogs are of the Cast Manganese rail bound type, such as are used on steam roads. We use five anti-creepers per 33 foot rail length.

Due to the superior signal and power systems, to the upkeep and maintenance of car equipment, and to the Transportation Division organization, the railroad has, since the beginning of operation, maintained a monthly "on time" performance of not less than 99.55 per cent. As a matter of fact the record for last year shows the following:

On time performance—99.91 per cent

Trains operated—769,303

Car miles operated—34,684,554

Total minutes detention (all causes)—1,512

Average minutes detention per interruption—5.07

Total failures—298,

making an average of 116,391 car miles operated per failure.

24.4 per cent of the time lost by detentions was due directly to passengers themselves, such as blocking and holding of doors, pulling emergency cord, ejection of disorderly passengers, suicides, and intoxicated persons falling from station platforms to trackway. In figuring this "on time" performance every late train is tabulated. It has been impressed upon the organization that not to include a late train is like cheating at solitaire.

The first interruption to service after the commencement of operation occurred on the morning of September 26, 1932, which, incidentally, happened to be the day of the funeral of the late Colonel John R. Slattery, who was Deputy Chief Engineer for the Board of Transportation. It made one feel that the railroad of its own accord decided to honor the Colonel. The interruption was caused by a power failure. A main bus insulator at the 99th Street substation failed, resulting in the loss of power between 119th and 91st Streets. I was on one of the trains that were caught between stations, and was indeed pleased to note how quickly the new men in the operating, power and maintenance organizations responded in correcting the trouble and handling the trains and passengers, which resulted in a minimum delay.

We have received many favorable comments on the practice of requiring trainmen on express trains to patrol their train on the long run between 59th and 125th Streets. This patrolling is mandatory at times when the Conductor of the train can get through the train without discommoding passengers. I was rather amused at an incident that took place on one of the express trains on that long run. At about 95th Street a male passenger hurriedly went from one car to another, and facing the passengers, in a very excited voice exclaimed: "A woman has fainted in the next car; has anyone a bottle of whiskey?" Two passengers immediately tendered the excited individual a bottle of whiskey. He grabbed one, uncorked it, drank about half, and returned it with thanks, saying that if there was anything in the world that made him sick to his stomach—it was to see a woman faint.

It is, of course, understood that unlike many other municipal enterprises the railroad is operating twenty-four hours a day, three hundred and sixty-five days a year, with the result that it is necessary to supervise and check every irregularity during the twenty-four hour period, a report and investigation of which is immediately made, so that conditions and practices can be corrected at their source. This includes all irregularities and unusual occurrences affecting the structure, the equipment, the personnel or the public.

Systematic inspection of the physical property has prevented breakdowns in service. As the record indicates tracks, signals and power are all operating with little or no trouble. All car equipment inspections are made at the 207th Street Yard, the terminus of the Washington Heights route. Regular inspections are made at 1,500 mile intervals. After each car has traveled 1,300 miles since the last inspection the Transportation Division gives notice and the Car Inspection Division withdraws it from service at the proper time. About eight days elapse between inspections, although cars not in continuous service run correspondingly longer. Every third period, or 4,500 miles, the car is given a semi-general inspection, and every sixth period, or 9,000 miles, a general inspection.

At the inspections the cars are placed over the pits in the inspection shed with the aid of flexible power leads, since there is no third rail in the building. Assignment boards are hung at the outside end of the first car to indicate that men are working and that the cars must not be moved. A metal tag bearing his name is hung by each inspector on the proper assignment board to indicate what work he is doing. Each inspector must remove his own tag personally. It is the safest method of knowing that he has completed his work and that the car may be moved.

At the 1,500 mile inspection period all working parts are checked and adjusted. Lubrication is done at this time only in the event that the check indicates it is needed.

The semi-general or 4,500 mile inspection constitutes a lubricating period, in addition to the items of the regular inspection.

At the general or 9,000 mile inspection the cars are received at the shed one-half hour before the regular working hours. The car cleaners open all covers and blow out dust and dirt so that when the inspectors begin work the parts are clean and the dust has subsided. These general inspections include all items covered at the regular and semi-general inspections, and in addition include a thorough checking, testing and cleaning of all mechanical and electrical parts and equipment.

Should an inspector at any inspection find a defect which cannot be immediately remedied the car is removed from service and sent to the repair shop for such work as is needed.

Up to now no overhauling has been done. Except for unusual defects uncovered at the inspection period, no work of this character has been necessary. Some of the cars have now run more than 170,000 miles and two cars have been sent to the shop to be torn down to determine what limits should be set for overhauling. This work is now in progress and when a review of the wear is completed a program for light repairs and general overhauling will be adopted.

(SLIDE No. 12—YARD)

(SLIDE No. 13—CAR)

This slide shows the type of car now in service on the Independent System, which is 60 feet 6 inches long over coupler faces, width 10 feet, height over all 12 feet 2 inches, and has one motor truck in which are mounted 2—190 horsepower motors, and 1 trailing truck with truck centers 44 feet 7 inches. The car weighs approximately 85,000 lbs. light, and has a seating capacity of 60 passengers, with standing room for over 200, giving a maximum loaded weight of approximately 124,000 lbs.

To compensate for this large difference between light and loaded weight, the car is equipped with a device known as the variable load valve, which maintains uniform acceleration and deceleration rates. This is accomplished by the variable resistance affecting the acceleration relay to increase or decrease the current to the motors. The acceleration rate is 1¾ miles per hour per second, and the deceleration rate is 2 miles per hour per second, for service application, and about 4 miles per hour per second for emergency.

All cars are equipped with the Westinghouse Airbrake Equipment known as the AMUE 5 equipment. Its principle features are the simultaneous operation of the brakes on each car regardless of how many cars in the train are controlled through the electric portion of the universal valve and the variable load valve, which was mentioned before.

This variable load valve, as its name implies, compensates for the variation in the live load in the car. It is actuated by the compression of the elliptic spring in the trailer truck each time the doors are opened and at that time is set for the succeeding acceleration period and stop. By a system of levers the brake cylinder pressure is changed from the service light car setting of 35 lbs. per square inch to the maximum service pressure of 50 lbs. per square inch. Emergency pressures are controlled similarly from 50 lbs. to 70 lbs.

You will note 4 side door openings, with 8 side doors that are operated by 5 air engines controlled from any selected operating position on the train by one man. These doors open in 1½ seconds and permit very rapid loading and unloading.

(SLIDE No. 14—OBLIQUE VIEW OF CAR)

(SLIDE No. 15—END OF CAR)

This is an end view of the car which shows the H 2 A automatic coupler, in which the air connections are made automatically.

The oblong section under the coupler shows where the train line connections for automatic control of the car doors, lights, heat, etc., are made when cars are coupled. This is done by means of 21 train line circuits and there are 39 contact buttons behind this cover which is shown in a closed position.

(SLIDE No. 16—INTERIOR OF CAR)

This is an interior view of the car and shows seating arrangements, as well as signs, fans, stanchions and an operating cab at the far end.

(SLIDE No. 17—CLOSE INTERIOR VIEW—END OF CAR)

This is a closer view of the end of the car, and on the left shows the coasting clock, from which a record of the coasting done each trip is obtained on a printed slip. The hand brake is shown mounted on the end sheet at the left of the door opening. On the right hand side is the operator's cab, on the back of which is mounted a fire extinguisher and the emergency cord to the Conductor's valve. This cord is also extended to the outside of the car, from which point it is available for the Conductor's use.

Road Car Inspectors are stationed at strategic points along the line to take care of emergency repairs. Often times minor troubles will occur enroute, and when trouble develops enroute the Motorman calls the Road Car Inspector by an authorized whistle signal, and in the majority of cases the Inspector makes running repairs while the train is moving. We have forty-seven such Inspectors distributed over the railroad.

The following slides show some of the odd features of our railroad:

(SLIDE No. 18—181st STREET STATION)

This shows the 181st Street Station which was constructed in a portion of a tunnel excavated in rock. Because of the limited width the platforms and stairways are necessarily narrow. A hanging mezzanine was constructed to relieve platform congestion and to expedite the movement of passengers to and from the exits. At one end of the station escalators carry the passengers to the street level. At the other end of the station a lateral tunnel serves to take the passengers out through the side of the hill. The entrance to that tunnel is shown on this slide:

(SLIDE No. 19—TUNNEL ENTRANCE)

The condition of the sidewalk was due to the construction of a new street which was then in progress.

(SLIDE No. 20—4th AVENUE STATION)

This slide shows the 4th Avenue Station in Brooklyn on a portion of the line which is elevated. A few blocks past this point the line again enters the ground.

(SLIDE No. 21—STATION DIAGRAM)
(SLIDE No. 22—STATION CONTROLS)
(SLIDE No. 23—EXPRESS STATION PLATFORM LEVEL)

The Station Division is one of the large operating units. Approximately 950 men are employed as Supervisors, Station Agents and Porters. The Independent System has received many testimonials commenting upon the cleanliness of stations, and the courtesy and efficiency of station employees.

In cleaning stations our aim is to serve the riding public by keeping stations safe and free from hazards, bright and clean in appearance and sanitary at all times with the least inconvenience and annoyance to passengers and at as small cost as can be justified by the results obtained.

To insure as close an approach as possible to our goal, all new Porters are given a thorough course of instruction in the field before being assigned to stations. After assignment to stations they are under constant supervision by Station Supervisors and Station Masters, their work being checked daily and further instructions given where needed. To guide them in the proper performance of their duties, schedules have been prepared for each station. These schedules specify the sequence of the various duties and designate the amount of time to be spent on each. In addition each Porter is supplied with a set of written instructions designed to keep before him at all times the basic principles of his work.

The safety and convenience of passengers and the cleanliness of stations go hand in hand. Where stairways, platforms, passageways, etc., are clean and free from water, snow, ice or other obstructions, the liability of accident is reduced to a minimum. Porters are so instructed and schedules are so framed as to effect the cleaning, first and frequently, of all areas of hazardous nature such as stairways, edges of platforms, base of turnstiles, etc. Much thought is given to traffic in relation to cleaning. Cleaning is done immediately before and immediately after concentrations of traffic, in order that the heavily used areas may be clean and safe at the time of heaviest use and to eliminate the necessity of endangering and inconveniencing our passengers by the use of brooms, brushes, pails and other equipment in their midst. Tile cleaning, column cleaning, sweeping and platform scrubbing in congested areas are accomplished as much as possible during the early morning hours when traffic is light. When work must be done in comparatively crowded areas, every precaution is taken and Porters are repeatedly cautioned to use their equipment with extreme care and with first thought for the safety of passengers.

Sanitary stations are striven for with a thought for future as well as present sanitation. Disinfectant is used freely not only in toilets but in the cleaning of various other parts of the stations. Certain sites on every station are used by inconsiderate passengers as convenient toilets, no spot on any station is safe from the early morning inebriates who can't hold their food, and every gutter and the base of every column are the targets for expectorators. These places are thoroughly and frequently cleaned, disinfected and deodorized. All sweeping is accompanied by the heavy use of damp sawdust to prevent the rise of dust and bacteria, and wherever possible, floor areas are periodically scrubbed and washed clean of dirt, dust, germs and odors. All waste and rubbish is disposed of as quickly as possible by work trains.

Economy is practiced in the supervision of labor and the careful selection and use of equipment. A great amount of time has been spent in the making of time studies and the preparation of schedules. It is known how much work each Porter can and should do, his schedule has been made out accordingly, and the supervision will not permit of great deviation from the work so laid out. Tools and equipment have been designed or selected with satisfactory performance and ultimate economy in mind. The care of equipment and the careful and economical use of expendable supplies has been drilled into each Porter.

It may interest you to know that in one year the Station Division uses:

588 corn brooms
212 push brooms
2,800 toilet and miscellaneous brushes
460 buckets
940 gallons of disinfectant
190 gallons of polish
17,000 pounds of pumice
41,000 pounds of soap
17,000 pounds of rock salt
30,000 pounds of sand
8,500 bushels of sawdust, and
37,000 packages of toilet paper

These items represent only a small part of the material that is necessary to be kept on hand at the Storehouse by the purchasing and storekeeper's departments. The storehouse consists of two floors at the north end of the Administration Building at 207th Street, an outside shed for the storing of bulk material and reels of cable, an oil and paint house, and coal hoppers. Branch storehouses are located at the Bronx Yard, Queens Yard and Power Division Headquarters. At the last inventory taken as of May 31, 1935, 12,897 items of material were found to be on hand, amounting to $477,756. To be prepared for any emergency, extra supplies and equipment, some of which involve a considerable investment, must be kept on hand to service all departments of the railroad.

The railroad is now operating a maximum of 811 cars in the morning peak hours, 2,132 trains and 124,634 car miles daily. There are approximately 145 single track and 35 route miles now in operation, and when the new lines are opened there will then be in operation approximately 54 route miles.

Express trains are operated at an average speed of twenty-five miles an hour, and local trains at nineteen point seven miles an hour, including all station stops between terminals. It is my understanding that this is the fastest subway in operation.

It is hardly necessasy to say that the public welcomes speedier transportation. No better indication of the public's response to rapid transit facilities can be found than in the liberal use of the Independent System immediately after it was placed in operation.

When the Bronx Line was placed in operation, extending from 145th Street to 205th Street, regardless of the fact that the Board had advertised how trains would operate, and the added fact that notices had been posted in cars, an unusual number of passengers boarded the wrong trains.

It is conceded by all that the Independent System is the most modern subway system in existence.

To my mind the most important thing in the operation of this railroad, regardless of its superior equipment, is the spirit of the men. Without that spirit the operation would not be successful. There are 3,408 of them. All through the twenty-four hours they go on and off duty to perform their specific tasks in the great machine producing transportation. At no time are they all on duty at the same time. At no time is it possible for them to be together as one unit, or to see them together. Yet they must co-operate so that the railroad shall function as a single unit. They know what public service means and they take pride in their work rendering that service.

The most important factor, however, in building good will is the service rendered by the employees of the railroad who come in contact with the public. Every department of the railroad may function 100 per cent and yet if those who are in contact with the public fail in their responsibilities, the good will of the public cannot be obtained.

Generally, a railroad has but two things to sell—service and scrap. The Independent System has sold its service, but VERY LITTLE SCRAP.

PRESIDENT: Gentlemen, we have listened to a most interesting paper, ably and clearly presented. For the next fifteen minutes the meeting is in your hands. I will not call on any one for remarks but will be glad to have you ask any questions that may come to your minds. Mr. Pfeifer has very kindly agreed to try to answer any questions you may wish to ask.

MR. C. O. DAMBACH: Having in mind the crossing accident that did not happen on the Independent Subway, have you had any serious train accidents on the Independent Subways?

MR. PFEIFER: With the exception of a few minor train accidents in the yards, no train accidents have occurred on the railroad. There have been no fatalities to passengers since the commencement of operation.

PROF. L. E. ENDSLEY: One of the pictures showed cars with four openings and eight doors. How long does the average train stand at the station?

MR. PFEIFER: The average station stop is 22 seconds. Many stops, of course, are made in less time.

MR. C. M. WHEELER: How many cars are in use on the Independent System?

MR. PFEIFER: 811 cars are required for actual daily operation. There are 865 cars now on the property. 435 cars are in the process of construction by three different car

ıanufacturers, which cars will be delivered in the very near
ᵤuture.

MR. JOHN B. WRIGHT: You spoke of trouble with
now in the city. On how much of your subway system do
ᵣou have snow conditions?

MR. PFEIFER: All of the railroad is underground with
ₕhe exception of the yards, and about a mile and a quarter
ₓtending from Carroll Street to Fourth Avenue Station,
ₕhich is on an elevated structure. All of the switches in the
ₐards are equipped with electric snow melting heaters, which
ₐave taken care of the situation very well. However, when
ₐ large snowstorm is anticipated, all of the cars stored in
ₒpen yards are placed under cover in the inspection sheds lo-
ₐated in the yards, and in the storage tracks in the subway
ₜtructure. Considerable trouble, of course, is experienced dur-
ₙng snowstorms, at the entrances to the stations, but this is
ₐared for by concentrating Porters, Maintenance of Way em-
ₗoyees and Trackmen on snow removal.

QUESTION: What was your arrangement for breakdown on your system during that electric current stop about
a week ago in New York?

MR. PFEIFER: The power for the operation of the
railroad is supplied under a contract with the New York Edison Company. At 4:16 p. m. on January 15, the electrical
energy supplied to all points north of 53rd Street on the
Washington Heights and Concourse Lines was interrupted as
the result of a failure in the Hell Gate power station of the
contractor. Restoration was effected on the Concourse and
Washington Heights Lines north of 145th Street to an extent
sufficient to permit resumption of revenue passenger traffic
on a restricted schedule at reduced speed by 7:30 p. m., and
along Central Park West to permit the restoration of the signal system to normal, and the resumption of regular train
schedules by 5:30 a. m. on January 16.

MR. W. R. GELLATLY: What equipment do you use
for wrecking equipment?

MR. PFEIFER: We have a number of automobile trucks
that are completely equipped to take care of any reasonable
breakdown in the Power, Maintenance of Way, and Transportation Divisions. In addition to this, we have a pump car

which is operated on the track, to take care of any flood conditions.

MR. A. B. SEVERN: As to cleaning the stations and the disposition of the waste, how do you take care of the trash that accumulates?

MR. PFEIFER: Refuse cans and paper receptacle cans are placed at certain locations on the station platforms, into which the Station Department and Maintenance of Way Department employees place the refuse collected. Passengers, of course, deposit their waste paper in the waste paper receptacles. This waste paper is collected, baled, and sold. We have an ingenious contrivance that is placed between tracks at the ends of stations, consisting of a wire screen about 8 inches deep and 24 inches wide, that collects most of the rubbish that is inadverently thrown from the platforms to the track by passengers. This collection is automatic and is caused by the suction of the train. This screen prevents refuse of this type from flying all over the railroad due to the suction of passing trains. Work trains operate over the road each night to collect all the rubbish from the stations.

QUESTION: You spoke of parallel traffic in comparison with your own traffic. May I ask what other traffic lines you parallel?

MR. PFEIFER: The Interborough Rapid Transit Company and the Brooklyn-Manhattan Transit Company.

QUESTION: How many people do you carry, and how dense is the traffic?

MR. PFEIFER: At the present time we are handling approximately 765 thousand passengers daily. The majority of this traffic, of course, is handled during the morning and evening peak hours of traffic, although there is a constant flow of traffic throughout the 24-hour period. During the peak periods of traffic, ten-car trains are operated, this service tapering off during the day commensurate with traffic requirements.

MR. FRANK J. LANAHAN: You have told us how you collect the garbage and the papers and all kinds of trash. How do you collect the money?

MR. PFEIFER: The money is received from patrons

through the medium of turnstiles. The coins are retrieved from the turnstiles, and bagged, by the Station Agents, and then deposited in a drop safe that is provided in each station booth. The Station Agent, of course, cannot open this safe. The money from the safe is collected by collectors from an armored truck that services the line.

MR. LANAHAN: What is your heaviest revenue station?

MR. PFEIFER: 34th Street. We handle approximately 150 thousand passengers a day at this station. The heaviest way station is 175th Street, where we handle approximately 50 thousand passengers a day.

MR. I. LAMONT HUGHES: You spoke of a record of the proportion of coasting that trains run. How is that done?

MR. PFEIFER: There is a coasting clock located in each car, which is electrically controlled by the propulsion of the motor. At the commencement of each run the motorman sets up the coasting clock, which records the amount of coasting that is done by each motorman on each trip. Coasting is done, of course, to save power. A record is kept of the amount of coasting done by each motorman. About 30 per cent of the entire time consumed is coasting.

QUESTION: What do you mean by competitive and non-competitive employees?

MR. PFEIFER: Of course, it is understood that the Independent System is municipally operated. Therefore, all employees engaged in the operation are municipal employees, under Civil Service rules. At the commencement of operation, and until January 1, 1935, practically all employees were in the non-competitive class, which means that the Board of Transportation examined and qualified the personnel for the various positions necessary for the operation of the railroad. Since January 1, 1935, all examinations for positions on the railroad are held by the Civil Service Commission, which promulgates a certified eligible list from which appointments are made in the order of that list.

PROF. L. E. ENDSLEY: I am sure this Club has enjoyed this talk and the ensuing discussion very much. It does show us what is necessary in a concentrated city traffic like that in New York. I have been personally very much interested for years in the operation of the New York subways and I know we all appreciate what Mr. Pfeifer has shown us tonight. So I would move you that we extend to Mr. Pfeifer a vote of thanks for his excellent discussion.

The motion prevailed by unanimous rising vote.

MR. PFEIFER: I thank you, and I want to express at this time the pleasure I have had in meeting a lot of railroad men and in being permitted to address this Railway Club of Pittsburgh.

PRESIDENT: If there is no other business, the meeting will stand adjourned. A lunch is prepared at each end of the room and we hope you will all stay and enjoy a social hour.

J. D. CONWAY, Secretary.

OFFICIAL PROCEEDINGS
RAILWAY CLUB OF PITTSBURGH
$1.00 Per Year   25¢ Per Copy

| Vol. XXXV. | FEBRUARY 27, 1936. | No. 4. |

RAILROAD RESEARCH PROBLEMS
By L. W. WALLACE, Director of Equipment Research,
Association of American Railroads, Chicago, Illinois

The proof of your interest

in the Club can be

enhanced

by securing a

NEW MEMBER.

Application form is available

in this magazine. Look

it up and

"ACT NOW."

OFFICIAL PROCEEDINGS

OF

The Railway Club of Pittsburgh

Organized October 18, 1901

Published monthly, except June, July and August, by the Railway Club of
Pittsburgh, J. D. Conway, Secretary, 515 Grandview Ave., Pittsburgh, Pa..

Entered as Second Class Matter February 6, 1915, at the Postoffice at Pittsburgh,
under the Act of March 3, 1879.

Vol. XXXV No. 4.	**Pittsburgh, Pa., Feb. 27, 1936**	$1.00 Per Year 25c Per Copy

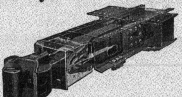

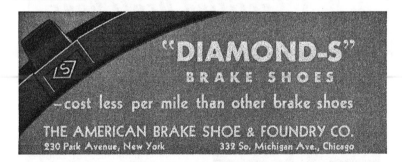

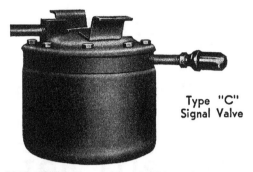

EQUIPMENT FOR RAILROADS

STATIONARY AIR COMPRESSORS   PORTABLE AIR COMPRESSORS

ROCK DRILLING EQUIPMENT   CONSTRUCTION AIR TOOLS

CENTRIFUGAL PUMPS   STEAM AND POWER PUMPS

DEEP WELL TURBINE PUMPS   SUMP AND DRAINAGE PUMPS

LOCOMOTIVE FEEDWATER HEATERS   STATIONARY FEEDWATER HEATERS

STEAM CONDENSERS   CONDENSER AUXILIARIES

DIESEL ENGINES   GAS ENGINES

*REFRIGERATION EQUIPMENT   *AIR CONDITIONING EQUIPMENT

V-BELT DRIVES   †LIQUID METERS

*Through subsidiary, CARBONDALE MACHINE CORPORATION
†Through subsidiary, WORTHINGTON-GAMON METER COMPANY

● *Complete descriptive literature available*

**WORTHINGTON PUMP AND MACHINERY CORPORATION
HARRISON, NEW JERSEY**

A-3580

INDEX—ADVERTISERS.

The Railway Club of Pittsburgh:

....19..........

Gentlemen:

Will you kindly consider my Application for Membership in your Club at the next meeting:

Name...

Title...

Company ....

My Address...

Recommended by...

OFFICIAL PROCEEDINGS
OF

The Railway Club of Pittsburgh

Organized October 18, 1901

Vol. XXXV No. 4.	Pittsburgh, Pa., Feb. 27, 1936	$1.00 Per Year 25c Per Copy

OFFICERS FOR 1935-1936

President
R. P. FORSBERG,
Chief Engineer, P. & L. E. R. R. Co., Pittsburgh, Pa.

First Vice President
E. A. RAUSCHART,
Mechanical Supt., Montour Railroad,
Coraopolis, Pa.

Secretary
J. D. CONWAY,
Railway Supply Manufacturers' Association,
Pittsburgh, Pa.

Second Vice President
G. M. SIXSMITH,
Supt., Pennsylvania Railroad,
Pittsburgh, Pa.

Treasurer
E. J. SEARLES,
Manager, Schaefer Equipment Co.,
Pittsburgh, Pa.

EXECUTIVE COMMITTEE:

FRANK J. LANAHAN, Chairman, President, Fort Pitt Malleable Iron Co., Pittsburgh, Pa.
A. STUCKI, Engineer, A. Stucki Company, Pittsburgh, Pa.
SAMUEL LYNN, Supt. Rolling Stock, P. & L. E. R. R., McKees Rocks, Pa.
D. F. CRAWFORD, Consulting Engineer, Pittsburgh, Pa.
G. W. WILDIN, Consulting Engineer, Westinghouse Air Brake Company, Pittsburgh, Pa.
W. S. McABEE, Vice Pres. & General Supt., Union Railroad Co., East Pittsburgh, Pa.
E. W. SMITH, Vice President, Pennsylvania Railroad, Pittsburgh, Pa.
LOUIS E. ENDSLEY, Consulting Engineer, 516 East End Avenue, Pittsburgh, Pa.
F. I. SNYDER, Vice President & General Manager, B. & L. E. R. R. Co., Pittsburgh, Pa.
C. O. DAMBACH, General Manager, P. & W. Va. Ry. Co., Pittsburgh, Pa.
R. H. FLINN, General Superintendent, Pennsylvania Railroad, Pittsburgh, Pa.

SUBJECT COMMITTEE:

D. W. McGEORGE, Chairman, Secretary, Edgewater Steel Company, Pittsburgh, Pa.
JOHN B. WRIGHT, Asst. Vice President, Westinghouse Air Brake Co., Wilmerding, Pa.
M. R. REED, General Supt. Motive Power, Pennsylvania Railroad, Pittsburgh, Pa.

ADVERTISING COMMITTEE:

E. A. FOARD, Chairman, Supt. Stations & Transfers, Pennsylvania R. R., Pittsburgh, Pa.
KARL BERG, Superintendent Motive Power, P. & L. E. R. R. Co., McKees Rocks, Pa.
H. E. PASSMORE, Representative, The American Hammered Piston Ring Co., Pgh., Pa.

RECEPTION AND ATTENDANCE COMMITTEE:

J. D. BELTZ, Chairman, Superintendent, B. & O. R. R. Co., Pittsburgh, Pa.
W. C. BUREL, Vice Chairman, Master Mechanic, Western Allegheny Railroad, Kaylor, Pa.
J. B. BAKER, Chief Engr. Maintenance of Way, Pennsylvania Railroad, Pittsburgh, Pa.
WALTER C. SANDERS, Gen. Mgr., Railway Div., Timken Roller Bearing Co., Canton, O.
G. A. BLACKMORE, President & Gen. Mgr., Union Switch & Signal Co., Swissvale, Pa.
J. S. LANAHAN, Vice President, Fort Pitt Malleable Iron Company, Pittsburgh, Pa.
J. A. WARFEL, Special Representative, Air Reduction Sales Co., Pittsburgh, Pa.
J. C. SHINGLEDECKER, Supervisor of Service Stations, The Pennzoil Co., Pittsburgh, Pa.
J. C. DILWORTH, Mgr. of Railroad Sales, Carnegie-Illinois Steel Corp., Pittsburgh, Pa.
G. H. BURNETTE, Assistant Chief Engineer, P. & L. E. R. R. Co., Pittsburgh, Pa.
W. R. TRIEM, Superintendent, Pennsylvania Railroad, Pittsburgh, Pa.
J. W. HOOVER, Asst. Chief of Transpn., Subsidiary Cos. U. S. Steel Corp., Pittsburgh, Pa.
J. W. JOHNSON, Superintendent, Railway Express Agency, Pittsburgh, Pa.
A. A. READ, Duquesne Slag Products Company, Pittsburgh, Pa.
C. P. SCHRECONGOST, Traffic Manager, Hillman Coal & Coke Company, Pittsburgh, Pa.

ENTERTAINMENT COMMITTEE:

J. PORTER GILLESPIE, Chairman, Asst. Gen. Supt., Lockhart Iron & Steel Co., Pgh., Pa.

FRANK E. WEIS, Vice Chairman, Transportation Clerk, Penna. R. R., Pittsburgh, Pa.

E. H. HOLMES, Sales Department, Fort Pitt Malleable Iron Co., Pittsburgh, Pa.

C. C. CLARK, Sales Manager Central District, Pressed Steel Car Co., McKees Rocks, Pa.

A. L. KESSLER, Clearance Clerk, Pennsylvania Railroad, Pittsburgh, Pa.

T. F. SHERIDAN, Asst. to S.M.P. and S.R.S., P. & L. E. R. R. Co., McKees Rocks, Pa.

JAMES NAGEL, Superintendent Transportation, Montour Railroad, Coraopolis, Pa.

FINANCE COMMITTEE:

J. L. O'TOOLE, Chairman, Asst. to Gen. Manager, P. & L. E. R. R. Co., Pittsburgh, Pa.

G. W. HONSBERGER, Transpn. Mgr., Westinghouse Electric & Mfg. Co., Pittsburgh, Pa.

F. J. RYAN, District Representative, Detroit, Toledo & Ironton Railroad, Pittsburgh, Pa.

C. E. CATT, Division Accountant, B. & O. R. R. Co., Pittsburgh, Pa.

J. W. BOYD, Superintendent, Monongahela Railway Company, Brownsville, Pa.

MEMBERSHIP COMMITTEE:

WILLIAM R. GELLATLY, Chairman, Pres., Superior Railway Products Corp., Pgh., Pa.

T. E. BRITT, Vice Chairman, Division Storekeeper, B. & O. R. R. Co., Pittsburgh, Pa.

A. B. SEVERN, General Manager, A. Stucki Company, Pittsburgh, Pa.

W. P. BUFFINGTON, Traffic Manager, Pittsburgh Coal Company, Pittsburgh, Pa.

R. S. BULL, Supt. Power & Inclines, Pittsburgh Railways Co., N. S., Pittsburgh, Pa.

A. F. COULTER, Master Car Builder, Union Railroad Co., East Pittsburgh, Pa.

T. R. DICKINSON, Purchasing Agent, B. & L. E. R. R. Co., Pittsburgh, Pa.

D. K. ORR, Road Master, Monongahela Railway Co., Brownsville, Pa.

C. M. WHEELER, Sales Engineer, Union Switch & Signal Company, Swissvale, Pa.

W. F. AMBROSE, Master Mechanic, Aliquippa & Southern Railroad, Aliquippa, Pa.

JOHN I. MULVEY, Traffic Manager, Hubbard & Company, Pittsburgh, Pa.

THOMAS R. FITZPATRICK, Freight Traffic Mgr., P. & L. E. R. R. Co., Pittsburgh, Pa.

P. W. HEPBURN, Sales Engineer, Gulf Refining Company, Pittsburgh, Pa.

W. B. MOIR, Chief Car Inspector, Pennsylvania Railroad, Pittsburgh, Pa.

C. W. TRUST, Assistant Traffic Manager, Carnegie-Illinois Steel Corp., Pittsburgh, Pa

PAST PRESIDENTS:

*J. H. McCONNELL	October,	1901, to October, 1903
*L. H. TURNER	November,	1903, to October, 1905
*F. H. STARK	November,	1905, to October, 1907
*H. W. WATTS	November,	1907, to April, 1908
*D. J. REDDING	November,	1908, to October, 1910
*F. R. McFEATTERS	November,	1910, to October, 1912
*A. G. MITCHELL	November,	1912, to October, 1914
*F. M. McNULTY	November,	1914, to October, 1916
*J. G. CODE	November,	1916, to October, 1917
*D. M. HOWE	November,	1917, to October, 1918
*J. A. SPIELMAN	November,	1918, to October, 1919
H. H. MAXFIELD	November,	1919, to October, 1920
FRANK J. LANAHAN	November,	1920, to October, 1921
SAMUEL LYNN	November,	1921, to October, 1922
D. F. CRAWFORD	November,	1922, to October, 1923
GEO. D. OGDEN	November,	1923, to October, 1924
A. STUCKI	November,	1924, to October, 1925
F. G. MINNICK	November,	1925, to October, 1926
G. W. WILDIN	November,	1926, to October, 1927
E. J. DEVANS	November,	1927, to October, 1928
W. S. McABEE	November,	1928, to October, 1929
E. W. SMITH	November,	1929, to October, 1930
LOUIS E. ENDSLEY	November,	1930, to October, 1931
*JOHN E. HUGHES	November,	1931, to October, 1932
F. I. SNYDER	November,	1932, to October, 1933
C. O. DAMBACH	November,	1933, to October, 1934
R. H. FLINN	November,	1934, to October, 1935

*—Deceased.

Meetings held fourth Thursday of each month except June, July and August.

PROCEEDINGS OF MEETING
FEBRUARY 27th, 1936

The meeting was called to order by President R. P. Forsberg at the Fort Pitt Hotel at 8 o'clock P. M.

Registered attendance, 234, as follows:

MEMBERS

Adams, Frank W.
Aivalotis, John
Arnold, J. J.
Aulbach, A. J.
Baker, W. E.
Balzer, C. E.
Barr, H. C.
Barr, S. T.
Barth, E. H.
Barton, E. E.
Bauer, F. C.
Beatty, R. N.
Beitsch, George F.
Bell, R. A.
Berg, Karl
Beswick, R. M.
Bone, H. L.
Boyd, John
Boyd, John R.
Bradley, J. P.
Brown, E. F.
Britt, T. E.
Buchanan, C. C.
Buck, L. L.
Buffington, W. P.
Campbell, F. R.
Carlson, L. E.
Catt, C. E.
Chaffin, H. B.
Clark, E. C.
Clarke, A. C.
Conway, J. D.
Coombe, A. B.
Cowen, Harry E.
Crawford, D. F.
Cree, W. M.
Cruikshank, J. C.
Cunningham, J. D.
Dambach, C. O.
Davis, Charles S.

Dean, W. A.
Dean, W. H.
Dickson, K. B.
Diven, J. B.
Duffley, F. M.
Dunham, C. W.
Eckels, W.
Egbert, J. A.
Emery, E.
Endsley, Prof. Louis E.
Evans, Charles S.
Farmer, C. C.
Ferguson, J. H.
Fike, James W.
Foard, E. A.
Follett, W. F.
Forsberg, R. P.
Frauenheim, Pierce H.
Freshwater, F. H.
Fry, L. H.
Fults, J. H.
Funk, Ellsworth J.
Furch, G. J.
Galbraith, James R.
Geiser, W. P.
Gilg, Henry F.
Glaser, C. J.
Glaser, J. P.
Goda, P. H.
Goodwin, A. E.
Gray, M. L.
Groves, W. C.
Grunden, B. C.
Haller, Nelson M.
Hansen, William C.
Hayward, C.
Heimbach, A. E.
Hoover, J. W.
Huber, H. G.
Holtzworth, C. H.

Hoopes, R. E.
Hornefius, S. R.
Hutchinson, George, Jr.
Johnson, J. W.
Keller, R. E.
Kennedy, G. N.
Kentlein, John
Kessler, A. L.
King, E. C.
Kirk, W. B.
Klein, S. J.
Kohl, Leo H.
Krahmer, Edward F.
Kruse, J. F. W.
Lanahan, Frank J.
Lanahan, J. S.
Lauderbaugh, M.
Leonard, P. J.
Lincoln, R. B.
Logan, J. W., Jr.
Long, R. M.
Lowe, William T.
Maliphant, C. W.
Masterman, T. W.
Matthews, R. J.
Megee, C. R.
Merk, Joseph S.
Misner, George W.
Mitchell, F. K.
Mitchell, W. S.
Mittelstadter, H. E.
Moir, W. B.
Molyneaux, D. S.
Moore, D. O.
Moser, G. B.
Mulvey, John I.
Myers, Arnold
McCune, J. C.
McDowell, C. G.
McLaughlin, H. B.
McOsker, C. T.
McQuiston, C. A.
McTighe, B. J.
Nathan, W. S.
Nichols, S. A.
Nies, E. L.
Noonan, Daniel
Oehlschlager, W. A.
Orbin, Joseph N.
Osborne, Raymond S.
O'Sullivan, John J.
Paisley, F. R.

Palmer, E. A.
Phillips, T. H.
Porter, H. N.
Posteraro, S. F.
Prichard, H. R.
Purchard, Paul
Redding, P. E.
Redding, R. D.
Reed, M. R.
Reifsnyder, J. W.
Rensch, R. H.
Reynolds, A. C.
Rief, Joseph
Roberts, E. L.
Robertson, A. S.
Roney, H. E.
Rowles, H. N.
Rumbarger, F. A.
Rupp, E. S.
Rutter, H. E.
Sarchet, Roger
Schako, E. J.
Schweinsberg, C. E.
Searles, E. J.
Semmer, M. R.
Servais, Francis W.
Severn, A. B.
Shellenbarger, H. M.
Sheridan, T. F.
Shingledecker, John C.
Shuster, W. W.
Simpkins, Fred E.
Slater, A. H.
Smith, Charles F.
Smith, Folger M.
Smith, Robert B.
Sterling, C. C.
Stevens, L. V.
Stevens, R. R.
Stewart, C. D.
Stocker, H. F.
Stoffregen, Louis E.
Sudell, D. W.
Sutherland, Lloyd
Teerkes, C. A.
Terry, Edward
Thomas, George P.
Thomas, Theo. T.
Thornton, A. W.
Tracey, J. B. A.
Trax, L. R.
Triem, W. R.

85

Trumpeter, W. C.
Tryon, I. D.
Van Blarcom, W. C.
Van Horne, C. F.
Van Nort, C. W.
Van Woert, F. E.
Van Wormer, George M.
Wagoner, K. J.
Waxler, Brice
Weaver, W. Frank
Weis, Frank E.
West, Troy
White, A. F.
Wikander, O. R.
Wilkinson, W. E.
Wilson, James R.

Wright, John B.

VISITORS

Baldinger, H. C.
Breneman, R. P.
Bryant, L. J.
Clegg, W. H.
Conley, E. F.
Cronin, J. R.
Davis, B. A.
Fry, Roy A.
Gramner, J. I.
Griest, E. E.
Hildenbauer, L. B.
Hoover, Frank L.
Hunter, B. F.
Keller, N. T.
Lewis, S. B.
Lloyd, D. W.
Maichle, F. M.
Martin, G. C.
Moore, M. K.
McClory, L. H.
Oyen, Finn
Priest, H. M.
Ramsey, Dennis W.
Robinson, H. J.
Sanderson, S. L.
Stavros, P.
Street, C. K.
Vandivort, R. E.
Voucht, E. E.
Wallace, L. W.
Ward, C. H.
Weis, Mrs. F. E.

Winton, C. A.

PRESIDENT: The first order of business is the roll call. You have signed registration cards as you came in which gives a record of the attendance and we will, therefore, forego the roll call.

Next in order is the reading of the minutes of the last meeting. Those minutes have been published in the January Proceedings, which is in your hands, so, with your permission, we will dispense with the reading of the minutes.

The next order of business will be the proposals for membership and I will ask the Secretary to read the names of those proposed for membership in our Club.

SECRETARY: We have the following proposals for membership

Boyd, John, Clerk, J. T. & A. Hamilton Company, 1432 Arnold Street, Pittsburgh (20), Pa. Recommended by Brice Waxler.
Brown, Earl F., Electrical Supervisor, P. & L. E. R. R. Co., Terminal Station, Pittsburgh, Pa. Recommended by A. E. Heimbach.
Dunham, C. W., Union Switch & Signal Company, 1219 Braddock Avenue, Edgewood, Pittsburgh, Pa. Recommended by K. E. Kellenberger.

Forst, J. F., Supervisor of Track, P. & L. E. R. R. Co., 3103 Fourth Avenue, Beaver Falls, Pa. Recommended by F. R. Paisley.

Harig, George J., District Freight Agent, Nelson Steamship Company, Oliver Building, Pittsburgh, Pa. Recommended by J. I. Mulvey.

Harwig, C. G., Engineer, Union Switch & Signal Company, 1023 Mifflin Avenue, Wilkinsburg, Pa. Recommended by C. M. Wheeler.

Hess, Charles A., Sales Department, Edgewater Steel Company, P. O. Box 478, Pittsburgh, Pa. Recommended by O. R. Wikander.

Kirkland, Norman L., Partner, Acme Printing & Stationery Company, 1475 Greenmont Avenue, Dormont, Pittsburgh, Pa. Recommended by John I. Mulvey.

Klein, S. J., Assistant Traffic Manager, P. & W. Va. Ry. Co., Wabash Building, Pittsburgh, Pa. Recommended by C. O. Dambach.

Lanken, C. C., President-Treasurer, Lincoln Electric Railway Sales Company, Marshall Building, Cleveland, Ohio Recommended by E. A. Rauschart.

Livingston, W. C. Regional Storekeeper, Pennsylvania Railroad, 1125 Savannah Avenue, Edgewood, Pittsburgh, Pa. Recommended by W. B. Moir.

McMillan, J. G., Secretary, The M. N. Landay Company, Clark Building, Pittsburgh, Pa. Recommended by Lloyd Sutherland.

Nathan, W. S., General Manager, Construction Specialties Company, Oliver Building, Pittsburgh, Pa. Recommended by J. D. Conway.

Olson, A. O., General Agent, C. & N. W. Ry. Co., Oliver Building, Pittsburgh, Pa. Recommended by C. W. Trust.

Pringle, W. D., Sales Engineer, W. S. Tyler Company, 6648 Wilkins Avenue, Pittsburgh, Pa. Recommended by W. R. Gellatly.

Reese, R. H., General Agent, Green Bay & Western Railroad, Gulf Building, Pittsburgh, Pa. Recommended by John I. Mulvey.

Rode, Harry, Platform Foreman, P. & L. E. and P. R. R. Co.'s, 21 Elton Avenue, Pittsburgh, Pa. Recommended by J. W. McElravy.

Shippert, Frank, Yard Foreman, P. & L. E. R. R. Co., 1738 Edgebrook Avenue, Pittsburgh, Pa. Recommended by J. W. Elravy.

Squibb, L., Auditor Station Accounts, P. & L. E. R. R. Co., Terminal Building, Pittsburgh, Pa. Recommended by Arthur Shield.

Timmis, A. F., Foreman of Carpenters, P. & L. E. R. R. Co., 1195 Island Avenue, McKees Rocks, Pa. Recommended by J. A. Noble.

Tyler, Buford W., Jr., Division Engineer, Pittsburgh Division, Pennsylvania Railroad, Pennsylvania Station, Pittsburgh, Pa. Recommended by G. M. Sixsmith.

Yorke, P. H., General Agent, Great Northern Railway, Oliver Building, Pittsburgh, Pa. Recommended by G. M. Sixsmith.

PRESIDENT: If there are any of the gentlemen present, whose names have just been read, will you kindly stand in order that we may associate your face with the name.

Gentlemen, we welcome you into the fraternity and membership of our Club and hope you will enjoy that association as much as we will enjoy your membership.

Mr. Secretary, do we have an communications?

SECRETARY: One of the sad features at some of our meetings is the announcement of the death of members of the Club and tonight I have to report the death of E. H. Skiles, Agent, Pennsylvania Railroad, who became a member of the Club on November 22, 1934, and passed away December 29, 1935.

PRESIDENT: A suitable memorial will appear in the next issue of the Proceedings.

I am glad to see a representative attendance tonight because we have a good speaker and a good subject. We have been fortunate in securing as our speaker this evening Mr.

L. W. Wallace, Director, Equipment Reserach Division, Association of American Railroads, Chicago, Ill., who will address us upon the subject, "Railroad Research Problems." Mr. Wallace:

RAILROAD RESEARCH PROBLEMS

By L. W. WALLACE, Director of Equipment Research,
Association of American Railroads, Chicago, Illinois

Mr. Chairman and Members of The Railway Club of Pittsburgh: I have spent several most pleasant hours in Pittsburgh today. They have been pleasant because of the great courtesy extended to me by Mr. Reed and others members of your Club. They have also been pleasant because of the opportunity of having a short visit with two long time and appreciated friends—Mr. D. F. Crawford and Professor Louis E. Endsley.

It has been a delightful day. Now comes the only hardship so far as I am concerned—I hope not so hard for you.

Pittsburgh is renowned for many good reasons. One of them is the 57 varieties of one of your prominent manufacturers. It may be that these 57 varieties have suggested 57 conceptions as to what constitutes research. However, the numerous varieties of thought concerning research are not as well founded as the varieties of products to which reference has been made.

We find in an article which appeared in The Journal of Engineering Education that in the realm of research, some stress the first syllable and look with contempt upon those who emphasize the second syllable. In academic circles you are told, in great confidence, that there is a wild eyed professor across the campus who calls commercial testing research. You are also told that Professor Smith thinks he is engaged in research because he is discovering what everybody knows. We are told there are those who spend their time with cosmic rays and test tubes who point with ridicule to those who travel to far-and-out-of-the-way places to search the ruins of past civilizations for facts concerning those civilizations. We are told that some of those who sit for hours with their eyes glued to the microscope or telescope look with derision upon those who ascend to the stratosphere and those who descend to the lower regions of the sea.

We know there are those who work with guinea pigs and

electrons, and who study the breeding habits of bees and other insects who do not consider that the railroad chemist, physicist, metallurgist or engineer do research. Those people rather sneer and say that laboratory and road investigations of the performance of cars, locomotives, and their appliances are merely commercial testing. They love that word commercial. Each time they use it their jaws smack with delight and that ends it as far as they can understand. There are men in each of the groups mentioned, as well as in other groups. who say, according to the type of research to which he is glued, that because the railroad chemist, metallurgist or engineer may not use a guinea pig, or a male or a female bee, or go up in the air or sink to the depth of the sea, that therefore they do no research work and consequently the railroads have never enjoyed the advantages of research. Such babbling of tongues relating to what constitutes research, its types, its field of application, and its technique, is absurd and childish. It is just as absurd to think that research is something elusive, fantastic or mysterious, and that its appropriate and only environment is the cloister. There is noththing uncanny or impracticable connected with research, nor is there any limitation as to what or where it may be apphed.

The process of research of whatever type and regardless of when, where or to what applied, is nothing more nor less than an *organized, diligent investigation to discover facts*. The facts to be discovered may relate to the stars, the fish, the color of the eyes of snakes, the habits of human kind, the performance of a locomotive, or to a myriad other things. Daily we apply the process of research because daily we are concerned with the facts of life.

In a large degree, research is an attitude of mind, that attitude which prompts one eternally to be asking the question "Why?", which does not permit one to close his mind, which leads one to ascertain what other people are doing in other lines of work and adopting what is adaptable to his own work. It is that attitude which recognizes that nothing is static—that change is the law of the universe and he who would win must constantly be changing his methods of procedure.

There is needed a standardized classification of the types of research. Such classification might clarify the situation and remove some of the existing confusion. It would certainly contribute to a better understanding and appreciation of research. That there may be no confusion as to what is meant by research in this discussion I shall, with some danger of being challenged, define research and three types thereof.

I shall repeat: *Research is an organized, diligent investigation to discover facts.* There are three types of research, namely, fundamental, creative and applied. Other designating words might be used with as much logic. I prefer those selected. It is recognized that in this classification, as is the case with all classification systems, there are twilight zones between the types of research where lines of demarcation are indistinct.

TYPE I—Fundamental Research.

The word fundamental means "of or pertaining to the foundation or basis." As a noun it means "a principle which serves as the ground work of a system." Therefore the primary objective of fundamental research is to discover the basic principles underlying the universe and the circumstances of life. The principles so formulated serve as the groundwork of a system. The work of the astronomers, some physicists, chemists, methematicians, engineers, and others, fall within this type of research. They are not primarily interested in adding to the financial assets of the world, but rather their interest is to broaden intellectual horizons. That the results they achieve often have a material value is unquestioned. This work is indispensable to the progress of mankind, for in order to utilize the resources of the universe we must understand the laws governing its elements.

TYPE II—Creative Research.

The word creative means "having the power or quality of creating: originative; productive". The primary objective of creative research, therefore, is to discover, invent or produce new materials, new processes, new equipment, or to find new uses for existing materials. This type of research is characterized by the work of some chemists, physicists, engineers and others which work is largely based upon the principles discovered by those engaged in fundamental research. The results of creative research express themselves in new types of materials or substances, as Dow metal, Bakelite, Duco, radio tubes, a variety of equipment and a myriad of other things.

In creative research the financial incentive plays a more

important role than in the case of fundamental research. This type of research may be designated as producers research, through which means producers are enabled to manufacture and sell new and improved commodities. Notwithstanding the financial-incentive aspect of this type of research, there often flows from it a large measure of data which does directly contribute to an understanding of the basic principles underlying the universe and to the broadening of intellectual horizons.

TYPE III—Applied Research.

The word applied means "to put to practical use; also sometimes, concerned with concrete problems rather than with fundamental principles". Therefore the primary objective of applied research is to determine ways and means of adapting to concrete problems the knowledge, materials, equipment and processes made available by fundamental and creative research. In other words, the primary objective is to determine what basic principles, new materials, equipment and processes may be applied to the solution of concrete problems in order that increased efficiency and economy may be realized in daily operations. It is a process through which the user or purchaser intelligently selects the materials, processes and equipment best adaptable to his purposes and needs.

As far as the well-being of the human race is concerned this type of research is just as necessary, valuable and commendable as either of the other two types of research. They form a trilogy, to use a literary term. Between the three there is an unbroken two-way traffic. There is passed down from one to the other indispensable fuel which each independently uses as required. Likewise there is passed up from one to the other information as to what are the requirements of the human race which is constantly struggling with the mundane affairs of life. This interchange of information serves as a spur to workers in each type of research to strive to bring forth additional knowledge, materials and equipment. Each type of research is necessary for the advancement of the intellectual, social, spiritual and economic status of the human race.

RAILROAD INDUSTRY

Where is the place of the railroad in such a research pattern? Before this question can be answered it is advisable to define the function of the railroad industry. It is neither a research agency nor a manufacturer. It is true that a few railroads in the United States do some manufacturing, but these are noticeable exceptions. Even these do not produce any large proportion of those things they use. The railroad industry has very wisely left the manufacture of those things which it uses to those whose primary function is the production of commodities. Therefore for the more than 70,000 individual commodities, including such things as pins, needles, locomotives, rails and bridges, used by the industry, it, as a buyer, goes into the market and makes purchases the same as an individual who purchases a sack of flour, an automobile, or a suit of clothes. The railroad industry has depended and continues to depend upon the metallurgical industry for metals and alloys, the heavy chemical industry for chemicals, the automotive and aeronautic industries for automobiles, trucks, and aeroplanes, the paint and dye industry for paints, lacquers and dyes, the textile industry for towels, sheets and upholstery fabrics, the manufacturers of cars and locomotives for those products, the electric industry for generators, motors and other electrical equipment, the food and drug industries for foods and drugs, the telephone and telegraph industries for telephone and telegraph equipment, the wood industries for ties, poles and bridge timbers, the manufacturers of explosives and insecticides for powder, dynamite and insecticides, and the manufacturers of air conditioning equipment for the equipment used in making passenger cars more habitable and comfortable. Because of the long-standing sound policy of the railroad industry to buy and not to manufacture the commodities it uses, it is one of the best and most sought after customers.

And again, as a result of this sound policy there is today a large and important railway supply industry. The interests and activities of this industry, which in some form represents all the industries hereinbefore mentioned, are so closely tied in with those of the railroad industry it is exceedingly difficult to tell where the research and development of one ends and the other begins. This is true because in a large measure the several different branches of the railway supply industry were started and continued to be operated by men who, while engaged in railway operations saw the need for some new material, device or process and after developing something to meet the observed need to the point of manufacture have left the railroad and organized a company to manufacture and sell to the railroads the developed commodity. Thus it is that in all of those industries named are to be found many executives, chemists, engineers, designers and research men who started their professional careers in the railroad industry and who in their present positions are devoting their efforts to those matters which will enable the railroads to perform with greater efficiency and economy.

There come to mind some men who are or who have been so situated. One of the most remarkable records made in the automobile industry during the last 15 years is that of Mr. Walter Chrysler who prior to entering the automobile industry, had spent most, if not all of his professional life in the mechanical departments of the railroads.

Mr. R. B. White, after many years of railroad service, resigned the presidency of the Central Railroad of New Jersey, about five years ago, to accept the presidency of the Western Union Telegraph Company, which of course has a very close relationship with the railroad industry.

Thomas A. Edison started as a newsboy on a railroad, then became a railroad telegraph operator, from which start he rose to great eminence. The results of his work have been of great value to the railroad industry. Because of his work and that of other scientific men and inventors the railroads have electric lights, electric and Diesel-electric locomotives.

The long and successful careers of such men as George Westinghouse, and George M. Pullman were so early, closely and intimately associated with the railroad industry, it matters not whether they, as railroad employees, developed the air brake and the Pullman car respectively. Their life work as suppliers of railway requirements was in each case devoted to the large and broad aims of the railway industry. Their contacts were so intimate and constructive for so many years, the railroad industry is clearly entitled to claim them as its own.

The foregoing brief discussion of the railway supply industry should suffice to show that the railroad industry as a buyer has been fortunate, as from its ribs, so to speak, there have been created many men and agencies who because of intimate relationships growing out of experience, have been able to anticipate railway needs and in co-operation with the railroads have produced the required materials, equipment and processes as the railroads could absorb them.

As in research there is a trilogy, so with the railway industry and all those manufacturing interests mentioned, there is a duality of purposes and objectives which contribute immeasurably to the advancement of each.

These many relationships mean that of the hundreds of millions of dollars spent annually for research by such industries as the steel, chemical, electric, textile, railway supply, and others, a measurable amount is spent directly in response to the needs of the railroad industry and therefore it benefits very directly because of such expenditures. Again, this means in a very real sense that the railroad industry has working for it, indirectly, it is admitted, a very large research personnel. In the last analysis the railroad industry pays a measurable amount of the cost of such research as is devoted to developing the commodities it uses in the price it pays for such commodities.

Such relationships and facts as the foregoing are generally not known or are not understood, or are purposely disregarded by many who proclaim that the railroads are dead from the neck up and that there is very little life in the lower extremities. Some of such discussion is due either to a misunderstanding of the appropriate place of the railroad industry in the research pattern, or to a lack of a rational conception of what constitutes research.

Again it is advisable to repeat that the railroad industry is a purchaser and user of materials and equipment and not a producer of them. Its primary and only function is that of serving the public by operating transportation facilities. Its duty is to provide comfortable, dependable, and safe transportation at a reasonable cost. To discharge this duty the railroad industry finds it necessary to conduct only that character of research requisite to determine what types of materials and equipment may be used in its operations with the greatest efficiency, economy and safety. The railroad industry has found that its purposes are served by conducting that type of research which the bus, truck and airway transportation agencies, as purchasers, conduct to determine the efficiency, economy and safety of operation of the types of vehicles they use. Therefore the place of the railroad industry in the research pattern is the same as that of all purchasers who buy materials and equipment for their own use and that is applied research.

The place of the railroad industry in the research pattern is essentially and necessarily applied research. This is also true of all others who purchase materials and equipment for their individual use in the sense the railroads do. Therefore it is neither a fair nor a correct comparison to compare the applied research expenditures of the railroad industry with the creative research expenditure of a self-contained manufacturing industry which makes such expenditures for the purpose of developing commodities for sale. Both the requirements and purposes are entirely different in the two cases. and necessarily the amount and justification of the expenditures are very unlike. A fair comparison would be to consider the expenditures for applied research made by the manufacturing industry to determine the need, economy, efficiency and safety of the materials and facilities it uses as plant. equipment. Another comparison which would more nearly approach fairness and correctness than many of those made would be to add to the expenditures of the railroad industry for applied research those of the railroad supply industry for creative research. All of the latter are made for the avowed and only purpose of supplying the railroads with better materials and equipment. The sum spent by both the railroad and railway supply industries annually for research is very large and is undoubtedly as large as that of many other industries. Even such a total would not include a reasonable proportion of the creative research expenditures of that long and important list of industries which sell commodities to the railroad industry. The amount spent for creative research in the development of the more than 70,000 commodities which the railroads buy and use must be a rather staggering amount.

The railroad industry need make no apologies for what it has done in the applied research. Over a long span of years many of the railroads have maintained well organized and equipped test departments. In addition, through numerous organizations within and associated with the industry a great amount of research has been and is being done. The results flowing from such efforts have been of a creative and applied character and it may be that a few crumbs have even dropped into the basket which is holding all human knowledge, for there is an undeniable interdependence and interrelation between all sciences, all industries and all knowledge:

The foregoing analysis concerning the types of research and the place of the railroad industry in the pattern is founded upon the following background of experience:

For fourteen years I was directly and indirectly associated with the railroad industry. Then the World War came and I went into other lines of activity and for eighteen years was so engaged. Owing to the circumstances then surrounding me I came to know little more about what had happened to the railroads during these eighteen years than the average interested citizen. In February, 1935, I took up the responsibilities of the Director of Equipment Research, Association of American Railroads. A year of intense interest and activity has passed. In that year I surveyed the field for the purpose of learning what had happened, what was happening and what would likely happen regarding railroad research. I did this in order to have a clear conception of my duties and as to the directions in which I should move as Director of Equipment Research. During the course of the survey I confronted such confusion and cross-currents relating to research as has been discussed in this paper. I soon realized it would be necessary to develop some rational reasoning as to what constitutes research as well as to the appropriate place of the railroad industry in the research pattern. Where such thinking led me has been presented in the fore part of this discussion. I know there are those who will take issue with me. There will be those who will undoubtedly say that I have endeavored to claim for the railroad industry some men and some accomplishments to which the industry is not entitled. I am going to reply to that right now. The most of such challenges will be in the class with that old question, "which came first, the chicken or the egg?"

It is now my purpose briefly to report upon what I have found out as to what has happened over the last 20 years, what is happening and what is likely to happen with respect to railroad research problems.

STATE OF MIND

One of the first and most stimulating facts that I found was the state of mind prevailing among railroad executives, scientists, engineers and other employees. There is a seething ferment of thought and action within the industry. Never have I experienced in any realm such an eagerness and alertness as now characterizes railroad men. They are eager to apply any new procedure which will enable the railroads to make available better transportation. Economy, efficiency, comfort, dependability and safety are the clarion action words of the industry. This attitude has found expression in many important directions—only a few of which can be mentioned here. Among some of these expressions of the alert, far-seeing and courageous attitude of mind which characterizes the railroad industry are these:

It has found expression in the expenditure during the worst economic depression of our national history of something like $40,000,000 for the air conditioning of railroad passenger cars since 1932.

It has found expression is an unknown but very large expenditure for new trains, into the construction of which has gone the best that science, engineering and industry have made available.

It has found expression in replacing the American Railway Association and other railroad associations with the Association of American Railroads, an organization broader in scope, clothed with more authority and so manned that it may more adequately, efficiently and satisfactorily deal with the problems of the industry.

It has found expression in providing within the setup of the Association a better and more effective means for co-operation between the railroads themselves and between the railway industry and those industries which serve the railroads with regard to matters of common concern—and this is particularly true with regard to research. This new alignment emphasizes the fact that the railroad industry, like other industries, has a full appreciation of the value of research and like other industries it has provided a means for an extension of this effort through which quicker and better results may be obtained.

It has found expression in exceedingly important improvements in the design, construction and operation of both freight and passenger equipment.

The general construction of some of the new passenger equipment is familiar to you. However the Zephyr types of trains do not give the complete story, because so-called conventional or standard equipment has gone through a very decided transformation within the last twenty years. The passenger cars of today, in appearance, serviceableness and comfort, are very unlike those of twenty years ago. And in view of

97

the active studies now in progress we may confidently expect many improvements in the years immediately ahead. All of which means that the "conventional" or "standard" car as spoken of by the railroad men is not so designated because of its age, nor, as some seem to think there have been no improvements for many, many years. When the experienced railroad man says "standard car" he means that design which was last adopted as the optimum. He knows that the optimum today may be quite different from the optimum of tomorrow, which will then be the "standard car". In the railroad industry standardization does not mean rigidity but rather flexible reasoned progress.

The point may be illustrated by the present A. A. R. light weight steel box car, which was adopted as a standard four years ago, only after the most careful study by a committee of experienced car engineers. This committee gave due consideration to the merits of all light weight metals recommended for car construction by the producers of such metals. Upon the basis of such consideration it designed, built and tested the cars under full load. Only after careful study and testing of the cars in the fire of operating conditions were they declared satisfactory. Thus there came into being the present standard car. This standard car has lost no teeth and it has no gray hair because of age. It probably will never have gray hair as the "standard A. A. R. car" because the railway supply industry is endeavoring to produce something even better and lighter. Since December first a series of tests have been under way on a box car made of corten steel, welded throughout and having a smaller area of center sill than the above standard car, and weighing approximately 8,000 lbs. less. This car is being put through hard knocks similar to those which it will get in service. In a few weeks it will be known whether corten, of the dimensions and in the manner used, and whether welding as applied in this case, are suitable. The results also will tell a story as to the merits of such light weight and cross-sectional area of the center sill as used in this car. Thus the railroad industry will determine whether this design or some other design will be its "standard car" tomorrow.

STEEL ALLOYS

We are told that the metallurgists have developed over ten thousand alloys. We know that the railroad industry has always been quick to consider the merits of the new alloys as they have been developed. We know that within the last three or four years railroad companies have built experimental passenger and freight cars of the newer steels and alloys. At this very hour cars are under observation and test, in the construction of which practically all alloys recommended by the producers because of their light weight, rust-resisting and abrasion-resisting qualities are used. We know that many of the moving parts of locomotives built since 1920 are constructed of aluminum and other light alloys. We know that no small amount of research is in process now for the purpose of determining to what degree other alloys may be successfully used in locomotive construction. These activities clearly show that the industry is alert to the possibilities and it is utilizing proven methods of determining whether the alloys have the chemical and physical properties necessary to meet the exacting requirements.

LOCOMOTIVES

There are those who say that the steam locomotive of today is essentially the same locomotive *"in principle"* that Stephenson used in 1829. Of course what the foregoing statement implies depends entirely upon what is meant by *"in principle"* as used in this connection. I could say that the man of today *"in principle"* is essentially the same as the prehistoric man, if I meant by *"in principle"* that each man had a head, stomach, heart, lungs, legs, arms and some other appurtenances. But if I meant by *"in principle"* that the man of today has no broader intellectual horizon, no better knowledge of the facts of life, no better concept of ethical values and social amenities than the prehistoric man, and even if I only meant that he had no more command of his physical and mental faculties than the prehistoric man, you would just laugh, and rightly so. Is it not just as laughable and ridiculous for some to say that the locomotive of today is essentially the same in principle as the locomotive of 1829, unless he means by *"in principle"* that the locomotive of today, as did the one of 1829, has a boiler, some wheels, a frame and cylinders, disregarding entirely all the developments, refinements, appliances and performance which characterize the modern locomotives.

It would be an interesting experience for some railroad to invite some of those who say there has been no change *"in principle"* in the locomtives and cars in 100 years to be its guests for a night and day. Over night give them a comfortable bed and good rest. In the morning, serve them a wholesome breakfast. After breakfast when it would be hoped that the eyes of the guests are wide open and their brains reasonably clear of cobwebs and fatigue, take them to a museum to see cars and locomotives used 50 and 100 years ago. Then show them some of the equipment of 10 years ago, and some of the present day standard equipment. It would be hoped that by such visual education the guests would recognize that progressively the railroad industry has taken a practical advantage of all that fundamental, creative and applied research has offered and there is at least a slight difference in principle between the cars and locomotives of 100 years ago and those of the 1930's.

Then before the guests are too tired, let them look at the record. They would find the record shows a great deal more than they ever knew before. They would find such facts as the following with respect to the progress made in increasing the power of the average locomotive. From 1916 to 1934 the tractive power of the average steam locomotive has been raised from 33,188 pounds to 47,712 pounds, an increase of 44%.

The record shows that the distance between stops for the 1910 locomotive was 40 miles, the 1920 was 60 miles and the 1930, 85 miles. The rejuvenated locomotive has more than twice the stamina of the 1910 locomotive, as measured in the miles traveled between drinks.

The record shows that a few years ago on the Illinois Central Railroad, locomotives were changed every 100 to 150 miles. Formerly four locomotives were used to move a passenger train from Chicago to Memphis, a distance of 500 miles. Now only one locomotive is used for the same run. This record is typical of that of many, if not all railroads.

The record shows that the average running speed of the 1910 locomotive was 20 M.P.H., that of 1920, 33 M.P.H. and that of the 1930 freight locomotive 42 miles per hour.

The record shows that in passenger service there are steam locomotives running at 80 miles and 90 miles per hour and capable of sustained speeds for some distance at the rate of 100 to 110 miles per hour.

The record shows that the draw bar horse power of the 1910 locomotive was 1240, the 1920, 2000, and the 1930, 3600

—a mere three-fold increase. And there are locomotives in operation with 4000 to 5000 draw bar horse power.

The record shows that coal consumed per draw bar horsepower per hour is 40% less for the 1930 than for the 1910 locomotive, and for the 1920 locomotive, is 30% less than for the 1910.

The record shows that the pounds of coal consumed per 1000 gross ton miles is 24% less for the 1930 than for the 1910 locomotive and 22% less than for the 1920 locomotive.

The record shows that in freight service in 1922 the fuel consumption was 163 lbs. per 1000 gross ton miles, that in 1931 it was 119 lbs., or a reduction of 27% in nine years. In the same nine years the reduction of the consumption of coal in passenger service was 19%.

The record shows that the savings made in the 1929 fuel bill, due to the increase in efficiency of its use which had been effected since 1920, was $91,300,000; and the saving made in the fuel bill for the same reason over a period of 12 years ending in 1932, amountd to almost $630,000,000.

In the light of the record, the old boys of 1829 and 1910 were evidently the world's greatest loafers, or else some very fundamental developments have taken place. The old arms, legs and hearts of the prehistoric man are certainly strutting these days. The truth is, old man locomotive of 1829 would not recognize his descendants of 1929. It is doubtful whether he could find even a few familiar birthmarks, such changes have the processes of evolution wrought. The experienced railroad men and the keen and open-minded observer know that the great contrasts which the record discloses are due to fundamental and far reaching developments.

CARS

The guests are now to be shown the record pertaining to freight and passenger cars. They are by now undoubtedly conscious of the fact that the type of management and methods which produced such locomotive records as they have just seen, would obviously have similar records relating to cars.

The record shows that both the freight and passenger cars of 100 years ago were all wood in construction. Even in the passenger car of 75 years ago heat and light were far from adequate, and provision for bodily comfort and necessities was wholly lacking.

The record shows there were no sleeping cars 100 years ago, and that the sleeping car of 50 years ago, as compared with that of today, was as different as an ox cart is different from the most luxurious automobile.

The record shows that the passenger equipment today, and not including the latest models of streamlined equipment, is as different in points of design, types of materials used and appointments, from those of 20 years ago as the automobile of 1936 is different from the automobile of 1920.

PASSENGER TRAINS

The record shows this as to the speed of passenger service: Between Washington and New York there are being operated over the Pennsylvania Railroad 44 electric-powered trains per day at the rate of 225 miles in 225 minutes. In addition, there are 34 other trains serving New York and Washington and intermediate points, making the run of 225 miles in four hours and ten minutes.

The record shows that six round trips per day, at a speed of 44 miles in 44 minutes are being made between Boston and Providence by the Diesel-powered comet of the New York, New Haven and Hartford Railroad.

The record shows that the Abraham Lincoln, a steam-powered train of the Chicago and Alton is running between St. Louis and Chicago, a distance of 280 miles in five and one-half hours—an approximate average rate of 52 miles an hour.

The record shows that the "400" train, steam-powered, of the Chicago and North Western Railroad, is running 410 miles at the rate of 63 miles per hour, including stops.

The record shows that the "Hiawatha", steam-powered train of the Milwaukee Road pulls a train of 8 cars between Chicago and the Twin Cities, a distance of 410 miles, at an average running speed, including stops, of 65 miles per hour.

The record shows that the Diesel-electric-powered train of the Santa Fe Railroad Company ran from San Francisco to Chicago in a few minutes over 39 hours.

The record shows also that a passenger train was operated a distance of 5 miles at the average speed of 115 miles per hour in 1904. Therefore a speed of 100 miles per hour is no unusual experience with the railroad industry.

The record shows that in 1934 the passenger business of the railroads totaled 18,033,309,000 passenger miles and in 1935 there was an increase of over 360,000,000 passenger miles.

The record shows that in 1935 there was not one passenger fatality in 18,393,975,180 passenger miles.

The record shows that on the basis of the unit cost of railway operation in 1920, the cost of the business done by the railroads in 1929 would have been greater than it actually was by $1,212,000,000. In 1920 the railroads were being operated by the government. Inasmuch as government operation is always more expensive than private operation some may say the above comparison is not a fair one. Therefore turn to 1923, when the railroads were privately operated, and the record shows that had the unit cost of 1923 prevailed in 1929 the cost of operation in 1929 would have been $521,003,000 greater than it actually was.

FREIGHT TRAIN

The record shows the following improvements in freight train operations due to better management, methods and equipment:

An important factor in the improved railway service is the increase in the average speed of freight trains. For example, miles per freight train hour averaged 10.3 miles in 1920, 11.1 miles in 1922 and 15.9 miles in 1934, an increase in 1934 over 1920 of 54.4%. These averages represent the running time between divisions and terminals, including delays encountered while en route.

As another example, gross ton miles per freight train hour averaged 14,877 in 1920, 16,188 in 1922 and 28,041 in 1934, an increase in 1934 over 1920 of 88.5%.

The record shows many freight trains are being operated with the regularity and dependability of passenger trains, and in many cases almost as fast.

The record shows that the average cost per 1000 revenue ton miles of freight traffic has been reduced from $10.66 in 1920 to $6.48 in 1933.

STREAMLINING

There are some other matters about which I wish to speak.

One of the present day fads is streamlining. Everything is being streamlined from ladies' hats to locomotives. Streamlining has its place and value, but the streamlining of a pile

103

of brick or of slow-moving things just does not make sense. It is understood that no real benefits are realized from streamlining until speeds of 60 miles per hour or more are reached. There are many things being streamlined which never move at any such speed. There are other things being streamlined which move at 60 miles per hour or more for only relatively short distances and periods of time. Therefore except when used for artistic advertising and styling purposes it would seem that no small amount of the present streamlining is plain ballyhoo.

Streamlining in its proper place is used to reduce atmospheric resistance to the motion of bodies or vehicles. The railroad industry has been aware of this from the beginning. Therefore it is exceedingly interesting and not surprising to know that in April, 1896, Dr. Goss, who was to the railroad industry what Drs. Steinmetz and Pupin were to the electric and telephone industries, presented a paper before the Western Railway Club in which he gave an account of his experiments to determine the atmospheric resistance to the motion of railway trains. These experiments were conducted with models of railway cars in what would now be called a wind tunnel. The director of one of the best known aeronautical laboratories told me in 1935 that notwithstanding the improvements in instruments, research technique, and other facilities for conducting wind tunnel experiments, since Dr. Goss' work in 1896, the principles Dr. Goss formulated on the basis of his research are sound today, and that aeronautic science has found nothing to justify questioning their validity. It would seem therefore, that Dr. Goss originally formulated the principles which govern streamlining of aeroplanes, automobiles and railroad trains.

In May and August, 1900, tests were made with the streamlined "Adams Windsplitter" train on the Baltimore and Ohio, speeds of 85 miles per hour being attained.

It is obvious from the foregoing that the railroad industry had an understanding of the atmospheric resistance to the motion of trains, and at least one railroad had experimented with streamlining before the first automobile chugged its wearisome way along the sandy road, or the first aeroplane had more than fluttered its faltering wings.

TRAIN BRAKES

The records which have been reviewed disclose the

marked increase in train schedules, train tonnage, and distances between stops that has taken place within the last twenty years. These operating conditions gave rise to the need for an improved air brake for freight equipment. In 1925 the A.R.A. (now the A.A.R.) initiated a long series of laboratory and road tests so patterned as to provide data upon which to base an improvement in freight car brake equipment. These series of tests extended over ten years and cost the Association alone $2,800,000. Undoubtedly the manufacturers spent a like amount. As a result of this endeavor a tremendous improvement in braking action has taken place. Freight trains, even when only partially supplied with the new equipment can be stopped more quickly, smoothly and safely than with the old equipment.

BLOCK SIGNALS

In step with other phases of railway operation, the block signaling and automatic train control systems have been markedly improved. While the first patents on block signaling were issued to English inventors, the first American interlocking machines were designed by Mr. Toucey and Mr. Buchanan, general superintendent and superintendent respectively of the New York and Hudson River Railroad.

The first power interlocking device using all electrically operated apparatus was developed by Mr. Taylor, a telegraph operator of the Baltimore and Ohio.

The first conception of automatic train control was by Mr. Voght, of the Pennsylvania Railroad.

The car retarder system for hump classification yards was invented and first installed by Mr. Hanauer, President of the Indiana Harbor Belt Railway.

Over the years the manufacturers of these types of equipment, and this is universally true of the manufacturers of all railway supplies, have closely co-operated with the railroad men in developing and manufacturing their inventions.

It will be observed that the present day control systems are the results of long years of effort and the participation of many men within the railroad industry. This is true of all devices used by the railroads for seldom indeed is a new invention serviceable, regardless of who may have been the inventor. To make a new invention serviceable requires years of painstaking attention by those who use the invention. Consequently, in the final analysis, it would be difficult indeed to assign credit because those who have made the invention a practicable, dependable device have been those on the job who had to make it work. This has been true, not only of block signals, but of air brakes, electric locomotives, car wheels, vestibule buffers, shock absorbers, and the myriad of other things the railroads use.

In this matter, as in the case of atmospheric resistance, streamlining, and in other instances, the railroad industry has developed something of use to other industries and the general public. Modifications of the principles and facilities used to control train movements have been and are being applied to control the movement of automobile traffic in the hope of reducing the tremendous number of injuries and fatalities due to such traffic.

Another illustration of the extent to which railroads go in their efforts to make available transportation facilities which embody speed, comfort, convenience, reliability and safety is the research work of the Pennsylvania Railroad in connection with the electrification of its line between New York and Washington.

To realize the foregoing objectives, exhaustive track and locomotive tests were made to obtain accurate data not previously available. To make such tests a special section of test track was built. The rails were laid on steel ties and a pressure-reading instrument was placed at the ends of every other tie. The instruments were so constructed that when the wheel flanges of passing locomotives caused pressure against the rail, a hardened steel ball was forced against a soft plate. The impressions so made upon the soft steel plate were carefully measured and the results charted. Thus a graphic picture of the side swings of the locomotive wheels and the pressure exerted against the rails was obtained.

During the same time the foregoing tests were in process, other tests were being made to determine the side forces developed at the hubs of the driving wheels and measuring devices were attached to the locomotive at different places to obtain records of pressure movements throughout the locomotive. Thus through long, tedious and expensive efforts to secure the facts, which is research, the Pennsylvania Railroad has perfected its equipment and is providing the public with fast, comfortable and safe service. This is merely typical of what is taking place throughout the country.

LOCOMOTIVE WHISTLES

Many would perhaps be surprised to know that the railroad industry within the last two years engaged the active co-operation of the Bell Telephone Laboratories and Electrical Research Products, Inc., to make studies of the carrying and tone characteristics of locomotive whistles. Likewise that Dr. Arthur L. Foley of Indiana University has made similar studies for some of the railroads. Thus the industry has used the best scientific skill and facilities available in order to see if the tone qualities of locomotive whistles could be improved.

CRANK PINS, AXLES, BEARINGS AND LUBRICATION

We have found that owing to the use of higher boiler pressures and temperatures, increased speed and longer runs, there have arisen new problems relating to crank pins, axles, bearings and lubrication. The Division of Equipment Research has been instructed to prepare a comprehensive research program relating to these matters. It is known that a successful solution of such problems as may exist will require the tapping of all existing scientific data and practical experience and will also require calling upon the best metallurgists, physicists, and oil chemists and other technical men for direct assistance, and the utilizing of the best available laboratory equipment.

Another problem relates to boiler construction and boiler waters and treatment. Involved in this problem are the relative merits of the new alloy steels, their characteristics with respect to fatigue and caustic embrittlement and other like metallurgical and chemical questions. There is also involved a critical examination of inspection methods and the possibility of developing an instrument for locating initial cracks in locomotive boilers while in service. The instrument visualized would be something like the Sperry rail detector which is used for detecting fissures in rails. A program of this character has been formulated.

STRESSES IN TRACK

An important research program has been under way continuously since 1927 with respect to stresses in railroad track.

RAIL FISSURES

A companion and a closely associated program of research is the one relating to rail fissures. This program has been continuously pursued since 1931. The expense is being borne approximately share and share alike by the railroad industry and the manufacturers of steel rails. This is a typical example of how a great deal of the research work relating to the development of materials and equipment is conducted and paid for. This work, like that of stresses in the track, is being done by Drs. Talbot and Moore. Through them the highest of scientific skill and experience is being brought to bear upon these problems.

Some years ago the railroads solicited and secured the interest of Dr. Elmer Sperry with respect to rail defects. With the co-operation of the railroad industry Dr. Sperry designed and built a successful machine for detecting defects in steel rails while in place in the road bed of the railroads. A number of the railroads now operate their own detector cars and many other railroads have service contracts with the Sperry Company. These detector cars are operated over thousands of miles of railroad tracks each year. Thus defects are detected before rail failures occur. This avoids the heavy expense incident to such failures and contributes to that safety of operation for which the railroads have always striven.

The foregoing activity relating to rail stresses and fissures is in keeping with the noted work of Dr. P. H. Dudley of the New York Central Lines, and that of Dr. Charles B. Dudley and W. C. Cushing of the Pennsylvania Railroad. Dr. P. H. Dudley completed and reported upon an exhaustive research program relating to rails and wheels in 1881. He established a fundamental datum line for all scientific workers since. Throughout the history of the railroad industry in this country such eminent metallurgists, chemists and engineers as Drs. P. H. Dudley, Charles B. Dudley, Elmer Sperry, W. F. M. Goss, S. W. Parr and John F. Stevens have given content, form and direction to the solving of the engineering and scientific problems which from time to time have confronted the railroad industry.

In the present period we find men of like professional attainments being used by the railroad industry. Reference has been made to Drs. Talbot and Moore of the University of Illinois. There are many others who are being consulted frequently. Among these are Drs. Edward C. Schmidt, A. E. White, H. M. Gillet, A. G. Christie and Herman Von Schrenk.

There is also a Research Advisory Board of the Association consisting of Drs. A. A. Potter, Harold G. Moulton and Karl Compton. Neither of the foregoing lists are intended to be all-inclusive. Many other names could be added but those given should suffice to show that long prior to the turn of the century and since, the railroad industry has followed the practice of utilizing the best scientific talent available at any given period. This simply means that if the best scientific job has not been done at a given time it was due to the fact that the railroads could not command, at the time, the scientific skill and facilities requisite for the task in hand.

A further illustration of the effort of the railroad industry to follow research procedure is the fact that it has maintained at Purdue University for many years laboratory equipment for testing brake shoes, car wheels, air brake equipment and draft gears. Frequently this and other equipment has been used for other purposes than those named. The industry has frequently used the Purdue Locomotive Testing Laboratory, built in 1891, the first in the world. Since 1891 there has been almost a continuous flow of experimental data from this laboratory having a direct bearing upon the design, construction, operation and performance of locomotives and their appurtenances. This has been true also of the more recently constructed locomotive laboratories of the University of Illinois and the Pennsylvania Railroad. This locomotive laboratory work has been supplemented by an innumerable number of locomotive road tests with dynamometer cars attached in which was housed the latest scientific instruments required to obtain a complete and accurate record of the locomotive and train performance. No other vehicle used in transportation has received as exhaustive, continuous and expensive scientific study as the locomotive. It has, since 1890 certainly, if not before, been put through all the trying paces that the most demanding proving ground could subject it. The locomotive laboratories and road tests were the original proving grounds for transportation equipment.

Notwithstanding the paces through which the locomotive has been put, and its greatly improved performance, there are being formulated *now* additional proving ground tests to determine the merits of the mental creations of yesterday of some of the best experienced minds within and allied with the railroad industry. Thus the process of evolution continues not only with respect to the locomotive but also in

109

relation to each of the 70,000 commodities the railroad industry purchases and uses.

The Division of Equipment Research realizes that, as has been done throughout the history of the railroad industry, it will have to be constantly alert to all new developments whenever and in whatever field of human endeavor they may occur. It also realizes it must maintain the closest possible contacts with all that body of data and experience that fundamental, creative and applied research have accumulated and use it many times for many reasons.

The Division realizes that it would be thoroughly impracticable and inadvisable to have a staff and laboratory facilities adequate in size and quality to deal with the great number of research problems which it will be expected to and must consider. The Division will therefore maintain a relatively small staff and will purchase only such special equipment as may be needed and not available in some laboratory. As each problem arises it will enlist the services of the best talent and facilities available for such research. Thus there will continue to be brought to bear upon the railroad research problems the highest degree of scientific and professional talent. Today two of the leading metallurgical research institutions are working on problems assigned to them. Three of the large technical institutions are likewise working on assigned problems.

The research program on the air conditioning of railroad passenger cars recently authorized is being so organized that the best research facilities of manufacturers, railroads and technical universities will be used.

This method of procedure is an old story to the railroad industry. The only new feature is that the Division of Equipment Research provides a means whereby co-operative effort may be broadened and expedited, and whereby there may be better correlation and more definite integration. These are important factors and will measurably contribute to enabling the railroads to make additional advances in the economy, efficiency, dependability, comfort and safety of the service it renders the public.

Statements have been made that the railroad industry is on the way out; that it has served its day; that its equipment, practice and performance are obsolete; that it is blind to the developments of science and engineering; and that it is unconscious of and unconcerned with the circumstances and requirements of this period. Nothing could be farther from the truth. Instead, the railroad industry stands on the threshold of one of the most active and fruitful eras of its history.

No one need have any fears for the railroad industry is not on the way out. It is not on the way out because, largely through research over a long period of years, the steam railroads have been made into the most adequate, dependable, economical and safe means of transportation for the mass movement of goods and people, to be found in this country.

PRESIDENT: We have just listened to a most outstanding and highly interesting paper presented by a gentleman whom nature has endowed with a splendid speaking voice, making it unnecessary for him to use the amplifier, and he, I am sure, has been distinctly heard and understood by each one in this large room.

As Mr. Wallace was speaking, I instinctively compared the quality of his voice and the character of the material he has given to us with another speaker, of whom I once heard. This man had a very weak, thin voice, that carried badly, his pronunciation was especially poor and indistinct, and the character of the material he was delivering was worse, if possible, than the quality of his voice and the degree of his pronunciation combined. He had been speaking for about ten minutes when someone in the rear of the room shouted, "Louder, louder." Instantly an old man who was sitting in one of the front seats arose and turning to the rear of the room said, "Can't you hear what this man is saying?" "No sir," said a young man, "I cannot." "Well then," said the old man, "Sit down and thank God that you can't."

Following the procedure I adopted when I became President of this Club, I will not call on anyone for remarks. Mr. Wallace has kindly consented to attempt to answer any questions you may ask him relative to his paper, so for the next fifteen minutes the meeting is in your hands.

MR. E. EMERY: I would like to ask Mr. Wallace, with the 70,000 odd articles the railroads purchase, what method or means the Division of Equipment Research is using to keep in touch with scientific and engineering developments which may be of value to the railroads? It looks to me as though they have a pretty good sized job.

MR. WALLACE: The entire task confronting the Division is a large one, and one of the necessary phases of the work is that of knowing what other individuals or agencies have done and are doing on the subjects in which we are interested. This enables us to profit by the experience of others, prevents us from repeating their mistakes, and avoids duplication of effort. I have on my staff a woman with a background of education and experience which is a combination of scientific, technical, industrial and library research. It is her duty to keep in touch with scientific and technical literature through all reliable engineering and scientific indices, and to secure copies or make abstracts of reports and articles which are useful in connection with the projects in which we are actually engaged, and those contemplated in the future. It is often necessary for her to make translations of foreign articles if they contain information of value to us. In short this member of my staff acts as a technical secretary; it is her function to know the sources of authoritative information on all subjects relating to railway equipment research; the field includes physics, chemistry, metallurgy, and the various branches of engineering.

MR. C. O. DAMBACH: We would be interested in knowing something about what is to be done with the research program on air conditioning as authorized by the Board of Directors of the A.A.R. What is to be the character of the program and how is it to be accomplished?

MR. WALLACE: The Division of Equipment Research was instructed to make a comprehensive study of air conditioning of passenger cars. The situation is about like this: the railroads have spent some $40,000,000 for air conditioning passenger equipment since 1932. They are using with many variations the three basic types of air conditioning systems, namely, the compressor, steam ejector, and the ice systems. Which of these basic systems is the most effective in producing a comfortable travel environment at an economical investment, operating and maintenance cost is the question. The answer to this question should serve as a valuable guide for all future installations.

In an effort to find a sound and helpful answer to the question the Division will pursue two lines of study—one laboratory, the other road. The laboratory work will be directed towards ascertaining the relative efficiency and economy of each of the elements which compose an air conditioning system and the over-all performance of the several being used. Through the courtesy of Mr. Daniel Willard, President of the Baltimore and Ohio Railroad, laboratory facilities for such purpose have been made available at the Mt. Clare Shops of the Baltimore and Ohio in Baltimore, Md.

Road investigations will be made to determine the actual conditions of temperature, humidity and air movement now prevailing on the air conditioned trains throughout the country. This effort will also include the determination of the character and extent of any mechanical trouble experienced in operating and maintaining the several systems.

The laboratory and road work will be so correlated that they will give a composite picture as to the relative performance of the several elements of an air conditioning system, as well as of the different systems used. On the basis of such an analysis we should be able more intelligently to select that system which will best meet specific operating conditions.

MR. KARL BERG: It appears to be the custom of the times for the railroads, as we know them to come in and correlate with other means of transportation, and I would like to ask if it is the intention of the Division to extend its activity in such questions, as for instance, Highway Transportation? What is to be your general procedure in doing the work?

MR. WALLACE: The Division is operating under a charter at the moment which specifies that it shall give consideration to research problems relating to car, locomotive and shop equipment of common concern. Inasmuch as the railroads do use automobiles, trucks and aeroplanes it is conceivable that the Division may be instructed to conduct research relating to such transportation vehicles. The economic and policy factors concerning the relationship of rail and highway transport do not come within the charter stipulations of the Division. Such questions are the responsibility of other subdivisions of the Association, such as the Bureau of Railway Economics and Dr. Duncan, the economist of the Association.

MR. D. F. CRAWFORD: Before asking the question I have in mind. May I express my appreciation of the excellent paper just presented. The subject recalls much personal experience. Every time a railroad made a test it was doing applied research, and it was my privilege to take part in some tests and to direct many investigations that led to much more than the mere determination of the problem of the moment. Such work is certainly research.

Of course our staff and equipment was not always of the type contemplated by Mr. Wallace—I remember an "Air Conditioning" test of the eighties. Some Pennsylvania Railroad passenger cars were equipped with a ventilating system, with intakes at the ends of the car, conduits to discharge the air under the seats, and exhaust ventilators in the roof. In addition to making anemometer readings, chemical analysis of the air, etc. On at least one trip, one of the cars was loaded with shop men, of which I was one, all smoking as hard as we could, and a run made from Altoona to Gallitzin to ascertain what might be expected in practice. Many cars were built having this, the best ventilating system available at the time. Crude perhaps, but effective research.

The question I would like to ask. By whom will the various problems mentioned be initiated—by the railroads, by the manufacturers, or by some of us outsiders?

MR. WALLACE: I could not help but smile at Mr. Crawford classifying of himself as an outsider. Mr. Crawford, you can never be an "outsider" to the railroad industry.

After a careful study of the problems of research I submitted a program to the Board of Directors in June, 1935, in which I outlined seven or eight projects for study by the Division of Equipment Research. There was also submitted a list of subjects under the heading "Contemplated". I was gald to be able to state to the Board that every subject listed had been submitted by a railroad official or by a railroad group, that it had not been necessary for the Division to pull problems out of the air. I am confident that the Division will be kept fully occupied in conducting research on subjects submitted by the railroad officials and committees of the industry. This is a very wholesome and promising fact.

MR. O. R. WIKANDER: I think all here would be glad to hear more about how the Division of Equipment Research will handle its work.

MR. WALLACE: I indicated something of the policy a few minutes ago, but will be glad to elaborate on it. The general plan of research as outlined for the air conditioning of passenger equipment is to be followed in most cases. The plan, in brief, will consist of the following steps:

1. A careful survey will be made to determine existing conditions.

2. An analysis will be made of such information to determine, if possible, what factors were really responsible for the problem.

3. A laboratory or road program of research will be projected of such character as will give promise of throwing more light on the problem and producing more factual information.

4. The results of the laboratory and road work will be used as a basis for recommendations designed to correct the difficulties and to increase efficiency and economy.

There was submitted to the Division a number of reports relating to a locomotive boiler explosion. There was involved in this questions relating to boiler water, boiler washouts and the character and behavior of steels used in locomotive boiler construction. The Division enlisted the co-operative interest of one of the outstanding independent metallurgical research agencies to aid it in studying the problem. The Division also secured the opinion of three capable locomotive men. Out of such studies came specific recommendations. It is recommended that two research programs be undertaken—one to determine the relative merits of the several steels offered for locomotive boiler construction and the other a study of inspection methods, coupled with the thought that there may be developed an instrument for detecting cracks in locomotive boilers while in service.

If these two studies should be authorized the Division would engage the research agency consulted to do the work. The matter of boiler washout is still under consideration. It is anticipated that a specific study of this subject will be recommended.

Such recommendations are made to the Board of Directors of the Association with a rather complete statement of the case, general outline of what is to be done and the results anticipated, with an estimate of time and cost involved. If the Board approves, the Division proceeds along lines similar to that of air conditioning.

MR. W. P. BUFFINGTON: I would like to ask, what is to be the relationship between the activities of your Division and those of the Mechanical Division and other such Divisions of the Association?

MR. WALLACE: I will tell you my own conception first, or my own wish. I hope the committees of the Mechanical Division, as well as all committees concerned with rolling stock and shop equipment will come to regard the Equipment Research Division as their expert staff. The Division could serve a most useful purpose in such a relationship. A service of this character would enable the committees to do a quicker and more complete job for the very obvious reason that the members of the committees are very busy men. Many demands are made upon them—such as associated with their daily work. Of necessity they have difficulty in finding an opportunity to give to committee work the amount of time required. The Division, as a staff, could greatly relieve these busy men of detail so when the committee meets it could devote its time to a consideration of the broad and important questions involved. Through such procedure the value of committee work could be expedited and enhanced and at the same time the demands made upon the members be reduced.

It is very gratifying to be able to say that some of the committee are using the Division in such fashion. Since December the Division has been participating in some impact tests of a steel box car as the agent of the Car Construction Committee. The Division will make a report to this Committee.

Last week the Division submitted a report to the Committee on Locomotive Construction relating to a revision of Cole's Ratios. This report was prepared and submitted in response to a request of the Committee.

Through such helpful means both the work of the Division and that of the committees may be expedited and the value thereof enhanced.

PRESIDENT: Gentlemen, I regret very much the time has arrived when we will have to close our meeting. I informed you when I took this office that I would not call on any one for remarks but Mr. Wallace has spoken tonight of some relationship he had with Professor Endsley, while at Purdue, so I am going to call on Professor Endsley and give him a chance to say something in rebuttal.

PROFESSOR LOUIS E. ENDSLEY: I always have something to say when I hear a man whom I have known for thirty years, as I have Mr. Wallace, tell us in a very interesting and concise way what his department of The American Association of Railways is doing and hopes to do. I don't think there is going to be any doubt about what his department will do for the railroads.

We are going to have the railroads for a good many years and I think everyone here has a little more pride in his work than he possibly had before hearing Mr. Wallace's talk, as he has told us in a very excellent manner some of the improvements which have been made by the railroads in the last fifteen years.

I move, Mr. President, that we offer the speaker, Mr. L. W. Wallace, a rising vote of thanks for coming here tonight and telling us what research is, what it is doing and what it can do for the railroads.

PRESIDENT: All in favor of the motion kindly rise. Gentlemen, a lunch is prepared on tables at each end of the room and we hope you will all stay and enjoy a little fellowship.

If there is no further business, the meeting will stand adjourned.

J. D. CONWAY, Secretary.

In Memoriam

E. H. SKILES

Joined Club November 22, 1934

Died December 29, 1935

if you want to cut Driving Costs use The Perfect Partners

THE PENNZOIL COMPANY
OIL CITY, PENNSYLVANIA

OFFICIAL PROCEEDINGS
RAILWAY CLUB OF PITTSBURGH

$1.00 Per Year   25¢ Per Copy

Vol. XXXV.   MARCH 26, 1936.   No. 5.

OWING TO FLOOD CONDITIONS OUR MARCH, 1936, MEETING WAS CANCELLED. THIS ISSUE IS PRESENTED IN LIEU OF REGULAR PROCEEDINGS.

The proof of your interest

in the Club can be

enhanced

by securing a

NEW MEMBER.

Application form is available

in this magazine. Look

it up and

"ACT NOW."

OFFICIAL PROCEEDINGS

OF

The Railway Club of Pittsburgh

Organized October 18, 1901

Published monthly, except June, July and August, by the Railway Club of
Pittsburgh, J. D. Conway, Secretary, 515 Grandview Ave., Pittsburgh, Pa..

Entered as Second Class Matter February 6, 1915, at the Postoffice at Pittsburgh,
under the Act of March 3, 1879.

| Vol. XXXV
No. 5 | Pittsburgh, Pa., Mar. 26, 1936 | $1.00 Per Year
25c Per Copy |

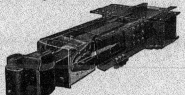

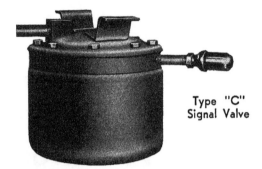

INDEX—ADVERTISERS.

NOTE—This form to be filled out in full by typewriter or printed and mailed to J. D. Conway, Secretary, 1941 Oliver Building, Pittsburgh, Pa. Membership fee, including dues, is $3.00 for each fiscal year or part thereof, except those proposed in September or October. Those proposed in these months will be credited upon payment for the following fiscal year. Dues are payable in advance.

The fiscal year ends with the month of October.

The Railway Club of Pittsburgh:

_____19____

Gentlemen:

Will you kindly consider my Application for Membership in your Club at the next meeting:

Name_____

Title_____

Company_____

My Address_____

_____

Recommended by_____

OFFICIAL PROCEEDINGS

OF

The Railway Club of Pittsburgh

Organized October 18, 1901

Vol. XXXV No. 5	Pittsburgh, Pa., Mar. 26, 1936	$1.00 Per Year 25c Per Copy

OFFICERS FOR 1935-1936

President
R. P. FORSBERG,
Chief Engineer, P. & L. E. R. R. Co., Pittsburgh, Pa.

First Vice President
E. A. RAUSCHART,
Mechanical Supt., Montour Railroad,
Coraopolis, Pa.

Secretary
J. D. CONWAY,
Railway Supply Manufacturers' Association,
Pittsburgh, Pa.

Second Vice President
G. M. SIXSMITH,
Supt., Pennsylvania Railroad,
Pittsburgh, Pa.

Treasurer
E. J. SEARLES,
Manager, Schaefer Equipment Co.,
Pittsburgh, Pa.

EXECUTIVE COMMITTEE:

FRANK J. LANAHAN, Chairman, President, Fort Pitt Malleable Iron Co., Pittsburgh, Pa.
A. STUCKI, Engineer, A. Stucki Company, Pittsburgh, Pa.
SAMUEL LYNN, Supt. Rolling Stock, P. & L. E. R. R., McKees Rocks, Pa.
D. F. CRAWFORD, Consulting Engineer, Pittsburgh, Pa.
G. W. WILDIN, Consulting Engineer, Westinghouse Air Brake Company, Pittsburgh, Pa.
W. S. McABEE, Vice Pres. & General Supt., Union Railroad Co., East Pittsburgh, Pa.
E. W. SMITH, Vice President, Pennsylvania Railroad, Pittsburgh, Pa.
LOUIS E. ENDSLEY, Consulting Engineer, 516 East End Avenue, Pittsburgh, Pa.
F. I. SNYDER, Vice President & General Manager, B. & L. E. R. R. Co., Pittsburgh, Pa.
C. O. DAMBACH, General Manager, P. & W. Va. Ry. Co., Pittsburgh, Pa.
R. H. FLINN, General Superintendent, Pennsylvania Railroad, Pittsburgh, Pa.

SUBJECT COMMITTEE:

D. W. McGEORGE, Chairman, Secretary, Edgewater Steel Company, Pittsburgh, Pa.
JOHN B. WRIGHT, Asst. Vice President, Westinghouse Air Brake Co., Wilmerding, Pa.
M. R. REED, General Supt. Motive Power, Pennsylvania Railroad, Pittsburgh, Pa.

ADVERTISING COMMITTEE:

E. A. FOARD, Chairman, Supt. Stations & Transfers, Pennsylvania R. R., Pittsburgh, Pa.
KARL BERG, Superintendent Motive Power, P. & L. E. R. R. Co., McKees Rocks, Pa.
H. E. PASSMORE, Representative, The American Hammered Piston Ring Co., Pgh., Pa.

RECEPTION AND ATTENDANCE COMMITTEE:

J. D. BELTZ, Chairman, Superintendent, B. & O. R. R. Co., Pittsburgh, Pa.
W. C. BUREL, Vice Chairman, Master Mechanic, Western Allegheny Railroad, Kaylor, Pa.
J. B. BAKER, Chief Engr. Maintenance of Way, Pennsylvania Railroad, Pittsburgh, Pa.
WALTER C. SANDERS, Gen. Mgr., Railway Div., Timken Roller Bearing Co., Canton, O.
G. A. BLACKMORE, President & Gen. Mgr., Union Switch & Signal Co., Swissvale, Pa.
J. S. LANAHAN, Vice President, Fort Pitt Malleable Iron Company, Pittsburgh, Pa.
J. A. WARFEL, Special Representative, Air Reduction Sales Co., Pittsburgh, Pa.
J. C. SHINGLEDECKER, Supervisor of Service Stations, The Pennzoil Co., Pittsburgh, Pa.
J. C. DILWORTH, Mgr. of Railroad Sales, Carnegie-Illinois Steel Corp., Pittsburgh, Pa.
G. H. BURNETTE, Assistant Chief Engineer, P. & L. E. R. R. Co., Pittsburgh, Pa.
W. R. TRIEM, Superintendent, Pennsylvania Railroad, Pittsburgh, Pa.
J. W. HOOVER, Asst. Chief of Transpn., Subsidiary Cos. U. S. Steel Corp., Pittsburgh, Pa.
J. W. JOHNSON, Superintendent, Railway Express Agency, Pittsburgh, Pa.
A. A. READ, Duquesne Slag Products Company, Pittsburgh, Pa.
C. P. SCHRECONGOST, Traffic Manager, Hillman Coal & Coke Company, Pittsburgh, Pa.

ENTERTAINMENT COMMITTEE:

J. PORTER GILLESPIE, Chairman, Asst. Gen. Supt., Lockhart Iron & Steel Co., Pgh., Pa.
FRANK E. WEIS, Vice Chairman, Transportation Clerk, Penna. R. R., Pittsburgh, Pa.
E. H. HOLMES, Sales Department, Fort Pitt Malleable Iron Co., Pittsburgh, Pa.
C. C. CLARK, Sales Manager Central District, Pressed Steel Car Co., McKees Rocks, Pa.
A. L. KESSLER, Clearance Clerk, Pennsylvania Railroad, Pittsburgh, Pa.
T. F. SHERIDAN, Asst. to S.M.P. and S.R.S., P. & L. E. R. R. Co., McKees Rocks, Pa.
JAMES NAGEL, Superintendent Transportation, Montour Railroad, Coraopolis, Pa.

FINANCE COMMITTEE:

J. L. O'TOOLE, Chairman, Asst. to Gen. Manager, P. & L. E. R. R. Co., Pittsburgh, Pa.
G. W. HONSBERGER, Transpn. Mgr., Westinghouse Electric & Mfg. Co., Pittsburgh, Pa.
F. J. RYAN, District Representative, Detroit, Toledo & Ironton Railroad, Pittsburgh, Pa.
C. E. CATT, Division Accountant, B. & O. R. R. Co., Pittsburgh, Pa.
J. W. BOYD, Superintendent, Monongahela Railway Company, Brownsville, Pa.

MEMBERSHIP COMMITTEE:

WILLIAM R. GELLATLY, Chairman, Pres., Superior Railway Products Corp., Pgh., Pa.
T. E. BRITT, Vice Chairman, Division Storekeeper, B. & O. R. R. Co., Pittsburgh, Pa.
A. B. SEVERN, General Manager, A. Stucki Company, Pittsburgh, Pa.
W. P. BUFFINGTON, Traffic Manager, Pittsburgh Coal Company, Pittsburgh, Pa.
R. S. BULL, Supt. Power & Inclines, Pittsburgh Railways Co., N. S., Pittsburgh, Pa.
A. F. COULTER, Master Car Builder, Union Railroad Co., East Pittsburgh, Pa.
T. R. DICKINSON, Purchasing Agent, B. & L. E. R. R. Co., Pittsburgh, Pa.
D. K. ORR, Road Master, Monongahela Railway Co., Brownsville, Pa.
C. M. WHEELER, Sales Engineer, Union Switch & Signal Company, Swissvale, Pa.
W. F. AMBROSE, Master Mechanic, Aliquippa & Southern Railroad, Aliquippa, Pa.
JOHN I. MULVEY, Traffic Manager, Hubbard & Company, Pittsburgh, Pa.
THOMAS R. FITZPATRICK, Freight Traffic Mgr., P. & L. E. R. R. Co., Pittsburgh, Pa.
P. W. HEPBURN, Sales Engineer, Gulf Refining Company, Pittsburgh, Pa.
W. B. MOIR, Chief Car Inspector, Pennsylvania Railroad, Pittsburgh, Pa.
C. W. TRUST, Assistant Traffic Manager, Carnegie-Illinois Steel Corp., Pittsburgh, Pa

PAST PRESIDENTS:

*J. H. McCONNELL	October,	1901, to October, 1903
*L. H. TURNER	November,	1903, to October, 1905
*F. H. STARK	November,	1905, to October, 1907
*H. W. WATTS	November,	1907, to April, 1908
*D. J. REDDING	November,	1908, to October, 1910
*F. R. McFEATTERS	November,	1910, to October, 1912
*A. G. MITCHELL	November,	1912, to October, 1914
*F. M. McNULTY	November,	1914, to October, 1916
*J. G. CODE	November,	1916, to October, 1917
*D. M. HOWE	November,	1917, to October, 1918
*J. A. SPIELMAN	November,	1918, to October, 1919
H. H. MAXFIELD	November,	1919, to October, 1920
FRANK J. LANAHAN	November,	1920, to October, 1921
SAMUEL LYNN	November,	1921, to October, 1922
D. F. CRAWFORD	November,	1922, to October, 1923
GEO. D. OGDEN	November,	1923, to October, 1924
A. STUCKI	November,	1924, to October, 1925
F. G. MINNICK	November,	1925, to October, 1926
G. W. WILDIN	November,	1926, to October, 1927
E. J. DEVANS	November,	1927, to October, 1928
W. S. McABEE	November,	1928, to October, 1929
E. W. SMITH	November,	1929, to October, 1930
LOUIS E. ENDSLEY	November,	1930, to October, 1931
*JOHN E. HUGHES	November,	1931, to October, 1932
F. I. SNYDER	November,	1932, to October, 1933
C. O. DAMBACH	November,	1933, to October, 1934
R. H. FLINN	November,	1934, to October, 1935

*—Deceased.

Meetings held fourth Thursday of each month except June, July and August.

Pittsburgh, Pa., April 6, 1936.

To the Members and Advertisers:

You no doubt will be interested and should be given some explanation as to why no meeting was held by the Club on the scheduled date of March 26, 1936. You, of course, would know there was a reason and no doubt would in your own mind know this had to do with the recent flood experienced not only in our city but pretty generally throughout the State.

Our speaker was to be Mr. E. W. P. Smith, Consulting Engineer, The Lincoln Electric Company, Cleveland, Ohio, subject, "Applied Welding with Particular Reference to Railroads." We were able, however, to get him word of the postponement of meeting by telegraph. Conditions were such that it would have been so much later than the scheduled date of meeting before we could arrange for it that it, therefore, seemed advisable to cancel the meeting for the month of March. In explanation of this, the printer of our Official Proceedings has his plant in the inundated section of the city and was unable to print our card notice covering the mail list advising of cancellation of the meeting. There were other conditions aside from this, and important as well, why no meeting could be held. The Fort Pitt Hotel, where our meetings are held had water in the meeting room to the depth of four feet and in addition were without light, power or heat and it was several days following the scheduled meeting date before these facilities were available.

I might give a few particulars coming under personal knowledge or observation at the time of the flood, although many, if not all of you, have learned much through the press:

What is known as the Triangle, which includes the principal hotels and shopping district, was practically all under water, in places as high as the second story of some of these buildings. The official record shows that the flood reached its peak of 46.0 feet at 9:00 o'clock P. M., Wednesday, March 18. To give a better conception, in comparison with other floods at Pittsburgh, a record showing the various floods beginning back as far as 1762 up to and including March 18, 1936, will be found on another page in this issue.

As stated at the beginning of this story, I may briefly sketch some of the observations: Troops were called into the city and many citizens deputized to police the city in

FIG. 1.—Showing side view of Pittsburgh & Lake Erie Passenger Station. Boat rescuing mail on first floor.

FIG. 2.—Another side view of Pittsburgh & Lake Erie Passenger Station.

addition to the regular police force. It was difficult to get into the triangle unless some very good reasons could be given for so doing. All the lines and arteries in the outlying districts were patrolled. I was able to get to my office in the Oliver Building on Wednesday morning, this building being in the triangle section and got to my office on the

FIG. 3.—Showing washed out track of P. R. R. Co. iust west of Johnstown, Pa.
(By courtesy of the Railway Age)

nineteenth floor, where word was passed that it might be expected at any time that all power, light, heat, etc., would fail. The tenants were so informed and most all left the building. I took the elevator for the ground floor, got as far as the ninth floor when the power failed and fortunately at a floor level. I walked from there to the bottom. On Friday morning I came to the building but all facilities at that time were

FIG. 4.—Two large steel barges, loaded with coal, left on main line P. & L. E. tracks near Pittsburgh station.

unavailable. Any of those having business of sufficient importance were permitted to walk, if they chose to do so. I had an important errand to my office and walked the nineteen stories, both ways, and if one does not think this is a task they have but to try it.

Our railroads suffered to an extent that would be perhaps hard to arrive at any definite figure. Loaded cars of freight, passenger cars, including all classes, and locomotives, as well as storage warehouses, were left helpless as there had not been sufficient notice that the water was going to reach such a height. I could see box cars standing on the tracks with water to the roof. The Pittsburgh & Lake Erie Railroad had water in the main waiting room to a depth of four feet. Three locomotives were seen just out of the station with water to the top of the boilers. A short distance from the passenger station two very large modern steel barges, loaded with coal, were left on the four main tracks when the river receded and were removed, however, within some two or three days when the water had left the tracks.

I have been informed that the office of one of the officials of the Montour Railroad, some ten miles out of the city, moved out with the flood and landed on the Pennsylvania

FIG. 5.—Four locomotives of Pennsylvania Railroad undermined and toppled into river at Conemaugh, Pa., stopped erosion which would have undercut and wrecked the engine house there. (By courtesy of the Railway Age)

tracks on the opposite side of the river in the vicinity of Conway Yards. This might be considered a real interchange in railroading.

I have learned that the Pennsylvania Railroad also fell heir to one of the large steel barges of coal, left high and dry on their right of way some distance from the river.

One could travel in most any direction of the city, among the smaller streams as well as the three principal rivers, the

Monongahela, Allegheny and Ohio, and find residences moved from their foundations and lodged on the property of others. To add to the trouble a number of large fires broke out and explosions took place, with the Fire Department practically helpless.

One of the most remarkable things that might be mentioned is the quick recovery of stores, office buildings, cleaning of streets, etc. While some of the main streets were

FIG. 6.—Tons of perishable produce were fouled and destroyed as the swollen Allegheny River flowed deeply through the Pennsylvania's large produce terminal at Pittsburgh. (By courtesy of the Railway Age)

sunken in places, that has practically all been cleaned up and repaired. At this writing, April 6, one could hardly believe the vast transformation that has taken place. It is true that some of the buildings are only operating a part of their elevators, which is true of this building, but the work is being speeded up to the extent that it will be but a few days when that will be remedied.

The Red Cross, Salvation Army, churches and other institutions are entitled to much praise for the aid and assistance rendered in taking care of sufferers.

One might go on and on and still leave much unsaid. Believing that what is here said may be of some little interest to the members and expressing appreciation for your forbearance, I am,　　　　　Sincerely,

　　　　　　　　　　J. D. CONWAY, Secretary.

NOTICE

OUR NEXT MEETING WILL BE HELD ON THE REGULAR DATE, APRIL 23, 1936, AT THE FORT PITT HOTEL, PITTSBURGH, PA. YOU WILL BE ADVISED FORMALLY BY POSTAL CARD LATER IN CONFIRMATION. WE WILL HAVE THE SAME SPEAKER SCHEDULED TO ADDRESS THE CLUB AT OUR POSTPONED MEETING OF MARCH 26, 1936—MR. E. W. P. SMITH, CONSULTING ENGINEER, THE LINCOLN ELECTRIC COMPANY, CLEVELAND, O., SUBJECT, "APPLIED WELDING WITH PARTICULAR REFERENCE TO RAILROADS."

HISTORICAL ITEM OF SOME INTEREST

The Club was organized October 18, 1901, there were 49 members enrolled on that date, and it was decided to leave the charter open until the following meeting, held November 15, 1901, and the membership was increased to 201. Of those who where charter members our record shows at this time nine of them still holding membership; the names of the nine are as follows:

J. Alexander Brown, Vice President and Manager,
    The Railway Equipment and Publication Company,

J. D. Conway, Secretary-Treasurer,
    The Railway Supply Manufacturers' Association,

R. P. Forsberg, Chief Engineer,
    Pittsburgh & Lake Erie Railroad Company,

N. S. Reeder,
    Pressed Steel Car Company,

A. Stucki, Engineer,
    A. Stucki Company,

R. S. Suydam, President,
    M. B. Suydam Company,

H. G. Taylor, President,
    Ball Chemical Company,

John L. Tucker, "Retired" Trainmaster,
    Pennsylvania Railroad,

Roy V. Wright, Secretary,
    Simmons-Boardman Publishing Company.

RECORD OF FLOODS IN THE OHIO RIVER
AT PITTSBURGH, PA.
Flood stage is 25 feet
Elevation of zero of the river gage is 694 feet above sea level; U.S.G.S. datum.

Year	Day of Month		Stage at Pittsburgh	Year	Day of Month		Stage at Pittsburgh
1762	January	9	39.2	1895	January	8	29.0
1763	March	9	41.1	1896	July	26	26.2
1809	April	10	37.1	1897	February	24	32.7
1810	November	9	35.2	1898	March	24	32.1
1813	January	....	32 2	1899	March	6	25.2
1816	February	....	36.2	1900	November	27	30.9
1932	February	10	38.2	1901	April	7	25.3
1840	February	1	30.0	1901	April	21	30.7
1846	March	15	28.2	1901	December	16	29.0
1847	February	2	30.1	1902	March	1	35.6
1847	December	12	27.2	1903	February	5	27.2
1848	December	22	26.2	1903	March	1	32.1
1851	September	20	34.1	1904	January	23	33.2
1852	April	6	28.2	1904	March	4	30.1
1852	April	19	35.1	1904	March	8	26.4
1858	May	27	29.2	1905	March	22	32.2
1859	April	28	25.2	1905	December	4	26.7
1860	April	12	32.9	1907	January	20	26.5
1860	November	4	25.2	1907	March	15	38.7
1861	September	29	34.2	1907	March	20	25.6
1862	January	21	33.2	1908	February	16	33.9
1862	April	22	28 6	1908	March	20	30.5
1865	March	4	27.7	1909	February	25	25.5
1865	March	18	34.6	1909	May	1	25.4
1867	February	15	25.2	1910	January	19	26.0
1867	March	13	26.7	1910	March	1	25.2
1868	March	18	25.2	1911	January	15	27.0
1873	December	14	28.9	1911	January	31	28.4
1874	January	8	25.4	1912	March	22	31.3
1876	September	19	28.2	1913	January	9	34.5
1877	January	17	27.8	1913	January	12	29.5
1878	December	11	27.7	1913	March	28	33.6
1881	February	11	26.4	1913	November	17	25.4
1881	June	10	30.3	1915	February	3	31.6
1883	February	5	28.0	1915	December	19	25.8
1883	February	8	31.2	1917	January	23	28.4
1884	February	6	36.5	1917	March	13	26.3
1885	January	17	26.2	1918	February	21	30.3
1886	April	7	26.0	1918	March	15	29.1
1887	February	12	25.2	1919	January	3	26.0
1887	February	27	25.2	1920	March	13	28.3
1888	July	11	25.2	1921	November	29	28.6
1888	August	22	29.2	1924	January	4	30.6
1889	June	1	27.2	1924	March	30	32.4
1890	March	23	27.5	1924	May	13	29.6
1890	May	24	25.2	1927	January	23	29.7
1891	January	3	26.4	1927	December	14	30.4
1891	February	18	34.5	1929	February	27	25.3
1892	January	15	26.2	1933	March	15	29.6
1893	February	8	27.2	1934	March	6	25.8
1893	February	11	25.2	1935	March	13	26.3
1894	May	22	26.4	1936	March	18	46.0

The river gage was lowered 3.2 feet March 1, 1926. All gage readings hereon prior to that date have been corrected to agree with the present gage readings.

HERE'S YOUR TICKET!

for better mileage

"THE PERFECT PARTNERS"

PENNZIP GASOLINE
PENNZOIL MOTOR OIL

THE PENNZOIL COMPANY . . . . OIL CITY, PA.

OFFICIAL PROCEEDINGS
LWAY CLUB OF PITTSBURGH

$1.00 Per Year   25¢ Per Copy

Vol. XXXV.   APRIL 23, 1936.   No. 6.

APPLIED WELDING WITH PARTICULAR REFERENCE TO RAILROADS

By E. W. P. SMITH, Consulting Engineer,
The Lincoln Electric Company, Cleveland, Ohio.

The proof of your interest

in the Club can be

enhanced

by securing a

NEW MEMBER.

Application form is available

in this magazine. Look

it up and

"ACT NOW."

The

Published
Pittsburgh

Entered as Second

The I

COLUME
NEW Y

OFFICIAL PROCEEDINGS

OF

The Railway Club of Pittsburgh

Organized October 18, 1901

Published monthly, except June, July and August, by the Railway Club of
Pittsburgh, J. D. Conway, Secretary, 515 Grandview Ave., Pittsburgh, Pa..

Entered as Second Class Matter February 6, 1915, at the Postoffice at Pittsburgh,
under the Act of March 3, 1879.

| Vol. XXXV
No. 6 | Pittsburgh, Pa., Apr. 23, 1936 | $1.00 Per Year
25c Per Copy |

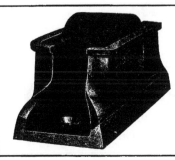

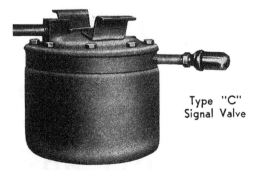

EQUIPMENT FOR RAILROADS

STATIONARY AIR COMPRESSORS	PORTABLE AIR COMPRESSORS
ROCK DRILLING EQUIPMENT	CONSTRUCTION AIR TOOLS
CENTRIFUGAL PUMPS	STEAM AND POWER PUMPS
DEEP WELL TURBINE PUMPS	SUMP AND DRAINAGE PUMPS
LOCOMOTIVE FEEDWATER HEATERS	STATIONARY FEEDWATER HEATERS
STEAM CONDENSERS	CONDENSER AUXILIARIES
DIESEL ENGINES	GAS ENGINES
*REFRIGERATION EQUIPMENT	*AIR CONDITIONING EQUIPMENT
V-BELT DRIVES	†LIQUID METERS

*Through subsidiary, CARBONDALE MACHINE CORPORATION
†Through subsidiary, WORTHINGTON-GAMON METER COMPANY

● *Complete descriptive literature available*

**WORTHINGTON PUMP AND MACHINERY CORPORATION
HARRISON, NEW JERSEY**

A-3580

INDEX—ADVERTISERS.

NOTE—This form to be filled out in full by typewriter or printed and mailed to J. D. Conway, Secretary, 1941 Oliver Building, Pittsburgh, Pa. Membership fee, including dues, is $3.00 for each fiscal year or part thereof, except those proposed in September or October. Those proposed in these months will be credited upon payment for the following fiscal year. Dues are payable in advance.

The fiscal year ends with the month of October.

The Railway Club of Pittsburgh:

_____19____

Gentlemen:

Will you kindly consider my Application for Membership in your Club at the next meeting:

Name_____

Title_____

Company_____

My Address_____

Recommended by_____

OFFICIAL PROCEEDINGS

OF

The Railway Club of Pittsburgh

Organized October 18, 1901

Vol. XXXV No. 6	**Pittsburgh, Pa., Apr. 23, 1936**	$1.00 Per Year 25c Per Copy

ENTERTAINMENT COMMITTEE:

J. PORTER GILLESPIE, Chairman, Asst. Gen. Supt., Lockhart Iron & Steel Co., Pgh., Pa.
FRANK E. WEIS, Vice Chairman, Transportation Clerk, Penna. R. R., Pittsburgh, Pa.
E. H. HOLMES, Sales Department, Fort Pitt Malleable Iron Co., Pittsburgh, Pa.
C. C. CLARK, Sales Manager Central District, Pressed Steel Car Co., McKees Rocks, Pa.
A. L. KESSLER, Clearance Clerk, Pennsylvania Railroad, Pittsburgh, Pa.
T. F. SHERIDAN, Asst. to S.M.P. and S.R.S., P. & L. E. R. R. Co., McKees Rocks, Pa.
JAMES NAGEL, Superintendent Transportation, Montour Railroad, Coraopolis, Pa.

FINANCE COMMITTEE:

J. L. O'TOOLE, Chairman, Asst. to Gen. Manager, P. & L. E. R. R. Co., Pittsburgh, Pa.
G. W. HONSBERGER, Transpn. Mgr., Westinghouse Electric & Mfg. Co., Pittsburgh, Pa.
F. J. RYAN, District Representative, Detroit, Toledo & Ironton Railroad, Pittsburgh, Pa.
C. E. CATT, Division Accountant, B. & O. R. R. Co., Pittsburgh, Pa.
J. W. BOYD, Superintendent, Monongahela Railway Company, Brownsville, Pa.

MEMBERSHIP COMMITTEE:

T. E. BRITT, Chairman, Division Storekeeper, B. & O. R. R. Co., Pittsburgh, Pa.
A. B. SEVERN, General Manager, A. Stucki Company, Pittsburgh, Pa.
W. P. BUFFINGTON, Traffic Manager, Pittsburgh Coal Company, Pittsburgh, Pa.
R. S. BULL, Supt. Power & Inclines, Pittsburgh Railways Co., N. S., Pittsburgh, Pa.
A. F. COULTER, Master Car Builder, Union Railroad Co., East Pittsburgh, Pa.
T. R. DICKINSON, Purchasing Agent, B. & L. E. R. R. Co., Pittsburgh, Pa.
D. K. ORR, Road Master, Monongahela Railway Co., Brownsville, Pa.
C. M. WHEELER, Sales Engineer, Union Switch & Signal Company, Swissvale, Pa.
W. F. AMBROSE, Master Mechanic, Aliquippa & Southern Railroad, Aliquippa, Pa.
JOHN I. MULVEY, Traffic Manager, Hubbard & Company, Pittsburgh, Pa.
THOMAS R. FITZPATRICK, Freight Traffic Mgr., P. & L. E. R. R. Co., Pittsburgh, Pa.
P. W. HEPBURN, Sales Engineer, Gulf Refining Company, Pittsburgh, Pa.
W. B. MOIR, Chief Car Inspector, Pennsylvania Railroad, Pittsburgh, Pa.
C. W. TRUST, Assistant Traffic Manager, Carnegie-Illinois Steel Corp., Pittsburgh, Pa

PAST PRESIDENTS:

*J. H. McCONNELL..October, 1901, to October, 1903
*L. H. TURNER..November, 1903, to October, 1905
*F. H. STARK..November, 1905, to October, 1907
*H. W. WATTS..November, 1907, to April, 1908
*D. J. REDDING..November, 1908, to October, 1910
*F. R. McFEATTERS..November, 1910, to October, 1912
*A. G. MITCHELL..November, 1912, to October, 1914
*F. M. McNULTY..November, 1914, to October, 1916
*J. G. CODE..November, 1916, to October, 1917
*D. M. HOWE..November, 1917, to October, 1918
*J. A. SPIELMAN..November, 1918, to October, 1919
H. H. MAXFIELD..November, 1919, to October, 1920
FRANK J. LANAHAN..November, 1920, to October, 1921
SAMUEL LYNN..November, 1921, to October, 1922
D. F. CRAWFORD..November, 1922, to October, 1923
GEO. D. OGDEN..November, 1923, to October, 1924
A. STUCKI..November, 1924, to October, 1925
F. G. MINNICK..November, 1925, to October, 1926
G. W. WILDIN..November, 1926, to October, 1927
E. J. DEVANS..November, 1927, to October, 1928
W. S. McABEE..November, 1928, to October, 1929
E. W. SMITH..November, 1929, to October, 1930
LOUIS E. ENDSLEY..November, 1930, to October, 1931
*JOHN E. HUGHES..November, 1931, to October, 1932
F. I. SNYDER..November, 1932, to October, 1933
C. O. DAMBACH..November, 1933, to October, 1934
R. H. FLINN..November, 1934, to October, 1935
*—Deceased.

Meetings held fourth Thursday of each month except June, July and August.

PROCEEDINGS OF MEETING
APRIL 23, 1936

The regular monthly meeting was called to order at the Fort Pitt Hotel at 8:00 o'clock P. M.

Registered attendance, 303, as follows:

MEMBERS

Allen, Earl M.
Ambrose, W. F.
Armstrong, J. L.
Aulbach, A. J.
Babcock, F. H.
Baker, W. E.
Balph, M. Z.
Balzer, C. E.
Barr, H. C.
Bauer, F. C.
Beam, E. J.
Beaver, R. C.
Beeson, H. L.
Beitsch, George F.
Beltz, J. D.
Berg, Karl
Beswick, R. M.
Brandt, George F.
Brant, William J.
Braun, O. F.
Britt, T. E.
Burel, W. C.
Burnette, G. H.
Buzzerd, J. P.
Cannon, T. E.
Carr, T. W.
Carson, John
Chaffin, H. B.
Chalker, A. R.
Chilcoat, H. E.
Christy, F. X.
Clements, Frank C.
Coakley, J. A., Jr.
Conway, J. D.
Coombe, A. B.
Cowen, Harry E.
Crawford, Burt H.
Cruikshank, J. C.
Cummings, Peter
Cunningham, J. D.
Dalrymple, R. W.

Dalzell, W. E.
Dambach, C. O.
Davies, James
Davin, W. E.
Davis, Charles S.
Dean, E. E.
Devine, J. C.
Dierker, R. H.
Donovan, L. T.
Duffley, F. M.
Dunham, C. W.
Egly, M. J.
Emery, E.
Enders, I. O.
Endsley, Louis E.
Fike, J. W.
Finegan, T. A.
Flinn, R. H.
Forsythe, George B.
Fralic, C. F.
Frauenheim, A. M.
Frauenheim, Pierce H.
Freshwater, F. H.
Furch, George J.
Galbraith, James R.
Gardner, George R.
George, R. H.
George, W. J.
Gillespie, J. Porter
Glaser, C. J.
Glaser, J. P.
Goldstrom, G. E.
Goodwin, A. E.
Greek, Joseph
Green, M. E.
Griest, E. E.
Gross, John
Groves, W. C.
Grunden, B. C.
Haller, Nelson M.
Hamilton, J. K.

Hansen, William C.
Harper, G. C.
Hassler, E. S.
Hayward, Carlton
Heed, H. L.
Hemma, Charles H.
Herring, J. R.
Hess, Charles A.
Hilstrom, A. V.
Hocking, Harry A.
Holland, S. E.
Holmes, E. H.
Honsberger, G. W.
Hoover, J. W.
Hopper, George
Hornefius, S. R.
Huff, A. B.
Huston, F. T.
Hutchinson, G. C., Jr.
Jahnke, Karl W.
Jennings, A. S.
Johnson, J. W.
Johnson, Le Vere H.
Kaup, H. E.
Keck, L. M.
Keller, R. B.
Kelly, Leo J.
Keller, R. E.
Kentlein, John
Kirk, W. B.
Knable, G. E.
Kroske, J. F.
Lanahan, Frank J.
Lanahan, J. S.
Larsen, W. E.
Laurent, Joseph A.
Lavine, Ralph D.
Lee, L. A.
Leet, C. S.
Lincoln, J. J.
Lincoln, R. B.
Longstreth, Willis L.
Lynn, Samuel
Marble, A. E.
Marsh, Ernest A.
Mayer, G. E.
Millar, C. W.
Mills, O. B.
Misner, George W.
Mitchell, J. G.
Mitchell, W. S.
Morgan, A. L.

Mulligan, Michael
Musgrove, W. W.
Myers, R. H.
McHugh, C. A.
McIntyre, R. C.
McGeorge, D. W.
McKay, N. H.
McKim, Hollis
McNamee, W.
McTighe, B.
Nathan, W. S.
Neff, John P.
Nichols, S. A.
Nieman, Harry L.
Noonan, Daniel
O'Leary, J. J.
O'Sullivan, J. J.
Paisley, F. R.
Phillips, T. H.
Porter, H. N.
Posteraro, S. F.
Purchard, Paul
Reed, M. R.
Redding, R. D.
Rensch, R. H.
Rief, Joseph
Rowan, J. R.
Rowles, H. N.
Rupp, E. S.
Rushneck, G. L.
Rutter, H. E.
Ryan, D. W.
Ryan, Frank J.
Sarchet, Roger
Satterfield, A. T.
Schadt, A. D.
Schaffer, W. E.
Schrecongost, C. P.
Searles, E. J.
Severn, A. B.
Shepherd, W. B.
Sheridan, T. F.
Shuster, W. W.
Smith, E. E.
Smith, Folger M.
Smith, Robert B.
Snyder, F. I.
Stevens, L. V.
Stocker, H. F.
Stoffregen, Louis E.
Stucki, A.
Sudell, D. W.

Suffern, R. J.
Sullivan, R. J.
Sutherland, Lloyd
Swank, W. E.
Taggart, J. G.
Thomas, George P.
Thomas, T.
Thornton, A. W.
Tipton, G. M.
Tracey, J. B. A.
Trax, L. R.
Tryon, I. D.
Tucker, John L.
Unger, Dr. J. S.
Van Nort, C. W.
Van Wormer, George M.

Vowinkel, Fred F.
Waxler, Brice
Weis, F. E.
Weniger, Oscar S.
Werner, L. A.
West, Troy
Whipple, A. L.
Wikander, O. R.
Wildin, G. W.
Wilkinson, W. E.
Winslow, George W.
Winter, Paul S.
Wright, Edward W.
Wright, John B.
Yohe, J. K., Jr.
Young, J., Jr.

VISITORS

Averill, E. A.
Balzer, Charles, Jr.
Banks, J. L.
Bieler, Oscar
Blackstock, W. H.
Boring, J. R.
Bossinger, A. H.
Bossinger, H. L.
Brodie, Stuart B.
Bruce, B. C.
Bryson, G. V.
Burkhard, A.
Coleman, A. D.
Conway, James G.
Corcoran, J. J.
Crossland, P. B.
Dalzell, W. E., Jr.
Enza, P. L.
Evans, F. H.
Flood, John F.
Foster, George J.
Funk, M. S.
Geist, Eugene
Glass, Frank D.
Glenn, Joseph
Gloss, A. G.
Gross, R. R.
Hankins, Cyrus
Hamilton, H. M.
Hartnett, T. R.
Henderson, Reed R.
Hildebrand, L. B.
Hydosky, S. J.
Jackson, E. W.

Johnson, R. A.
Keeney, John H.
Kelin, A. W.
Kelly, Frank J.
Kelly, W. J.
Kephart, R. D.
Kernahan, R. H.
Larmer, J. W.
Lewis, S. B.
Livingston, E. M.
Longstreth, Wendell L.
Maichle, F. M.
Marcoff, E.
Meskell, Aulden
Milberger, Fred
McClory, L. H.
McGregor, S. S.
McKinley, H. J.
Osterrieder, A. J.
Osterrieder, J. S.
Oswald, Louis W.
Oyen, F.
Pagett, V.
Pastre, R. E.
Patterson, Robert
Persons, W. R.
Peterson, S. M.
Posteraro, Alfred
Radtke, J. E.
Rider, R. W.
Sly, Harmon
Smith, E. S.
Smith, E. W.
Smith, E. W. P.

Smith, Sion B.
Steele, Charles
Storek, E. M.
Sutherland, O. C.
Tramblie, H. I.
Vakovac, V. P.
Vandivort, R. E.
Vitale, Michael

Vollmer, W. K.
Washabaugh, George A.
Weis, Mrs. F. E.
White, H. E.
White, R. E.
Williams, A. G.
Wilson, A. R.
Wilson, George F.

Winton, C. A.

The business meeting was preceded with the customary musical program, which this evening took the form of a community sing, led by Mr. Frank E. Weis, with Mrs. Weis at the piano.

SECRETARY: We regret very much the absence of our President, Mr. R. P. Forsberg, but no more so I am sure than he does. His presence is required at the Directors' Meeting of the Pittsburgh & Lake Erie Railroad in New York, and being a good soldier he answers the call of duty.

In his absence I am going to assume the authority, in your behalf, of calling to the chair our senior past President, Mr. Lanahan.

MR. FRANK J. LANAHAN: You are all sorry, I know, that Mr. Forsberg could not be with us tonight, and he, himself, was extremely disappointed that due to circumstances and conditions over which he had no control, he had to relinquish his good intention of 100 per cent attendance during his tenure of office.

Our First Vice President, Mr. Rauschart, is this evening requisitioned by a convention here in Pittsburgh of Methodist Bishops. The outstanding event of this gathering of religious in our city, is a dinner being held at this present moment in Syria Mosque, and in company with Mrs. Rauschart, Ed is doing proper honor to the occasion. This afternoon did he telephone to me, asking that I explain his absence and tender the membership at large, his excuse.

Second Vice President, Mr. Sixsmith, also being absent, it looks as though you will have to put up with me tonight as your presiding officer. It gives me a thrill to look into your faces again, because ordinarily occupying a seat in the back of the room, I have had the experience of gazing at your collective necks, and frankly, that is not altogether inspiring. But, I must realize I am not on this elevated platform to

131

indulge in levity, so we will proceed with the routine business of the meeting.

First on the order of business is the roll call. As you all have signed the registration cards on entrance, that can be dispensed with now. Next comes the reading of the minutes of the last meeting. There are no minutes, for there was no meeting held in March, instead we had the historical St. Patrick's Day Flood. This deluge of water has been explicitedly explained to the gathering in the terse but complete story sent to you by our Secretary, embodied in the last issue of the "Proceedings". In perusing the interesting pages depicting the condition of inundated Pittsburgh, with particular reference to the Fort Pitt Hotel and this room in which we are assembled, one can freely visualize the reason for skipping the scheduled March meeting. The photographs and word pictures that Mr. Conway presents are particularly fine and I venture the opinion that Carnegie Museum would be glad to preserve in their file the historical data embraced in this issue.

The next order of business is the reception of new members. I will ask that the Secretary please read the list of names, and in accordance with our custom, the new members are asked to rise as their names are called and to kindly remain standing until the list is completed and thus afford us the pleasure of viewing each singly before welcoming them as a group.

SECRETARY: We have the following list of proposals for membership:

Bacon, J. L., Manager of Sales, Valve Pilot Corporation, 230 Park Avenue, New York, N. Y. Recommended by R. M. Long.

Griest, E. E., Vice President and General Manager, Fort Pitt Malleable Iron Company, P. O. Box 505, Pittsburgh, Pa. Recommended by Frank J. Lanahan.

Hamilton, Joseph K., Examiner, Labor and Wage Bureau, Pennsylvania Railroad, Pennsylvania Station, Pittsburgh, Pa. Recommended by Roger Sarchet.

Johnson, Stephen, Jr., Chief Engineer, Bendix Westinghouse Automotive Air Brake Company, 5001 Center Avenue, Pittsburgh, Pa. Recommended by J. B. Wright.

Kerr, James P., M.D., Comptroller, City of Pittsburgh, Wabash Building, Pittsburgh, Pa. Recommended by C. O. Dambach.

Nabors, W. F., Scale Inspector, P. & L. E. R. R. Co., 7122 Schoyer Avenue, Swissvale, Pa. Recommended by J. A. Noble.

Peterson, E. J., Foreman of Carpenters, P. & L. E. R. R. Co., 2004 Bailey Avenue, McKeesport, Pa. Recommended by J. A. Noble.

Pohlman, A., Steam Engineer, Jones & Laughlin Steel Corporation, Aliquippa, Pa. Recommended by R. M. Long.

Sanders, C. R., Supervisor, Pennsylvania Railroad, 411 Duquesne Avenue, Trafford, Pa. Recommended by W. B. Moir.

Small, Walter J., Sales Engineer, Dodge Steel Company, 6501 Tacony Street, Philadelphia, Pa. Recommended by E. A. Rauschart.

CHAIRMAN: Gentlemen, it is our privilege to welcome you into the membership of this Club.

SECRETARY: Since our last meeting we have received information of the death of two of our members:

William C. Seiss, Retired Pennsylvania Railroad Employee, Philadelphia, Pa., died March 6, 1936, and Joseph S. Merk, Statistical Clerk, P. & L. E. R. R. Co., Pittsburgh, Pa., died April 6, 1936.

CHAIRMAN: An appropriate memorial minute will appear in the next issue of the "Proceedings".

If there are no Reports of Officers or Committees, we will proceed to the order of New Business. Under this designation, I regret to announce that the head of one of our very important Committees, Mr. William R. Gellatly, Chairman of the Membership Committee, is ill and upon the advice of his physician, he feels it encumbent upon him to temporarily retire, and has recommended as a successor, the Vice Chairman, Mr. T. E. Britt. The Executive Committee has taken cognizance of Mr. Gellatly's suggestion, and realizing an inevitable situation, has taken favorable action on the substitution of Mr. Britt, and the matter now comes before you for action.

ON MOTION, the resignation of Mr. Gellatly is accepted, with sincere regret, and Mr. T. E. Britt is elected Chairman of the Membership Committee to succeed him.

CHAIRMAN: If there is no further business to come before the meeting, we will proceed with the paper of the evening. The subject is "Applied Welding with Particular Reference to Railroads". There is probably nothing today in commercial life that is more pertinent, nor has any industry made more progress in a comparatively few years, than welding. The gentleman who will present the subject tonight is thoroughly competent to depict this latest contribution in mechanical achievement. He represents one of the outstanding companies in the welding field, the Lincoln Electric Company of Cleveland, Ohio, as its consulting engineer. It is my privilege to introduce him to you, Mr. E. W. P. Smith.

APPLIED WELDING WITH PARTICULAR REFERENCE TO RAILROADS
By E. W. P. SMITH, Consulting Engineer,
The Lincoln Electric Company, Cleveland, Ohio.

Mr. Chairman and Gentlemen of The Railway Club of Pittsburgh: Your Chairman mentioned that the Company ··

with which I am connected is in a commercial line. It is, but my talk is not going to be commercial. .I will not present to you a series of discussions which you might take from any one of our catalogues. I want to keep it on the basis of a study of the science of welding. We freely admit the superiority of our product, so that is that, and we may go at once to the consideration of welding.

Again. as a sort of preliminary statement or basis of our discussion, if I may be a little personal, two things disturb me greatly. One of them is to have somebody come before an audience such as this and undertake to tell it how to run the railroads, insofar as welding is concerned. It has been demonstrated for a good many years that railroads are successful and are operating and doing a good job. The character and experience of men necessary to do that job must be there with an amount of brains, ability and energy, which if applied to welding will reduce welding problems to much simpler terms. All is necessary is to get through that veil of mystery which exists in the minds of so many people. For a speaker to say "This is what you must do,"—I cannot see that at all.

The other item is where there is presented to a man certain facts which are demonstrated, either by himself or somebody else, and he is not governed by those facts. I was once talking about welding and a chap kept asking me question after question until he had me in a corner because I could not find out what he was driving at and could not answer. Some one spoke up and said, "That was thirteen years ago." That kind of thing disturbs me, that is, where facts of thirteen years ago are used as the basis of suggestions or design at the present time. You can go back not so many years, as time goes, through a considerable period in the development of welding, and find the statement that $\frac{1}{8}''$ electrode is the biggest electrode that you can use. You know today that is not so.

It seems to me that first attitude is not only an insult to intelligence and experience but a total disregard of that experience. And the second is a total lack of present day facts. I want to give you some of those facts.

For instance, one of the most prevalent things we run into is where somebody wants to buy something, say an electrode, and he begins with "How much is it?" We will say 8 cents a pound. Another fellow comes along with one that is 12 cents a pound. I am an outsider and I do not know much about running railroad trains, but I notice service is the big word. We in the welding industry call that service life. It can be demonstrated that the cost of an electrode is only a small part of the cost involved in getting service life out of a piece of equipment. There are various other items entering into that cost. We have the labor to consider, the characteristics of the electrode, the speed at which it can be deposited. When we finally get to the real answer it is a question of what that will do for us to keep our trains running and keep our costs down. I do not suppose the average man thinks of it in just that way. I have seen the work done in welding on railroads. And if it was possible to get a general picture of the amount of experience and ability and plain hard work that goes into keeping those trains running the average man would come to a realization of the tremendous amount of ability which is used on these railroads. And I can say that for a good many other industries. Glass factories, silk factories, most any product. So we step on a railroad train and do not think of the ability that is involved in running that train.

What I want to present to you are a few facts in relation to electrodes and a little bit of some of the applications, which are not always directly applicable to railroads but which will show what kind of work can be done, and then something about special electrodes. The idea is this, whether it be a frame, for example, that you want to fix up, or fabricate a system in relation to a frame, you want to know when you make those joints the characteristics of the joints. You want to know that the joint has an ultimate strength, a yield point, a fatigue and impact value at least equal to the plate. If it does not have these you are not particularly interested, and rightly so.

There may be some other special problems in your own field that offer a tremendous field for special service. It may be a cutting surface, abrasion, friction, impact, all those enter into it, and you can apply a special surface by means of an electrode on to a material that is lower in cost, at a very material saving in total cost when your working surface is relatively small, such as applying a cutter edge on a tool. Naturally I took time to check up on some examples on railroads on the basis of welding. You find for example that you have the finest example in the world for the control of expansion and contraction in a wheel center; another is the case of frames. You have all sorts of loads where fatigue and impact are important. Take all these things that you are doing in your shops and line them up and classify them according to load or service requirements and you will find it a great help in classifying your welding knowledge in accordance with these experiences. Arrange all those facts. You have we will say a fatigue load. What do you have to do to keep down fatigue failures? You must have a certain distribution of stress. It does not necessarily follow that if you have a load and an area and divide the load by the area that is your unit stress. I can show where you can divide a load by an area and the variation may actually be considerable from the maximum stress to the average stress. That may be where the difficulty lies. Then you have an impact. The stresses will be so high and of such short duration they will cause a failure because the metal does not have time to move. So we are interested in ductility. Another one is the question of yield point. High yield point, high ductility, and the consequent cost reduction you can get. Take an ordinary gondola car in a riveted construction, you will have 600 pounds of rivet heads in the car. If you weld the car you can save about 3,000 pounds. As a matter of fact it is over that. That means that on a 100 car train you have 150 tons more pay load. That is quite attractive. Figure that at 2½ cents a pound and it runs into quite a saving.

If you tell us what characteristics you have to have we can get them. If we cannot, we can tell you how far we can go and you can judge whether the use of that particular set up is justified.

That is what I mean in the case of using your experience. I know it may not be unusual for a speaker, due to his enthusiasm and limited view to make statements which are a little far fetched. As a result you may lose faith in certain methods and schemes. Think of all the welds in a train failing at once what a beautiful lot of scrap iron you would have. You must combine your experience and knowledge with welding.

I want to show a few slides illustrative of some of the characteristics which we can get by means of some of these special electrodes and then some comparisons of different types of electrodes to indicate possibly another scheme of fabrication or another slant on the possible different applica-

136

tions of welding to your problem. I do not want to try to tell you just what should be done, because that is very difficult. If you will read, as you have, some articles you will find a statement something like this. If we were permitted to do this job by welding we could save a lot more money, but we are not permitted to do it. There may be regulations that do not permit it to be done. But in this case there is no combination of experience and welding. I want to give you a few of the characteristics which I think will be applicable to a great many of your problems and which you can solve by this method of combination.

It is common knowledge that molten steel has an affinity for oxygen and nitrogen. When exposed to the air molten steel enters into chemical combination with these elements of the air to form oxides and nitrides in the steel. These impurities in the steel tend, to weaken and embrittle it as well as lessen its resistance to corrosion.

In the ordinary arc using bare or lightly coated electrode, the molten globules which pass from the electrode to the work are exposed to the ambient atmosphere which contains chiefly oxygen and nitrogen. The molten base metal is also exposed to these elements. They combine with the molten metal, forming oxides and nitrides in the weld metal. Hence the consequent weakening and embrittlement as mentioned earlier.

If the metal during the fusion process is completely protected from contact with the ambient atmosphere, the injurious chemical combination cannot take place. This is achieved by shielding the arc.

An arc may be shielded by enveloping it with an inert gas, which will not enter into the chemical combination with the molten metal and at the same time prevent its contact with the elements of the air. Welds made with a shielded arc are largely free of oxides and nitrides and are therefore composed of metal having superior physical characteristics to that deposited by an ordinary arc.

In previous slides has been shown the difference in the grain structure of the metal and that this is reflected in the physical characteristics is evident by this slide. The upper test coupon shows the weld in the middle of the coupon machined down flush with the rest of the coupon. Note that the material itself broke outside of the weld and at some distance from the weld. Note also that the unshielded arc as made by the bare or lightly coated electrode, broke in the weld. The tensile strength of shielded arc weld metal will vary from 65,000 to 85,000 pounds per square inch, while the tensile strength of the ordinary arc weld metal will be from 40,000 to 55,000 pounds per square inch. Mild steel plate such as these welds were made in will develop a tensile strength of from 55,000 to 65,000 pounds per square inch.

This shows tensile specimens of all-weld metal, which is a standard basis of comparison. All-weld metal specimens are prepared by depositing metal in a groove and then machining out a portion which will contain entirely all weld metal. These are turned to a diameter of approximately ½-inch. The upper specimen shows such a tensile test specimen made with Fleetweld, which gave a tensile strength of well over 70,000 pounds per square inch. The lower shows an all weld metal specimen made with the bare or lightly coated type of electrode, which broke at 49,000 pounds per square inch. This same type of specimen is used as a measure of the ductility of weld metal. It will be noted that there is a decided necking in the case of the Fleetweld or shielded arc type of specimen which is absent in the lower specimen. Two inches are measured off in the specimen and carefully marked, the specimens are then pulled and the elongation measured. In the case of the shielded arc specimen this will range from 20 to 30%, and in some cases higher, particularly if the weld is stress relieved or annealed. In the case of the bare or lightly coated electrode, the elongation will be from 5 to 10%.

This slide shows graphically the difference in ductility between the welds made with the shielded arc—such electrode as Fleetweld, and the welds made with the bare or lightly

SLIDE No. 3

coated rod. These specimens were made by butt welding
heavy plate and the plate was then bent using the weld as a
fulcrum point. Note that the specimen on the left, made with
the shielded arc, was bent to 180 degrees without any ill
effect on the weld, even though the outside fibres were elon-
gated 47%. Note also that the specimen on the left shows

SLIDE No. 4

a crack which occurred when the elongation on the outside fibres was only 23%.

This slide also shows the relative ductility between the shielded arc and the unshielded arc type of welds. The lower bead, or the one with the crack, was laid on a plate of steel with the bare or lightly coated type of rod, and the upper weld was also made at the same time with the shielded arc type or rod, such as Fleetweld, then plate bent cold. It will be noticed that the weld made with the shielded arc took this test without any sign of failure, whereas the other type of weld cracked badly.

This slide shows a number of specimens made up of all weld metal by the shielded arc, using electrode such as Fleetweld. The upper specimen is a standard tensile specimen of all weld metal which withstood a tension of over 70,000 pounds per square inch. Note the necking down of the specimen and its elongation indicating ductility. The specimen in the lower middle is a typical fatigue resistance specimen.

SLIDE No. 5 (Showing weld metal sample bent cold and forged)

These specimens are made up consisting of weld metal cut from welded joints and set up in rotating beam machines and subjected to reverse stresses. This specimen carried a maximum stress on the outside fibres of approximately 30,000 pounds, and was subject to 10,000,000 reversals without failure. This is compared with a similar fatigue specimen made with the ordinary arc with the bare or lightly coated electrode of 12,000 to 15,000 pounds stress on the outside fibre. The specimen at the lower left shows a fatigue specimen after having been fatigued, or put through 10,000,000 reversals, with 30,000 pounds per square inch stress on the outside fibres and then bent cold through 180 degrees without sign of failure.

The specimen at the lower right shows an impact resistance test specimen. Impact resistance test showing the resistance in foot pounds definitely establishes the superiority of weld metal made with the shielded arc over that produced

with the unshielded arc. The impact resistance of this specimen made with the shielded arc will run from 50 to 80 foot
pounds (Izod). The impact resistance of mild steel will
usually run from 40 to 80 foot pounds (Izod).

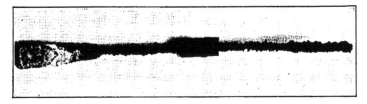

SLIDE No. 6

Effects of corrosion on the weld metal and parent metal
must be duly considered in determining the proper method
or process of arc welding to employ in the fabrication of
products which are subjected to acid fumes, weather conditions, or which are to be buried in the ground. Rate of
deterioration due to corrosion is usually a determining factor
in the sale of an arc welded product whose use requires exposure to the action of corrosive agents.

Corrosive effects on welds made with shielded and unshielded arc can be readily ascertained after immersion of the
welds in a solution of sulphuric acid. This slide shows a
sample of steel plate welded with shielded arc electrode, using
electrode of the Fleetweld type, and then immersed for 230
hours in a 20% solution of sulphuric acid. Note the condition of the weld metal in the center of each specimen and
compare this with the weld metal to be shown on the next
slide. Note also that the plate is practically eaten away
while the weld is largely intact.

SLIDE No. 7

This slide also shows the effect of corrosion. The weld
at the top was made with a bare or lightly coated type of
electrode, the weld at the bottom being made with the heavily

141

coated type such as Fleetweld, utilizing the shielded arc. The specimen was then subjected to a 72-hour immersion in 50% solution of hydrochloric acid. Note that the welds made with the bare or lightly coated type of electrode are badly eaten, while the welds made with the shielded arc type of electrode are practically intact. It can be seen also that the parent plate is beginning to be attacked.

This is a typical specimen of bend test across the shielded arc weld. Elongation of the outside fibres of the weld metal was 43%. Note that no cracks appear at the top of this weld or any sign of failure.

This lide shows the injury of a two-story warehouse in Florida after one of their little blows. The operators on top there are cutting apart the steel. Not one weld failed or was broken in the entire installation.

This member is made up of two channels of plate at the top and bottom and was deformed by dropping a weight five feet, ten feet, fifteen feet, until the deformation shown resulted. Notice that while the weld metal and the steel is bent and deformed considerably, there is no fracture in either.

This illustrates the ingenious application of welding. This type frame work supports a bucket in the center of the frame work and it also serves as an air receiver, thus saving the weight of the additional tank.

A pressure vessel operating at 250 pounds fabricated by the Shielded Arc process.

Illustrating the gear fabricated by welding, mill housing; charging machine; support for mill housing; several views of the gears, mill housings, supports, bases, etc., which all illustrate the use of steel in the fabrication of these parts. I asked the General Master Mechanic doing this work, why he did not weld up some of these parts after they were broken and his reply was that there was no sense in that at all because when he made them out of steel he knew that they would last.

This illustrates the application of a cutting edge to an ordinary piece of steel. This cutting edge can be ground and then used as a tool in the regular way; the Rockwell hardness running up to 62 to 64 degrees. Several illustrations of the application of this process of applying cutting edges to machine tools were given. Lathes, boring mills, shapers and cutters of various types and sizes were illustrated.

One of the most important characteristics of welding is the superior physical results obtained. It is necessary in some cases to be able to inspect a weld. The following simple method, under the subject of "Weld Inspection" will be found helpful.

There are a number of methods of inspection of welding. Of those various methods the simplest of course, is that of visual inspection.

It takes a man of experience and good observation to arrive at any conclusions which are satisfactory, when visual inspection is made. However, there is one characteristic of visual inspection of welds which is true of a welded joint and of no other type joint, and that is, that you see the inside of the joint when you are making it.

Another scheme of inspection which is used, perhaps the next method, is that of the stethoscope. The method is the same as used by a doctor when examining your lungs. By tapping gently along the welded seam with a light hammer and listening with the stethoscope, a change in the sound shows when a fault is reached. It is, of course, necessary that the operator be trained in the use of a stethoscope so that he can get this difference in the change of sound and therefore know when the defect has been located, but due to the fact that it showed up this way, it would seem that the method was satisfactory. The equipment is simple and rather inexpensive.

The next method is the magnetic method. If a flux is passed through the weld and the metal adjacent thereto, if the metal is a pattern on some iron filings or powder sifted on a piece of paper. If, however, there is a fault, this pattern will be very materially changed and therefore, the fault may be located.

Another scheme along the same line is to have the welded joint subjected to flux and have a meter indicating a deflection caused by this flux. If there is any variation in the flux, the deflection of the meter varies. This has been used especially in connection with pipe inspection.

X-ray, of course, is perhaps the best known. This is essentially a shadow process. The cracks, holes and porosity being indicated on the negative which is placed on one side of the weld and mechanism on the other. It has, of course, certain limitations as to the thickness of the material. It is used and required in the Class 1 of the A. S. M. E. Boiler Code.

Another method somewhat similar to the X-ray inspection is that of the gamma ray. The gamma ray is a radium emanation and has the properties that it penetrates the thicker work more rapidly than does the X-ray and it is therefore used in cases where the X-ray would take a very long exposure.

None of the above, with the exception of visual inspection, can be so very easily or cheaply done.

We hear the statement made that "You don't know what is inside of a weld. The only way you can tell is to break it and then if you break it you have got to do it all over again." But they forget that you can see the inside of this joint while it is being made and that it is the only type of joint which can be seen on the inside.

Then there is the question of human element, personal element, and all that sort of thing. Is there any operation any fabrication process which does not involve a personal element? With the ability to see and know what you are doing, there is absolutely no excuse for poor welds. There may be reasons for it such as poor steel, wrong kind of electrode, wrong technique, or something of that sort, but there is no excuse or alibi which should go. If it is properly done, under proper supervision, the welds must come out right.

Now it's really a very simple matter to learn how to judge the characteristics of a weld. We will assume of course, that the set-up is correct, that is, correct polarity, correct current, arc length and speed, and that a good machine and good electrodes are being used. The problem under discussion concerns therefore, only the variables over which the operator has control—that is, the "human element."

How then can you tell about these variables? There are four things which should be watched. These are:
1. The burn-off of the electrode.
2. The fusion and penetration.
3. The piling up of the bead on the work or the forming of the bead on the work.
4. The sound of the arc.

Those four tell-tale signs indicate to the operator just what the trouble is or if they are as they should be, that the weld is sound. In regard to penetration and fusion, a word of explanation may be necessary. Fusion is the melt-

144

ing and joining of the metal. Penetration is the depth to which the parent metal is melted or penetrated by the operation of the arc. Proper penetration means that the parent metal is melted to a degree sufficient to result in all of the weld metal deposited being clean and of good quality but it is not any greater than is absolutely necessary to get good fusion. There are cases, of course, where penetration is imperative, say in a case of a butt joint where the edges are not scarfed, a rod which penetrates deeply is very helpful. On the other hand, in the case of a scarf joint the minimum penetration, is necessary. In both cases good fusion, that is, a good joint must be obtained.

Ordinarily, with proper penetration you get good fusion.

The experiments which are outlined below should be done in your own shop, by you, or at least carefully witnessed by yourself. Merely reading these notes will not be sufficient.

The method of investigation is to vary only one factor at a time—and then study the effect of the variation of that one factor.

SHIELDED ARC ELECTRODES

CURRENT VARIATIONS

With a normal current, the arc sound has a sputtering hiss with somewhat irregular cracking. The fusion is well defined and deep, the coating burns deeply and there is no overlap. Now if the current is reduced too low the arc sound has a very irregular sputtering and slight cracking, the fusion is shallow and the bead is on top of the plate. An increase of current to a value which is too high results in irregular explosive sounds and the fusion is deep and long, the coating is consumed irregularly and a broad thin bead with good fusion is obtained.

ARC VOLTAGE VARIATIONS

Supposing now that we reduce the voltage to too low a value, we will get a hiss or steady sputter. The fusion is fair, the coating touches the molten metal, does not have an opportunity to be transformed into gas and therefore, porus beads result. The bead is on the plate and rather broad. On the other hand if we increase the voltage to too high a value, we will get a soft hiss with few crackles. The fusion is wide and deep, the electrode has drops on the end, which splutter about and finally drop into the crater. The bead is wide and there is considerable splatter.

SPEED VARIATIONS

Assuming now that we consider the speed variations. The sound, of course, is normal, but with the speed low there is a fair crater, the electrode performance is normal but the bead is wide and considerably overlapped and the base metal and the bead are heated over a considerable area. Note that this corresponds to the heating of the electrode part way up when you have low speed on the bare electrode. If the speed is increased too high then we have normal arc sound, rather small crater, the performance of the electrode is normal but the bead itself is small and undercut. This bead size and undercut vary with the speed and the current. It is to be noted that in the case of the shielded arc that only in one case, that is, where the voltage is too low is the quality of the weld metal particularly undesirable. In all other cases the deposit of weld metal, that is the actual metal deposited, is a satisfactory quality, however, the joint is not particularly good in those cases where you might have undercutting or overlap but the weld metal itself is good.

There is, therefore, indicated a method whereby a weld may be inspected while it is being made and assurance given that the quality of the joint is of character desired. It is obvious that these methods of test and inspection outlined above require proper supervision and procedure control.

There is one item which should be considered very carefully and that is, the method of inspection to be specified.

A prospective purchaser discussing the fabrication of certain machines comes to the question of inspection. He is told that there is Class 1 and Class 2 and so on and immediately says "I want the best there is, and that is Class 1." Now it is obviously a waste of money and time to insist on Class 1 inspection in all cases. The method of inspection and supervision must be in accordance with the requirements of the design. Do not misunderstand this statement. X-ray inspection is a wonderful scheme of inspecting welds. It is very necessary in a good many cases, but in a good many cases it is not necessary. The cost to the customer is unduly increased merely because he insists on having what he thinks is the best there is, and calls for Class 1. There must be a co-ordination of the requirements of the design and the specification for inspection such that it will produce a piece of equipment which will have an adequate service life at a cost which will be acceptable to the customer.

I gave you these illustrations purposely from installations other than railroads to illustrate the fact that you can take your general conditions, whatever they may be, apply proper welding, electrodes and procedure to your problem, resulting in a reduction in cost because it is not always necessary to use a high quality of metal throughout. We do not have any good term for that. Some call it hard surfacing. You have two general characteristics of these deposited surfaces. One is hard as deposited. It may run from a relatively fair hardness up to as high as 62C64C Rockweld. The other is soft relatively when deposited and becomes hard as it is worked.

You have those two general characteristics of surfacing, and the characteristics of the loads against this surfacing. Is it a high friction load? Is it abrasive, or is it impact, or is it a combination of them? You have in the case of your usual tye of electrode the usual strengths, 65,000 to 70,000 pounds, and a high tensile, 85,000 and on up. And we are going far up. We have some welds over 100,000 pounds, as far as ultimate tensile is concerned. You have as applied, to these particular materials various kinds of loads. We do not find straight tension failure. I have not found any good examples of pure tension failure. They are generally reported as due to lack of ductility but are really due to high fatigue. We have tension and compression and shear in those types of loads and any combination of those. When we know what those combinations are and how they occur in our mechanism then we can apply our welding procedure to meet those load conditions regardless of what they are in the most satisfactory way to give the ultimate service life, and that will be measured in dollars and cents. The result will be that we will get the greatest service life for the lowest number of dollars. I thank you.

CHAIRMAN: Mr. Smith says he is through. My dear Sir, you are far from that, for one of the principal features of these meetings of the Railway Club of Pittsburgh, is the opportunity of asking questions, and you, Mr. Speaker, will be subject to a whole lot of interrogating.

There are many men in this audience tonight interested in the science of welding which the speaker stated has been revolutionized in the last thirteen years. Am sure a genial gentleman like Mr. Smith will be gracious enough to lend from his scientific knowledge and broad experience, assistance to any member who has, to him, what seems a complex problem. So, fire your queries and don't be backward.

CHAIRMAN: During this pause I might mention that Mr. Forsberg has some moving pictures of the happenings to the Pittsburgh & Lake Erie Railroad that were taken during the period of the high water here last March. These will be shown, at the close of the discussion of Mr. Smith's paper. Particularly interesting are they, presenting among other things the paradox of large coal barges on the tracks of a railroad. Now, are there any more questions for Mr. Smith on welding? Do not be afraid to ask them.

MR. A. STUCKI: I would like to ask Mr. Smith one question. He spoke of facing tools on their cutting surfaces. Have you ever faced punches in that way?

MR. SMITH: Yes. It is not as simple in every case as you suggest. But you can surface cutting edges with this material and then grind it. If it becomes necessary to put on multiple beads there is some heat treatment advisable for the reason that the material as deposited is subject to a certain heat action because of welding and this heat is not always uniform. We make it uniform by heat treating. That is not a serious heat treatment, however.

MR. C. O. DAMBACH: About thirteen years ago we had a welding man here and he spoke of a skyscraper that was welded. What has been done in the last thirteen years in that line? Have you seen any skyscrapers welded since then?

MR. SMITH: Some 300 buildings in the country are welded. There is in Dallas a fourteen story building. In San Francisco a welded building that stood up in the last shake. It was designed for earthquake. The first put up by other than the welding industry was put up in 1927 or 1928. Another is the Electro-Motive Corporation shop. It is well worth while seeing. There is this difficulty in construction work that, much as we like to think of these things as being easy, that the personnel is not always readily available for such welding. It is a matter of education. We do not have them for welding in as great numbers as we do for riveting. If you are considering a structure welded or riveted do not take the bids as indicative of comparative costs. Due to the lack of trained personnel to a great extent it is still largely a matter of developing personnel.

MR. PAUL PURCHARD: You mentioned the izod as a unit of measurement. Will you kindly define that term?

MR. SMITH: There are several schemes—one is a special test piece about .4 inches square and it has a slot milled in it. A weight that swings on a pendulum from a predetermined height hits that piece and bends it over. By means of instruments we can get a record of the foot-pounds used to bend the sample over. This is resistance to impact which is measured. In welding material this is from 45 to 70 footpounds (izod). There is no particular comparison with tensile strength.

IMPACT TEST

The impact test is designed to be a measure of the ability of a metal to withstand suddenly or rapidly applied stress such as shock or hammer blows, etc.

This test is of course a comparative one, that is, the actual results mean nothing in the field. Test specimens are very carefully made and field jobs would be very different. However, it does serve as a comparison of materials.

There are two general methods of making such a test. One is known as Izod, the other as the Charpy. Both utilize the principle of a falling pendulum striking a test specimen, specially prepared and breaking it. The amount of energy required to break the specimen being a measure of its resistance to shock. This is given in both Izod and Charpy in foot pounds.

However, the test specimens in the two methods are different and the method of holding the specimen and striking the blow are different so that the results are not comparable and results of one system cannot be translated into the other.

We will describe briefly the Izod system. A specimen of pure weld metal is prepared as follows:

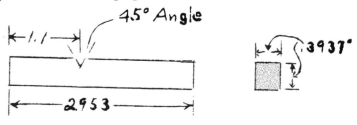

This specimen is then set up in a vise-like arrangement and a weight allowed to swing against the specimen—this pendulum or swinging weight breaks the specimen at the notch and swings on a bit.

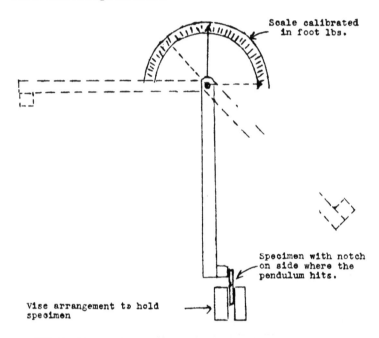

Scale calibrated in foot lbs.

Specimen with notch on side where the pendulum hits.

Vise arrangement to hold specimen

When the pendulum falls and hits the specimen it has a certain amount of energy in it, breaking the specimen absorbs some of the energy and retards the swing. How much it is retarded indicates the amount of energy it has taken to break the specimen. For convenience a pointer is attached to the top which indicates the values, on a calibrated scale.

Specimens made of bare or lightly coated electrode have an Izod value of from about 10 to 15 foot pounds. Specimens made from Fleetweld have a value of from 50 to 80 foot pounds.

Charpy values for bare or lightly coated are generally about 4 to 8 ft. lbs. and Fleetweld about 30 tc 50.

Again we say that this test is only a comparative test on various materials and this test should be used with others on other physical qualities to indicate the real value of an electrode.

MR. H. E. CHILCOAT: We do a lot of welding of light structures. One of the difficulties we have is in welding the structure out of shape. You do not get that in the rivets. The only way we can feel safe to overcome that is to hold the shapes in a jig. What is the answer to that? Just to hold it in shape?

MR. SMITH: That is the answer. Part would be in the sequence of welding. I give you two general rules. Always weld toward the open edge of a plate, and never cross another weld. You can not always keep these rules but follow them if you possibly can. But you are faced with the fact that in the plate you are using you do not know anything about how it was heated or cooled. You do not want that distortion and one way is to hold it in a jig. Another way is to put on a protection to keep the heat confined to a relatively small space. For instance think what is the relative co-efficient of expansion and contraction of grey iron as compared with steel? How is stainless steel compared with steel, or as compared with aluminum or anything else. Cast iron and steel.

MR. CHILCOAT: A normalizing process is necessary to get a good structure?

MR. SMITH: Not always. We have a railroad job— the design of some trucks for high speed trains and the furnace was not big enough to take the whole structure. I suggested to them that inasmuch as they did not know anything about the stresses involved, anneal the parts separately, then weld and forget about it. They did and it worked. There was a piece of equipment with a capacity of around 700,000 pounds that was welded. And it did not fail.

MR. CHILCOAT: Is there much of that done in actual practice, much normalizing done in ordinary light structures?

MR. SMITH: Not in ordinary light structures, no. You forget about the heat that went into the plate or shapes at the mill and the cooling. If the stresses were serious in all cases we would be in trouble. But what happens is this: The highly stressed part takes a permanent set. It moves along the horizontal part of the elastic curve, which horizontal part is much greater than the vertical part, so the other parts have time to adjust themselves to this changed condition. If done at air temperature it is mechanical stress welding.

If part is heated the same thing occurs but at lower stresses due to change in steel.

CHAIRMAN: Now that we have gotten into scientific fields, we will turn to a gentleman who is eminently qualified to speak in that language, Dr. Unger.

DR. JOHN S. UNGER: Mr. Chairman and gentlemen: It seems your Chairman has elected me to describe the Izod impact machine. I will do that in the atmosphere that is being stressed today in the political situation, to illustrate which I will tell two stories. Two men were busy working on a church and had been working quite some weeks. One day one said to the other, "Pat, this is a mighty fine Catholic church we are building. It will be a credit to the Pope." You are wrong. It is an Episcopal church." "What! An Episcopal church? What is an Episcopalian?" "He is a good Catholic that voted the Republican ticket."

For the other political story, it seems that a murder had been committed and the murderer had been tried and convicted and sentenced to be hung at one o'clock at night. The warden called him about fifteen minutes before the time and he was not able to proceed with the execution until the exact time set. So he said to the man, "You have fifteen minutes more time. Is there anything you would like to say?" No, he did not think he had anything to say. At that, one of the official witnesses said, "Gentlemen, as the chief performer hasn't anything to say, I would like to speak to you about the political situation in our ward." So he went on to speak about five minutes and the man that was going to be hung turned to the warden and said: "Warden, if it doesn't make any difference to you, I would like to go ahead with the hanging."

CHAIRMAN: After the clear and explicit definition of the Izod, it is problematic as to any indebtedness for that scientific discourse. May I say, however, as a Catholic, I am strongly of the opinion that the Republican of whom Dr. Unger spoke, will have to go to Purgatory for a long time to expiate that sin?

PROF. LOUIS E. ENDSLEY: Mr. President and Gentlemen: I think all of us have enjoyed very much this discussion of electric welding. I have attempted to keep up with what has been done, for the railroads more especially, and there has been a lot of electric welding around the railroads as you know. The very first remarks of the speaker, that the railroads by this electric welding would get a better job and save 3,000 lbs in weight. If that can be done it is a mighty fine thing. We would all like to have the benefit of that 3,000 lbs. lighter non-paying load.

We have all enjoyed this meeting tonight and the splendid illustrations along with the talk of what can be done with welding if done correctly and under correct supervision. I would therefore move that this meeting show to the speaker our appreciation by a rising vote of thanks.

The motion was duly seconded and unanimously adopted.

CHAIRMAN: And now, through the courtesy of Mr. Forsberg, there will be shown the flood pictures and the effect of the high water on the P. & L. E. Railroad.

J. D. CONWAY, Secretary.

In Memoriam

WILLIAM C. SEISS,
Joined Club March 23, 1917
Died March 6, 1936

JOSEPH S. MERK,
Joined Club January 23, 1936
Died April 6, 1936

This is the last meeting until September 24th.

* * * * *

We might remark you are given a breathing spell.

* * * * *

No doubt you have in mind some plans outlined to put in the time.

* * * * *

There will at least be variation and much of it, for—

* * * * *

"Now is the time for all good men to come to the aid of their country", and

* * * * *

We will get the Pro and Con how we must do it—"mostly Con."

* * * * *

All this aside—Here's extending to each of you the wish that you have full enjoyment during the Summer Months.

THE SECRETARY.

Try the perfect partners

PENNZIP

GASOLINE

PENNZOIL

MOTOR OIL

if you want to save money

•

THE PENNZOIL COMPANY

Chamber of Commerce Building, Pittsburgh, Pa.

OFFICIAL PROCEEDINGS
RAILWAY CLUB OF PITTSBURGH

$1.00 Per Year   25¢ Per Copy

Vol. XXXV.   MAY 28, 1936.   No. 7.

AIR BRAKE DEVELOPMENTS FOR RAILROAD REQUIREMENTS OF THE PRESENT DAY

By J. C. McCUNE, Assistant Director of Engineering,
Westinghouse Air Brake Company, Wilmerding, Pa.

The proof of your interest

in the Club can be

enhanced

by securing a

NEW MEMBER.

Application form is available

in this magazine. Look

it up and

"ACT NOW."

OFFICIAL PROCEEDINGS

OF

The Railway Club of Pittsburgh

Organized October 18, 1901

Published monthly, except June, July and August, by the Railway Club of
Pittsburgh, J. D. Conway, Secretary, 515 Grandview Ave., Pittsburgh, Pa..

Entered as Second Class Matter February 6, 1915, at the Postoffice at Pittsburgh,
under the Act of March 3, 1879.

Vol. XXXV No. 7	**Pittsburgh, Pa., May 28, 1936**	$1.00 Per Year 25c Per Copy

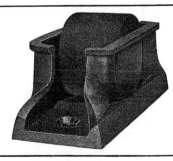
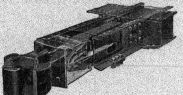

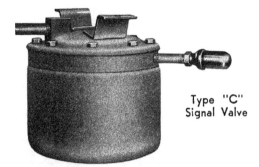

INDEX—ADVERTISERS.

NOTE—This form to be filled out in full by typewriter or printed and mailed to J. D. Conway, Secretary, 1941 Oliver Building, Pittsburgh, Pa. Membership fee, including dues, is $3.00 for each fiscal year or part thereof, except those proposed in September or October. Those proposed in these months will be credited upon payment for the following fiscal year. Dues are payable in advance.

The fiscal year ends with the month of October.

The Railway Club of Pittsburgh:

_____19____

Gentlemen:

Will you kindly consider my Application for Membership in your Club at the next meeting:

Name_____

Title_____ .._____

Company_____

My Address_____

_____

Recommended by_____

OFFICIAL PROCEEDINGS

OF

The Railway Club of Pittsburgh

Organized October 18, 1901

Vol. XXXV No. 7	Pittsburgh, Pa., May 28, 1936	$1.00 Per Year 25c Per Copy

ENTERTAINMENT COMMITTEE:

J. PORTER GILLESPIE, Chairman, Asst. Gen. Supt., Lockhart Iron & Steel Co., Pgh., Pa.
FRANK E. WEIS, Vice Chairman, Transportation Clerk, Penna. R. R., Pittsburgh, Pa.
E. H. HOLMES, Sales Department, Fort Pitt Malleable Iron Co., Pittsburgh, Pa.
C. C. CLARK, Sales Manager Central District, Pressed Steel Car Co., McKees Rocks, Pa.
A. L. KESSLER, Clearance Clerk, Pennsylvania Railroad, Pittsburgh, Pa.
T. F. SHERIDAN, Asst. to S.M.P. and S.R.S., P. & L. E. R. R. Co., McKees Rocks, Pa.
JAMES NAGEL, Superintendent Transportation, Montour Railroad, Coraopolis, Pa.

FINANCE COMMITTEE:

J. L. O'TOOLE, Chairman, Asst. to Gen. Manager, P. & L. E. R. R. Co,. Pittsburgh, Pa.
G. W. HONSBERGER, Transpn. Mgr., Westinghouse Electric & Mfg. Co,. Pittsburgh, Pa.
F. J. RYAN, District Representative, Detroit, Toledo & Ironton Railroad, Pittsburgh, Pa.
C. E. CATT, Division Accountant, B. & O. R. R. Co., Pittsburgh, Pa.
J. W. BOYD, Superintendent, Monongahela Railway Company, Brownsville, Pa.

MEMBERSHIP COMMITTEE:

T. E. BRITT, Chairman, Division Storekeeper, B. & O. R. R. Co., Pittsburgh, Pa.
A. B. SEVERN, General Manager, A. Stucki Company, Pittsburgh, Pa.
W. P. BUFFINGTON, Traffic Manager, Pittsburgh Coal Company, Pittsburgh, Pa.
R. S. BULL, Supt. Power & Inclines, Pittsburgh Railways Co., N. S., Pittsburgh, Pa.
A. F. COULTER, Master Car Builder, Union Railroad Co., East Pittsburgh, Pa.
T. R. DICKINSON, Purchasing Agent, B. & L. E. R. R. Co., Pittsburgh, Pa.
D. K. ORR, Road Master, Monongahela Railway Co., Brownsville, Pa.
C. M. WHEELER, Sales Engineer, Union Switch & Signal Company, Swissvale, Pa.
W. F. AMBROSE, Master Mechanic, Aliquippa & Southern Railroad, Aliquippa, Pa.
JOHN I. MULVEY, Traffic Manager, Hubbard & Company, Pittsburgh, Pa.
THOMAS R. FITZPATRICK, Freight Traffic Mgr., P. & L. E. R. R. Co., Pittsburgh, Pa.
P. W. HEPBURN, Sales Engineer, Gulf Refining Company, Pittsburgh, Pa.
W. B. MOIR, Chief Car Inspector, Pennsylvania Railroad, Pittsburgh, Pa.
C. W. TRUST, Assistant Traffic Manager, Carnegie-Illinois Steel Corp., Pittsburgh, Pa.

PAST PRESIDENTS:

*J. H. McCONNELL...October, 1901, to October, 1903
*L. H. TURNER...November, 1903, to October, 1905
*F. H. STARK...November, 1905, to October, 1907
*H. W. WATTS..November, 1907, to April, 1908
*D. J. REDDING..November, 1908, to October, 1910
*F. R. McFEATTERS..November, 1910, to October, 1912
*A. G. MITCHELL...November, 1912, to October, 1914
*F. M. McNULTY...November, 1914, to October, 1916
*J. G. CODE...November, 1916, to October, 1917
*D. M. HOWE...November, 1917, to October, 1918
*J. A. SPIELMAN..November, 1918, to October, 1919
H. H. MAXFIELD..November, 1919, to October, 1920
FRANK J. LANAHAN...November, 1920, to October, 1921
SAMUEL LYNN ....November, 1921, to October, 1922
D. F. CRAWFORD..November, 1922, to October, 1923
GEO. D. OGDEN..November, 1923, to October, 1924
A. STUCKI ....November, 1924, to October, 1925
F. G. MINNICK...November, 1925, to October, 1926
G. W. WILDIN..November, 1926, to October, 1927
E. J. DEVANS...November, 1927, to October, 1928
W. S. McABEE..November, 1928, to October, 1929
E. W. SMITH..November, 1929, to October, 1930
LOUIS E. ENDSLEY..November, 1930, to October, 1931
*JOHN E. HUGHES..November, 1931, to October, 1932
F. I. SNYDER...November, 1932, to October, 1933
C. O. DAMBACH..November, 1933, to October, 1934
R. H. FLINN..November, 1934, to October, 1935

*—Deceased.

Meetings held fourth Thursday of each month except June, July and August

PROCEEDINGS OF MEETING
MAY 28th, 1936

The meeting was called to order at the Fort Pitt Hotel at 8 o'clock, P. M., with President R. P. Forsberg in the chair.

Registered attendance 230, as follows:

MEMBERS

Adams, F. W.
Aivalotis, John
Allen, Earl M.
Allison, John
Ambrose, W. F.
Baker, W. E.
Balzer, C. E.
Barth, E. H.
Baumann, E. G.
Beam, E. J.
Beltz, J. D.
Berghane, A. L.
Bergman, C. R.
Best, D. A.
Bishop, M. L.
Bradley, J. P.
Brandt, George F.
Britt, T. E.
Brown, E. F.
Buchanan, C. C.
Buck, L. L.
Buffington, W. P.
Burnett, C. E.
Campbell, F. R.
Carr, T. W.
Chilcoat, H. E.
Connelly, J. T.
Conway, J. D.
Coombe, A. B.
Cotter, G. L.
Courtney, Harry
Cowen, H. E.
Crenner, Joseph A.
Cunningham, R. I.
Davis, Charles S.
Dean, E. E.
Dean, Robert W.
Dean, W. A.
Dempsey, A.
Dickinson, B. F.
Diven, J. B.

Dunham, C. W.
Durnell, W. E.
Endsley, Louis E., Prof.
Emery, E.
Evans, Charles S.
Fair, J. M.
Ferguson, George
Ferguson, R. G.
Flinn, R. H.
Forsberg, R. P.
Fralic, C. F.
Frauenheim, A. M.
Furch, George J.
Gilbert, William J.
Gilg, Henry F.
Gillespie, J. Porter
Glaser, C. J.
Glaser, J. P.
Goda, P. H.
Goldstrom, G. E.
Greek, Joseph
Griest, E. E.
Grieve, Robert E.
Gross, John
Groves, W. C.
Grunden, B. C.
Haller, Nelson M.
Hamsher, W. Edgar
Hansen, William C.
Harper, G. C.
Hassler, E. S.
Heed, H. L.
Heinzenberger, Arthur E.
Hemma, C. H.
Henderson, George L.
Hepburn, P. W.
Hilstrom, A. V.
Holmes, E. H.
Hood, A. N.
Hoones, R. E.
Hopper, George

Huber, H. G.
Huff, A. B.
Hutchinson, G. C., Jr.
Irwin, R. D.
Johnson, J. R.
Kearfott, W. E.
Keck, L. M.
Kemmerer, R. R.
Kennedy, G. N.
Kentlein, John
Kusick, Harry F.
Lanahan, Frank J.
Lanahan, J. S.
Larson, W. E..
Leet, C. S.
Logan, J. W., Jr.
Long, R. M.
Longdon, Clyde V.
Longstreth, W. L.
Mahaney, A. R.
Masterman, T. W.
Maxwell, Thomas
Metzgar, C. L.
Misner, George W.
Mitchell, F. K.
Mitchell, W. S.
Morgan, A. L.
Muir, R. Y.
Murray, S.
Murray, T. A.
Musgrove, W. W.
McCrossin, C. D.
McCully, D. L.
McFetridge, W. S.
McHugh, C. A.
McLaughlin, H. B.
McPherson, A. R.
McQuiston, C. A.
Nagel, James
Nash, R. L.
Nathan, W. S.
Nichols, Samuel A.
Nies, E. L.
Orchard, Charles
O'Sullivan, John J.
Overholt, B. C.
Paisley, F. R.
Perreas, S. J.
Peters, R. F.
Plunkett. James, Jr.
Porter, H. N.

Posteraro, S. F.
Prichard, Hugh R.
Purchard, Paul
Ralston, J. A.
Redding, P. E.
Renshaw, W. B.
Reymer, Charles H.
Roberts, E. L.
Rushneck, G. L.
Rutter, H. E.
Ryan, Frank J.
Schako, E. J.
Schmitt, Andrew
Searles, E. J.
Severn, A. B.
Shellenbarger, H. M.
Sheridan, T. F.
Showalter, Joseph
Sixsmith, G. M.
Smith, A. H.
Smith, Folger M.
Smith, G. M.
Steiner, P. E.
Stevens, R. R.
Stevenson, W. M.
Stewart, C. D.
Stucki, A.
Swope, B. M.
Sudell, D. W.
Sutherland, Lloyd
Thomas, Theodore
Thornton, A. W.
Tipton, G. M.
Tomasic, N. M., Jr.
Tracey, J. B. A.
Trax, L. R.
Tucker, John L.
Uhar, John J.
Van Vranken, S. E.
Van Woert, F. E.
Van Wormer, George M.
Von Pein. A. N.
Wallace, H. A.
Ward, N. H.
Weniger, Oscar S.
West, Troy
Wheeler, C. M.
Wilson, J. R.
Wright, John B.
Yarnall, Jesse
Young, J., Jr.

Yohe, J. K., Jr.

VISITORS

Bach, William F.
Balla, J. A.
Balobok, J. M.
Barnhart, C. H.
Bayer, Francis C.
Breneman, Richard R.
Brown, Homer
Brown, R. J.
Carrow, T. H.
Chapman, W. K.
Clausen, Harold C.
Davis, W. B.
Diven, I. C.
Failor, Charles W.
Fowler, W. E., Jr.
Hammond, Albert
Hastings, W. S.
Henricks, E. H.
Hoerath, J. J.
Horaz, Austin L.
Jack, George R.
Joseph, David B.

Lewis, S. B.
Long, Ray W.
Longstreth, Wendell L.
Mullin, A. C.
McConnel, F. B.
McKenna, J. B.
McKenna, J. T.
McTighe, M. L.
Neff, Paul F.
Pavian, H. C.
Redman, H. W.
Robinson, H. J.
Scheuerle, Andrew
Scheuerle, Lojas
Scheuerle, Rudolph
Scheuerle, Walter
Smith, George M.
Smith, Sion B.
Terkelsen, Bernhard
Wallace, O. T.
Westinghouse, George T.
Williamson, G. B.

Young, James L.

The meeting was preceded by a community sing, led by Mr. Frank E. Weis, with Mrs. Weis at the piano.

PRESIDENT: It was a matter of deep regret to me that I was unable to attend the last meeting of our Club. When I assumed the office of President I made a mental resolve that nothing but sickness or death would prevent my making a perfect attendance record during my term of office but "The best laid plans of mice and men gang aft a-gley." A business engagement in New York, the date of which I was unable to change, prevented my attending our meeting. I, therefore, requested Mr. Frank Lanahan to be responsible for the conduct of that meeting and it is my advice that he personally conducted the exercises in his usual inimitable manner.

The first order of business is the calling of the roll, but as each one of you signed the registry card as you entered the room, we may dispense with the roll call.

The next order is the reading of the minutes of the last meeting. These minutes will appear in print in the next issue of the Proceedings, which you will receive in the next few days, and with your permission we will dispense with the reading of the minutes.

The next order is the reception of proposals for membership. The Secretary will read the list.

SECRETARY: The delay in the Proceedings was from causes entirely beyond the control of the Secretary, which I deeply regret.

We have the following proposals for membership:

Baker, Dale, Car Foreman, B. & O. R. R. Co., 443 Boyd Street, Pitcairn, Pa. Recommended by T. E. Britt.

Boyland, William E., Train Master, B. & O. R. R. Co., 109 Green Street, Connellsville, Pa. Recommended by T. E. Britt.

Burchell, R. W., Wreckmaster, B. & O. R. R. Co., 232 Glencaldah Street, Hazelwood, Pittsburgh, Pa. Recommended by T. E. Britt.

Burnett, C. E., Engineer, Anchor Sanitary Company, 213 Water Street, Pittsburgh, Pa. Recommended by T. E. Britt.

Capps, W. P., Stoker Supervisor, B. & O. R. R. Co., Care Mechanical Engineer, Mt. Clare Shops, Baltimore, Md. Recommended by T. E. Britt.

Dean, Robert W., Asst. Car Foreman, B. & O. R. R. Co., 4124 Stanley Street, Pittsburgh, Pa. Recommended by T. E. Britt.

Douglass, William H., Locomotive Engineer, P. & L. E. R. R. Co., 309 East Fifth Avenue, Homestead, Pa. Recomemnded by W. T. Karnes.

Downing, N. H., Engine House Foreman, B. & O. R. R. Co., 1617 Monongahela Avenue, Swissvale, Pa. Recommended by T. E. Britt.

Eberle, E. J., Air Brake Foreman, B. & O. R. R. Co., 3014 Vernon Avenue, Brentwood, Pittsburgh (10), Pa. Recommended by T. E. Britt.

Gainer, Alva, Supply Car Storekeeper, B. & O. R. R. Co., 5151 Blair Street, Hazelwood, Pittsburgh, Pa. Recommended by T. E. Britt.

Heinzenberger, Arthur E., Assistant Car Foreman, B. & O. R. R. Co., 315 Shaw Avenue, McKeesport, Pa. Recommended by T. E. Britt.

Kearfoot, W. E., Assistant Engineer Maintenance of Way, B. & O. R. R. Co., 231 Martin Avenue, Mt. Lebanon, Pittsburgh, Pa. Recommended by T. E. Britt.

Kerr, Alexander D., Apprentice Engineer, Pennsylvania Railroad, Middletown, Ohio. Recommended by J. M. Fair.

Perreas, S. J., Carman, B. & O. R. R. Co., 2224 Starkamp Street, Brookline, Pittsburgh, Pa. Recommended by T. E. Britt.

Peters, R. F., Car Foreman, B. & O. R. R. Co., 7339 Race Street, Pittsburgh, Pa. Recommended by T. E. Britt.

Plunkett, James, Jr., Car Foreman, B. & O. R. R. Co., 4714 Monongahela Street, Pittsburgh, Pa. Recommended by T. E. Britt.

Sherrard, H. M., District Motive Power Inspector, B. & O. R. R. Co., Care Master Mechanic Office, Newark, Ohio.

Terwilliger, Walter, Clerk, P. & L. E. R. R. Co., 418 Broadway Street, Glassport, Pa. Recommended by W. T. Karnes.

Watson, W. R., Locomotive Engineer, P. & L. E. R. R. Co., 408 Monongahela Avenue, McKeesport, Pa. Recommended by W. T. Karnes.

Williams, I. R., Agent, B. & O. R. R. Co., 5488 Howe Street, East End, Pittsburgh, Pa. Recommended by G. M. Tipton.

PRESIDENT: In accordance with our custom I will ask those who are present on the list that has been read to stand and give us your names, that we may recognize you and give you an appropriate welcome. (Several stood and gave their names).

We welcome you into the fellowship of our Club and hope you will find your association with us both pleasant and profitable.

Are there any communications, Mr. Secretary? If not,

I believe it would be perfectly proper and right for me to announce that we learned with deep grief this afternoon of the death of Mr. Earl Stimson, Chief Engineer Maintenance of the Baltimore and Ohio Railroad. He was one of the outstanding railroad engineers of this country and I think it eminently fitting that we should make note of his passing at this time, though he was not associated immediately with this Club.

We now come to the paper of the evening. The speaker is a representative of the largest air brake manufacturing company in the world. And speaking of the Westinghouse Air Brake Company as the largest air brake manufacturing company in the world brings to my mind the fact that Pittsburgh has a number of other largest manufacturing industries in the world, and I have taken time to compile a list of them, and to get that information on the record and before you I am going to read it.

Pittsburgh possesses the *World's Only* manufacturer of forged steel sheets.

The *World's Largest* food products company of its kind.

The *World's Largest* operating unit in the steel industry.

The *World's Largest* manufacturers of steel rolls.

The *World's Largest* manufacturers of aluminum.

The *World's Largest* manufacturers of air brakes.

The *World's Largest* manufacturers of plate glass.

The *World's Largest* by-product coke plant.

The *World's Largest* manufacturers of refractories.

The *World's Largest* manufacturers of plumbing fixtures.

The *World's Largest* manufacturers of rolling mill machinery.

The *World's Second Largest* independent steel company.

The *World's Second Largest* electrical equipment company.

America's Largest manufacturer of bolts, nuts and rivets.

America's Largest independent oil company.

America's Largest commercial coal producer.

America's Largest wrought iron pipe company.

America's Largest stainless steel company.

If you feel as I do you are proud of living in a city that leads the world in so many of the largest manufacturing and industrial establishments.

I intend during the summer, if I have time, to compile some information relative to the contribution our steam rail-

roads make to the Pittsburgh District, and I hope to have
something of that kind to give to you at the September or
October meeting.

The gentleman who is to talk to us this evening is, as
you know, from the Westinghouse Air Brake Company. As
I came into the room this evening I found that we had in
the audience the grandson of George Westinghouse, George
Westinghouse III. I asked him if he would say a word to
us, but he said he would prefer not to do that, so I am going
to ask Mr. Westinghouse to kindly rise and let us give him
a good round of applause.

(Mr. Westinghouse responded in a few fitting words).

PRESIDENT: We are to have the pleasure of hearing
a paper presented by Mr. J. C. McCune, Assistant Director
of Engineering, Westinghouse Air Brake Company, Wilmerding, Pa., entitled "Air Brake Developments for Railroad Requirements of the Present Day." I take pleasure in presenting to you Mr. McCune.

AIR BRAKE DEVELOPMENTS FOR RAILROAD
REQUIREMENTS OF THE PRESENT DAY

By J. C. McCUNE, Assistant Director of Engineering,
Westinghouse Air Brake Company, Wilmerding, Pa.

In order that air brake development may result in practical devices, of utility and value to railroads, railroad conditions and requirements must be closely studied. Such studies
disclose trends in railroad operation which suggest improvements in old devices or the need for completely new devices.
When brake development is thus indicated, it should be
carried on as expeditiously as possible in order that improved
devices may be available as soon as the railroads actually
require them. When improved railroad practices, as at present, are being rapidly effected, continued air brake development is inevitable.

It is a matter of great concern to the national welfare
that railroad operation be continuously made more efficient,
which, in turn, will require further air brake development.
Obviously, efficient conduct of railroad operations is demanded
to meet the new competition arising on water, land and air.
But the most efficient operation possible is required, not only
because of the new competition, but also because of the

tremendously important place the American railroad system occupies in our domestic economy. Full economic recovery cannot be obtained by the American people until the American railroad system achieves a fair measure of financial prosperity.

Since the railroad system is so important to our national economy, it is imperative that its efficiency be continuously improved, insofar as this is possible. Improvements can be conceived in the imagination which, at the time, may be practically unattainable. If conditions as they have previously existed are continuously changed for the better, improvement, in the practical sense, exists. Improvements in one industry may be measured against improvement in another industry to ascertain if progress, at a reasonable rate, is being made.

By common consent, the automobile industry is regarded by the American people as alert, efficient, progressive and capable. Perhaps the improvements, associated in the public mind as synonymous with the automotive industry, may be grouped under six heads: (1) increase in power; (2) increase in speed; (3) increase in comfort or capacity; (4) increase in economy of operation; (5) improved appearance; and (6) reduced cost. It is of interest to examine what the railroads have done in these respects.

Since the railroads are an old industry, great improvement may be deduced by taking a time interval extending far enough back into the past. Many comparisons have lately been based upon 1926 as a normal year. Consequently, comparisons will be made between 1926 and 1934, the most recent year for which complete statistics are available. It should be noted that the depression years make up a very considerable portion of this interval.

Considering an increase in power, it is found that the tractive effort of the average steam locomotive has increased from 41,886 lbs. to 47,712 lbs. or 13.9%. An increase in average power of almost 14% in eight years is thought to be a most creditable accomplishment, especially when attention is given to the fact that a large number of very old locomotives remain in service.

The increase in average speed has been noteworthy. Between terminals, the average freight train speed in 1926 was 11.9 M.P.H.; in 1934, 15.9 M.P.H., an increase of 33.6%. The full significance of this statement is, probably, not immediately comprehended. It means that, on the average, every freight train operated in the United States in the year 1934 reached its destination in three-fourths of the time required for the same trip in 1926. In 1926, American railroads were admired throughout the world for their efficiency. To improve a performance, generally recognized as excellent, to the degree indicated is certainly an achievement of high order.

The increase in capacity of freight cars, having in mind the limitations in new car purchasing caused by the depression, is also a reason for commendation. The average capacity in 1926 was 45.1 tons; in 1934, 48.0 tons, an increase of 6.4%.

Operating economies accomplished in this same period were also outstanding. In 1926, one hundred thirty-seven (137) pounds of coal would move one ton of freight one thousand miles, along with locomotive, tender and cars; in 1934, one hundred twenty-two (122) pounds would give the same performance, an increase in fuel economy of 10.9%.

The appearance of passenger cars has been improved, not only in respect to their exterior appearance as with streamlined cars, but with more conventional equipment, in connection with seats, upholstery, finish, etc. Air conditioning has added greatly to the comfort of passenger travel.

The automotive industry has been widely acclaimed because of its policy of continuously reducing the price of its product. Thus the wholesale price of the average automobile in 1926 was $695 (Automotive Industries February 22, 1936); in 1934, $530, a reduction in price of 23.8%. The railroads have been extensively criticized because of their alleged failure to reduce prices and they have been compared, most unfavorably, with the automotive industry. To repeat a familiar cry, "Let us look at the record." According to the I.C.C., the average charge in 1926 for transporting one passenger one mile was 2.936 cents; in 1934, 1.918 cents, a reduction of 34.7%. Again, the charge in 1926 for moving one ton of freight one mile was 1.081 cents; in 1934, .978 cents, a reduction of 9.5%. Charges in 1936 will make a still more favorable comparison with 1926. It must also be remembered that, on the whole, passenger and freight charges have been declining for the past one hundred years.

To permit the above mentioned reductions in charges, it was necessary for the railroads to cut operating costs, for the system as a whole. Because of the decline in passenger

161

traffic, the cost of carrying one passenger one mile increased from 3.402 cents to 3.733 cents or 9.7%. On the other hand, the cost of transporting one ton of freight one mile decreased from .778 cents to .658 cents or 15.4%. That railroad managements were able to effect such reductions in the cost of transporting freight must not only be a source of gratification to them, but should also be a source of gratification to every citizen for a completely bankrupt railroad system would entail unpredictable consequences.

From all of the foregoing, it is apparent that the prosperity of the railroad industry is of vital concern to the country; that the efficiency of railroad operations has been substantially improved in recent years; that railroad managements throughout the country are pursuing alert, aggressive and forward looking policies; that as a result, further marked improvement in railroad operation is to be expected; and that air brake development must envisage such improvements.

IMPORTANCE OF THE AIR BRAKE

The air brake is now so much a matter of course to this generation that even a railroad audience is inclined to minimize its importance. Perhaps the importance of the air brake is demonstrated most forcibly by the career of its inventor, George Westinghouse. At 21, Mr. Westinghouse was a young veteran of the Civil War, newly married, seeking to establish himself; at 23, he was famous among American railroad men; at 26, he was introducing his brake in England; at 30, he was world famous and had already equipped 38% of all American passenger locomotives and cars with his brake; in middle age, he had a great American business with branch plants in England, France, Germany, Italy, Russia and Australia. Truly, the world-wide and immediate acceptance of his invention measured its importance. It is confidently believed that recent developments to meet changed railroad conditions have even increased the importance of the air brake as a factor in railroading.

THE "AB" BRAKE

The "AB" brake for freight service is now well known. Its importance in efficient operation of modern freight trains is so great, however, that some comments appear called for.

The remarkable accomplishment of the steam railroads in reducing, from 1926 to 1934, by 15.4% the cost of moving one ton of freight one mile has already been cited. It is of the utmost importance that this reduction in cost be continued because, apart from a revival of traffic, the prosperity of the railroad system depends upon it. Toward this end, the "AB" brake can make important contributions.

The outstanding feature of the "AB" brake is that by its use, and solely because of its use, the continuing operation of long trains is made possible. Many railroad systems have improved bridges, tunnels, roadway, terminal facilities and have purchased high power locomotives, all to permit moving a greater tonnage train at a higher speed. In 1926, the operation of a freight train for one hour produced 20,692 gross ton miles of freight transportation; in 1934, 28,041, an increase of 35.5%. The cost of operating a freight train for one hour, presumably, did not greatly change between 1926 and 1934. Increasing the output 35.5% obviously meant a great reduction in cost of train operation per gross ton-mile. Such savings must not only be retained but must be further increased if the railroad system is to prosper, and one essential to this end is that freight cars be equipped with "AB" brakes.

At the same time that the railroads have increased the length and tonnage of freight trains operating at a relatively high speed, they have developed "overnight" freight service between many important cities. This kind of service involves relatively short freight trains running at what have, heretofore, been considered passenger speeds. The "AB" brake is also of great value in this sort of operation, for reasons which will appear later.

The marked tendency in present railroad operation, both passenger and freight, is to increase the schedule speed, which obviously means a still greater increase in the maximum speed. It seems a reasonable assumption that this increase in speed will increase the need for and the use of the air brake in freight service. Previously, the air brake was not applied for long periods on many freight trains. But when the speed has been increased, it would appear more necessary than in the past to apply the air brake to reduce the speed at grade crossings, special work, bad order track, curves, restrictive signal indications, etc. This increased use of the air brake will bring out more markedly two important improvements effected in the "AB" brake.

The first of these improvements relates to the functioning of the brake. When a train is equipped with "AB" brakes, the engineman can approach closer at speed to the low speed zone before he makes a brake application, because "AB" brakes will apply more rapidly, uniformly and positively than "K" brakes; he can regain speed in less time because the "AB" brakes will release more rapidly, uniformly and positively than "K" brakes. He can approach a caution zone more confidently because he is aware that he can make an emergency application, at any time, to compensate for an error in judgment. The enumeration of these items does not bring out their importance. These functions assist in getting a train over the road, which is the very essence of successful railroading.

Not only does the "AB" brake assist in train movement because of its rapid, positive and uniform action, but also because it eliminates severe running of the slack, heretofore such a baffling problem in the handling of long freight trains. Doing away with violent slack action not only reduces possible equipment damage, but also indirectly speeds up train movement. For with "K" equipment, many slow-downs are accomplished by drifting, because of the fear of causing damage. With "AB" brakes, on the other hand, slow-downs can be brought about by application of the air brakes, since no undesired consequences are to be anticipated, and since, with "AB" brakes, running releases are possible, an extremely important operating advantage. The result is that the train can make better time over the road.

The second improvement refers to the much greater reliability of the "AB" brake as compared with the "K" brake. Greater use of the air brake in freight service will emphasize this reliability. When an engineman makes a service application, he wishes his brakes to apply positively and reliably but not in emergency; when he releases, he desires all brakes to release and not to "drag" or "stick". With the "AB" brake, the engineman can expect, with assurance, that the result he desires will follow his manipulation of the brake valve. This reliability of the "AB" brake is important from another viewpoint. Not many years ago, it was possible to operate freight trains with 15% of the brakes inoperative. Now 100% of the brakes must be functioning. Consequently, if a brake becomes defective en route, there may be not only direct switching charges but also the much greater cost of delaying the movement of an entire train. In this respect, the reliable performance of the "AB" brake over long periods of time, must be of great value to the railroads.

EMPTY AND LOAD BRAKES

Another development affecting freight service is that of empty and load brakes, which automatically adjust themselves to empty or to load position. Brief consideration will disclose that empty and load brakes for freight service are becoming increasingly necessary, especially in view of modern freight car development.

The standard "AB" brake or the old "K" brake are known as "single capacity" brakes. This means that the brake develops the same brake shoe pressure, whether the car is empty or loaded. Since the retarding force is produced by the shoe pressure, the retarding force remains constant irrespective of the load. Obviously, the effect of this retarding force is less, the greater the load. The gross weight of the car is frequently four times the tare weight. The rate of retardation produced on the empty car is, consequently, four times that produced on the fully loaded car. There seems no reason to question that, in such a situation, there is either too much empty brake or too little load brake. An empty and load brake—a double capacity brake—clears the situation.

Perhaps a concrete example will be of interest. It can be readily calculated that when the coefficient of friction is 15% and the brake rigging efficiency 80%, a braking ratio of 16.7% is needed to just balance the acceleration due to gravity on a 2% grade. In order to obtain 16.7% braking ratio on a loaded car, the gross to tare ratio must not exceed 3.59, if the braking ratio on the empty car is 60%. Under the conditions assumed, the brake on a car with a gross to tare ratio of 3.6 is insufficient to overcome the acceleration due to gravity on a 2% grade, with 50 lbs. pressure developed in the brake cylinder. Obviously, such a car could not be controlled, apart from being stopped. Brake cylinder pressures in excess of 50 lbs. must therefore be realized if the car is to descend the grade under control, unless other cars in the train with lower gross to tare ratio compensate for the inadequate brake on this car. This situation can be entirely overcome by the application of empty and load brakes for then the load braking ratio can be given an adequate value.

The gross to tare ratio of new freight cars has been increasing for many years and quite recently the increase has been marked because of the introduction of freight cars, manufactured from lighter materials than heretofore employed . The lower the gross to tare ratio, the more effective the brake on the loaded car. Manifestly, with an increase in the average gross to tare ratio, the control of loaded freight trains will be impaired unless empty and load brakes are employed. The average gross to tare ratio is increasing, not only because new cars have such a high ratio, but perhaps even more importantly, because many older cars with a much lower ratio are being rapidly retired. An increase in average speed and greater use of the air brake, as previously mentioned, along with an increase in average gross to tare ratio, implies that the use of empty and load brakes, in general freight service, merits serious consideration. As emphasized previously, the prime concern of the railroads is a reduction in operating costs and anything which contributes to the more expeditious movement of freight trains and therefore lessened cost is of interest.

Empty and load brakes were first introduced more than a quarter of a century ago. Their general application was handicapped by several limitations, among which may be mentioned a manual change-over and great weight, cost and complication.

With a manual change-over, a trainman was required to set the brake either in empty or in load position. It was evidently impossible to instruct all trainmen, who might come in contact with the car anywhere, when and how to make the necessary adjustment. There was thus no guarantee that the benefits of the empty and load brake would be realized in general service and there was even probability that the brake might be improperly adjusted. All this is overcome by the introduction of the automatic change-over. With this arrangement, whenever the air pressure is restored after it has been depleted (as by setting off the car on a loading track), a mechanism on the truck is caused to move an amount proportionate to the car load, as measured by the deflection of the truck springs. According to what this movement may be, the brake is set either for empty or for load. Before the air pressure is completely restored, the mechanism mentioned is cut out so that vibratory motions of the truck do not cause it to wear. This combination provides that the advantages of the empty and load brake will always be obtained, even though the car may leave its home line and be handled by employees who are totally unacquainted with empty and load brakes.

The original empty and load brakes were heavy, complicated and costly, largely because of a multiplicity of reservoirs. The adoption of a new principle of operation has radically reduced weight, complication and cost. Pressure is developed in a brake cylinder because a quantity of compressed air from the auxiliary reservoir is admitted to it. The pressure developed, for a given quantity of air, is proportional to the cylinder volume; that is, the larger the volume, the less the pressure.

With the new empty and load brake, as most recently applied, the volume of the empty cylinder is reduced, because it is an 8″ cylinder instead of a 10″. The reduction in volume of the empty cylinder is compensated for by connecting to it, in empty position, an additional volume. The two volumes together equal the volume of a standard 10″ cylinder, so that in empty position, the brake operates as does any single capacity brake.

When the brake is set for load position, the additional volume is disconnected from the empty cylinder and in its place is substituted a load cylinder. The load cylinder is supplied with a clutch, which permits full travel of the push rod but reduces the travel of the piston itself. Hence its volume is less than that of the conventional cylinder. The volume of the empty and the load cylinder together equal that of a standard 10″ cylinder. Consequently, the proper pressure is developed in both empty and in load cylinders for a given brake pipe reduction.

Three important advantages are secured on account of this principle of operation. First, a single standard auxiliary reservoir can be used (except on the very heaviest cars). This reduces weight, complication and cost. Second, the air consumption of the new empty and load brake is the same as that of a standard single capacity brake, something never before achieved and quite important. Third, a standard "AB" valve is employed as a triple valve. This last advantage is particularly noteworthy since it permits a car to move freely in interchange and yet, though an empty and load car, the operating valve is entirely familiar to all who have to do with it.

The new empty and load brake bears the same name as the original and yet has little resemblance to it, either in principle of operation or construction. It is obvious that consideration of the new brake should not be prejudiced by recollection of its predecessor's limitations.

NO. 8-ET EQUIPMENT

It has been mentioned that, between 1926 and 1934, the tractive effort of the average steam locomotive increased 14%. The increase was caused, of course, not only by the purchase of new locomotives but also by the retirement of old locomotives of low tractive effort. But the remarkable performance of which the modern locomotive is capable is widely known. It is a magnificent machine of which the locomotive builders and the railroads may be justly proud because of its sustained high speed, increased starting ability, higher horsepower output, improved economy, great availability for service, capability for long engine runs, and reliability when on the road.

It is somewhat ironical that, until recently, this great machine, representative of the best modern engineering, was furnished with brakes which were first introduced into service in 1906. It is a tribute to the original designing skill that these brakes were capable of a sufficiently efficient performance to permit their continued use over this period of years. But brakes for locomotives of much higher efficiency are now available.

This new locomotive brake equipment is designated the No. 8-ET and has important improvements for both freight and passenger service. Basically, the principle of operation is the same as that used so successfully these many years with the No. 6-ET Equipment. But changed conditions since the introduction of the No. 6 Equipment have necessitated the addition of several new features.

The operation of long freight trains has previously been discussed. Brake pipe leakage with these long trains detrimentally affects air brake operation. For brake pipe leakage causes the brake pipe pressure at the rear of these long trains to be less than that at the head end. Hence, when the supply of air to the brake pipe is cut off, as by lapping the brake valve, the higher pressure at the front endeavors to equalize with the lower pressure at the rear. The result, when a brake application is made, is that the brakes at the head end apply with excessive force as compared with those at the rear. This action is productive of considerable shock. It is overcome, in the No. 8-ET Equipment, by incorporating what is called a "first service position" in the brake valve. This position provides for admitting air, automatically, at the head end, as required, to prevent the head end pressure dropping too rapidly. By this means, smooth handling of long freight trains is assured.

The locomotive is an important factor in stopping long freight trains smoothly with an emergency application. For the weight of the locomotive is the equivalent of a considerable number of empty cars and this weight is concentrated at the very head end of the train. If the locomotive stops too suddenly, after an emergency application, it clearly forms a "bumping post" for the remainder of the train. This condition is overcome in the No. 8-ET Equipment by providing means for use with long trains which synchronizes the action of the locomotive brakes, in an emergency application, with the car brakes. In passenger service, this means is not needed because of the much more effective car brakes.

The locomotive is not only a very heavy unit, but also its internal resistance is very different from that of the cars, particularly passenger cars. Since brake applications are initiated at the locomotive, there has always been difficulty in obtaining smooth slack action. Various modifications, over a period of ten years or more, were made in the No. 6-ET Equipment in an attempt to secure improved operation, these modifications finally culminating in the "6-E" Distributing Valve. The 8-ET Equipment takes care of the requirements in a much more complete and positive manner by providing, through a special mechanism, that the locomotive brakes shall always develop braking forces in harmony with the car brakes.

The No. 8-ET Equipment is arranged to handle large volumes of air, needed by the braking requirements of the modern large locomotive. It has effective provision against brakes "creeping on," always a source of trouble with the No. 6-ET Equipment. It has protection against broken pipes to a much greater degree than was attained with the No. 6-ET Equipment. In addition to all these new features, the equipment is so constructed that it will operate reliably in service over long periods of time. The maintenance record now being made by the No. 8-ET Equipment is little short of remarkable in view of the dirt, water, and heat always associated with a locomotive. In every way, the No. 8-ET Equipment is worthy of a place on the modern locomotive.

"HSC" EQUIPMENT

Undoubtedly, the general public has been more impressed with the new high speed streamlined trains than with any other innovation lately made in the railroad field. The good will created by this very modern development has been of substantial value to the railroads.

These trains have inaugurated a new era in passenger train braking because operation on a new principle is being perfected, which, eventually, should result in much improved braking performance. It is well known that, for the same pressure, the friction of brake shoes is less at high speeds than at low speeds. Since the retarding force is produced by this friction, the rate of retardation at high speeds is less than at low speeds. For instance, a brake shoe pressure which produces a rate of retardation of 1 M.P.H. per second at high speed might produce a rate of retardation of 2 M.P.H. per second at very low speed.

It is essential that high speeds be reduced as quickly as possible, after an emergency brake application is initiated, if short stops are to result. Thus, at 100 M.P.H., a train travels 1,167 ft. in ten seconds. But 1,200 ft., for many years, has been taken as the objective in a stop from 60 M.P.H. Consequently, if the 100 M.P.H. stop is not to be several times as long as the 60 M.P.H. stop, it is vital that a high rate of retardation be set up as quickly as possible. Obviously, this requires that the brake shoe pressure at high speed be high to compensate for low friction and then be automatically reduced as the speed decreases, to prevent wheel sliding at the lower speeds.

It will be recalled that this was the function of the high speed reducing valve, introduced into service about 1894. The high speed reducing valve operated on a time basis, irrespective of the initial velocity. As cars became heavier and speeds higher, it was found that the device was not required because the friction of the brake shoes did not markedly increase because of the effect of heat upon them. But the modern brake shoe is much more heat resistant and, in addition, the shoe pressure, with the new trains at high speed, has been very much increased. Consequently, automatic protection against wheel sliding with these new light weight, high speed trains is not secured.

170

The device, which has been applied to these high speed trains, to permit the use of high retardation rates at high speeds and yet prevent wheel sliding at low speeds is known as the "Decelakron". It is an inertia device, set to operate when a certain rate of retardation is exceeded. Clearly, if the train is stopping too rapidly, the wheels may slide. The action of the "Decelakron" is to prevent the train stopping at a rate of retardation in excess of a predetermined value. If the retardation increases due to an increase in brake shoe friction, the "Decelakron" acts to reduce the brake shoe pressure.

The new high speed trains in operation to date, equipped with the "Decelakron", have been completely articulated and are not intended to train with conventional equipment. For this reason they have been fitted with what is basically electro-pneumatic straight air brake equipment, non-interchangeable with standard air brakes. Some of the streamlined high speed trains under construction are intended, at times, to operate on high speed schedules, when hauled by detachable locomotives. Their brake equipment must be suitable for operation with standard brakes. As a result, these trains are not now being equipped with a "Decelakron" but instead with a speed governor which adjusts the maximum braking ratio to the speed.

All of the foregoing has emphasized efforts to increase the rate of retardation obtainable at high speeds. It is obvious that the efficiency of high speed braking will be thereby improved. It is likewise clear that this is a very necessary condition for the continued successful operation of high speed trains.

CONCLUSION

In this paper an attempt has been made to demonstrate that the steam railroads are of vital consequence to this country; that forward looking railroad managements, the country over, are steadily bringing about improvement in railroad service; that air brake developments not only assist in this improvement but are necessitated by it; and that some particular air brake developments, discussed in general outline, show that research in air brakes is at least maintaining the effectiveness of the air brake in meeting the newer and greater demands placed upon it by continued railroad development.

PRESIDENT: Gentlemen, you have listened to a most able and a most interesting presentation of a paper that is of real importance to us and it brings up to date our information relative to the air brake. We are under a deep debt of gratitude to Mr. McCune for the service he has rendered. For the next twelve or fifteen minutes the meeting is in your hands. I will ask if you will not volunteer to ask Mr. McCune any questions or make any statements relative to the subject that you may wish. May we hear from you promptly.

MR. HENRY F. GILG: I was very much interested in the paper because at one time I worked for the Air Brake Company. I am very much pleased to know that we have George Westinghouse III here tonight. He favors his grandfather to some extent. I worked for the Air Brake Company in 1884.

I would like to ask Mr. McCune whether the K train can be handled successfully with the 8-ET brake.

MR. McCUNE: That is a very good question. I did not stress that as much as I should have done. The 8-ET equipment can be used very successfully with the K equipment. It will help the K equipment to do better work.

MR. HARRY COURTNEY: How about the AB train, is it necessary to have a train completely equipped with AB brakes?

MR. McCUNE: Very fortunately it is not necessary to have a train completely equipped with AB brakes, because if that were the case, it would be quite a few years before the benefits of the AB brake would be realized. The more AB equipment you have, the greater the gain realized.

MR. H. P. BENDER: On these new trains running at very high speed do you recall how these brakes work as compared with the heavier trains.

MR. McCUNE: Very fortunately the light weight of these super-speed trains is of help. In stopping a train the energy to be dissipated increases as the square of the speed. If the train is running 120 miles an hour as compared with 60, the weight being the same, the energy that must be dissipated is four times as great. The energy goes up as the square of the speed, but only directly as the weight. Cutting the weight in half, the kinetic energy to be dissipated is cut in half.

PROF. L. E. ENDSLEY: One of the points that the speaker brought out this evening is—the empty and load brake, the railroads must give serious consideration to this. He did not emphasize it but it is a fact that freight equipment is going to be built lighter, and the need for empty and load brake is going to be greater. And I am also very glad that the new empty and load brake is automatic in its change over from empty to load.

I am confident that we will have, in the very near future, freight cars that carry a load four times their weight and under this condition the 60% brake shoe pressure, when the car is empty, will only be 12% when the car is loaded. There is another thing which he mentioned but did not go into detail, which I would like to have him amplify on this empty and load brake, using the same amount of air as the present brake.

MR. McCUNE: I think probably you all realize how difficult it is to get full air pressure at the rear of a long train. Consequently the less air the equipment requires the easier it is to maintain a fairly uniform pressure throughout the train. The early form of empty and load brakes increased the air requirement quite considerably. This new form requires the same air as the present standard AB 10" equipment. Consequently, the matter of air supply with the new empty and load brakes remains unchanged from what it has been with standard 10" equipment.

MR. H. E. COWEN: AB valve in emergency position, then giving to full release. Would there be a possibility of the emergency parts sticking as sometimes happens with the K type of triple?

MR. McCUNE: The AB brake is provided with a special valve which insures that the brake will positively release. With the K equipment, the release differential may be three or four pounds, but with the AB valve, there is a small valve contained within the complete structure which prevents the release differential from exceeding about 1½ lbs., so that it assures a positive release.

MR. T. W. CARR: In connection with the empty and load brakes on freight cars, I would like to ask Mr. McCune this question: Are empty and load brakes an advantage in level road service?

MR. McCUNE: I am glad you asked that question. A great many people think of empty and load brakes only in connection with grade operation. The gross to tare ratio is constantly increasing; on the one hand because the gross to tare ratio is so high with new cars, and on the other hand, because so many of the old cars with low gross to tare ratio are being retired. The result is that the average gross to tare ratio on almost any freight train is higher than it was some years back and all the time the ratio is further increasing. The braking ratio is cut down by the gross to tare ratio. With a braking ratio of 60% and a gross to tare ratio of 4 to 1, the braking ratio on the loaded car is only 15%, which is not a very high braking ratio. It is evident that loaded trains in the future will be more difficult to control than they were in the past.

The maximum speed of the freight train is constantly increasing and, as I said before, this calls for greater use of the air brake, and yet with single capacity brakes, continuously they are becoming less effective. To meet modern conditions their effectiveness should be increased, and this is the purpose of the empty and load brake.

MR. H. E. CHILCOAT: At such high speeds co-efficient of friction between the shoe and the wheel must be very low. Has anything been done in connection with these high speed streamlined trains to improve this condition?

MR. McCUNE: The braking ratio for emergency stops on conventional trains is 150%. Some of these high speed trains will have a braking ratio of 300%. The brake shoe load on such a train will be three times the weight on the wheel.

As you increase the pressure, the co-efficient of friction decreases, so you have to increase the pressure further, not only to compensate for the increase in speed, but also for the increased shoe load.

MR. CHILCOAT: There is a limit to where you can go with that?

MR. McCUNE: That is so, there is.

MR. CHILCOAT: The loss in co-efficient of friction due to the generation of heat between the shoe and the wheel at high speeds at one time was a serious matter with the old heavy cars and resulted in the eventual application of the clasp type of brake which largely I believe solved the difficulty. However, with the still higher speeds of these streamlined trains and the correspondingly higher braking percentages, this question of generation of heat between the shoe and wheel might again become a serious matter unless something has been done to overcome or offset it.

MR. McCUNE: Since that time the brake shoe has been changed. The reinforced brake shoe will stand up under a condition where the old shoe would begin to disintegrate.

MR. E. EMERY: We have certainly had a very interesting and instructive paper. Mr. McCune has brought to us clearly and very forcibly what the Air Brake Company has been doing to stop the trains; however, it is the sincere wish of all present that trains could be kept moving more than they have of recent years.

Anticipate that the Air Brake Company has carried these developments on with the faith that the railroads will soon return to prosperous times.

The railroads with increased business, for reasons as outlined in the paper, will need better control of their trains, and the Air Brake Company has anticipated that need.

I would like to move, Mr. President, that the Club give Mr. McCune a rising vote of thanks for his comprehensive paper on this important subject.

The Motion was seconded and prevailed by unanimous vote.

PRESIDENT: Mr. Gillespie and Mr. Weis have arranged a real musical treat for us and I am going to turn the meeting over to them at this time.

The following program was then presented:

Scheuerle Brothers—Instrumental Quartet:
(from Pitcairn Shops, P. R. R.)

Walter Scheuerle—First Trumpet
Lojas Scheuerle—Second Trumpet
Rudolph Scheuerle—Trombone
Andrew Scheuerle—Xylophone

1—Little Girl of My Heart ....Quartet
2—I Love You Truly..Quartet

3—Old Black Joe.............Xylophone Solo—Andrew Scheuerle
    Repaz Band................Xylophone Solo—Andrew Scheuerle
4—Lost ....Quartet

The Railway Club Male Quartet:
        Ray Long—First Tenor
        Lafe Bishop—Second Tenor
        Gus Goldstrom—Baritone
        George Jack—Basso
1—The Stein Song
2—Annie Laurie
3—The Bumble Bee
4—Just A Dream of You.

PRESIDENT: I suspect some of us have paid the price of our Annual Dues to the Railway Club of Pittsburgh to listen to a performance no more enjoyable or creditable than the one we have just heard. We are deeply grateful to the Scheuerle Brothers Instrumental Quartet, The Railway Club of Pittsburgh Quartet, Mr. Porter Gillespie, Mr. Frank Weis, and last but by no means least to the talented accompanist, Mrs. Weis. I suggest that we show our appreciation by giving them a rousing round of applause.

When we adjourn it will be to meet again on September 24th, 1936. The Entertainment Committee, the Reception and Attendance Committee and the Subject Committee have all contributed so much to the success of our meetings that I cannot forebear a tribute to their splendid accomplishment. These three committees working as a whole will prepare a program for our September meeting, something in the nature of an open field day, to be held at one of the Country Clubs in the vicinity, and while public announcement will be made later, we will have golf and bridge and horseshoe pitching and sports of that kind and we are looking forward to a general good time. I wish for each one of you a most pleasant and profitable vacation. We will now adjourn to the tables and an hour of good-fellowship.

                    J. D. CONWAY, Secretary.

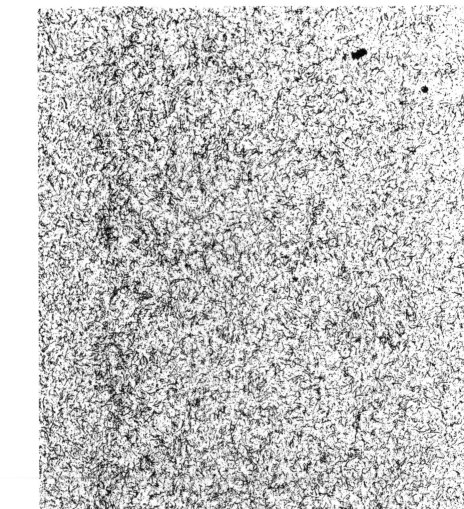

If

you want more miles
per Gallon.... get

PENNZIP GASOLINE
PENNZOIL MOTOR OIL

*Perfect Partners for
Smoother Mileage*

THE PENNZOIL COMPANY

Chamber of Commerce Building, Pittsburgh, Pa.

OFFICIAL PROCEEDINGS
RAILWAY CLUB OF PITTSBURGH

$1.00 Per Year   25¢ Per Copy

Vol. XXXV.	SEPTEMBER 24, 1936.	No. 8.

THE OIL INDUSTRY IN ITS RELATION TO THE RAILROADS
By R. J. S. PIGOTT, Staff Engineer, Gulf Research and Development
Corporation, Pittsburgh, Pa.

The proof of your interest

in the Club can be

enhanced

by securing a

NEW MEMBER.

Application form is available

in this magazine. Look

it up and

"ACT NOW."

OFFICIAL PROCEEDINGS

OF

The Railway Club of Pittsburgh

Organized October 18, 1901.

Published monthly, except June, July and August, by the Railway Club of
Pittsburgh, J. D. Conway, Secretary, 515 Grandview Ave., Pittsburgh, Pa..

Entered as Second Class Matter February 6, 1915, at the Postoffice at Pittsburgh,
under the Act of March 3, 1879.

| Vol. XXXV No. 8 | Pittsburgh, Pa., Sept. 24, 1936 | $1.00 Per Year 25c Per Copy |

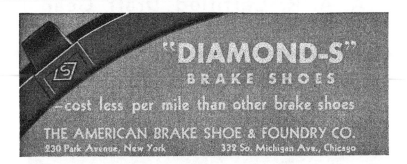

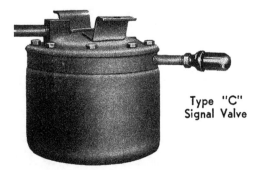

INDEX—ADVERTISERS.

NOTE—This form to be filled out in full by typewriter or printed and mailed to J. D. Conway, Secretary, 1941 Oliver Building, Pittsburgh, Pa. Membership fee, including dues, is $3.00 for each fiscal year or part thereof, except those proposed in September or October. Those proposed in these months will be credited upon payment for the following fiscal year. Dues are payable in advance.

The fiscal year ends with the month of October.

The Railway Club of Pittsburgh:

....19........

Gentlemen:

Will you kindly consider my Application for Membership in your Club at the next meeting:

Name..

Title..

Company..

My Address..

....

Recommended by..

OFFICIAL PROCEEDINGS

OF

The Railway Club of Pittsburgh

Organized October 18, 1901

Vol. XXXV No. 8	Pittsburgh, Pa., Sept. 24, 1936	$1.00 Per Year 25c Per Copy

ENTERTAINMENT COMMITTEE:

J. PORTER GILLESPIE, Chairman, Asst. Gen. Supt., Lockhart Iron & Steel Co., Pgh., Pa.
FRANK E. WEIS, Vice Chairman, Transportation Clerk, Penna. R. R., Pittsburgh, Pa.
E. H. HOLMES, Sales Department, Fort Pitt Malleable Iron Co., Pittsburgh, Pa.
C. C. CLARK, Sales Manager Central District, Pressed Steel Car Co., McKees Rocks, Pa.
A. L. KESSLER, Clearance Clerk, Pennsylvania Railroad, Pittsburgh, Pa.
T. F. SHERIDAN, Asst. to S.M.P. and S.R.S., P. & L. E. R. R. Co., McKees Rocks, Pa
JAMES NAGEL, Superintendent Transportation, Montour Railroad, Coraopolis, Pa.

FINANCE COMMITTEE:

J. L. O'TOOLE, Chairman, Asst. to Gen. Manager, P. & L. E. R. R. Co., Pittsburgh, Pa.
G. W. HONSBERGER, Transpn. Mgr., Westinghouse Electric & Mfg. Co., Pittsburgh, Pa.
F. J. RYAN, District Representative, Detroit, Toledo & Ironton Railroad, Pittsburgh, Pa.
C. E. CATT, Division Accountant, B. & O. R. R. Co., Pittsburgh, Pa.
J. W. BOYD, Superintendent, Monongahela Railway Company, Brownsville, Pa.

MEMBERSHIP COMMITTEE:

T. E. BRITT, Chairman, Division Storekeeper, B. & O. R. R. Co., Pittsburgh, Pa.
A. B. SEVERN, General Manager, A. Stucki Company, Pittsburgh, Pa.
W. P. BUFFINGTON, Traffic Manager, Pittsburgh Coal Company, Pittsburgh, Pa.
R. S. BULL, Supt. Power & Inclines, Pittsburgh Railways Co., N. S., Pittsburgh, Pa.
A. F. COULTER, Master Car Builder, Union Railroad Co., East Pittsburgh, Pa.
T. R. DICKINSON, Purchasing Agent, B. & L. E. R. R. Co., Pittsburgh, Pa.
D. K. ORR, Road Master, Monongahela Railway Co., Brownsville, Pa.
C. M. WHEELER, Sales Engineer, Union Switch & Signal Company, Swissvale, Pa.
W. F. AMBROSE, Master Mechanic, Aliquippa & Southern Railroad, Aliquippa, Pa.
JOHN I. MULVEY, Traffic Manager, Hubbard & Company, Pittsburgh, Pa.
THOMAS R. FITZPATRICK, Freight Traffic Mgr., P. & L. E. R. R. Co., Pittsburgh, Pa.
P. W. HEPBURN, Sales Engineer, Gulf Refining Company, Pittsburgh, Pa.
W. B. MOIR, Chief Car Inspector, Pennsylvania Railroad, Pittsburgh, Pa.
C. W. TRUST, Assistant Traffic Manager, Carnegie-Illinois Steel Corp., Pittsburgh, Pa.

PAST PRESIDENTS:

*J. H. McCONNELL	October, 1901, to October, 1903
*L. H. TURNER	November, 1903, to October, 1905
*F. H. STARK	November, 1905, to October, 1907
*H. W. WATTS	November, 1907, to April, 1908
*D. J. REDDING	November, 1908, to October, 1910
*F. R. McFEATTERS	November, 1910, to October, 1912
*A. G. MITCHELL	November, 1912, to October, 1914
*F. M. McNULTY	November, 1914, to October, 1916
*J. G. CODE	November, 1916, to October, 1917
*D. M. HOWE	November, 1917, to October, 1918
*J. A. SPIELMAN	November, 1918, to October, 1919
H. H. MAXFIELD	November, 1919, to October, 1920
FRANK J. LANAHAN	November, 1920, to October, 1921
*SAMUEL LYNN	November, 1921, to October, 1922
D. F. CRAWFORD	November, 1922, to October, 1923
GEO. D. OGDEN	November, 1923, to October, 1924
A. STUCKI	November, 1924, to October, 1925
F. G. MINNICK	November, 1925, to October, 1926
G. W. WILDIN	November, 1926, to October, 1927
E. J. DEVANS	November, 1927, to October, 1928
W. S. McABEE	November, 1928, to October, 1929
E. W. SMITH	November, 1929, to October, 1930
LOUIS E. ENDSLEY	November, 1930, to October, 1931
*JOHN E. HUGHES	November, 1931, to October, 1932
F. I. SNYDER	November, 1932, to October, 1933
C. O. DAMBACH	November, 1933, to October, 1934
R. H. FLINN	November, 1934, to October, 1935

*—Deceased.

Meetings held fourth Thursday of each month except June, July and August.

PROCEEDINGS OF MEETING
SEPTEMBER 24, 1936

The meeting was called to order at the Fort Pitt Hotel at 8:00 o'clock, with President R. P. Forsberg in the chair.

Registered attendance 195. The following gentlemen registered:

MEMBERS

Adams, F. W.
Adams, W. A.
Allen, Earl M.
Allison, John
Ambrose, W. F.
Aulbach, Albert J.
Barr, H. C.
Baker, W. E.
Balzer, C. E.
Baumann, E. G.
Beam, E. J.
Beeson, H. L.
Beitsch, George F.
Berg, Karl
Bergman, C. R.
Boyd, J. W.
Bradley, J. P.
Britt, T. E.
Bruce, S. S.
Burel, W. C.
Burnette, G. H.
Campbell, F. R.
Cannon, T. E.
Carey, C. D.
Carr, T. W.
Chalker, A. R.
Cipro, Thomas
Clausen, Harold C.
Conway, J. D.
Coombe, A. B.
Courtney, H.
Cowen, H. E.
Crawford, B. H.
Crede, W. A.
Cree, W. M.
Cushman, P. J.
Dalzell, W. E.
Dambach, C. O.
Davis, Charles S.
Dean, R. W.
Dickinson, B. F.

Diven, J. B.
Donovan, L. T.
Duffley, F. M.
Durnell, W. E.
Emery, E.
Fitz Simmons, E. S.
Flinn, R. H.
Fox, George W.
Frauenheim, A. M.
Frauenheim, Pierce H.
Freshwater, F. H.
Forsberg, R. P.
Fults, J. H.
Furch, George J.
Galbraith, James R.
Gardner, George R.
Gariepy, L. H.
George, W. J.
Geiser, W. P.
Gilg, Henry F.
Gillespie, J. Porter
Glaser, C. J.
Glaser, J. P.
Goldstrom, G. E.
Goodwin, A. E.
Griest, E. E.
Grieve, Robert E.
Groves, W. C.
Haller, Nelson M.
Hansen, William C.
Hassler, E. S.
Hemma, Charles H.
Hepburn, P. W.
Hilstrom, A. V.
Holland, S. E.
Holmes, E. H.
Hornefius, S. R.
Huston, F. T.
Keller, R. B.
Kentlein, John
Krause, Harry A.

Kroske, J. F.
Lanahan, Frank J.
Lanahan, J. S.
Lincoln, J. J., Jr.
Loder, C. C.
Logan, J. W., Jr.
Long, R. M.
Lowe, William T.
Maliphant, C. W.
Masters, William C.
Millar, C. W.
Mitchell, W. S.
Morgan, A. L.
Murray, Stewart
McIntyre, R. C.
Nichols, Samuel A.
Noonan, Daniel
Orbin, Joseph N.
Osborne, Raymond S.
Overholt, B. C.
Paisley, F. R.
Peirce, W. B.
Phillips, T. H.
Pohlman, A.
Pringle, Paul V.
Purchard, Paul
Redding, P. E.
Reymer, Charles H.
Rief, Joseph
Rudd, W. B.
Rushneck, G. L.
Rutter, H. E.
Ryan, D. W.
Schako, E. J.
Sekera, C. J.

Severn, A. B.
Shellenbarger, H. M.
Sheridan, T. F.
Sixsmith, G. M.
Smith, Folger M.
Smith, Robert B.
Steiner, P. E.
Sterling, C. C.
Stoecker, J. P.
Stoffregen, L. E.
Stucki, A.
Sudell, D. W.
Sutherland, L.
Taylor, H. D.
Taylor, Joseph M.
Terry, Edward
Thomas, George P.
Thomas, T.
Thornton, A. W.
Tipton, G. M.
Tomasic, N. M., Jr.
Tracey, J. B. A.
Troxell, H. K.
Unger, Dr. J. S.
Van Blarcom, W. C.
Van Horne, C. F.
Van Vranken, S. E.
Von Pein, A. N.
Wheeler, C. M.
White, H. A.
Winslow, G. W.
Woods, G. M.
Woodward, R.
Wynne, F. E.
Yohe, J. K., Jr.

VISITORS

Adams, W. C.
Balla, J. A.
Beckett, Russell
Bonner, Col. Joseph C.
Chalker, H. S.
Coleman, J. H., Jr.
Daly, C. F.
Davis, William B.
Dunkerly, E. R.
Edsall, S. D.
Fulton, K. H.
Gardner, George R., Jr.
Heer, Walter
Hepburn, W. B.

Hildebrand, L. B.
Holt, James
Jenkins, C. B.
Kamenske, Ernest
Knoell, Charles J.
Kothe, C. A.
Lewis, S. B.
Lovett, S. C.
Lowndes, T. H.
Marshall, L. L.
McIlroy, J.
Oldham, Ronald W.
Pigott, R. J. S.
Pigott, William S.

Provost, C. T.   Smith, E. R.
Provost, William J.   Smith, George M.
Rider, H. C.   Smith, Sion B.
Robinson, H. J.   Terkelsen, B.
Schenck, J. H.   TreDemcy, J. C.
Schott, O. E.   Williams, A. G.
Severn, John J.   Wimer, H. B.
                    Zell, Harry A.

Before opening the business meeting an enjoyable musical program was presented by four instrumental entertainers.

PRESIDENT: The first order of business is the roll call, but the system we have devised of requesting you to sign your names on the registration cards and depositing them at the door as you enter removes that necessity and we will accordingly dispense with it.

The minutes of the last meeting were printed in the last issue of the Official Proceedings which you received some months ago. We will, therefore, forego the reading of those minutes.

We now come to the announcement of applications for membership in our Club. We usually credit the fairer sex with being bargain hunters and enjoying a bargain sale above all other pastimes. I am hoping tonight that we have some of that spirit among the sterner sex and that the bargain sale of membership tickets in our Club, that obtains for the next two months, is going to be a real attraction. In other words, those who join our Club during the months of September and October, will not be annoyed by the collector until October 31, 1937. I hope that a hint to the wise will be sufficient. Mr. Secretary, will you kindly read the names of the applicants for membership that you have. The Secretary read the following list of proposals for membership:

Clausen, Harold C., Mechanical Engineer, Union Switch & Signal Company, Althea Road, R. D. No. 1, Wilkinsburg, Pittsburgh, Pa. Recommended by C. M. Wheeler.

Dixon, C. R., District Sales Manager, North American Refractories Company, Oliver Building, Pittsburgh, Pa. Recommended by T. E. Britt.

Failor, Charles H., General Engineer, Union Switch & Signal Company, 107 Elmore Road, Forest Hills, Pa. Recommended by C. M. Wheeler.

Fulton, K. H., Sales Manager, Ball Chemical Company, Fulton Building, Pittsburgh, Pa Recommended by T. E. Britt.

Gariepy, L. H., Gang Foreman, Pennsylvania Railroad, Freeport, Pa. Recommended by G. J. Furch.

Meagher, Maurice E., Railway Equipment Representative, Peter E Meagher, Roosevelt Hotel, Pittsburgh, Pa. Recommended by W. B. Moir.

Sayre, Herschel A , Principal Assistant Engineer, Union Railroad Company, 103 Summer Avenue, Forest Hills Borough, Wilkinsburg, Pa. Recommended by A. F. Coulter.

Scott, J. M., General Superintendent, B. & O R. R. Co., Pittsburgh, Pa. Recommended by T. E. Britt.

Sperry, C. E., Engineer, Detroit Lubricator Company, 40 West 40th Street, New York, N. Y. Recommended by Karl Berg.

Taylor, John T., District Manager, E. F. Houghton & Company, 215 Beverly Road, Mt. Lebanon, Pittsburgh, Pa. Recommended by T. E. Britt.

PRESIDENT: As is our custom, I will request any of the new members, whose names have just been read and who are present, to stand in order that we may welcome you into the fellowship of our Club. (Several of those proposed for membership stood).

We trust you will find your association with us as pleasant and as profitable as we expect to find it on our part.

At this point the Secretary, upon request of the President, read the following communication from the Traffic Club of Pittsburgh:

THE TRAFFIC CLUB
of Pittsburgh

Mr. R. P. Forsberg,
Railway Club of Pittsburgh,
c/o Pittsburgh & Lake Erie Railroad,
Pittsburgh, Pa.

Dear Sir:

For many years past, it has been the practice to hold the Annual Dinner of The Traffic Club of Pittsburgh on the first Thursday in March. However, at a recent meeting of the Club, it was decided to advance this date so that the 1937 Annual Dinner will be held on Friday, January 22nd.

I am writing you at this time with the thought in mind that, if entirely consistent and possible, any important meetings, hearings, etc., which may occur around that time, be set for such other dates as will not interfere with the above.

Very truly yours,
FRANK J. RYAN,
Secretary.

SECRETARY CONWAY: Since our last meeting we have received information of the death of the following members of our Club:

Frederick Kerby, "Retired", B. & O. R. R. Co., Cumberland, Md., died May 18, 1936.

Samuel Lynn, Superintendent Rolling Stock, P. & L. E. R. R. Co., died August 8, 1936.

John M. Mogan, Assistant General Yard Master, P. & L. E. R. R. Co., died September 23, 1936.

J. G. Platt, President and General Manager, Hunt-Spiller Manufacturing Corporation, Boston, Mass., died July 26, 1936.

J. C. Whitridge, President and General Manager, Buckeye Steel Castings Company, Columbus, O., died July 29, 1936.

PRESIDENT: A suitable memorial minute, honoring the memory of those who have passed on since our last meeting, will appear in the next issue of the Proceedings. I note the second name on the list just read is that of a Past President of our Club. Mr. Samuel Lynn, a man who held the real interests of our Club at heart at all times. I, therefore, feel that it is right and fit and proper that I should call upon some member of our Club at this time to say just a few words in honor of his memory. I see before me a man who enjoyed a life long association with him, both in our Club affairs and other activities, and I will ask him to kindly come to the platform and say a few words—Mr. Frank J. Lanahan.

MR. FRANK J. LANAHAN: Mr. President, a special honor do I deem it that the pleasure is mine of paying tribute to one who not alone was held in highest esteem by me, but as well, a feeling that is shared by every member of this organization. We do ourselves honor in honoring the memory of our dear departed friend, Mr. Sam Lynn. He was the fourteenth President of our Club, and that was fourteen years ago. Strangely enough he is the fourteenth President who has taken the Long Trail, two other chief executives serving since Mr. Lynn's term expired, have gone to the Great Beyond. There are only two who served previous to him who are with us tonight.

Mr. Lynn was a delightful companion. Of no man do I know who was held in higher esteem. Am sure none of you ever met in your contacts with men from day to day, anyone who exhibited that admirable virtue of humility to the extent that he did, and yet, that he was a leader in so many organizations attest the honor and respect in which he was held by his fellowmen. When the poet wrote these appropriate lines, I think he must have had in mind a man of his qualities:

"True worth is in being, not seeming
And in doing each day that goes by
Some little good, not in dreaming
Of the great things to do by and by."

His memory will be long revered, his services to this Club ever remembered, and I am sure we all feel a sorrow beyond expression in the passing of Mr. Lynn.

PRESIDENT: Thank you Mr. Lanahan.

PRESIDENT: We next come to the "Reports of Officers or Committees." If you are familiar with the provisions of our Constitution, you will recall that Section 2 of Article VI prescribes that the President will appoint a Nominating Committee, consisting of five members, three of whom must be regularly elected members of the Executive Committee, who shall at the September meeting recommend nominations for all offices to be filled at the annual meeting.

In accordance with that provision, I appointed such a Committee, consisting of Messrs. Frank J. Lanahan, F. I. Snyder, R. H. Flinn, J. W. Johnson and T. E. Britt. I will, at this time, request Mr. Lanahan, the Chairman of that Committee, to submit his report.

REPORT OF NOMINATING COMMITTEE

For President—E. A. Rauschart.

For First Vice President—G. M. Sixsmith.

For Second Vice President—J. D. Beltz.

For Secretary—J. D. Conway.

For Treasurer—E. J. Searles.

Executive Committee (Eleven to Nominate):
Frank J. Lanahan, A. Stucki, D. F. Crawford, G. W. Wildin, W. S. McAbee, E. W. Smith, Louis E. Endsley, F. I. Snyder, C. O. Dambach, R. H. Flinn, R. P. Forsberg.

Subject Committee (One to Nominate):
(3 Years) G. H. Burnette, Assistant Chief Engineer, P. & L. E. R. R., Pittsburgh, Pa.

Reception and Attendance Committee (Seven to Nominate):
(3 Years) J. W. Boyd, Superintendent, Monongahela Railway Company, Brownsville, Pa.

(3 Years) Thomas E. Cannon, General Superintendent, Pittsburgh & West Virginia Railroad, Pittsburgh, Pa.

(3 Years) T. W. Carr, Superintendent of Rolling Stock, P. & L. E. R. R., McKees Rocks, Pa.

(3 Years) D. C. Carroll, Assistant Agent, Pennsylvania Railroad, Pittsburgh, Pa.

(3 Years) S. G. Down, Vice President, Westinghouse Air Brake Company, Wilmerding, Pa.

(3 Years) Harry C. Graham, Pittsburgh Screw & Bolt Corporation, Pittsburgh, Pa.

(3 Years) J. W. Schad, Division Master Mechanic, B. & O. R. R., Glenwood, Pittsburgh, Pa.

(3 Years) George S. West, Superintendent of Pittsburgh Division, Pennsylvania Railroad, Pittsburgh, Pa.

Finance Committee (Two to Nominate):

(3 Years) J. B. Diven, Superintendent Motive Power, Pennsylvania Railroad, Pittsburgh, Pa.

(3 Years) M. A. Smith, General Manager, P. & L. E. R. R., Pittsburgh, Pa.

Membership Committee (Three to Nominate):

(3 Years) F. H. Eaton, Sales Engineer, American Car & Foundry Company, Pittsburgh, Pa.

(3 Years) C. W. Gottschalk, Assistant Traffic Manager, Jones & Laughlin Steel Corporation, Pittsburgh, Pa.

(3 Years) Lloyd Sutherland, General Storekeeper, P. & L. E. R. R., McKees Rocks, Pa.

NOMINATING COMMITTEE
Frank J. Lanahan, Chairman,
F. I. Snyder,
R. H. Flinn,
T. E. Britt,
J. W. Johnson.

PRESIDENT: You understand, I am sure, that a large number of members of our various Committees are elected for terms of more than one year, and the names just read by Mr. Lanahan are those who will fill the vacancies that occur on the various Committees this year by reason of the expiration of their term of office or other causes. You understand further that any member of the Club has the privilege of placing in nomination the name of any member for any office. Are there any other nominations? If not, the Chair will entertain a motion that the nominations close. On motion the nominations were closed.

PRESIDENT: Mr. Lanahan, may I thank you and each member of your Committee for the time and thought you have given to this work. The outcome speaks for itself.

May I say to you that the members of this Committee spent three hours in the preparation of this report. The committee has endeavored to maintain an equal balance in the official family of the Club among the various railroads in this district and the industries. Thus when a man goes off from one railroad we try to fill the vacancy with a man from the same railroad, and a man who goes off from an industry we endeavor to fill the vacancy with a man from that same industry. We have, therefore, endeavored to preserve the balance between the railroads and the industries as it has existed in the past. If there is no further business we will have the presentation of the paper of the evening. Anything that is of interest to the railroads is of interest to this Club, and there is in this country an industry that has a vital relation to the railroads, namely the oil industry, and I feel, therefore, we are fortunate in having with us tonight two gentlemen well qualified to present this all important subject. We are going to first show two reels of pictures taken in the oil fields and refineries. After that Mr. Charles D. Carey, one of our members and a representative of the Railroad Sales Department of the Gulf Oil Company, will give us some interesting figures on petroleum and define a few terms which may help you to better understand what the speaker of the evening has to say. When he has completed his talk, I will request Mr. Carey to introduce Mr. R. J. S. Pigott, Staff Engineer of the Gulf Research and Development Corporation, Pittsburgh, who will address us upon the subject—"THE OIL INDUSTRY AND ITS RELATION TO RAILROADS". Mr. Carey.

MR. CHARLES D. CAREY: Mr. President and fellow Members of the Railway Club of Pittsburgh and guests: First we are going to show you two reels of pictures which concern the oil industry and which we hope will give you a clearer picture of the workings of that industry. (Moving pictures shown).

As Mr. Forsberg said, I am going to attempt to give you some figures and some explanations that may help a little in interpreting what the speaker of the evening will say to you about lubricating oils and other things that will be of vital interest to the railroad men.

The first question that naturally comes to anybody is what is petroleum? It is a very complex combination of hydrocarbons. Just as sugar and wood, so petroleum oils are hydrocarbons and the principal job of the refiners is to separate and combine those hydrocarbons so that certain portions are suitable for lubricating oils and others for kerosene, gasoline, napthas, etc.

Now in order to use these hydrocarbons, which are the base elements in petroleum, there are certain impurities in the form of sulphur and nitrogen and oxygen, in amounts up to about 3%, that have to be removed. There are three general types of petroleum, classified in America as the paraffine base, the asphaltic base and the mixed base oil. The oils that we know best in this section of Pennsylvania are those oils which are taken from the ground throughout the Appalachian fields through New York, Pennsylvania and West Virginia. Other fields are called the Midcontinent petroleum fields, including parts of Texas, Oklahoma, Kansas, Arkansas and nothern Louisiana, and the Coastal fields, including southern Texas and southern Louisiana. The coastal field oils are an asphaltic base and the midcontinent field oils a mixture of paraffine and asphaltic base oils.

Now as to the production of petroleum in the United States. In 1935 there was taken from the ground in the United States 966,243,000 barrels of crude petroleum, substantially a billion barrels at 42 gallons to the barrel. Out of that total of a billion barrels, 427,127,000 barrels were motor fuel or approximately 44% of all the petroleum taken from the fields in the United States in a year was made into motor fuel; 55,813,000 barrels were kerosene, that is 5.8% of all the crude taken from the ground; 355,125,000 barrels was gas oil and fuel oil, or 36.7% of all the crude, and 27,-771,000 barrels were lubricating oil, about 2.9% of the total crude. That is a very small percentage. Not because we would not like to have more but that is all the lubricating oil we can get out of a billion barrels, less than 3%, and that is why lubricating oils are more expensive than gasoline.

The railroads of the United States used approximately 53,000,000 barrels of fuel oil and gasoline in a year. For that 53,000,000 barrels they paid approximately $34,000,000, which added to the $9,000,000 worth of lubricants which they bought in a year makes a total of railroad purchases in the United States of about $43,000,000. On the other hand the petroleum industry pays to the railroads of the United States in freight for hauling petroleum products $224,000,000 annually, so that for every dollar which the petroleum industry gives to the railroads the railroads give back to the petroleum industry somewhere between 19 cents and 20 cents.

Now I am going to explain some of the terms which Mr. Pigott will use when he talks to you. One of the terms you hear most frequently particularly in talking about lubricating oil is viscosity. Viscosity is expressed usually by the letters S.U.V. and a number following the letters. The S.U.V. is an abbreviation for Saybold Universal Viscosity, which means that if you take 3.66 cubic inches of oil and heat that oil to 100° Fahrenheit and allow that oil to run through an orifice which is about 1/16" in diameter and count the number of seconds it takes for that oil to go through that orifice, then you have the S.U.V. of that oil at that particular temperature. Heat it to 210°F. and it will run through very much faster and you call that the S.U.V. at 210°F. The S.U.V. number which you assign to the oil is the number of seconds it takes to run through the orifice.

There are very heavy oils, the kind you use in the differential of your automobile for instance, that are so heavy they would take too long to run through an orifice 1/16" in diameter, so we select another designation, Furol viscosity, which is the number of seconds it takes an oil at a given temperature to run through an ⅛" orifice. The same oil through the orifice twice as large in diameter will go through about ten times as fast. Furol and S.U.V. viscosities are about in the ratio of 10 to 1.

A few words about gravity. That is a word you often hear and you hear it expressed for instance as 34 or 36 gravity. The reason why we do not use the Baume Hydrometer which is ordinarily used in other gravity tests of liquids is that the Beaume instrument for measuring gravity is one instrument for liquids lighter than water, and another for liquids heavier than water. By changing the formula slightly we have the A.P.I. gravity measurement which means the American Petroleum Institute. They are almost the same. The formula for the Beaume gravity is 140 over the specific gravity at 60° minus 130. The A.P.I. formula is 141.5 over the specific gravity minus 131.5. One instrument serves the purpose for all petroleums.

Flash Test: If a given quantity of oil is heated slowly with fire until vapor starts to come off so that if you pass a match over the top of that oil you get little flashes over that oil, that is the flash point of the oil. The fire test of that oil is the temperature at which the distilled gases burn continuously.

What do we mean by S.A.E. numbers? You ask for 30. What you mean is 30 S.A.E. What does that mean? It means that the automobile engineers wanted to lay down some kind of limitation for the viscosity of the oil. It does not tell a thing about the oil except viscosity. It may be paraffine or asphalt, high flash or low flash, but this S.A.E. number only means viscosity. Oil may differ in viscosity from 30 to 70 seconds in the same S.A.E. number according to the standards of the different firms manufacturing the oil.

You no doubt will pardon me if I give you a few figures about Gulf. The things we live with and see every day become very commonplace and we lose that sense of appreciation and admiration that we have for things way off. Just a niblick shot from the place where we are holding this meeting the principal executive offices of one of the largest oil companies in the world are located. Gulf operates eight modern refineries which refine approximately 64,000,000 barrels of crude oil annually. The refineries are located at Port Arthur, Texas; Fort Worth, Texas; Sweetwater, Texas; Staten Island, New York; Philadelphia, Pennsylvania; Pittsburgh, Pennsylvania; Toledo, Ohio, and Cincinnati, Ohio. The combined capacity of these refineries is in excess of 200,000 barrels of oil per day.

Gulf operates 6,150 wells, producing annually about 64,-000,000 barrels of oil. It operates in most of the principal oil fields in Texas, Oklahoma, Kansas, Arkansas, Louisiana, and New Mexico, and also has interests in Kentucky, Michigan and California. In foreign fields Gulf has considerable production in Venezuela and Mexico.

Gulf owns and operates a fleet of six motor ships, thirty-five steamships, six ocean barges, four ocean going tugs, and a number of river, harbor and lake vessels. It operates 2,000 tank cars and 1,250 tank trucks. It markets 650 petroleum products in 29 states through 1,000 distributing plants and

35,000 retail outlets in the United States. Through its foreign subsidiaries Gulf markets in Central and Western Europe and in the Scandinavian Peninsula.

Gulf, by the way, paid in 1935 $53,080,344 in gasoline taxes which it collected from you and other motorists in its marketing territory. The railroads of the United States paid in the same time $240,000,000 in taxes.

Gulf employs about six hundred chemists and research engineers who conduct extensive research work to improve petroleum products and enlarge their uses, and now I want to introduce to you the Staff Engineer of the Gulf Research and Development Corporation, Mr. R. J. S. Pigott, the speaker of the evening.

The Oil Industry In Its Relation To The Railroads

By R. J. S. PIGOTT, Staff Engineer, Gulf Research and Development Corporation, Pittsburgh, Pa.

Conditions:

The conditions under which lubrication must be provided in railroad operation are, as a general rule, quite severe and difficult in fulfillment. Due to the limitations in weights and dimensions, loading of most bearings in railroad service is relatively high and the speed (by this I mean the rubbing speed of the bearing) varies from fairly high values down to zero. Shock is generally present and the temperature range is extreme, varying from temperatures as low as –40 deg. fahr. to 110 deg. fahr. ambient with actual temperatures in the journal running as high as 300 deg. In addition, most of these bearings fall in the class known as "imperfect film" lubrication, as distinguished from the "perfect film" or "flood" lubrication generally obtaining, for example, in the automobile; or the "plastic" lubrication such as occurs with greases. In addition to the foregoing difficulties, dirt and abrasives are usually present to more than the average degree and although design has protected the bearings to a limited extent, such a situation cannot be fully corrected.

Waste Packed Journals:

By far the largest number of bearings consists of waste packed journals. This type of bearing is a very old one and in some respects it is rather primitive. It would certainly be desirable to change to more improved types of journal. The great difficulty in this case is that of enormous cost to the railroad for changes due to the fact that this type of journal is used in immense numbers. The whole system is at present set up to handle the waste packed journal rather than something else. Even the advent of the roller bearing has not been able to displace the waste packed journal to any extent because, aside from high cost, the roller bearing, while having many advantages particularly those of low starting effort, is very much more sensitive in some respects to the extreme conditions occurring in railroad operation.

The main force which feeds oil up through the waste to the surface of the journal is surface tension of the oil, resulting in the phenomenon known as "capillarity". The viscosity of the oil tends to retard the flow. Surface tension of most liquids in commercial use does not vary very greatly and it is obvious then that, as any given oil is chilled by a reduction of temperature, the viscosity increases very rapidly. As a consequence, the rate of feed through the waste is greatly changed, being lowest in cold weather and highest in hot weather. In addition the presence of foreign liquids, such as moisture condensed in the box, may affect rate of feed by displacing oil from the fibers in the waste, particularly in the case of cottons. This again may alter the rate of feed of lubricant to the journal surface.

Other less important factors are the contact pressure of the waste against the journal, and its general springiness so that it can maintain the contact. Again, the character of the waste may alter the behavior of the journal bearing considerably. Waste grab, or the picking up of threads, varies with the quality and make-up of the waste and very often misbehavior of the waste is blamed upon oil. There seems to be a general tendency to conclude as a result of experimental investigation that more wool should be used in the mixtures. Since oil changes its viscosity roughly as about the cube of the Fahrenheit temperature, it can be seen that, just as in the automobile, it would be desirable to change the viscosity of the oil between summer and winter (at least it would be very desirable from the oil manufacturer's point of view) because otherwise the variation of viscosity is very great. However, from the railroad's point of view it is desirable if possible to use a single lubricant for winter and summer. I can hardly put it too strongly that the attempt to use a single oil for so large a range of temperature makes the problem of lubrication a very difficult one to solve satisfactorily for all conditions. The practice generally used at present of adding light oils for winter and heavier oils for summer is one that should be continued. If we could once get an oil that had a very small variation of viscosity with temperature, this problem would be solved very neatly, but there is no hope at present of developing any such oil. It would appear, from examination of such experimental work as has been carried on so far, that too much attention has been paid to imitating as nearly as possible, the actual operating conditions of a journal under test in actual practice. As a result the differences in behavior are hard to run down to a single cause, as there are too many variables occurring at once in such a test. We purpose to carry out experiments on rates of feed of oil at different viscosities through different kinds of waste, to test for the behavior of the waste in allowing threads to be picked up on the journal, to determine the effect of viscosity index on the general behavior of the oil in the waste whether beneficial or otherwise, and finally to temperature and pressure search the journal brasses to see just what is going on at the bearing surface. All of this represents an extensive program but it is felt that permanently satisfactory and reliable results in the choice and make-up of oils will not be attained until this has been done. Following this detailed work we would then purpose to go back to the overall tests imitating the actual operation. It is just possible that of the many proposals which have been made for modifying the waste packed journal with intent to improve lubrication, one might result in some final design that would be acceptable to the railroads and provide at the same time a very much better device for feeding oil.

Theories of Lubrication:

There are three classes of lubrication which are quite distinct from each other and which present an entirely different mathematical set-up for analysis. In the hydrodynamic lubrication, ordinarily called the "fluid" or "perfect film" region, it matters very little what the lubricant is so long as it is a liquid. In the fluid region lubrication, lubrication can be obtained with water, sugar and water, or in fact anything that has definite viscosity, does not corrode the bearing, and can be kept in the same condition over a period of time. Of course that usually means the only material which fulfills all of these requirements is oil. But in the hydrodynamic region the properties of the oil, aside from corrosion or breakdown due to time of service, only involve viscosity and density. The other factors involved in determining the carrying capacity of the bearing are the rubbing speed, and the actual clearance of the bearing. In the hydrodynamic region, the ability of the bearing to carry load is determined largely by the pressure required to squirt the oil out from the clearance space so that the bearing is actually supported on a film of liquid and ordinarily no metallic contact whatever takes place. As an example of this class of bearing, one can consider the high speed steam turbine type. In these bearings, the rubbing speed is quite high, in the neighborhood of 150 to 200 ft. per second, and the bearing is usually a full circle fit. In this case the clearance is partly determined by the oil conditions. I know of one instance, for example, where a 10,000 kw. turbine operating at quite moderate speed was found to climb about 0.010 in. as it got up speed. This meant that the clearance was established by the resistance of the oil film to shear and actually lifted the entire rotor clear of the bearing in normal operation by a measurable amount. The class of bearing just described usually involves fairly thin oils and the loads must be kept moderate. The reason for this condition is that while the high viscosity oil at the high rubbing speed of these bearings would give very great load-carrying capacity, the heat generated by shearing this thick oil at the high rubbing speed of the bearing would be so great as to burn it up and as a consequence, as the rubbing speeds go up and the clearances are small, the oil viscosity must be reduced in order to obtain a reasonable heat generation which can be conducted away from the bearing satisfactorily. As a result the use of the thinner oil to cut down this heat generation results in reduction of the load that the bearing may carry. Such bearings are seldom designed for much more than 200 lb. per sq. in.

The second class in which lubrication falls is the "thin" or "imperfect film" region. In this type of bearing the lubricant is not supplied in a flood, but in any case the bearings are apt to be heavily loaded and running at slower speed. In order to maintain any kind of a film and keep the metallic contact down to such an amount as will not involve overheating, it is necessary to use the higher viscosity oils. In the extreme case, we reach the very slow speed, very heavily loaded bearing, such as used in mill roll necks and similar duties in which oil of heavy body is necessary, or we must resort to grease.

Greases form the third class, namely "plastic" lubrication. The mathematics of the hydrodynamic region or "perfect film" lubrication has been extensively developed over the last 50 years and while not absolutely complete is in very satisfactory shape so that a bearing may be designed for this class of lubrication with reasonably good security that it will work when built. Thin film region and the plastic region have not been solved mathematically at all as yet, and a great deal of work will be needed on these two classes before we shall be in satisfactory position for reliable designing. One step made within the last few years in the thin film region where an oil is to be used, for example in the hypoid and worm gears, is the development of the oils and greases known as E.P. (Extreme Pressure) lubricants. These lubricants consist of oils or greases to which some compound has been added, usually a sulphur or chlorine compound, which produces a new effect on the rubbing surface. This effect is not wholly understood at the present time but the indications are that it is the formation of a sulphide film on the rubbing surface, which seems to give them the ability to pass each other under high loads without galling or scuffing. As a rule, the necessity of using an E.P. lubricant would indicate that the design of the apparatus is not entirely satisfactory, but there are some cases where the use of these newly developed oils and greases is absolutely necessary because the inherent nature of the design involves very high loading at the rubbing surfaces. One of these cases is the hypoid gear. It is possible that in the near future some of the E.P. lubricants might be of use in railroad work because there are many conditions in the thin film region of lubrication where an E.P. lubricant would definitely be of help.

Test Programs:

Up to the present time most of the test investigations on railroad bearings have been limited to two classes; namely, the operation of the bearings with oils to be rated, in dynamometer-type testing machines, by means of which the friction factor is measured; and those machines in which the bearing is operated under steady load for long periods of time to determine the amount of wear. Neither of these types of machine can give the whole story. Of course, the friction factor is the most familiar unit in bearing tests but it is really in many respects of very little value. The friction factor is merely measure of the force required to rotate the bearing under any set of conditions, given as a fraction of the total load on the bearing. Now it has been found with numerous experiments that the friction factor varies in the same bearing and with the same oil, with speed, load, ambient temperature, and the actual physical condition of the bearing. As a result the information it can give on the behavior of any particular oil is extremely vague and quite hard to interpret. Under rigorously duplicated conditions it can be of considerable value, but it must be borne in mind that even when the ambient temperature surrounding the bearing is kept the same, the temperature of the oil in the bearing is not the same at different speeds or different loads and it is largely the combination of viscosity and rubbing speed that determines the friction factor. Most tests on bearings have taken no account whatever of the actual temperature of the oil in the bearing and in fact this is not even a constant at different places in the bearing. Wear or life test machines are of course useful in determining rather authoritatively the behavior of a particular design of bearing under any given conditions. But where the wear of the bearing is unsatisfactory, the wear test will often not tell what is the cause of the failure. Maybe the load is too high for the oil used, or maybe it is only that the heat conduction from the test bearing is unsatisfactory and the oil is not given a chance to work properly. Many railroad bearings showing unsatisfactory performance have nothing inherently wrong with them except that the heat generated by the operation of the bearing is given no opportunity to get out without raising the temperature of the oil and bearing too high. Such bearings can be converted to satisfactory operation by adequate cooling. For example, artificial cooling is practically always employed in the case of the high speed large turbine, simply because the bearing cannot be operated at all without artificial cooling as the rate of heat generated is very high. More recent test programs on railroad bearings of various types have included the simulation of the actual operation such as start, run, and stop programs, and similar approximations of the operating conditions. However, these tests are all up to the present run on the two types of machine mentioned above, chiefly the dynamometer type, and it would appear that this is not going to be enough to get the answers. It will be necessary, in addition to the friction factor and wear machines, to add to one or both types means for measuring temperature and pressure all over the bearings, and position of the journal in the brass, as well as the friction factor. One thing that attracts attention immediately in the ordinary car journal is the fact that the bearing has a very poor chance to get rid of its heat since the only contact is with the brass around less than a quarter of the circumference and this brass is mounted with several loose joints between it and the structures which should ordinarily cool it. All of these points have to be considered in finding out why a bearing will or will not run satisfactorily or why one oil is better than another for the purpose.

Testing Equipment:

The dynamometer testing equipment has hitherto been developed in about four different types, the earliest generally exemplified by the Thurston machine, later redesigned in the Kingsbury machine, which might be termed the "double loading" type. In this a full bearing in halves is loaded by pressing the two halves against the journal from opposite sides by means of a suitably mounted spring. The first objection appears plain, i.e., nobody ever uses such a bearing—that is to say, one which is loaded from two directions at once—and therefore any analysis of the results is rendered very difficult because it does not bear any very close relation to an actual bearing. About seven different machines of this type have been built and commercially used.

The next type is the single-loading type which is nearer to the conditions occurring in an actual bearing. In this case the bearing proper is loaded by means of springs, a lever system, or a hydraulic cylinder. However, both in this type as well as in the preceding, the actual bearing itself is used as the dynamometer element and the friction of the bearing tends to rotate it upon the shaft, producing a force which can be measured by means of a lever arm or some similar device. However, the drawback is that if one wishes to measure the position of the journal in the bearing, or to make a pressure or temperature search, addition of the necessary apparatus destroys the sensitivity of the dynamometer at once and the results become very uncertain. About six different types of this machine have been commercially used and are still being used.

A third type which is very largely academic in nature and can only be used with reasonable security in the development of basic mathematical analysis is the step type, in which a rotating shaft is loaded endwise on a stationary plate, and the tendency of the plate to rotate with the shaft is used as the dynamometer element. Another form of this machine is in the use of vertical pins, several of which may be rotated on a spider around a central shaft. The objection to this type of step machine is that the bearing surfaces are not at liberty to assume the correct angle of slope to produce an oil film under normal bearing conditions and consequently the results are extremely difficult to interpret. It can easily be seen why any test machine which is imitating a real bearing must have two surfaces free to assume their proper angle to each other. For example in a journal bearing it is well known that the shaft is not displaced downward, (that is, in the direction of the load), but travels sideways in the journal and assumes an eccentricity which is determined by the speed, viscosity of the oil, clearances of the bearing, and its length relative to diameter and the load on the bearing. In fact, such a shaft only rotates centrally with the bearing when there is no load whatever on it. At all other times it is eccentric in the bearing. Two or three of these designs of step bearing test machines have been commercially used to a very limited extent.

The last class developed rather recently consists of a rolling hard steel wheel bearing against a flat block, or two rolling steel wheels rotating against each other in the opposite direction. This type of machine gives theoretically a line contact for the bearing surface. Actually its results mean very little because the only thing it can possibly represent is a gear tooth contact. It certainly does not represent any known bearing, not even a roller bearing. Two of these machines have been used, one of them quite extensively, in the automobile industry, but the type is fortunately falling into a position of considerable doubt as to value.

New Methods:

When we were faced with the problem of developing a reliable method of testing oils for use in any given bearing, we had to start from the ground up. The first requirement was that the bearing to be tested should be a real one and not some imitation of bearing, so we designed our first machine large enough to take an actual railway car journal full size, just as used in the car. In order to imitate the normal conditions as closely as possible, it is loaded and cooled in about the same way, it can be oscillated axially just as a car axle oscillates in the journal, and the test journal box is mounted solidly to the frame so that the addition of any thermocouples or pressure leads does not interfere with the dynamometer reading for friction. In addition we took considerable pains to increase the precision of the measurement. This machine has no knife edges whatever but is suspended upon steel tapes or fulcrum plates which have very small angles of swing, no noticeable friction, and the advantage that one knows exactly what their condition is. In short, they are either in perfect condition or broken; there is no intermediate state. Where knife edges are used, dirt or a damaged knife edge may be interfering with the precision without any very easy means of detecting the condition. As a result, this machine will show a variation of less than 0.01 lb. on the torque arm at a load of 20,000 lbs. on the bearing. The precision appears to be, therefore, from 5 to 10 times as high as that of any machine previously built. Two or three methods of measuring position of the journal in the box are being developed, the first and simplest of course being by means of accurate dial micrometers. It may seem as if all of this effort in developing such a machine was more or less hair-splitting, but this is not true. The trouble with nearly all bearing testing hitherto is that the lack of precision in the test machine has scattered the results to such an extent as to make them unreliable or difficult to spot in any regular curve. Provision is available for making a complete temperature and pressure search of the bearing. The beauty of this arrangement is that any kind of a bearing may be tested in this machine. We simply make up stub shafts to take the actual bearing and mount the whole structure on the dynamometer cradle. This costs a little more money for change-over on different tests but should prove invaluable, especially when testing under imperfect film conditions or grease lubrication. Even if a mathematical analysis of the results cannot be made, we can at least utilize the results

196

of such tests in the design of a similar bearing without having to interpret them to any extent.

The first set-up in this machine involved a synchronous motor drive with eight speeds provided through a gear box so that in running the tests we would have no difficulty in holding the speeds exactly constant. For later work involving acceleration and deceleration a variable speed motor or variable speed drive will be used. A further advantage of this type of machine is that it can be made in several other sizes, right down to a bench machine which can be very conveniently used for academic investigations developing the theory of lubrication in the now-unknown regions as well as for such practical tests as outlined above.

Temperatures:

In order to take care of the effect of temperature upon the operation of bearings, such as continually occurs in railroad use, we have two methods of procedure. One is to make the tests at room temperature but change the viscosity of the oil, and this will be largely used in determining the effect of viscosity change, per se; the other method is by the enclosure of a test bearing in a refrigerating chamber, and simulating the actual cold weather conditions found in practice but using one oil in this case throughout the varying temperature range. While we feel that the variation of the viscosity of the oil on tests run at room temperature will give us nearly all the information we need, it is felt that such a program would have to be backed by actual operation with the normal single oil under the actual low temperatures, particularly in view of the fact that railroad men as a rule have been taught by bitter experience to regard academic tests as being somewhat unsafe until checked by tests under the actual oprating conditions. Personally, the writer is wholly in sympathy with this attitude because it is so easy to assume that a condition has been imitated when actually it has not. The safest thing to do is to apply the actual conditions. It is believed that we are at the beginning of an era of considerable discovery in the way to apply lubricants to railway bearings and it should be quite evident by this time that the old cut-and-try methods of determining not only suitable lubricants but suitable designs are no longer good enough for the industry, and that more refined methods of investigation (involving a good deal of money, when all is said and done), will have to be the future course.

(Slides were given at this point. A few selected photographs from which these slides were made can be furnished if desired).

PRESIDENT: We have seen on the screen and listened to two speakers on the most interesting topic of the refining of oil. Though the hour is late, for the next ten minutes we will turn the meeting over to you and you may ask any questions you may wish relative to the paper of the evening and the two gentlemen, I am sure, will satisfactorily answer them.

MR. J. B. DIVEN: At the refinery down on Neville Island there is a tank which is spherical in shape where all the others are cylindrical with a flat top. Why is that?

MR. PIGOTT: The spheroidal tanks, such as the Horton-sphere, are used so that liquids can be stored under pressure, which cannot be done in the case of a stationary sided flat roof tank. Ordinarily storage tanks with stationary sides and flat roofs will not stand over a few ounces of pressure without blowing the roof out. Spheroidal tanks, however, can be designed under operating pressures of 5 to 50 lbs., although most of those used in liquids are operated under rather low pressures. Spheroidal tanks are used also for storing gas under pressure. It is naturally the best form to withstand pressure without pulling out of shape.

MR. EARL M. ALLEN: We hear a lot about S.A.E. What does that mean?

MR. CAREY: I explained that to some extent. S.A.E. refers to the range of viscosity. S.A.E. 30 means a range of viscosity anywhere from 30 to 75. S.A.E. means Society of Automobile Engineers, and it refers to a standard which they have set up.

MR. A. STUCKI: The speaker said that oil in sealed turbine bearings lasted for years in constant service. Yet we are told by many automobile manufacturers to change the oil every 500 miles. From that I judge it is not because the oil loses its life, but rather it must be on account of impurities passing the piston rings, or otherwise entering the oil, which determines renewals. Therefore, it looks to me that the request of changing the oil after a certain mileage is incorrect, because it depends on the condition of each car. Am I correct?

MR. PIGOTT: The reason for changing oil in the automobile engine is largely based on the very wide variety of conditions under which it is operated. In the steam turbine such as used in the major power stations, the same oil is used for a period of years, as a rule. The turbine is started up and put on the line, and runs for hours and sometimes for days, without any appreciable change in conditions on the oil. There is little change in temperature, little contact with air, and almost no chance for water to get in; consequently the formation of sludges and acid is very low. If we could get these conditions in the automobile engine, we would run the oils something like the same length of time. It is the cold starts that are largely responsible for change of oil, although of course quality of the oil has an important bearing on the life in the crank-case. Assuming that you are using a high grade stable oil in the summer-time when the engine never starts very cold, and if fairly long average trips are made so that the engine is hot for considerable periods, you can run a high grade oil from 2,000 to 4,000 miles without risk. It is to be remembered that in burning the fuel more water vapor is produced by weight than gasoline entering the engine and some of this always reaches the crank-case. If the engine is run hot for a sufficient time this water vapor is reevaporated from the crank-case and the oil left much as it was at the start. On the other hand if the owner of the automobile is a salesman making many short runs, and many stops and starts in winter, the amount of water vapor reaching the crank-case is enormously increased and does not boil off again because the engine does not become hot for long enough periods to reevaporate it and gradual accumulation of water in the crank-case will occur. The extreme case is that of milk wagons, which start and stop all day long and make perhaps 8 to 12 miles a day total. Under these conditions in winter they can get a crank-case full of water in a week. Water is in itself not especially objectionable but it does induce sludge and acid formation. Since we have been ventilating crank-cases of automobiles we have increased the tendency to sludge from other causes than water (largely oxidation) and have decreased the dilution during cold operation both by water and by heavy ends of the gasoline, but also reevaporate them faster. It is a difficult matter for the oil companies, or indeed the automobile manufacturers, to specify the length of time which you should run the oil in your car. It is without doubt safe for the average driver to change his oil about every 500 miles in winter, but in summer with a high grade oil he does not need to change oftener than 1,000 miles and for many cases providing a high grade oil is used, it need be changed in summer-time only every 2,000 or 3,000 miles. However, if cheap oils are used it is not safe to run them so long. The 500 miles in winter is still probably fairly safe but the oils are not stable enough to be good after 1,000 miles, even in summer. You can judge of the time to change your oil best by examining its condition as it comes out of the crank-case. If it still appears to have good body or viscosity and looks fairly clean, continue to use it a little longer and you can make up your own table of changes by examining what you take out of the crank-case.

MR. W. M. CREE: Mr. Carey, how deep are oil wells generally?

MR. CAREY: Oil is found at almost any depth. Sometimes and in certain places it comes out of the ground without a well at all. The deepest well I know of anywhere is a well drilled recently by Gulf. It is approximately two miles deep.

QUESTION: Mr. Carey, you mentioned something about the consumption of oil being in the neighborhood of a billion barrels per year. Is there plenty of oil in the ground for the country's future needs?

MR. CAREY: New oil fields are being discovered with capacities about equal to the rate of consumption at the present time. The known reserves so far discovered are about fifteen billion barrels. The future supply of oil depends upon whether or not the discovery of new fields keeps pace with the consumption.

MR. J. S. LANAHAN: Mr. Carey, I have heard that there are large deposits in the shales of the Northwest of the United States. Will you say a few words about that?

MR. CAREY: There is a known potential of perhaps fifteen billion barrels of oil in the shales of the Northwest. It is a strange fact that the so-called oil in the shales of the

Northwest is not oil until the shales are treated, principally by the application of heat. Oil does not exist in the shales in the same form that it does exist in the wells as we know them. It is entirely possible that the shale deposits will never be worked for oil because of the expense involved. It is probable that oil will be produced synthetically from the hydrogenation of coal before many years.

QUESTION: How does one increase the production from a well?

MR. PIGOTT: The subject is a complicated one. At the present time there is very much less demand for increasing the production from wells on account of the fact that proration is generally in control. There are several ways to increase production. In the old wells where the sand is not clogged in any way but pressure has declined to the point where the well will not produce as much as in its early life, the method used is to repressure. This may be done either by pumping dry gas from the gasoline plants back into the formation through an old well whose production is so low that it can be turned into an input well without much loss. This gas goes back into the formation and by building up again the gas pressure which formerly subsisted, will raise the production on the wells in the neighborhood of the input well. Repressuring may also be done by pumping water into the formation, particularly where the oil is being produced by water drive. The effect is much the same as in repressuring with gas. If the reduction in capacity of the well is due to paraffin, the remedy is clean out the well either with chemicals or by scraping. If the sand is clogged with salts, chiefly carbonates and sulphates, dropped out of the liquids in the well, (mainly of course with salt water), the remedy is to use inhibited hydrochloric acid to dissolve salts deposited in the pores of the sand around the well bore. The hydrochloric acid used in this case is inhibited with various chemicals so as to prevent attack upon the tubing and casing, but leave it free to attack the carbonates and sulphates which have been deposited in the pores of the sand.

MR. LLOYD SUTHERLAND: This has been a very enjoyable as well as instructive meeting, and as an expression of our appreciation I would move a vote of thanks to be extended to Mr. Pigott and to Mr. Carey.

201

The motion was duly seconded and prevailed by unanimous vote.

There being no further discussion, ON MOTION the meeting was adjourned to the lunch tables.

J. D. CONWAY, Secretary.

In Memoriam

FREDERICK KERBY,
Joined Club September 13, 1918
Died May 18, 1936

SAMUEL LYNN,
Joined Club December 28, 1903
Died August 8, 1936

JOHN M. MOGAN,
Joined Club February 24, 1927
Died September 23, 1936

J. G. PLATT,
Joined Club October 22, 1909
Died July 26, 1936

J. C. WHITRIDGE,
Joined Club May 22, 1924
Died July 29, 1936

IT'S

"CLEAR TRACK AHEAD"

with

PENNZIP
GASOLINE

PENNZOIL
MOTOR OIL

*Perfect Partners for
Smoother, Safer Mileage*

THE PENNZOIL COMPANY

**Chamber of Commerce Building
Pittsburgh, - - - - - Pa.**

OFFICIAL PROCEEDINGS

RWAY CLUB OF PITTSBURGH

$1.00 Per Year   25¢ Per Copy

Vol. XXXV.	OCTOBER 22, 1936.	No. 9.

ANNUAL MEETING—ELECTION OF OFFICERS
LIST OF MEMBERS

The proof of your interest

in the Club can be

enhanced

by securing a

NEW MEMBER.

Application form is available

in this magazine. Look

it up and

"ACT NOW."

OFFICIAL PROCEEDINGS

OF

The Railway Club of Pittsburgh

Organized October 18, 1901

Published monthly, except June, July and August, by the Railway Club of
Pittsburgh, J. D. Conway, Secretary, 515 Grandview Ave., Pittsburgh, Pa..

Entered as Second Class Matter February 6, 1915, at the Postoffice at Pittsburgh,
under the Act of March 3, 1879.

Vol. XXXV No. 9	**Pittsburgh, Pa., Oct. 22, 1936**	$1.00 Per Year 25c Per Copy

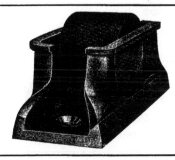

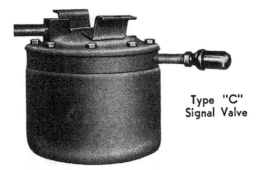

INDEX—ADVERTISERS.

NOTE—This form to be filled out in full by typewriter or printed and mailed to J. D. Conway, Secretary, 1941 Oliver Building, Pittsburgh, Pa. Membership fee, including dues, is $3.00 for each fiscal year or part thereof, except those proposd in September or October. Those proposed in these months will be credited upon payment for the following fiscal year. Dues are payable in advance.

The fiscal year ends with the month of October.

The Railway Club of Pittsburgh:

_____19___

Gentlemen:

Will you kindly consider my Application for Membership in your Club at the next meeting:

Name_____

Title_____

Company_____

My Address_____

_____

Recommended by_____

OFFICIAL PROCEEDINGS
OF

The Railway Club of Pittsburgh

Organized October 18, 1901

| Vol. XXXV No. 9 | Pittsburgh, Pa., Oct. 22, 1936 | $1.00 Per Year 25c Per Copy |

OFFICERS FOR 1935-1936

President
R. P. FORSBERG,
Chief Engineer, P. & L. E. R. R. Co., Pittsburgh, Pa.

First Vice President
E. A. RAUSCHART,
Mechanical Supt., Montour Railroad,
Coraopolis, Pa.

Secretary
J. D. CONWAY,
Railway Supply Manufacturers' Association,
Pittsburgh, Pa.

Second Vice President
G. M. SIXSMITH,
Supt., Pennsylvania Railroad,
Pittsburgh, Pa.

Treasurer
E. J. SEARLES,
Manager, Schaefer Equipment Co.,
Pittsburgh, Pa.

EXECUTIVE COMMITTEE:

FRANK J. LANAHAN, Chairman, President, Fort Pitt Malleable Iron Co., Pittsburgh, Pa.
A. STUCKI, Engineer, A. Stucki Company, Pittsburgh, Pa.
D. F. CRAWFORD, Consulting Engineer, Pittsburgh, Pa.
G. W. WILDIN, Consulting Engineer, Westinghouse Air Brake Company, Pittsburgh, Pa.
W. S. McABEE, Vice Pres. & General Supt., Union Railroad Co., East Pittsburgh, Pa.
E. W. SMITH, Vice President, Pennsylvania Railroad, Pittsburgh, Pa.
LOUIS E. ENDSLEY, Consulting Engineer, 516 East End Avenue, Pittsburgh, Pa.
F. I. SNYDER, Vice President & General Manager, B. & L. E. R. R. Co., Pittsburgh, Pa.
C. O. DAMBACH, General Manager, P. & W. Va. Ry. Co., Pittsburgh, Pa.
R. H. FLINN, General Superintendent, Pennsylvania Railroad, Pittsburgh, Pa.

SUBJECT COMMITTEE:

D. W. McGEORGE, Chairman, Secretary, Edgewater Steel Company, Pittsburgh, Pa.
JOHN B. WRIGHT, Asst. Vice President, Westinghouse Air Brake Co., Wilmerding, Pa.
M. R. REED, General Supt. Motive Power, Pennsylvania Railroad, Pittsburgh, Pa.

ADVERTISING COMMITTEE:

E. A. FOARD, Chairman, Supt. Stations & Transfers, Pennsylvania R. R., Pittsburgh, Pa.
KARL BERG, Superintendent Motive Power, P. & L. E. R. R. Co., McKees Rocks, Pa.
H. E. PASSMORE, Representative, The American Hammered Piston Ring Co., Pgh., Pa.

RECEPTION AND ATTENDANCE COMMITTEE:

J. D. BELTZ, Chairman, Superintendent, B. & O. R. R. Co., Pittsburgh, Pa.
W. C. BUREL, Vice Chairman, Master Mechanic, Western Allegheny Railroad, Kaylor, Pa.
J. B. BAKER, Chief Engr. Maintenance of Way, Pennsylvania Railroad, Pittsburgh, Pa.
WALTER C. SANDERS, Gen. Mgr., Railway Div., Timken Roller Bearing Co., Canton, O.
G. A. BLACKMORE, President & Gen. Mgr., Union Switch & Signal Co., Swissvale, Pa.
J. S. LANAHAN, Vice President, Fort Pitt Malleable Iron Company, Pittsburgh, Pa.
J. A. WARFEL, Special Representative, Air Reduction Sales Co., Pittsburgh, Pa.
J. C. SHINGLEDECKER, Supervisor of Service Stations, The Pennzoil Co., Pittsburgh, Pa.
J. C. DILWORTH, Mgr. of Railroad Sales, Carnegie-Illinois Steel Corp., Pittsburgh, Pa.
G. H. BURNETTE, Assistant Chief Engineer, P. & L. E. R. R. Co., Pittsburgh, Pa.
W. R. TRIEM, Superintendent, Pennsylvania Railroad, Pittsburgh, Pa.
J. W. HOOVER, Asst. Chief of Transpn., Subsidiary Cos. U. S. Steel Corp., Pittsburgh, Pa.
J. W. JOHNSON, Superintendent, Railway Express Agency, Pittsburgh, Pa.
A. A. READ, Duquesne Slag Products Company, Pittsburgh, Pa.
C. P. SCHRECONGOST, Traffic Manager, Hillman Coal & Coke Company, Pittsburgh, Pa.

ENTERTAINMENT COMMITTEE:

J. PORTER GILLESPIE, Chairman, Asst. Gen. Supt., Lockhart Iron & Steel Co., Pgh., Pa.
FRANK E. WEIS, Vice Chairman, Transportation Clerk, Penna. R. R., Pittsburgh, Pa.
E. H. HOLMES, Sales Department, Fort Pitt Malleable Iron Co., Pittsburgh, Pa.
C. C. CLARK, Sales Manager Central District, Pressed Steel Car Co., McKees Rocks, Pa.
A. L. KESSLER, Clearance Clerk, Pennsylvania Railroad, Pittsburgh, Pa.
T. F. SHERIDAN, Asst. to S.M.P. and S.R.S., P. & L. E. R. R. Co., McKees Rocks, Pa.
JAMES NAGEL, Superintendent Transportation, Montour Railroad, Coraopolis, Pa.

FINANCE COMMITTEE:

J. L. O'TOOLE, Chairman, Asst. to Gen. Manager, P. & L. E. R. R. Co., Pittsburgh, Pa.
G. W. HONSBERGER, Transpn. Mgr., Westinghouse Electric & Mfg. Co., Pittsburgh, Pa.
F. J. RYAN, District Representative, Detroit, Toledo & Ironton Railroad, Pittsburgh, Pa.
C. E. CATT, Division Accountant, B. & O. R. R. Co., Pittsburgh, Pa.
J. W. BOYD, Superintendent, Monongahela Railway Company, Brownsville, Pa.

MEMBERSHIP COMMITTEE:

T. E. BRITT, Chairman, Division Storekeeper, B. & O. R. R. Co., Pittsburgh, Pa.
A. B. SEVERN, General Manager, A. Stucki Company, Pittsburgh, Pa.
W. P. BUFFINGTON, Traffic Manager, Pittsburgh Coal Company, Pittsburgh, Pa.
R. S. BULL, Supt. Power & Inclines, Pittsburgh Railways Co., N. S., Pittsburgh, Pa.
A. F. COULTER, Master Car Builder, Union Railroad Co., East Pittsburgh, Pa.
T. R. DICKINSON, Purchasing Agent, B. & L. E. R. R. Co., Pittsburgh, Pa.
D. K. ORR, Road Master, Monongahela Railway Co., Brownsville, Pa.
C. M. WHEELER, Sales Engineer, Union Switch & Signal Company, Swissvale, Pa.
W. F. AMBROSE, Master Mechanic, Aliquippa & Southern Railroad, Aliquippa, Pa.
JOHN I. MULVEY, Traffic Manager, Hubbard & Company, Pittsburgh, Pa.
THOMAS R. FITZPATRICK, Freight Traffic Mgr., P. & L. E. R. R. Co., Pittsburgh, Pa.
P. W. HEPBURN, Sales Engineer, Gulf Refining Company, Pittsburgh, Pa.
W. B. MOIR, Chief Car Inspector, Pennsylvania Railroad, Pittsburgh, Pa.
C. W. TRUST, Assistant Traffic Manager, Carnegie-Illinois Steel Corp., Pittsburgh, Pa

PAST PRESIDENTS:

*J. H. McCONNELL..October, 1901, to October, 1903
*L. H. TURNER...November, 1903, to October, 1905
*F. H. STARK..November, 1905, to October, 1907
*H. W. WATTS..November, 1907, to April, 1908
*D. J. REDDING..November, 1908, to October, 1910
*F. R. McFEATTERS..November, 1910, to October, 1912
*A. G. MITCHELL...November, 1912, to October, 1914
*F. M. McNULTY..November, 1914, to October, 1916
*J. G. CODE...November, 1916, to October, 1917
*D. M. HOWE...November, 1917, to October, 1918
*J. A. SPIELMAN...November, 1918, to October, 1919
H. H. MAXFIELD..November, 1919, to October, 1920
FRANK J. LANAHAN...November, 1920, to October, 1921
*SAMUEL LYNN..November, 1921, to October, 1922
D. F. CRAWFORD..November, 1922, to October, 1923
*GEO. D. OGDEN..November, 1923, to October, 1924
A. STUCKI...November, 1924, to October, 1925
F. G. MINNICK...November, 1925, to October, 1926
G. W. WILDIN..November, 1926, October, 1927
E. J. DEVANS..November, 1927, October, 1928
W. S. McABEE..November, 1928, October, 1929
E. W. SMITH...November, 1929, October, 1930
LOUIS E. ENDSLEY..November, 1930, October, 1931
*JOHN E. HUGHES...November, 1931, October, 1932
F. I. SNYDER..November, 1932, October, 1933
C. O. DAMBACH...November, 1933, to October, 1934
R. H. FLINN...November, 1934, to October, 1935
*—Deceased.

Meetings held fourth Thursday of each month except June, July and August.

PROCEEDINGS OF MEETING
OCTOBER 22, 1936

The annual meeting was called to order at the Fort Pitt Hotel at 8:00 o'clock P. M., with President R. P. Forsberg in the chair.

Attendance, as shown by registration cards, 537 persons, thirty-one of whom neglected to sign cards handed in at door:

MEMBERS

Adams, W. A.
Armstrong, C. B.
Aulbach, A. J.
Babcock, F. H.
Balla, J. A.
Barclay, J. R.
Barr, H. C.
Baumann, C. G.
Beall, C. R.
Beam, E. J.
Beatty, Raymond N.
Beeson, H. L.
Beitsch, George F.
Beltz, J. D.
Bender, H. P.
Bergman, C. R.
Beswick, R. M.
Bishop, H. E.
Boyd, John R.
Bradley, J. W.
Braun, O. F.
Brennan, J. T.
Britt, T. E.
Brown, C. C.
Brown, E. F.
Buchanan, C. C.
Burel, W. C.
Burnette, G. H.
Callahan, F. J.
Campbell, F. R.
Campbell, J. Alan
Campbell, W. T.
Cannon, T. E.
Carlson, H. E.
Carr, T. W.
Carroll, D. C.
Carson, John
Carter, E. D.
Catt, C. E.

Cavanaugh, J. J.
Chalker, A. R.
Christy, F. X.
Clokey, John
Conway, J. D.
Coombe, A. B.
Courtney, H.
Cree, W. M.
Cruikshank, J. C.
Cudworth, H. D.
Cunningham, J. Donald
Cunningham, R. I.
Curley, W. J.
Curtis, V. K.
Dalzell, W. E.
Dambach, C. O.
Davidson, J. C.
Davies, James
Davin, W. E.
Davis, Charles S.
Davis, John W.
Day, T. R.
Dean, R. W.
Dean, W. H.
Dean, W.
Dehne, G. C.
Devine, J. C.
Dillon, A. L.
Diven, J. B.
Donovan, L. T.
Dugan, G. R.
Duffley, F. M.
Durnell, W. E.
Edwards, Walter
Emery, E.
Evans, Charles S.
Falkner, A. J.
Fay, Hon. Frank L.
Fieldson, P. H.

Fike, James W.
Fischer, John J.
Fitzpatrick, T. R.
Fitz Simmons, E. S.
Fleckenstein, August
Flinn, R. H.
Forsberg, R. P.
Fox, George W.
Fralic, C. F.
Frauenheim, A. M.
Frauenheim, Pierce H.
Freshwater, F. H.
Friend, E. F.
Fults, J. H.
Furch, G. J.
Galbraith, James R.
Galloway, W. R., Jr.
Gardner, George R.
Gardner, K. C.
Gariepy, L. H.
Gatfield, Philip
George, W. J.
Gilg, Henry F.
Gilespie, J. Porter
Glaser, C. J.
Glaser, J. P.
Glenn, J. H.
Goda, P. H.
Goldstrom, G. E.
Goodwin, A. E.
Goron, F. W.
Griest, E. E.
Grieve, Robert E.
Gross, John
Groves, W. C.
Guinnip, M. S.
Haler, Nelson M.
Hamilton, W. H.
Hamsher, W. E.
Hansen, William C.
Harper, G. C.
Harper, J. T.
Hassler, E. S.
Heimbach, A. E.
Heinz, W. J.
Hepburn, R. W.
Herpst, R. C.
Hess, Charles A.
Higginbottom, S. B.
Hill, J. A.
Hilstrom, A. V.
Holland, S. E.

Holmes, E. H.
Holtzworth, C. H.
Hoopes, R. E.
Hoover, J. W.
Horne, John S.
Huber, H. G.
Huff, A. B.
Hunt, C. T.
Huston, F. T.
Hutchinson, G. C., Jr.
Hykes, W. H.
Irvin, R. K.
Irwin, R. D.
Jados, Walter T.
Johnson, Ira S.
Johnson, LeVere H.
Kearfott, W. E.
Kennedy, F. J.
Kennedy, G. N.
Kentlein, John
Kerr, Dr. James P.
Kimling, Carl
Klassen, F. G.
Klein, S. J.
Kondej, Henry
Kramer, W. E.
Kramer, W. H.
Kroske, J. F.
Kruse, J. F. W.
Kusick, Harry F.
Lanahan, Frank J.
Larson, W. E.
Lavine, Ralph D.
Lees, Thomas
Leet, C. S.
Leonard, C. W.
Leonard, P. J.
Lewis, N. F.
Lincoln, J. J., Jr.
Livingston, W. C.
Loder, C. C.
Long, R. M.
Longstreth, W. L.
Maliphant, C. W.
Masters, W. C.
Maxwell, Thomas
Mayer, L. I.
Meagher, Maurice E.
Megee, C. R.
Meinert, Henry J.
Menk, C. W.
Metzger, C. L.

Millar, C. W.
Miller, John
Mills, O. B.
Misner, George W.
Moir, W. B.
Morgan, A. L.
Morgan, Homer C.
Murray, C. C.
Murray, T. A.
Musgrove, W. W.
McCandless, William A.
McCormick, E. S.
McCrea, J. G.
McGeorge, D. W.
McIntyre, R. C.
McKay, N. H.
McKim, Hollis
McKinley, A. J.
McKinley, John T.
McKinstry, C. H.
McLaughlin, H. B.
McMillan, A. P.
McPherson, A. R.
McQuiston, C. A.
McTighe, B. J.
Nagel, James
Nash, R. L.
Nathan, W. S.
Nieman, H. L.
Nies, E. L.
Noble, J. A.
O'Leary, Jeremiah J.
Orbin, G. N.
Overholt, B. C.
Paisley, F. R.
Pearl, W. W.
Peel, J. E., Jr.
Peirce, W. B.
Pevler, H. H.
Phillips, R. A.
Phillips, T. H.
Pickard. S. B.
Pillar, Michael
Pohlman, A.
Porter, H. N.
Posteraro, S. F.
Pringle, Paul R.
Prinkey, C. M.
Purcell, E. J.
Purchard, Paul
Rankin, B. B.
Rauschart, E. A.

Rief, Joseph
Riley, O. W.
Rizzo, C. M.
Roberts, E. L.
Robertson, A. S.
Rupp, E. S.
Rutter, H. E.
Ryan, D. W.
Ryan, Frank J.
Sarchet, Roger
Sayre, H. A.
Schadt, A. D.
Schaffer, W. E.
Schako, E. J.
Schauers, R. W.
Schiller, Joseph, Jr.
Schmitt, Andrew
Schrecongost, C. P.
Searles, E. J.
Seibert, W. L.
Seidel, John, Jr.
Sekera, C. J.
Servais, F. W.
Severn, A. B.
Shaw, M. H.
Shellenbarger, H. M.
Sheridan, T. F.
Showalter, Joseph
Shuster, W. W.
Smith, Folger M.
Smith, Robert B.
Snyder, F. I.
Snyder, Joseph J.
Stack, John E.
Stamets, William K.
Steiner, P. E.
Stevens, L. V.
Stewart, C. D.
Stewart, C. G.
Stillwagon, C. K.
Stocker, H. F.
Stoffregen, L. E.
Strople, G. H.
Stucki, A.
Sullivan, R. J.
Sutherland, Lloyd
Swank, W. E.
Taylor, J. T.
Ternent. H. J.
Terry, Edward
Thomas, Theodore
Thompson, H. C.

Tipton, G. M.
Tobasco, P.
Tomasic, Nich. M., Jr.
Tracey, J. B. A.
Trautman, H. J.
Tucker, John L.
Tyler, B. W., Jr.
Uhar, John J.
Unger, Dr., J. S.
Urtel, E. J.
Van Horne, C. F.
Van Vranken, S. E.
Van Woert, F. E.
Vollmer, Karl L.
Vowinkel, Fred F.
Weis, Frank E.

Welton, Alvin A.
West, G. S.
West, Troy
Westerman, M. A.
Wikander, O. R.
Williams, David L.
Wilson, James R.
Wilson, W. S.
Wilson, W. Stuart, Jr.
Winslow, George W.
Woodward, Robert
Wright, Edward W.
Wright, J. B.
Yohe, J. K., Jr.
Yorke, P. H.
Young, F. C.

VISITORS

Aiton, John C.
Alberts, J. F.
Anderson, C. A.
Andrews, R. P.
Argel, A. J.
Arnold, J. G.
Bageley, G. P.
Baker, George N.
Barrie, J. S.
Bell, R. P.
Berkoben, Charles, Jr.
Bigatts, Gus
Bitzel, H. J.
Bochert, C. G.
Bovard, William L.
Brown, R. J.
Bryant, L. J.
Burgess, T. S.
Burgess, W. C.
Butzler, C. A.
Cahill, Arthur B.
Carroll, J. F.
Cashdollar, Roy G.
Clark, C. J.
Colclaser, L. A.
Cole, J. A.
Collers, M. L.
Condon, W. H., Jr.
Connell, J. R.
Coonev, Charles J.
Corn. David H.
Cowell, A. P.
Cramer, J. H.

Curley, J. M.
Dalzell, William, Jr.
Davis, William B.
Deitwiler, Ward
Dennis, J. G.
Doherty, T. J.
Ebersberger, F.
Edsall, S. D.
Eichhorn, T. F.
Eichner, John
Elles, C. D.
Elmer, W. T.
Faison, L. H.
Ferguson, James H., Jr.
Fleming, Robert J.
Fletcher, Albert
Ford, R. C.
Forger, F. D.
Forrester, J. B.
Friend, R. A.
Frump, Perry
Garrity, John
Gelston, George A.
Gillen, J. B.
Gollmer, H. C.
Gower, Robert
Grimm, W. R.
Guff, Gerald P.
Guidotti, Harry
Gumz, Fred A.
Gykis, J. A.
Harbourt, C. W.
Harper, Paul S.

206

Harris, E. W.
Hastings, W. S.
Heer, Walter
Heeth, James
Helly, C. R.
Henderson, G.
Henry, M. A.
Hewlett, H. D.
Higgs, David
Hobson, Dillinger R.
Hockenberry, H. D.
Holland, Alex.
Hostetter, H. G.
Hurray, Charles A.
Imhoff, George H.
Jacob, Arthur
Jones, G. L.
Jones, W. M.
Kerstein, G. A.
Kessler, M.
Kettering, Benjamin M.
King, William R.
Kneebone, Percy M.
Larson, E. R.
Lenzinger, W. M.
Lewis, Benjamin
Lewis, S. B.
Lower, R. C.
Lyons, J. C.
Macoubry, R. J.
Mayhall, J.
Meyer, August P.
Meixner, M. J.
Miller, Bernard B.
Miller, L. P.
Miller, Paul
Moeller, Frank J.
Montgomery, James
Moody, E. H.
Moore, D. M.
Morford, R. F.
Morrison, Glenn W.
Morse, F. L.
Murawski, Andrew
McAllister, James
McCollum, O. R.
McCoy, G. L.
McHugh, E. C.
McHugh, R. E.
McKenna, J. T.
McKenna, J. V.
McKinley, L. C.

McKinstry, C. M.
McPherson, K. W.
McVicker, J. W.
McWilliams, M. E.
Nagel, James, Jr.
Nieman, H. L., Jr.
Noble, Robert F.
O'Hagan, J. E.
Ornig, Thomas F.
Parsons, F. W.
Pederson, M. A.
Penn, William
Peoples, James
Perrear, S. J.
Pillar, John
Pillar, Joseph
Pohlmeyer, H. M.
Porter, J. V.
Rainey, John G.
Rauschart, Frederick
Record, J. F.
Reill, John J.
Reuter, Paul C.
Rider, C. E.
Rider, H. C.
Robeck, George B.
Robinson, H. L.
Roddy, E. B.
Rosse, Harry
Rowles, C. B.
Salisbury, H. R.
Schako, C. E.
Severn, Harry A.
Severn, John J.
Seymour, Theodore C.
Sheldon, Fred B.
Sheppard, A. B.
Shoemaker, Fred
Skiles, Harry
Smillie, Thomas
Smith, Sion B.
Snyder, H. C.
Stayduhar, T. A.
Stewart, William
Stopp, W. R.
Stritzinger, Frank R.
Terkelsen, Bernard
Thomas, Benjamin
Thomson, C. F.
Tomlinson, J. H.
Turner, E. H.
Turner, W. J.

Van Male, E. G.
Vasco, O. O.
Vito, M. D.
Vogel, E. E.
Vossil, P.
Walton, H. R.
Ward, W. J.
Weber, Alfred
Wedge, C. A.

Weitzel, C. E.
Weitzel, H. W.
White, J. J.
Winkler, A. H.
Wolf, Joseph
Young, James L.
Zaker, Mott M.
Zell, Harry A.
Zimmerman, Chester

PRESIDENT: Gentlemen, this, as you know, is the annual meeting of our Club and we have in consequence a large amount of business to transact. I will, therefore, endeavor to eliminate all unnecessary details and we will proceed at once with our work.

Inasmuch as we have a record of the evening's attendance on the registration cards you have signed, and as the printed proceedings containing the Minutes of the last meeting will reach you in a few days, we will dispense, with your consent, with those items.

We next come to applications for membership. Mr. Secretary, will you kindly read the names of any applicants we have.

SECRETARY: We have the following proposals for membership:

Ainsworth, John R., Special Apprentice, Westinghouse Air Brake Company, 353 Marguerite Avenue, Wilmerding, Pa. Recommended by C. W. Maliphant.

Balla, J. A., Assistant Supervisor Telegraph and Signals, Pennsylvania Railroad, Pittsburgh, Pa. Recommended by G. M. Sixsmith.

Bender, H. P., Mechanical Engineer, P. & L. E. R. R. Co., 921 Fordham Avenue, Pittsburgh, Pa. Recommended by T. W. Carr.

Campbell, J. Alan, Special Apprentice, Westinghouse Air Brake Company, 353 Marguerite Avenue, Wilmerding, Pa. Recommended by C. W. Maliphant.

Carter, E. D., Lineman, Union Railroad Company, 1305 Meadow Street, McKeesport, Pa. Recommended by T. E. Britt.

Cudworth, H. D., Apprentice, Westinghouse Air Brake Company, 423 Peebles Avenue, Wilkinsburg, Pa. Recommended by R. L. Nash.

Davidson, John C., Branch Manager, General Cable Corporation, Koppers Building, Pittsburgh, Pa. Recommended by V. K. Curtis and G. H. Burnette.

Dugan, G. R., City Passenger Agent, B. & O. R. R. Co., Union Trust Building, Pittsburgh, Pa. Recommended by T. E. Britt.

Hill, John A., Manager, Independent Pneumatic Tool Company, 803 Wabash Building, Pittsburgh, Pa. Recommended by T. E. Britt.

Hodges, R. C., Assistant Car Foreman, B. & O. R. R. Co., 3100 Gaylord Avenue, Dormont, Pittsburgh, Pa. Recommended by T. E. Britt.

Hunker, G. F., Assistant Division Manaer, Gulf Oil Corporation, Gross Street and P. R. R., Pittsburgh, Pa. Recommended by J. D. Conway.

Hunt, C. T., Assistant Engine House Foreman, Pennsylvania Railroad, 6014 Stanton Avenue, Pittsburgh, Pa. Recommended by W. B. Moir.

Jados, Water T., Westinghouse Air Brake Company, 104 Clara Street, Wilmerding, Pa. Recommended by C. W. Maliphant.

Kondej, Henry, Test Engineer, Westinghouse Air Brake Company, 571½ East End Avenue, Pittsburgh, Pa. Recommended by C. W. Maliphant.

Leonard C. W., Salesman, Independent Pneumatic Tool Company, Wabash Building, Pittsburgh, Pa. Recommended by T. E. Britt.

Lewis. N. F., Test Engineer, Westinghouse Air Brake Company, 523 North Avenue, Wilkinsburg, Pa. Recommended by C. W. Maliphant.

Metcalf, George E., Locomotive Engineer, Montour Railroad Company, 717 School Street, Coraopolis, Pa. Recommended by T. E. Britt.

Pevler, H. H., Division Enigneer, Pennsylvania Railroad, 1444 North Euclid Avenue, Pittsburgh, Pa. Recommended by G. S. West.

Purcell, Edward J., Westinghouse Air Brake Company, 353 Marguerite Avenue, Wilmerding, Pa. Recommended by C. W. Maliphant.

Shaw, M. H., Gang Foreman, Stores Department, B. & O. R. R. Co., 4712 Monongahela Avenue, Pittsburgh, Pa Recommended by T. E. Britt.

Stack, J. E., Superintendent, Pittsburgh Coal Company, 210½ Olympia Street, Mt. Washington, Pittsburgh, Pa. Recommended by T. E. Britt.

Welton, Alvin A, Special Apprentice Westinghouse Air Brake Company, 353 Marguerite Avenue, Wilmerding, Pa. Recommended by C. W. Maliphant.

Williams, David L., Salesman, G. W. Griffin Company, P. O. Box 1322, Pittsburgh, Pa. Recommended by M. S. Guinnip.

PRESIDENT: I will request those in the audience, whose names have just been called, to kindly stand. Gentlemen, this is the last time I expect to have the privilege of officially welcoming new members into our midst, and for that reason I extend to each one of you an especially warm and hearty welcome.

SECRETARY: Since our last meeting we have received notice of the death of Mr. George D. Ogden, Assistant Vice President—Traffic, Pennsylvania Railroad, New York, N. Y., a past President of the Club, which occurred on October 4, 1936, and have received the following acknowledgment for floral tribute sent by the Club:

"Ithan, Pa.,

"My dear Mr. Conway:

"Mother and I deeply appreciate the beautiful basket of flowers. Will you express for us to The Railway Club of Pittsburgh our thanks for their very kind thought of us at this time.

"Very sincerely,
"(Signed)   Katherine Ogden Souder."

PRESIDENT: As before stated, this is our annual meeting and we will proceed at this time to have submitted to us the annual reports of our Officers and Chairmen of the various Committees. We will first have the report of our Treasurer, Mr. Searles.

TREASURER'S REPORT

Pittsburgh, Pa., October 22, 1936.

To the Officers and Members of
The Railway Club of Pittsburgh.

Gentlemen:

I herewith submit my report for the year ended October 22, 1936:

ON HAND AND RECEIPTS

Cash on hand, October 24, 1935...................$1,892.48

Moneys received from J. D. Conway, Secretary, from October 24, 1935, to October 22, 1936.. 4,702.70

Interest on Bonds... 88.75

Total Receipts $6,683.93

DISBURSEMENTS

Paid on Vouchers No. 862 to 890, inclusive................ 5,485.58

Cash Balance $1,198.35

RESOURCES

Two U. S. Treasury Bonds, $1,000.00 each, bearing interest at $2\frac{7}{8}$ per cent...........$2,000.00

One U. S. Treasury Bond, $1,000.00, bearing interest at $3\frac{1}{8}$ per cent, at purchase price 949.39

Cash Balance 1,198.35

Total Resources $4,147.74

E. J. SEARLES, Treasurer.

APPROVED:

EXECUTIVE COMMITTEE,
FRANK J. LANAHAN, Chairman.

PRESIDENT: We will next have the report of our Secretary, Mr. Conway.

SECRETARY'S REPORT

Pittsburgh, Pa., October 22, 1936.

To the Officers and Members of
The Railway Club of Pittsburgh.

Gentlemen:

The following is a summary of membership and financial statement for the fiscal year ended October 22, 1936:

Membership reported last year......................... 1,157

Received into membership during year..................... 282

————— 1,439

Suspended	10
Resigned	31
Loss of address	-6
Deaths reported during year	11
	58

Present membership 1,381

Of the above membership four are honorary. They are: D. C. Buell, D. F. Crawford, Samuel O. Dunn and John A. Penton.

DECEASED MEMBERS

Name	Died
C. A. Croft	November 25, 1935
Daniel F. Downes	October 31, 1935
Frederick Kerby	May 18, 1936
Samuel Lynn	August 8, 1936
Joseph S. Merk	April 6, 1936
John M. Mogan	September 23, 1936
George D. Ogden	October 4, 1936
J. G. Platt	July 26, 1936
William C. Seiss	March 6, 1936
E. H. Skiles	December 29, 1935
J. C. Whitridge	July 29, 1936

RECEIPTS

In hands of Treasurer at close of last year	$4,841.87	
From advertisements	1,006.50	
From dues	3,114.00	
From sale of Proceedings	11.69	
Smoker tickets and dinner October 24, 1935	532.00	
Miscellaneous sources	38.51	
Interest on Bonds	88.75	
		$9,633.32

DISBURSEMENTS

Printing Proceedings, notices, mailing, etc.	$2,321.60
Luncheons, cigars, postage, etc.	916.56
Reporting meetings	180.00
Dinner, Entertainment, Smoker, etc., October 24, 1935	781.75
Salaries and advertising expense	1,100.65

Moving pictures	42.00	
Messenger service, affidavits, etc.	16.50	
Premium on Bonds—Treasurer and Secretary	14.00	
Floral pieces	20.00	
Various entertainment at meetings	53.00	
Incidentals	39.52	
		$5,485.58

Net Balance at Close of Year $4,147.74

NOTE:—Balance is made up of $1,198.35 cash and two U. S. Treasury Bonds, $1,000.00 each, $2\frac{7}{8}$ per cent interest, and one $1,000.00 U. S. Treasury Bond, $3\frac{1}{8}$ per cent interest, at cost of $949.39.

J. D. CONWAY, Secretary.

APPROVED:

EXECUTIVE COMMITTEE,
FRANK J. LANAHAN, Chairman.

We have audited the accounts of the Secretary and Treasurer, for the year ended October 31, 1936, and find them correct as reported.

FINANCE COMMITTEE,
J. L. O'TOOLE, Chairman,
G. W. HONSBERGER,
C. E. CATT.

PRESIDENT: I note in the list of members who have passed on since our last meeting the names of two Past Presidents of our Club. At our last meeting I requested one of the members of our Club to say a few words in honor of the memory of Mr. Samuel Lynn,, Past President, whose death occurred a short time before that meeting. I selected the speaker on account of the long and close personal and business relations he had enjoyed with Mr. Lynn. Tonight, we mourn the death of another Past President, Mr. George D. Ogden. It happens that Mr. Frank J. Lanahan enjoyed the same close personal relations with Mr. Ogden that he did with Mr. Lynn, and I am, therefore, going to request him to come to the platform and say a few words in honor of the memory of George D. Ogden, and when he has completed his remarks I will ask every one in the audience to rise and stand with bowed heads in reverent contemplation for one minute as a silent tribute to the memory of the members of our Club who have passed over "THE GREAT DIVIDE" since our last annual meeting.

MR. FRANK J. LANAHAN: Gentlemen: Inasmuch as the achievements you have heard tonight from the different Committee Chairmen covering the past year, reflect the work of the Executive Committee, it would be simply repetition to go into further detail, so in lieu of that, on behalf of the Executive body, congratulations are freely extended to the membership as a whole on the accomplishments of the past year and to point to the bright hopes for the future from the friendly spirit of co-operation declared by our new officers. In this connection, may I call to your attention, the declaration made in this same exuberant spirit to us twelve months ago? It emanated from the gentleman who occupies the chair now, and who on that occasion had just been designated as our President. This is what that gentleman said on the occasion of his inauguration:

"Boys, I have no axe to grind, no fish to fry, no pet scheme to advance, I have no interest in the work of our Club for the ensuing year higher than an honest purpose and a sincere desire to serve you as your President, as you want your President to serve you, and, 'May my tongue cleave to the roof of my mouth, and my right hand forget its cunning', if I ever knowingly prove unworthy of possessing the friendship of such an aggregation of men."

That was the platform and the declaration of principle of which our President took office one year ago tonight. By no stretch of the imagination can there be even an incipient thought of repudiation, but on the contrary, there has been a consistent performance of an honest purpose, and a sincere desire to conform to the wants of the collective membership.

Cultured and refined, sympathetic, cordial and kindly have been the dominating characteristics of the gentleman who tonight completes his term as President. All too swiftly has the time flown by, for tonight there comes the parting, and it is my province to say "Good-bye." Happy and contented have we been under the regime of President Forsberg. During the entire year there has been not one incident to mar the serenity of his official procedure. In recognition of the time honored custom of the organization, feasible evidence is tendered to the retiring chief of the regard and esteem in which he is held by those who compose the bone and sinue of the Railway Club of Pittsburgh. Acting for them and in their behalf, it is with unadultered personal pleasure that I tender to you, Mr. President, this beautiful case of silverware, embracing knives, forks, spoons, carvers, etc., and hope that it' may adorn the table at your domicile and be the occasion of perpetual joy to you and your good wife. The pattern is known as St. Dunstan who was the patron saint of the early jewelry-smiths of London. There is a legend that when the devil tempted the holy man, that he picked up a pair of hot tongs and pulled the nose of his satanic majesty. May I express the wish that your table may ever be ladened with plenty, and that the congenial and happy occupants of the family chairs may have an increasing appreciation as the years go by, for this St. Dunstan silver, which is the tie that cements your memory, with the events that have endeared the Club and each member individually to the cockles of your warm affectionate nature.

PRESIDENT: Next is the report of the Subject Committee, Mr. McGeorge.

(Mr. McGeorge came to the platform with an enormous scrap book, a City Directory, and several large rolls of manuscript. The President reminded Mr. McGeorge that he had requested the Chairmen to be brief in the submission of their reports, and Mr. McGeorge retorted that he desired to "examine the record").

REPORT OF SUBJECT COMMITTEE

MR. D. W. McGEORGE: "Mr. President and fellow members of The Railway Club of Pittsburgh:

"During the past year, your Subject Committee has digressed from the precedents established in former years in that they have provided some speakers whose subjects were broader than the particular railroad field in which we are interested. It is believed that the speaker on an economic subject and another speaker on the subject of the subways of New York were well received and it is our suggestion that the practice of having a few outsiders is a good one. Please allow us to remind you that while it is generally supposed that the attendance record depends to a large extent on the type of speakers, nevertheless a good attendance is a great help in securing good speakers. In other words, if you want your Subject Committee to provide you with good speakers, you should give them your help by attending the meetings.

"I wish to take this opportunity to thank the other members of our Committee for the hard work they have freely contributed during the past year. I thank you.

"D. W. McGEORGE, Chairman."

PRESIDENT: We will now listen to the report of the Advertising Committee, Mr. Foard.

REPORT OF ADVERTISING COMMITTEE

Report read by Secretary, as Mr. Foard was unable to attend the meeting.

Your Advertising Committee, during the past year, found that it was rather difficult to secure any new advertising and, of course, we did the next best thing—that was to hold the advertisements we had previously secured.

Total number of advertisers—October, 1935................. 34
Total number of advertisers—October, 1936................. 32
Total amount of advertising—October, 1935.............$1,040
Total amount of advertising—October, 1936.............$ 965

Yours very truly,

E. A. FOARD, Chairman,
KARL BERG,
H. E. PASMORE.

PRESIDENT: Next we will have the report of the Reception and Attendance Committee, Mr. Beltz.

REPORT OF RECEPTION AND ATTENDANCE COMMITTEE

Mr. President and Fellow Members of the Railway Club:

As Chairman of the Reception and Attendance Committee I do not have any flowery report to make. The attendance has been fairly good during the past year notwithstanding the fact that many of our members have been very busy, due to increased business, which interfered with their attending the meetings regularly.

The Reception Committee has endeavored to receive both members and guests in a most cordial way, and to see that they were properly taken care of.

I wish, at this time, to thank the members of the Committee who so ably assisted in this work, and assure them that their services are appreciated.

J. D. BELTZ, Chairman.

PRESIDENT: We will now have the report of the Entertainment Committee, Mr. Gillespie.

MR. J. PORTER GILLESPIE: The Entertainment Committee have no report to make at this time, for in a very few minutes they will be put on the spot. I would like, however, to take this opportunity to thank the other members of the Committee for their co-operation, and particularly Mr. and Mrs. Frank Weis for the splendid way in which they have led the singing.

PRESIDENT: The last report of the Committee Chairmen is that of the Membership Committee, Mr. Britt.

REPORT OF MEMBERSHIP COMMITTEE

Mr. President and Members of
The Railway Club of Pittsburgh:

On behalf of the Membership Committee I wish to make the following report for the year ending October 22, 1936:

During the past year we have offered 282 new members. We have lost 58 by resignation, suspension, death, and loss of address—leaving a net gain of 224. We started out the year with 1,157 members and we now have 1,381. Taking into consideration the Coldest Winter since Valley Forge, the Greatest Flood since Noah's time, and the fact that only eight meetings were held during the year, we feel that we have done a pretty good job.

I would like to take this opportunity, on behalf of the members of the Membership Committee, to thank Mr. William R. Gellatly, who was our Chairman the major portion of the year, for his interest and co-operation, which, to a large extent, made this report so favorable. We are sorry that it was necessary for him to relinquish the Chairmanship on account of sickness and hope that he gains a complete recovery as quickly as possible.

We have some members that are delinquent in the payment of their dues, due prior to October 22, 1936. We requested the Secretary in mailing out the ballots the first of October, to insert a statement indicating the amount of delinquent dues, and a letter inviting everyone to remain with us.

The response has been good up to this time, but we earnestly request all those delinquent to send in their dues as soon as possible.

The Membership Committee requests that each member read the sign on the table, "ONE GET ONE," and try to live up to it by bringing in at least one new member during the next fiscal year. We will then have a Railway Club twice as large as we now have.

The Secretary has tabulated the total membership as of October 22, 1936, including the members welcomed in tonight, and with your permission I would like to read it:

	Members
Pennsylvania Railroad	309
Pittsburgh & Lake Erie Railroad	221
Baltimore & Ohio Railroad Company	118
Pittsburgh & West Virginia Railway Company	29
Bessemer & Lake Erie Railroad Company	28
Union Railroad Company	29
Montour Railroad Company	20
Monongahela Railway Company	13
Donora Southern Railroad Company	7
Aliquippa & Southern Railroad Company	6
Monongahela Connecting Railroad Company	4
Alton & Southern Railroad Company	2
P. C. & Y. Ry Co.	2
Pittsburgh, Lisbon & Western Railroad Company	2
Pittsburgh & Shawmut Railroad Company	2
Allegheny & South Side Railway Company	1
Chicago Great Western Railway Company	1
Chicago & North Western Railway Company	1
Delaware & Hudson Railroad Company	1
Delaware, Lackawanna & Western Railroad Company	1
Detroit, Toledo & Ironton Railroad Company	1
Green Bay & Western Railroad	1
Great Northern Railway Company	1
Lake Terminal Railroad Company	1
Pittsburgh, Shawmut & Northern Railroad Company	1
Southern Pacific Lines	1
Union Pacific System	1
Unity Railways Company	1
Western Allegheny Railroad Company	1

Respectfully submitted,

THOMAS E. BRITT, Chairman.

PRESIDENT: The next order of business is the report of the Tellers of Election, and with your permission I will request our Secretary, Mr. Conway, to read that report.

SECRETARY: The Report of the Tellers is as follows:

PRESIDENT—E. A. Rauschart, Mechanical Supt., Montour Railroad Co., Coraopolis, Pa.

FIRST VICE PRESIDENT—G. M. Sixsmith, Superintendent, Pennsylvania Railroad, Pittsburgh, Pa.

SECOND VICE PRESIDENT—J. D. Beltz, Superintendent, B. & O. R. R. Co., Pittsburgh, Pa.

SECRETARY—J. D. Conway, The Railway Supply Manufacturers' Association, Pittsburgh, Pa.

TREASURER—E. J. Searles, Manager, Schaefer Equipment Company, Pittsburgh, Pa.

EXECUTIVE COMMITTEE

Frank J. Lanahan, (Chairman), President, Fort Pitt Malleable Iron Co., Pittsburgh, Pa.

A. Stucki, Engineer, A. Stucki Company, Pittsburgh, Pa.

D. F. Crawford, Consulting Engineer, Pittsburgh, Pa.

G. W. Wildin, Consulting Engineer, Westinghouse Air Brake Co., Pittsburgh, Pa.

W. S. McAbee, Vice Pres. and Gen. Supt., Union Railroad Co., East Pittsburgh, Pa.

E. W. Smith, Vice President, Pennsylvania Railroad, Pittsburgh, Pa.

Louis E. Endsley, Consulting Engineer, 516 East End Avenue, Pittsburgh, Pa.

F. I. Snyder, Vice Pres. and Gen. Mgr., B. & L. E. R. R. Co., Pittsburgh, Pa.

C. O. Dambach, General Manager, P. & W. Va. Ry. Co., Pittsburgh, Pa.

R. H. Flinn, General Superintendent, Pennsylvania Railroad, Pittsburgh, Pa.

R. P. Forsberg, Chief Engineer, P. & L. E. R. R. Co., Pittsburgh, Pa.

SUBJECT COMMITTEE*

M. R. Reed, (Chairman), Gen. Supt. Mo. Power, Pennsylvania Railroad, Pittsburgh, Pa.

G. H. Burnette, Asst. Chief Engineer, P. & L. E. R. R. Co., Pittsburgh, Pa.

D. W. McGeorge, Secretary, Edgewater Steel Company, Pittsburgh, Pa.

RECEPTION AND ATTENDANCE COMMITTEE*

J. W. Johnson, (Chairman), Superintendent, Railway Express Agency, Pittsburgh, Pa.

W. C. Burel, (Vice Chairman), Master Mechanic, Western Allegheny Railroad, Kaylor, Pa.

J. W. Boyd, Superintendent, Monongahela Railway Company, Brownsville, Pa.

Thomas E. Cannon, General Supt. Equipment, P. & W. Va. Ry. Co., Pittsburgh, Pa.

T. W. Carr, Supt. Rolling Stock, P. & L. E. R. R. Co., McKees Rocks, Pa.

D. C. Carroll, Asst. Agent, Pennsylvania Railroad, Pittsburgh, Pa.

S. G. Down, Vice President, Westinghouse Air Brake Co., Wilmerding, Pa.

Harry C. Graham, Pittsburgh Screw & Bolt Corporation, Pittsburgh, Pa.

J. W. Schad, Division Master Mechanic, B. & O. R. R. Co., Pittsburgh, Pa.

George S. West, Division Superintendent, Pennsylvania Railroad, Pittsburgh, Pa.

*In addition to the newly elected members, the complete committees are shown above, including those previously elected and whose terms of office have not yet expired.

J. W. Hoover, Asst. Chief of Transportation, Subsidiary Cos., U. S. Steel Corporation, Pittsburgh, Pa.

A. A. Read, Duquesne Slag Products Co., Pittsburgh, Pa.

C. P. Schrecongost, Traffic Manager, Hillman Coal & Coke Co., Pittsburgh, Pa.

J. A. Warfel, Special Representative, Air Reduction Sales Co., Pittsburgh, Pa.

J. C. Shingledecker, Supervisor Service Stations, The Pennzoil Co., Pittsburgh, Pa.

J. C. Dilworth, Manager Railroad Sales, Carnegie-Illinois Steel Corporation, Pittsburgh, Pa.

ENTERTAINMENT COMMITTEE*

J. Porter Gillespie, (Chairman), Asst. Gen. Supt., Lockhart Iron & Steel Co., Pittsburgh, Pa.

Frank E. Weis, (Vice Chairman), Transportation Clerk, Pennsylvania Railroad, Pittsburgh, Pa.

James Nagel, Supt. Transportation, Montour Railroad, Coraopolis, Pa.

E. H. Holmes, Sales Department, Fort Pitt Malleable Iron Co., Pittsburgh, Pa.

C. C. Clark, Sales Manager, Central District, Pressed Steel Car Co., Pittsburgh, Pa.

A. I. Kessler, Clearance Clerk, Pennsylvania Railroad, Pittsburgh, Pa.

T. F. Sheridan, Asst. to S. M. P. & S. R. S., P. & L. E. R. R. Co., McKees Rocks, Pa.

FINANCE COMMITTEE*

M. A. Smith, (Chairman), General Manager, P. & L. E. R. R. Co., Pittsburgh, Pa.

J. B. Diven, Supt. Motive Power, Pennsylvania Railroad, Pittsburgh, Pa.

F. J. Ryan, District Representative, Detroit, Toledo & Ironton R. R., Pittsburgh, Pa.

C. E. Catt, Division Accountant, B. & O. R. R. Co., Pittsburgh, Pa.

G. W. Honsberger, Transportation Manager, Westinghouse Electric and Manufacturing Company, Pittsburgh, Pa.

ADVERTISING COMMITTEE*

E. A. Foard, (Chairman), Supt. Stations and Transfers, Pennsylvania Railroad, Pittsburgh, Pa.

Karl Berg, Supt. Motive Power, P. & L. E. R. R. Co., McKees Rocks, Pa.

H. E. Passmore, Representative, The American Hammered Piston Ring Co., Pittsburgh, Pa.

MEMBERSHIP COMMITTEE*

T. E. Britt, (Chairman), Division Storekeeper, B. & O. R. R. Co., Glenwood Shops, Pittsburgh, Pa.

C. M. Wheeler, (Vice Chairman), Sales Engineer, Union Switch & Signal Co., Swissvale, Pa.

F. H. Eaton, Sales Engineer, American Car & Foundry Co., Pittsburgh, Pa.

C. W. Gottschalk, Asst. Traffic Manager, Jones & Laughlin Steel Corporation, Pittsburgh, Pa.

Lloyd Sutherland, General Storekeeper, P. & L. E. R. R. Co., McKees Rocks, Pa.

Thomas R. Fitzpatrick, Freight Traffic Manager, P. & L. E. R. R. Co., Pittsburgh, Pa.

P. W. Hepburn, Sales Engineer, Gulf Refining Co., Pittsburgh, Pa.

W. B. Moir, Chief Car Inspector, Pennsylvania Railroad, Pittsburgh, Pa.

C. W. Trust, Asst. Traffic Manager, Carnegie-Illinois Steel Corporation, Pittsburgh, Pa.

William R. Gellatly, President, Superior Railway Products Corporation, Pittsburgh, Pa.

R. S. Bull, Supt. Power and Inclines, Pittsburgh Railways Co., N. S., Pittsburgh, Pa.

A. F. Coulter, Master Car Builder, Union Railroad Co., East Pittsburgh, Pa.

T. R. Dickinson, Purchasing Agent, B. & L. E. R. R. Co., Pittsburgh, Pa.

D. K. Orr, Road Master, Monongahela Railway Co., Brownsville, Pa.

W. F. Ambrose, Master Mechanic, Aliquippa & Southern Railroad, Aliquippa, Pa.

John I. Mulvey, Traffic Manager, Hubbard & Co., Pittsburgh, Pa.

PRESIDENT: Gentlemen, I sincerely congratulate you upon the splendid line of capable Officers and Committeemen you have selected to guide the affairs of our Club during the coming year.

I am especially pleased to know that E. A. Rauschart is to act as the Commander-in-Chief, and "Ed." I predict for you a most successful administration. In looking over the list of Past Presidents of our Club I note it has been many years since we have had a representative from the Mechanical Department, and I am glad to see proper recognition given to that branch of the railroad organization. "Ed." in the presence of this large audience, I pledge to you my whole hearted support and if I can, at any time, be of service, you will find me 100 per cent responsive. I know the boys would like to have a word from you, and I am going to ask you to come to the platform and at least say, hello!

MR. E. A. RAUSCHART: Mr. President and fellow members of the Railway Club of Pittsburgh: I want to thank you one and all for the honor of being elected to the highest office of this Club, as President. I assure you that with your help during the coming year, we may have a much larger and better Railway Club. I trust that my wish will be fully realized. I thank you.

PRESIDENT: Thank you "Ed." We know that you mean every word you have said.

PRESIDENT: Our First Vice President-elect is another most happy selection. I am going to tell him before this audience, at this time, something I have never said to him before. You know the President from his chair on the platform has an opportunity of seeing about everything worth while that transpires in the audience during the conduct of the meeting, and I have sat here evening after evening and watched "Six" effectively taking care of this and that, and I have always felt more secure in my place when I realized I had that kind of support. "Six", I fancy the boys would like to have a word from you, and I will ask you to come to the platform and tell us some of the things you have on your mind.

MR. G. M. SIXSMITH: Mr. Old President, Mr. New President, members of the Railway Club of Pittsburgh and friends: Before starting on what I thought I would like to say on this occasion, I want to thank Mr. Forsberg for his kind expression as to my usefulness to this Club during the past year. I hope my boss, Rufus Flinn, is in the room at the moment and remembers the incident. (That interruption sounds like Mr. Nieman; is Charlie Nieman in the room?— no response).

I realize, tempered with proper dignity and the necessity for transacting some little business, this meeting tonight is primarily a fun-making affair, and I feel that any delay in getting to that part of the program will be just that much time lost. But, even at the risk of your getting a little bit bored, I would like to say just one thing and I say it in all sincerity—the Railway Club of Pittsburgh has been good to me. You have honored me with several offices in your organization, and I have been well repaid for any effort I may have made to further the interests of this club. You have now elected me First Vice-President, which I deeply appreciate, and it is not hard for me to promise that I will do everything I can to assist in making this a bigger and better club to belong to, because, after all, you cannot find a better club anywhere, and I pledge to the officers my full support, and particularly do I pledge to our New President, Mr. Rauschart, my best and every effort in making his reign as head of our club successful during the coming year.

PRESIDENT: Thank you "Six." I also place my full stamp of approval upon the selection you have made for your Second Vice President, and I am especially pleased to note that you have given deserved recognition to the Baltimore and Ohio Railroad Company. We have a large number of members from that Company, and in my opinion you have made a splendid selection in the election of Mr. J. D. Beltz. Mr. Beltz, may we have a word from you.

(Mr. Beltz stood in the audience and bowed his acknowledgment).

PRESIDENT: At the request of its Chairman, I have purposely placed the report of the Executive Committee at the last, and I will now request Mr. Frank J. Lanahan to submit his report which, as before stated, will conclude the reports of the evening, Mr. Lanahan.

MR. FRANK J. LANAHAN: Mr. President and Fellow Members: It is not at all strange in view of the recent sad happening in my little family, that I should be the one called upon to pay tribute to the memory of those of our membership who are no longer with us by reason of death. Two especially, among the names that have been read, were honored by this organization with the gift of the highest office within the Club's disposal, both having served as President. George Ogden and Sam Lynn will ever be revered as beloved friends. It was at the last meeting that note was made of the snuffing out of the candle where Past-President Lynn was concerned, and tonight it is the memory of George Ogden, who was the fifteenth president of this organization, that we commemorate. During this present month, the sixth of October, a goodly number of George's associates of the Club, journeyed to Homer City, a little country town in Indiana County, where in the silence of sorrowing friends, and midst beautiful rural surroundings of flowers, trees and shrubbery, he was laid away to rest. George Ogden was a genial, happy individual, one whose constant effort was to please his fellowmen. Those who knew him best loved him most; his memory will long be cherished by those who enjoyed his intimate acquaintance. Particularly appropriate is the little stanza of poetry of which George was fond:

"Not how did he die, but how did he live,
Not what did he gain, but what did he give?
These are the units to measure the worth
Of a man as a man, regardless of birth.

Not what was his station, but had he a heart
And how did he play his God-given part?
Was he ever ready with word of good cheer
To bring back the smile and banish the tear?

Not what was his Church, or what was his Creed
But was he ever ready to help those truly in need?
Not what did the piece in the paper say,
But how many were really sorry when he passed away?"

PRESIDENT: Mr. Lanahan and my co-laborers in The Railway Club of Pittsburgh, I am fully conscious, at this time, of my absolute inability to summon to my use words, that even in a small measure, would properly express my appreciation of all that your friendship, all that your fellowship have been to me in the years that have passed, that expression culminating at this hour in the presentation of this most handsome remembrance and the words of commendation of your spokesman, all of which I feel are far, far in excess of anything that I deserve.

Boys, this gift will be used and appreciated by my wife, myself, our children and our children's children to the third and fourth generations, and it will serve to keep ever alive the fact that at one time you honored me with the office of President of our Club.

I have really had a most pleasant year, the work having been made easy for me by the splendid response you always made to my every request, no band of men could have given more loyal support to anyone than you have accorded to me during the past twelve months.

Our organization primarily devotes its thoughts and its energies to the betterment and improvement of the steam railroads of this and other countries, but I feel sometimes that perchance it is doing a larger, a more comprehensive piece of work. In other words, I am sure that the acquantances we have made, the friendships we have formed, and the subjects we have discussed within the boundaries of our Club, have helped the older men to stabilize and the younger members to form those traits that make the kind of American citizens we very sorely need in our country today.

I say to you in all candor and sincerity that when I consider the thought and the conditions that obtain in so many parts of the world today, I say in all reverence, "Thank God for The Railway Club of Pittsburgh." It is no small, no inconsequential thing for 1,381 men to be banded together with a high purpose and a worthy aim before them.

I distinctly recall the excerpts Mr. Lanahan has just read from the minutes of our last annual meeting. I did say a year ago, "I have no axe to grind, no fish to fry, no pet scheme to advance. I have no interest in the work of our Club higher than an honest purpose and a sincere desire to serve you as your President, as you want your President to serve you." Tonight I lay down that responsibility, saying that I have made an honest, though, in some respects, a futile effort to fulfill that pledge.

Again, from the very bottom of my heart, I thank you for this handsome remembrance| Good night, and may God bless you one and all. The program of the evening will now be turned over Mr. Porter Gillespie, Chairman of the Entertainment Committee. After the entertainment we will repair to the Gold Room where luncheon will be served.

In keeping with the usual high standard of entertainment always provided by the Entertainment Committee, J. Porter Gillespie, Chairman, announced that this was to be Amateur Night at the Railway Club and introduced Frank Weis who acted as "Major Bowes" for the evening.

With Jerry Mayhall at the piano the contest opened with Bertha Mae Stockhausen, blues singer, who immediately captivated the audience with her charming personality. Elmer Bianco, age 12 years, next gave a remarkable performance as a banjoist and was followed by Robert and Virginia Moore, colored dancing team who brought down the house with a clever routine and intricate individual steps. John Larkin, imitator, gave delightful imitations of Boake Carter, Al Smith and Walter Winchell and included a number of local news flashes concerning club members which made a great hit with the boys. Louis Ross, bell hop from the William Penn Hotel, gave a fine account of himself as a tenor after which Jeanne Langer, Carnegie schoolgirl, did a tap dance on roller skates which brought forth a wave of applause sufficient to award her the second prize money.

The "Major" next brought to the microphone Milo Milanovitch, long and lanky, who got the bell but continued with his comedy song as if nothing had happened. Pretty Frances Nessler, whose telephone number was carefully noted by "The Major" for the records of the Chairman of the Entertainment Committee (?), gave her interpretation of "Some of These Days." Then came the Three Buddies, instrumentalists, followed by Harlem Leon, colored dancer of the Bill Robinson type. Next the first prize winners were the four Ragamuffins, school boy hill billies from Braddock who stole the show beyond any question of doubt with their fast clever comedy and versatility. They were called back for a number of encores and truly deserved the winners spoils. Last but not least, but only after a number of unsuccessful attempts to locate him, Peter Goode, colored baritone, was induced to sing "Shine" as only Peter Goode can sing it.

The judges, being unable to determine the winner of the third prize requested Robert and Virginia Moore, dancing team, and Harlem Leon, tap dancer, to again compete but still finding it impossible to determine which of the acts got the most applause, decided to give each a prize much to the satisfaction of the audience as well as the contestants.

J. D. CONWAY, Secretary.

CONSTITUTION

ARTICLE I

The name of this organization shall be "THE RAILWAY CLUB OF PITTSBURGH."

ARTICLE II

OBJECTS

The objects of this Club shall be mutual intercourse for the acquirement of knowledge by reports and discussion, for the improvement of railway operation, construction, maintenance and equipment, and to bring into closer relationship men employed in railway work and kindred interests.

ARTICLE III

MEMBERSHIP

SECTION 1. The membership of this Club shall consist of persons interested in any department of railway service or kindred interests, or persons recommended by the Executive Committee upon the payment of the annual dues for the current year.

SEC. 2. Persons recommended by the Executive Committee and by unanimous vote of all members present at any regular meeting of the Club may be made an Honorary Member and shall be entitled to all the privileges of membership and not be subject to the payment of dues or assessments.

ARTICLE IV

OFFICERS

The officers of this Club shall consist of a President, First Vice President, Second Vice President, Secretary, Treasurer and an Executive Committee of seven or more members, elected at the Annual Meeting of the Club, for a term of one year. There shall be a Finance Committee of five or more members; a Membership Committee of twelve or more members; an Entertainment Committee of seven or more members; a Reception and Attendance Committee of twelve or more members; a Subject Committee of three or more members; and an Advertising Committee of three or more members; all elected at the Annual Meeting, the term of office to be specified, but in no case to exceed three years. Chairmen and Vice Chairmen of these committees where not named on the ballot will be elected from among the elected members by the Executive Committee.

ARTICLE V

DUTIES OF OFFICERS

SECTION 1. The President shall preside at all regular or special meetings of the Club and perform all duties pertaining to a presiding officer; also serve as a member of the Executive Committee.

SEC. 2. The First Vice President, in the absence of the President, will perform all the duties of that officer; the Second Vice President, in the absence of the President and First Vice President, will perform the duties of the presiding officer. The First and Second Vice Presidents shall also serve as members of the Executive Committee.

SEC. 3. The Executive Committee will exercise a general supervision over the affairs of the Club and authorize all expenditures of its funds.

SEC. 4. The Secretary will attend all meetings of the Club or Executive Committee, keep full minutes of their proceedings; preserve the records and documents of the Club, accept and turn over all moneys received to the Treasurer at least once a month, draw cheques for all bills, when approved by a majority of the Executive Committee present at any meeting of the Club or Executive Committee meeting. He shall have charge of the publication of the Club Proceedings and perform other routine work pertaining to the business affairs of the Club under direction of the Executive Committee.

SEC. 5. The Treasurer shall receipt for all moneys received from the Secretary, and deposit the same in the name of the Club within thirty days in a bank approved by the Executive Committee. All disbursements of the funds of the Club shall be by check signed by the Secretary and Treasurer.

SEC. 6. The Subject Committee will arrange programs and select speakers for the regular meetings of the Club and perform such other duties as may be assigned them by the President or First and Second Vice Presidents, working in conjunction with the Entertainment Committee as may be required. The Chairman of the Subject Committee will serve as an advisory member of the Executive Committee.

SEC. 7. The Membership Committee will actively engage in building up and maintaining the list of active members of the Club and perform such other duties as may be assigned them by the President or First and Second Vice Presidents. The Chairman of this Committee will serve as an advisory member of the Executive Committee.

SEC. 8. The Advertising Committee will solicit advertisements for the Official Proceedings and perform such other duties as may be assigned them by the President or First and Second Vice Presidents. The Chairman of this Committee will serve as an advisory member of the Executive Committee.

SEC. 9. The Reception and Attendance Committee will receive members, guests and visitors at the meetings and generally assist in promoting social intercourse and good fellowship, securing attendance of the members, and performing such other duties as may be assigned them by the President or First and Second Vice Presidents. The Chairman of this Committee will serve as an advisory member of the Executive Committee.

SEC. 10. The Entertainment Committee will perform such duties as may be assigned them by the President or First and Second Vice Presidents, and such other duties as may be proper for such a committee.

SEC. 11. The Finance Committee will perform the duties of an auditing committee to audit the accounts of the Club at the close of a term or at any time necessary to do so and perform such other duties as may be assigned them by the President or First and Second Vice Presidents.

ARTICLE VI

ELECTION OF OFFICERS

SECTION 1. The officers shall be elected at the regular annual meeting as follows, except as otherwise provided for:

SEC. 2. The President will appoint a Nominating Committee of five members, three of whom must be regularly elected members of the Executive Committee, who shall at the September meeting recommend nominations for all offices to be filled at the annual meeting and these, together with any other nominations which may be made from the floor under proper procedure, will be printed and mailed as a letter-ballot to all of the members of the Club, not less than twenty days previous to the Annual Meeting, by the elective members of the Executive Committee. Each member may express his choice for the several offices to be filled by properly marking the letter-ballot and returning it to the Chairman of the Executive Committee.

SEC. 3. The elective members of the Executive Committee will present to the President the names of the members receiving the highest number of votes for each office, together with the number of votes received.

SEC. 4. The President will announce the result of the ballot and declare the election.

SEC. 5. Should two or more members receive the same number of votes, it shall be decided by a vote of the members present, by ballot.

ARTICLE VII

AMENDMENTS

Amendments may be made to this Constitution by written request of ten members, presented at a regular meeting and decided by a two-thirds vote of the members present at the next regular meeting.

BY-LAWS

ARTICLE I

MEETINGS

SECTION 1. The regular meetings of the Club shall be held at Pittsburgh, Pa., on the fourth Thursday of each month, except June, July and August, at 8 o'clock P. M.

SEC. 2. The annual meeting shall be held on the fourth Thursday of October each year.

SEC. 3. The President may, at such times as he deems expedient, or upon request of a quorum, call special meetings.

ARTICLE II

QUORUM

At any regular or special meeting twenty-five members shall constitute a quorum.

ARTICLE III

DUES

SECTION 1. The annual dues of members shall be Two Dollars, payable in advance on or before the fourth Thursday of September each year. .

SEC. 2. The annual subscription to the printed Proceedings of the Club shall be at the published price of One Dollar. Each member of the Club shall pay for both dues and subscription. Dues and subscription paid by members proposed at the meetings in September or October shall be credited for the following fiscal year.

SEC. 3. At the annual meeting members whose dues and subscription are unpaid shall be dropped from the roll after due notice mailed them at least thirty days previous.

SEC. 4. Members suspended for non-payment of dues shall not be reinstated until all arrearages have been paid.

ARTICLE IV

1. Roll call.
2. Reading of the minutes of preceding meeting.
3. Reception of new members.
4. Announcements and communications.
5. Appointment of committees.
6. Reports of officers or committees.
7. Unfinished business.
8. New business.
9. Election of officers.
10. Presentation of program and discussion.
11. Adjournment.

ARTICLE V

PUBLICATIONS

SECTION 1. The Proceedings or such portion as the Executive Committee may approve shall be published (standard size, 6x9 inches) and mailed to the members of the Club or other similar clubs with which exchange is made.

ARTICLE VI

The stenographic report of the meetings will be confined to resolutions, motions and discussions of papers unless otherwise directed by the presiding officer.

ARTICLE VII

AMENDMENTS

These By-Laws may be amended by written request of ten members, presented at a regular meeting, and a two-thirds vote of the members present at the next meeting.

In Memoriam

GEORGE D. OGDEN,

Joined Club October 27, 1921

Died October 4, 1936.

MEMBERS

Adams, Charles E.,
Superintendent,
Pennsylvania Railroad,
Pennsylvania Station,
Pittsburgh, Pa.

Adams, Frank W.,
Local Storekeeper,
B. & O. R. R.,
486 Ashby St.,
Hays, Pittsburgh, Pa.

Adams, Walter A.,
Clerk,
P. & L. E. R. R.,
230 Ohio Ave.,
Glassport, Pa.

Adrian, J. H.,
Clerk,
Pennsylvania Railroad,
1931 Noblestown Road,
Pittsburgh, Pa.

Ainsworth, John R.,
Special Apprentice,
Westinghouse Air Brake Co.,
353 Marguerite Ave.,
Wilmerding, Pa.

Aivalotis, John,
Assistant Car Foreman,
B. & O. R. R. Co.,
Midway, Pa.

Allderdice, Norman,
Sales Representative,
General American Transp.
Corp.,
P. O. Box 46,
Sewickley, Pa.

Allen, Earl M.,
Engineer (Signal),
Union Switch & Signal Co.,
1318 Lancaster Ave.,
Pittsburgh (18), Pa.

Allen, Harvey,
Mechanical Engineer,
347 Columbia Ave.,
West View,
Pittsburgh, Pa.

Allison, John,
Sales Engineer,
Pgh. Steel Foundry Corp.,
Glassport, Pa.

Ambrose, W. F.,
M. M., Aliquippa & So. R. R.,
1301 Meadow St.,
Aliquippa, Pa.

Ament, F. Chalmer,
Train Service Inspector,
Pgh. Div., Penna. R. R.,
6932 Standish St.,
Pittsburgh (6) Pa.

Anderegg, G. W.,
Electrician,
P. & L. E. R. R. Co.,
814 Freeland St.,
Pittsburgh, Pa.

Anderson, Burt T.,
Asst. to President,
Union Switch & Signal Co.,
Swissvale, Pa.

Anderson, G. S.,
Foreman,
Pennsylvania System,
Box 19, Penna. Station,
Pittsburgh, Pa.

Anderson, H. N.,
Division Engineer,
B. & O. R. R.,
2 Victory Blvd.,
Tompkinsville, S. I., N. Y.

Anderson, J. G.,
Inspector Bridges & Buildings
Pennsylvania Railroad,
623 Market Street,
Freeport, Pa.

Anderson, M. M.,
Personnel Manager,
Aluminum Co. of America,
Gulf Building,
Pittsburgh, Pa.

Anne, George E.,
Representative,
American Brake Shoe &
Foundry Co.,
R. D. 2,
Hollidaysburg, Pa.

Arensberg, F. L.,
President,
Vesuvius Crucible Co.,
Box 29,
Swissvale, Pa.

Armstrong, C. B.,
Railway Sales Manager,
Central Division,
Air Reduction Sales Co.,
332 South Michigan Ave.,
Chicago, Ill.

Armstrong, Joseph G., Jr.,
Asst. to Manager of Sales,
Carnegie Steel Company,
Carnegie Building,
Pittsburgh, Pa

Armstrong, J. L.,
Foreman P. P. & Elec.,
Pennsylvania Railroad,
2 Grandview Avenue,
Crafton, Pittsburgh, Pa.

Arnold, C. C.,
Water Service Inspector,
P. & L. E. R. R. Co.,
Room 506 Terminal Bldg.,
Pittsburgh, Pa.

Arnold, J. J.,
Sales Dept.,
Pressed Steel Car Co.,
McKees Rocks, Pa.

Ashley, F. B.,
Vice President,
Pruett Schaffer Chemical Co.,
Tabor St.,
Corliss Station,
Pittsburgh, Pa.

Ater, Byron F.,
Assistant Secretary,
Y. M. C. A.,
P. & L. E. R. R. Co.,
Newell, Pa.

Atkins, T. Earl,
Branch Manager,
The Pennzoil Company,
Chamber of Commerce
Building,
Pittsburgh, Pa.

Aulbach, A. J.,
Yardmaster, P. & L. E. R. R.,
318 Quincy Ave.,
Mt. Oliver Station,
Pittsburgh, Pa.

Babcock, F. H.,
Safety Agent,
P. & L. E. R. R.,
221 Magnolia Ave.,
Mt. Lebanon,
Pittsburgh, Pa.

Bacon, J. L.,
Manager of Sales,
Valve Pilot Corporation,
230 Park Avenue,
New York, N. Y.

Baer, Harry L.,
Pres., Water Treatment Co.
of America,
1536 Madison Ave.,
N. S., Pittsburgh, Pa.

Bailey, F. G.,
Mech. Engr., Truck Dept.,
Standard Steel Car Corp'n.,
P. O. Box 839,
Butler, Pa.

Bailey, J. C.,
Car Service Agent,
B. & L. E. R. R.,
350 Main St.,
Greenville, Pa.

Baily, J. H.,
Vice President,
Edgewater Steel Co.,
P. O. Box 478,
Pittsburgh, Pa

Bain, Clarence R.,
Triple Valve Repairer,
P. & L. E. R. R. Co.,
532 Russellwood Ave.,
McKees Rocks, Pa.

Bair, J. K.,
Locomotive Engineer,
Union Railroad,
415 Osborne St.,
Turtle Creek, Pa

Baker, Dale,
Car Foreman,
B. & O. R. R. Co.,
443 Second St.
Pitcairn, Pa.

Baker, George N.,
Chief Clerk to V. P. & G. M.,
B. & L. E. R. R.,
P. O. Box 456,
Pittsburgh, Pa.

Baker, J. B.,
Chief Engr., M. of W.,
Pennsylvania Railroad,
Pennsylvania Station,
Pittsburgh, Pa.

Baker, W. E.,
Supervisor,
Pennsylvania Railroad,
51 McMunn Avenue,
Crafton, Pittsburgh, Pa.

Bakewell, Donald C.,
Vice President,
Continental Roll & Steel
Foundry Co.,
Grant Bldg.,
Pittsburgh, Pa.

Balbaugh, John G.,
Sales Engineer,
Pittsburgh Valve Foundry &
Construction Co.,
26th St. & A. V. Ry.,
Pittsburgh, Pa.

Ball, Fred M.,
District Manager,
Franklin Ry. Sup. Co., Inc.,
Broad St. Station Bldg.,
Philadelphia, Pa.

Ball, George L.,
Secretary and Treasurer,
Ball Chemical Co.,
230 S. Fairmont Ave.,
Pittsburgh, Pa.

Balla, J. A.,
Asst. Supervisor T. & S.,
Pennsylvania Railroad,
Pittsburgh, Pa.

Balph, M. Z.,
Assistant Engineer,
P. & L. E. R. R.,
3308 Sixth Ave.,
Beaver Falls, Pa.

Balsley, J. I.,
Asst. General Foreman,
B. & O. R. R. Co.,
406 Zara Street,
Knoxville,
Pittsburgh, Pa.

Balzer, C. E.,
Inspector of Tests,
P. & L. E. R. R.,
3432 Allendale St.,
Pittsburgh, Pa.

Bancroft, A. G.,
Vice President,
Union Metal Products Co.,
310 Michigan Ave.,
Chicago, Ill.

Bandi, John E.,
Bill Clerk, P. C. & Y. R. R.,
1115 Criss St.,
Pittsburgh, Pa.

Barclay, J. R.,
Cost Engineer,
P. & L. E. R. R.,
4 Oakwood Road,
Crafton, Pittsburgh, Pa.

Barkley, Sherwood W.
Triple Valve A.B. Tester,
P. & L. E. R. R. Co.,
Box 126, R. D. No. 1,
McKees Rocks, Pa.

Barnett, George,
Salesman,
W. W. Lawrence & Co.,
West Carson St.,
Pittsburgh, Pa.

Barney, Harry,
President-Treasurer,
Barney Machinery Co., Inc.,
2410 Koppers Bldg.,
Pittsburgh, Pa.

Barnhart, B. F.,
Road Foreman of Engines,
B. & L. E. R. R.,
9 Shady Ave.,
Greenville, Pa.

Barr, H. C.,
Agent, P. & L. E. R. R.,
131 Sycamore St.,
Pittsburgh (11), Pa.

Barr, S. T.,
Air Brake Instructor,
Pennsylvania Railroad,
Pennsylvania Station,
Pittsburgh, Pa.

Barth, E. H.,
Triple Valve Repairer,
P. & L. E. R. R. Co.,
1119 Faust Street,
Pittsburgh (4), Pa.

Barton, E. E.,
Asst. Local Treasurer,
P. & L. E. R. R. Co.,
1718 Ridge Avenue,
Coraopolis, Pa

235

Bash, J. E.,
District Inspector,
R. R. Perishable Inspection
Agency,
P.R.R. Produce Terminal,
Pittsburgh, Pa.

Batchelar, E. C.,
Manager, The Motch &
Merryweather Mach'y Co.,
1315 Clark Bldg.,
Pittsburgh, Pa.

Batson, J. F.,
Asst. Master Mechanic,
Pennsylvania Railroad,
Pitcairn, Pa.

Bauer, F. C.,
Assistant Agent,
Railway Express Agency,
480 Antenor Ave.,
Overbrook,
Pittsburgh, Pa.

Bauer, R. B.,
General Yard Master,
P. & L. E. R. R. Co.,
Dickerson Run, Pa.

Baughman, G. W.,
100 West Hutchinson St.,
Edgewood,
Pittsburgh, Pa.

Baumann, Edward G.,
Supervisor Tel. & Signals,
Pennsylvania Railroad,
East Waldheim Road,
Aspinwall, Pa

Beall, C. R.,
Asst. Chief Engineer,
Union Switch & Signal Co.,
Braddock Avenue,
Swissvale, Pa.

Beam, E. J.,
Car Builder, Penna. System,
577 Fourth St.,
Pitcairn, Pa.

Beattie, J. A.,
1090 Shady Ave.,
Pittsburgh, Pa.

Beatty, Raymond N.,
Conductor,
Pennsylvania Railroad,
1207 Allegheny Ave.,
N. S. Pittsburgh, Pa.

Beaver, J. D.,
General Supt.,
P. S. & N. R. R.,
St. Marys, Pa.

Beaver, R. C.,
Asst. Mechanical Engineer,
B. & L. E. R. R.,
122 West Main St.,
Greenville, Pa.

Beeson, H. L.,
Engine House Foreman,
Monongahela Ry. Co.,
202 Riverview Terrace,
West Brownsville, Pa.

Beitsch, George F.,
Gang Foreman,
Pennsylvania Railroad,
1110 Allegheny Street,
New Brighton, Pa.

Bell, D. H.,
Engineer of Car Design,
Pittsburgh Railways Co.,
435 Sixth Ave.,
Pittsburgh, Pa.

Bell, R. A.,
Clerk,
P. & L. E. R. R. Co.,
325 Mathews Ave.,
Carrick, Pittsburgh, Pa.

Bell, W. T.,
Inspector Train Service,
Pennsylvania Railroad,
Pennsylvania Station,
Pittsburgh, Pa.

Beltz, J. D.,
Superintendent,
B. & O. R. R.,
2915 Belrose Ave.,
South Hills,
Pittsburgh, Pa.

Bender, H. P.,
Mechanical Engineer,
P. & L. E. R. R. Co.,
921 Fordham Ave.,
Pittsburgh, Pa.

Berg, Karl,
Supt. Motive Power,
P. & L. E. R. R.,
6319 Morrowfield Ave.,
Pittsburgh, Pa.

Berghane, A. L.,
  Mechanical Expert,
    Westinghouse Air Brake Co.,
      Wilmerding, Pa

Bergman, Carl R.,
  Supervisor—Track,
    Pennsylvania Railroad,
      222 Emerson Ave.,
        Aspinwall, Pa.

Bessolo, A. J.,
  Asst. Gen. Traf. Mgr.,
    Gulf Refining Co.,
      Gulf Building,
        Pittsburgh, Pa.

Best, C. Thomas,
  President,
    American Shim Steel Co.,
      1304 Fifth Ave.,
        New Kensington, Pa.

Best, D. A.,
  Test Engineer,
    Westinghouse Air Brake Co.,
      Wilmerding, Pa.

Best, Rankin M.,
  Clerk,
    P. & L. E. R. R. Co.,
      Monaca, Pa.

Beswick, Richard M.,
  Tester,
    Westinghouse Air Brake Co.,
      514 Chicora Street,
        East McKeesport, Pa.

Bickett, M. A.,
  Freight Agent,
    P. & L. E. R. R. Co.,
      303 Boyles Ave.,
        New Castle, Pa.

Bier, C. D.,
  Salesman,
    Garlock Packing Co.,
      Maloney Building,
        Boulevard of Allies,
          Pittsburgh, Pa.

Biggerstaff, James M.,
  Electrical Foreman,
    P. & L. E. R. R. Co.,
      P. O. Box 48,
        Wireton, Pa.

Bingham, W. C.,
  Proprietor,
    Bingham Metal Co.,
      Law & Finance Bldg.,
        Pittsburgh, Pa.

Binyon, Thomas E.,
  Telegraph & Telephone Engr.,
    Pennsylvania Railroad,
      Pennsylvania Station,
        Pittsburgh, Pa.

Bishop, H. G.,
  Asst. Road Fore. of Engines,
    Pennsylvania Railroad,
      422 North Highland Ave.,
        Pittsburgh, Pa.

Bishop, M. L.,
  A. R. A. Clerk,
    P. & W. Va. Ry. Co.,
      126 Sanford St.,
        20th Ward,
          Pittsburgh, Pa.

Bisi, Charles W.,
  Asst. Road Fore. of Engines,
    Pennsylvania Railroad,
      615 Calvin Avenue,
        Buffalo, N. Y.

Bittner, George,
  Asst. Engine House Foreman,
    Pennsylvania Railroad,
      Twenty-eighth St.,
        Pittsburgh, Pa.

Blackmore, G. A.,
  President,
    Union Switch & Signal Co.,
      Swissvale, Pa.

Blair, John R.,
  Asst. Mgr. of Sales,
    Pittsburgh Steel Co.,
      P. O. Box 118,
        Pittsburgh, Pa.

Blest, Minot C.,
  Chief Engineer,
    Pressed Steel Car Co.,
      McKees Rocks, Pa.

Boden, A. S.,
  Traffic Manager,
    Coal Control Assn.,
      Western Pennsylvania,
        Oliver Bldg.,
          Pittsburgh, Pa.

Boggs, L. S.,
  825 N. Negley Ave.,
    Pittsburgh, Pa.

Bone, H. L.,
  General Mechanical Engr.,
    Union Switch & Signal Co.,
      Swissvale, Pa

237

Bonhoff, E. L.,
Engine House Foreman,
Pennsylvania Railroad,
718 Blackburn Road,
                    Sewickley, Pa.

Booth, W. F.,
Asst. Superintendent,
B. & O. R. R. Co.,
B. & O. Station,
                    Pittsburgh, Pa.

Borg, John Edw.,
Chief Draftsman,
Julian Kennedy,
232 Martsolf Ave.,
                    West View, Pa.

Bosley, Norman D.,
Gang Leader,
P. & L. E. R. R. Co.,
R. D. — Poplar Street,
                    McKees Rocks, Pa.

Bottomly, E. S.,
Chief Joint Inspector,
P. R. R., B. & O.,
Rdg. and W. M.,
P. O. Box 646,
                    Martinsburg, W. Va.

Bowden, Foster S.,
Supervisor—Track,
Pennsylvania Railroad,
136 Como Ave.,
                    Buffalo, N. Y.

Bowden, T. C.,
Coal Inspector,
B. & L. E. R. R.,
97 S. Mercer St.,
                    Greenville, Pa.

Bowen, C. R.,
Pennsylvania Railroad,
3265 Raleigh Ave.,
Dormont,
                    Pittsburgh, Pa.

Bowery, Frank J.,
Chief Estimator, F. C. D.,
P. S. C. Co.,
214 Birmingham Ave.,
                    Avalon, Pa.

Boyd, John,
Clerk,
J. T. & A. Hamilton Co.,
1432 Arnold St.,
                    Pittsburgh (20), Pa.

Boyd, John R.,
Designing Engineer,
P. & L. E. R. R. Co.,
P&LE Terminal Bldg.,
                    Pittsburgh, Pa.

Boyd, J. W.,
Superintendent,
Monongahela Railway Co.,
                    Brownsville, Pa.

Boyd, Samuel S.,
Asst. Supervisor,
Union Railroad Co.,
551 Fourth Street,
                    Pitcairn, Pa.

Boyland, William E.,
Train Master,
B. & O. R. R. Co.,
109 Green Street,
                    Connellsville, Pa.

Bradley, Howard J.,
Field Engineer,
Monongahela Railway Co.,
556 Pearl Street,
                    Brownsville, Pa.

Bradley, J. P.,
General Agent,
Railway Express Agency,
Inc.,
926 Penn Avenue,
                    Pittsburgh, Pa.

Bradley, W. C.,
C. C. to Gen'l. Supt.,
Union R. R.,
260 Cascade Road,
                    Wilkinsburg, Pa.

Brady, T. Jos.,
President,
Powell Coal Co.,
303 Kearsage St.,
Mt. Washington Sta.,
                    Pittsburgh, Pa.

Brandt, George F.,
Triple Valve Repairer,
P. & L. E. R. R. Co.,
925 Woodward Ave.,
                    McKees Rocks, Pa.

Brant, Wm. J.,
709 East Ohio St.,
                    N. S., Pittsburgh, Pa.

238

Braun, Otto F.,
Gen. Mach. Shop Foreman,
P. & L. E. R. R.,
R. D. 1—Herbst Road,
Coraopolis, Pa.

Brennan, John T.,
Assistant Vice President,
Greenville Steel Car Co.,
Greenville, Pa.

Brewer, H. W.,
Supt. of Shops,
B. & O. R. R. Co.,
Du Bois, Pa.

Brice, A. E.,
Special Representative,
Gulf Refining Co.,
Gulf Building,
Pittsburgh, Pa.

Bricker, O. F.,
Mgr., Transp'n. Advertising,
Westinghouse Electric &
Mfg. Co.,
East Pittsburgh, Pa.

Britt, T. E.,
Division Storekeeper,
B. & O. R. R.,
2818 Clermont Ave.,
Pittsburgh, (10), Pa.

Brown, C. C.,
Rep., Dearborn Chemical Co.,
Farmers Bank Bldg.,
Pittsburgh, Pa.

Brown, C. E.,
Yard Master,
Pennsylvania Railroad,
245 Clifton Ave.,
Mingo Junction, Ohio

Brown, Earl F.,
Electrical Supervisor,
P. & L. E. R. R. Co.,
Terminal Station,
Pittsburgh, Pa.

Brown, F. M.,
Supt., P. & L. E. R. R.,
Pittsburgh, Pa.

Brown, J. Alexander,
424 W. 33rd St.,
Eleventh Floor,
New York, N. Y.

Brown, John T., Jr.,
Supt., Federated Metal Corp.,
6667 Woodwell St.,
Pittsburgh, Pa.

Browne, Bard,
Asst. to Vice President,
The Superheater Co.,
60 East 42nd St.,
New York, N. Y.

Bruce, S. S.,
General Traffic Manager,
The Koppers Co.,
Koppers Bldg.,
Pittsburgh, Pa.

Brunnings, George H.,
District Manager,
American-Hawaiian
Steamship Co.,
Gulf Building,
Pittsburgh, Pa.

Bryant, Jess H.,
Station Agent,
Pennsylvania Railroad,
Vandergrift, Pa.

Buchanan, Charles C.,
Engineer,
Union Switch & Signal Co.,
Swissvale, Pa.

Bucher, Fred J.,
Electrical Engineer,
Hillman Coal & Coke Co.,
First National Bank
Bldg.,
Pittsburgh, Pa.

Buck, E. R.,
Asst. Master Mechanic,
Pennsylvania Railroad,
1214 25th Avenue,
Altoona, Pa.

Buck, L. L.,
Engineer,
Union Switch & Signal Co.,
441 Olymuia Road,
Mt. Washington,
Pittsburgh, Pa.

Buckbee, W. A.,
The Superheater Co.,
Nyack, N. Y.

Buckwalter, T. V.,
Vice President,
Timken Roller Bearing Co.,
Canton, Ohio.

Buell, D. C.,
Director, The Railway Educational Bureau,
1809 Capitol Ave.,
Omaha, Neb

Buffington, W. P.,
Traffic Manager,
Pittsburgh Coal Co.,
P. O Box 146,
Pittsburgh, Pa

Buhrmester, H. C.,
Chief Clerk, Eastern Div.,
Pennsylvania Railroad,
3418 Clearfield St.,
Pittsburgh, Pa.

Bull, R. S.,
Supt. Power & Inclines,
Pittsburgh Railways Co.,
600 Sandusky St.,
N. S., Pittsburgh, Pa.

Burchell, R. W.,
Wreck Master,
B. & O. R. R. Co.,
232 Glencaladh Street
Hazelwood, Pittsburgh, Pa.

Burel, W. C.,
Master Mechanic,
Western Allegheny R. R.,
Kaylor, Pa

Burk, G. C.,
Engine House Foreman,
Pennsylvania Railroad,
Blairsville, Pa.

Burkhart, A. E.,
Foreman, Car Department,
Pennsylvania Railroad,
260 Woodlawn Road,
Steubenville, Ohio

Burkhart, G. A.,
Engine House Foreman,
Monongahela Railway Co.,
P. O. Box 97,
Hiller, Pa.

Burnett, C. E.,
Engineer,
Anchor Sanitary Co.,
213 Water Street,
Pittsburgh, Pa.

Burnette, G. H.,
Asst. Chief Engineer,
P. & L. E. R. R.,
Terminal Building,
Pittsburgh, Pa.

Burriss, W. C.,
Inspector,
Westinghouse Air Brake Co.,
Wilmerding, Pa.

Butcher, F. M.,
Captain of Police,
Pennsylvania Railroad,
Pennsylvania Station,
Pittsburgh, Pa

Buzzerd, J. P.,
Signal Supervisor,
B. & O. R. R. Co.,
318 Rochelle Street,
Pittsburgh (10), Pa

Byers, Thomas,
General Agent,
Delaware & Hudson R. R.,
Koppers Bldg.,
Pittsburgh, Pa.

Byrne, William L.,
W. L. Byrne Co.,
4 Smithfield St.,
Pittsburgh, Pa

Byron, Robert J.,
Asst. Foreman,
Pennsylvania Railroad,
4050 Cambronne St.,
Pittsburgh, Pa.

Cable, H. E.,
District Engineer,
National Aluminate Corp.,
150 South Euclid Ave.,
Bellevue, Pittsburgh, Pa.

Cadwallader, W. H.,
Vice Pres. & Gen. Mgr.,
Union Switch & Signal Co.,
Swissvale, Pa.

Cage, Charles A.,
Gen. Fore., Mech. Dept.,
B. & O. R. R. Co.,
213 Kimberly Avenue,
Somerset, Pa.

Callahan, D. E.,
Asst. Div. Engineer,
Pennsylvania Railroad,
210 Grant Ave.,
Bellevue, Pa.

Callahan, F. J.,
Gang Leader,
Montour Railroad,
1109 Chartiers Ave.,
McKees Rocks, Pa.

Callahan, Lawrence H.,
Yardmaster, P. & L. E. R. R.,
600 Monongahela Ave.,
McKeesport, Pa.

Campbell, Edward D.,
Traffic Manager,
B. & L. E. R. R.,
P. O. Box 536,
Pittsburgh, Pa.

Campbell, F. R.,
Shop Foreman,
Donora Southern Railroad
Co.,
664 Thompson Ave.,
Donora, Pa.

Campbell, J. Allen,
Special Apprentice,
Westinghouse Air Brake Co.,
353 Marguerite Ave.,
Wilmerding, Pa.

Campbell, W. T.,
Secretary & Treasurer,
Montour Railroad,
Oliver Building,
Pittsburgh, Pa.

Cannon, T. E.,
Gen. Supt. Equipment,
P. & W. Va. Ry.,
Wabash Bldg.,
Pittsburgh, Pa.

Capps, W. P.,
Stoker Supervisor,
B. & O. R. R. Co.,
c/o Mechanical Engin'r.,
Mt. Clare Shops,
Baltimore, Md.

Cardwell, J. R.,
President,
Cardwell Westinghouse Co.,
332 S. Michigan Ave.,
Chicago, Ill.

Carey, Charles D.,
Railway Sales,
Gulf Refining Company,
Gulf Bldg.,
Pittsburgh, Pa.

Carlson, H. E.,
Engineer Computer,
P. & L. E. R. R.,
700 Eighteenth Ave.,
Beaver Falls, Pa.

Carlson, Lawrence E.,
Westinghouse Air Brake Co.,
904 Munsey Bldg.,
Washington, D. C.

Carmack, John L.,
Crane & Shovel Foreman,
Union Railroad,
111 Comrie Ave.,
Braddock, Pa.

Carmody, J. J.,
Agent,
Pennsylvania Railroad,
228 Chestnut St.,
Kittanning, Pa.

Carothers, J. A.,
President,
Pittsburgh Tool-Knife
& Mfg. Co.,
7501 Thomas Blvd.,
Pittsburgh, Pa.

Carpenter, J. F.,
Agent,
P. & L. E. R. R. Co.,
Monaca, Pa.

Carr, John S.,
President,
John Carr Coal Co.,
Adamsburg, Pa.

Carr, T. W.,
Supt. Rolling Stock,
P. & L. E. R. R.,
400 Island Ave.,
McKees Rocks, Pa.

Carran, E. W.,
President,
E. W. Carran & Sons,
Covington, Ky.

Carrick, J. E.,
Asst. Yard Master,
Pennsylvania Railroad,
Elrama Ave.,
Elrama, Pa.

Carroll, D. C.,
Asst. Agent,
Pennsylvania Railroad,
Eleventh & Etna Sts.,
Pittsburgh, Pa.

Carroll, Edw. John,
Train Dispatcher,
P. & W. Va. Ry. Co.,
307 Fifth Ave.,
Carnegie, Pa.

Carson, John,
 Foreman Pattern Shop,
 Ft. Pitt Malleable Iron Co.,
 1705 Morningside Ave.,
  Pittsburgh, Pa.

Carter, E. D.,
 Lineman,
 Union Railroad Co.,
 1305 Meadow Street
  McKeesport, Pa.

Carter, John D.,
 General Agent,
 Union Pacific System,
 Oliver Building,
  Pittsburgh, Pa.

Carter, S. T.,
 417 Fourth Avenue,
  Parnassus, Pa.

Cartwright, Wm. E.,
 Vice President,
 National Bearing Metals
  Corp.,
 928 Shore Ave.,
  N. S., Pittsburgh, Pa.

Case, H. D.,
 Live Stock Agent,
 Pennsylvania Railroad,
 34 Fourth St.,
  Aspinwall, Pa.

Casey, John F.,
 Chairman of the Board,
 John F. Casey Co.,
 P. O. Box 1888,
  Pittsburgh, Pa.

Cashdollar, C. J.,
 Foreman, Pgh. 11th St.,
 Pennsylvania Railroad,
 40 North Harrison Ave.,
  Bellevue, Pa.

Catt, C. E.,
 Division Accountant,
 B. & O. R. R.,
 B. & O. Passenger
  Station,
  Pittsburgh, Pa.

Cavanaugh, T. J.,
 Chief Special Agent,
 P. & W. Va. Ry. Co.,
 Wabash Building,
  Pittsburgh, Pa.

Chaffin, H. B.,
 M. M.,
 Pennsylvania Railroad,
 1523 Fulton Road, N.W.,
  Canton, Ohio

Chalker, A. R.,
 Engineer,
 Atwood-Bradshaw Corp.,
 473 Dawson Ave.,
  Bellevue, Pa.

Chase, Daniel K.,
 Superintendent,
 Pennsylvania Railroad,
 Pennsylvania Station,
  Pittsburgh, Pa.

Chesley, J. O.,
 Mgr., Development Division,
 Aluminum Co. of America,
 Gulf Building,
  Pittsburgh, Pa.

Chilcoat, H. E.,
 General Manager of Sales,
 Koppel Industrial Car &
  Equipment Co.,
  Koppel, Pa.

Chipley, G. R.,
 Traveling Freight Agent,
 Pennsylvania Railroad,
 Pennsylvania Station,
  Pittsburgh, Pa.

Chittenden, A. D.,
 Supt. Transportation,
 B. & L. E. R. R.,
 P. O. Box 536,
  Pittsburgh, Pa.

Christfield, J. G.,
 Mechanical Engineer,
 American Rolling Mill Co.,
  Butler, Pa.

Christianson, A.,
 Chief Engineer,
 Standard Steel Car Co.,
  Butler, Pa.

Christner, L.,
 Electrician,
 B. & O. R. R. Co.,
 2709 Queensboro Ave.,
  Brookline, Pittsburgh, Pa.

Christopher, Nicholas,
 Sales Manager,
 Meadow Gold Dairies, Inc.,
 Forbes & Boyd Sts.,
  Pittsburgh, Pa.

Christy, F. X.,
Inspector,
Pennsylvania Railroad,
1628 Duffield St.,
Pittsburgh, Pa.

Christy, G. J.,
Electrician,
Gardner Sign Co.,
1628 Duffield St.,
Pittsburgh, Pa.

Christy, W. A.,
Assistant Chief Clerk,
P. & L. E. R. R. Co.,
299 Fiftetenth St.,
Monaca, Pa.

Christy, P. J.,
Asst. District Manager,
Chicago Pneumatic Tool Co.,
237 North 12th St.,
Philadelphia, Pa.

Cipro, Thomas,
Gang Foreman,
Union Railroad Co.,
R. D. No. 1,
Turtle Creek, Pa.

Clardy, W. J.,
Transportation Engineer,
Westinghouse Elec. &
Mfg. Co.,
East Pittsburgh, Pa.

Clark, C. C.,
Sales Manager, Central Dist.,
Pressed Steel Car Co.,
Grant Building,
Pittsburgh, Pa.

Clark, E. C.,
Clerk,
Pennsylvania Railroad,
77 Kendall Ave.,
Bellevue, Pittsburgh, Pa.

Clark, H. C.,
Supervising Agt.—Div. Opr.,
Pennsylvania Railroad,
411 Center Ave.,
Verona, Pa.

Clark, R. A.,
General Manager,
Mellon-Stuart Company,
Oliver Building,
Pittsburgh, Pa.

Clarke, A. C.,
Asst. Chief Engineer,
B. & O. R. R. Co.,
Maloney Building,
Pittsburgh, Pa.

Clausen, Harold C.,
Mechanical Engineer,
Union Switch & Signal Co.,
Althea Road, R. D. No. 1,
Wilkinsburg, Pgh., Pa.

Clemens, E. G.,
General Foremans Clerk,
B. & O. R. R. Co.,
140 Parkfield Street,
Pittsburgh (10), Pa.

Clements, B. A.,
President,
American Arch Co., Inc.,
60 E. 42nd Street,
New York City, N. Y.

Clements, Frank C.,
Foreman,
P. & L. E. R. R.,
844 Island Ave.,
McKees Rocks, Pa.

Clokey, John,
Assistant Trainmaster,
Pennsylvania Railroad,
Sixteenth Street,
Pittsburgh, Pa.

Clowes, W. K.,
Freight Agent,
Pennsylvania Railroad,
P.R.R. Produce Terminal,
Pittsburgh, Pa.

Coakley, J. A.,
Gen. Traffic Manager,
Subsidiary Companies of
U. S. Steel Corp.,
Carnegie Building,
Pittsburgh, Pa.

Coakley, John A., Jr.,
Vice President and Secretary,
Lincoln Electric Railway
Sales Co.,
Marshall Bldg.,
Cleveland, Ohio.

Cochran, Harry A.,
Traffic Manager,
A. M. Byers Company,
Clark Building,
Pittsburgh, Pa.

Code, C. J.,
Division Engineer,
Pennsylvania Railroad,
42 East Steuben St.,
Crafton,
Pittsburgh, Pa.

Coffin, C. W. Floyd,
Vice President,
Franklin Railway Supply
Co., Inc.,
60 E. 42nd St.,
New York, N. Y.

Colbert, J. T.,
General Superintendent,
Pittsburgh & Shawmut R. R.,
Kittanning, Pa.

Conneely, E. K.,
Manager of Railroad Sales,
Republic Steel Corporation,
3 Linden Place,
Sewickley, Pa.

Connelly, John T.,
General Foreman,
B. & O. R. R. Co.,
1705 Hays Street,
Swissvale, Pa.

Connolly, R. D.,
Metallurgical Dept.,
Carnegie-Illinois Steel Corp.,
317 N. Dallas Ave.,
Pittsburgh, Pa.

Conway, J. D.,
Sec'y-Treas., Railway Supply
Manufacturers' Association,
1941 Oliver Bldg.,
Pittsburgh, Pa.

Cook, Sidney J.,
Vice-President,
Egan-Webster Co., Inc.,
Grant Bldg.,
Pittsburgh, Pa.

Coombe, A. B.,
Supt., F. C. D.,
Pressed Steel Car Co.,
1515 Quail Ave.,
Bellevue, Pa.

Cooper, A. H.,
Manager,
Savarins, Inc.,
220 Jefferson Drive,
Mt. Lebanon,
Pittsburgh, Pa.

Copeland, T. A.,
General Yard Master,
P. & L. E. R. R. Co.,
677 McKee Avenue,
Monessen, Pa.

Cotter, George L.,
District Engineer,
Westinghouse Air Brake Co.,
Wilmerding, Pa.

Coulter, A. F.,
Supt. of Rolling Stock,
Union R. R. Company,
East Pittsburgh, Pa.

Courtney, Harry,
Shop Supt., P. & L. E.,
520 Giffin Ave.,
Mt. Oliver Sta.,
Pittsburgh, Pa.

Covert, G. W., Jr.,
Assistant to President,
Montour Railroad,
Oliver Bldg.,
Pittsburgh, Pa.

Cowen, Harry E.,
Triple Valve Tester,
P. & L. E. R. R. Co.,
1115 Adon Street,
Pittsburgh (4), Pa.

Cox, George P.,
Supervisor,
Monongahela Railway Co.,
Union Street,
Brownsville, Pa.

Cox, W. E.,
Asst. Superintendent,
Monongahela Connecting
R. R.,
2535 Brownsville Road,
Pittsburgh, Pa

Craig, W. J.,
District Boiler Inspector,
B. & O. R. R.,
3507 Powhattan St.,
Baltimore, Md

Crawford, Alvin B.,
Sales Dept.,
Continental Roll & Steel
Foundry Co.,
Grant Bldg.,
Pittsburgh, Pa.

244

Crawford, A. M.,
Supvr. Tel. & Signals,
Pennsylvania Railroad,
30th Street Station,
Philadelphia, Pa.

Crawford, Burt H.,
Clerk,
Pennsylvania Railroad,
316 Fisk Avenue,
Bellevue, Pittsburgh, Pa.

Crawford, D. F.,
Consulting Engineer,
5243 Ellsworth Ave.,
Pittsburgh, Pa.

Crede, Wm. A.,
Chief Train Clerk,
Office of Supt. Transp'n,
Pennsylvania Railroad,
1605 Clark St.,
Wilkinsburg, Pa.

Cree, W. M.,
Salesman,
Edgewater Steel Co.,
P. O. Box 478,
Pittsburgh, Pa.

Creighton, D. M.,
Engineers' Field Man,
P. & L. E. R. R. Co.,
Kennedy Place,
New Brighton, Pa.

Creighton, W. R.,
Captain of Police,
Pennsylvania Railroad,
83 Valeview Drive,
Kennywood Park, Pa.

Crenner, Jos. A.,
District Manager,
Dearborn Chemical Co,
Farmers Bank Building,
Pittsburgh, Pa.

Crissman, L. N.,
Sales Engineer,
Electric Storage Battery Co.,
1015 Cochran Road,
Mt. Lebanon,
Pittsburgh, Pa.

Critchfield, W. P.,
Supervisor—Track,
Pennsylvania Railroad,
287 North Walnut St.,
Blairsville, Pa.

Critchlow, J. N.,
Sales Department,
Union Steel Casting Co.,
62nd & Butler Sts.,
Pittsburgh, Pa

Cromwell, H. T.,
Asst. Supt. Shops,
B. & O. R. R.,
Glenwood Shops,
Pittsburgh, Pa

Cross, J. H.,
Coal & Ore Agent,
Pennsylvania Railroad,
Union Trust Bldg.,
Cleveland, Ohio.

Crouse. John L.,
Transportation Sales,
Westinghouse Elec. &
Mfg. Co.,
East Pittsburgh, Pa.

Crow, C. C.,
Freight Agent,
Pennsylvania Railroad,
1477 Davenport Ave.,
Cleveland, Ohio

Crowell, F. C.,
Foreman, Car Dept.,
Pennsylvania Railroad,
1120 Piedmont Ave.,
Canton, Ohio.

Cruikshank, J. C.,
Div. Engr., P. & W. Va. Ry.,
439 Wabash Bldg.,
Pittsburgh, Pa.

Cudworth, H. D.,
Apprentice,
Westinghouse Air Brake Co.,
423 Peebles Ave.,
Wilkinsburg, Pa.

Cummings, Peter,
Engineer,
U. S. Chromium Co.,
Pitt & Wallace Sts.,
Wilkinsburg, Pa.

Cunningham, J. Donald,
Sales Engineer,
Southern Wheel Co.,
1510 Grace Ave.,
Lakewood, Ohio.

Cunningham, J. L.,
Asst. to Gen. Supt. Mo. Power,
Pennsylvania Railroad,
1009 Penna. Station,
Pittsburgh, Pa.

Cunningham, R. I.,
Mech. Expert, W. A. B. Co.,
606 Hampton Ave.,
Wilkinsburg, Pa.

Cunningham, W. P.,
Shop Inspector,
P. & L. E. R. R. Co.,
McKees Rocks, Pa.

Curley, Walter J.,
President,
Penna.-Conley Tank Car Co.,
Koppers Building,
Pittsburgh, Pa.

Curtis, V. K.,
Sales Representative,
Copperweld Steel Co.,
515 Berkshire Ave.,
Pittsburgh, Pa.

Cushman, P. J.,
Foreman, Car Department,
Pennsylvania Railroad,
91 Union Ave.,
Crafton, Pittsburgh, Pa.

Dailey, F. J.,
Lubrication Engineer,
Socony-Vacuum Oil Co.,
30 Clyde Ave.,
Jamestown, N. Y.

Daley, C. A.,
Engineer M. of W.,
Air Reduction Sales Co.,
60 East 42nd St.,
New York, N. Y.

Dalrymple, R. W.,
Metallurgical Engineer,
Jones & Laughlin Steel Corp.
J. & L. Building,
Pittsburgh, Pa.

Dalzell, J. C.,
Chief Clerk, Auditor Freight
Accounts,
P. & L. E. R. R. Co.,
307 Natchez St.,
Pittsburgh, Pa.

Dalzell, W. E.,
Asst. Planner,
Pressed Steel Car Co.,
1014 Milton St.,
Coraopolis, Pa.

Dambach, C. O.,
General Manager,
P. & W. Va. Ry.,
Wabash Bldg.,
Pittsburgh, Pa.

Damrau, Edward A.,
District Manager,
The Okonite Co.,
Gulf Bldg.,
Pittsburgh, Pa.

Danforth, G. H.,
Contracting Engineer,
J. & L. Steel Corpn.,
3rd Ave. and Ross St.,
Pittsburgh, Pa.

Danielson, W. D.,
Asst. Supervisor of Track,
P. & L. E. R. R. Co.,
113 Duquesne Ave.,
Dravosburg, Pa.

Darr, Elsworth E.,
Yard Master,
P. & L. E. R. R.,
235 Meridan St.,
Mt. Washington,
Pittsburgh, Pa.

Darrah, C. B,
Supvr. Telegraph & Signals,
Pennsylvania Railroad,
612 Pennsylvania Stattion,
Pittsburgh, Pa.

Daugherty, W. A.,
Gang Fore., Car Dept.,
Union Railroad,
Box 237,
North Bessemer, Pa.

Davidson, John C.,
Branch Manager,
General Cable Corp.,
Koppers Building,
Pittsburgh, Pa.

Davies, Benjamin S.,
General Secretary,
Y. M. C. A.,
2685 Wilson Ave.,
Campbell, Ohio.

Davies, James,
General Auditor,
Alton & Southern R. R.,
Gulf Building,
Pittsburgh, Pa.

Davin, John P.,
W/B Clerk,
B. & O. R. R. Co.,
1814 Belleau St.,
N. S., Pittsburgh, Pa.

Davin, W. E.,
Road Master,
P. & L. E. R. R.,
P. & L. E. Terminal Bldg.,
Pittsburgh, Pa.

Davis, Chas. S.,
Traffic Manager.
Standard Tin Plate Co.
Canonsburg Pa.

Davis, E. B.,
Asst. Yard Master,
Pennsylvania Railroad,
Brilliant, Ohio.

Davis, John W.,
General Manager,
Penn Iron & Steel Co.,
Creighton, Pa.

Dawson, V. N.,
District Storekeeper,
B. & O. R. R. Co.,
B. & O. Station,
Pittsburgh, Pa.

Day, Tom R.,
Chief Draftsman,
Pennsylvania Railroad,
179 Steuben Street,
Crafton, Pittsburgh, Pa.

Day, U. G.,
Yard Master,
Pennsylvania Railroad,
4200 Noble St.,
Bellaire, Ohio.

Deakins, H. H.,
Chief Clerk,
Supt. Freight Transp.,
Pennsylvania Railroad,
Pennsylvania Station,
Pittsburgh, Pa.

Dean, E. E.,
Car Foreman,
B. & O. R. R. Co.,
1218 Evergreen Ave.,
Millvale, Pa.

Dean, Robert W.,
Asst. Car Foreman,
B. & O. R. R. Co.,
4124 Stanley Street,
Pittsburgh, Pa.

Dean, William A.,
Signal Supervisor,
P. & L. E. R. R. Co.,
1515 Grandin Avenue,
Dormont, Pittsburgh, Pa.

Dean, W. H.,
Division Storekeeper,
B. & O. R. R. Co.,
1224 Sycamore St.,
Connellsville, Pa

Dehne, G. C.,
Asst. to Vice President,
W. A. B. Co.,
Wilmerding, Pa

Dempsey, Alex.,
Clerk to M. C. B.,
P. & W. Va. Ry. Co.,
1104 Bidwell St.,
N. S., Pittsburgh, Pa.

Denehey, Robert H.,
Publicity Representative,
Pennsylvania Railroad,
Pennsylvania Station,
Pittsburgh, Pa.

Dennis, J. G.,
Freight Train Master,
Pennsylvania Railroad,
324 Pennsylvania Sta.,
Pittsburgh, Pa.

Derr, A. I.,
Asst. to President,
P. & W. Va. Ry.,
Wabash Bldg.,
Pittsburgh, Pa.

Deutsch, Albert G.,
Yard Master,
P. & L. E. R. R. Co.,
512 Ninth Street,
Monessen, Pa.

Devine, John C.,
Asst. Yard Master,
Pennsylvania Railroad
243 South Pacific Ave.,
Pittsburgh, Pa.

Dickinson, B. F.,
Engineer Tel. & Signals,
Pennsylvania Railroad,
Pennsylvania Station,
Pittsburgh, Pa.

Dickinson, F. W.,
Retired, M. C. B.,
B. & L. E. R. R. Co.,
117 Clinton St.,
Greenville, Pa.

Dickinson, T. R.,
Purchasing Agent,
B. & L. E. R. R.,
Union Trust Bldg.,
Pittsburgh, Pa.

Dickson, K. B.,
Manager, Bureau of
Equipment Inspection,
Carnegie Steel Co.,
227 Oakview Ave.,
Edgewood, Pa.

Dierker, R. H.,
Agent,
B. & O. R. R. Co.,
R. D. 2,
Allison Park, Pa.

Dietrich, W. S.,
Vice-President,
Greenville Steel Car Co.,
Greenville, Pa.

Diettrich, John J.,
President,
J. J. Diettrich & Son,
417 Chartiers Ave.,
McKees Rocks, Pa.

Dihle, James E.,
Locomotive Engineer,
P. & L. E. R. R.,
Fourth Ave.,
Beaver Falls, Pa.

Diller, Clark,
Representative,
Gustin-Bacon Mfg. Co.,
1021 Filbert St.,
Philadelphia, Pa.

Dillon, Arthur L.,
Engineer Computer,
P. & L. E. R. R. Co.,
77 Hawthorne Ave.,
Crafton, Pittsburgh, Pa.

Dillon, H. W.,
Sales Engineer,
Paxton-Mitchell Company.
312 Main Street,
South Amboy, N. J.

Dindinger, Charles C.,
Agent,
P. & L. E. R. R. Co.,
487 Duquesne Drive,
Mt. Lebanon, Pa.

Dipper, F. W.,
Cashier,
P. & L. E. R. R. Co.,
Churchview Avenue,
Carrick, Pittsburgh, Pa.

Dittman, George
General Foreman,
P. & L. E. R. R. Co.,
100 Roycraft Ave.,
Mt. Lebanon, Pittsburgh, Pa.

Dilworth, John C.,
Mgr. of Railroad Sales,
Carnegie-Illinois Steel Corp.,
Carnegie Bldg.,
Pittsburgh, Pa.

Diven, J. B.,
Supt. Motive Power,
Pennsylvania Railroad,
Pennsylvania Station,
Pittsburgh, Pa.

Dixon, Charles P.,
Asst. Train Master,
Pennsylvania Railroad,
156 North Spring St.,
Blairsville, Pa.

Dixon, C. R.,
District Sales Manager,
N. Americ'n Refractories Co.
Oliver Building,
Pittsburgh, Pa.

Dixon, Joseph M.,
Asst. Yard Master,
Pennsylvania Railroad,
110 California Ave.,
Oakmont, Pa.

Dobson, F. L.,
General Fuel Manager,
Pennsylvania Railroad,
Philadelphia, Pa.

Doggett, A. L.,
Freight Traffic Manager,
B. & O. R. R. Co.,
Oliver Bldg.,
Pittsburgh, Pa.

Donovan, J. J.,
Gen. Fore., P. & L. E. R. R.,
426 Jones St.,
Belle Vernon, Pa.

Donovan, Lawrence T.,
Car Inspector,
Pennsylvania Railroad,
146 Noble Ave.,
Crafton, Pittsburgh, Pa.

Douglass, William H.,
  Locomotive Engineer,
    P. & L. E. R. R. Co.,
    309 E. Fifth Avenue,
                Homestead, Pa.

Down, S. G.,
  Vice President,
    Westinghouse Air Brake Co.,
                Wilmerding, Pa.

Downing, J. A.,
  District Freight Claim Agent,
    Pennsylvania Railroad,
    1013 Penn Avenue,
                Pittsburgh, Pa.

Downing, N. H.,
  Engine House Foreman,
    B. & O. R. R. Co.,
    1617 Monongahela Ave.,
                Swissvale, Pa.

Doyle, Timothy E.,
  Foreman Painter,
    Montour Railroad,
    1125 First Ave.,
                Coraopolis, Pa.

Draper, Thos.,
  President, Draper Mfg. Co.,
                Port Huron, Mich.

Duffley, F. M.,
  Machinery Inspector,
    P. & L. E. R. R. Co.,
    902 Liberty Street,
                McKees Rocks, Pa.

Dugan, G. R.,
  City Passenger Agent,
    B. & O. R. R. Co.,
    Union Trust Bldg.,
                Pittsburgh, Pa.

Dunbar, Harold F.,
  Sales Manager, McConway
    & Torley Corp.,
    48th St. & A. V. R. R.,
                Pittsburgh, Pa.

Dunham, C. W.,
  Union Switch & Signal Co.,
    1219 Braddock Ave.,
    Edgewood, Pittsburgh, Pa.

Dunlop, Robert J., Jr.,
  Terminal Foreman,
    Montour Railroad Co.,
    R. D. 1,
                Willock, Pa.

Dunn, J. W.,
  Foreman, Mechanical Dept.,
    B. & O. R. R. Co.,
    244 Trowbridge St.,
    Hazelwood, Pittsburgh, Pa.

Dunn, Samuel O.,
  Editor, Railway Age Gazette,
    105 W. Adams St.,
                Chicago, Ill.

Durell, W. A.,
  Movement Director,
    Pennsylvania Railroad,
    Pennsylvania Station,
                Pittsburgh, Pa.

Durnell, W. E.,
  T. & S. Signals,
    Pennsylvania Railroad,
    218 Buffalo Street,
                Freeport, Pa.

Duryea, O. C.,
  President,
    O. C. Duryea Corp.,
    30 East 42nd St.,
                New York, N. Y.

Dusenberry, S. H.,
  Engine House Foreman,
    P. & L. E. R. R. Co.,
    P. O. Box 532,
                Newell, Pa.

Eagan, Daniel F.,
  Rules Examiner,
    Pennsylvania Railroad,
    252 Humbolt Blvd.,
                Buffalo, N. Y.

Easler, E. H.,
  Chief Clerk to Superintendent,
    Monongahela Railway Co.,
    11 Third Avenue,
                Brownsville, Pa.

East, Louis P.,
  Live Stock Supervisor,
    Pittsburgh Joint Stock
      Yards Co.,
    21 N. W. Fifth St.,
                Richmond, Ind.

Eaton, Fred'k. H.,
  Sales Engineer,
    American Car & Foundry
      Co.,
    Farmers Bank Bldg.,
                Pittsburgh, Pa.

Eberle, E. J.,
Air Brake Foreman,
B. & O. R. R. Co.,
3014 Vernon Avenue,
Brentwood, Pgh. (10), Pa.

Eckels, Wilber,
Representative,
Cardwell Westinghouse Co.,
332 So. Michigan Ave.,
Chicago, Ill.

Edgett, Joseph W.,
Sales Engineer,
Walworth Company,
703 Gulf Bldg.,
Pittsburgh, Pa.

Edmiston, R. J.,
Special Representative,
U. S. Graphite Co.,
Fulton Bldg.,
Pittsburgh, Pa.

Edmonston, George F.,
Supervisor Labor & Wage,
Pennsylvania Railroad,
Pennsylvania Station,
Pittsburgh, Pa.

Edwards, H. F.,
Road Foreman of Engines,
Monongahela Railway Co.,
South Brownsville, Pa.

Edwards, W.,
Section Stockman,
Stores Dept.,
B. & O. R. R. Co.,
4714 Sylvan Avenue,
Hazelwood, Pittsburgh, Pa.

Egbert, J. A.,
President,
Railway Products Co.,
Gulf Building,
Pittsburgh, Pa.

Egly, M. J.,
Chief Clerk to Gen. Mgr.,
Pennsylvania Railroad,
Pennsylvania Station,
Pittsburgh, Pa.

Eichenlaub, W. C.,
Sales Manager,
Pittsburgh Steel Foundry
Corp.,
Glassport, Pa.

Eiland, C. L.,
General Foreman,
Pullman Co.,
2915 Voelkel Ave.,
Dormont,
Pittsburgh, (16) Pa.

Eisenman, William H.,
Day Agent,
Pullman Co.,
7423 Race St.,
Pittsburgh, Pa.

Ekey, J. S.,
Engineer of Bridges,
B. & L. E. R. R.,
4 College Ave.,
Greenville, Pa.

Ellis, C. B.,
Apartment 6-F,
Bellefield Dwellings,
Pittsburgh, Pa.

Ely, J. L.,
Supervising Agent,
Pittsburgh Division,
Pennsylvania Railroad,
Pennsylvania Station,
Pittsburgh, Pa.

Emerick, J. B.,
Sales Representative,
Garlock Packing Co.,
256 Beverly Road,
Pittsburgh, Pa.

Emery, E.,
Railway Supplies,
6511 Darlington Road,
Pittsburgh, Pa.

Emery, L. F.,
General Foreman,
P. & L. E. R. R. Co.,
180 Marion Avenue,
Struthers, Ohio.

En Dean, J. F.,
Inspecting Engineer,
P. & L. E. R. R.,
436 Edgemont St.,
Knoxville,
Pittsburgh, Pa.

Enders, I. O.,
Superintendent Labor &
Wage,
Pennsylvania Railroad,
Pennsylvania Station,
Pittsburgh, Pa.

Endsley, Louis E., Prof.,
Consulting Engineer,
516 East End Ave.,
Pittsburgh, Pa.

Escott, Charles M.,
Clerk,
Jones & Laughlin Steel Corp.,
J. & L. Building.
Pittsburgh, Pa.

Evans, Charles S.,
Chief Car Service Clerk,
Donora Southern Railroad
Company,
Box 133,
Fayette City, Pa.

Evans, David F.,
District Manager,
The Duff-Norton Mfg. Co.,
250 Parke Ave.,
New York, N. Y.

Evans, Robert E.,
Yardmaster,
Pennsylvania Railroad,
814 Norwich St.,
South Hills Station,
Pittsburgh, Pa.

Failor, Charles W.,
General Engineer,
Union Switch & Signal Co.,
107 Elmore Road,
Forest Hills, Pa.

Fair, J. M.,
Engineer M. & W.,
Pennsylvania Railroad,
Pennsylvania Station,
Pittsburgh, Pa.

Falkner, Andrew J.,
Clerk,
B. & O. R. R.,
4014 Coleman St.,
Pittsburgh, Pa.

Farlow, George B.,
Division Engineer,
B. & O. R. R.,
Smithfield & Water Sts.,
Pittsburgh, Pa.

Farmer, C. C.,
Director of Engineering,
W. A. B. Co.,
Wilmerding, Pa.

Farrell, G. R.,
Sales Agent,
Nat'l Mall. & Steel Cstgs. Co.,
10600 Quincey Ave.,
Cleveland, Ohio

Farrington, Robert J.,
General Foreman,
P. & L. E. R. R.,
R. D. 1, Herbst Road,
Coraopolis, Pa.

Fay, Frank L., Hon.,
Chairman of the Board,
Greenville Steel Car Co.,
Greenville, Pa.

Feidt, J. J.,
Chief Clerk—Operating Dept,
P. & L. E. R. R. Co.,
863 Marshall Avenue,
N. S., Pittsburgh, Pa.

Ferguson, George,
Air Brake Instructor,
Pennsylvania Railroad,
3719 Mahoning Road, N.E.,
Canton, Ohio.

Ferguson, James H., Jr.,
Draftsman,
Union Railroad Co.,
1435 Foliage St.,
Wilkinsburg, Pa.

Ferguson, R. G.,
Electrician,
Pennsylvania Railroad,
1938 East St.,
N. S., Pittsburgh, Pa.

Fieldson, P. H.,
Asst. Master Car Builder,
P. & L. E. R. R.,
220 Greydon Ave.,
McKees Rocks, Pa.

Fike, James W.,
Division Operator,
Pennsylvania Railroad,
2236 Valera Ave.,
Mt. Oliver, Pittsburgh, Pa.

Finegan, Leo,
Eastern Sales Manager,
Flannery Bolt Co.,
Keystone Hotel,
Pittsburgh, Pa.

Finegan, Thomas A.,
Wreck Foreman,
Eastern Division,
Pennsylvania Railroad,
P. O. Box 702,
Conway, Pa.

Fischer, G. E.,
Clerk, Union Railroad,
2202 Hampton St.,
Swissvale, Pa.

Fischer, John G.,
Chief Rate Clerk,
B. & O. R. R. Co.,
109 Shady Drive, West,
Mt. Lebanon, Pittsburgh, Pa.

Fisher, E. M.,
Asst. R. F. of E.,
Penna. Railroad System,
909 E. Washington St.,
New Castle, Pa.

Fitzgerald, T.,
Vice President & Gen. Mgr.,
Pittsburgh Railways Co.,
435 Sixth Ave.,
Pittsburgh, Pa.

Fitzpatrick, T. R.,
Freight Traffic Manager,
P. & L. E. R. R.,
Terminal Bldg.,
Pittsburgh, Pa.

Fitzsimmons, Edward J.,
City Manager,
City Ice & Fuel Co.,
5550 Claybourne St.,
Pittsburgh, Pa.

Fitz Simmons, E. S.,
Vice President,
Flannery Bolt Co.,
Bridgeville, Pa.

Flaherty, Michael,
Yard Master,
Pennsylvania Railroad,
145 Wildon Ave.,
Steubenville, Ohio.

Flaherty, P. J.,
Pres. and General Mgr.,
Johnson Bronze Co.,
So. Mill Street,
New Castle, Pa.

Flanigan, A. C.,
Freight Agent,
P. & L. E. R. R. Co.,
McKees Rocks, Pa.

Flannery, J. Rogers,
Flannery Bolt Co.,
Flannery Bldg.,
Pittsburgh, Pa.

Fleckenstein, August,
P. W. Insp'r., P. & L. E. R. R.,
1108 Crucible St., 20th Wd.,
Pittsburgh, Pa.

Flick, Samuel H.,
Asst. Yard Master,
Pennsylvania Railroad,
429 Biddle Ave.,
Wilkinsburg, Pa.

Flinn, R. H.,
General Superintendent,
Pennsylvania Railroad,
Pennsylvania Station,
Pittsburgh, Pa.

Flocker, R. M.,
General Passenger Agent,
Pennsylvania Railroad,
Pennsylvania Station,
Pittsburgh, Pa.

Foard, Edwin A.,
Supt. Stations & Transfers,
Pennsylvania Railroad,
Pennsylvania Station,
Pittsburgh, Pa.

Folan, J. V.,
Clerk,
Pennsylvania Railroad,
7720 St. Lawrence Ave.,
Swissvale, Pa.

Follett, W. F.,
Asst. Superintendent,
Aliquippa & Southern
R. R. Co.,
652 Highland Ave.,
Aliquippa, Pa.

Forbriger, E. A.,
Dist. M. of W. Storekeeper,
B. & O. R. R. Co.,
4333 Winterburn St.,
Pittsburgh, Pa.

Forsberg, R. P.,
Chief Engineer,
P. & L. E. R. R.,
P. & L. E. Terminal Bldg.,
Pittsburgh, Pa.

Forst, J. F.,
 Supervisor of Truck,
 P. & L. E. R. R. Co.,
 3103 Fourth Avenue,
 Beaver Falls, Pa

Forsyth, D. B.,
 Chief Clerk to Engr. M. W.,
 P. & L. E. R. R. Co.,
 P&LE Terminal Bldg.,
 Pittsburgh, Pa.

Forsythe, G. B.,
 Foreman, Car Dept.,
 Pennsylvania Railroad,
 Baden, Pa.

Fortescue, Charles L.,
 Consulting Transmission Engr.
 Westinghouse Electric &
 Mfg. Co.,
 East Pittsburgh, Pa.

Foster, F. L.,
 Supt. Frt. Transportation,
 P. & L. E. R. R.,
 Pittsburgh, Pa.

Foulk, R. S.,
 Asst. Train Master,
 Division Operator,
 Pennsylvania Railroad,
 653 Sherwood Ave.,
 Corliss Station, Pittsburgh, Pa.

Fowler, W. E.,
 President,
 Pgh., Lisbon & Western
 R. R.,
 P. O. Box 688,
 Youngstown, Ohio.

Fownes, James A.,
 Vice Pres. & Treas.,
 Gem Manufacturing Co.,
 1229 Goebel St.,
 N. S., Pittsburgh, Pa.

Fox, George W.,
 Secretary,
 Davis Brake Beam Co.,
 146 Second Ave.,
 Westmont,
 Johnstown, Pa.

Fox, M. C.,
 Supervisor—Track,
 Pennsylvania Railroad,
 Wheeling, W. Va.

Fralic, C. F.,
 Section Stockman,
 B. & O. R. R. Co.,
 3470 Beechview Blvd.,
 Pittsburgh, Pa.

Frauenheim, A. M.,
 Vice President,
 Auto-Tite Joints Co.,
 7501 Thomas Blvd.,
 Pittsburgh, Pa.

Frauenheim, Pierce H.,
 Purchasing Agent,
 Auto-Tite Joints Co.,
 7501 Thomas Blvd.,
 Pittsburgh, Pa.

Freshwater, F. H.,
 Sales Engineer,
 Koppel Industrial Car
 & Equipment Co.,
 Farmers Bank Bldg.,
 Pittsburgh, Pa.

Friend, Edward F.,
 Asst. Chief Clerk,
 Traffic Department,
 Pittsburgh Coal Co.,
 Oliver Bldg.,
 Pittsburgh, Pa.

Fry, Lawford H.,
 Railway Engineer,
 Edgewater Steel Co.,
 P. O. Box 478,
 Pittsburgh, Pa.

Fulks, B. M.,
 Movement Director,
 Pennsylvania Railroad,
 428 Center Ave.,
 Carnegie, Pa.

Fulton, K. H.,
 Sales Manager,
 Ball Chemcial Co.,
 Fulton Building,
 Pittsburgh, Pa.

Fults, John H.,
 Union National Bank,
 Wood Street,
 Pittsburgh, Pa.

Funk, E. J.,
 General Foreman,
 P. & L. E. R. R. Co.,
 42 Laclede Street,
 Pittsburgh, Pa.

Furch, George J.,
Gang Fore., Penna. R. R. Co.,
319 Fifth St.,
Freeport, Pa.

Gainer, Alva,
Supply Car Storekeeper,
B. & O. R. R. Co.,
5115 Blair Street,
Hazelwood, Pittsburgh, Pa.

Galbraith, James R.,
Fire Marshal,
P. & L. E. R. R. Co.,
500 Rossmore Ave.,
Brookline, Pittsburgh, Pa.

Galinis, J. W.,
Draftsman,
Pennsylvania R. R. Co.,
709 Broadway,
East McKeesport, Pa.

Galloway, W. R.,
Division Trainmaster,
B. & O. R. R. Co.,
B. & O. Station,
Pittsburgh, Pa.

Gallowich, Louis J.,
Car Inspector,
Pennsylvania Railroad,
3 Matson St.,
N. S., Pittsburgh, Pa.

Gandy, R. H.,
Mechanical Draftsman,
B. & O. R. R. Co.,
Baptist Rd., R. D. 1,
Library, Pa.

Gardiner, Jas. E.,
Spl. Rep. Schaefer Equipt. Co.,
Koppers Bldg.,
Pittsburgh, Pa.

Gardner, George R.,
Chief Clerk—Traffic Dept.,
Pittsburgh Coal Co.,
1024 Oliver Bldg.,
Pittsburgh, Pa.

Gardner, K. C.,
Vice President,
Greenville Steel Car Co.,
Greenville, Pa.

Gariepy, L. H.,
Gang Foreman,
Pennsylvania Railroad,
Freeport, Pa.

Gatens, A. J.,
Asst. Chief Clerk,
P. & L. E. R. R. Co.,
302 South Pacific Ave.,
E. E., Pittsburgh, Pa.

Gates, C. F.,
Asst. Chief Clerk,
P. & L. E. R. R.,
Pittsburgh, Pa.

Gatfield, Philip I.,
Mechanic,
Keystone Sand & Supply Co.,
219 Zara St.,
Knoxville,
Pittsburgh, Pa.

Gauvey, Fred J.,
Captain of Police,
Pennsylvania Railroad,
Pennsylvania Station,
Pittsburgh, Pa.

Geiser, W. P.,
Supervisor Track,
Pennsylvania Railroad,
610 Dick Street,
Carnegie, Pa.

Gellatly, Wm. R.,
President,
Superior Railway Products
Corp.,
Thomas Boulevard,
Pittsburgh, Pa.

Gemmell, R. W.,
Railway Engineer,
Westinghouse Electric &
Mfg. Co.,
East Pittsburgh, Pa.

George, R. H.,
Assistant Engineer,
P. & L. E. R. R.,
Terminal Building,
Pittsburgh, Pa.

George, W. J.,
Asst. Sales Manager,
Edgewater Steel Co.,
P. O. Box 478,
Pittsburgh, Pa.

Gilbert, William J.,
Supervisor—Track,
Pennsylvania Railroad,
New Kensington, Pa.

Gilg, Henry F.,
Railway Supplies,
1424 Orchlee St.,
N. S., Pittsburgh, Pa.

Gillespie, J. Porter,
Asst. General Supt.,
Lockhart Iron & Steel Co.,
P. O. Box 1165,
Pittsburgh, Pa.

Gillespie, John M.,
Vice President,
Lockhart Iron & Steel Co.,
P. O. Box 1243,
Pittsburgh, Pa.

Gillum, J. S.,
Supt., Mon. Div.,
Pennsylvania Railroad,
Pennsylvania Station,
Pittsburgh, Pa.

Glaser, C. J.,
Statistical Clerk,
B. & O. R. R. Co.,
302 Winston Street,
Pittsburgh, Pa.

Glaser, J. P.,
Auditor Disbursements,
P. & L. E. R. R.,
909 Bellaire Ave.,
Pittsburgh, Pa.

Gleeson, Harry L.,
Sales Agent,
The Lorain Division.
Carnegie-Illinois Steel
Corporation,
Frick Bldg.,
Pittsburgh, Pa.

Glenn, J. H.,
Master Mechanic,
P. & W. Va. Ry. Co.,
20 Obey St.,
Pittsburgh, Pa.

Goble, A. S.,
Baldwin Locomotive Works,
Paschall Station,
Philadelphia, Pa.

Goda, P. H.,
Foreman, P. R. R.,
311 South Ave.,
Wilkinsburg, Pa.

Goff, J. P.,
T. M., P. & L. E. R. R.,
615 Montour St.,
Coraopolis, Pa.

Goldcamp, C. F.,
Sales Department,
Jones & Laughlin Steel
Corporation,
Third & Ross St.,
Pittsburgh, Pa.

Goldstrom, G. E.,
Draftsman,
P. & W. Va. Ry.,
1305 Highman St.,
Pittsburgh, Pa

Goodwin, A. E.,
Tool Designer,
Westinghouse Electric &
Mfg. Co.,
602 Marion Ave.,
Forest Hills, Wilkinsburg, Pa.

Gordon, C. M.,
Asst. to General Auditor,
P. & L. E. R. R. Co.,
995 Second Street,
Beaver, Pa.

Gorman, Charles,
1301 Adams St.,
N. S., Pittsburgh, Pa.

Goron, F. W.,
General Foreman,
P. & L. E. R. R.,
Dickerson Run, Pa.

Goss, Richard C.,
District Sales Manager,
Ohio Brass Company,
Oliver Building,
Pittsburgh, Pa.

Gottschalk, C. W.,
Asst. Traffic Manager,
Jones & Laughlin Steel Corp.,
J. & L. Building,
Pittsburgh, Pa.

Graf, Benjamin,
Foreman, M. E. Dept.,
Pennsylvania Railroad,
1425 Straka St.,
Pittsburgh, Pa.

Graham, A. C.,
Traffic Manager,
Youngstown Sheet and
Tube Company,
Stambaugh Bldg.,
Youngstown, Ohio.

Graham, Chas. J.,
Vice President,
Pressed Steel Car Co., Inc.,
Grant Bldg.,
Pittsburgh, Pa

Graham, Harry C.,
Pittsburgh Screw & Bolt Corp.
P. O. Box 72,
Pittsburgh, Pa.

Graham, H. E.,
Asst. to Pres. & Gen. Traf. Mgr.
Jones & Laughlin Steel Corp.,
3rd Ave. & Ross St.,
Pittsburgh, Pa.

Graham, Herbert W.,
General Metallurgist,
Jones & Laughlin Steel Corp.,
J. & L. Building,
Pittsburgh, Pa.

Gray, C. C.,
General Freight Agent,
Western Maryland Railway
Company,
Koppers Bldg.,
Pittsburgh, Pa.

Gray, Guy M.,
S. M. P.,
B. & L. E. R. R. Co.,
Greenville, Pa

Gray, H. H.,
Division Freight Agent,
Pennsylvania Railroad,
Pennsylvania Station,
Pittsburgh, Pa.

Gray, M. L.,
Vice President,
Union Switch & Signal Co.,
Swissvale, Pa.

Gray, T. H.,
Master Carpenter,
Pennsylvania Railroad,
Pennsylvania Station,
Pittsburgh, Pa.

Greek, Joseph,
Section Foreman,
P. & W. Va. Ry. Co.,
812 Logan St.,
Carnegie, Pa.

Green, M. E.,
Asst. Chief Clerk to
Vice President,
P. & L. E. R. R. Co.,
P&LE Terminal Bldg.,
Pittsburgh, Pa.

Gregory, Walter H.,
Machinist,
P. & L. E. R. R. Co.,
123 Owen Street,
McKees Rocks, Pa.

Grier, M. L.,
Accountant,
Alton & Southern Railroad,
Gulf Building,
Pittsburgh, Pa.

Griest, E. E.,
Vice Pres. & Gen. Mgr.,
Fort Pitt Malleable
Iron Co.,
P. O. Box 505,
Pittsburgh, Pa.

Grieve, Robert E.,
Passenger Train Master,
Pennsylvania Railroad,
740 East End Ave.,
Pittsburgh, Pa.

Grimshaw, F. G.,
Works Mgr., P. R. R.,
Altoona, Pa.

Gross, John,
Captain of Police,
B. & O. R. R. Co.,
625 Churchview Avenue
Extension,
Pittsburgh (10), Pa.

Groves, Walter C.,
Chief Engineer,
Donora Southern R. R. Co.,
Donora, Pa.

Grunden, B. C.,
Commercial Agent,
Railway Express Agency,
Inc.,
926 Penn Avenue,
Pittsburgh, Pa.

Guinnip, M. S.,
Sales Engineer,
Ingersoll-Rand Co.,
706 Chamber of Commerce
Building,
Pittsburgh, Pa.

Gunnison, Walter L.,
Representative,
Enterprise Railway
Equipment Co.,
59 E. Van Buren St.,
Chicago, Ill.

Guy, W. S.,
Traffic Manager,
U. S. Steel Corp.,
Subsidiaries, E. D.,
614 Carnegie Bldg.,
Pittsburgh, Pa.

Haase, L. R.,
District Boiler Inspector,
B. & O. R. R. Co.,
7358 Whiple pSt.,
Swissvale Branch,
Pittsburgh, Pa

Hackett, C. M.,
Division Boiler Maker Fore.,
Pennsylvania Railroad,
618 Pennsylvania Ave.,
Oakmont, Pa.

Hackett, S. E.,
President,
Jones & Laughlin Steel Corp.,
J. & L. Building,
Pittsburgh, Pa.

Haggerty, J. F.,
General Foreman,
B. & O. R. R. Co.,
1602 Chelton Ave.,
Brookline, Pittsburgh, Pa.

Hague, James R.,
Clerk,
P. & L. E. R. R. Co.,
5120 Second Avenue,
Pittsburgh, Pa.

Haller, C. T.,
President,
Colonial Supply Co.,
217 Water St.,
Pittsburgh, Pa.

Haller, Nelson M.,
Sup'r. Scrap and Reclamation,
P. & L. E. R. R.,
3678 Middletown Road,
Corliss Station,
Pittsburgh, Pa.

Hamilton, Joseph K.,
Examiner, Labor & Wage
Bureau,
Pennsylvania Railroad,
Pennsylvania Station,
Pittsburgh, Pa.

Hamilton, W. H.,
Supt., of Roadway &
Structures,
Montour Railroad Co.,
1711 State Ave.,
Coraopolis, Pa.

Hamsher, W. E.,
Mechanical Representative,
Hennessy Lubricator Co.,
245 East King St.,
Chambersburg, Pa.

Hance, R. H,
Supervising Agent.-
Div. Operator,
Pennsylvania Railroad,
Pennsylvania Station,
Pittsburgh, Pa.

Hancock, Milton L.,
Office Engineer,
Westinghouse Air Brake Co.,
557 Broadway Extension,
East McKeesport, Pa.

Handloser, Bertram F.,
General Superintendent,
Dilworth Porter Division,
Republic Steel Corp.,
4th & Bingham Sts.,
Pittsburgh, Pa.

Hankey, E. B.,
Asst. Gen. Freight Agent,
Pennsylvania Railroad,
Pennsylvania Station,
Pittsburgh, Pa.

Hankey, E. B., Jr.,
General Manager,
Penna. Truck Lines, Inc.,
1013 Penn Avenue,
Pittsburgh, Pa

Hankins, F. W.,
Asst. Vice President—
Chief of Motive Power,
Pennsylvania Railroad,
Broad St. Station Bldg.,
Philadelphia, Pa.

Hansen, Wm. C.,
Sales Engr., A. Stucki Co.,
419 Oliver Bldg.,
Pittsburgh, Pa.

Harbaugh, Chas. P.,
Wreck Master,
Union Railroad,
East Pittsburgh, Pa.

Hardy, James E.,
Agent,
P. & L. E. R. R. Co.,
303 Monongahela Ave.,
Otto, McKeesport, Pa.

Harger, M. L.,
Foreman Car Repairs,
P. & L. E. R. R. Co.,
Newell, Pa.

Harig, George J.,
District Freight Agent,
Nelson Steamship Co.,
Oliver Building,
Pittsburgh, Pa.

Harman, H. H.,
Engineer—Track,
B. & L. E. R. R.,
Greenville, Pa.

Harper, A. M.,
Manager of Sales,
Carnegie-Illinois Steel Corp.,
Carnegie Bldg.,
Pittsburgh, Pa.

Harper, G. C.,
General Supt.,
Montour Railroad,
1711 State Ave.,
Coraopolis, Pa.

Harper, J. T.,
Asst. to Mech. Supt.,
Montour Railroad,
R. F. D. No. 1,
McKees Rocks, Pa.

Harper, James W.,
Medical Examiner,
Pennsylvania Railroad,
5121 Bayard St.,
Pittsburgh, Pa.

Harper, James W., Jr.,
Locomotive Engineer,
Montour Railroad Co.,
1610 Vance Ave.,
Coraopolis, Pa.

Harris, J. P.,
Chief Clerk to Div. Engr.,
B. & O. R. R. Co.,
3429 Meadowcroft Ave.,
South Hills Branch,
Pittsburgh, Pa.

Harrison, Albert,
Chemist,
Union Railroad Co.,
1227 Bell Ave.,
North Braddock, Pa.

Harter, Arnold,
Asst. Fore., W. A. B. Co.,
353 Marguerite Ave.,
Wilmerding, Pa.

Hartnett, C. J.,
Supervisor of Tracks,
P. & L. E. R. R. Co.,
610 Arlington Ave.,
McKeesport, Pa.

Harwig, C. G.,
Engineer,
Union Switch & Signal Co.,
1023 Mifflin Avenue,
Wilkinsburg, Pa.

Haser, A. J.,
Funeral Director,
512 Chartiers Ave.,
McKees Rocks, Pa.

Hassler, E. S.,
Car Foreman,
Pennsylvania Railroad,
5526 Beverly Place,
Pittsburgh, Pa.

Hauser, G. Bates,
Engineer, Development Div.,
Aluminum Co. of America,
New Kensington, Pa.

Hawkes, T. L.,
Pennsylvania Railroad,
625 West 169th St.,
New York, N. Y.

Hawkins, J. M.,
District Sales Manager,
Elwell-Parker Electric Co.,
Investment Bldg.,
Pittsburgh, Pa.

Hawkins, Paul R.,
Pullman-Standard Car
Mfg. Co.,
P. O. Box 928,
Pittsburgh, Pa.

Hays, Harry E.,
R. F. of E.,
Pennsylvania Railroad,
3148 Huxley St.,
Corliss Station,
Pittsburgh, Pa.

Hayward, Carlton,
C. C. to Gen. Supt. Motive
Power,
Pennsylvania Railroad,
7412 Penfield Place,
Pittsburgh, Pa.

Heed, H. L.,
Agent, 26th St. Terminal,
Railway Express Agency,
Inc.,
5742 Howe Street,
Pittsburgh, Pa.

Heffelfinger, A. E.,
Sales Engineer,
The Symington Co.,
230 Park Ave.,
New York City.

Heimbach, A. E.,
Asst. Signal-Telegraph Engr.,
P. & L. E. R. R.,
Terminal Annex Bldg.,
Pittsburgh, Pa.

Heinz, W. J.,
Mgr. Central R. R. Dept.,
Ingersoll-Rand Company,
Williamson Building,
Cleveland, Ohio.

Heinzenberger, Arthur E.,
Assistant Car Foreman,
B. & O. R. R. Co.,
315 Shaw Avenue,
McKeesport, Pa.

Hektner, Joel,
Asst. Engr., Ry. Division,
Timken Roller Bearing Co.,
Canton, Ohio.

Helfrich, F. A.,
Chief Electrician,
B. & O. R. R. Co.,
404 Olympia Road,
Pittsburgh, Pa.

Hellriegel, W. H.,
Traffic Representative,
P. & W. Va. Ry.,
Wabash Bldg.,
Pittsburgh, Pa.

Hemma, Charles H.,
Draftsman,
P. & L. E. R. R. Co.,
1210 Valley Street,
McKees Rocks, Pa.

Henderson, Geo. L.,
Engr., P. & L. E. R. R.,
228 Sheridan Ave.,
New Castle, Pa.

Henning, C. C.,
Asst. Gen. Metallurgist,
Jones & Laughlin Steel
Corp.,
J. & L. Building,
Pittsburgh, Pa.

Henry, C. J.,
Division Engineer,
Pennsylvania Railroad,
30 Burbank Terrace,
Buffalo, N. Y.

Hepburn, P. W.,
Sales Engineer,
Gulf Oil Corporation,
6963 Frankstown Ave.,
Pittsburgh, Pa.

Herpst, R. C.,
Sales Agent,
American Steel Foundries,
29 De Foe Street,
N. S., Pittsburgh, Pa.

Herring, John R.,
Conductor,
P. & L. E. R. R. Co.,
Moredale St.,
South Hills Branch,
Pittsburgh, Pa.

Herrold, A. E.,
M. M. & M. C. B.,
Mon. Conn. R. R.,
3915 Winterburn Ave.,
Pittsburgh, Pa.

Hervey, R. S.,
Auditor, Freight Accounts,
P. & L. E. R. R.,
722 Main St.,
Coraopolis, Pa.

Hess, Charles A.,
Sales Department,
Edgewater Steel Co.,
P. O. Box 478,
Pittsburgh, Pa.

Hewes, John, Jr.,
Transportation Assistant,
B. & O. R. R.,
B. & O. Passenger Station,
Pittsburgh, Pa.

Hicks, W. A.
Vice President,
Penn Iron & Steel Co.,
Creighton, Pa

Higginbottom, S. B.,
Supervisor Tel. & Sigs.,
Pennsylvania Railroad,
Pennsylvania Station,
Pittsburgh, Pa.

Higgins, George A.,
Asst. Manager of Sales,
Carnegie Steel Co.,
Carnegie Bldg.,
Pittsburgh, Pa.

Hilbert, Rudolph F.
Engineer,
Fort Pitt Spring Co.,
833 Neely Heights,
Coraopolis, Pa.

Hill, George W.,
Blacksmith Foreman,
B. & O. R. R. Co.,
310 Twenty-sixth Street,
McKeesport, Pa.

Hill, John A.,
Manager,
Independent Pneumatic Tool
Co.,
Wabash Bldg.,
Pittsburgh, Pa.

Hilstrom, Anton V.,
Foreman,
P. & L. E. R. R.,
R. D. 3, Box 226-B,
Coraopolis, Pa.

Hocking, Harry A.,
Representative,
Air Reduction Sales Co.,
60 East 42nd St.,
New York, N. Y.

Hodge, Edwin, Jr.,
President,
Pittsburgh Forgings Co.,
Gulf Bldg.,
Pittsburgh, Pa.

Hodges, A. H.,
District Master Mechanic,
B. & O. R. R. Co.,
3100 Gaylord Ave.,
Dormont. Pittsburgh, Pa.

Hodges, R. C.,
Assistant Car Foreman,
B. & O. R. R. Co.,
3100 Gaylord Ave.,
Dormont, Pittsburgh, Pa.

Hoffstot, H. P.,
President,
Koppel Industrial Car &
Equipment Co.,
Farmers Bank Bldg.,
Pittsburgh, Pa.

Hofmann, Eugene L.,
Asst. Passenger Train Master,
Pennsylvania R. R.,
411 Todd Street,
Wilkinsburg, Pa.

Hohn, George W.,
Track Supervisor,
B. & L. E. R. R.,
538 East Pearl St.,
Butler, Pa.

Holiday, Harry,
Works Manager,
The American Rolling
Mill Company,
Butler, Pa.

Holland, S. E.,
Asst. Div. Engr., Pgh. Div.,
Pennsylvania Railroad.
318 West St.,
Wilkinsburg, Pa.

Holmes, E. H.,
Sales Department,
Ft. Pitt Malleable Iron Co.,
3662 Middletown Road,
Corliss Station,
Pittsburgh, Pa.

Holmes, J. R.,
Movement Director,
Pennsylvania Railroad,
35 Schley Ave.,
Ingram, Pa.

Holtzworth, C. H.,
Chief Clerk, Engineering Dept.,
B. & O. R. R. Co.,
Maloney Building,
Pittsburgh, Pa.

Honsberger, G. W.,
Transportation Manager,
Westinghouse E. & M. Co.,
Gulf Building,
Pittsburgh, Pa.

Hood, A. N.,
Freight Agent,
P. & L. E. R. R. Co.,
831 Neely Heights Ave.,
Coraopolis, Pa.

Hook, Charles H.,
  Asst. on Engineering Corps,
  Pennsylvania Railroad,
  1216 Brownsville Road,
      Pittsburgh (10), Pa

Hoon, F. R.,
  Supervising Agent,
  Pennsylvania Railroad,
  7225 McCurdy Place,
      Ben Avon, Pa.

Hoop, J. H.,
  Freight Agent,
  P. & L. E. R. R. Co.,
  413 Eleventh Street,
      Beaver Falls, Pa.

Hoopes, R. E.,
  Agent,
  Pennsylvania Railroad,
      Donora, Pa.

Hoover, Jacob W.,
  Asst. Chief of Transportation,
  Subsidiary Co.'s, U. S. Steel
  Corp.,
  816 Carnegie Bldg.,
      Pittsburgh, Pa.

Hopper, George,
  Chief Clerk to Terminal Agent
  B. & O. R. R. Co.,
  Grant & Water Sts.,
      Pittsburgh, Pa.

Horne, John S.,
  Gang Foreman,
  Pass. Car Insprs.,
  Pennsylvania Railroad,
  427 So. Pacific Ave.,
      Pittsburgh, Pa.

Hornefius, S. Reed,
  Movement Director,
  Pennsylvania Railroad,
  Pennsylvania Station,
      Pittsburgh, Pa.

Hovey, Otis W.,
  Engineer, Railway Research
  Bureau,
  U. S. Steel Corporation,
  Frick Building,
      Pittsburgh, Pa.

Howard, L. F.,
  Chief Engineer,
  Union Switch & Signal Co.,
      Swissvale, Pa.

Howe, Harry,
  Engr. of Ry. Equipment,
  Manganese Steel Forge Co.,
  Richmond & Castor Ave.,
      Philadelphia, Pa.

Huber, H. G.,
  Assistant Foreman,
  Pennsylvania Railroad,
  Pennsylvania Station,
      Pittsburgh, Pa.

Huff, A. B.,
  Foreman,
  Pennsylvania Railroad,
  209 Midland Ave.,
      Carnegie, Pa.

Huggans, A. V.,
  Agent,
  P. & L. E. R. R. Co.,
  1211 Berkshire Ave.,
      Pittsburgh, Pa.

Hughes, E. H.,
  Asst. Manager of Sales,
  Steel Construction Dept.,
  Jones & Laughlin Steel
  Corp.,
  311 Ross Street,
      Pittsburgh, Pa.

Hughes, I. Lamont,
  Woodland Road,
      Pittsburgh, Pa.

Hughes, L. H.,
  Supervisor, Eastern Demurrage & Storage Bureau,
  Pennsylvania Railroad,
  427 Vermont Ave.,
      Rochester, Pa.

Humphrey, A. L.,
  Chairman of Executive Com.,
  Westinghouse Air Brake Co.,
      Wilmerding, Pa.

Hunker, G. F.,
  Assistant Division Manager,
  Gulf Oil Corporation,
  Gross St. & P. R. R.
      Pittsburgh, Pa.

Hunt, C. T.,
  Asst. Engine House Foreman,
  Pennsylvania Railroad,
  604 Stanton Ave.,
      Pittsburgh, Pa

Hunt, Francis M., Jr.,
Supvr. Station Service,
Pennsylvania Railroad,
Pennsylvania Station,
Pittsburgh, Pa.

Hunt, Lawrence,
General Foreman,
Tank Car Department,
Pressed Steel Car Co.,
McKees Rocks, Pa.

Hunt, Roy A.,
President,
Aluminum Co. of America,
Gulf Building,
Pittsburgh, Pa.

Hursh, Samuel R.,
Division Superintendent,
Penna. Railroad Co.,
Wilmington, Del.

Huston, Frederick T.,
Master Mechanic,
Pennsylvania Railroad,
611 Pennsylvania Station,
Pittsburgh, Pa.

Hutchinson, George, Jr.,
District Sales Manager,
The Duff-Norton
Manufacturing Co.,
P. O. Box 1889,
Pittsburgh, Pa.

Hykes, W. H.,
Assistant Trainmaster,
Penna. R. R. Co.,
526 Sixth St.,
Oakmont, Pa.

Ingman, E. B.,
Patrolman,
B. & O. R. R. Co.,
131 Tipton St.,
Pittsburgh, Pa.

Inks, S. W.,
Master Mechanic,
Monongahela Railway Co.,
South Brownsville, Pa.

Irvin, Robert K.,
Conductor,
P. & L. E. R. R. Co.,
427 South Main St.,
Pittsburgh, Pa.

Irwin, Robert D.,
Foreman,
Westinghouse Air Brake Co.,
521 Holmes St.,
Wilkinsburg, Pa.

Israel, E. J., Jr.,
Industrial Agent,
Pennsylvania Railroad,
Pennsylvania Station,
Pittsburgh, Pa.

Jados, Walter T.,
Westinghouse Air Brake Co.,
104 Clara St.,
Wilmerding, Pa.

Jahnke, Karl W.,
Piece Work Inspector
P. & L. E. R. R. Co.,
238 Singer Avenue,
McKees Rocks, Pa.

James, J. H,.
Purchasing Agent,
P. & L. E. R. R.,
Pittsburgh, Pa.

Jarden, Carroll,
Railway Representative,
Sherwin-Williams Co.,
105 South Water Street,
Philadelphia, Pa.

Jarres, Frank A.,
Local Storekeeper,
B. & O. R. R. Co.,
392 West Fairview St.,
Somerset, Pa.

Jenkins, G. A.,
Patrolman,
B. & O. R. R. Co.,
362 Flowers Avenue,
Pittsburgh, Pa.

Jenness, D. H.,
R. F. of E., Penna. R. R.,
620 Sheridan Ave.,
Pittsburgh, Pa.

Jennings, A. S.,
Gen. Coal Freight Agent,
Pennsylvania Railroad,
Pennsylvania Station,
Pittsburgh, Pa.

Jennings, John E.,
Yard Master,
P. & L. E. R. R. Co.,
44 Aliquippa Street,
Monessen, Pa.

John, William,
Freight Claim Agent,
P. & L. E. R. R. Co.,
202 Dewey St.,
Edgewood, Swissvale P. O., Pa.

Johnson, E. A.,
15 North Euclid Ave.,
Bellevue, Pa.

Johnson, George T.,
Vice President, The
Buckeye Steel Castings Co.,
South Parsons Ave.,
Columbus, Ohio

Johnson, I. S.,
Resident Material Inspector,
The Pennsylvania Railroad,
Room 402, 1013 Penn Ave.,
Pittsburgh, Pa.

Johnson, J. W.,
Superintendent,
Railway Express Agency,
926 Penn Ave.,
Pittsburgh, Pa.

Johnson, Le Vere H.,
Executive Secretary,
Penna. Railroad Y. M. C. A.,
28th St. & Liberty Ave.,
Pittsburgh, Pa.

Johnson, Nelson E.,
Gang Leader,
P. & L. E. R. R. Co.,
1429 Summit St.,
McKees Rocks, Pa.

Johnson, Perry,
Asst. Train Master,
Pennsylvania Railroad,
1011 James Street,
N. S., Pittsburgh, Pa.

Johnson, Stephen, Jr.,
Chief Engineer,
Bendix Westinghouse
Automotive Air Brake Co.,
5001 Center Avenue,
Pittsburgh, Pa.

Johnson, Wm. M.,
Gen. Superintendent,
B. & L. E. R. R.,
Greenville, Pa.

Johnston, A. E.,
Asst. Gen. Freight Agent,
Pennsylvania Railroad,
Pennsylvania Station,
Pittsburgh, Pa.

Johnston, J. T.,
Asst. to Supy'r of Wage
Schedules,
P. & L. E. R. R. Co.,
1418 Fourth Ave.,
Beaver Falls, Pa.

Johnston, Samuel,
Asst. Comptroller,
Gulf Refining Co.,
Gulf Bldg.,
Pittsburgh, Pa.

Jones, Edward W.,
Correction Clerk,
B. & O. R. R. Co.,
2410 Glenroy Street,
Pittsburgh, Pa.

Jones, George, Sr.,
General Boiler Foreman,
B. & O. R. R. Co.,
605 Hazelwood Avenue,
Pittsburgh, Pa.

Jones, H. W.,
General Superintendent,
Pennsylvania Railroad,
Indianapolis, Ind.

Jones, L. E.,
Engr. to Vice President,
Carnegie-Illinois Steel Corp.,
Carnegie Bldg.,
Pittsburgh, Pa.

Jones, Louis E.,
Department Manager,
American Steel Foundries,
North Wrigley Bldg.,
Chicago, Ill.

Jones, William M.,
Clerk, Union Railroad,
5020 Glenwood Ave.,
Hazelwood Sta.,
Pittsburgh, Pa.

Joyce, P. H.,
Trustee,
C. G. W. R. R.,
122 So. Michigan Ave.,
Chicago, Ill.

Kamerer, R. W.,
General Agent,
P. & L. E. R. R. Co.,
Terminal Bldg.,
Pittsburgh, Pa.

Kane, Henry S.,
Freight Agent,
Pennsylvania Railroad,
433 Library Ave.,
Carnegie, Pa.

Kapp, A. C.,
General Foreman,
B. & L. E. R. R.,
R. F. D. No. 1,
Verona, Pa.

Karnes, W. T.,
General Foreman,
P. & L. E. R. R.,
330 Ohio Ave.,
Glassport, Pa.

Kashner, W. C.,
Asst. Train Master,
Pennsylvania Railroad,
1041 Fourth St.,
Beaver, Pa.

Kaup, Harry E.,
General Superintendent,
Pressed Steel Car Co.,
McKees Rocks, Pa.

Kavanagh, D.,
Storekeeper,
Union Railroad,
East Pittsburgh, Pa.

Kearfott, W. E.,
Asst. Engineer M. of W.,
B. & O. R. R. Co.,
231 Martin Avenue,
Mt. Lebanon, Pittsburgh, Pa.

Keck, L. M.,
Agent, Junction Transfer,
B. & O. R. R. Co.,
Liberty & 32nd Sts.,
Pittsburgh, Pa.

Keeney, A. R.,
Foreman Foundry,
Union Switch & Signal Co.,
4803 Cypress Street,
Pittsburgh, Pa.

Kellenberger, K. E.,
Advertising Manager,
Union Switch & Signal Co.,
Swissvale, Pa.

Keller, R. B.,
Supervisor,
Air Reduction Sales Co.,
942 California Ave.,
Avalon, Pittsburgh, Pa.

Keller, R. E.,
Lead Car Inspector,
P. & L. E. R. R.,
560 Stokes Ave.,
Braddock, Pa.

Kellerman, Dewey W.,
Clerk,
Pennsylvania Railroad,
1430 Nixon St.,
N. S., Pittsburgh, Pa.

Kelly, Eugene V.,
Yard Master,
P. & L. E. R. R. Co.,
313 Oneida Street,
Duquesne Heights,
Pittsburgh, Pa.

Kelly, H. B.,
Gen. R. F. of E.,
P. & L. E. R. R.,
3115 Ashlyn St.,
Corliss Station,
Pittsburgh, Pa.

Kelly, J. P.,
Asst. Superintendent,
P. & L. E. R. R.,
922 School St.,
Coraopolis, Pa.

Kelly, Leo J.,
Superintendent,
Fort Pitt Mall. Iron Co.,
3036 Bergman St.,
Pittsburgh, Pa.

Kemmerer, R. R.,
General Engineer,
Union Switch & Signal Co.,
8012 St. Lawrence Ave.,
Swissvale, Pa.

Kemp, Archie,
Engineer,
Pennsylvania Railroad,
1506 Twentieth St.,
Altoona, Pa.

Kempton, J. W.,
Gen. Sec'y, Y. M. C. A.,
P. & L. E. R. R.,
Newell, Pa.

Kennedy, A. R.,
Traffic Manager,
Pittsburgh Steel Co.,
Union Trust Bldg.,
Pittsburgh, Pa.

Kennedy, F. J.,
Auditor Pass. Accounts,
P. & L. E. R. R.,
Box 206,
New Brighton, Pa.

Kennedy, G. N.,
Foreman,
Pennsylvania Railroad,
575 So. Negley Ave.,
House No. 14,
Pittsburgh, Pa.

Kentlein, John,
Chief Draftsman,
H. K. Porter Co.,
49th & Harrison Sts.,
Pittsburgh, Pa.

Kern, Roy S.,
Chairman,
Coal, Coke & Iron Ore Com.,
Wabash Building,
Pittsburgh, Pa.

Kerr, Alexander D.,
Asst. Supervisor,
Pennsylvania Railroad,
Mansfield, Ohio.

Kerr, Charles, Jr.,
Railway Engineer,
Westinghouse Electric &
Mfg. Co.,
231 Elm St.,
Edgewood, Swissvale P. O,. Pa.

Kerr, Clark R.,
Asst. Car Foreman,
Union Railroad Co.,
East Pittsburgh, Pa.

Kerr, James P., M. D.,
Chief Surgeon,
P. & W. Va. Ry. Co.,
Wabash Building,
Pittsburgh, Pa.

Kessler, A. L.,
Clearance Clerk,
Pennsylvania Railroad,
402 Knox Avenue.
Pittsburgh, Pa.

Keys, A. H.,
Dist. Master Car Builder,
B. & O. R. R. Co.,
1651 Potomac Ave.,
Dormont,
Pittsburgh, Pa.

Kilborn, W. T.,
President,
Flannery Bolt Co.,
Bridgeville, Pa.

Kim, J. B.,
Gang Foreman,
Pennsylvania Railroad,
7354 Hamilton Ave.,
Pittsburgh, Pa.

Kimling, Carl,
Asst. Mgr., Central Warehouse,
P. & L. E. R. R.,
85 Harwood St.,
Pittsburgh, Pa.

King, C. F., Jr.,
District Engineer,
Westinghouse Elec. & Mfg.
Company,
3001 Walnut St.,
Philadelphia, Pa.

King, E. C.,
Route Agent,
Railway Express Agency,
Inc.,
5801 Rippey Street,
Pittsburgh, Pa.

King, J. C.,
Yard Master,
Pennsylvania Railroad,
2200 Nance Ave.,
Wheeling, W. Va.

Kirby, D. D.,
President,
Kirby Trans. & Storage Co.,
2538 Smallman St.,
Pittsburgh, Pa.

Kirk, Charles C.,
Supervisor Reg. Express,
Pennsylvania Railroad,
Pennsylvania Station,
Pittsburgh, Pa.

Kirk, W. B.,
Test Engineer,
Westinghouse Air Brake Co.,
412 Arlington Ave.,
East McKeesport, Pa.

Kirkland, Norman L.,
Partner,
Acme Printing & Stationery
Company,
1475 Greenmont Ave.,
Dormont, Pittsburgh,
Pa.

Kiskadden, H. L.,
Clerk,
Pennsylvania Railroad,
115 Stewart Ave.,
Freeport, Pa.

Klassen, Fred G.,
Traveling Engineer,
P. & W. Va. Ry.,
Carnegie, Pa.

Kleber, P. C.,
Gang Leader,
P. & L. E. R. R. Co.,
803 Eighth St.,
McKees Rocks, Pa.

Klein, J. W.,
  President & General Manager,
  Pittsburgh Refrigeration Co.,
  1115 Penn Ave.,
                  Pittsburgh, Pa.

Klein, Nicholas P.,
  Foreman Car Repairs,
  Pennsylvania Railroad,
  50 South 33rd St.,
                  Pittsburgh, Pa.

Klein, S. J.,
  Asst. Traffic Manager,
  P. & W. Va. Ry. Co.,
  Wabash Building,
                  Pittsburgh, Pa.

Kleinhans, Harry,
  President,
  H. Kleinhans Co.,
  419 Union Trust Bldg.,
                  Pittsburgh, Pa.

Knable, G. Elkins,
  Manager Structural and
  Plate Division,
  Carnegie-Illinois Steel
    Corp.,
    Carnegie Bldg,.
                  Pittsburgh, Pa.

Knoff, R. A.,
  National Railroad Adjustment
  Board, First Div.,
  220 South State St.,
                  Chicago, Ill.

Knoke, H. C.,
  Secretary to District
  Master Mechanic,
  B. & O. R. R. Co.,
  1518 Kelton Ave.,
  Dormont, Pittsburgh, Pa.

Knox, Wm. J.,
  112 Second Ave.,
                  DuBois, Pa.

Koch, C. W.,
  Clerk,
  P. & L. E. R. R. Co.,
  1257 Clairhaven St.,
                  Pittsburgh, Pa.

Kohl, H. J.,
  Gen. Car Foreman,
  P. & L. E. R. R.,
  1106 Tweed St.,
                  Pittsburgh, Pa.

Kohl, Leo H.,
  S. W. District Secretary,
  State R. R., Y. M. C. A.,
  241 Whipple St.,
                  Swissvale, Pittsburgh, Pa.

Kondej, Henry,.
  Test Engineer,
  Westinghouse Air Brake Co.,
  571½ East End Ave.,
                  Pittsburgh, Pa.

Krahmer, Edward F.,
  Supvr. Agt.—Div. Opr.,
  Pennsylvania Railroad,
  Pennsylvania Station,
                  Pittsburgh, Pa.

Kramer, F. E.,
  P. & W. Va. Ry. Co.,
  3260 Beaconhill Ave.,
  Dormont,
                  Pittsburgh, Pa.

Kramer, W. H.,
  Train Rider,
  B. & O. R. R. Co.,
  203 Maytide Street,
                  Carrick, Pittsburgh, Pa.

Kramer, William E.,
  Representative,
  Acme Steel Co.,
  3674 Middletown Road,
  Corliss Station,
                  Pittsburgh, Pa.

Kraus, Raymond E.,
  Mechanical Draftsman,
  P. & L. E. R. R.,
  241 Dickson Ave.,
  Ben Avon,
                  Pittsburgh, Pa.

Krause, Harry A.,
  Gang Fore., Penna. R. R. Co.,
  160 Race Street,
  . Edgewood, Pittsburgh, Pa.

Kroen, Vincent,
  Supervisor Express Service,
  Pennsylvania Railroad,
  Pennsylvania Station,
                  Pittsburgh, Pa.

Kromer, Wm. F.,
  Mechanical Engineer,
  H. K. Porter Co.,
  108 Tenth St.,
                  Aspinwall, Pa.

Kroske, J. F.,
Mgr., P. T. Sales,
Ingersoll-Rand Co.,
706 Chamber of Commerce
Building,
Pittsburgh, Pa.

Kruse, J. F. W.,
Superintendent,
Hubbard & Co.,
528 Washington Ave.,
Oakmont, Pa.

Kuhn, Samuel H.,
Office Engineer,
Pennsylvania Railroad,
51 Division St.,
Crafton, Pittsburgh, Pa.

Kulp, J. G.,
Train Master,
Pennsylvania Railroad,
810 Rebecca Ave.,
Wilkinsburg, Pa.

Kusick, Harry F.,
Engineer,
Union Switch & Signal Co.,
Swissvale, Pa.

Lackner, Ray A.,
District Sales Manager,
Penna. Forge Corp.,
5724 Bartlett St.,
Pittsburgh, Pa.

Lanahan, Frank J.,
President, Fort Pitt Malleable
Iron Co.,
P. O. Box 492,
Pittsburgh, Pa.

Lanahan, J. S.,
Vice President, Fort Pitt
Malleable Iron Co.,
127 Elysian Ave.,
Pittsburgh, Pa.

Landis, W. C.,
Asst. Works Manager,
Westinghouse Air Brake Co.,
Wilmerding, Pa.

Langhurst, R. O.,
Gang Leader,
P. & L. E. R. R. Co.,
1502 Orchlee St.,
N. S., Pittsburgh, Pa.

Lanken, C. C.,
President-Treasurer,
Lincoln Electric Railway
Sales Company,
Marshall Building,
Cleveland, Ohio.

Lanning, Edward H.,
Acting Gang Foreman,
Pennsylvania Railroad,
6832 McPherson Blvd.,
Pittsburgh, Pa.

Lanning, J. Frank,
President,
J. Frank Lanning & Co.,
327 First Ave.,
Pittsburgh, Pa.

Largent, J. R.,
Ticket Agent,
P. & L. E. R. R. Co.,
P&LE Station,
Pittsburgh, Pa.

Larsen, O. C.,
Secretary-Treasurer,
The North American
Coal Corp.,
Wabash Building,
Pittsburgh, Pa.

Larson, W. E.,
Vice President, Superior
Railway Products Corp.,
7501 Thomas Blvd.,
Pittsburgh, Pa.

Lauderbaugh, Moss,
Freight Agent,
P. & L. E. R. R. Co.,
16 Fifth Street,
Ellwood City, Pa.

Laurent, Jos. A.,
Gen. Fore. Fin. Dept.,
Fort Pitt Mall. Iron Co.,
206 Bruce St.,
McKees Rocks, Pa.

Lavine, Ralph D.,
Chief Rate & Div. Clerk,
P. & L. E. R. R. Co.,
324 Ophelia St.,
Pittsburgh, Pa.

Lawler, Joseph A.,
Sup't Trans.,
Carnegie Steel Co.,
Edgar Thomson Works,
Braddock, Pa.

Lawrence, Norman M.,
Superintendent E. & A.
Division,
Pennsylvania Railroad,
322 E. Lincoln Ave.,
New Castle, Pa.

Layng, Frank R.,
Chief Engineer,
B. & L. E. R. R.,
Greenville, Pa.

Lear, E. J.,
Hostler,
B. & O. R. R. Co.,
713 Freeland St.,
Pittsburgh, Pa.

Leban, J. L.,
Asst. District Supt.,
Pullman Co.,
1434 Gulf Bldg.,
Pittsburgh, Pa.

Lee, L. A.,
Secretary, General
Safety Committee,
P. & L. E. R. R.,
645 Bigelow Street,
Pittsburgh, Pa.

Lees, Thomas,
Reymer & Brothers, Inc.,
123 Bascom St.,
Pittsburgh, (14) Pa.

Leet, C. S.,
Asst. Gen. Mgr.,
B. & L. E. R. R.,
P. O. Box 536,
Pittsburgh, Pa.

Leiper, C. I.,
Gen. Mgr., Central Region,
Pennsylvania Railroad,
Pennsylvania Station,
Pittsburgh, Pa.

Leonard, C. W.,
Salesman,
Independent Pneumatic Tool
Co.,
Wabash Building,
Pittsburgh, Pa.

Leonard, J. F.,
Engineer, Bridges & Bldgs.,
Pennsylvania Railroad,
Pennsylvania Station,
Pittsburgh, Pa.

Leonard, P. J.,
General Foreman,
B. & O. R. R. Co.,
5220 Holmes Street,
Pittsburgh, Pa.

Lewis, Herbert,
Vice President & Secretary,
The Durametallic Corp.,
24 Commerce St.,
Newark, N. J.

Lewis, N. F.,
Test Engineer,
Westinghouse Air Brake Co.,
523 North Avenue,
Wilkinsburg, Pa.

Lincoln, John J.,
District Manager,
Air Reduction Sales Co.,
1116 Ridge Ave.,
N. S., Pittsburgh, Pa.

Lincoln, R. B.,
Director of Weld Testing,
Pittsburgh Testing
Laboratory,
Locust & Stevenson Sts.,
Pittsburgh, Pa.

Lippold, Hermann H.,
Coal Freight Agent,
Pennsylvania Railroad,
Pennsylvania Station,
Pittsburgh, Pa.

Litty, J. H.,
Extra Agent, Eastern Div.,
Pennsylvania Railroad,
Pennsylvania Station,
Pittsburgh, Pa.

Livingston, W. C.,
Regional Storekeeper,
Pennsylvania Railroad,
1125 Savannah Ave.,
Edgewood, Pittsburgh, Pa.

Lloyd, J. A.,
General Freight Agent,
Pittsburgh Railways Co.,
Exposition Building,
Pittsburgh, Pa.

Lloyd, John,
Asst. General Superintendent
Edgar Thomson Works,
Carnegie-Illinois Steel
Corp.,
Braddock, Pa.

Loder, C. C.,
Representative,
Plibrico Jointless Fire-
brick Co.,
298 Duquesne Way,
Pittsburgh, Pa.

Loeffler, George O.,
District Representative,
Climax Molybdenum Co.,
905 Union Trust Bldg.,
Pittsburgh, Pa.

Logan, J. W., Jr.,
Engineer,
Union Switch & Signal Co.,
Swissvale, Pa.

Long, Alfred J.,
Movement Director,
Pennsylvania Railroad,
1828 Pioneer Ave.,
Pittsburgh, Pa.

-Long, R. M.,
"Retired" Air Brake
Inspector and Instructor,
P. & L. E. R. R.,
3118 Pioneer Ave.,
South Hills Branch,
Pittsburgh, Pa.

Long, Walter,
Walter Long Mfg. Co.,
1313 Burgham St.,
S. S., Pittsburgh, Pa.

Longdon, Clyde V.,
Asst. Engineer,
T. & E. D. Dept.,
Westinghouse Air Brake
Company,
R. D. 1, Box 260,
Turtle Creek, Pa.

Longstreth, W. L.,
Road Foreman of Engines,
Conemaugh Div.,
Pennsylvania Railroad,
301 Delaware Ave.,
Oakmont, Pa.

Looman, F. W.,
Freight Agent,
Pennsylvania Railroad,
Canton, Ohio

Lortz, Elmer A.,
Safety Engineer,
Pressed Steel Car Co.,
3924 Winshire St.,
N. S., Pittsburgh, Pa.

Loucks, William V.,
Yard Master,
Pennsylvania Railroad,
207 North Walnut St.,
Blairsville, Pa.

Lowe, William T.,
General Freight Agent,
American Window Glass Co.,
117 Hemphill St.,
N. S., Pittsburgh, Pa.

Lowery, J. V.,
Passenger Train Master,
Pennsylvania Railroad,
707 Nevin Ave.,
Sewickley, Pa.

Lowry, Wm. F., Jr.,
Sales Agent,
American Car &
Foundry Co.,
Farmers Bank Bldg.,
Pittsburgh, Pa.

Luce, W. A.,
Master Mechanic,
Pittsburgh, Lisbon &
Western R. R. Co.,
Darlington, Pa

Lundeen, Carl J.,
Asst. Mechanical Engr.,
P. & L. E. R. R.,
400 Island Ave.,
McKees Rocks, Pa

Lunz, G. J.,
Chief Clerk, Freight Traffic
Department,
P. & L. E. R. R. Co.,
Terminal Bldg.,
Pittsburgh, Pa.

Lustenberger, L. C.,
Asst. to Vice Pres. & Gen.
Mgr. of Sales,
Carnegie Steel Co.,
Subsidiaries,
R. F. D. No. 4,
Millvale Branch,
Pittsburgh, Pa.

Lutz, Harry,
Supvr. Tel. & Signals,
Pennsylvania Railroad,
499 Roosevelt Ave.,
Bellevue, Pa.

Lynn, William,
General Car Foreman,
P. & L. E. R. R.,
1521 Ridge Ave.,
Coraopolis, Pa.

MacDonald, George F.,
Chief Clerk to Chief Engineer,
P. & L. E. R. R. Co.,
Pittsburgh, Pa.

MacDonald, William C.,
Special Agent, Contracts,
Penna. R. R. Co.,
254 Allison Ave.,
Emsworth, Pa.

MacElveny, A. W.,
General Traffic Manager,
Schenley Products Co.,
20 West 40th St.,
New York, N. Y.

Machin, Norman H.,
Gang Foreman,
Pennsylvania Railroad,
359 Reno Street,
Rochester, Pa.

Mackert, A. A.,
450 Caldwell Ave.,
Wilmerding, Pa.

Mahaney, A. R.,
Transportation Apprentice,
Pennsylvania Railroad,
Amber Club, Wellesley Ave.,
E. E., Pittsburgh, Pa.

Maliphant, C. W.,
Test Dept.,
W. A. B. Co.,
101 Herman Ave.,
Wilmerding, Pa.

Malone, Creed,
General Yard Master,
Monongahela Railway Co.,
Morgantown, W. Va.

Mann, Henry S.,
District Sales Manager,
Standard Stoker Co., Inc.,
1801 McCormick Bldg.,
Chicago, Ill.

Mannion, M. F.,
Office Asst. to Chief Engr.,
B. & L. E. R. R.,
96 North High St.,
Greenville, Pa.

Manson, Arthur J.,
Asst. Sales Manager,
Westinghouse Electric &
Mfg. Co.,
700 Braddock Ave.,
East Pittsburgh, Pa.

Marble, A. E.,
Metallurgical Dept.,
Jones & Laughlin Steel
Corp.,
Third Ave. & Ross St.,
Pittsburgh, Pa.

Marble, Robert A.,
Structural Engineer,
Carnegie Steel Co.,
Carnegie Bldg.,
Pittsburgh, Pa.

Marquis, G. E.,
Chief Train Master,
P. & L. E. R. R. Co.,
702 Sixth Avenue,
New Brighton, Pa.

Marsh, E. A.,
Car Foreman,
B. & O. R. R. Co.,
2830 Louisiana St.,
Dormont, Pgh., Pa.

Mason, W. N.,
General Yard Master,
P. & L. E. R. R. Co.,
936 Atlantic Ave.,
Monaca, Pa.

Masterman, T. W.,
Asst. to Chief Design Engr.,
Westinghouse Air Brake Co.,
1249 McClure Ave.,
East McKeesport, Pa.

Masters, W. C.,
Sales Engineer,
Flannery Bolt Co.,
Bridgeville, Pa.

Matchneer, Wm. W.,
Sales Engineer,
Buckeye Steel Castings Co.,
Columbus, Ohio.

Matthews, R. J.,
Salesman,
Edgewater Steel Co.,
P. O. Box 478,
Pittsburgh, Pa.

270

Matuseski, Robert R.,
Gang Foreman,
Pennsylvania Railroad,
Pittsburgh, Pa.

Maxfield, Col. H. H.,
S. M. P., Southern Div.,
Pennsylvania Railroad,
402 Pennsylvania Bldg.,
Wilmington, Del.

Maxwell, R. E.,
Wheel Engineer,
Carnegie Steel Co.,
Carnegie Bldg.,
Pittsburgh, Pa.

Maxwell, Thomas,
Foreman Tool & Equipment
Design Department,
Westinghouse Air Brake
Co.,
933 Milton Street,
Pittsburgh, Pa.

May, Herbert A.,
Vice President,
Union Switch & Signal Co.,
Swissvale, Pa.

May, J. D.,
Yard Master,
Pennsylvania Railroad,
1410 Penn Ave.,
Steubenville, Ohio.

Mayer, George E.,
Photographer,
P. & L. E. R. R. Co.,
Terminal Annex Bldg.,
Pittsburgh, Pa.

Mayer, L. I.,
Westinghouse Air Brake Co.,
1228 Fifth Ave.,
East McKeesport, Pa.

Meagher, Maurice E.,
Railway Equip. Rep.,
Peter Meagher,
Roosevelt Hotel,
Pittsburgh, Pa.

Megee, Caleb R.,
District Manager,
Car Service Division,
Association of American
Railroads,
1103 Penna. Station,
Pittsburgh, Pa.

Meinert, Henry, J.,
Locomotive Inspector,
Montour Railroad,
11 Geneva St.,
Etna, Pa.

Mekeel, David L.,
Consulting Engineer,
Jones & Laughlin Steel Corp.
J. & L. Building,
Pittsburgh, Pa.

Mellon, Curtis B.,
Asst. Foreman,
Pennsylvania Railroad,
124 Noll Ave.,
Ingram, Pa.

Mellor, C. L.,
Vice President,
Barco Manufacturing Co.,
1801 Winnemac Ave.,
Chicago, Ill.

Menaglia, Victor A.,
District Sales Manager,
S K F Industries,
Grant Bldg.,
Pittsburgh, Pa.

Menk, C. W.,
Agent,
Pennsylvania Railroad,
New Kensington, Pa.

Meredith, A. R.,
Real Estate Agent,
Pennsylvania Railroad,
Pennsylvania Station,
Pittsburgh, Pa.

Merz, G. L.,
Asst. Fore., Pgh. 11th St.,
Pennsylvania Railroad,
500 Curtin Ave.,
Pittsburgh, Pa.

Metcalf, George E.,
Locomotive Engineer,
Montour Railroad Co.,
717 School St.,
Coraopolis, Pa.

Metzgar, Herbert T.,
Storehouse Foreman,
B. & O. R. R. Co.,
5301 Gertrude St.,
Hazelwood, Pittsburgh, Pa

Metzgar, C. L.,
  Secretary,
    Auto-Tite Joints Co.,
    7501 Thomas Blvd.,
        Pittsburgh, Pa.

Micheals, John H.,
  Yard Master,
    Pennsylvania Railroad,
    1550 Marlborro Ave.,
        Wilkinsburg, Pa.

Millar, Clarence W.,
  Mgr. Order Dept.,
    Pressed Steel Car Co.,
        McKees Rocks, Pa.

Miller, Henry,
  General Manager,
    Fort Pitt Spring Company,
    Box 1377,
        Pittsburgh, Pa.

Miller, J. F.,
  Sales Engineer,
    Carnegie Steel Co.,
    Carnegie Bldg.,
        Pittsburgh, Pa.

Miller, John,
  General Car Foreman,
    Montour Railroad,
    5127 Blair St.,
        Hazelwood, Pa.

Miller, R. C.,
  General Superintendent,
    Pennsylvania Railroad,
    Pennsylvania Station,
        Pittsburgh, Pa.

Miller, R. E.,
  General Engineer,
    Westinghouse Air Brake Co.,
        Wilmerding, Pa.

Miller, R. H.,
  General Freight Agent,
    Pennsylvania Railroad,
    Pennsylvania Station,
        Pittsburgh, Pa.

Miller, S. H.,
  Secretary & Treasurer,
    Fort Pitt Chemical Co.,
    26th & Smallman Sts.,
        Pittsburgh, Pa.

Miller, W. J.,
  Storekeeper,
    Pennsylvania Railroad,
    349 Moyhend St.,
        Springdale, Pa.

Milliken, Roy C.,
  Asst. Yard Master,
    Pennsylvania Railroad,
    Box 125,
        Allegheny River Bldg.,
            Verona, Pa.

Mills, C. C.,
  General Manager,
    Unity Railways Co.,
    Union Trust Bldg.,
        Pittsburgh, Pa.

Mills, O. B.,
  Stationery Storekeeper,
    Pennsylvania Railroad,
    11th St. Freight Station,
        Pittsburgh, Pa.

Minnick, F. G.,
  37 North Bryant Street,
    Bellevue, Pittsburgh, Pa.

Misklow, C. J.,
  C. C. to Asst. Train Master,
    P. & W. Va. Ry.,
    7 Division St.,
        Crafton, Pittsburgh, Pa.

Misner, George W.,
  Westinghouse Air Brake Co.,
    304 Arlington Ave.,
        East McKeesport, Pa.

Mitchell, A. T.,
  Chief Smoke Inspector,
    Pennsylvania Railroad,
    413 McNair St.,
        Wilkinsburg, Pa.

Mitchell, Frank K.,
  Signal Inspector,
    P. & L. E. R. R.,
    240 East End Ave.,
        Beaver, Pa.

Mitchell, J. G.,
  Sub-Storekeeper,
    Union Railroad,
        East Pittsburgh, Pa.

Mitchell, W. S.,
  Signal Inspector,
    P. & L. E. R. R.,
    540 River Road,
        Beaver, Pa.

Mittelstadter, Howard,
  Foreman,
    P. & L. E. R. R. Co.,
    1139 Wisconsin Ave.,
    Dormont,
        Pittsburgh, Pa.

Mohn, Louis,
District Manager,
Garlock Packing Co.,
339 Blvd. of Allies,
Pittsburgh, Pa.

Moir, W. B.,
Chief Car Inspector,
Pennsylvania Railroad,
1009 Penna. Station,
Pittsburgh, Pa

Molyneaux, Dawes S.,
Sales Engineer,
Ft. Pitt Spring Co.,
Box 917,
Pittsburgh, Pa.

Montague, C. F.,
Master Carpenter,
Monongahela Division,
Pennsylvania Railroad,
Pennsylvania Station,
Pittsburgh, Pa.

Montgomery, J. L.,
Assistant Auditor,
Union Railroad,
Frick Bldg. Annex,
Pittsburgh, Pa.

Moore, Donald O.,
Mgr. of Traffic Div.,
Chamber of Commerce,
Chamber of Com. Bldg.,
Pittsburgh, Pa.

Morgan, A. L.,
Supt. on Special Duty,
Penna. R. R. Co.,
24 Maple Ave.,
Woodlawn,
Wheeling, W. Va.

Morgan, Homer C.,
613 Frederick St.,
McKees Rocks, Pa

Morris, J. M.,
President & Gen. Mgr.,
The Lake Terminal R. R. Co.
McKeesport Connecting
R. R.,
Frick Bldg.,
Pittsburgh, Pa

Morris, W. F., Jr.,
Vice President,
Weirton Steel Co.,
Grant Bldg.,
Pittsburgh, Pa.

Morse, J. W.,
Asst. T. M.-Asst. R. F. of E.,
Pennsylvania Railroad,
303 North 4th St.,
Youngwood, Pa.

Morton, R. A.,
Machine Shop Foreman,
B. & O. R. R. Co.,
236 Johnstone Ave.,
Hazelwood, Pittsburgh, Pa.

Moser, G. B.,
Clerk,
Pittsburgh, Chartiers &
Youghiogheny Ry.,
P&LE Terminal Annex
Bldg.,
Pittsburgh, Pa.

Moulis, F. J.,
Cash Clerk,
B. & O. R. R. Co.,
1412 Alton St.,
Beechview,
Pittsburgh, Pa.

Mowery, George B.,
Gen. Fore., Allegheny Shops,
B. & O. R. R. Co.,
101 Hazelwood Ave.,
Pittsburgh, Pa.

Mowry, John W.,
Salesman,
Scully Steel Products Co.,
1281 Reedsdale St.,
Pittsburgh, Pa.

Muir, Robert Y.,
Master Car Builder,
P. & W. Va. Ry. Co.,
1237 Hillsdale Ave.,
Dormont,
Pittsburgh, Pa.

Mulligan, Michael,
Engine House Foreman,
Monongahela Railway Co.,
315 Water Street,
South Brownsville, Pa.

Mulvey, John I.,
Traffic Manager,
Hubbard & Co.,
6301 Butler St.,
Pittsburgh, Pa.

Munn, Alex D.,
First Aid Inspector,
P. & L. E. R. R.,
Box 307,
Glenwillard, Pa.

Murphy, Martin,
 General Yard Master,
 P. & L. E. R. R. Co.,
 316 Jucunda St.,
 Knoxville, Pittsburgh, Pa.

Murray, Charles C.,
 Asst. C. C. to Storekeeper,
 B. & O. R. R. Co.,
 5312 Gertrude St.,
 Pittsburgh, Pa.

Murray, Stewart,
 Salesman,
 Joseph Dixon Crucible Co.,
 6615 Northumberland St.,
 Pittsburgh, Pa.

Murray, Thomas A.,
 Stenographer,
 P. & L. E. R. R. Co.,
 Terminal Bldg.,
 Pittsburgh, Pa.

Murray, T. J.,
 Track Supervisor,
 Pennsylvania Railroad,
 Homestead, Pa.

Muse, Thos. Charles,
 Traveling Car Agent,
 P. & L. E. R. R.,
 253 Fourth St.,
 Beaver, Pa.

Musgrove, W. W.,
 Piece Work Inspector,
 P. & L. E. R. R.,
 Box 301,
 Glenwillard, Pa

Mussey, Delavan S.,
 Engineer, Development Div.,
 Aluminum Co. of America,
 Wearever Bldg.,
 New Kensington, Pa

Myer, Charles R.,
 Engine House Foreman,
 Pennsylvania Railroad,
 529 Hill Avenue,
 Wilkinsburg, Pa

Myers, Arnold,
 Equipment Inspector,
 B. & L. E. R. R. Co.,
 217 Woodlawn Ave.,
 Munhall, Pa.

Myers, Robert H.,
 Sales Manager,
 American Shim Steel Co.,
 1304 Fifth Avenue,
 New Kensington, Pa.

McAbee, W. S.,
 Vice Pres. & Gen. Supt.,
 Union Railroad,
 664 Linden Avenue,
 East Pittsburgh, Pa.

McAndrew, R. E.,
 General Storekeeper,
 B. & L. E. R. R.,
 Greenville, Pa.

McBride, Gordon P.,
 Supervisors' Field Man,
 P. & L. E. R. R. Co.,
 Terminal Bldg.,
 Pittsburgh, Pa.

McCandless, William A.,
 Passenger Trainman,
 Pennsylvania Railroad,
 206 Alwine Ave.,
 Greensburg, Pa.

McCarthy, F. W.,
 Supt. Road Operation,
 Pittsburgh Railways Co.,
 435 Sixth Ave.,
 Pittsburgh, Pa.

McCarthy, Frank C.,
 Fitter,
 Mesta Machine Company,
 307½ Fiske Street,
 Pittsburgh, Pa.

McCartney, John H.,
 District Manager,
 Gustin-Bacon Mfg. Co.,
 1021 Filbert St.,
 Philadelphia, Pa

McCauley, William,
 Road Foreman of Engines,
 Pennsylvania Railroad,
 1013 Savannah Ave.,
 Wilkinsburg, Pa

McClintock, John D.,
 Manager, Injector Dept.,
 Wm. Sellers & Co., Inc.,
 1600 Hamilton St.,
 Philadelphia, Pa.

McComb, R. J.,
Sales Manager,
Woodings-Verona Tool
Works,
648 Peoples Gas Bldg.,
Chicago, Ill.

McConnell, Frank P.,
Yard Master,
P. & L. E. R. R.,
2101 Arlington Ave.,
Pittsburgh, Pa.

McCorkle, J. B.,
General Freight Agent,
Pennsylvania Railroad,
Pennsylvania Station,
Pittsburgh, Pa.

McCormick, E. S.,
Train Master,
Pennsylvania Railroad,
'c' 511 Sixth St.,
Oakmont, Pa.

McCowin, John,
Signal Supervisor,
P. & L. E. R. R. Co.,
236 Ann St.,
McKeesport, Pa.

McCrea, James G.,
Brakeman,
Pennsylvania Railroad,
811 Franklin Ave.,
Wilkinsburg, Pa.

McCready, R. E.,
General Foreman,
Water Supply,
P. & L. E. R. R. Co.,
296 Park Street,
Beaver, Pa.

McCrossin, C. D.,
Tel. & Sig. Foreman,
Pennsylvania Railroad,
204 Emerson Ave.,
Aspinwall, Pa.

McCuen, J. T.,
Salesman,
Motch & Merryweather
Machinery Co.,
Clark Building,
Pittsburgh, Pa.

McCully, D. L.,
Supervisor,
Westinghouse Air Brake Co.,
8001 Westmoreland Ave.,
Edgewood, Pa.

McCune, J. C.,
Asst. Director Engineering,
Westinghouse Air Brake Co.,
Wilmerding, Pa.

McDowell, C. G.,
Chief Route Agent,
Railway Express Agency,
Inc.,
708 Summerlea St.,
Pittsburgh, Pa.

McElravy, J. W.,
Terminal Agent,
P. & L. E. R. R.,
Terminal Annex Bldg.,
S. S., Pittsburgh, Pa.

McFetridge, W. S.,
Principal Asst. Engineer,
B. & L. E. R. R. Co.,
Greenville, Pa.

McGaughey, J. V.,
Asst. Road Fore. of Engines,
Pennsylvania Railroad,
313 South Avenue,
Wilkinsburg, Pa.

McGeary, E. J.,
Superintendent,
B. & L. E. R. R.,
P. O. Box 471,
Greenville, Pa.

McGeorge, D. W.,
Secretary,
Edgewater Steel Co.,
P. O. Box 478,
Pittsburgh, Pa.

McGervey, William P., Jr.,
Asst. to President,
Union Steel Casting Co.,
62nd & Butler Sts.,
Pittsburgh, Pa.

McGuirk, John J.,
Div. Car Foreman,
B. & O. R. R. Co.,
414 Moore Ave.,
Knoxville,
Pittsburgh, Pa.

McHail, J. L.,
Agent,
Pennsylvania Railroad,
904 McClure St.,
Homestead, Pa.

McHugh, C. A.,
Train Master,
P. & W. Va. Ry.,
21 Cannon St.,
Crafton, Pa.

McIntyre, R. C.,
Supt. Motive Power,
Union Railroad,
East Pittsburgh, Pa.

McKalip, W. B.,
Agent,
Pennsylvania Railroad,
Tarentum, Pa.

McKay, N. H.,
President,
U. S. Chromium Corp.,
1100 Pitt St.,
Wilkinsburg, Pa.

McKedy, H. V.,
Rep., Railway Dept.,
The Patterson, Sargent Co.,
135 East 42nd St.,
New York, N. Y.

McKee, Frederick C.,
Pres., Winfield R. R.,
2215 Oliver Bldg.,
Pittsburgh, Pa.

McKibbin, J. S.,
Local Treasurer,
P. & L. E. R. R. Co.,
3111 Wainbell Avenue,
Dormont, Pgh. (16), Pa.

McKim, Hollis,
Office Manager,
Edgewater Steel Company,
P. O. Box 478,
Pittsburgh, Pa.

McKinley, Archie J.,
Chief Motive Power Inspector
P. & L. E. R. R.,
613 Broadway Ave.,
McKees Rocks, Pa.

McKinley, John T.,
Stenographer,
P. & L. E. R. R.,
403 Woodward Ave.,
McKees Rocks, Pa.

McKinstry, C. H.,
Asst. Research Engineer,
W. A. B. Co.,
46 Sprague St.,
Wilmerding, Pa

McKinzie, Edward,
General Yard Master,
P. & W. Va. Ry.,
1524 Alabama Ave.,
Dormont,
Pittsburgh, Pa.

McKisson, R. W.,
Sales Agent,
American Steel Foundries,
410 N. Michigan Ave.,
Chicago, Ill.

McLain, J. E.,
Special Representative,
Bethlehem Steel Co.,
1214 Oliver Bldg.,
Pittsburgh, Pa.

McLaughlin, Howard B.,
R. F. of E.,
P. & L. E. R. R.,
2401 Alwyn St.,
Pittsburgh, (16) Pa.

McLean, J. L.,
Representative,
Barco Mfg. Co.,
12980 Edgewater Drive,
Cleveland, Ohio

McMillan, A. P.,
Boiler Foreman,
P. & W. Va. Ry.,
520 Washington Ave.,
Carnegie, Pa.

McMillan, J. G.,
Secretary,
The M. N. Landay Co.,
Clark Building,
Pittsburgh, Pa

McMillen, Harry,
Car Inspector,
P. & L. E. R. R.,
P. O. Box 378,
Braddock, Pa.

McMullen, Clark E.,
Inspector Transportation,
P. & L. E. R. R. Co.,
P. & L. E. Terminal Bldg.,
Pittsburgh, Pa.

McNamee, William
District Manager,
Briggs & Turivas Co.,
41 Marion St.,
Crafton, Pa.

McNary, Frank R.,
Movement Supervisor,
Pennsylvania Railroad,
Pennsylvania Station,
Pittsburgh, Pa.

McNeal, A. R.,
Asst. Fore., Pgh. 11th St.,
Pennsylvania Railroad,
West Railroad St.,
Heidelberg, Pa.

McPherson, A. R.,
Train Master,
Montour Railroad,
1706 Ridge Avenue,
Coraopolis, Pa.

McQuillen, J. J.,
President,
The Durametallic Corp.,
24 Commerce St.,
Newark, N. J.

McQuiston, C. A.,
Commercial Agent,
Railway Express Agency,
Inc.,
926 Penn Avenue,
Pittsburgh, Pa.

McTighe, B. J.,
Hubbard & Co.,
5253 Carnegie Ave.,
Pittsburgh, Pa.

McVicker, Allen,
Agent,
P. & L. E. R. R. Co.,
P. O. Box 36,
West Pittsburgh, Pa.

McWilliams, J. B.,
President,
Railway Maintenance
Corporation,
Box 1888,
Pittsburgh, Pa.

Nabors, W. F.,
Scale Inspector,
P. & L. E. R. R. Co.,
7122 Schoyer Avenue,
Swissvale, Pa.

Nagel, James,
Supt. Transportation,
Montour Railroad,
1711 State St.,
Coraopolis, Pa.

Nash, R. L.,
Test Engr., Test Division,
Westinghouse Air Brake Co.,
Wilmerding, Pa

Nathan, W. S.,
General Manager,
Construction Specialties Co
Oliver Building
Pittsburgh, Pa.

Neff, Charles,
Yard Master,
Pennsylvania Railroad,
127 Fairfield Ave.,
New Castle, Pa

Neff, John P.,
Vice President,
American Arch Co.,
60 E. 42nd St.,
New York, N Y.

Nelson, King R. H.,
Asst. Director of Exhibits,
American Sheet & Tin
Plate Co.,
Morrowfield Apartments,
Pittsburgh, Pa.

Nestor, T. E.,
Division Engineer,
Pennsylvania Railroad,
Pennsylvania Station,
Pittsburgh, Pa.

Nethken, H. W.,
Vice President—Traffic,
Pgh. & West Va. R. R.,
405 Wabash Bldg.,
Pittsburgh, Pa

Newell, J. P., Jr.,
Asst. Div. Engr., Middle Div.
Pennsylvania Railroad,
Altoona, Pa.

Newman, S. A.,
Asst. Dist. Sales Mgr.,
Gulf Refining Co.,
Gross St. & P. R. R.,
Pittsburgh, Pa.

Nichols, Samuel A.,
129 East Kennedy Ave.,
N. S., Pittsburgh, Pa

Nieman, Charles J.,
Secretary-Treasurer,
Penn Iron & Steel Co.,
Creighton, Pa.

Nieman, H. L.,
Gang Foreman,
P. & L. E. R. R.,
208 Copeland St.,
McKees Rocks, Pa.

Nies, E. L.,
Chief Clerk,
Railway Express Agency,
926 Penn Avenue,
Pittsburgh, Pa.

Niklaus, C. G.,
Head Clerk,
Pennsylvania Railroad,
1600 Evergreen Ave.,
Millvale, Pa.

Noble, Jesse A.,
Supv'r Bridges & Bldgs.,
P. & L. E. R. R.,
1643 Broadway,
McKees Rocks, Pa.

Noonan, Daniel,
Sales Representative,
Air Reduction Sales Co.,
1116 Ridge Ave.,
N. S., Pittsburgh, Pa.

Norris, J. L.,
R. F. of E., B. & O. R. R.,
4818 Chatsworth St.,
Pittsburgh, Pa.

Oberlin, A. C.,
Auditor,
Schaefer Equipment Co.,
Koppers Building,
Pittsburgh, Pa.

Obley, J. S.,
File Clerk,
P. & L. E. R. R. Co.,
Greenock, Pa.

O'Connor, Edward L.,
Manager,
Savon Sales Co.,
4746 Mossfield St.,
Pittsburgh, Pa.

O'Connor, M. J.,
Rep., Dearborn Chemical Co.,
Farmers Bank Bldg.,
Pittsburgh, Pa.

Oehlschlager, W. A.,
Engineer,
Union Switch & Signal Co.,
Swissvale, Pa.

Ogden, F. A., Jr.,
Railway Sales & Traffic,
Pittsburgh Steel
Foundry Corp.,
27 Kingston Ave.,
Crafton, Pa.

O'Leary, Jeremiah J.,
Machinist, Penna. System,
132 Fourth St.,
Oakmont, Pa.

Olson, A. O.,
General Agent,
C. & N. W. Ry. Co.,
Oliver Building,
Pittsburgh, Pa.

Orbin, George N.,
Retired,
Engineman, B. & O. R. R.,
2945 Glenmore Avenue,
Dormont, Pittsburgh, Pa.

Orbin, Joseph N.,
District Manager,
Oliver Iron & Steel Corp.,
10th and Murial Sts.,
Pittsburgh, Pa

Orchard, Charles,
5849 Hobart St.,
Pittsburgh, Pa.

Orr, D. K.,
Road Master,
The Monongahela Ry. Co.,
Brownsville, Pa.

Osborne, Raymond S.,
Mechanical Engineer,
Sewickley, Pa.

O'Sullivan, John J.,
Pipe Fitter, P. & L. E. R. R.,
1130 Wayne Ave.,
McKees Rocks, Pa.

O'Toole, J. L.,
Asst. to Gen. Manager,
P. & L. E. R. R.,
Pittsburgh, Pa

Overholt, Bruce C.,
Tel. & Sig. Foreman,
Pennsylvania Railroad,
205 Buffalo St.,
Freeport, Pa.

Paisley, F. R.,
Engineer Maintenance of Way
P. & L. E. R. R. Co.,
Pittsburgh, Pa.

Palmer, E. A.,
Manager,
Light Traction Section,
Transportation Dept.,
Westinghouse Elec. &
Mfg. Company,
East Pittsburgh, Pa.

Park, Charles L.,
Salesman,
Goodall Rubber Co.,
522 Second Ave.,
Pittsburgh, Pa.

Parkhill, Ray T.,
Chief Demurrage Clerk,
B. & O. R. R. Co.,
1615 Columbus Avenue,
N. S., Pittsburgh, Pa.

Passmore, H. E.,
Representative,
The American Hammered
Piston Ring Co.,
5668 Darlington Road,
Pittsburgh, Pa.

Paul, Lesley C.,
Manager, Publicity Bureau,
W. E. & Mfg. Co.,
217 Woodside Road,
Forest Hills Boro.,
Pittsburgh, (21) Pa.

Paul, William C.,
Plant Manager,
American Chain Co., Inc.,
First St. & P.&L.E.R.R.,
Braddock, Pa.

Payne, J. R.,
Salesman,
J. B. Sipe & Co.,
Pittsburgh, Pa.

Peabody, Reuben T.,
Railroad Sales Assistant,
Air Reduction Sales Co.,
60 East 42nd St.,
New York, N. Y.

Pearl, W. W.,
Section Stockman, Stores
Dept., B. & O. R. R. Co.,
R. D. 2, Box 411,
Connellsville, Pa

Peebles, A. T.,
Chief Clerk.
P. R. R. Produce Terminal,
Pennsylvania Railroad,
Twenty-first Street,
Pittsburgh, Pa.

Peel, Joseph E., Jr.,
Movement Director,
Pennsylvania Railroad,
81 Evans Ave.,
Ingram, Pa.

Pehrson, A. K.,
Mechanical Engineer,
Pressed Steel Car Co.,
McKees Rocks, Pa.

Peirce, W. B.,
Works Manager,
Flannery Bolt Co.,
Bridgeville, Pa.

Penton, John A.,
Pres., The Penton Pub. Co.,
Cleveland, Ohio

Perreas, S. J.,
Carman,
B. & O. R. R. Co.,
2224 Starkamp Street,
Brookline, Pittsburgh, Pa.

Peters, L. A.,
Train Rider,
B. &. O. R. R. Co.,
4829 Liberty Ave.,
Pittsburgh, Pa

Peters, R. F.,
Car Foreman,
B. & O. R. R. Co.,
7339 Race Street,
Pittsburgh, Pa.

Peterson, E. J.,
Foreman Carpenters,
P. & L. E. R. R. Co.,
2004 Bailey Avenue,
McKeesport, Pa.

Pevler, H. H.,
Division Engineer,
Pennsylvania Railroad,
1444 N. Euclid Ave.,
Pittsburgh, Pa.

Phillips, Robert A.,
Purchasing Agent,
Safety First Supply Co.,
Glenfield, Pa

Phillips, T. H.,
Boiler Maker,
P. & L. E. R. R. Co.,
632 Woodward Avenue,
McKees Rocks, Pa

Phillips, W. A.,
Asst. Gen. Pass. Agent,
Pennsylvania Railroad,
Pennsylvania Station,
Pittsburgh, Pa.

Phillips, William E.,
President, Pgh. Branch,
The Multi Stamp Co.,
381 Freeport Road,
Blawnox, Pa.

Pickard, S. B.,
Chief Electrician,
P. & L. E. R. R.,
R. D. No. 3,
Coraopolis, Pa.

Pillar, Michael,
Piece Work Inspector,
P. & L. E. R. R.,
206 Jane St.,
McKees Rocks, Pa.

Pinkerton, C. J.,
Industrial Sales Manager,
The Watson Standard Co.,
225 Galveston Ave.,
N. S., Pittsburgh, Pa.

Plunkett, James, Jr.,
Car Foreman,
B. & O. R. R. Co.,
4714 Monongahela St.,
Pittsburgh, Pa.

Poe, C. F.,
Timekeeper,
B. & O. R. R. Co.,
1309 Brookline Blvd.,
Pittsburgh, Pa

Pohlman, A.,
Steam Engineer,
Jones & Laughlin Steel
Corp.,
Aliquippa, Pa.

Pollock, J. H.,
Boiler Foreman,
Montour Railroad,
1341 Fourth Ave.,
Coraopolis, Pa.

Porter, H. N.,
Piece Work Inspector,
P. & L. E. R. R.,
Box 5,
Glenwillard, Pa.

Porterfield, W. B.,
Shop Superintendent,
B. & O. R. R. Co.,
25 Rosemont Ave.,
Mt. Lebanon, Pgh., Pa.

Posteraro, S. F.,
Frt. Cashier,
B. & O. R. R.,
Grant and Water Sts.,
Pittsburgh, Pa.

Powell, H. C.,
Asst. Foreman Car Dept.,
Pennsylvania Railroad,
362 Ohio Ave.,
Rochester, Pa.

Powell, Lloyd G.,
Erection Foreman,
B. & O. R. R. Co.,
2820 West Liberty Ave.,
Brookline, Pittsburgh, Pa.

Prinkey, Clyde M.,
Clerk,
B. & O. R. R. Co.,
B. & O. Passenger Station,
Pittsburgh, Pa.

Pringle, H. C.,
Vice Pres. and Supt.,
Mon. Con. R. R.,
25 Lakemont Drive,
Pittsburgh (16), Pa.

Pringle, J. L.,
Freight Train Master,
Pennsylvania Railroad,
513 Pennsylvania Sta.,
Pittsburgh, Pa.

Pringle, P. V.,
Commercial Engineer,
Westinghouse Air Brake Co.,
1236 McClure Ave.,
East McKeesport, Pa

Pringle, W. D.,
Sales Engineer,
W. S. Tyler Co.,
6648 Wilkins Avenue,
Pittsburgh, Pa.

Provost, S. W.,
Representative,
American Locomotive Co.,
Terminal Tower Bldg.,
Cleveland, Ohio

Pry, E. B.,
Supt. Tel. & Signals,
Pennsylvania Railroad,
Pennsylvania Station,
Pittsburgh, Pa.

Purcell, Edward J.,
Westinghouse Air Brake Co.,
353 Marguerite Ave.,
Wilmerding, Pa.

Purchard, Paul,
Registered Professional
Engineer,
Park Bldg.,
Pittsburgh, Pa.

Pye, David W.,
President,
Tuco Products Corp.,
30 Church St.,
New York, N. Y.

Queer, Thomas H.,
Sales Engineer,
Pittsburgh Coal Company.,
Oliver Building,
Pittsburgh, Pa.

Quinn, W.,
Section Stockman,
Stores Dept.,
B. & O. R. R. Co.,
2208 Lynnbrook Ave.,
Brookline, Pittsburgh, Pa.

Ralston, John A.,
Manager,
Railroad Research Bureau,
Subsidiary Mfg. Co.'s of
U. S. Steel Corp.,
Frick Bldg. Annex,
Pittsburgh, Pa.

Rambo, Jay B.,
Asst. Road Foreman of
Engines,
Pennsylvania Railroad,
3129 Chestnut St.,
Camp Hill, Pa.

Rambo, M. H.,
Station Inspector,
Pennsylvania Railroad,
Pennsylvania Station,
Pittsburgh, Pa.

Rankin, B. B.,
Gen. Auditor,
P. & L. E. R. R.,
1502 Park Blvd.,
Dormont, Pittsburgh, Pa

Rankin, R. E.,
Manager,
Pgh. Repair & Supply Dept.,
Goodman Mfg. Co.,
1011 California Ave.,
Avalon, Pittsburgh, Pa.

Raser, George B.,
R. D. No. 1,
Millville,
Columbia Co., Pa.

Rauschart, E. A.,
Mechanical Supt.,
Montour Railroad,
948 Greenfield Ave.,
Pittsburgh, Pa.

Raymer, I. S.,
Signal-Telegraph Engineer,
P. & L. E. R. R.,
959 Fourth Street,
Beaver, Pa.

Read, A. A.,
Duquesne Slag Products Co.,
Diamond Bank Bldg.,
Pittsburgh, Pa.

Ream, A. H.,
S. M. P. & E.,
P. & S. R. R.,
Brookville, Pa.

Reardon, M. J.,
General Yard Master,
P. & L. E. R. R. Co.,
Vance Avenue,
Coraopolis, Pa.

Rebstock, J. B.,
Chief Clerk, Div.,
P. R. R. Co.,
Penna. Station,
Pittsburgh, Pa.

Record, J. Fred,
Supt. of Production,
Westinghouse Air Brake Co.
Wilmerding, Pa.

Redding, R. D.,
General Foreman,
P. & L. E. R. R. Co.,
Campbell, Ohio

Reed, E. S.,
Supt. Pass. Transp'n.
P. R. R. Co.,
Penna. Station,
Pittsburgh, Pa.

Reed, M. R.,
Gen. Supt. Mo. Power,
Pennsylvania Railroad,
Pennsylvania Station,
Pittsburgh, Pa.

Reeder, N. S.,
Pressed Steel Car Co.,
80 Broad St.,
New York, N. Y.

Reese, R. H.,
General Agent,
Green Bay & Western R. R.,
Gulf Building,
Pittsburgh, Pa.

Reeve, George,
Foreman Electrical Dept.,
Ft. Pitt Malleable Iron Co.,
330 Woodward Ave.,
McKees Rocks, Pa.

Regan, W. J.,
Mechanical Engineer,
McConway & Torley Corp.,
48th St. & A. V. Ry.,
Pittsburgh, Pa.

Reifsnyder, J. W.,
Engineer of Tests,
Pgh. Testing Laboratory,
P. O. Box 1115,
Pittsburgh, Pa.

Reno, D. A.,
Yard Master,
P. R. R. Co.,
3011 Zephyr Ave.,
Corliss Station,
Pittsburgh, Pa.

Rensch, R. H.,
Sales Engineer,
General Electric Co.,
Brightwood, R. D. 1,
Library, Pa.

Renshaw, W. B.,
Representative,
Westinghouse Air Brake Co.,
Wilmerding, Pa

Reymer, C. H.,
Special Representative,
Oliver Iron & Steel Corp'n.,
So. 10th & Muriel Sts.,
Pittsburgh, Pa

Reynolds, A. C.,
Buyer,
Aluminum Co. of America,
Gulf Building,
Pittsburgh, Pa.

Richardson, E. F.,
Asst. to Engr., of
Motive Power,
B. & L. E. R. R.,
57 Chambers Ave.,
Greenville, Pa.

Richardson, Fred,
Freight Rep.,
P. R. R. Co.,
Penna. Station,
Pittsburgh, Pa.

Richardson, H. R.,
Suprv. of Wage Schedules,
P. & L. E. R. R.,
Pittsburgh, Pa

Rief, Joseph,
O. S. & D. Clerk,
B. & O. R. R. Co.,
328 Mathews Ave.,
Station 10, Pittsburgh, Pa.

Riley, O. W.,
Chief Clerk to Storekeeper,
B. & O. R. R. Co.,
2606 Belmar Place,
Swissvale, Pa.

Rizzo, C. M.,
Agent, P. & W. Va. Ry.,
Box 331,
Castle Shannon, Pa.

Roberts, E. L.,
Chief Clerk,
Donora Southern R. R. Co.,
567 McKean Ave.,
Donora, Pa.

Robertson, A. S.,
Traffic Manager,
Montour Railroad,
8 Market St.,
Pittsburgh, Pa.

Robinson, G. H.,
Machinery Inspector,
P. & L. E. R. R. Co.,
531 Chatauqua St.,
Pittsburgh, Pa.

Robinson, John M.,
  Engineer,
    Westinghouse Elec. &
      Mfg. Co.,
        Nuttall Works,
          200 McCandless Ave.,
            Pittsburgh, Pa.

Robinson, Lester L.,
  Dist. Mo. Power Inspector,
    B. & O. R. R.,
      1521 Orangewood Ave.,
        Pittsburgh, Pa.

Robinson, W. H.,
  Chief Delivery Clerk,
    B. & O. R. R. Co.,
      668 Boggs Avenue,
        Pittsburgh, Pa.

Robison, Ernest N.,
  District Passenger Agent,
    P. & L. E. R. R. Co.,
      Terminal Bldg.,
        Pittsburgh, Pa.

Rode, Harry,
  Platform Foreman,
    P. & L. E. - P. R. R. Cos.,
      21 Elton Avenue,
        Pittsburgh, Pa.

Rodeniser, B. H.,
  Supt. Transportation,
    Meadow Gold Dairies, Inc.,
      6418 Jackson Street,
        Pittsburgh, Pa.

Rodkey, C. C.,
  Cap't. of Police,
    P. R. R. Co.,
      3001 Graham Blv'd.
        Wilkinsburg, Pa.

Rogers, Robert E.,
  Coal Freight Representative,
    P. & L. E. R. R. Co.,
      Terminal Bldg.,
        Pittsburgh, Pa.

Rohyans, A. V.,
  Clerk,
    Pennsylvania Railroad,
      262 Center Ave.,
        Emsworth, Pittsburgh, Pa.

Roney, H. E.,
  Circuit Supervisor,
    P. & L. E. R. R.,
      3111 College Ave.,
        Beaver Falls, Pa.

Root, E. E.,
  Master Mechanic,
    D. L. & W. R. R. Co.,
      458 N. Arlington Ave.,
        East Orange, N. J.

Rose, A. J.,
  Salesman,
    Greenville Steel Car Co.,
      Greenville, Pa.

Ross, C. R.,
  Asst. Supervisor Operating,
    Expenditures,
      P. R. R. Co.,
        Broad St. Suburban
        Station,
          Philadelphia, Pa

Rossell, R. T.,
  President, B. & L. E. R. R.,
    Union Trust Building,
      Pittsburgh, Pa.

Rowan, J. R.,
  Salesman,
    J. B. Ford Sales Company,
      P. & L. E. Annex Bldg.,
        Pittsburgh, Pa.

Rowles, H. N.,
  Asst. Train Master,
    Pennsylvania Railroad,
      1466 Greenmont Ave.,
        South Hills,
          Pittsburgh, Pa.

Roy, L. E.,
  Gang Foreman,
    Pennsylvania Railroad,
      117 Peebles Street,
        Wilkinsburg, Pa.

Rudd, W. B.,   ·
  General Engineer,
    Union Switch & Signal Co.,
      Swissvale, Pa.

Rumbarger, F. A.,
  Sales Manager,
    The Browning Crane &
      Shovel Co.,
        1639 Oliver Bldg.,
          Pittsburgh, Pa.

Rupp, Edwin S.,
  Asst. Div. Accountant,
    B. & O. R. R. Co.,
      228 Lelia St.,
        Pittsburgh (11), Pa.

Rushneck, George L.,
Draftsman,
P. & L. E. R. R.,
McKees Rocks, Pa.

Rutter, Harley E.,
Electrician,
Duquesne Light Co.,
101 Grandview Ave.,
Mt. Washington Sta.,
Pittsburgh, Pa.

Ryan, D. W.,
C. C. Order Dept.,
Fort Pitt Malleable Iron Co.,
3138 Landis St.,
Pittsburgh, Pa.

Ryan, Frank J.,
District Representative,
Detroit, Toledo & Ironton
R. R.,
Wabash Bldg.,
Pittsburgh, Pa

Ryan, James H.,
Mgr., Tank Car Dept.,
Gulf Refining Co.,
Gulf Bldg.,
Pittsburgh, Pa.

Rys, C. F. W.,
Chief Metallurgical Engr.,
Carnegie-Illinois Steel Corp.,
Carnegie Bldg.,
Pittsburgh, Pa.

Sager, Ray I.,
Yard Master,
P. & L. E. R. R. Co.,
419 Green Street,
South Brownsville, Pa.

Saltic, Thomas,
Foreman,
Ft. Pitt Malleable Iron Co.,
321 Russellwood Ave.,
McKees Rocks, Pa

Sample, W. E.,
Supervisor Loco. Operation,
B. & O. R. R.,
211 Newburn Drive,
Mt. Lebanon,
Pittsburgh, Pa.

Sanders, C. R.,
Supervisor,
Pennsylvania Railroad,
411 Duquesne Avenue,
Trafford, Pa.

Sanders, Colonel Walter C.,
Gen. Mgr., Ry. Div.,
Timken Roller Bearing Co.,
Canton, Ohio

Sanner, B. H.,
Clerk,
P. & L. E. R. R. Co.,
Terminal Bldg.,
Pittsburgh, Pa.

Sarchet, Roger,
Chief Clerk,
Labor & Wage Bureau,
Pennsylvania Railroad,
Pennsylvania Station,
Pittsburgh, Pa.

Satterfield, A. T.,
Section Stockman-Stores
Dept.,
B. & O. R. R. Co.,
2918 Claremont Ave.,
Brentwood,
Pittsburgh, Pa.

Sauer, George L.,
Freight Agent,
P. & L. E. R. R.,
McKeesport, Pa.

Sayre, Herschel A.,
Principal Asst. Engineer,
Union Railroad Co.,
103 Sumner Avenue,
Forest Hills Boro.,
Wilkinsburg, Pa.

Schad, J. W.,
Division Master Mechanic,
B. & O. R. R. Co.,
Glenwood, Pittsburgh, Pa.

Schadt, Alton D.,
Clerk-Office V. P. & G. M.,
B. & L. E. R. R.,
7338 Whipple St.,
Pittsburgh (18), Pa.

Schaefer, Frederic,
Schaefer Equipment Co.,
Koppers Bldg.,
Pittsburgh, Pa.

Schaeffer, F. E.,
Secretary,
Union Spring & Mfg. Co.,
New Kensington, Pa.

Schaffer, G. F.,
Asst. Storekeeper,
B. & O. R. R. Co.,
307 Winston St.,
Pittsburgh, Pa.

Schaffer, W. E.,
Back Shop Foreman,
P. & W. Va. Ry.,
242 Boden Ave.,
Carnegie, Pa.

Schako, E. J.,
Shop Superintendent,
Superior Railway Products
Corp.,
7501 Thomas Blvd.,
Pittsburgh, Pa.

Schaller, Andrew J.,
Asst. Supervisor,
Pennsylvania Railroad,
808 Coleman Ave.,
Johnstown, Pa.

Schauers, Robert W.,
Gen. Fore., Stores Dept.,
B. & O. R. R. Co.,
495 Muldowney Ave.,
Lincoln Place, Pa.

Scheline, William A.,
Gang Foreman,
Pennsylvania Railroad,
2200 Holyoke St.,
N. S., Pittsburgh, Pa.

Schenck, S. B.,
Special Engineer,
B. & L. E. R. R. Co.,
18 Rosedale Ave.,
Greenville, Pa.

Schiller, John,
Cond'r., P. & W. Va. R. R.,
601 Beechwood Ave.,
Carnegie, Pa.

Schiller, Joseph, Jr.,
Rate Clerk,
B. & O. R. R. Co.,
Grant & Water Streets,
Pittsburgh, Pa.

Schmied, Fred J.,
Foreman,
Railway Service & Supply
Corporation,
302 Russellwood Ave.,
McKees Rocks, Pa.

Schmitt, Andrew,
Car Inspector,
B. & O. R. R. Co.,
2650 Veteran Street,
N. S. Pittsburgh, Pa.

Schmitt, Raymond F.,
Clerk,
Mon. Con. R. R. Co.,
1531 Hoff St.,
N. S., Pittsburgh, Pa.

Schoch, A. J.,
Application Engineer,
Westinghouse Elec. &
Mfg. Co.,
5863 Hobart St.,
Pittsburgh, Pa.

Schoen, W. H., Jr.,
Vice President,
Pgh. Knife & Forge Co.,
Park Building,
Pittsburgh, Pa.

Schrader, A. P.,
Asst. to Mgr. Transp'n.
Sales,
Westinghouse Elec. &
Manufacturing Co.,
East Pittsburgh, Pa.

Schramm, G. N.,
Metallurgical Dept.,
Sheet and Strip Div.,
Carnegie-Illinois Steel
Corporation,
Frick Bldg. Annex,
Pittsburgh, Pa.

Schrecongost, C. P.,
Traffic Manager,
Hillman Coal & Coke Co.,
First Nat. Bank Bldg.,
Pittsburgh, Pa.

Schultz, H. P.,
General Yard Master,
P. & L. E. R. R. Co.,
2714 Fifth Avenue,
Beaver Falls, Pa.

Schweinsberg, C. E.,
Joint Chief Clerk,
P&LE-PRR Warehouse
& Transfer Station,
213 West Canal St.,
N. S., Pittsburgh, Pa.

Scott, J. M.,
General Superintendent,
B. & O. R. R. Co.,
Pittsburgh, Pa.

Scudder, D. F.,
District Superintendent,
The Pullman Company,
Gulf Bldg.,
Pittsburgh, Pa.

Searles, E. J.,
Manager,
Schafer Equipment Co.,
Koppers Bldg.,
Pittsburgh, Pa.

Seibert, Wm. L.,
Engine House Foreman,
P. & L. E. R. R.,
327 Russellwood Ave.,
McKees Rocks, Pa.

Seidel, John, Jr.,
Chief Clerk,
P. & L. E. R. R. Co.,
Terminal Bldg.,
Pittsburgh, Pa.

Seitz, Warren W.,
Circuit Engr., T.&S. Dept.,
Pennsylvania Railroad,
1559 Montier St.,
Wilkinsburg, Pa.

Sekera, Charles J.,
Tester, Engine Dept.,
Westinghouse Air Brake Co.,
1108 Oak Ave.,
Turtle Creek, Pa.

Seltman, O. W.,
Cashier
P. R. R. Co.,
11th & Etna Sts.,
Pittsburgh, Pa.

Semmer, M. R.,
Salesman,
Air Reduction Sales Co.,
281 Dixon Ave.,
South Hills Branch,
Pittsburgh, Pa.

Sersch, J. G.,
Supt. of Police,
P. R. R. Co.,
3 Eastern Ave.,
Aspinwall, Pa.

Servais, F. W.,
Signal Stockman-Stores
Dept.,
B. & O. R. R. Co.,
400 Johnston Avenue,
Hazelwood,
Pittsburgh, Pa.

Severn, A. B.,
General Manager,
A. Stucki Co.,
419 Oliver Bldg.,
Pittsburgh, Pa.

Sexton, E. M.,
Railroad Sales Manager,
Air Reduction Sales Co.,
60 East 42nd St.,
New York, N. Y.

Shackelford, L. P.,
Asst. Yard Master,
P. R. R. Co.,
3305 Main St.,
Homestead Park, Pa.

Shafer, J. S.,
Safety Inspector,
Union Railroad,
Linden Ave.,
East Pittsburgh, Pa.

Shaffer, R. G.,
Agent,
Pennsylvania Railroad,
Box 97,
Emlenton, Pa.

Sharpless, G. G.,
Mgr. Pgh. Joint Stock Yards
Co.,
Herrs Island,
Pittsburgh, Pa.

Shaw, George M.,
Sales Representative,
Pullman-Standard Car
Mfg. Co.,
Box 266,
Baltimore, Md.

Shaw, M. H.,
Gang Foreman, Stores Dept.,
B. & O. R. R. Co.,
4712 Monongahela Ave.,
Pittsburgh, Pa.

Shellenbarger, Herbert M.,
Com. Engr., W. A. B. Co.,
1624 Dellrose Ave.,
Carrick, Pittsburgh, Pa.

Shepherd, W. B.,
Asst. General Traffic Manager
Aluminum Co. of America,
Gulf Building,
Pittsburgh, Pa.

Sheridan, Thomas F.,
Asst. to S. M. P. & S. R. S.,
P. & L. E. R. R.,
McKees Rocks, Pa.

Sherlock, D. V.,
President,
Union Steel Casting Co.,
62nd & Butler Sts.,
Pittsburgh, Pa.

Sherrard, H. M.,
Dist. Motive Power Inspector,
B. & O. R. R. Co.,
c/o Master Mech. Office,
Newark, Ohio.

Shield, Arthur,
Asst. Auditor Freight Acct's.
P. & L. E. R. R.,
1230 Penn Ave.,
New Brighton, Pa.

Shields, J. C.,
Office Manager,
Carnegie-Illinois Steel Corp.,
Carnegie Bldg.,
Pittsburgh, Pa.

Shingledecker, John C.,
Superv'r of Service Stations,
The Pennzoil Co.,
C. of C. Bldg.,
Pittsburgh, Pa.

Shippert, Frank,
Yard Foreman,
P. & L. E. R. R. Co.,
1738 Edgebrook Ave.,
Pittsburgh, Pa.

Shira, William A.,
Yard Master,
P. & L. E. R. R. Co.,
134 Euclid Avenue,
New Castle, Pa.

Showalter, Joseph,
Boiler Maker Foreman,
Aliquippa & Southern
R. R. Co.,
116 Carrol St.,
Aliquippa, Pa.

Shuck, Wm. C.,
Salesman,
Lockhart Iron & Steel Co.,
P. O. Box 1165,
Pittsburgh, Pa.

Shull, George S.,
President,
Safety First Supply Co.,
Brady Bldg.,
Pittsburgh, Pa.

Shultz, Leo W.,
Clerk,
P. R. R. Co.,
836 Florence Ave.,
Avalon, Pa.

Shumaker, John W.,
Capt. of Police,
P. R. R. Co.,
1401 Jeffers St.,
Pittsburgh, Pa.

Shuman, Forrest R.,
Movement Director,
P. R. R. Co.,
405 Franklin St.,
Wilkinsburg Station,
Pittsburgh, Pa.

Shuster, C. A.,
Agent,
Pennsylvania Railroad,
Box 46,
Red Bank, Pa.

Shuster, William W.,
Road Master,
P. & W. Va. Ry. Co.,
Pittsburgh, Pa.

Simons, Philip,
Traffic Manager,
Copperweld Steel Co.,
1033 East End Ave.,
Pittsburgh (21), Pa.

Simpkins, Fred E.,
Freight Movement Director,
P. R. R. Co.,
915 Ross Ave.,
Wilkinsburg, Pa.

Simpson, Clifford E.,
Asst. General Freight Agent,
P. & L. E. R. R. Co.,
329 Stratford Avenue,
Pittsburgh (6), Pa.

Simpson, Walter B.,
Salesman,
A. M. Byers Company,
Clark Building,
Pittsburgh, Pa.

287

Sipe, C. P.,
Supervisor,
Pennsylvania Railroad,
Federal Street Station,
N. S., Pittsburgh, Pa.

Sipe, D. A.,
Supervisor Track,
Pennsylvania Railroad,
6373 Stanton Avenue,
Pittsburgh, Pa.

Sixsmith, G. M.,
Superintendent,
Pennsylvania Railroad,
Room 211, Penna. Station,
Pittsburgh, Pa.

Sladden, F. T.,
G. F. A., P. & L. E. R. R.,
Terminal Building,
Pittsburgh, Pa.

Slagle, Charles E.,
Fore. Produce Yard,
P. R. R. Co.,
114 View St.,
Oakmont, Pa.

Slater, A. H.,
Chief Clerk to Gen. Supt.,
Pennsylvania Railroad,
Pennsylvania Station,
Pittsburgh, Pa.

Slick, Frank F.,
General Superintendent,
Edgar Thomson Works,
Carnegie-Illinois Steel
Corp.,
Braddock, Pa.

Small, Walter J.,
Sales Engineer,
Dodge Steel Co.,
6501 Tacony Street,
Philadelphia, Pa.

Smith, A. H.,
Sales Engineer,
Kerite Insulated Wire &
Cable Co.,
30 Church Street,
New York, N. Y.

Smith, Charles F.,
103 Sixth St.,
Pittsburgh, Pa.

Smith, Daniel J.,
Executive Assistant,
U. S. Steel Corporation,
Room 1517,
71 Broadway,
New York, N. Y.

Smith, E. E.,
General Passenger Agent,
P. & L. E. R. R. Co.,
Terminal Bldg.,
Pittsburgh, Pa.

Smith, E. W.,
Vice President,
Pennsylvania Railroad,
Pennsylvania Station,
Pittsburgh, Pa.

Smith, Folger M.,
Traffic Manager,
Federal Laboratories, Inc.,
185 Forty-first St.,
Pittsburgh, Pa.

Smith, G. C.,
Assist. Yard Master,
P. R. R. Co.,
8 Center Avenue,
Aspinwall, Pa.

Smith, Gilbert M.,
Gang Foreman,
Pennsylvania Railroad,
376 Pennsylvania Ave.,
Rochester, Pa.

Smith, J. Frank,
Gang Foreman,
Union Railroad,
141 Brown Ave.,
Turtle Creek, Pa

Smith, M. A.,
General Manager,
P. & L. E. R. R.,
Pittsburgh, Pa.

Smith, M. S.,
Storekeeper,
Monongahela Railway Co.,
South Brownsville, Pa.

Smith, Robert B.,
Transportation Sales,
Westinghouse E. & M. Co.,
East Pittsburgh Pa

Smith, T. R.,
Sales Representative,
Oakite Products, Inc.,
Hotel Lorraine,
422 N. Highland Ave.,
Pittsburgh, Pa.

Smith, Theodore F.,
Secretary and Asst. Treas.,
Oliver Iron & Steel Corp.,
S. 10th and Muriel Streets,
Pittsburgh, Pa.

Sneckenberger, E. R.,
Yard Master,
P. & L. E. R. R.,
803 Emerson Ave.,
New Castle, Pa.

Snitehurst, James G.,
Engine House Foreman,
Pennsylvania Railroad,
109 N. Sprague Ave.,
Bellevue,
Pittsburgh, Pa.

Snyder, F. I.,
Vice Pres. & General Mgr.,
B. & L. E. R. R. Co.,
Box 536,
Pittsburgh, Pa.

Snyder, J. J.,
Coal Freight Agent,
P. & L. E. R. R.,
Pittsburgh, Pa.

Snyder, Jesse L.,
Yard Master,
P. R. R. Co.,
216 N. Linden Ave.,
Pittsburgh, Pa.

Sparks, Hynes,
Sales Department,
The Symington Co.,
230 Park Ave.,
New York, N. Y.

Spencer, Albert C.,
Supervisor Train Service,
P. R. R. Co.,
Penna. Station,
Pittsburgh, Pa.

Sperry, C. E.,
Engineer,
Detroit Lubricator Co.,
40 West 40th St.,
New York, N. Y.

Squibb, L.,
Auditor Station Accounts,
P. & L. E. R. R. Co.,
Terminal Building,
Pittsburgh, Pa.

Stack, J. E.,
Superintendent,
Pittsburgh Coal Co.,
210½ Olympia St.
Mt. Washington, Pgh., Pa.

Stackhouse, R. K.,
Gen. Supt. Stations, Transfers,
Penna. R. R.,
1636 Broad St. Station
Building,
Philadelphia, Pa.

Stamets, William K.,
4026 Jenkins Arcade,
Pittsburgh, Pa.

Stamm, B. B.,
Draftsman,
Pullman-Standard Car Mfg.
Co.,
410 McKinley Ave.,
Butler, Pa.

Stapleton, H. B.,
General Agent.
P. & L. E. R. R. Co.,
Brownsville, Pa.

Starke, H. F.,
General Agent,
Southern Pacific Lines,
Gulf Building,
Pittsburgh, Pa.

Stayman, Ralph J.,
Gen. Mgr. of Warehouses,
Jones & Laughlin Steel
Corp.,
J. & L. Building,
Pittsburgh, Pa.

Stebler, W. J.,
Vice President,
Pennsylvania Conley Tank
Car Co.,
Koppers Building,
Pittsburgh, Pa.

Steding, Henry L.,
Special Duty Engineman,
P. R. R. Co.,
East Brady, Pa.

Steiner, P. E.,
Maintainer T. & S.,
Pennsylvania Railroad.
P. O. Bldg., Market St.,
Freeport, Pa.

Stephen, James
Foreman, Carpenter Shop,
Montour Railroad,
620 Vine St.,
Coraopolis, Pa.

Stephens, E. C.,
Conductor,
Pennsylvania Railroad,
1613 Alverado Avenue,
Pittsburgh, Pa.

Sterling, C. C.,
Engine House Foreman,
Union R. R.,
339 Albert St.,
Turtle Creek, Pa.

Stevens, Ernest,
Asst. Head Clerk, A.F.A. Dept.,
P. & L. E. R. R. Co.,
P&LE Terminal Bldg.,
Pittsburgh, Pa.

Stevens, L. V.,
President,
Stoker Parts Co.,
P. O. Box 903,
Pittsburgh, Pa.

Stevens, R. R.,
Asst. Design Engineer,
Westinghouse Air Brake
Co.,
Elmore Road,
Wilkinsburg, Pa.

Stevenson, H. G.,
Engineering Department,
Hillman Coal & Coke Co.,
First National Bank
Bldg.,
Pittsburgh, Pa.

Stevenson, R. F.,
C. C., Pgh. Eleventh St.,
P. R. R. Co.,
365 College Ave.,
Oakmont, Pa.

Stevenson, W. M.,
Dist. Rep., Railway Dept.,
Crucible Steel Co. of
America,
1258 East 55th St.,
Cleveland, Ohio.

Stewart, C. D.,
Chief Engineer,
Westinghouse Air Brake
Co.,
Wilmerding, Pa.

Stewart, C. G.,
Leading Draftsman,
P. & L. E. R. R. Co.,
Wildwood, Pa.

Stewart, J. C.,
Freight Agent,
Pennsylvania Railroad,
Eleventh St. Station,
Pittsburgh, Pa.

Stewart, J. D.,
Supt. Rolling Mills,
Jones & Laughlin Steel Corp.,
27th & Carson Sts.,
Pittsburgh, Pa.

Stiles, Lawson A.,
Baggage Agent,
P. & L. E. R. R.,
P. & L. E. Terminal,
Pittsburgh, Pa.

Stillwagon, Charles K.,
Superintendent,
Davis Brake Beam Co.,
R. D. 5, Box 80,
Johnstown, Pa.

Stiver, Joseph R.,
Conductor,
B. & O. R. R.,
116 Cypress St.,
Punxsutawney, Pa.

Stocker, H. F.,
President,
H. F. Stocker & Co.,
Clark Building,
Pittsburgh, Pa.

Stoecker, J. P.,
Transportation Assistant,
Pittsburgh Steel Co.,
Union Trust Bldg.,
Pittsburgh, Pa.

Stoffregen, Louis E.,
Draftsman,
P. & L. E. R. R.,
804 Southern Ave.,
Mt. Washington,
Pittsburgh, Pa.

Stone, E. C.,
  Assistant to President,
  Philadelphia Company,
  435 Sixth Avenue,
      Pittsburgh, Pa.

Storer, N. W.,
  Consulting Rwy. Engineer,
  Westinghouse Elec. &
  Manufacturing Co.,
      East Pittsburgh, Pa.

Strahl, Herman,
  Chief Clerk, Auditor Freight
  Accts.,
  P. & L. E. R. R. Co.,
      Pittsburgh, Pa.

Streamer, A. C.,
  Manager, Switchgear Div.,
  West. Elec. & Mfg. Co.,
  5 Newport Road,
      Wilkinsburg, Pa.

Strople, George H.,
  Track Supervisor,
  B. & O. R. R. Co.,
      Callery, Pa.

Stucki, A.,
  Engineer,
  419 Oliver Bldg.,
      Pittsburgh, Pa.

Stuebing, A. F.,
  Railroad Mechanical
  Engineer,
  United States Steel
  Corpn.,
  71 Broadway,
      New York, N. Y

Suckfield, G. A.,
  Asst. Chief Engr., F. C. D.,
  Pressed Steel Car Co.,
      McKees Rocks, Pa.

Sudell, Donald W., †
  Lubrication Engineer,
  Crew-Levick Company,
  738 Brookline Boulevard,
      Pittsburgh, Pa.

Suffern, R. J.,
  Asst. R. F. of E.,
  P. R. R. Co.,
  3500 Allendale St.,
  Corliss Station.
      Pittsburgh, Pa.

Sullivan, Ambrose, W.,
  Sales Agent,
  American Locomotive Co.,
  Plaza Bldg.,
      Pittsburgh, Pa.

Sullivan, P. W.,
  Asst. to Gen. Mgr.,
  Pennsylvania Railroad,
  Pennsylvania Sta.,
      Pittsburgh, Pa.

Sullivan, Robert J.,
  Examiner,
  Pennsylvaina Railroad,
  Pennsylvania Station,
      Pittsburgh, Pa.

Sutherland, Lloyd,
  Gen. Storekeeper,
  P. & L. E. R. R.,
  124 Greydon Ave.,
      McKees Rocks, Pa.

Sutter, A. A.,
  Lieut. of Police,
  B. & O. R. R. Co.,
  2044 Redrose Ave.,
      Carrick, Pittsburgh, Pa.

Sutton, K. B.,
  Chemist,
  P. & L. E. R. R. Co.,
  1056 Hiland Ave.,
      Coraopolis, Pa.

Suydam, R. S.,
  President,
  M. B. Suydam Co.,
  Island & Preble Aves.,
      N. S., Pittsburgh, Pa.

Swank, W. E.,
  Chief Clerk to Freight Agent,
  B. & O. R. R. Co.,
  38 Cowan Street,
      Pittsburgh, Pa.

Swanson, Carl A.,
  C. C. to Gen. Mgr.,
  P. & L. E. R. R.,
  468 Irvin Ave.,
      Rochester, Pa.

Swope, Bruce M.,
  Supt. Motive Power,
  Pennsylvania Railroad,
  3955 Bigelow Blvd.,
      Pittsburgh, Pa.

Sykes, **Arthur H.,**
Asst. Baggage Agent,
P. & L. E. R. R.,
707 Florida Ave.,
Mt. Lebanon,
Pittsburgh, Pa.

Sylvester, H. G.,
Freight Agent,
P. & L. E. R. R. Co.,
Monessen, Pa.

Taggart, J. G.,
Transitman,
P. & L. E. R. R. Co.,
719 Thirty-fifth St.,
Beaver Falls, Pa.

Taggart, Ross E.,
Field Engineer,
P. & L. E. R. R.,
2733 Amman Street,
South Hills Branch,
Pittsburgh, Pa.

Taplin, Frank E.,
Chairman of Board,
P. & W. Va. Ry. Co.,
Union Trust Bldg.,
Cleveland, Ohio.

Tate, James B.,
Purchasing Agent.
Pressed Steel Car Co.,
McKees Rocks, Pa.

Tate, M. K.,
Manager Railway Division,
Lima Locomotive Works,
Inc.,
Lima Trust Bldg.,
Lima, Ohio.

Taylor, H. G.,
Pres., Ball Chemical Co.,
Fulton Bldg.,
Pittsburgh, Pa.

Taylor, Harry D.,
Captain of Police,
P. R. R. Co.,
7140 Meade St.,
Homestead, Pgh., Pa.

Taylor, John T.,
District Manager,
E. F. Houghton & Co.,
215 Beverly Road,
Mt. Lebanon, Pgh., Pa.

Taylor, Joseph M.,
Sales Dept.,
Ball Chemical Co.,
1201 Fulton Bldg.,
Pittsburgh, Pa.

Teerkes, Charles A.,
Freight Agent,
P. & L. E. R. R. Co.,
Aliquippa, Pa.

Ternent, Harry J.,
Sec. Stockman,
B. & O. R. R. Co.,
840 North Ave.,
North Braddock, Pa.

Terry, Edward,
Salesman,
Safety First Supply Co.,
Brady Building,
Pittsburgh, Pa.

Terwilliger, Walter,
Clerk,
P. & L. E. R. R. Co.,
418 Broadway St.,
Glassport, Pa.

Teufel, W. O.,
Master Mechanic,
P. R. R. Co.,
118 W. Hutchinson Ave.,
Edgewood, Pittsburgh, Pa.

Thiele, Fred,
Asst. General Yardmaster,
P. & L. E. R. R. Co.,
543 Woodward Avenue,
McKees Rocks, Pa.

Thomas, Frank B.,
General Engineer,
W. A. B. Co.,
606 Walnut St.,
Irwin, Pa.

Thomas, George P.,
President,
Thomas Spacing Machine
Co.,
Etna Branch P. O.,
Pittsburgh, Pa.

Thomas, Harold N.,
Auto-Tite Joints Co.,
5908 Rural St.,
Pittsburgh, Pa.

Thomas, T. T.,
Foreman,
Union Railroad Co.,
422 Albert St.,
Turtle Creek, Pa.

Thompson, H. C.,
Salesman,
Air Reduction Sales Co,
Grandview Ave.,
Glenshaw, Pa.

Thompson, Harry T.,
District Manager,
Thermit Department,
Metal & Thermit Corp.,
1514 North Ave., West,
N. S., Pittsburgh, Pa.

Thompson, Howard A.,
General Engineer,
Union Switch & Signal Co.,
311 W. Swissvale Ave.,
Edgewood,
Swissvale P. O., Pa

Thornton, A. W.,
Resident Engineer,
P. & L. E. R. R.,
Terminal Bldg.,
Pittsburgh, Pa.

Thunell, Frederick G.,
Rate Clerk,
B. & O. R. R. Co.,
301 Marie Ave.,
Avalon, Pittsburgh, Pa.

Timmis, A. F.,
Foreman of Carpenters,
P. & L. E. R. R. Co.,
1195 Island Avenue,
McKees Rocks, Pa.

Tipton, George M.,
Terminal Agent,
B. & O. R. R.,
Grant and Water Sts.,
Pittsburgh, Pa.

Tobasco, P.,
Section Stockman,
B. & O. R. R. Co.,
295 Baldwin Road,
Hays, Pittsburgh, Pa.

Todd, A. H.,
Agent,
P. & L. E. R. R. Co.,
706 Lincoln St.,
Monongahela, Pa.

Todd, Wm. B.,
Vice President,
J. & L. Steel Corp'n.,
J. & L. Bldg.,
Pittsburgh, Pa

Tomasic, Nicholas M., Jr.,
Locomotive Mechanic,
Pennsylvania Railroad,
412 Tintsman St.,
Turtle Creek, Pa

Touceda, Prof. Enrique,
Consulting Engineer,
Malleable Iron Research
Institute,
943 Broadway,
Albany, N, Y.

Toussaint, R.,
Chief of Police,
P. & L. E. R. R.,
Pittsburgh, Pa

Tovey, G. F.,
Asst. Train Master,
Aliquippa & Southern R. R.,
1213 Boundry St.,
Aliquippa, Pa.

Tracey, J. B. A.,
Chief Clerk Div.,
P. R. R. Co.,
Penna. Station,
Pittsburgh, Pa.

Trainer, M. N.,
Vice President,
American Brake Shoe &
Foundry Co.,
230 Park Ave.,
New York N. Y.

Trautman, Harry J.,
Yard Superintendent,
Briggs & Turivas,
R. D. No. 2,
Coraopolis, Pa.

Trax,, Louis R.,
Inspector,
Union Railroad,
520 James St.,
Turtle Creek, Pa.

Triem, W. R.,
Gen. Supt. of Telegraph,
Pennsylvania Railroad,
Philadelphia, Pa.

Troxell, Henry K.,
Railroad Sales Dept.,
Carnegie-Illinois Steel
Corp.,
Carnegie Bldg.,
Pittsburgh, Pa

Trump, Perry,
Chief Clerk, Car Dept.,
B. & O. R. R. Co.,
229 Winston Street,
Pittsburgh, Pa.

Trumpeter, W. C.,
Chief Clerk,
P. & L. E. R. R. Co.,
917 Indiana Ave.,
Monaca, Pa.

Trust, C. W.,
Asst. Traffic Mgr.,
U. S. Steel Corp.
Subsidiaries,
Carnegie Bldg.,
Pittsburgh, Pa.

Tryon, I. D.,
Freight Agent,
P. &. W. Va. Ry. Co.,
Fourth & Liberty,
Pittsburgh, Pa.

Tucker, Jas. W.,
Division Storekeeper,
B. & O. R. R.,
Box 166,
Chillicothe, Ohio.

Tucker, John L.,
"Retired" Trainmaster,
Pennsylvania Railroad,
5514 Center Ave.,
Pittsburgh, Pa.

Turner, A. L.,
Extra Agent,
P. R. R. Co.,
334 School St.,
Springdale, Pa.

Turner, C. B.,
Vice-President,
South Penn Oil Company,
Chamber of Commerce
Building,
Pittsburgh, Pa.

Turner, F. M.,
General Superintendent,
A. & S. S. R. R. Co.,
Cor. 10th and Muriel Sts.,
S. S., Pittsburgh, Pa.

Tuttle, C. L.,
Mech. Engr., B. & L. E. R. R.,
15 Shady Ave.,
Greenville, Pa.

Tyler, Buford W., Jr.,
Div. Engr., Pittsburgh Div.,
Pennsylvania R. R.,
Pennsylvania Station,
Pittsburgh, Pa.

Tyrie, Robert M.,
Road Foreman of Engines,
Montour Railroad,
815 Ferree St.,
Coraopolis, Pa.

Uhar, John J.,
Auditor,
Penn Iron & Steel Co.,
Creighton, Pa.

Unger, Dr. J. S.,
5538 Aylesboro Avenue,
Pittsburgh, Pa.

Urtel, E. J.,
Asst. Division Storekeeper,
B. & O. R. R.,
3908 Brownsville Road,
Brentwood,
Pittsburgh, Pa..

Van Blarcom, Warren C.,
Vice President, Aliquippa &
Southern R. R.,
Aliquippa, Pa.

Van Horne, C. F.,
Applied Engineering Dept.,
Air Reduction Sales Co.,
92 Sheridan Ave.,
Bellevue, Pa.

Van Nort, C. W.,
Supt., Wilkes-Barre Div.,
Pennsylvania Railroad,
Sunbury, Pa.

Van Vranken, S. E.,
Vice President,
Soap & Chemical Inc.,
319 Federal St.,
N. S., Pittsburgh, Pa.

Van Woert, F. E.,
Vice Pres. & Gen. Supt.,
Donora Southern R. R.
Co.,
137 Ida Avenue,
Donora, Pa.

Villee, R. E.,
Chief Clerk,
P. & L. E. R. R. Co.,
344 Kambach St.,
Mt. Washington,
Pittsburgh, Pa

Volkert, E. L.,
Supervisor Transportation,
Railway Express Agency,
Inc.,
26th & Liberty Ave.,
Pittsburgh, Pa.

Vollmer, Karl L.,
Steam Engineer,
Spang-Chalfant Co.,
106 W. Undercliff St,.
Etna, Pa.

Von Pein, A. N.,
Traffic Manager,
Oliver Iron & Steel Corp.,
1001 Muriel St.,
S. S., Pittsburgh, Pa.

Vowinkel, Fred F.,
Salesman,
J. & L. Steel Corp'n.,
J. & L. Bldg.,
Pittsburgh, Pa.

Wagoner, Karl J.,
Asst. Engineer, Engineering
Dept.
B. & O. R. R. Co.,
Maloney Bldg.,
Pittsburgh, Pa.

Wait, William Bell,
President,
Valve Pilot Corporation,
230 Park Ave.,
New York, N. Y.

Wallace, H. A.,
Engineer,
Union Switch & Signal Co.,
Swissvale, Pa.

Wallace, W. E.,
Section Foreman,
P. & L. E. R. R.,
452 Motheral Ave.,
Monessen, Pa.

Walsh, J. J.,
Special Agent,
P. R. R. Co.,
Penna. Station,
Pittsburgh, Pa.

Walter, E. R.,
Movement Director,
P. R. R. Co.,
1504 Foliage St.,
Wilkinsburg, Pa.

Walter, H. L.,
Freight Representative,
Pennsylvania Railroad,
Pennsylvania Station,
Pittsburgh, Pa.

Walton, W. K.,
C. C. Coal Freight Traffic
Dept.,
P. R. R. Co.,
Penna. Station,
Pittsburgh, Pa.

Ward, Norval H.,
Air Brake Instructor,
P. & L. E. R. R. Co.,
3031 Glenmawr Ave.,
Pittsburgh (4), Pa.

Warfel, John A.,
Special Representative,
Air Reduction Sales Co.,
1116 Ridge Ave.,
N. S., Pittsburgh, Pa.

Wark, J. M.,
Foreman,
Pennsylvania Railroad,
202 Lincoln Ave.,
Swissvale Branch,
Pittsburgh, Pa.

Warner, E. O.,
District Sales Manager,
National Malleable &
Steel Casting Co.,
1617 Pennsylvania Blvd.,
Philadelphia, Pa.

Waterman, Edwin H.,
Car Foreman, Union R. R.,
Monongahela Jct. Shop,
East Pittsburgh, Pa.

Watson, W. R.,
Locomotive Engineer.
P. & L. E. R. R. Co.,
408 Monongahela Ave.,
McKeesport, Pa.

Watt, Herbert J.,
District Sales Manager,
Jones & Laughlin Steel
Corporation,
500 Fifth Avenue,
New York, N. Y.

Watt, R. Nevin,
Sales Manager,
Standard Steel Works Co.,
Burnham, Mifflin Co., Pa.

Waxler, Brice,
Clerk, Pay Roll Dept.,
Pennsylvania Railroad,
37 Haldane Street,
Crafton, Pittsburgh, Pa.

Weaver, W. Frank,
Storekeeper,
The Pullman Co.,
2726 Twelfth St., N. E.,
Washington, D. C

Webb, William W.,
Manager,
National Carloading Corpn.,
1013 Penn Ave.,
Pittsburgh, Pa

Weber, Robert J.,
Central Station Manager,
Westinghouse Electric
& Mfg. Co.,
Gulf Building,
Pittsburgh, Pa

Webster, H. D.,
392 S. Main St.,
Greenville, Pa.

Webster, R. L.,
Agent,
Fruit Growers Express Co.,
21st & Pike St.,
Pittsburgh, Pa

Weis, Frank E.,
Transportation Clerk,
Pennsylvania Railroad,
26 East Crafton Blvd.,
Pittsburgh, Pa.

Welch, E. M.,
Service Engineer,
Dearborn Chemical Co.,
2615 Mackinaw Ave.,
Pittsburgh, Pa.

Weldon, Dewey,
Asst. Train Master,
P. R. R. Co.,
255 Brighton Road,
Bellevue, Pittsburgh, Pa.

Welton, Alvin A.,
Special Apprentice,
Westinghouse Air Brake Co.,
353 Marguerite Ave.,
Wilmerding, Pa.

Weltz, E. E.,
Asst. Agt., 23rd St. Station,
P. & L. E. R. R. Co.,
2218 Lutz Street,
Pittsburgh, Pa.

Wendt, Edwin F.,
Consulting Engr.,
Union Trust Bldg.,
Washington, D. C.

Weniger, Oscar S.,
Sales Engineer,
Electric Storage Battery Co.
Union Trust Bldg.,
Pittsburgh, Pa.

Wenzel, J. Louis,
Asst. Manager, Tool Dept.,
Hubbard & Company,
6301 Butler Street,
Pittsburgh, Pa.

Werner, L. A.,
Chief Clerk,
P. & L. E. R. R. Co.,
3608 Mayfair St.,
McKeesport, Pa.

West, George S.,
Division Superintendent,
Pennsylvania Railroad,
Pittsburgh, Pa.

West, Troy,
Draftsman,
Union Railroad Co.,
1713 Tonette St.,
Swissvale, Pa.

Westerman, F. R.,
Asst. Treasurer,
P. & W. Va. Ry. Co.,
Wabash Bldg.,
Pittsburgh, Pa.

Westerman, M. A.,
Sales Department,
Edgewater Steel Co.,
P. O. Box 478,
Pittsburgh, Pa.

Weygandt, J. H.,
Asst. Yard Master,
P. R. R. Co.,
313 Anton St.,
Monongahela, Pa.

Wheeler, Charles M.,
Sales Engineer,
Union Switch & Signal Co.,
Swissvale, Pa.

Whipkey, Daniel L.,
Relief Yard Master,
P. & L. E. R. R. Co.,
P. O. Box 444,
Newell, Pa.

Whipple, A. L.,
District Sales Manager,
Standard Stoker Co., Inc.,
350 Madison Ave.,
New York City

White, A. F.,
Time Clerk,
P. & L. E. R. R. Co.,
47 Haberman Ave.,
Pittsburgh, Pa.

White, Herbert A.,
Sales Mgr., Pgh. Dist.,
National Bearing
Metals Corp.,
928 Shore Ave.,
N. S., Pittsburgh, Pa.

Whitehouse, E. L.,
Station Agent,
P. R. R. Co.,
Ford City, Pa.

Wikander, Oscar R.,
Mechanical Engineer,
Ring Spring Dept.,
Edgewater Steel Co.,
900 South Negley Ave.,
Pittsburgh, Pa.

Wildin, G. W.,
Consulting Engineer,
Westinghouse Air Brake
Company,
Westinghouse Bldg.,
Pittsburgh, Pa.

Wilkins, Harry,
203 Allegheny Ave.,
Emsworth,
Pittsburgh, Pa.

Wilkinson, F. C.,
Superintendent,
Penna. Railroad,
621 South Bowman Ave.,
Merion,
Montgomery Co., Pa.

Wilkinson, William E.,
Assistant Foreman,
The Pullman Company,
4819 Broad Street,
Pittsburgh, Pa.

Wilkoff, Louis E.,
Vice President,
Youngstown Steel Car Corp.
Box 268,
Niles, Ohio.

Williams, David L.,
Salesman,
G. W. Griffin Co.,
P. O. Box 1322,
Pittsburgh, Pa.

Willilams, I. R.,
Agent,
B. & O. R. R. Co.,
5438 Howe Street,
E. E. Pittsburgh, Pa.

Williams, J.,
Yardmaster,
P. R. R. Co.,
Fifth St.,
West Elizabeth, Pa.

Williams, O. J.,
Movement Supervisor,
P. R. R. Co.,
816 Ivy St.,
E. E., Pittsburgh, Pa.

Williamson, A. G.,
Engineer,
Union Switch & Signal Co.,
721 Washington Ave.,
Carnegie, Pa.

Williamson, E. F.,
Movement Director, Supt.
Passenger Transportation,
Pennsylvania Railroad,
609 Dick Street,
Carnegie, Pa.

Wilson, J. N.,
President,
Aliquippa & Southern
R. R. Co.,
311 Ross Street,
Pittsburgh, Pa.

Wilson, James M.,
Sales Engineer,
Metal & Thermit Corp'n.,
2961 Stafford St.,
Corliss Station,
Pittsburgh, Pa.

Wilson, James R.,
Draftsman,
P. R. R. Co.,
Penna. Station,
Pittsburgh, Pa.

Wilson, W. S.,
Div. Engineer,
Conemaugh Div.,
P. R. R. Co.,
233 Dalzell Ave.,
Ben Avon, Pa.

Wilson W. Stuart,
Rate Clerk,
Pennsylvania Railroad,
725 Florence Ave.,
Avalon, Pittsburgh, Pa.

Wilt, Howard H.,
Sales Representative,
Carnegie Steel Co.,
Carnegie Bldg.,
Pittsburgh, Pa.

Winslow, George W.,
Manager,
Ingersoll-Rand Co.,
Chamber of Commerce
Building,
Pittsburgh, Pa.

Winslow, Sidney H.,
Service Engineer,
Franklin Rwy. Supply Co.,
1105 Biltmore Ave.,
S. H. B., Pittsburgh, Pa.

Winter, P. S.,
Master Car Builder,
B. & L. E. R. R.,
42 First Ave.,
Greenville, Pa.

Wisegarver, F. H.,
Train Master,
P. R. R. Co.,
63 Bradford Ave.,
Crafton, Pittsburgh, Pa.

Withrow, R. C.,
Sales Engineer,
Freedom Oil Works Co.,
Brighton Heights,
New Brighton, Pa.

Wittmann, Edward A.,
Loco. Boiler Inspector,
Montour Railroad,
1402 Straka St.,
Corliss Station,
Pittsburgh, Pa.

Wolcott, L. M.,
Asst. Train Master,
P. R. R. Co.,
1326 Willsley Avenue,
Steubenville, Ohio.

Wolf, William M.,
Chief Clerk, A. F. A. Dept.,
P. & L. E. R. R. Co.,
358 La Marido St.,
Pittsburgh, Pa.

Wood, John H.,
Operator & Wire Chief,
P. & L. E. R. R.,
1613 Chelton Avenue,
Pittsburgh (16), Pa.

Woods, G. M.,
Ry. Engineer,
W. Elec. & Mfg. Co.,
East Pittsburgh, Pa.

Woodward, Robert,
Machinist, P. R. R. Co.,
314 George St.,
Turtle Creek, Pa.

Woollen, A. H.,
Engineer,
Development Division,
Aluminum Company of
America,
New Kensington, Pa.

Wright, C. W.,
Vice President,
Pullman-Standard Car Mfg.,
Co.,
Gulf Bldg.,
Pittsburgh, Pa.

Wright, E. W.,
Asst. to President,
Ft. Pitt Malleable Iron Co.,
5442 Baywood St.,
Pittsburgh, Pa.

Wright, Harold C.
Asst. Master Mechanic,
Pennsylvania Railroad,
414 Willow Place,
Edgewood, Pittsburgh, Pa.

Wright, John B.,
Assistant Vice President,
W. A. B. Co.,
Wilmerding, Pa.

Wright, O. L.,
District Manager,
The Joyce-Cridland Co.,
421 Chestnut St.,
Philadelphia, Pa.

Wright, Roy V.,
  Secretary,
    Simmons-Boardman
    Publishing Co.,
    30 Church St.,
      New York, N. Y.

Wuerthele, Howard A.,
  Clerk,
    B. & O. R. R. Co.,
    1239 McNeilly Ave.,
    Dormont, Pittsburgh, Pa.

Wurts, T. C.,
  Heavy Traction Section Head,
    Westinghouse Elec. &
    Mfg. Co.,
      East Pittsburgh, Pa.

Wyke, John W.,
  Road Foreman of Engines,
    Union Railroad,
      East Pittsburgh, Pa.

Wynne, F. E.,
  Section Engr.,
    Ry Engr'g. Dept.,
    Westinghouse Elec.,
    & Mfg. Co.,
      East Pittsburgh, Pa.

Yarnall, Jesse,
  Asst. Yard Master,
    Pennsylvania Railroad,
    123 Race St.,
      Edgewood, Pa.

Yeardley, H.,
  Gang Fore., Car Dept.,
    Pennsylvania Railroad,
    2662 Center St.,
    Ingram,
      Pittsburgh (5), Pa.

Yohe, C. M.,
  Vice President,
    P. & L. E. R. R.,
      Pittsburgh, Pa.

Yohe, J. K.,
  Train Master,
    Monongahela Railway Co.,
      Brownsville, Pa.

Yohe, J. K., Jr.,
  Supervisor's Field Man,
    P. & L. E. R. R. Co.,
    2215 Hawthorne St.,
      Pittsburgh (18), Pa.

Yorke, P. H.,
  General Agent,
    Great Northern Railway,
    Oliver Building,
      Pittsburgh, Pa.

Young, F. C.,
  Credit Manager,
    Westinghouse Air Brake Co.,
      Wilmerding, Pa.

Young, J., Jr.,
  Engine House Foreman,
    P. R. R. Co.,
    4073 Cambronne St.,
      N. S., Pittsburgh, Pa.

Zearley, J. P.,
  Asst. Supervisor-Track,
    Pennsylvania Railroad,
    202 So. Braddock Ave.,
      Pittsburgh, Pa.

Ziegler, S. L.,
  Gang Foreman,
    Pennsylvania Railroad,
    8 Salter St.,
      N. S., Pittsburgh, Pa.

Zitzman, N. E.,
  Chief Clerk to S. F. T.,
    P. & L. E. R. R.,
    Terminal Bldg.,
      Pittsburgh, Pa.

STATEMENT OF THE OWNERSHIP, MANAGEMENT, CIRCULATION, ETC., REQUIRED BY THE ACT OF CONGRESS OF MARCH 3, 1933

Of Official Proceedings of The Railway Club of Pittsburgh, published Monthly, except June, July and August, at Pittsburgh, Pa., for October 1, 1936.

STATE OF PENNSYLVANIA ⎫
COUNTY OF ALLEGHENY ⎬ SS:
⎭

Before me, a Notary Public, in and for the State and county aforesaid, personally appeared, J. D. Conway, Secretary, who, having been duly sworn according to law, deposes and says that he is the Editor of the Official Proceedings—Railway Club of Pittsburgh.

Publisher, Official Proceedings—The Railway Club of Pittsburgh.

Editor, J. D. Conway, 515 Grandview Avenue, Pittsburgh, Pa., (19th Ward.)

Managing Editor, J. D. Conway, 515 Grandview Avenue, Pittsburgh, Pa., (19th Ward.)

Business Manager, J. D. Conway, 515 Grandview Avenue, Pittsburgh, Pa., (19th Ward.)

Official Proceedings—The Railway Club of Pittsburgh.

President, R. P. Forsberg, Pittsburgh, Pa.

Vice President, E. A. Reuschart, Coraopolis, Pa.

Secretary, J. D. Conway, Pittsburgh, Pa.

Treasurer, E. J. Searles, Pittsburgh, Pa.

Known Bondholders—None.

J. D. CONWAY, Secretary.

Sworn to and subscribed before me this 24th day of September, 1936.

[Seal]   EMMA LEA MONTGOMERY, Notary Public.
(My commission expires February 21, 1939)

OFFICIAL PROCEEDINGS
WAY CLUB OF PITTSBURG

$1.00 Per Year   25¢ Per Copy

Vol. XXXVI.   NOVEMBER 19, 1936.   No. 1.

Co-operation Between Railroad Purchasing and Stores Departments and Industries

By U. K. HALL, General Purchasing Agent, Union Pacific Railroad Company, Omaha, Nebraska.

The proof of your interest

in the Club can be

enhanced

by securing a

NEW MEMBER.

Application form is available

in this magazine. Look

it up and

"ACT NOW."

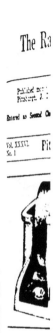

The Ra

Published by
Pittsburgh 2.

Entered as Second Cl

Vol. XXXVI.
No. 1   Pit

The Bu

OFFICIAL PROCEEDINGS

OF

The Railway Club of Pittsburgh

Organized October 18, 1901

Published monthly, except June, July and August, by the Railway Club of
Pittsburgh, J. D. Conway, Secretary, 515 Grandview Ave., Pittsburgh, Pa..

Entered as Second Class Matter February 6, 1915, at the Postoffice at Pittsburgh,
under the Act of March 3, 1879.

| Vol. XXXVI.
No. 1 | Pittsburgh, Pa., Nov. 19, 1936 | $1.00 Per Year
25c Per Copy |

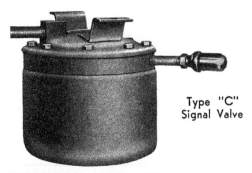

Type "C"
Signal Valve

A SUPERIOR AIR SIGNAL VALVE

Signals Always Distinct—No Interference or Overlapping
Consistently Positive Operation—Long or Short Trains
Wear Does Not Affect Consistent Operation
Maintenance Costs Are Very Low

Westinghouse Air Brake Company

GENERAL OFFICE AND WORKS — WILMERDING, PA.

Malleable
CASTINGS
OF UNIFORM QUALITY
ARE PERMANENT

CURRENT AVERAGE TESTS
For 12 Months
910 Consecutive Heats

	Tensile Strength Lbs. per sq. in.	Yield Point Lbs. per sq. in.	Elong. % in 2 in.
HIGH	61370	40420	28.1
LOW	56490	37210	22.6
AVERAGE	58344	38494	25.9

This Trade-mark is your security on Railroad Car Castings

Send Blue Prints for Estimates

Fort Pitt Malleable Iron Company
PITTSBURGH, PA.

INDEX—ADVERTISERS.

NOTE—This form to be filled out in full by typewriter or printed and mailed to **J. D. Conway, Secretary, 1941 Oliver Building, Pittsburgh, Pa.** Membership fee, including dues, is $3.00 for each fiscal year or part thereof, except those propsed in September or October. Those proposed in these months will be credited upon payment for the following fiscal year. Dues are payable in advance.

The fiscal year ends with the month of October.

The Railway Club of Pittsburgh:

....19.........

Gentlemen:

Will you kindly consider my Application for Membership in your Club at the next meeting:

Name...

Title...

Company ....

My Address..

....

Recommended by...

OFFICIAL PROCEEDINGS

OF

The Railway Club of Pittsburgh

Organized October 18, 1901

Vol. XXXVI No. 1	Pittsburgh, Pa., Nov. 19, 1936	$1.00 Per Year 25c Per Copy

OFFICERS FOR 1936-1937

President
E. A. RAUSCHART,
Mechanical Superintendent, Montour Railroad Co., Coraopolis, Pa

First Vice President
G. M. SIXSMITH,
Supt., Pennsylvania Railroad,
Pittsburgh, Pa.

Secretary
J. D. CONWAY,
Railway Supply Manufacturers' Association,
Pittsburgh, Pa.

Second Vice President
J. D. BELTZ,
Supt., B. & O. R. R Co,
Pittsburgh, Pa.

Treasurer
E. J. SEARLES,
Manager, Schaefer Equipment Co,
Pittsburgh, Pa.

EXECUTIVE COMMITTEE:

FRANK J. LANAHAN, Chairman, President, Fort Pitt Malleable Iron Co., Pittsburgh, Pa.
A. STUCKI, Engineer, A. Stucki Company, Pittsburgh, Pa.
D. F. CRAWFORD, Consulting Engineer, Pittsburgh, Pa.
G W. WILDIN, Consulting Engineer, Westinghouse Air Brake Company, Pittsburgh, Pa.
W. S. McABEE, Vice Pres. & General Supt., Union Railroad Co., East Pittsburgh, Pa.
E. W. SMITH, Vice President, Pennsylvania Railroad, Pittsburgh, Pa.
LOUIS E. ENDSLEY, Consulting Engineer, 516 East End Avenue, Pittsburgh, Pa.
F. I. SNYDER, Vice President & General Manager, B. & L. E. R. R. Co., Pittsburgh, Pa.
C. O. DAMBACH, General Manager, P. & W. Va. Ry. Co., Pittsburgh, Pa.
R. H. FLINN, General Superintendent, Pennsylvania Railroad, Pittsburgh, Pa.
R. P. FORSBERG, Chief Engineer, P. & L. E. R R. Co., Pittsburgh, Pa

SUBJECT COMMITTEE:

M. R. REED, Chairman, Gen. Supt. Motive Power, Pennsylvania Railroad, Pittsburgh, Pa.
G. H. BURNETTE, Asst. Chief Engineer, P. & L. E. R. R. Co., Pittsburgh, Pa.
D W McGEORGE, Secretary, Edgewater Steel Company, Pittsburgh, Pa.

RECEPTION AND ATTENDANCE COMMITTEE:

J. W. JOHNSON, Chairman, Superintendent, Railway Express Agency, Pittsburgh, Pa
W. C. BUREL, Vice Chairman, Master Mechanic, Western Allegheny Railroad, Kaylor, Pa.
J. W. BOYD, Superintendent, Monongahela Railway Company, Brownsville, Pa.
THOMAS E. CANNON, General Supt. Equipment, P. & W. Va. Ry. Co., Pittsburgh, Pa
T. W. CARR, Superintendent Rolling Stock, P. & L. E. R. R. Co., McKees Rocks, Pa.
D. C. CARROLL, Assistant Agent, Pennsylvania Railroad, Pittsburgh, Pa.
S. G. DOWN, Vice President, Westinghouse Air Brake Company, Wilmerding, Pa.
HARRY C. GRAHAM, Pittsburgh Screw & Bolt Corporation, Pittsburgh, Pa.
J. W. SCHAD, Division Master Mechanic, B. & O. R. R. Co., Pittsburgh, Pa.
GEORGE S. WEST, Division Superintendent, Pennsylvania Railroad, Pittsburgh, Pa.
J. W. HOOVER, Asst. Chief of Transpn., Subsidiary Cos. U S. Steel Corp., Pittsburgh, Pa.
A. A. READ, Duquesne Slag Products Company, Pittsburgh, Pa.
C. P. SCHRECONGOST, Traffic Manager, Hillman Coal & Coke Company, Pittsburgh, Pa
J. A. WARFEL, Special Representative, Air Reduction Sales Company, Pittsburgh, Pa.
J. C. SHINGLEDECKER, Supervisor of Service Stations, The Pennzoil Co., Pittsburgh, Pa.
J. C. DILWORTH, Manager Railroad Sales, Carnegie-Illinois Steel Corp., Pittsburgh, Pa.

ENTERTAINMENT COMMITTEE:

J PORTER GILLESPIE, Chairman, Asst. Gen. Supt., Lockhart Iron & Steel Co., Pgh., Pa
FRANK E. WEIS, Vice Chairman, Transportation Clerk, Penna. R. R., Pittsburgh, Pa.
JAMES NAGEL, Superintendent Transportation, Montour Railroad, Coraopolis, Pa.
E. H. HOLMES, Sales Department, Fort Pitt Malleable Iron Co., Pittsburgh, Pa.
C. C. CLARK, Sales Manager, Central District, Pressed Steel Car Co., Pittsburgh, Pa.
A. I. KESSLER, Clearance Clerk, Pennsylvania Railroad, Pittsburgh, Pa.
T. F. SHERIDAN, Asst. to S.M.P. and S R.S., P. & L..E. R. R. Co., McKees Rocks, Pa

FINANCE COMMITTEE:

M. A. SMITH, Chairman, General Manager, P. & L. E. R. R Co., Pittsburgh, Pa
J. B. DIVEN, Superintendent Motive Power, Pennsylvania Railroad, Pittsburgh, Pa.
F. J. RYAN, District Representative, Detroit, Toledo & Ironton Railroad, Pittsburgh, Pa.
C E. CATT, Division Accountant, B. & O. R. R. Co., Pittsburgh, Pa.
G. W. HONSBERGER, Transpn. Mgr., Westinghouse Electric & Mfg. Co., Pittsburgh, Pa.

ADVERTISING COMMITTEE:

E. A. FOARD, Chairman, Supt. Stations & Transfers, Pennsylvania R. R., Pittsburgh, Pa.
KARL BERG, Superintendent Motive Power, P. & L E. R. R. Co., McKees Rocks, Pa.
H. E. PASSMORE, Representative, The American Hammered Piston Ring Co., Pgh., Pa.

MEMBERSHIP COMMITTEE:

T. E. BRITT, Chairman, Div. Storekeeper, B. & O. R. R. Co., Glenwood Shops, Pgh., Pa.
C. M. WHEELER, Vice Chairman, Sales Engr., Union Switch & Signal Co., Swissvale, Pa.
F. H. EATON, Sales Engineer, American Car & Foundry Co., Pittsburgh, Pa.
C. W. GOTTSCHALK, Asst. Traffic Manager, Jones & Laughlin Steel Corp., Pgh., Pa.
LLOYD SUTHERLAND, General Storekeeper, P. & L. E. R R. Co., McKees Rocks, Pa.
THOMAS R. FITZPATRICK, Freight Traffic Mgr., P. & L. E. R. R. Co., Pittsburgh, Pa.
P W. HEPBURN, Sales Engineer, Gulf Refining Company, Pittsburgh, Pa
W. B. MOIR, Chief Car Inspector, Pennsylvania Railroad, Pittsburgh, Pa
C W. TRUST, Assistant Traffic Manager, Carnegie-Illinois Steel Corp., Pittsburgh, Pa.
WILLIAM R. GELLATLY, President, Superior Railway Products Corp., Pittsburgh, Pa.
R. S. BULL, Supt. Power & Inclines, Pittsburgh Railways Co., N. S., Pittsburgh, Pa.
A. F. COULTER, Master Car Builder, Union Railroad Co., East Pittsburgh, Pa
T. R. DICKINSON, Purchasing Agent, B. & L. E. R. R. Co., Pittsburgh, Pa.
D. K. ORR, Road Master, Monongahela Railway Co., Brownsville, Pa.
W. F. AMBROSE, Master Mechanic, Aliquippa & Southern Railroad, Aliquippa, Pa.
JOHN I. MULVEY, Traffic Manager, Hubbard & Company, Pittsburgh, Pa.

PAST PRESIDENTS:

*J. H. McCONNELL	October,	1901, to October, 1903
'L. H. TURNER	November,	1903, to October, 1905
*F. H. STARK	November,	1905, to October, 1907
*H. W. WATTS	November,	1907, to April, 1908
'D. J. REDDING	November,	1908, to October, 1910
'F. R. McFEATTERS	November,	1910, to October, 1912
⚬A. G. MITCHELL	November,	1912, to October, 1914
'F. M. McNULTY	November,	1914, to October, 1916
*J. G. CODE	November,	1916, to October, 1917
'D. M. HOWE	November,	1917, to October, 1918
*J. A. SPIELMAN	November,	1918, to October, 1919
H. H. MAXFIELD	November,	1919, to October, 1920
FRANK J. LANAHAN	November,	1920, to October, 1921
*SAMUEL LYNN	November,	1921, to October, 1922
D. F. CRAWFORD	November,	1922, to October, 1923
*GEO. D. OGDEN	November,	1923, to October, 1924
A. STUCKI	November,	1924, to October, 1925
F. G. MINNICK	November,	1925, to October, 1926
G. W. WILDIN	November,	1926, to October, 1927
E. J. DEVANS	November,	1927, to October, 1928
W. S. McABEE	November,	1928, to October, 1929
E. W. SMITH	November,	1929, to October, 1930
LOUIS E. ENDSLEY	November,	1930, to October, 1931
*JOHN E. HUGHES	November,	1931, to October, 1932
F. I. SNYDER	November,	1932, to October, 1933
C. O. DAMBACH	November,	1933, to October, 1934
R. H. FLINN	November,	1934, to October, 1935
R. P. FORSBERG	November,	1935, to October, 1936

*—Deceased.

Meetings held fourth Thursday of each month except June, July and August

PROCEEDINGS OF MEETING
NOVEMBER 19, 1936

The meeting was called to order at the Fort Pitt Hotel at 8 o'clock P. M. with President E. A. Rauschart in the chair.

Registered attendance 209, as follows:

MEMBERS

Adams, F. W.	Durnell, W. E.
Allen, Earl M.	Emery, E.
Ambrose, W. F.	Endsley, Prof. Louis E.
Arnold, J. J.	Fair, J. M.
Ashley, F. B.	Ferguson, George
Baker, W. E.	Flinn, R. H.
Balzer, C. E.	Follett, W. F.
Beam, E. J.	Foltz, C. D.
Beeson, H. L.	Forsberg, R. P.
Berghane, A. L.	Fralic, C. F.
Beswick, R. M.	Frauenheim, A. M.
Blair, John R.	Frauenheim, Pierce H.
Britt, T. E.	Fry, L. H.
Buckwalter, T. V.	Fulton, K. H.
Buffington, W. P.	Geiser, W. P.
Burel, W. C.	George, W. J.
Buzzerd, J. P.	Gilg, Henry F.
Campbell, F. R.	Gillespie, J. Porter
Campbell, W. T.	Glaser, J. P.
Cannon, T. E.	Goble, A. S.
Carey, C. D.	Goda, P. H.
Carroll, D. C.	Goodwin, A. E.
Carter, E. D.	Groves, W. C.
Carter, John D.	Haller, Nelson M.
Cavanaugh, T. J.	Hayward, Carlton
Conway, J. D.	Heed, H. L.
Crawford, B. H.	Heinzenberger, A. E.
Cree, W. M.	Hemma, Charles H.
Crenner, Joseph A.	Hepburn, P. W.
Cruikshank, J. C.	Hess, Charles A.
Cudworth, H. D.	Hilstrom, A. V.
Cunningham, J. D.	Holmes, E. H.
Cunningham, R. I.	Huston, F. T.
Dambach, C. O.	Hutchinson, G. C., Jr.
Davis, John W.	James, J. H.
Dawson, J. N.	Johnson, J. W.
Daugherty, W. A.	Jordan, J. W.
Dean, R. W.	Kentlein, J.
Donovan, L. T.	Lanahan, Frank J.
Down, S. G.	Larson, W. E.
Dunham, C. W.	Lewis, N. F.
Durell, W. A.	Lincoln, R. B.

Little, J. G.
Livingston, W. C.
Long, R. M.
Lowe, William T.
Lowry, William F., Jr.
Lundeen, C. J.
Maliphant, C. W.
Mayer, G. E.
Miller, John
Miller, R. H.
Mills, O. B.
Misner, George W.
Moir, W. B.
Morgan, A. L.
Morgan, Homer C.
Mulvey, J. I.
Murray, C. C.
Murray, Stewart
Myers, Arnold
McAndrews, R.
McGeorge, D. W.
McIntyre, R. C.
McKim, Hollis
McKinley, John T.
McNamee, William
McTighe, B. J.
Nieman, Charles J.
Noonan, Daniel
O'Leary, J. J.
Palmer, E. A.
Pollock, Joseph H.
Posteraro, S. F.
Prinkey, C. M.
Purcell, E. J.
Reed, M. R.
Renshaw, W. B.
Rider, C. E.
Riley, O. W.

Roberts, E. L.
Rowan, J. R.
Rupp, E. S.
Ryan, D. W.
Schako, E. J.
Schmitt, Andrew
Severn, A. B.
Sheridan, T. F.
Shingledecker, John C.
Showalter, Joseph
Sixsmith, G. M.
Slater, A. H.
Smith, Robert B.
Steiner, P. E.
Stephen, James
Stephens, E. C.
Stevens, L. V.
Stoffregen, Louis E.
Stucki, A.
Sutherland, L.
Taylor, Joseph M.
Thompson, F. H.
Trax, L. R.
Tryon, Ira D.
Uhar, John J.
Unger, Dr. J. S.
Urtel, E. J.
Van Blarcom, W. C.
Van Vranken, S. E.
Vowinkel, Fred F.
Welton, Alvin A.
Wenzel, J. Louis
West, Troy
Westerman, M. A.
Wikander, O. R.
Wildin, G. W.
Woodings, Robert T.
Wright, John B.

Yohe, J. K., Jr.

VISITORS

Belleville, R. R.
Brungess, F. H.
Buckwalter, E. P.
Cole, Philip
Delaney, Robert
Ellicott, C. R.
Forrester, W. A.
Galloway, Harold R.
Gayetty, C. H.

Hakanson, Martin
Hall, C. B.
Harris, R. C.
Hatton, T. E.
Hilgert, T. J.
Holwell, Claude H.
Homer, W. M. C.
Hubbard, John W.
Jaboon, V. P.

Kelly, Frank J.
Kinnear, C. W.
Lais, G. J.
Latshaw, T. R.
Leech, B. E.
Leech, George R.
Lewis, S. B.
Lindberg, W. N.
Moore, J. W.
Moran, F. S.
Morrison, A. A.
Mulligan, H. J.
McKean, W. A.
O'Leary, J. P.
Pitman, C. A.

Poe, C. F.
Regath, Gus
Robertson, M. L.
Robinson, H. J.
Scranton, R. A.
Smith, Sion B.
Sommers, W. C.
Stanford, Tex.
Teskey, Walter J.
Tinker, J. H.
Walsh, C. E.
Walther, G. W.
Wimer, H. B.
Young, C. D.
Zell, Harry A.

Prior to the opening of the business meeting an enjoyable musical program was presented by a quartette and accompanist from the waiters of the Fort Pitt Hotel.

PRESIDENT RAUSCHART: As you have all signed registration cards we will dispense with the roll call.

The minutes of the last meeting are in the printer's hands, and unless there is objection we will dispense with the reading of the minutes of the last meeting.

Mr. Secretary, are there any announcements?

SECRETARY: We have the following proposals for membership:

Barrie, James S., Material Inspector, New York Central Lines, 130 Elmont Street, Crafton, Pittsburgh, Pa. Recommended by H. Courtney.

Bixler, Warren, Secretary-Treasurer, Foster-Bixler Fuel Company, Grant Building, Pittsburgh, Pa. Recommended by G. M. Sixsmith.

Burnside, G. M., Boiler Inspector, Monongahela Railway Company, 1025 Second Street, South Brownsville, Pa. Recommended by H. L. Beeson

Connors, John M., Assistant to Car Foreman, Montour Railroad Company, 87 Aztec Way, Mt Washington, Pittsburgh, Pa. Recommended by Thomas F. Sheridan

Germerodt, Oscar C., Chief Clerk to Mechanical Superintendent, Montour Railroad Company, 1412 Ridge Avenue, Coraopolis, Pa. Recommended by Thomas F. Sheridan

Gillie, H. C., Electric Welder, Monongahela Railway Company, Pearl Street, Brownsville, Pa. Recommended by H L. Beeson

Harper, J. S., Locomotive Engineer, Montour Railroad Company, 205 Orchid Street, Neville Island, Pittsburgh, Pa Recommended by T E. Britt

Harris, Edward W., Air Brake Foreman, Montour Railroad Company, 615 East Carson Street, Pittsburgh, Pa. Recommended by Thomas F. Sheridan.

Jordan, J. W., Salesman, Kansas City Works, Edgewater Steel Company, 706 Midland Building, Kansas City, Mo. Recommended by Charles J. Nieman.

Little, John G., Assistant to Vice President, Simmons-Boardman Publishing Company, Terminal Tower, Cleveland, O Recommended by T E Cannon and Chas. J. Nieman

Noonan, W. C., Superintendent Car Service, P. & W. Va. Ry. Co , Wabash Building, Pittsburgh, Pa. Recommended by C O Dambach

Pitcher, C. C., Assistant Superintendent, B & O. R R. Co , B & O. Station, Pittsburgh, Pa. Recommended by T. E. Britt.

Porter, J. V., Locomotive Air Brake Inspector, Montour Railroad Company, 1528 Hiland Avenue, Coraopolis, Pa. Recommended by Thomas F. Sheridan.

Rider, C. E., Timekeeper, B. & O. R R. Co., 25 Craighead Street, Mt. Washington, Pittsburgh, Pa. Recommended by T. E. Britt.

PRESIDENT: Following the precedent of the previous administration, I will ask those present whose names have just been read to stand that we may know you and welcome you.

SECRETARY: We have unfortunately to announce at most meetings the death of some member or members. Since our last meeting we have received information of the death of Mr. W. A. Skellie, who died March 23rd, 1935. He became a member of this Club on January 26, 1933.

PRESIDENT: An appropriate memorial minute will appear in the next issue of the Proceedings.

Is there any further business, before we proceed to the paper of the evening? If not, it gives me great pleasure at this time to introduce to you a speaker who is well known to the majority of our members, and I can assure you that you are going to listen to a very wonderful address. Mr. U. K. Hall, General Purchasing Agent of the Union Pacific Railroad Company, Omaha, Nebraska, will speak to you upon the subject, "Co-operation Between Railroad Purchasing and Stores Departments and Industries." Mr. Hall.

Co-operation Between Railroad Purchasing and Stores Departments and Industries

By U. K. HALL, General Purchasing Agent, Union Pacific Railroad Company, Omaha, Nebraska.

Mr. President, Members of the Railway Club of Pittsburgh and Friends: I am delighted to be here tonight. I have had a wonderful day. More than that, I have had two fine meals and they did not cost me a cent! I visited a fine steel plant this morning and a fine airbrake plant this afternoon. When you can learn something about two great industries by visiting their plants you are really accomplishing something. So I have had a very profitable day and a very pleasant day, and I am glad indeed to be here with you tonight.

I am just wondering, however, if I may not be somewhat in the position of the speaker when the chairman of the meeting turned to him and said, "Had we better let the men enjoy themselves a little longer or do you want to begin your talk now?"

At a gathering such as this, I believe it is well for us to identify ourselves, find out who we are, what we represent, or stand for.

It is an undeniable fact, and one which I believe is generally recognized by the majority of thinking people, that the railroads are the very life-blood of the nation, for although there are other means of transportation, still if the railroads failed to function, our vast country would soon be reduced to want and suffering. Moreover, in addition to their public service, the railroads represent one of the largest customers of the basic industries of the country. Therefore we have a right to be proud of our association with such a necessary industry, and by this industry I mean not only the railroads but the allied industries that make the operation of railroads possible. Furthermore, as the railroads prosper, industry prospers, and if carloadings fall and earnings fail, the reaction on industry is very noticeable, and in direct proportion.

If we are to succeed, there is one outstanding and important factor that we must recognize, that is, "Co-operation" and this will be the theme of my talk this evening.

There is no one individual, I care not who he may be, how strong or how competent, who can alone succeed in any large organization. He must have the co-operation not only of his own employes but of those interested or necessary in the operation of his property. Without doubt, one of the greatest factors in the success of any organization is the spirit of the men employed by that organization. If we want to succeed in our task, we must be ready and willing to do all we can, not only the tasks assigned to us but the things over and above these that we can study out for ourselves. We all know individuals who can readily and efficiently do tasks assigned to them, but this is not enough; we must reach out and make a place for ourselves; we must ask and solve the question, "What is there for me to do?"

In the Acts of the early Apostles, we read of a very dynamic character, Saul of Tarsus, or as he afterwards became known, Paul the Apostle. This man Saul started out one morning on a very momentous mission or journey. Going to Damascus, about noon suddenly there shone from heaven a bright light round about him, brighter than the noon-day sun. As Saul fell to the ground, he heard a voice saying: "Saul, Saul, why persecutest thou me?" And he answered, "Who art thou, Lord?" And then the answer, "I am Jesus of Nazareth whom thou persecutest." And then Saul asked a question which has rung down through the ages since, and one which comes to us here tonight and will every day of our lives, and one which if answered right will help us all in our daily tasks, especially in this great question of co-operation. The question Saul asked was, "What will thou have me to do, Lord?"

Let us ask this same question; what will thou have me to do; what is there for me to do; where do I fit into this great scheme of things? So with the idea of doing the right thing I believe it is well for us tonight to consider this great question.

Naturally, being a purchasing agent with a lifetime of Stores Department background, it is difficult for me to approach any discussion of the material handling situation without first harking back to the fundamental organization, namely, the Stores Department. Every individual here tonight connected with railroads or allied industries, is somewhere or in some way, vitally affected by the influence and activities of the Stores Departments of our railroads. There isn't a train that can be operated, a track or construction gang or an office organization that could function, if the Stores Department fell down on the job. The railroads cannot operate without materials and supplies. The using departments are naturally too busy in taking care of their own problems to bother with the material end and the Stores Department must therefore see to it that the using departments are not handicapped by shortages or mishandling. On the other hand, the Purchasing and Stores Department always have before them the question of stock turn-over, in other words, it is their duty to see that not only do they have sufficient materials on hand, but always with an eye to the amount of the material investment.

The Stores Department is interested in the procuring, storing, distributing and salvaging of material. The problem of the Stores Department is therefore that it must provide for and maintain materials in sufficient quantities to meet all requirements for the using departments, and to accomplish this it must have the co-operation of all the users of material, regardless of the department.

I am not going into any detail of the Stores Department organization, this not being my present subject, but I do want to stress how the Stores Department can co-operate with other departments to bring about unified success. No stockman or storekeeper can intelligently handle requirements of his particular group or store without daily personal contact with various mechanics, foremen and supervisors at the point where he is located. Storekeeping to be handled in an intelligent manner, is a complex problem. At times there is a spurt or epidemic in the consumption of given materials, and unless the stores representatives are closely in touch with the users as above mentioned, they will find they are out of materials when required, or they will become stampeded and order materials far in excess of immediate needs. Therefore, the competent stores man should not wait for the using department to contact the stores forces, but they should always endeavor to be in touch so far as possible with the users of all material.

With regard to Maintenance of Way Department materials handled for this department on the line, by direct shipment to point of use, or by supply train, Stores Department should endeavor to co-operate, see that the materials are shipped in such a manner as to be there in logical order, for instance, in erecting a building, naturally first material required is the form lumber and sand, cement, gravel, plumbing goods; shipment of material for the roof and finishing materials to follow later; in the matter of major repair programs requiring certain fabricated steel shapes, these shapes which may be required first, naturally should be shipped first. At other times, it is necessary to move all materials for the job at one time. This requires full co-operation of the Stores Department to see that the material is shipped complete or in its logical order to avoid delay to gangs as they are moved to the job and not delay their work account of material shortage. This same proposition applies with equal respect to erection of signal lines and other construction work.

With reference to the salvaging of material, it is one of the major duties of the Stores Department, who have charge of scrap accumulations from all departments, to see that the only materials which are disposed of as scrap are those disposed of by reason of being worn out, destroyed beyond repair or are obsolete. When serviceable materials are found in cars at scrap docks, the supervisor in charge instantly recognizes there is something wrong which needs correction and he notifies Storekeeper and immediate contact should be made with department from which serviceable materials in scrap have been received; not in the spirit of criticism but rather with the intent of correcting such condition.

Another factor of Stores Department co-operation is the delivery of materials from stores and material yards to point of use. At larger store points stores delivery system is provided for the benefit of the Mechanical Department. This delivery system not only includes handling material to and from stores to shops but covers movement between various departments of the shops and between shops and roundhouses. There is a foreman or leader in charge of stores delivery where the terminal is large enough to warrant and this supervisor is invaluable in watching to see materials are at the various machines ready for machining and he keeps a check during the day to determine when equipment will be finished at one machine and ready for movement to another or movement to point of consumption. This entire service is one of distinct co-operation.

With reference to the operating department of the railroad, during normal times or when seasonal business is at its height all Operating Departments are taxed to see that power is maintained and in service, yards are taxed to capacity and switch engines are utilized to the maximum in making up and breaking trains and at such times full co-operation of Stores Department is essential with yard points to see movement of switch engines is reduced to the minimum. By reason of the volume of business and necessity of quick movement of materials, it is necessary for the General Store to make numerous LCL shipments and from the nature of such material frequently it is left in the car and the car switched to the store. This not only delays the supplies but also causes congestion at the store. While it will cause more work on the part of the store during such rush times this material should be unloaded at the freight house as it is received in cars with commercial material and Stores

Department truck haul such materials, which will eliminate considerable yard switching.

CO-OPERATION WITH THE STORES DEPARTMENT BY THE USING DEPARTMENTS

Supervisors of the using departments also have a duty to perform in contacting the Stores Department and should do so daily. The shop superintendent knows what work is lined up for his shop and he should keep the storekeeper advised at all times so that materials can be received and delivered to the point of use accordingly. For example, when authority has been obtained to start a certain program, the supervisor should furnish the storekeeper full facts. If unusual conditions are ahead with which they are familiar, they should give the storekeeper an opportunity to be able to meet such condition by giving him all the advance information they can. Unfortunately, this is an opportunity for co-operation that is often overlooked.

In the handling of cars, the Car Service Department require the cars for movement of commercial lading; the Superintendent complains that they take up trackage room needed for switching and the yardmaster claims the Stores Department cars and engines have him sewed up. This can be overcome by asking, and receiving, from the Division Superintendent and his Yardmaster, certain tracks for storing Company material cars, and then see to it that the cars are always placed on those tracks, release them promptly, and turn cars back to commercial service. The railroad cannot operate without adequate material and supplies and these cannot be moved without cars. Therefore, in the proper spirit of co-operation it is up to the operating department to handle such cars promptly, and the Stores Department to release them just as quickly.

PURCHASING AND STORES DEPARTMENT

On the subject of co-operation between the Purchasing and Stores Departments, it is generally recognized today that there is practically little or no division of responsibility between these two departments; in fact, many railroads today have a co-ordinated department. However, the Stores Department should place purchase requisitions or information for replenishment of stock in sufficient time to allow the proper and orderly method of purchasing and securing such materials, and the Purchasing Department should endeavor to place orders as promptly as possible and keep the storekeeper fully advised as to delivery date.

In the co-operation of the Purchasing Agent with the using departments, it is my opinion that it is not up to the Purchasing Agent to endeavor to dictate to the users as to the character of material that should be ordered, except where the mutual interests of the railroad's general policy is involved. In this I realize that my position may be at variance with some of the other Purchasing Agents, nevertheless I feel keenly that the heads of the using departments are the ones most vitally interested in the operating expenses of their department, they are technical experts and know what is necessary and what is best suited to their needs. I feel therefore that the using departments are the ones to specify any special machines or equipment, and in conjunction with the laboratory or test department, to specify the character of materials to be ordered. It is then up to the Purchasing Agent to secure to the best advantage the materials and supplies that in the judgment of the using departments are best suited to their needs.

THE PURCHASING AGENT

There are variations in all human beings, therefore there are variations in Purchasing Agents, for after all, Purchasing Agents are human beings. However, despite the differences in methods, practices and procedure, the average purchasing agent of today believes in playing square, moreover, to lay the cards on the table and to look at both sides of any situation. It is absolutely necessary to have thorough co-operation not only in our own organization, but with those with whom we deal daily. The Purchasing Agent has an equal right to expect just as fair and square treatment from salesmen as the salesmen have a right to expect fair and square treatment from the purchasing agent. No purchasing agent can make a success of his job unless he has the sympathetic co-operation of those calling on him daily in an endeavor to sell their products. All departments of a railroad and industry are so interwoven that it is generally recognized that the one cannot successfully function without the aid and co-operation of the other. The purchasing agent expects fair treatment from his callers. What is fair treatment? Personally, I feel that in offering prices or rendering bids on the general run of material, the purchasing agent has a right to expect the first bid to be the lowest and the only figure that the seller has to offer. I do not believe in receiving a price and then haggling or working towards reduction. My own personal opinion is that the most satisfactory way to purchase material is to have all of our friends realize the prices they offer are the prices at which they will either receive or lose the order. This is as fair to one as to the other. Friendships are of tremendous value, not only in our personal lives but in our official actions and no man can succeed without friendly contacts. However, the purchasing agent does not expect the salesman, because of being a friend of his, to thus figure on having an advantage over his competitors, or expect his friendship to secure for him confidential information as to prices offered by his competitors. This is the wrong use of friendship.

Incidentally, real friendship is too valuable a possession to put on a monetary basis. Such friendship, if sincere and honest, tends toward a more mutual understanding and settlement of our joint problems.

The purchasing agent who encourages suggestions as to substitutions, improvements or changes in specifications, by permitting firms to demonstrate or submit samples, will be benefitted thereby, and at least have the satisfaction of knowing that he is getting his money's worth, and no doubt the percentage of changes for the better would be sufficient to more than offset the effort. Furthermore, his willingness to co-operate with the suppliers would give them an incentive to continue their efforts to serve.

In all fairness to concerns to whom price inquiries are mailed, descriptions of materials should be complete with definite specifications, so that there will be no opportunity to quote a low price on an article of inferior quality. It is our practice where necessary to submit samples or request that representative samples be furnished when it is impossible to show the exact material required.

The Purchasing Agent has found that his duties embrace something else rather than the browbeating and chiseling of peddlers. He has come to the realization that his duties are manifold and important to his company, involving a knowledge of the materials he uses and buys, market conditions confronting his suppliers which includes raw materials and finished products, and their anticipated price changes and delivery prospects.

With the constant change in development of industries, new materials and devices are constantly being marketed and it is the added duty of the purchasing agent to investigate such devices and materials to see if they can be used to advantage by his company, and the expert advice of the technicians of his own organization is often not sufficient in such a broad scope of activities, and he can never become oversaturated with the knowledge of the important phases of his own business.

Our railroad has listed in its stock books approximately eighty thousand items which are regularly stocked and purchased and in addition, special materials and items of equipment are necessary for the operation of the property. In spite of the continuous standardization and simplification which enables us to reduce stock items, research and advances in transportation, particularly in recent years, such as the introduction of diesel powered streamline trains, air conditioning equipment, etc., have over-balanced any reduction in items and they continue to increase numerically. In a broad sense, there is something to know about all these items. They are secured from a myriad of sources, all of whom sell and we buy.

This emphasizes my thought that the purchasing agent must of necessity, if not by nature, seek unlimited co-operation, not only with the technical and using departments of his own organization, but he must seek and grant this cooperation with the men who represent his sources of supply for all materials. He never knows when he will require information and services from some source or other.

How can he best establish a relationship with the supplier so as to result in a business association of mutual benefit? I believe in fostering an acquaintance with representatives of our sources and this acquaintance need not necessarily be secured by back-slapping or entertaining; the granting of a kind and courteous reception generally is responded to in a like manner. The salesman from the time he enters our reception room is entitled to prompt and courteous attention; he should not be expected to wait for an interview beyond the limits of necessity and when received, should be given a full opportunity to express the purpose of his visit.

My own experience has been that in general the type of

men now selling us materials are of high caliber, sincere and honest; they have a knowledge of the products which they sell and they are in fact specialists in their particular line. They are possessed with complete knowledge of the goods which they handle, their process of manufacture, and they should be and generally are, acquainted with business conditions in their territories, any contemplated change in prices, and the demands for materials and supplies which would affect deliveries. They should also be thoroughly acquainted with any new products in their line, their use, and have a knowledge of the economies that can be effected by their introduction. There are exceptions to this type of a sales representative, but, in general, the individual who is selling today is fully informed as to his materials and is in a position to impart this knowledge to the purchaser, which is of great value to the purchasing agent and permits him to better perform his duties.

Through the course of years and continued calls of salesmen on the purchasing agent, there exists an acquaintanceship and mutual personal understanding of individuals which cannot help but produce a business relationship which is frank and fair to both parties, resulting in a natural co-operation which is of infinite value. I thoroughly believe that such a mutual relationship can be established with dignity and without partiality or favor. The business of buying is, or course, not a personal matter; the Purchasing Agent represents his corporation first and foremost and he is expected to purchase to the best advantage for his company, considering all factors such as price, quality, reliability of source and delivery. The sales representative on the other hand is likewise not in a personal enterprise—he represents his company and as he represents it he establishes a reputation for his employer.

As stated, we believe that a sales representative is entitled to courteous and prompt reception. He is also entitled to a full hearing in order that he may present properly his materials or specialities which he has to offer and if he sells an item which must necessarily be passed on by the using department, he should be permitted to contact this department under the direction and full co-operation of the purchasing agent. If he is bidding on any special items, he should obviously be furnished with complete specifications, drawings, etc.; so as to permit of an intelligent bid. He should likewise be possessed with the thorough understanding that he will be given every consideration equal to that of his competitors, but that regardless of personalities or friendship, he is not entitled to any undue consideration or confidential information.

I believe further that a source of supply should attempt, through every reasonable effort, to follow up the use of their material. If the items involved require any special instructions as to use, the manufacturer should service such devices to see that the utmost utility is obtained.

Placing of an order should not close a transaction insofar as the salesman is concerned.

With little difference in prices quoted, and the fact that deliveries are much slower than they have been, we are compelled at times to place orders with firms offering the best deliveries, and co-operation on the part of the representatives in having shipments of material made as promised will go a long way toward getting them orders at this time when material is being used in larger quantities than during the past four or five years.

In many instances there are occasions where delivery is of utmost importance and we have found too frequently after the placing of an order with definite specified delivery, which was given consideration in the placing of that order, that the sales representative does not recognize his responsibility in seeing that his concern follows through the production of the goods so as to meet the delivery requirement of the customer, such delays in a great many cases resulting in a material loss to the customer. Further, on the other hand, and as previously mentioned, the customer should be informed wherever possible of price advances so that he can protect himself on materials where it is deemed advisable. He should be informed of general market conditions within the specific industry and where special information may be desired, such as prices for estimating purposes or special materials required for an unusual purpose, the co-operation of salesman and firm he represents is very important. We have all had frequent experiences where prices have been reduced voluntarily by manufacturers when conditions would permit; again, we have had price advances called to our attention that would permit us to stock certain items of material at a distinct saving. Manufacturers who establish such policies cannot help but impress the customer with their spirit of fairness and co-operation, and I believe this results in a mutually profitable relationship.

Further, the purchasing agent desires an established source of supply. There is nothing to be gained by merely changing from one establishment to another unless there is an advantage from the purchasing agent's standpoint, that is, a better price or improved quality. Some salesmen suggest that a certain firm has had the business long enough and they feel it is their turn to secure a share of the railroad's business. This is not, from our viewpoint, a sufficient reason for a change. We would rather have the reputation of staying with an established source of supply as long as they produce the goods at satisfactory price, quality, live up to their delivery promises and follow up the use of their materials.

Briefly summarized, I again desire to pay a tribute to the character of the salesmen who contact us daily. It is well understood there are many mutual problems which we must work out together. Neither party, the Purchasing Agent nor the supply man, in this co-operative work, can be divorced one from the other. Both I am sure, realize the necessity of co-operation as the keynote of mutual success.

There is however, a still greater problem, in the co-operation of the purchasing power of railroads and industry, and one which they must work out together, namely, the joint reaction on the public generally.

According to "Yearbook of Railroad Information", compiled by the Committee on Public Relations of the Eastern Railroads, of the average dollar of operating revenues received by the Class I railways, 45c was spent for labor and 22.1c for fuel, materials and supplies, or 67.1c for these two items alone.

Does the public realize the importance of railroad prosperity to the general business of the nation? In order to bring out specific cases and to emphasize the subject further, let me quote examples from the road with which I have the honor and privilege of being employed. Almost every conceivable item of material that is produced is used to a more or less extent by our railroad. These materials embrace goods from chemicals to foodstuffs, radios and furniture to medicinal and hospital supplies, as well as all lines of durable goods; in other words, practically everything that the average consumer purchases as the necessities of life, and in addition, maintenance and heavy materials peculiar to a railroad's requirements. It is therefore obvious that all forms of industry are directly benefitted by the Union Pacific purchases. These materials are all purchased largely in the States in which we operate, and from there react to the great industrial centers generally.

What has been said of the Union Pacific, which is quoted for an example only, applies equally well to every other railroad, and every purchasing agent here tonight could repeat the same statements for his road for the States in which they operate.

It is therefore very evident that every community is vitally interested in the welfare of the railroads, and they all profit largely thereby.

What is the result of these enormous expenditures? I believe the answer is obvious. The railroad dollar as explained, aside from fixed charges, represents mainly wages and materials and supplies. Expenditures for materials and supplies in territory tributary to our own lines in turn represent more labor and wages and contribute largely to the economic welfare of these communities.

The railroad industry as a whole represents the largest users of material. Thus, there is no State in the Union that is not vitally affected by railroad purchases and therefore by railroad prosperity. Great manufacturing and distributing centers such as we are in tonight, are to a large extent dependent upon the purchasing power of the railroads. When the railroads prosper, they prosper. In time of depression, when the railroads cannot buy, their factories will run largely on a limited basis.

In this matter of co-operation, therefore, the question comes back to us—have you and I representing the railroads and allied industry, fully informed ourselves as to this situation, and are we in a position to intelligently discuss with representatives of the public, the importance of the railroads and their allied industries?

There is no question but what the railroads need the sympathetic friendship and co-operation of not only shippers but the public generally. The railroads need a better break in general legislation affecting the railroads. The question is: Do you and I know these facts sufficiently to present them in an intelligent discussion? For instance, in order to bring the situation directly home, are we informed regarding the huge sums which the railroads contribute in salaries and wages, as well as purchases, in our various communities? Do we know the amount of taxes that are paid in our communities? Does the public fully realize the good service being rendered by railroads in both transportation of passengers and in the shipment of materials and supplies? Do your neighbors realize that in the year 1935 the railroads purchased materials to the value of $612,500,000, an average of $51,000,000 per month?

Are we failthful to our trust and responsibility? Are we able to co-operate with our people, with our friends and neighbors, presenting intelligently important facts appertaining to our industry? We all realize the tremendous importance of public opinion, and we have all realized the antagonistic attitude of the public towards the railroads, based principally on the old and out-of-date sentiments of the "public be damned". We know this policy by the railroads has been entirely reversed. We know that the railroads are endeavoring to serve and to please the public. We believe today there is a silver lining that the public has a better understanding of railroad problems and are reacting more to the railroad's side of the question.

However, there is still a tremendous task ahead of us and one that will never be fully accomplished, but if we are all informed as to the answers to these various problems, the more intelligently we can discuss them.

Where do you come into the picture? Where do I come into the picture? Is there something that you should do; that I should do?

There is nothing we can do in this great co-operative effort today that is more necessary and more important than to take this message out to the public. The power of public opinion is the greatest force in the life of our country today, and we who should have this information ought to take it out to the public. Why are we interested in the railroad situation? I can tell you why I am. I have a family to support. I am interested that I may receive the best salary I can earn to protect and give the advantages and comforts of life to those who are dependent on me. We have no reason to be ashamed of the endeavor to do the most we can for those who are dependent upon us.

Another reason: We all realize that the railroads are so necessary for the upbuilding of the country that we should do what we can as l o y a l, patriotic American citizens to further the interests of the railroads in order to further the economic welfare of our country and for national defense. We know there is not any government in the world that can operate the American railroads like private ownership. Therefore we should know all the facts and do the best we can to present those facts to the public to keep away some of the things that may be staring us in the face. We need to be loyal and faithful to the interests that employ us. There is no greater thing in the world than loyalty and there is no limit to what loyalty will accomplish. Turn back the pages of history two thousand years and see a figure so humble he had no where to lay his head. But he had a wonderful message—a message needed by a sin-sick world. The accomplishment of his life work—of the promulgating of this great message—was left in the hands of twelve humble men, and had these men failed it is hard to visualize the result. But they did not fail—the Master's confidence in their loyalty was justified. Through sickness, privation, persecution, martyrdom, they stood fast, and their loyalty and co-operation carried the message, until today the story is known and Christianity encircles the world. What a tribute to loyalty, to co-operation, to intelligence. What is the spirit of we who are gathered here tonight? I hope that as we go forth, we will go determined to carry the gospel of good will towards the railroads by whom we are employed—that we go determined to do our part to be loyal and to justify the faith of those who employ us.

PRESIDENT: You have listened to a wonderful talk. I am not going to call on any individual, but I would like to have volunteers to say a few words or to ask any questions that may occur to you.

MR. W. C. BUREL: Could you tell us something about the Robinson-Patman Bill and what effect it is going to have on business and the railroads?

MR. HALL: I think I could answer that in this way. Considering this same subject, I went to our General Counsel and asked him if he had a copy of the Robinson-Patman Bill, and he said he had, and gave me the bill and his file about five inches thick, asking if I would please read it over and come back and tell him what it was all about. This question is a hard one to answer. About all we can do, is to wait and see what action is taken in the clarifying of the law before we can really know what the facts are. I do feel that the law was not intended to infringe on legitimate business, and I do not believe interruption to railroad business was really intended. We will therefore have to wait and see what further definite interpretation of the bill brings forth.

MR. A. STUCKI: Although I am a mechanical man, Mr. Hall's address on co-operation between the departments of Purchasing and Stores and the industries was very interesting and very elevating to me. He mentioned three specific points which interested me very much.

Prompt deliveries I realize are very essential, in fact imperative, in order to keep every one down the line moving as per schedule previously decided on.

I also appreciated Mr. Hall's broadminded remarks, when he said that the department using the materials or devices should pass on the merits of them, because that department will have to take care of the upkeep during the life in service. This, of course, means true economy to the railroad. It will help the Stores Department in their task. And, speaking especially of mechanical devices, if one device will answer for locomotives as well as cars, regardless of capacity, length, etc., it will again greatly simplify the Stores Department's proposition, in requiring them to keep only one in stock instead of two or more. Additional merit, co-operation and economy. Am I right?

PRESIDENT: I see Mr. S. G. Down of the Westinghouse Air Brake Company, in the audience. I wonder if we might hear a word from him?

MR. S. G. DOWN: We of Pittsburgh, "The Workship of the World," are greatly honored to have with us tonight Mr. U. K. Hall, who came all the way from Omaha to give us this most interesting address, which is quite different from the form of address we are accustomed to hear and which came right from the heart. I have had many contacts with Mr. Hall and he has expressed himself tonight just as he does to all who visit his office on business.

He struck a number of high points in his talk which I think it would be well to dwell on. In the first place, he has a full realization of the spirit of co-operation between

19

the railroads and the Railway Supply people because railroads cannot exist without the Supply Industry and we cannot exist without the railroads. Our fortunes go hand in hand. Just a few years ago, you will remember, we were all at a very low ebb and there was a feeling that the railroads were down and out, due to the various forms of competitive transportation such as buses, trucks, airplanes, waterways, etc. Today that would be the farthest from our thoughts. The railroads are coming into their own stronger than ever. Therefore, I suggest it is to our mutual interest to put our shoulder to the wheel and see that the public at large is informed concerning what modern railroad transportation has in store for them.

How many of us, for instance, know how low the fare is between New York and San Francisco? It would be well to look it up and find out. You may know someone who is contemplating a trip to California and encourage them to make the trip if you knew how low the rate is and the splendid facilities available for them.

Mr. Hall spoke at a luncheon this noon and told about the special service in effect on their new train, the "Challenger," consisting of coaches of the latest type, fast service, cars for women only with special attendants, etc., which service a great many people would take advantage of if they knew it existed. I believe all the members of the Supply Industry and those who work with us could do very much to encourage the use of this latest type of transportation.

Mr. Hall also spoke of the requirements on the part of the Purchasing and Stores Departments to keep the railroads operating. The railroad must carry on and that means that the Stores Department, regardless of what calamity may take place, must have the materials on hand to keep their railroad running. Further, they must be able to read the future and anticipate unusual requirements and also the increase in volume of business and the demand for supplies. A few months ago, I had occasion to speak before the Purchasing Agents' Annual Convention and referred to the apparent car shortage. All the cars available for car loading are now in use and they have almost reached the practical saturation point, and we hope this will continue as its increase means prosperity for all of us.

Mr. Hall spoke of Purchasing Agents being really human beings. I am sure you will agree that they are. It has been my pleasure for many years to contact these agencies and I find if you approach them with a knowledge of your product and the thought that you have something to give them which will help improve their service, you will find them in a very responsive mood. Where you occasionally find one who is a little cold, if you look down deep, you will find that you have not presented your subject in a proper manner. You must not only try to sell him something but you should try to sell him something you know is going to improve the service of his property and to do that you have to know your product. One of the weaknesses of a great many of our salesmen is that they approach the Purchasing Department with a price book and try to sell something out of that book and when asked just what the device will do or how much better it is than something else, they are not able to answer the question. They should be able to show just how their product will help the railroad service for in the last analysis the Purchasing Agent is responsible for the success of his company.

Mr. Hall spoke about the question of the lowest price. He does not buy on that alone. What he buys is service to his company. What is the difference if it is a fraction of a cent more or less? What he really buys is the service his company is going to get out of the particular thing he buys.

Another factor, and a very important factor, is this: They want to buy from a company they know is responsible, that is in a position to serve. "Readiness to serve" is a stock phrase of mine. That is the position the railroads are in. They are compelled to be ready to serve. The result is that they have thousands of cars standing on the side tracks right now ready and waiting to serve their patrons. And that is doubly true of the Supply Industry. Therefore, when we approach a Purchasing Agent, we must assure him that we are not only trying to sell him something but sell him a service and to stand back of that service. I am sure if we emphasize that particular point we will find very little difficulty in selling our product at a proper price and not necessarily at the lowest price. Those who do not have a substantial background must of necessity sell at a lower price to get any business at all.

I am going to close my remarks by expressing in behalf of the representatives of the Supply Industry our appreciation for the fine courtesy Mr. Hall has always extended o us, and I would like to suggest as an expression of appreiation of all the members, and friends present for the splenlid address given to us this evening by Mr. Hall a rising 'ote of thanks.

The motion was duly seconded and carried by unanimous 'ote.

PRESIDENT: Is there any further business? If not, he meeting will stand adjourned and we invite you to the ables where luncheon is prepared.

J. D. CONWAY, Secretary.

In Memoriam

W. A. SKELLIE

Joined Club January 26, 1933

Died March 23, 1935

OFFICIAL PROCEEDINGS
RAILWAY CLUB OF PITTSBURGH
$1.00 Per Year   25¢ Per Copy

| Vol. XXXVI. | DECEMBER 17, 1936. | No. 2. |

NOTES ON LOCOMOTIVE TESTING WITH A GLANCE AT HISTORY

By LAWFORD H. FRY, Railway Engineer, Edgewater Steel Company, Pittsburgh, Pa.

The proof of your interest

in the Club can be

enhanced

by securing a

NEW MEMBER.

Application form is available

in this magazine. Look

it up and

"ACT NOW."

OFFICIAL PROCEEDINGS

OF

The Railway Club of Pittsburgh

Organized October 18, 1901

Published monthly, except June, July and August, by the Railway Club of
Pittsburgh, J. D. Conway, Secretary, 515 Grandview Ave., Pittsburgh, Pa..

Entered as Second Class Matter February 6, 1915, at the Postoffice at Pittsburgh,
under the Act of March 3, 1879.

No. 2
Vol. XXXVI.
Pittsburgh, Pa., Dec. 17, 1936
$1.00 Per Year
25c Per Copy

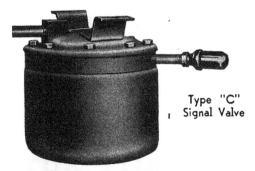

INDEX—ADVERTISERS.

NOTE—This form to be filled out in full by typewriter or printed and mailed to J. D. Conway, Secretary, 1941 Oliver Building, Pittsburgh, Pa. Membership fee, including dues, is $3.00 for each fiscal year or part thereof, except those proposed in September or October. Those proposed in these months will be credited upon payment for the following fiscal year. Dues are payable in advance.

The fiscal year ends with the month of October.

The Railway Club of Pittsburgh:

....19......

Gentlemen:

Will you kindly consider my Application for Membership in your Club at the next meeting:

Name...

Title...

Company...

My Address...

....

Recommended by...

OFFICIAL PROCEEDINGS

OF

The Railway Club of Pittsburgh

Organized October 18, 1901

Vol. XXXVI. No. 2	Pittsburgh, Pa., Dec. 17, 1936	$1.00 Per Year 25c Per Copy

OFFICERS FOR 1936-1937

President
E. A. RAUSCHART,
Mechanical Superintendent, Montour Railroad Co., Coraopolis, Pa.

First Vice President
G. M. SIXSMITH,
Supt., Pennsylvania Railroad,
Pittsburgh, Pa.

Secretary
J. D. CONWAY,
Railway Supply Manufacturers' Association,
Pittsburgh, Pa.

Second Vice President
J. D. BELTZ,
Supt., B. & O. R. R. Co.,
Pittsburgh, Pa.

Treasurer
E. J. SEARLES,
Manager, Schaefer Equipment Co.,
Pittsburgh, Pa.

EXECUTIVE COMMITTEE:

FRANK J. LANAHAN, Chairman, President, Fort Pitt Malleable Iron Co., Pittsburgh, Pa.
A. STUCKI, Engineer, A. Stucki Company, Pittsburgh, Pa.
D. F. CRAWFORD, Consulting Engineer, Pittsburgh, Pa.
G W. WILDIN, Consulting Engineer, Westinghouse Air Brake Company, Pittsburgh, Pa.
W. S. McABEE, Vice Pres. & General Supt., Union Railroad Co, East. Pittsburgh, Pa.
E: W. SMITH, Vice President, Pennsylvania Railroad, Pittsburgh, Pa.
LOUIS E. ENDSLEY, Consulting Engineer, 516 East End Avenue, Pittsburgh, Pa.
F. I. SNYDER, Vice President & General Manager, B. & L. E. R. R. Co, Pittsburgh, Pa.
C. O. DAMBACH, General Manager, P. & W. Ry. Co., Pittsburgh, Pa.
R. H. FLINN, General Superintendent, Pennsylvania Railroad, Pittsburgh, Pa.
R. P. FORSBERG, Chief Engineer, P. & L. E. R. R. Co., Pittsburgh, Pa.

SUBJECT COMMITTEE:

G. H. BURNETTE, Asst. Chief Engineer, P. & L. E. R. R. Co., Pittsburgh, Pa.
D. W. McGEORGE, Secretary, Edgewater Steel Company, Pittsburgh, Pa.

RECEPTION AND ATTENDANCE COMMITTEE:

J. W. JOHNSON, Chairman, Superintendent, Railway Express Agency, Pittsburgh, Pa.
W. C. BUREL, Vice Chairman, Master Mechanic, Western Allegheny Railroad, Kaylor, Pa.
J. W. BOYD, Superintendent, Monongahela Railway Company, Brownsville, Pa.
THOMAS E. CANNON, General Supt. Equipment, P. & W. Va. Ry. Co., Pittsburgh, Pa.
T. W. CARR, Superintendent Rolling Stock, P. & L. E. R. R. Co., McKees Rocks, Pa.
D. C. CARROLL, Assistant Agent, Pennsylvania Railroad, Pittsburgh, Pa.
S. G. DOWN, Vice President, Westinghouse Air Brake Company, Wilmerding, Pa.
HARRY C. GRAHAM, Pittsburgh Screw & Bolt Corporation, Pittsburgh, Pa.
J. W. SCHAD, Division Master Mechanic, B. & O. R. R. Co., Pittsburgh, Pa.
GEORGE S. WEST, Division Superintendent, Pennsylvania Railroad, Pittsburgh, Pa.
J. W. HOOVER, Asst. Chief of Transpn., Subsidiary Cos. U. S. Steel Corp., Pittsburgh, Pa.
A. A. READ, Duquesne Slag Products Company, Pittsburgh, Pa.
C. P. SCHRECONGOST, Traffic Manager, Hillman Coal & Coke Company, Pittsburgh, Pa.
J. A. WARFEL, Special Representative, Air Reduction Sales Company, Pittsburgh, Pa.
J. C. SHINGLEDECKER, Supervisor of Service Stations, The Pennzoil Co., Pittsburgh, Pa.
J. C. DILWORTH, Manager Railroad Sales, Carnegie-Illinois Steel Corp., Pittsburgh, Pa.

ENTERTAINMENT COMMITTEE:

J. PORTER GILLESPIE, Chairman, Asst. Gen. Supt., Lockhart Iron & Steel Co , Pgh., Pa.
FRANK E. WEIS, Vice Chairman, Transportation Clerk, Penna. R. R., Pittsburgh, Pa.
JAMES NAGEL, Superintendent Transportation, Montour Railroad, Coraopolis, Pa.
E. H. HOLMES, Sales Department, Fort Pitt Malleable Iron Co., Pittsburgh, Pa.
C. C. CLARK, Sales Manager, Central District, Pressed Steel Car Co., Pittsburgh, Pa.
A. I. KESSLER, Clearance Clerk, Pennsylvania Railroad, Pittsburgh, Pa.
T. F. SHERIDAN, Asst. to S.M.P. and S.R S., P. & L. E. R. R. Co., McKees Rocks, Pa.

FINANCE COMMITTEE:

M. A. SMITH, Chairman, General Manager, P. & L E. R. R. Co., Pittsburgh, Pa.
J. B. DIVEN, Superintendent Motive Power, Pennsylvania Railroad, Pittsburgh, Pa.
F. J. RYAN, District Representative, Detroit, Toledo & Ironton Railroad, Pittsburgh, Pa.
C. E. CATT, Division Accountant, B. & O. R. R. Co., Pittsburgh, Pa.
G. W. HONSBERGER. Transpn. Mgr., Westinghouse Electric & Mfg. Co., Pittsburgh, Pa.

ADVERTISING COMMITTEE:

H H HAUPT. Chairman, Gen. Supt., Motive Power, Pennsylvania Railroad, Pittsburgh, Pa.
KARL BERG, Superintendent Motive Power, P. & L E. R. R. Co., McKees Rocks, Pa.
H. E. PASSMORE, Representative, The American Hammered Piston Ring Co., Pgh., Pa.

MEMBERSHIP COMMITTEE:

T. E. BRITT, Chairman, Div. Storekeeper, B. & O. R. R. Co., Glenwood Shops, Pgh., Pa.
C. M. WHEELER, Vice Chairman, Sales Engr., Union Switch & Signal Co., Swissvale, Pa.
F. H. EATON, Sales Engineer, American Car & Foundry Co., Pittsburgh, Pa.
C. W. GOTTSCHALK, Asst. Traffic Manager, Jones & Laughlin Steel Corp., Pgh., Pa.
LLOYD SUTHERLAND, General Storekeeper, P. & L. E. R R. Co., McKees, Rocks, Pa.
THOMAS R. FITZPATRICK, Freight Traffic Mgr., P. & L. E. R. R. Co., Pittsburgh, Pa.
P. W. HEPBURN, Sales Engineer, Gulf Refining Company, Pittsburgh, Pa.
W. B. MOIR, Chief Car Inspector, Pennsylvania Railroad, Pittsburgh, Pa.
C. W. TRUST, Assistant Traffic Manager, Carnegie-Illinois Steel Corp., Pittsburgh, Pa.
WILLIAM R. GELLATLY, President, Superior Railway Products Corp., Pittsburgh, Pa.
R. S. BULL, Supt. Power & Inclines, Pittsburgh Railways Co., N. S., Pittsburgh, Pa.
A. F. COULTER, Master Car Builder, Union Railroad Co., East Pittsburgh, Pa.
T. R. DICKINSON, Purchasing Agent, B. & L. E. R. R. Co., Pittsburgh, Pa.
D. K. ORR, Road Master, Monongahela Railway Co., Brownsville, Pa.
W. F. AMBROSE, Master Mechanic, Aliquippa & Southern Railroad, Aliquippa, Pa.
JOHN I. MULVEY, Traffic Manager, Hubbard & Company, Pittsburgh, Pa.

PAST PRESIDENTS:

*J. H. McCONNELL	October, 1901, to October, 1903
*L. H. TURNER	November, 1903, to October, 1905
*F. H. STARK	November, 1905, to October, 1907
*H. W. WATTS	November, 1907, to April, 1908
'D. J. REDDING	November, 1908, to October, 1910
*F. R. McFEATTERS	November, 1910, to October, 1912
*A. G. MITCHELL	November, 1912, to October, 1914
*F. M. McNULTY	November, 1914, to October, 1916
*J. G. CODE	November, 1916, to October, 1917
°D. M. HOWE	November, 1917, to October, 1918
*J. A. SPIELMAN	November, 1918, to October, 1919
H. H. MAXFIELD	November, 1919, to October, 1920
FRANK J. LANAHAN	November, 1920, to October, 1921
*SAMUEL LYNN	November, 1921, to October, 1922
D. F. CRAWFORD	November, 1922, to October, 1923
*GEO. D. OGDEN	November, 1923, to October, 1924
A. STUCKI	November, 1924, to October, 1925
F. G. MINNICK	November, 1925, to October, 1926
G. W. WILDIN	November, 1926, to October, 1927
E. J. DEVANS	November, 1927, to October, 1928
W. S. McABEE	November, 1928, to October, 1929
E. W. SMITH	November, 1929, to October, 1930
LOUIS E. ENDSLEY	November, 1930, to October, 1931
*JOHN E. HUGHES	November, 1931, to October, 1932
F. I. SNYDER	November, 1932, to October, 1933
C. O. DAMBACH	November, 1933, to October, 1934
R. H. FLINN	November, 1934, to October, 1935
R. P. FORSBERG	November, 1935, to October, 1936

*—Deceased.

Meetings held fourth Thursday of each month except June, July and August.

PROCEEDINGS OF MEETING
DECEMBER 17, 1936

The meeting was called to order at the Fort Pitt Hotel at 8 o'clock P. M. with President E. A. Rauschart in the chair. Registered attendance, 173, as follows:

MEMBERS

Adams, Frank W.
Ainsworth, J. H.
Aulbach, A. J.
Babcock, F. H.
Balla, J. A.
Balph, M. Z.
Balzer, C. E.
Barr, H. C.
Barr, S. T.
Beam, E. J.
Beltz, J. D.
Best, D. A.
Beswick, R. M.
Bixler, Warren
Buffington, W. P.
Campbell, J. A.
Carey, C. D.
Carson, John
Cavanaugh, T. J.
Chalker, A. R.
Chilcoat, H. E.
Christy, F. X.
Cipro, Thomas
Clausen, Harold C.
Coombe, A. B.
Courtney, Harry
Crawford, Burt H.
Cree, W. M.
Crenner, Joseph A.
Crowell, F. C.
Cruikshank, J. C.
Davis, Charles S.
Dean, E. E.
Dean, W. A.
Donovan, L. T.
Downing, J. A.
Dunham, C. W.
Dunlop, R. J.
Emery, E.
Endsley, Prof. Louis E.

Failor, Charles W.
Ferguson, George
Ferguson, J. H.
Fisher, Earl H.
Flinn, R. H.
Forsberg, R. P.
Frauenheim, A. M.
Frauenheim, Pierce H.
Freshwater, F. H.
Fry, L. H.
Fulton, K. H.
Furch, George J.
Galbraith, James R.
Geiser, W. P.
George, W. J.
Gillespie, J. Porter
Goda, P. H.
Goodwin, A. E.
Haller, Nelson M.
Harris, E. W.
Hayward, C.
Hemma, Charles H.
Hepburn, P. W.
Hess, Charles A.
Hilstrom, A. V.
Holland, S. E.
Holmes, E. H.
Honsberger, G. W.
Huff, A. B.
Huston, F. T.
Irwin, R. D.
Jados, Walter T.
Johnson, Ira S.
Johnson, J. W.
Kemmerer, R. R.
Kentlein, John
Lanahan, Frank J.
Lanahan, J. S.
Larson, W. E.
Loder, C. C.
Lowry, William F., Jr.

Maliphant, C. W.
Masterman, T. W.
Meinert, H. J.
Miller, J.
Mitchell, W. S.
Misner, George W.
Moir, W. B.
Morgan, Homer C.
Mulligan, Michael
Murray, S.
McIntyre, R. C.
McKim, Hollis
McKinley, A. J.
McKinley, John T.
Nash, R. L.
Nies, E. L.
Paisley, F. R.
Peirce, W. B.
Pevler, H. H.
Pickard, S. B.
Prinkey, C. M.
Purchard, Paul
Ralston, J. A.
Rensh, R. H.
Reymer, Charles H.
Rider, C. E.
Rief, Joseph
Robertson, A. S.
Rushneck, G. L.

Rutter, H. E.
Ryan, D. W.
Searles, E. J.
Semmer, M. R.
Sheridan, Thomas F.
Shuster, W. W.
Sixsmith, G. M.
Smith, Folger M.
Smith, Robert B.
Stocker. H. F.
Stoffregen, Louis E.
Strahl, Herman
Sutherland, Lloyd
Taylor, H. D.
Taylor, J. M.
Terkelsen, Bernhard
Teskey, Dr. Walter J.
Teufel, W. O.
Thomas, George P.
Thomas, Theodore,
Tryon, Ira D.
Unger, Dr. J. S.
Van Vranken, S. E.
Von Pein, A. N.
Welton, A. A.
West, G. S.
West, Troy
Wildin, G. W.
Wilson, W. Stuart, Jr.
Yarnall, Jesse

Yohe, J. K., Jr.

VISITORS

Barber. W. H.
Carr, T. L.
Cornell, L. E.
Cover, H. T.
Dankmyer, F. C.
Davis, William B.
Donnelli, Fred, Jr.
Downing, R. W.
Edsall, E. D.
Gaston, Charles
Gelston, George A.
Geyer, J. V.
Gyekis. J. A.
Hansen, Henry L.
Jones, Henry C.
Keeney, John H.

Kimmich, K. J.
King, A. O.
Kouche, N. J.
Lewis, S. B.
Ord, George H.
Pascoe, R. L.
Pennington, Fred W.
Petersen, W. C.
Picard, A. J.
Reed, George P.
Reynolds, D. E.
Shaw, D. A.
Smith, Sion B.
Uakoval, Victor P.
Walther, George W.
Young, J. L.

24

Before taking up the business of the meeting a very enjoyable musical program was presented by "Three Guesses and Bill Cook," an instrumental and vocal quartette from the P. R. R. at Clairton (?).

President Rauschart then took up the business of the evening.

The call of the roll was dispensed with as those present signed registration cards at the door, giving a full record.

The reading of the minutes of the last meeting was by common consent dispensed with as the printed Proceedings have already been mailed to the members.

The following list of proposals for membership was read by the Secretary, and having been approved by the Executive Committee, were duly admitted to membership:

Ainsworth, J. H Sales Engineer. Carnegie-Illinois Steel Corporation, Carnegie Building, Pittsburgh, Pa. Recommended by W. B. Moir.

Bauer, Lawrence M., Car Repairer, Pennsylvania Railroad, 7217 Kedron Street, Pittsburgh, Pa. Recommended by H G. Huber

Bovard, William R., Clerk Office General Superintendent Motive Power, Pennsylvania Railroad, 1210 Fairdale Street, Pittsburgh, Pa. Recommended by W. B. Moir.

Clapper, H L., Superintendent Freight Transportation, Pennsylvania Railroad, Pennsylvania Station, Pittsburgh, Pa Recommended by W. B. Moir

Fisher Earl H., Sales Engineer, The Wine Railway Appliance Company, Box C, Station E Toledo, Ohio Recommended by E A. Rauschart.

Gibson, B. G. Assistant Master Mechanic, Pennsylvania Railroad, 494 Wayne Square, Beaver, Pa Recommended by W. B Moir.

Hamilton R. F., Safety Engineer, Monongahela Connecting Railroad, 2357 Brownsville Road Pittsburgh, Pa Recommended by A. E. Herrold

Haupt, H. H., General Superintendent Motive Power, Pennsylvania Railroad, Pennsylvania Station, Pittsburgh, Pa Recommended by W. B. Moir.

Leonard, George I., Fuel Distributor, Pennsylvania Railroad, Pennsylvania Station, Pittsburgh, Pa. Recommended by W B. Moir.

Lupton, E J, Salesman, The Sherwin-Williams Company, 601 Canal Road, Cleveland, Ohio Recommended by E. A. Rauschart.

Magner, John H., Clerk, B. & L. E. R R. Co., R. D. 6, Box 172, Mt. Oliver Station, Pittsburgh (10), Pa. Recommended by E. A. Rauschart

Mowry James G., Railway Representative, Pittsburgh Plate Glass Company, Rockefeller Plaza, New York N. Y. Recommended by E. A. Rauschart.

McGinnis, Crawford, District Sales Manager, The Pyle-National Company, Oliver Building, Pittsburgh, Pa. Recommended by R. M. Long

Ryan, John F., Special Representative, The Ramtite Company, 511 Overbrook Boulevard, Pittsburgh (10), Pa. Recommended by C. C. Loder.

Schonover, W. H. Asst. Superintendent Freight Transportation, Pennsylvania Railroad, Pennsylvania Station Pittsburgh, Pa. Recommended by W. B Moir.

Sommers William C, Asst. General Freight Agent, Pennsylvania Railroad, Pennsylvania Station Pittsburgh, Pa. Recommended by W. P. Buffington.

Terkelsen, B, R D. 3, Box 226-B, Coraopolis, Pa. Recommended by A. E. Goodwin.

Teskey, Dr. Walter J, Superintendent, Dream City Lines (Minature B. & O. R. R.), Empire Building, Pittsburgh, Pa. Recommended by C. E. Balzer.

Wiesen E S, Joint Agent, B. & L. E. and P. & W. Va. Ry., R. D. 6, Box 138-C, Mt. Oliver Station, Pittsburgh, Pa. Recommended by E. A. Rauschart.

Winring, Robert W, Yard Master, Montour Railroad Co., 821 Wood Street, Coraopolis, Pa. Recommended by E A. Rauschart.

Wood, T. M., Assistant Master Mechanic, Pennsylvania Railroad, 128 Dewey Street, Edgewood, Pittsburgh, Pa. Recommended by W. B. Moir.

PRESIDENT: As is our custom, I will ask those of the new members who are present to rise, that we may welcome you into our membership. And at the close of the meeting

I will ask the Reception Committee to take these gentlemen in charge and see that they meet the members personally.

As there are no communications or announcements, we will proceed at once to the paper of the evening. Mr. Lawford H. Fry, Railway Engineer, Edgewater Steel Company, Pittsburgh, Pa., will address us upon the subject, "Notes on Locomotive Testing with a Glance at History." As Mr. Fry has had a wide experience along this line of railroad work we are looking forward to a very interesting paper. I may also say that the speaker is from Pittsburgh, and it is not often that we have a Pittsburgh man as a speaker.

NOTES ON LOCOMOTIVE TESTING WITH A GLANCE AT HISTORY

By LAWFORD H. FRY, Railway Engineer, Edgewater Steel Company, Pittsburgh, Pa.

Gentlemen: I have been asked to talk to you tonight on Locomotive Testing.

The present time is particularly opportune for consideration of the subject. The railroads, after several years of hard sledding are entering a period of activity. One phase of this is the introduction of new forms of motive power. Those responsible are to be congratulated on the stimulating effect produced by the internal combustion engines and the light weight trains. The new equipment has made a useful place for itself but it seems quite certain that the steam locomotive will remain a vital factor in railroad motive power for many years to come. If this is to be true steam locomotive engineering cannot stand still. It must go forward and the road to be taken must be found by study and research. Locomotive testing is vitally necessary for future progress.

This is well recognized and it seems probable that before long the Association of American Railroads will formulate an extensive program of tests. Having this in mind I should like to say to you gentlemen here, and through our Club Proceedings to a wider audience, that if new tests are to be of full value they should be preceded by a thorough and intelligent study of the tests that have been already made.

The steam locomotive has been the subject of tests for over 100 years. In spite of this there is still disagreement, among those who should know better, over many basic facts which could and should be settled by existing test data. In many cases the situation is as though electrical engineers failed to accept Ohm's law and started every series of tests by finding out for themselves that current was proportional to electromotive force divided by resistance. Let me give you an instance. In December, 1898, before the Western Railway Club, Dr. W. F. M. Goss discussed the relation between boiler efficiency and the speed at which the engine was running. He presented an extensive series of test figures and concluded that in a given locomotive the boiler efficiency depended only on the rate at which the steam was produced. He said definitely that the boiler efficiency was not affected by the speed and cut-off at which the cylinders worked. This opinion has been confirmed by scores of tests since 1898, but in December, 1934, before the American Society of Mechanical Engineers, the point was discussed as though it were still in question.

Many other instances could be given to show that tests already made have not been sufficiently studied and assimilated.

My major theme tonight is that to see ahead it is first necessary to look back. It seems, therefore, appropriate to note some early instances of locomotive testing.

As a matter of background let me start at the beginning of things and remind you that the prototype of all our modern locomotives, George Stephenson's "Rocket", was put into service in 1830 after a series of successful tests in September, 1829. The occasion was the opening of the Liverpool and Manchester Railway. In the 1820's steam locomotives were hauling coal at slow speeds in the North of England, and had proven to be commercially successful. Some adventurous spirits, inspired undoubtedly by the profit motive, conceived the idea that the steam locomotive might be improved so that speeds of 10 or even 15 miles an hour would be possible and that passengers as well as goods could be handled. A line was projected and finally authorized between Manchester and Liverpool, two prosperous commercial cities 31 miles apart. George Stephenson, who had already acquired a sound reputation as a civil engineer and as a builder of coal road locomotives, was appointed chief engineer. The building of the road was not easy. It was necessary to cross Chat Moss, a quagmire on which neither man nor horse could walk. Liverpool had to be entered through a tunnel 2,240 yards long and at Mount Olive a two-mile cut was necessary through red sandstone, with a depth of as much as one hundred feet in some places. George Stephenson was not easily beaten and the road was built. It cost $4,000,000 and took four years to build. This was the first railroad built for general freight and passenger traffic and its completion was the occasion of the first competitive locomotive tests. The Directors had decided to purchase a steam locomotive and had offered a prize of 500 pounds for the most suitable locomotive. The requirements were that the locomotive must draw three times its own weight at 10 miles per hour. The interest taken was widespread. I quote from a contemporary account:

"Multifarious were the schemes proposed to the Directors for facilitating Locomotion. Communications were received from all classes of persons; from professors of philosophy down to the humblest mechanic; England, America, and Continental Europe were alike tributary. The friction of the carriages was to be reduced so low that a silk thread would draw them, and the power to be applied was to be so vast as to rend a cable asunder. Hydrogen gas and high pressure steam—columns of water and columns of mercury —a hundred atmospheres and a perfect vacuum — wheels within wheels to multiply speed without diminishing power— to the ne plus ultra of perpetual motion. Every scheme which the restless ingenuity or prolific imagination of man could devise was liberally offered to the Company; the difficulty was to choose and decide."

The competition for the prize was set for October 6, 1829. The contest appealed to the public as a sporting event and drew a large crowd. I quote an account of the meet from the Liverpool Courier for October 7, 1829:

"The Directors of the Liverpool and Manchester Railroad having offered, in the month of April last, a prize of 500 pounds for the best Locomotive Engine, the trial of carriages which had been constructed to contend for the prize commenced yesterday. The running ground was on the Manchester side of the Rainhill Bridge, at a place called Kenrick's Cross, about ten miles from Liverpool. At this place the Railroad runs on a dead level, and formed, of course, a fine spot for trying the comparative speed of the carriages. The directors had made suitable preparations for this important as well as interesting experiment of the powers of Locomotive Carriages. For the accommodation of the ladies who might visit the course (to use the language of the turf), a booth was erected on the south side of the Railroad, equi-distant from the extremities of the trial-ground. Here a band of music was stationed, and amused the company during the day by playing pleasing and favorite airs. The directors, each of whom wore a white ribbon in his button-hole, arrived on the course shortly after ten o'clock in the forenoon, having come from Huyton in cars drawn by Mr. Stephenson's Locomotive Steam Carriage, which moved up the inclined plane from thence with considerable velocity. Meanwhile, ladies and gentlemen in great numbers, arrived from Liverpool and Warrington, St. Helen's and Manchester, as well as from the surrounding country, in vehicles of every description. Indeed all the roads presented, on this occasion, scenes similar to those which roads leading to race-courses usually present during the days of sport. The pedestrians were extremely numerous and crowded all the roads which conducted into the race-ground. The spectators lined both sides of the road, for the distance of a mile and a half; and, although the men employed on the line, amounting to nearly 200, acted as special constables, with orders to keep the crowd off the course, all their efforts to carry their orders into effect were rendered nugatory, by the people persisting in walking on the ground. It is difficult to form an estimate of the number of individuals who had congregated to behold the experiment; but there could not, at a moderate calculation, be less than 10,000. Some gentlemen even went so far as to compute them at 15,000.

"Never, perhaps, on any previous occasion, were so many scientific gentlemen and practical engineers collected together in one spot as there were on the Railroad yesterday. The interesting and important nature of the experiments to be tried had drawn them from all parts of the kingdom, to be present at this contest of Locomotive Carriages, as well as to witness an exhibition whose results may alter the whole system of our existing internal communications, many and as important as they are, substituting an agency whose ultimate effects can scarcely be anticipated; for although the extraordinary change in our river and coast navigation, by steamboats, may afford some rule of comparison, still the effect of wind and waves, and a resisting medium, combine in vessels to present obstructions to the full exercise of the gigantic power which will act on a Railway unaffected by the seasons, and unlimited but by the demand for its application.

"There were only one or two public-houses in the vicinity of the trial-ground. These were, of course, crowded with company as the day advanced, particularly the Railroad Tavern, which was literally crammed with company. The landlady had very prudently and providently reserved one room for the accommodation of the better class visitors. The good lady will. we imagine,. have substantial reasons for remembering the trial of Locomotive Carriages, but there is nothing like making hay while the sun shines."

Five Competitors were entered who were officially described as follows:

No. 1. Messrs. Braithwaite and Ericson of London; The Novelty; copper and blue.

No. 2. Mr. Hackworth of Darlington; the Sans Pareil; green, yellow and black.

No. 3. Mr. Robert Stephenson; The Rocket; yellow and black. white chimney.

No. 4. Mr. Brandseth of Liverpool; The Cycloped; worked by a horse.

No. 5. Mr. Burstall of Edinburgh; The Perseverance; red wheels.

Of the five competitors only three actually appeared. The horse driven Cycloped made no appearance and Mr. Burstall's machine met with an accident on the way from Liverpool and was scratched. Of the three actual competitors the Novelty was the popular favorite because of its neat appearance and excellent workmanship. A series of breakdowns and lack of ability to maintain steam put it out of the running. Its designer Ericson was later to become famous as the designer of the Federal battleship Monitor. The Sans Pareil hauled its assigned loads but was judged to be inferior to the Rocket in design. performance and efficiency.

The Rocket was awarded the prize and by its showing established the steam locomotive as the motive power of the future. George Stephenson's common sense genius had produced a locomotive which pointed the path that locomotive designers have been following ever since. Following a suggestion made by Henry Booth. Stephenson used for the Rocket a multi-tubular boiler with firetubes surrounded by water. The firebox was nearly cubical and also surrounded by water. Thus was born the locomotive type boiler. The cylinders were set nearly horizontal driving directly through connecting rods. The cylinder exhaust was discharged up the stack to give a forced draft. Our modern locomotives are larger and more efficient, but the essential elements combined by Stephenson, fire-tube boiler, direct connected cylinders and the blast pipe are still the backbone of locomotive design.

Before going back to the more technical side of locomotive testing it may interest you to glance at a couple of early American tests or trials.

One of the earliest American engineers to study railroad operations in England was Horatio Allen, who was sent over by John B. Jervis, Chief Engineer of the Delaware and Hudson Canal and Railroad Company. Mr. Allen purchased four locomotives the first of which, the Stourbridge Lion, reached New York in May, 1829, and after being erected and tried under steam was shipped by canal boat to Honesdale, Pa. The local paper described the trial trip:

"On Saturday, August 8, 1829, the fire was kindled and steam raised and under the management of Mr. Horatio Allen the 'wonderful machine' was found capable of moving to the great joy of the crowd of excited spectators. After running it back and forth awhile Mr. Allen started it with no person accompanying—ran it with good speed across the bridge and up the railroad about one and a half miles. Here he reversed the engine and ran it back to the place of starting greeted by the shouting cheers of the people and the booming of cannon. Mr. Alva Adams, a mechanic, while assisting to fire the cannon had his arm so badly shattered that amputation became necessary. Mr. Allen later gave the following account of his trip: 'The circumstances which led to my being left alone on the engine were these: The road had been built in the summer, the structure was of hemlock-timber, and the rails, of large dimensions, notched on to caps placed far apart. The timber had cracked and warped, from exposure to the sun. After about five hundred feet of straight line, the road crossed the Lackawaxen Creek on a trestlework about thirty feet high, and with a curve of three hundred and fifty or four hundred feet radius. The impression was very general that the iron monster would either break down the road or that it would leave the track at the curve and plunge into the creek. My reply to such apprehension was, that it was too late to consider the probability of such occurrences; that there was no other course but to have the trial made of the strange animal which had been brought here at such great expense, but that it was not necessary that more than one should be involved in its fate; that I would take the first ride alone, and that the time would come when I should look back to this incident with great interest. As I placed my hand on the throttle-valve handle I was undecided whether I would move slowly or with a fair degree of speed; but believing that the road would prove safe, and preferring, if we did go down, to go down handsomely and without any evidence of timidity, I started with considerable velocity, passed the curve over the creek safely, and was soon out of hearing of the cheers of the large assemblage present. At the end of two or three miles, I reversed the valves and returned without accident to the place of starting, having thus made the first railroad trip by locomotive on the Western Hemisphere.'

"The Stourbridge Lion proving too heavy for the lightly built wooden track was never put into service and appears to be the only one of Mr. Allen's four English locomotives which was even tried. It was of the old grasshopper type soon to be obsolete, and while its appearance as the first steam locomotive to run on a railroad in the Western Hemisphere is historically interesting it was only an incident and the Lion left no cubs.

"Another historic incident is the appearance of the 'Best Friend' on the South Carolina Railway in November, 1830. This was the first locomotive built in America for actual service on a railroad. Its designer, Mr. E. L. Miller of Charleston, had attended the Rainhill trials the year before. His design was original but was not perpetuated though the locomotive was a success. The President's report to the directors said: 'On the fourteenth and fifteenth of December, 1830, the engine was tried and proved her force and efficiency to be double that contracted for; running at the rate of sixteen to twenty-one miles an hour with forty to fifty passengers in some four or five cars, and without the cars, thirty to thirty-five miles an hour.' "

The Best Friend ran successfully until June 17, 1831, when an involuntary test on the part of the fireman produced the world's first locomotive boiler explosion.

An account of this accident is given by Mr. Nicholas

W. Darrell, the first locomotive engineer of the Best Friend and later the first Superintendent of Machinery of the South Carolina Railroad. "When I ran the 'Best Friend' I had a Negro fireman to fire, clean and grease the machine. This Negro, annoyed at the noise occasioned by the blowing off the steam, fastened the valve-lever down and sat upon it, which caused the explosion, badly injuring him, from the effects of which he died afterward, and scalding me." On the next locomotive for this road, the safety-valve was placed "out of the reach of any person but the engineer."

I now come back to more direct contact with locomotive testing, but do not yet move ahead very far in time. The success of the Liverpool and Manchester Railway was striking and new locomotives were added. Progress in locomotive design was based on numerous tests. An interesting account of locomotive testing and locomotive theory has been left us by a Frenchman, Count F. M. G. de Pambour, who carried out a large number of tests and described them in a book first published in France in 1834. I quote the title page of the second English edition of his Treatise on Locomotive Engines, published in 1840.

A Practical Treatise on Locomotive Engines
A Work Intended
To Show The Construction, The Mode of Acting, And The Use of Those Engines for Conveying Heavy Loads on Railways: To Give The Means of Ascertaining, on an Inspection of The Machine, The Velocity With Which It Will Draw A Given Load, And The Effects it Will Produce under Various Circumstances: To Determine The Quantity of Fuel and Water It Will Require: To Fix The Proportions it Ought to Have, in Order to Answer Any Intended Purpose: Etc.
Founded on
A Great Many New Experiments,
made on a Large Scale, in a Daily Practice, on the Liverpool and Manchester, and Other Railways, with Many Different Engines, and Considerable Trains of Carriages.
To Which is Added,
An Appendix:
Showing The Expense of Conveying Goods, By Locomotive Engines on Railroads.
By the Comte F. M. G. De Pambour
Formerly a Student Of The Ecole Polytechnique, Late of The Royal Artillery, On The Staff In The French Service, Knight

of 'The Royal Order of The Legion D'Honneur, of The Royal Academy of Sciences of Berlin, Etc. During a Residence in England for Scientific Purposes.

A Second Edition.

Increased By a Great Many New Experiments and Researches.

London: John Neale.

1840.

In his first edition Pambour wrote:

"We have studied the subject with all the interest, and, we might say, with all the enthusiasm it excited in us. In fact, what a subject for admiration is such a triumph of human intelligence! What an imposing sight is a locomotive engine, moving without effort, with a train of 40 to 50 loaded carriages, each weighing more than ten thousand pounds! What are henceforth the heaviest loads, with machines able to move such enormous weights? What are distances, with motors which daily travel 30 miles in an hour and a half? The ground disappears, in a manner, under your eyes; trees, houses, hills, are carried away from you with the rapidity of an arrow; and when you happen to cross another train travelling with the same velocity, it seems in one and the same moment to dawn, to approach, and to touch you; and scarcely have you seen it with dismay pass before your eyes, when already it has again become like a speck disappearing at the horizon." Our feelings have changed very little since this was written. Pambour had in mind a ten-ton locomotive, but if the speeds be multiplied by three and the train loads by four the quotation might come from a Sunday feature article dealing with a present day Pacific type locomotive weighing 170 tons.

In spite of his flowery language Pambour had a scientific mind and made exhaustive practical tests. He measured train resistance, studied the evaporative capacity of various locomotive boilers and set up formulae for computing the dimensions of a locomotive for any given service. Pambour's work has the virtue of connecting the tests with a definite theory of locomotive operation. It represents a sound and systematic series of tests carried out when the science of locomotive engineering was young.

Since that day there have been innumerable tests of locomotives and based on such tests locomotive design has improved and the steam locomotive has grown in size and efficiency.

It is not possible to give a complete and detailed history of locomotive testing. The early tests have been quoted as a matter of antiquarian interest. I now jump to methods of testing which are important at the present day. Tests of locomotives may be made by one of three methods:

1. Road tests with regular trains.
2. Road tests at constant speed and cut-off.
3. Tests on a stationary locomotive testing plant.

Road tests with regular trains are useful mainly to check on the performance of a given locomotive. They serve to measure over-all coal and water consumption, to examine the relation between train loads and timing and to check tonnage rating assignments. It is not usually possible to obtain accurate information regarding the individual processes such as combustion, steam production and utilization of the steam. Tests with regular trains do not, therefore, provide the kind of information that is necessary if a scientific study of locomotive design is to be made. To obtain information of this type, a locomotive must be run under constant conditions of speed and cut-off for a considerable length of time. Such runs can be made on the road, under special conditions, or on a locomotive test plant. To use the road, either a long stretch of track with uniform gradient must be available, or some arrangement must be made so that the rolling resistance of the train behind the tender can be varied to offset any changes in resistance due to changes in grade. This use of a variable train resistance began in Russia over fifty years ago and has been developed and used very successfully in France and Germany in recent years. In the summer of 1883. Mr. L. Loevy, then Assistant Chief of Motive Power of the Southwestern Railway of Russia, ran a series of road tests with compound locomotives. In order to permit the test locomotive to operate with constant cut-off he put ahead of it another auxiliary locomotive which could pull or brake as needed. In 1900, Prof. Lomonossoff made running tests under uniform conditions on some of the long straight level stretches available in Russia.

In 1923 Professor Czeczott wished to carry out tests in Poland and, in the absence of straight level stretches of sufficient length, made use of a train of 10 cars with an auxiliary

35

locomotive. A further advance has been made in Germany and in France in the last few years. The cars have been discarded and the test train behind the dynamometer car consists only of one or more brake locomotives. These are regular engines run in reverse gear so that the cylinders act as an air compressor. Water is added to the air taken in through the exhaust pipe. This provides lubrication in the cylinders and keeps down the temperature. The steam chests are connected by a pipe fitted with valve so that compressed air can be exhausted to the atmosphere. The engineman on the test locomotive sets his throttle and reverse lever in the desired positions and sits back to watch the fireman keep the boiler pressure steady. On the brake locomotive the situation is reversed. The fireman carries a very light fire, but the engineman is busy. He is provided with a large scale speed indicator and it is his job to keep the needle steady. The resistance of the brake locomotive is controlled chiefly by the reverse lever. It has been found in Germany that a locomotive can deliver continuously a resistance equal to about one-tenth of its adhesive weight. At higher pulls there is a tendency to slip and the compression temperature gives trouble.

Brake locomotives have been used extensively in Germany and France in the last ten years. They provide a very convenient form of load for test purposes. The difficulties of assembling and dispersing a test train are avoided. At the same time, the results are comparable in accuracy and refinement with those obtainable on a stationary plant. While this is true and while road tests are necessary for measurement of the rolling friction of a locomotive, nevertheless, the stationary locomotive testing plant, as developed in this country, stands pre-eminent for the scientific study of locomotive operation.

In principle such a plant is very simple. The driving wheels of the locomotive are supported on rollers. The drawbar is hooked to a dynamometer. The throttle and reverse lever are set in the positions desired and a load applied to the carrying rollers by hydraulic brakes. By manipulating the brakes the load and speed are held constant. The locomotive runs under constant conditions and laboratory facilities are available for determining coal and water consumption, indicating the cylinders, measuring pressures and temperatures and making any other observations or measurements that may be desired.

The foregoing may sound as though a plant test of a locomotive were a simple matter. It will be found, however, that to get a two hundred ton locomotive to run smoothly on rollers requires engineering ability for the design, and considerable skill in manipulating the locomotive and the plant.

The first large scale locomotive testing plant was that of the Pennsylvania Railroad. This was exhibited in operation at the St. Louis exhibition in 1904. The plant in operation is an impressive sight. The drivers spin without getting anywhere, the exhaust makes an ear shattering noise and the whole engine sways and throbs. At St. Louis a Cole four-cylinder compound locomotive built by the American Locomotive Company ran at a speed of 75 miles an hour for sixty minutes continuously. Mr. F. J. Cole, the designer of the locomotive, was present. At the beginning of the test he was proud of his locomotive. As the engine continued to thunder away in one spot, surrounded by interested spectators, with the drivers turning more than five revolutions in a second, he began to figure what would happen if anything failed. By the end of the hour Mr. Cole was sitting at a table with his head in his hands. The engineer in charge reported, "Everything fine Mr. Cole, shall we keep on?" F. J. heaved a sigh of relief and said: "Shut her down, I'm no hog."

Let me turn back and give you a short history of the locomotive testing plant. As we know it today it is of American origin. Chronologically, however, the first locomotive testing plant was set up by Borodine in Russia in 1881 to measure the effect of steam jackets on the cylinders of compound locomotives. The locomotive was jacked up, the side rods removed and the main drivers belted to the main shaft of a machine shop. As only 90 horsepower could be absorbed the full power of the locomotive could not be developed. It had been planned to use Prony brakes to take up 250 to 300 horsepower but funds were lacking and the plant was abandoned in 1886.

The first locomotive testing plants to make real contributions to our knowledge of locomotive operating processes was designed and erected at Purdue University by Dr. W. F. M. Goss, who at that time had no knowledge of Borodine's work. A 4-4-0 locomotive weighing 85,000 pounds was installed and

Dr. Goss gives an interesting account of the job the students did in hauling this engine a mile and a half cross-country from the railroad to the plant. The plant was burned in 1894. In 1897 a more modern locomotive was obtained and in 1909 this was equipped with a superheater.

A great deal of useful research work was done. Light was thrown on the factors limiting horsepower and rates of combustion which were not well understood before the test plant results were available. Cylinder action was investigated and work was done on locomotive front-ends which influenced American practice for many years. This work contributed to the recommended practice for locomotive front-ends which was adopted by the A. R. M. M. Association in 1906. This was useful 30 years ago, but was gradually outgrown. It was revised this year as the result of a report made by D. S. Ellis and A. H. Fetters, to the Locomotive Construction Committee of the A. A. R. Mechanical Division. The next plant of importance in this country was that of the Pennsylvania Railroad. After the St. Louis exhibition closed at the end of 1904, it was transferred to its present location in Altoona. Our older members may remember that an account of the plant was given in a Pittsburgh Railway Club paper presented in May, 1916, by Mr. C. D. Young, now Vice President and then Engineer of Tests of the Pennsylvania Railroad. The Altoona plant was under Mr. Young's charge from November, 1911, to May, 1917. It has contributed a great deal of valuable information which could hardly have been obtained otherwise. Much of this information has been made available to those interested through the courtesy of the late Mr. J. T. Wallis and of the present Chief of Motive Power, Mr. F. W. Hankins. The plant has been used for testing electric as well as steam locomotives. The work done has had considerable influence on steam locomotive design.

A third important American locomotive testing plant was set up in 1914 at the University of Illinois under Dr. W. F. M. Goss as Dean of the College of Engineering and Professor E. W. Schmidt in charge of the Department of Railway Engineering. This plant has published some interesting test reports and should be in a position to do good work in the future.

As a matter of historical record a number of other locomotive test plants should be mentioned. In Russia the earliest plant was, as has been mentioned, closed in 1896. Ten years later, in 1906, a plant was installed at St. Petersburg. In 1912, a new and larger plant was planned, but was not completed until 1924.

I have received a number of bulletins on locomotive tests from my friend Professor Lomonossoff representing a large amount of work done in Russia. Unfortunately, my acquaintance with the Russian language is not sufficient for me to report to you on their contents. A fourth Russian plant was built in Germany to test some Diesel locomotives and has since, I believe, been shipped to Russia. My information on the Russian plants was given by my friends Dr. I. A. Lipetz and Professor Lomonossoff.

In America two plants of small capacity were installed, one by the Chicago and Northwestern Railway in 1894, which did some useful work on front-ends, and one at Columbia University in 1899. Both have been abandoned. In England the records show that a set of testing rollers to carry a locomotive and drive an air compressor were put up at the Swindon Shops of the London and Northwestern Railway about 1904. The record of work done is hardly sufficient to justify this being reckoned as a locomotive testing plant. Recently there has been a move in favor of building a modern plant in England. Plans have been drawn and Sir Nigel Gresley has proposed that the locomotive be tested in a wind tunnel to give the effect of speed. France and Germany both have modern locomotive testing plants. The German plant at Gruenewald was put into operation on June 17, 1930. It is equipped with three sets of carrying wheels to test a six coupled locomotive with 44,000 pounds on an axle. Speeds up to 100 km. (62.5 miles) per hour can be used. Froude hydraulic brakes are used to absorb the power. Special sanders are applied with an exhaust system to take away the used sand. This is intended to eliminate slipping which has been a source of difficulty on the American plants. To trap the sparks an elaborate double turbo separator followed by a cyclone collector is provided.

The French plant at Vitry, which is for the use of the seven large Railway systems of France, was put into operation July 27, 1933. Work on the designs extended from 1920 to 1929 and construction from 1930 to July, 1933. It is larger than the German plant having four pairs of carrying wheels for axle loads up to 66,000 pounds and speeds of 100 miles an hour. Each carrying axle drives a Froude hydraulic brake capable of absorbing up to 1900 horsepower. These brakes are said to be self-regulating so that when they are once set for the conditions of a given test they operate automatically holding the speed uniform to within plus or minus one per cent without further attention.

The difficulty of collecting all of the unburned fuel thrown out of the stack was realized by the French designer and it was decided not to provide any spark catcher. It has been found, however, that the long duct leading from the locomotive stack to the final outlet provided a natural trap.

Both French and German plants report that useful studies have been carried out, but I have not seen any detailed figures such as have been given out by the three American plants.

Now leaving the historical aspect, let us examine the ground gained and consider the possibilities of further advance.

The work done at Purdue and Altoona has thrown a great deal of light on the processes by which the locomotive boiler takes up the heat produced in the fire-box. The test plants have shown that as a heat absorbing mechanism the locomotive boiler works with very nearly uniform efficiency. The Purdue 4-4-0 locomotive in 1906, showed an average efficiency of heat absorption of 77 per cent. The P. R. R. Mountain type locomotive in 1926 averaged 82 per cent. In neither case did change in the rate of evaporation cause the efficiency of absorption to vary more than 2 per cent from the average figures. The over-all boiler efficiency varied from 50 to 80 per cent. Obviously any further advance in locomotive boiler efficiency must depend on improving the combustion rather than the heat absorption. Further test work along these lines would provide valuable information regarding the better utilization of various grades of coal. Such work should take into account the test data already provided by the testing plants. So far as the engine is concerned designers are committed to high superheat. It is worth noting that P. R. R. Bulletin No. 24, covering study of superheaters, gave for the first time, unobscured by other variables, authentic information as to the effect of superheat on steam consumption.

For the test plant in the future many possibilities for the better utilization of steam offer a field for study. But such study should begin with analysis of the detail figures already issued by Purdue, Altoona and Illinois. The test reports constitute a mine of information which has not been worked to the extent which it deserves. Many of the tests were made thirty years ago and some of the locomotives tested are obsolete. This is true, but it is equally true that certain basic principles underline the operation of all steam locomotives, and that it is often easier to arrive at these principles if tests from locomotives of widely differing types are compared.

In conclusion, gentlemen, may I re-affirm my opinion that the steam locomotive will be an important factor in railroad economy for many years to come, that it can be and will be improved and that for such improvement a basis of forward looking experiment is necessary. I further believe that any program of experiment should be very carefully studied in advance and that it should be directed to principles rather than to details and should be based on a very thorough study of existing test data. Success in the future is dependent on a correct comprehension of the past.

PRESIDENT: We thank you, Mr. Fry, for your very, very interesting paper. I am going to call on a few of our members who are more particularly interested in the subject of the paper, and first, Professor Endsley, himself a Purdue man and for a number of years connected with this Purdue testing plant.

PROF. L. E. ENDSLEY: It makes me feel a little old tonight to look back thirty-five years. It was thirty-five years ago that I took charge of the Purdue Locomotive Testing Plant and I was in charge of the locomotive testing work until 1914. During that time the front end tests referred to by Mr. Fry as the Master Mechancis front end were designed. Just a little about those tests I think might be of interest.

A New York Central locomotive of the Atlantic type with an 84" smoke box was used. It was decided that no coal burning engine could have a constant enough resistance in the fire box to the passage of air going through to get accurate results for the small changes in the front end and so the locomotive was equipped for the burning of oil. In burning oil we made certain size openings in the fire box that gave us a constant resistance.

We were so well equipped that tests could be run up to sixty miles an hour, shut down the locomotive, open the front end, get into the front end, change the draft pipes or some other change, close it up and repeat the cycle in one minute. It seems to be almost impossible, but we did it.

Those reports were all published in what was then called the American Engineer & Railroad Journal, now the Railway Mechanical Engineer, and it was very interesting indeed. While those tests only went up to that time, it did produce a front end that made steam in a great many locomotives.

The Purdue testing plant also did a wonderful work in proving that superheated steam must come. In 1908 I read a paper before the convention at Atlantic City and said that within twenty years switching engines would have superheated steam. I was laughed at. One superintendent of motive power, who has now long passed on, said, "I am building 50 locomotives today and not one of them is going to be superheated.

Two years later he came back and said, "I wish I had believed you and gone ahead at that time. I have now superheated twenty and wish the other thirty were also."

So we have discovered some facts in locomotive testing. What would we do without superheat? So I think that the story of the past should be studied, as Mr. Fry has pointed out, and it will enlighten us in the future development of our locomotive testing. I thank you.

PRESIDENT: Thank you, Mr. Endsley.

MR. E. EMERY: Mr. Fry's talk has been very interesting. But I understand on some European railroads they have been making extensive experiments for several years on both reciprocating engines and also turbine engines. Have you any data in regard to that?

MR. FRY: A number of designs differing greatly from the conventional locomotive design have been tried out in Europe. The Germans in particular have built several turbine locomotives, but so far as I know none have been really successful. Some ten years ago I had an interesting trip on their high pressure three-cylinder reciprocating locomotive with a double pressure boiler. The firebox portion of the boiler furnishes steam at 850 lbs. per sq. in. to a single high pressure cylinder. The exhaust from this is mixed with and superheated by steam at 250 lbs. per sq. in. from the tubular portion of the boiler.

In France four-cylinder compound locomotives with poppet valves have been put into service. Test reports show very economical performance for these engines.

In England the latest development is a non-condensing turbine locomotive which is reported to be working satisfactorily. Earlier condensing turbine locomotives gave considerable trouble, and the present experimental machine is being tried with a view to seeing whether the trouble was due to the turbine or to the condenser.

MR. R. H. FLINN: Mr. Chairman and Gentlemen: I think we have listened to a very interesting paper this evening. I do not care to try to add anything to it but I will say that I think Mr. Fry has adopted a verp happy method of presenting his point that from the experience of the past we may determine what should be the direction of our advance in the future. There is to be a constant development and it must be done in an intelligent and progressive manner, always looking to the possible competition of new things. But we must not forget the lessons of the experience of the past and of applying those lessons in the developments of the future. I would move as an expression of our appreciation to Mr. Fry for his delightfully interesting paper a rising vote of thanks.

The motion was duly seconded and prevailed by unanimous rising vote.

PRESIDENT: Mr. Fry, the Club extends to you its sincere appreciation. If there is no further business, the meeting will stand adjourned. Lunch will be served as usual.

J. D. CONWAY, Secretary.

OFFICIAL PROCEEDINGS
RAILWAY CLUB OF PITTSBURGH

$1.00 Per Year   25¢ Per Copy

| Vol. XXXVI. | JANUARY 21, 1937. | No. 3. |

"BOULDER DAM"

By MR. R. A. KIRKPATRICK, Special Representative,
Union Pacific Railroad Company

The proof of your interest

in the Club can be

enhanced

by securing a

NEW MEMBER.

pplication form is available

in this magazine. Look

it up and

"ACT NOW."

OFFICIAL PROCEEDINGS

OF

The Railway Club of Pittsburgh

Organized October 18, 1901

Published monthly, except June, July and August, by the Railway Club of
Pittsburgh, J. D. Conway, Secretary, 515 Grandview Ave., Pittsburgh, Pa..

Entered as Second Class Matter February 6, 1915, at the Postoffice at Pittsburgh,
under the Act of March 3, 1879.

| No. 3 Vol. XXXVI. | Pittsburgh, Pa., Jan. 21, 1937 | $1.00 Per Year 25c Per Copy |

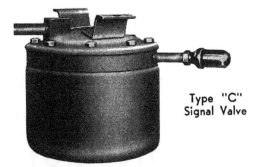

KOPPERS SERVES the RAILROADS

KOPPERS PRODUCTS AND WHERE THEY APPLY IN THE RAILROAD FIELD	TREATED TIMBER, TIES, POSTS, ETC.	ROOFING MATERIALS	PISTON RINGS	COAL	WATER-PROOFING MATERIALS	BITUMINOUS PAINTS	TARMAC ROAD MATERIALS	FAST'S COUPLINGS	CREOSOTE	CYLINDER AND VALVE PACKING	WEED KILLERS	INSECTICIDES AND DISINFECTANTS	PLATE WORK	CAR FERRIES, RAILROAD BARGES, ETC.
ROADBEDS	A								D		F			
LOCOMOTIVES		D	C	B	D	D				C		F		
STATIONS	A	D	C	B	D	D			D			F		
SHOPS	A			B	D	D		E	D			F	E&G	
BRIDGES	A				D	D	D		D				E&G	
TUNNELS	A				D	D	D						E&G	
DRIVEWAYS	A				D	D	D				F			
POWER HOUSES	A	D	C	B	D	D		E	D	C			E&G	
STRUCTURAL	A	D			D	D			D				E&G	
GRADE CROSSINGS	A						D							
CATTLE PENS	A	D			D	D			D			F		
RAILROAD MARINE OPERATIONS	A	D	C	B	D	D			D	C		F	E&G	H

A—The Wood Preserving Corporation, Pittsburgh, Pa.   B—The Koppers Coal Company, Pittsburgh, Pa.   C—American Hammered Piston Ring Division, Baltimore, Md.   D—Tar and Chemical Division, Pittsburgh, Pa.   E—Bartlett Hayward Division, Baltimore, Md.   F—The White Tar Company of New Jersey, Inc.   G—Western Gas Division, Fort Wayne, Ind.   H—The Maryland Drydock Company, Baltimore, Md.

INDEX—ADVERTISERS.

The Railway Club of Pittsburgh:

_____19____

Gentlemen:

Will you kindly consider my Application for Membership in your Club at the next meeting:

Name ....

Title...

Company..

My Address...

....

Recommended by..

OFFICIAL PROCEEDINGS

OF

The Railway Club of Pittsburgh

Organized October 18, 1901

No. 3
Vol. XXXVI. | **Pittsburgh, Pa., Jan. 21, 1937** | $1.00 Per Year
25c Per Copy

OFFICERS FOR 1936-1937

President

E. A. RAUSCHART,

Mechanical Superintendent, Montour Railroad Co., Coraopolis, Pa.

First Vice President
G. M. SIXSMITH,
Supt., Pennsylvania Railroad,
Pittsburgh, Pa.

Secretary
J. D. CONWAY,
Railway Supply Manufacturers' Association,
Pittsburgh, Pa.

Second Vice President
J. D. BELTZ,
Supt., B. & O. R. R. Co.,
Pittsburgh, Pa

Treasurer
E. J. SEARLES,
Manager, Schaefer Equipment Co.,
Pittsburgh, Pa.

EXECUTIVE COMMITTEE:

FRANK J. LANAHAN, Chairman, President, Fort Pitt Malleable Iron Co,. Pittsburgh, Pa
A. STUCKI, Engineer, A. Stucki Company, Pittsburgh, Pa.
D. F. CRAWFORD, Consulting Engineer, Pittsburgh, Pa.
G W. WILDIN, Consulting Engineer, Westinghouse Air Brake Company, Pittsburgh, Pa
W. S. McABEE, Vice Pres. & General Supt., Union Railroad Co., East Pittsburgh, Pa
E. W. SMITH, Vice President, Pennsylvania Railroad, Pittsburgh, Pa.
LOUIS E. ENDSLEY, Consulting Engineer, 516 East End Avenue, Pittsburgh, Pa.
F. I. SNYDER, Vice President & General Manager, B. & L. E. R. R. Co., Pittsburgh, Pa
C. O. DAMBACH, General Manager, P. & W. Va. Ry. Co., Pittsburgh, Pa
R. H. FLINN, General Superintendent, Pennsylvania Railroad, Pittsburgh, Pa
R P. FORSBERG, Chief Engineer, P. & L. E R. R Co., Pittsburgh, Pa

SUBJECT COMMITTEE:

G. H. BURNETTE, Asst. Chief Engineer, P. & L. E. R. R. Co., Pittsburgh, Pa
D W. McGEORGE, Secretary, Edgewater Steel Company, Pittsburgh, Pa.

RECEPTION AND ATTENDANCE COMMITTEE:

J W. JOHNSON, Chairman, Superintendent, Railway Express Agency, Pittsburgh, Pa.
W. C. BUREL, Vice Chairman, Master Mechanic, Western Allegheny Railroad, Kaylor, Pa
J. W. BOYD, Superintendent, Monongahela Railway Company, Brownsville, Pa.
THOMAS E. CANNON, General Supt. Equipment, P. & W. Va. Ry. Co., Pittsburgh, Pa
T. W. CARR, Superintendent Rolling Stock, P. & L. E. R. R. Co., McKees Rocks, Pa.
D. C. CARROLL, Assistant Agent, Pennsylvania Railroad, Pittsburgh, Pa.
S. G. DOWN, Vice President, Westinghouse Air Brake Company, Wilmerding. Pa
HARRY C. GRAHAM, Pittsburgh Screw & Bolt Corporation, Pittsburgh, Pa.
J. W. SCHAD, Division Master Mechanic, B. & O. R. R. Co., Pittsburgh, Pa.
GEORGE S. WEST, Division Superintendent, Pennsylvania Railroad, Pittsburgh, Pa.
J. W. HOOVER, Asst. Chief of Transpn., Subsidiary Cos. U. S. Steel Corp., Pittsburgh, Pa.
A. A. READ, Duquesne Slag Products Company, Pittsburgh, Pa.
C. P. SCHRECONGOST, Traffic Manager, Hillman Coal & Coke Company, Pittsburgh, Pa
J. A. WARFEL, Special Representative, Air Reduction Sales Company, Pittsburgh, Pa
J. C. SHINGLEDECKER, Supervisor of Service Stations, The Pennzoil Co., Pittsburgh, Pa.
J C. DILWORTH, Manager Railroad Sales, Carnegie-Illinois Steel Corp., Pittsburgh, Pa

ENTERTAINMENT COMMITTEE:

J. PORTER GILLESPIE, Chairman, Asst. Gen. Supt., Lockhart Iron & Steel Co., Pgh., Pa.
FRANK E. WEIS, Vice Chairman, Transportation Clerk, Penna. R. R., Pittsburgh, Pa
JAMES NAGEL, Superintendent Transportation, Montour Railroad, Coraopolis, Pa.
E. H. HOLMES, Sales Department, Fort Pitt Malleable Iron Co., Pittsburgh, Pa.
C. C. CLARK, Sales Manager, Central District, Pressed Steel Car Co., Pittsburgh, Pa.
A. I. KESSLER, Clearance Clerk, Pennsylvania Railroad, Pittsburgh, Pa.
T F. SHERIDAN, Asst. to S.M.P. and S.R.S., P. & L. E. R. R. Co., McKees Rocks, Pa.

FINANCE COMMITTEE:

M. A. SMITH, Chairman, General Manager, P. & L. E. R. R. Co., Pittsburgh, Pa
J. B. DIVEN, Superintendent Motive Power, Pennsylvania Railroad, Pittsburgh, Pa.
F. J. RYAN, District Representative, Detroit, Toledo & Ironton Railroad, Pittsburgh, Pa.
C. E. CATT, Division Accountant, B. & O. R. R. Co., Pittsburgh, Pa.
G. W. HONSBERGER, Transpn. Mgr., Westinghouse Electric & Mfg. Co., Pittsburgh, Pa.

ADVERTISING COMMITTEE:

H. H. HAUPT, Chairman, Gen. Supt., Motive Power, Pennsylvania Railroad, Pittsburgh, Pa
KARL BERG, Superintendent Motive Power, P. & L. E. R. R. Co., McKees Rocks, Pa.
H. E. PASSMORE, Representative, The American Hammered Piston Ring Co., Pgh., Pa

MEMBERSHIP COMMITTEE:

T. E. BRITT, Chairman, Div. Storekeeper, B. & O. R. R. Co., Glenwood Shops, Pgh., Pa.
C. M. WHEELER, Vice Chairman, Sales Engr., Union Switch & Signal Co., Swissvale, Pa.
F. H. EATON, Sales Engineer, American Car & Foundry Co., Pittsburgh, Pa.
C. W. GOTTSCHALK, Asst. Traffic Manager, Jones & Laughlin Steel Corp., Pgh , Pa
LLOYD SUTHERLAND, General Storekeeper, P. & L. E. R R. Co., McKees Rocks, Pa.
THOMAS R. FITZPATRICK, Freight Traffic Mgr., P. & L. E. R. R. Co., Pittsburgh, Pa.
P. W. HEPBURN, Sales Engineer, Gulf Refining Company, Pittsburgh, Pa.
W. B. MOIR, Chief Car Inspector, Pennsylvania Railroad, Pittsburgh, Pa.
C. W. TRUST, Assistant Traffic Manager, Carnegie-Illinois Steel Corp., Pittsburgh, Pa.
WILLIAM R. GELLATLY, President, Superior Railway Products Corp., Pittsburgh, Pa.
R. S. BULL, Supt. Power & Inclines, Pittsburgh Railways Co., N. S., Pittsburgh, Pa.
A. F. COULTER, Master Car Builder, Union Railroad Co., East Pittsburgh, Pa.
T. R. DICKINSON, Purchasing Agent, B. & L. E. R. R. Co., Pittsburgh, Pa.
D. K. ORR, Road Master, Monongahela Railway Co., Brownsville, Pa.
W. F. AMBROSE, Master Mechanic, Aliquippa & Southern Railroad, Aliquippa, Pa.
JOHN I. MULVEY, Traffic Manager, Hubbard & Company, Pittsburgh, Pa.

PAST PRESIDENTS:

*J. H. McCONNELL	October, 1901, to October, 1903
*L. H. TURNER	November, 1903, to October, 1905
*F. H. STARK	November, 1905, to October, 1907
*H. W. WATTS	November, 1907, to April, 1908
*D. J. REDDING	November, 1908, to October, 1910
*F. R. McFEATTERS	November, 1910, to October, 1912
*A. G. MITCHELL	November, 1912, to October, 1914
*F. M. McNULTY	November, 1914, to October, 1916
*J. G. CODE	November, 1916, to October, 1917
*D. M. HOWE	November, 1917, to October, 1918
*J. A. SPIELMAN	November, 1918, to October, 1919
H. H. MAXFIELD	November, 1919, to October, 1920
FRANK J. LANAHAN	November, 1920, to October, 1921
*SAMUEL LYNN	November, 1921, to October, 1922
D. F. CRAWFORD	November, 1922, to October, 1923
*GEO. D. OGDEN	November, 1923, to October, 1924
A. STUCKI	November, 1924, to October, 1925
F. G. MINNICK	November, 1925, to October, 1926
G. W. WILDIN	November, 1926, to October, 1927
E. J. DEVANS	November, 1927, to October, 1928
W. S. McABEE	November, 1928, to October, 1929
E. W. SMITH	November, 1929, to October, 1930
LOUIS E. ENDSLEY	November, 1930, to October, 1931
*JOHN E. HUGHES	November, 1931, to October, 1932
F. I. SNYDER	November, 1932, to October, 1933
C. O. DAMBACH	November, 1933, to October, 1934
R. H. FLINN	November, 1934, to October, 1935
R. P. FORSBERG	November, 1935, to October, 1936

*—Deceased.

Meetings held fourth Thursday of each month except June, July and August

PROCEEDINGS OF MEETING
JANUARY 21, 1937

The meeting was called to order at the Fort Pitt Hotel at 8:00 o'clock P. M., with Vice President G. M. Sixsmith in the chair.

Registered attendance, 209, as follows:

MEMBERS

Adams, Frank W.
Ainsworth, J. H.
Ainsworth, John R.
Allen, Earl M.
Ambrose, W. F.
Aulbach, A. J.
Balla, J. A.
Balph, M. Z.
Balzer, C. E.
Barney, Harry
Barr, H. C.
Barr, S. T.
Beltz, J. D.
Beswick, Richard M.
Black, C. R.
Bone, H. L.
Boyd, John R.
Britt, T. E.
Brown, E. F.
Burel, W. C.
Burnette, G. H.
Buzzerd, J. P.
Campbell, J. Alan
Carter, John D.
Cavanagh, T. J.
Chalker, A. R.
Chalker, Henry S.
Cipro, Thomas
Conway, J. D.
Coulter, A. F.
Critchlow, J. N.
Cruikshank, J. C.
Cudworth, H. D.
Dalzell, W. E.
Dambach, C. O.
Davis, Charles S.
Dean, E. E.
Dean, R. W.
Dickinson, B. F.
Diven, J. B.

Dunham, C. W.
Emery, E.
Endsley, Prof. Louis E.
Failor, Charles W.
Fair, J. M.
Ferguson, George
Ferguson, R. G.
Forsberg, R. P.
Fralic, C. F.
Fults, J. H.
Furch, George J.
George, W. J.
Glaser, J. P.
Goldstrom, G. E.
Goodwin, A. E.
Gray, T. H.
Griest, E. E.
Hackett, C. M.
Haller, Nelson M.
Hansen, William C.
Haupt, H. H.
Hayward, C. R.
Hayward, Carlton
Hellregel, W. H.
Hemma, Charles H.
Hess, Charles A.
Hocking, H. A.
Holmes, E. H.
Honsberger, G. W.
Hopper, George
Irvin, R. K.
Jados, W. J.
Johnson, J. W.
Kearfott, W. E.
Keck, L. M.
Keller, R. E.
Keller, R. B.
Kentlein, John
Kerr, C. R.
Kintner, J. B.

Kroske, J. F.
Lanahan, J. S.
Landis, William C.
Lauderbaugh, M.
Lee, L. A.
Lewis, Benjamin
Livingston, W. C.
Long, R. M.
Lupton, E. J.
Lundeen, C. J.
Mayer, L. I.
Millar, C. W.
Misner, George W.
Mitchell, W. S.
Moir, W. B.
Morgan, Homer C.
Murray, Stewart
McGeorge, D. W.
McKinley, John T.
McKinstry, C. H.
McNamee, W.
McTighe, B. J.
Nichols, Samuel A.
Nies, E. L.
Noonan, Daniel
Osborne, Raymond S.
Paisley, F. R.
Passmore, H. E.
Pehrson, A. K.
Peirce, W. B.
Poe, C. F.
Posteraro, S. F.
Prinkey, C. M.
Purchard, Paul
Rankin, B. B.
Reed, E. S.

Rider, C. E.
Rupp, E. S.
Rutter, H. E.
Ryan, D. W.
Schaller, Andrew J.
Schmitt, Andrew
Schmitt, Raymond F.
Searles, E. J.
Sekera, C. J.
Servais, Francis W.
Shellenbarger, H. M.
Sheridan, T. F.
Showalter, Joseph
Simons, Philip
Sixsmith, G. M.
Steiner, P. E.
Stevenson, W. M.
Sullivan, A. W.
Sutherland, Lloyd
Sutton, K. B.
Taylor, H. D.
Ternent, H. J.
Teskey, Dr. Walter J.
Thomas, George P.
Trautman, H. J.
Tryon, I. D.
Van Vranken, S. E.
Vollmer, Karl L.
Waterman, E. H.
West, Troy
Wheeler, C. M.
Wildin, George W.
Wilkinson, William E.
Wilson, J. M.
Wilson, James R.
Wilson, Jr., W. Stuart

Yohe, J. K., Jr.

VISITORS

Ackley, J. O.
Black, F. J.
Bletzinger, J. H.
Carthew, John W.,
Christman, Frederick M.
Clay, T. F.
Coons, Floyd A.
Corlett, W. H.
Crissman, R. M.
Crombie, C. R.
Davis, William B.
Edsall, S. D.

Emery, R. J.
Ewing, George S.
Flatly, William J.
Fowler, W. E., Jr.
Gordon, James P.
Gray, George R.
Hackett, Robert H.
Hallman, Charles
Jakovoc, V.
Johanek, George J.
Klein, S. C.
Klorer, C. P.

Koenig, Walter A.
Kouche, N. J.
Lawler, Herman
Lehew, Edwin C.
Lewis, S. B.
Lockard, W. N.
Meixner, J. Edward
Miller, L. P.
Muir, William
McGough, Harry
McKinstry, Clair M.
Nell, H.
Newman, John H.
Picard, A. J.
Reagan, P. H.
Richardson, G. S.

Richardson, L.
Rigdon, E. D.
Scott, Charles F.
Shaw, D. A.
Shelly, D. L.
Snodgrass, T. R.
Thomas, Robert W.
Voller, Norman
Vollmer, Paul F.
Warso, Michael M.
Weyman, Frank
Williams, W. S.
Wolff, H.
Wright, Grover
Zell, Harry A.
Zoog, Jerome H.

SECRETARY: Information has been conveyed to me that our President, Mr. E. A. Rauschart will be detained at his home on account of illness and I am sure we regret that he will not be able to be with us this evening, and from what information I have he will soon be out again. In the absence of the President, I will take the liberty of calling on our First Vice President, Mr. Sixsmith, to take the chair and conduct the meeting of the evening.

G. M. SIXSMITH: I feel sorry for you gentlemen to-night because under the circumstance that confronts us I am afraid you are going to have to take me whether you want to or not.

As Mr. Conway has told you, our President Mr. Rausch-art is under the weather, but I am glad to be able to say that based on information we have nothing of a serious nature is anticipated and I feel sure that Mr. Rauschart is as regretful as we are of his inability to be present on this occasion and conduct the meeting in person rather than by proxy as is now contemplated.

Mr. Lanahan, the Chairman of the Executive Committee, is likewise unable to be here, but not for the same reason I am glad to say.

Therefore, gentlemen, it is with a great deal of pleasure that I respond to Mr. Conway's invitation to preside, although I, of course, regret as you do the circumstances that make it necessary for me to do so.

You gentlemen have heard me say many times, I believe, that in my opinion this is a great club—a great organization to belong to. Just look at this attendance on a night like this. The continuous rains we have had and the troubles incident thereto, and the epidemic of sickness that prevails, and you will know what I mean. Under such conditions an attendance like we have here tonight speaks well for the importance of this Club and the future of this Club, and you may be sure is a source of great satisfaction to your officers who, after all, can succeed only in the administration of their duties according to the interest that prevails on the part of the membership—and I am glad to say that I see no lessening of that interest.

We will now proceed with the regular business of the club in the usual manner.

The call of the roll was dispensed with as those present signed registration cards at the door, giving a full record.

The reading of the minutes of the last meeting was, by common consent, dispensed with as the Proceedings have been printed and mailed to the members.

The following list of proposals for membership was read by the Secretary, and having been approved by the Executive Committee, were duly admitted to membership:

Black, C. R., Salesman, Westinghouse Electric & Manufacturing Company, Gulf Building. Pittsburgh, Pa. Recommended by G. W. Honsberger.

Brown, H. C., Salesman, Independent Pneumatic Tool Company, Wabash Building, Pittsburgh, Pa. Recommended by A. F. Coulter.

Gibson, Sam D., Salesman, Ingersoll-Rand Company, Chamber of Commerce Building. Pittsburgh, Pa. Recommended by J. F. Kroske.

Hayward, C. R., Insurance, 419 Highland Avenue, Aliquippa, Pa. Recommended by W. F. Ambrose.

Keeney, John H., Salesman, Air Reduction Sales Company, 1116 Ridge Avenue, N. S., Pittsburgh, Pa. Recommended by E. A. Rauschart.

Kessler, Bernard J., Clerk, Accounting Department, B. & O. R. R. Co., 901 Third Street, Versailles, McKeesport, Pa. Recommended by G. M. Prinkey.

Kintner, John B., Salesman, Union Steel Casting Company, 5649 Beacon Street, Pittsburgh, Pa. Recommended by William P. McGervey, Jr.

Lewis, Benjamin, 961 Main Street, Aliquippa, Pa. Recommended by W. F. Ambrose.

Miller, Carl A., Salesman, Ingersoll-Rand Company, Chamber of Commerce Building. Pittsburgh, Pa. Recommended by J. F. Kroske.

Willis, Paul, Vice President, J. S. Coffin, Jr. Company, 2304 West 19th Place, Blue Island, Ill. Recommended by Charles J. Nieman.

CHAIRMAN: Are there any communications or announcements, Mr. Secretary?

SECRETARY: Since our last meeting we have received information of the death of Charles L. Fortescue, Consulting Transmission Engineer, Westinghouse Electric & Manufacturing Company, which occurred on December 4, 1936.

CHAIRMAN: A suitable memorial minute will appear in the next issue of the Proceedings.

We are now down to the high spot of the evening—the presentation of an address by our guest speaker Mr. R. A. Kirkpatrick of the Union Pacific Railroad, and if you will refer to your cards sent out by the Secretary—if you have not already done so—you will observe that Mr. Kirkpatrick has more curlicues following his name than any other railroad man I know of. To my mind he appears more in the role of a College Professor.

However, your Subject Committee is to be congratulated on their selection and their ability to secure such a man to speak to us on such an outstanding and interesting subject as Boulder Dam. To me and no doubt to many of you Boulder Dam is largely a name only, and I miss my guess badly if we do not go away from here tonight much better informed on the Boulder Dam project and what it really is and will do. As for myself, I would not have missed this opportunity for anything and I am sure the evening is going to be well spent. Gentlemen, I now present to you Mr. Kirkpatrick of the Union Pacific Railroad, and the letters behind his name, to which I have already referred, go along with the introduction.

"BOULDER DAM"
By MR. R. A. KIRKPATRICK, Special Representative,
Union Pacific Railroad Company

Mr. Chairman and Gentlemen of the Railway Club of Pittsburgh:

Before beginning my story of the "Boulder Dam" this evening I wish to give to each of you the greetings and the very best wishes of our President, Mr. Carl R. Gray, of Omaha; also those of our Executive Vice President, Mr. W. M. Jeffers of Omaha, whose representative I happen to be. Particularly, do I bring these salutations to those assembled here tonight holding official positions with the various Railroads serving the community of Pittsburgh. I wish to request your Secretary, Mr. Conway, to convey to your good President, Mr. E. A. Rauschart, who, I have been informed, is confined to his home on account of illness, these greetings from the Executives of the Union Pacific Railroad Company with their sincere hope that he will enjoy a speedy and complete recovery from his illness.

Last September upon my return from a trip to Honolulu,

I stopped at a little city which had been constructed in the desert of southeastern Nevada, some six-and-one-half or seven years ago. The city bore the name of "Boulder City" because its existence was intimately connected with the building of the Boulder Dam. Looking out over the city from the hill upon which the administrative buildings had been constructed I recalled that, a year prior, the city had contained the homes of approximately 5,000 workers employed in the construction of Boulder Dam and that this number had been decreased to something less than 2,000 workers during the period of one year. This decrease in population was due to the fact that many of the men had completed their tasks in connection with the construction of the Dam and had moved away seeking employment on other projects, or had slipped back into the civic life of the various communities from which they were assembled.

Many interesting things had occurred in connection with various phases of this little city, none of which I think was more interesting, or of more benefit to the human race than that of the discovery made by the medical authorities in the treatment of heat prostration cases occuring early in the construction period of the dam. Seven miles to the southeast of the city lays the great Canyon of the Colorado River, in which Boulder Dam had been constructed. The intense heat of the desert climate caused those responsible for the health of the workers to look forward with apprehension and dread upon the thought of bringing some 5,000 workers, assembled from all parts of our Nation to work in the canyon during the heat of the summer months. The workers who were to be assembled at Boulder City would no doubt be largely green men who, in many instances, had never seen a desert and who knew nothing whatsoever of the oppression of desert heat. It was to be expected that many of these men would suffer heat prostration or sun-stroke during the summer seasons. With the coming of the summer months of July and August in the first year of the construction of the dam, the apprehensions of those in charge with respect to heat prostration began to materialize. The doctors in charge of heat prostration cases ascertained that the bodies of the heat prostrated men had been robbed of their salt content. This was due to the fact that the men had been working in the intense heat of the canyon, drinking large quantities of water, which being thrown off by the kidneys or in the form of perspiration, had flushed out the salt content of their bodies. An effort was made to restore this element by administering dosages of salt and, with the replacing of the salt content in the bodies of the heat prostration cases, a decided improvement in their condition was manifest. This led to the thought that possibly by giving the men salt while they were at work, so that the salt content of their bodies might not be disturbed, much of the danger of heat prostration might be avoided. Consequently, salt was placed in the drinking water used by the men while they were working on the job and according to a statement published by the Reclamation Bureau this treatment was so effective that during the period required to complete the dam, approximately five years, not a single death occurred from heat prostration. Today, I am informed this method of preventing heat prostration is being used in the deep mines of England and Australia and in many industries of our own country wherein men are required to work under high temperatures.

Many other things equally as interesting had occurred in the city. I am informed that the birth rate of this city is considerably higher than that of any similarly sized city in the United States. There are possibly several reasons for this but it isn't the one that you are thinking of (LAUGHTER). I am told that this high birth rate is due to "hero worship". As the story of the construction of the dam is brought out you will find the application of this "hero worship" idea.

The story of the "Boulder Dam" itself goes back a long, long time. Millions of years ago, probably ages before man came to live upon this earth, the area now known as the "Great American Desert" was covered by a mighty sea. On the floor of that sea there developed an immense, firery, burning ulcer of a sore—a submarine volcano. Out of the firery mouth of that ulcer there oozed oceans and oceans of lava which spead out over the floor of the sea covering hundreds and hundreds of square miles of area. In most places this lava is thousands of feet deep. Subsequent to the laying of this lava field, the earth's crust moved up through the waters of the sea into the sunlight and the sea itself drained away, leaving the old sea-bed much as we find it today. Eventually the Rocky Mountains were upheaved, their mighty tops being thrust high into the sky where great fields of ice and snow were formed, glistening in the sunlight. Seasons came, winters were followed by spring seasons in which warm currents of air heated in passing over the desert areas of Old Mexico, New Mexico and Arizona swept northward strik- ing and melting rapidly these great ice and snow fields. The waters resulting from the melting of this ice and snow, col- lected by a thousand tributaries, gave birth to a great river. In finding its way to the sea, this river worked itself across the desert country from the States of COLORADO, UTAH and WYOMING, southwesterly to the Gulf of California in Old Mexico. In reaching the Gulf of Mexico the river had to cut a deep channel or canyon across the field of lava of which I told you. Picking up immense loads of sand gathered in the desert country above the lava field, the river used this sand for scouring and cutting purposes and throughout the ages has worked continuously to make this canyon deeper and deeper where passing through the lava field. Today, the canyon, which, because of the dark lava coloring of the walls, is called "BLACK CANYON," is almost one-quarter of a mile wide across its top having walls that drop almost sheer from 1200 to 1400 feet, wedging together at the bottom where the river bed lies.

During the construction of the dam, tunnels were blasted through the canyon walls near water level and the river was diverted into these tunnels, thereby flowing around the site upon which it was desired to construct the dam, leaving the bed of the canyon exposed and dry so that the dam might be constructed. The sand and silt carried by the river through these tunnels was carefully measured and weighed and, for the period of the construction of the dam, approxi- mately 4½ years, the amount of sand and silt sliding through the tunnels under the flow of the river reached the astonish- ing average of 330 tons per minute. Gentlemen, this tremen- dous amount of sand and silt has been carried down the river not merely during the 4½-year-period required for the construction of the dam, but has continued during the mil- lions of years that preceded it. This sand and silt has been deposited at and near the mouth of the river in the upper or northerly end of the Gulf of California. Ages ago the Gulf of California extended much farther north than it now ex- tends. Through the continuous dumping of this great amount of sand and silt, the river built a mighty dam across the Gulf of California, as it then existed, forming a great lake laying north of the dam in the southern part of what is now the "STATE OF CALIFORNIA". The warm climate of that region eventually evaporated the water from this lake, leaving a low-lying valley which we now know as the "Imperial Valley of Southern California." Under normal conditions the river flowed into the Gulf of California and thence reached the sea. However, the depositing of this immense load of silt built up a great deltaic area which constantly grew higher and higher as fresh loads of sand were deposited upon it, the various mouths of the river spreading out and flowing over the top of the delta like the fingers of your hand. In order to maintain a gradient down which the river could flow, it has, through the settling of sand and silt, gradually built a ridge above this deltaic area and the river actually flows along on top of this ridge in much the same manner as the Mississippi River flows on top of a similar ridge built by it in LOUISIANA. Several times during the ages that have elapsed since the river started building this delta it has broken down its wall on the northerly side and emptied into the Imperial Valley. Just how many times this has occurred is not known but through these several inundations the surface of the Imperial Valley has been covered with a rich coating of fertile soil brought down by the river. In each instance, the river would eventually return to its normal course and empty into the Gulf of California.

The last of these inundations occurred in 1906, the river at that time in the flood stage followed an irrigation ditch that had been constructed from its bank into the Imperial Valley. Within a very short time the flood scoured this ditch into a great channel down which the river roared its way into the Imperial Valley. It is estimated that over $11,000,000 damage was caused by this flood, farms and homes being swept away or inundated with great loss in the matter of live stock and growing crops. Theodore Roosevelt, President, at that time knowing that the emergency caused by this flood was too great to be handled by the State of California or any local community, secured authority to expand a large amount of money for the purpose of damming the channel cut by the flood and thereby restoring the river to its normal course. Using every means at his command and assisted by various Departments of the Government, a tremendous effort extending over a course of months was made without success. The Federal Government eventually threw up its hands in despair, admitting that it did not have the means to dam the flood. Theodore Roosevelt then appealed to the management of the Southern Pacific Railway imploring the management to endeavor to stop the flood. The Southern Pacific Railway Company better organized for such emergencies than were the various Departments of the Federal Government: first developed a number of great gravel pits. Branch lines of railroad were constructed to these pits and derricks and steam shovels furnished by the Railway Company, loaded train load after train load of gravel which were dumped by the Railway Company into the channel cut by the river. I am informed that the Railway Company used every available car and engine not required in the normal operation of its railroad for this purpose; that it also used all bridging material and ties it then had or which it could procure, that in some instances it tore down depots and other station facilities in order to obtain material to be used in forming a dam across the new channel of the river. Eventually, the heroic efforts made by the Railway Company brought success, the river was dammed and turned back into its normal course. The Southern Pacific Railway Company had succeeded where the Federal Government had met defeat. Theodore Roosevelt then promised the management of the Southern Pacific Railway Company that the Federal Government would reimburse the Railway Company for all expenditures covering material, use of equipment, wages and other items incurred in the damming of the river. I am informed that this debt has never been paid, the Federal Government still owing the Railway Company several Million Dollars.

Theodore Roosevelt, in his fighting characteristic American manner, decided that there should be no more floods of this character which might inundate the Imperial Valley or other low-lying areas along the lower course of the Colorado River. A commission was appointed which, after careful study of the entire river course reported that deep canyons cut by the river through fields or hard rock or lava afforded locations in which dams might be builded of sufficient size to hold back and retain the flood water of the Colorado for several years if necessary and that by feeding the water through the dam in a steady stream throughout the year the liability of floods in the portion of the river below the site of the dam would be done away with. This plan of "flood control" was eventually adopted.

No sooner was the word passed out that the Federal

Government might assist in building a dam of this character, than each of the several States adjacent to or drained by the Colorado started a fight to have the dam constructed in a location which would give that particular State the lion's share of water to be impounded by the dam for agricultural purposes, and of the power which might be generated by the dam, for the development of its industries. For approximately twelve years the dirtiest, most disgusting, disgraceful political fight the West has ever known embroiled these States, each seeking to get the advantage of the others in the location of the dam.

That was the picture as it looked when the World War came. For several years during the period of the war we were too busily engaged in other things to consider the building of dams. However, when the war was ended and we got our feet back down on the ground again and began to look around to discover what might need our attention, we found that this dam had not as yet been constructed. By this time the population and development of the Imperial Valley had greatly increased making the imperative need of the dam much greater than it had ever been before.

Calvin Coolidge became President. In choosing the members of his official family, he appointed Dr. Elwood Mead, at that time Chief Engineer of the State of Wyoming, Commissioner of the newly formed Bureau of Reclamation, established in the Department of the Interior. Wyoming was one of the states which had been embroiled in that bitter political fight and Dr. Mead was fully acquainted with its various ramifications, its bitterness and distrust. Of much more importance he was also acquainted with the need for, and the possibilities and potentialities of the dam and carried to his new position in Washington a determination to build the dam if it was possible to do so. However, he did not have to work alone, valuable assistance came through the appointment of another Western man.

In choosing the members of his cabinet, Mr. Coolidge appointed a great engineer to the position of Secretary of Commerce. This man was Herbert Hoover, the Californian. California, too, was one of the states embroiled in this political fight and Herbert Hoover, likewise, was well acquainted with the conditions arising from it. As Secretary of Commerce, he succeeded in ironing out this dirty political fight. Under his advice the states formed a Commission, which Commission, with Mr. Hoover as Chairman, entered into a compact allocating the water to be impounded by the proposed dam and the power to be generated by it among the various states involved, leaving the site of the dam to be chosen by competent engineers. Each of the states embroiled with the exception of Arizona, signed this so-called "Colorado Compact". In the meantime, President Coolidge, assisted by Dr. Mead and Mr. Hoover had been working with Congress in an effort to secure funds to build the dam. Congress was not disposed to take money from the general tax funds of the nation, funds derived from taxes paid by the people of Pennsylvania, Ohio, Maine, Florida and other states of the nation to be used for the purpose of constructing a dam that would protect and be of benefit to only a small group of people located in the Imperial Valley and adjacent regions. In the first place, it did not appear to be just right and equitable. In the second place, perhaps, the river would never again break out of its normal bed and inundate these areas. Besides, in the event the river did break loose it might detour to the south instead of to the north, in which event, it would inundate a part of Old Mexico and would therefore be something for the Mexican Government to worry about rather than the Government of the United States.

After a great deal of consideration a plan was finally developed which would provide for the building of the dam. Money for paying the costs of constructing the dam could be raised, it was found, through the sale of electrical energy which might be generated at the dam. Congress agreed to appropriate sufficient funds to build the dam, providing the people of the Southwest who were to be benefitted through the construction of the dam would sell, in advance, enough elctrical power to guarantee the return to the Federal Treasury within a period of fifty years all the money necessary to build the dam.

This proposition did not scare the people of the Southwest. They have faith in the integrity of California, Arizona and New Mexico and they also had faith in the Colorado River. A campaign was organized for the purpose of selling this electrical power, and through this campaign enough power was sold, years in advance of its delivery, to the states themselves, various municipalities and other users of electrical power to guarantee the repayment to the Federal Government of the entire cost of constructing the dam within a period of thirty-five years instead of fifty years, as provided by Congress.

Careful surveys and studies of the various locations in the course of the river were made. Eventually "Black Canyon" was selected as the site for the dam. Congress then passed the enabling act authorizing the expenditure of One Hundred and Sixty-five Million Dollars ($165,000,000) the estimated cost of preparing the canyon, building the dam, constructing Boulder City and an ALL-AMERICAN Canal to carry water from the Colorado River into the Imperial Valley and adjacent areas for agricultural purposes.

Engineering parties arriving at the canyon for the purpose of making surveys found the walls of the canyon very rough. Great shoulders of rock hung precariously along the walls, and in many instances, great deposits of rubble and gravel and other loose materials had been deposited in pockets along the wall. It was impossible to start large bodies of men working on the floor of the canyon where they might be buried by falling rock or train loads of loose material, loosened by the jars of blasting or other causes. Accordingly, it was found necessary to get the canyon walls ready first. Boulder City was built so as to provide homes for the first group of men. Approximately 5,000 men were assembled at Boulder City, acclimated to the desert heat and taught in so far as it was possible, safety. When conditions were found ready some of these men were brought in shifts to the canyon to work upon the walls in cables suspended from anchors set in the lava back of the rim of the canyon. These men were armed with dynamite. electric drills, pick-axes. shovels, anything that could be used most effectively in blasting off the shoulders of rock and emptying the pockets of loose material, thundering the debris down into the canyon where it was scooped up by immense steam shovels, loaded on great trucks—trucks having a carrying capacity, I am told of 50 tons each—trucks that, in some instances had 17 forward shifts and 5 reverse shifts—and hauled up a highway to the rim of the canyon where it was thrown away. This work on the canyon walls required approximately 2½ years' time. During this period the men on the cables were gradually lowered day by day down the canyon walls, leaving a wall as solid and smooth as could be obtained under the circumstances. At the end of the 2½-year period these men were swinging near the floor of the canyon on cables approximating 1200 feet in length. During the summer time the heat of the canyon became so great that the men on the walls were worked only between 2 o'clock after midnight until 9 o'clock before noon. When the sun rose high enough in the heavens so that it shown down between the walls of the canyon, the walls became "bake ovens." I have been told that Dr. Mead starting at the top of the canyon was lowered down the walls on one of these cables, carrying an ordinary house thermometer with him. As he neared the canyon floor the thermometer exploded at 130 degrees Fahrenheit.

When the work of scaling the walls was completed the construction zone, a strip of wall 660 feet wide down each side of the canyon was surveyed in order that blueprints might be prepared. This job of surveying required approximately a year's time. I desire to say this to you Gentlemen, and I say it with all the fervor of my soul that, in my opinion, the greatest job of work ever done by the human family, and I will except nothing from this statement, the greatest job of work ever done by the human family, was the surveying of these canyon walls and rendering them into blueprints. An entire year was spent in surveying these two strips of canyon walls and during the entire year's time, not a man quit the job. Some of them were injured and some were, no doubt, fired, but there was not a quitter among them. They had the guts, the determination, the stick-to-itiveness to stay there and work under the conditions I have described to you in order that this great project might be carried through to completion. I can pay no higher tribute to the manhood of America or to the builders of the dam, or to the men who did the work than to say, "THESE MEN WERE HEROES".

In the meantime, the two tunnels I have mentioned had been blasted through the canyon walls; these tunnels were approximately 4,000 feet long. When everything was ready, a coffer dam was thrown across the river just below the upper portals of the tunnel and the river backing up behind the coffer dam eventually started flowing through the tunnels, leaving the floor of the canyon below the coffer dam exposed so that the construction of Boulder Dam itself might be begun.

Approximately 120 ft. of sand was found in the bed of the canyon, this was scooped up by steam shovels, loaded into trucks and hauled to the top of the canyon in the same manner as the debris taken from the canyon walls had been. The builders were then down to bed-rock and the construction of the dam proper could be started. Gravel for the concrete in the dam was secured from gravel pits located a short distance south of the canyon in the State of Arizona. This gravel was hauled by train-loads across the canyon into Nevada where it was run through a great washing and separation plant, which plant washed all earth, clay and other foreign matter out of the gravel and separated the aggregate into the various sizes required in the construction of the dam. An immense concrete mixing plant was constructed. Four great hoppers each containing large amounts of each of the four types of cement used formed a part of this mixing plant. Other similar hoppers held the various types of aggregate. The great machine was motivated by electricity brought in from California and, during the construction of the dam, mixed concrete requiring from 25 to 36 cars of cement per day. I have been informed that the machine on a number of occasions mixed concrete amounting to approximately 22,000 tons per day. Every known record in the matter of mixing and pouring concrete was broken during the construction of the dam.

In order that the chemical heat generated through the "setting" of such vast amounts of concrete might be removed without injury to the concrete content itself, the dam was built in numerous vertical columns varying in size from 25'x25' to 60'x60' on top. Concrete was poured on these columns in 5-foot layers. One such layer of concrete could be poured every 72 hours. Heat generated through the setting of this concrete was removed by a series of water pipes inserted in the concrete at the time it was poured. When the concrete started to set and through this chemical action generated heat, cold water from a gigantic refrigeration plant was pumped through these water pipes, taking the heat out of the concrete and permitting the block to set without cracking or other damage. This refrigeration plant had a capacity sufficient to produce 1,000 tons of ice from water at 32 degrees Fahrenheit in 24 hours.

The concrete was brought into the canyon principally in pails, these pails had a capacity of 16 tons of concrete each and were operated over cables carried across the canyon.

The dam, now completed, is of the "bow-gravity" type, bowing up-stream with the ends wedging in against the canyon walls in such manner that the greater the water pressure is on the up-stream face of the dam, the tighter, theoretically at least, the ends will fit against the side walls of the canyon.

The structure stands 727 feet high measured from the floor of the canyon. Let us visualize this height. Take for instance, a 15-story building and place it on the floor of the canyon. On top of this building you may place the Washington Monument and the top of the Monument will not reach to the top of the dam. The dam is 660 feet thick (up and down stream) in the bottom of the canyon—two city blocks of solid concrete in thickness. The down stream face of the dam swings in with a magnificent arc without decreasing the thickness as you near the top of the dam. At its top, the dam is 45 feet thick and 1,180 feet long, stretching from canyon wall to canyon wall.

As you walk out on the top of the dam you look down into the canyon on the up-stream side to find a beautiful lake of water filling up there. At the time of my visit to the dam last September this lake was approximately 390 feet deep and extended back up the canyon for a distance of almost 90 miles. When the lake is permitted to fill up so that a normal dam-load of water is obtained, if it were possible to divert the Colorado River into some other canyon so that no more water could come into the lake from the river, enough water would be impounded above the dam to cover the entire state of New York to a depth of one foot. This water would supply every man, woman and child living in the United States with 80,000 gallons of water at one time. This means that I could take every soul that lives upon this entire earth, North America, South America, Europe, Asia, Africa and the Isles of the Sea, every man, woman and child living today, out to that lake, give each of them 5,000 gallons of water at one time and send them home to take a drink. If the city of Los Angeles used a billion gallons of water a day it would take the city 29 years to empty that lake if we never put another drop of water in it.

And you asked the question "WHY". Why this dam? Why this mighty reservoir of water? You picture in your minds great irrigation projects, acres and acres of farm land brought under irrigation, and you form the conclusion that the dam was built for the purpose of irrigating land. But, you are wrong. Land will be irrigated from the waters of this lake. Approximately two million (2,000,000) acres will be placed under irrigation as soon as the distribution systems can be set-up. Ultimately, I have been told, ten million (10,-000,000) acres of land may be brought under irrigation through the developments of this project. Let me tell you, gentlemen, that 10,000,000 acres of land means thousands and thousands of homes, good homes, homes on irrigated farms where there is no drought, homes in a region where a crop can be harvested every month of the year, where crops can be harvested during the months of January, February and March as they are harvested here during the months of June, July, August and September. However, we would have built the dam if we never irrigated a single acre of land from its waters.

Then, looking into the canyon on the down-stream face of the dam, you find immense power houses being constructed. These power houses will be 20 stories high and will contain the most stupendous, the most gigantic power equipment ever assembled in any power plant on the face of the earth. When that power plant is operated to its fullest capacity it will provide a constant load of 1,800,000 horsepower of electrical energy. High tension wire lines, newly devised cables, will distribute this potential throughout the southwest. This power will build cities. It will motivate the machinery in hundreds of the greatest industries of our land. It will open up hundreds of mines that now lay in that desert and mountain country in locations too remote from civilization to be operated at the present time. These mines are rich in the finest metals to be found on the North American Continent, and their development will add materially to the natural wealth of our entire nation.

The dam was not constructed for the purpose of generating electricity. It was built for flood control purposes, and, after constructing it we would have been very very foolish not to have generated electricity. Likewise, we would have been very very foolish not to have irrigated land.

Mr. R. A. Kirkpatrick then showed still pictures illustrating various features connected with the construction of the dam and various phases of its construction.

CHAIRMAN: If you gentlemen feel as I do, and I believe you do by the profound interest displayed while Mr. Kirkpatrick was speaking, you are not only thrilled but spellbound, by this most interesting and instructive description of this tremendous undertaking. The planning and construction of Boulder Dam—certainly we now know what it is all about and the many interesting sidelights that have been described have made the whole picture a complete presentation. Now you know what I had in mind when I said that our Subject Committee was to be congratulated that it selected Boulder Dam as the subject for tonight and its ability to bring Mr. Kirkpatrick here to present it. With all this water coming down from above, and the rivers around us overflowing, it is an appropriate subject at the moment.

Now before calling on Professor Endsley for such closing remarks as he may desire to make, I would like to say to Mr. Kirkpatrick that we of the Railway Club of Pittsburgh appreciate the greetings that he brought to us from Mr. C. R. Gray and Mr. W. M. Jeffers of his company, both of whom are known to many of us here in Pittsburgh, and in the name of our President and on behalf of the membership of this Club I wish you would take back to Mr. Gray and Mr. Jeffers a friendly greeting from the Railway Club of Pittsburgh and an expression of our unanimous appreciation that it was made possible for you to be with us on this occasion. You may say to them if you will that this Club has over 1,400 members, and every railroad and industrial corporation in Pittsburgh and vicinity is well represented in membership.

Now gentlemen we are coming to the end of a happy get-together but I feel that I cannot close the meeting without extending to Mr. Rauschart a word of regret from you and me that circumstances in the way of illness forced his absence tonight, and the hope he will be well again soon and be with us on all future occasions.

If there is nothing else that any person would like to bring before the meeting, I will say that immediately following adjournment lunch, as usual, will be served at both ends of the room, and we will now here from Professor Endsley.

PROF. LOUIS E. ENDSLEY: I am sure that everyone here tonight is glad that he came, for we have all heard a very interesting description of the Boulder Dam, and I move, Mr. Chairman, that the Club extend a rising vote of thanks to Mr. Kirkpatrick for his very excellent talk to us.

The motion was duly seconded and prevailed by unanimous rising vote.

There being no further business, upon motion, adjourned.

J. D. CONWAY, Secretary.

In Memoriam

CHARLES L. FORTESCUE

Joined Club February 23, 1933

Died December 4, 1936

DON'T BE "CRANKY"

Be Wise!

for Quick Starts use Pennzip and Pennzoil

Ole Man Winter holds all the trumps against you when you neglect to keep you car in shape for cold weather driving. You can tell he's won a trick when your battery hardly turns the motor over—or when you have to push or tug on the gear shift lever. But his most costly toll of all is the wear that takes place in your motor—**the wear** you can't see or feel.

Wise motorists play two cards that win trouble-free motoring all winter long. They fill their crankcases with Pennzoil motor oil and their tanks with Pennzip gasoline. These perfect partners for winter driving start motors quickly—keep down wear and repairs — and give you better mileage. Get both at your nearest Pennzip dealer.

THE PENNZOIL COMPANY

Chamber of Commerce Bldg. . . . Pittsburgh, Pa.

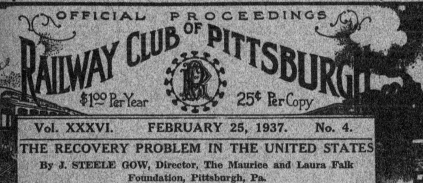

OFFICIAL PROCEEDINGS
RAILWAY CLUB OF PITTSBURGH
$1⁰⁰ Per Year   25¢ Per Copy

Vol. XXXVI.   FEBRUARY 25, 1937.   No. 4.

THE RECOVERY PROBLEM IN THE UNITED STATES
By J. STEELE GOW, Director, The Maurice and Laura Falk Foundation, Pittsburgh, Pa.

The proof of your interest

in the Club can be

enhanced

by securing a

NEW MEMBER.

Application form is available

in this magazine. Look

it up and

"ACT NOW."

OFFICIAL PROCEEDINGS

OF

The Railway Club of Pittsburgh

Organized October 18, 1901

Published monthly, except June, July and August, by the Railway Club of
Pittsburgh. J. D. Conway, Secretary, 515 Grandview Ave., Pittsburgh, Pa..

Entered as Second Class Matter February 6, 1915, at the Postoffice at Pittsburgh,
under the Act of March 3, 1879.

| No. 4 Vol. XXXVI. | Pittsburgh, Pa., Feb. 25, 1937 | $1.00 Per Year 25c Per Copy |

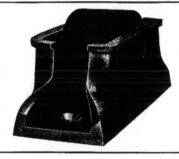

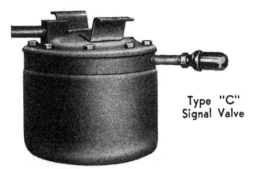

KOPPERS SERVES the RAILROADS

KOPPERS PRODUCTS AND WHERE THEY APPLY IN THE RAILROAD FIELD	TREATED TIMBER, TIES, POSTS, ETC.	ROOFING MATERIALS	PISTON RINGS	COAL	WATER-PROOFING MATERIALS	BITUMINOUS PAINTS	TARMAC ROAD MATERIALS	FAST'S COUPLINGS	CREOSOTE	CYLINDER AND VALVE PACKING	WEED KILLERS	INSECTI-CIDES AND DISINFEC-TANTS	PLATE WORK	CAR FERRIES, RAILROAD BARGES, ETC.
ROADBEDS	A								D		F			
LOCOMOTIVES		D	C	B		D				C				
STATIONS	A	D	C	B	D	D			D			F		
SHOPS	A	D	C	B	D	D		E	D			F	E&G	
BRIDGES	A				D	D	D		D				E&G	
TUNNELS	A				D	D	D		D				E&G	
DRIVEWAYS	A				D	D	D				F			
POWER HOUSES	A	D	C	B	D	D		E	D	C			E&G	
STRUCTURAL	A	D			D	D			D				E&G	
GRADE CROSSINGS	A						D							
CATTLE PENS	A	D			D	D			D			F		
RAILROAD MARINE OPERATIONS	A	D	C	B	D	D			D	C		F	E&G	H

A—The Wood Preserving Corporation, Pittsburgh, Pa.   B—The Koppers Coal Company, Pittsburgh, Pa.   C—American Hammered Piston Ring Division, Baltimore, Md.   D—Tar and Chemical Division, Pittsburgh, Pa.   E—Bartlett Hayward Division, Baltimore, Md.   F—The White Tar Company of New Jersey, Inc.   G—Western Gas Division, Fort Wayne, Ind.   H—The Maryland Drydock Company, Baltimore, Md.

INDEX—ADVERTISERS.

NOTE—This form to be filled out in full by typewriter or printed and mailed to J. D. Conway, Secretary, 1941 Oliver Building, Pittsburgh, Pa. Membership fee, including dues, is $3.00 for each fiscal year or part thereof, except those proposd in September or October. Those proposed in these months will be credited upon payment for the following fiscal year. Dues are payable in advance.

The fiscal year ends with the month of October.

The Railway Club of Pittsburgh:

_____19____

Gentlemen:

Will you kindly consider my Application for Membership in your Club at the next meeting:

Name_____

Title_____

Company_____

My Address_____

_____

Recommended by_____

OFFICIAL PROCEEDINGS

OF

The Railway Club of Pittsburgh

Organized October 18, 1901

Vol. XXXVI. No. 4	Pittsburgh, Pa., Feb. 25, 1937	$1.00 Per Year 25c Per Copy

OFFICERS FOR 1936-1937

President
E. A. RAUSCHART,
Mechanical Superintendent, Montour Railroad Co., Coraopolis, Pa.

First Vice President
G. M. SIXSMITH,
Supt., Pennsylvania Railroad,
Pittsburgh, Pa.

Secretary
J. D. CONWAY,
Railway Supply Manufacturers' Association,
Pittsburgh, Pa.

Second Vice President
J. D. BELTZ,
Supt., B. & O. R. R. Co.,
Pittsburgh, Pa.

Treasurer
E. J. SEARLES,
Managei, Schaefer Equipment Co.,
Pittsburgh, Pa.

EXECUTIVE COMMITTEE:

FRANK J. LANAHAN, Chairman, President, Fort Pitt Malleable Iron Co., Pittsburgh, Pa
A. STUCKI, Engineer, A. Stucki Company, Pittsburgh, Pa.
D. F. CRAWFORD, Consulting Engineer, Pittsburgh, Pa.
G W. WILDIN, Consulting Engineer, Westinghouse Air Brake Company, Pittsburgh, Pa
W. S. McABEE, Vice Pres. & General Supt., Union Railroad Co., East Pittsburgh, Pa
E. W. SMITH, Vice President, Pennsylvania Railroad, Pittsburgh, Pa.
LOUIS E. ENDSLEY, Consulting Engineer, 516 East End Avenue, Pittsburgh, Pa.
F. I. SNYDER, Vice President & General Manager, B. & L. E. R. R. Co., Pittsburgh, Pa
C. O. DAMBACH, General Manager, P. & W. Va. Ry. Co., Pittsburgh, Pa.
R. H. FLINN, General Superintendent, Pennsylvania Railroad, Pittsburgh, Pa.
R. P. FORSBERG, Chief Engineer, P. & L. E. R. R. Co., Pittsburgh, Pa.

SUBJECT COMMITTEE:

D. W. McGEORGE, Chairman, Secretary, Edgewater Steel Company, Pittsburgh, Pa.
G. H. BURNETTE, Asst. Chief Engineer, P. & L. E. R. R. Co., Pittsburgh, Pa

RECEPTION AND ATTENDANCE COMMITTEE:

J. W. JOHNSON, Chairman, Superintendent, Railway Express Agency, Pittsburgh, Pa
W. C. BUREL, Vice Chairman, Master Mechanic, Western Allegheny Railroad, Kaylor, Pa
J. W. BOYD, Superintendent, Monongahela Railway Company, Brownsville, Pa.
THOMAS E. CANNON, General Supt. Equipment, P. & W. Va. Ry. Co., Pittsburgh, Pa
T. W. CARR, Superintendent Rolling Stock, P. & L. E. R. R. Co., McKees Rocks, Pa
D. C. CARROLL, Assistant Agent, Pennsylvania Railroad, Pittsburgh, Pa.
S. G. DOWN, Vice President, Westinghouse Air Brake Company, Wilmerding, Pa
HARRY C. GRAHAM, Pittsburgh Screw & Bolt Corporation, Pittsburgh, Pa.
J. W. SCHAD, Division Master Mechanic, B. & O. R. R. Co., Pittsburgh, Pa.
GEORGE S. WEST, Division Superintendent, Pennsylvania Railroad, Pittsburgh, Pa.
J. W. HOOVER, Asst. Chief of Transpn., Subsidiary Cos. U. S. Steel Corp., Pittsburgh, Pa
A. A. READ, Duquesne Slag Products Company, Pittsburgh, Pa.
C. P. SCHRECONGOST, Traffic Manager, Hillman Coal & Coke Company, Pittsburgh, Pa
J. A. WARFEL, Special Representative, Air Reduction Sales Company, Pittsburgh, Pa.
J. C. SHINGLEDECKER, Supervisor of Service Stations, The Pennzoil Co., Pittsburgh, Pa
J. C. DILWORTH, Manager Railroad Sales, Carnegie-Illinois Steel Corp., Pittsburgh, Pa

ENTERTAINMENT COMMITTEE:

J. PORTER GILLESPIE, Chairman, Asst. Gen. Supt., Lockhart Iron & Steel Co., Pgh., Pa.
FRANK E. WEIS, Vice Chairman, Transportation Clerk, Penna. R. R., Pittsburgh, Pa.
JAMES NAGEL, Superintendent Transportation, Montour Railroad, Coraopolis, Pa.
E. H. HOLMES, Sales Department, Fort Pitt Malleable Iron Co., Pittsburgh, Pa.
C. C. CLARK, Sales Manager, Central District, Pressed Steel Car Co., Pittsburgh, Pa
A. I. KESSLER, Clearance Clerk, Pennsylvania Railroad, Pittsburgh, Pa.
T. F. SHERIDAN, Asst. to S.M.P. and S.R.S., P. & L. E. R. R. Co., McKees Rocks, Pa.

FINANCE COMMITTEE:

M. A. SMITH, Chairman, General Manager, P. & L. E. R. R. Co., Pittsburgh, Pa.
J. B. DIVEN, Superintendent Motive Power, Pennsylvania Railroad, Pittsburgh, Pa.
F. J. RYAN, District Representative, Detroit, Toledo & Ironton Railroad, Pittsburgh, Pa.
C. E. CATT, Division Accountant, B. & O. R. R. Co., Pittsburgh, Pa.
G. W. HONSBERGER, Transpn. Mgr., Westinghouse Electric & Mfg. Co., Pittsburgh, Pa.

ADVERTISING COMMITTEE:

H. H. HAUPT, Chairman, Gen. Supt., Motive Power, Pennsylvania Railroad, Pittsburgh, Pa
KARL BERG, Superintendent Motive Power, P. & L. E. R. R. Co., McKees Rocks, Pa.
H. E. PASSMORE, Representative, The American Hammered Piston Ring Co., Pgh., Pa.

MEMBERSHIP COMMITTEE:

T. E. BRITT, Chairman, Div. Storekeeper, B. & O. R. R. Co., Glenwood Shops, Pgh., Pa
C. M. WHEELER, Vice Chairman, Sales Engr., Union Switch & Signal Co., Swissvale, Pa.
F. H. EATON, Sales Engineer, American Car & Foundry Co., Pittsburgh, Pa.
C. W. GOTTSCHALK, Asst. Traffic Manager, Jones & Laughlin Steel Corp., Pgh., Pa.
LLOYD SUTHERLAND, General Storekeeper, P. & L. E. R R. Co., McKees Rocks, Pa.
THOMAS R. FITZPATRICK, Freight Traffic Mgr., P. & L. E. R. R. Co., Pittsburgh, Pa.
P. W. HEPBURN, Sales Engineer, Gulf Refining Company, Pittsburgh, Pa.
W. B. MOIR, Chief Car Inspector, Pennsylvania Railroad, Pittsburgh, Pa.
C. W. TRUST, Assistant Traffic Manager, Carnegie-Illinois Steel Corp., Pittsburgh, Pa
WILLIAM R. GELLATLY, President, Superior Railway Products Corp., Pittsburgh, Pa.
R. S. BULL, Supt. Power & Inclines, Pittsburgh Railways Co., N. S., Pittsburgh, Pa.
A. F. COULTER, Master Car Builder, Union Railroad Co., East Pittsburgh, Pa.
T. R. DICKINSON, Purchasing Agent, B. & L. E. R. R. Co., Pittsburgh, Pa.
D. K. ORR, Road Master, Monongahela Railway Co., Brownsville, Pa.
W. F. AMBROSE, Master Mechanic, Aliquippa & Southern Railroad, Aliquippa, Pa
JOHN I. MULVEY, Traffic Manager, Hubbard & Company, Pittsburgh, Pa.

PAST PRESIDENTS:

*J. H. McCONNELL	October,	1901, to October, 1903
*L. H. TURNER	November,	1903, to October, 1905
*F. H. STARK	November,	1905, to October, 1907
*H. W. WATTS	November,	1907, to April, 1908
*D. J. REDDING	November,	1908, to October, 1910
*F. R. McFEATTERS	November,	1910, to October, 1912
*A. G. MITCHELL	November,	1912, to October, 1914
*F. M. McNULTY	November,	1914, to October, 1916
*J. G. CODE	November,	1916, to October, 1917
*D. M. HOWE	November,	1917, to October, 1918
*J. A. SPIELMAN	November,	1918, to October, 1919
H. H. MAXFIELD	November,	1919, to October, 1920
FRANK J. LANAHAN	November,	1920, to October, 1921
*SAMUEL LYNN	November,	1921, to October, 1922
D. F. CRAWFORD	November,	1922, to October, 1923
*GEO. D. OGDEN	November,	1923, to October, 1924
A. STUCKI	November,	1924, to October, 1925
F. G. MINNICK	November,	1925, to October, 1926
G. W. WILDIN	November,	1926, to October, 1927
E. J. DEVANS	November,	1927, to October, 1928
W. S. McABEE	November,	1928, to October, 1929
E. W. SMITH	November,	1929, to October, 1930
LOUIS E. ENDSLEY	November,	1930, to October, 1931
*JOHN E. HUGHES	November,	1931, to October, 1932
F. I. SNYDER	November,	1932, to October, 1933
C. O. DAMBACH	November,	1933, to October, 1934
R. H. FLINN	November,	1934, to October, 1935
R. P. FORSBERG	November,	1935, to October, 1936

*—Deceased.

Meetings held fourth Thursday of each month except June, July and August.

PROCEEDINGS OF MEETING
FEBRUARY 25, 1937

The meeting was called to order at the Fort Pitt Hotel at 8:00 o'clock, P. M., with President E. A. Rauschart in the chair.

Registered attendance, 203, as follows:

MEMBERS

Adams, Frank W.
Ainsworth, J. H.
Allen, Earl M.
Anderson, G. S.
Anne, George E.
Ashley, F. B.
Aulbach,, A. J.
Babcock, F. H.
Baer, Harry L.
Baer, S. T.
Baker, William E.
Bailey, J. C.
Balph, M. Z.
Balzer, C. E.
Barnhart, B. F.
Barr, H. C.
Baughman, G. W.
Beall, C. R.
Beltz, J. D.
Bender, H. P.
Berg, K.
Black, C. R.
Britt, T. E.
Buchanan, C. C.
Buzzerd, J. P.
Callahan, F. J.
Campbell, W. T.
Carroll, D. C.
Cavanaugh, T. J.
Christy, F. X.
Cipro, Thomas
Clardy, W. J.
Clausen, H. C.
Conway, J. D.
Courtney, H.
Cudworth, H. D.
Cunningham, J. D.
Davis, Charles S.
Dean, E. E.
Dickinson, T. R.

Dickson, K. B.
Dunha, C. W.
Eaton, Frederick H.
Emery, E.
Endsley, Louis E.
Failor, Charles W.
Farlow, G. B.
Forsberg, R. P.
Fralic, C. F.
Fulton, K. H.
Galbraith, James R.
Geiser, W. P.
George, W. J.
Gilg, Henry F.
Gillespie, J. Porter
Glaser, J. P.
Goda, P. H.
Goldstrom, G. E.
Griest, E. E.
Groves, W. C.
Guinnip, M. S.
Hansen, William C.
Harman, H. H.
Heed, H. L.
Hepburn, P. W.
Herpst, R. C.
Hess, Charles A.
Hill, Jack
Hilstrom, A. V.
Honsberger, G. W.
Huff, A. B.
Hunt, L.
Hutchinson, G. C., Jr.
Irvin, R. K.
James, J. H.
Johnson, Ira S.
Johnson, J. W.
Johnson, W. M.
Kearfott, W. E.
Kentlein, John

Klassen, F. G.
Lanahan, Frank J.
Lanahan, J. S.
Landis, William C.
Lewis, N. F.
Loder, C. C.
Lowndes, T. H.
Lowry, William F., Jr.
Maliphant, C. W.
Mann, Henry S.
Manson, A. J.
Millar, C. W.
Mills, C. C.
Mills, O. B.
Misner, George W.
Mitchell, W. S.
Moir, W. B.
Moore, D. O.
Morgan, A. L.
Morgan, Homer C.
Mulligan, Mitchael
Myers, Arnold
McGeorge, D. W.
McKim, Hollis
McKinley, John T.
McKisson, R. W.
McTighe, B. J.
Nathan, W. S.
Nies, E. L.
Osborne, Raymond S.
O'Sullivan, John J.
Paisley, F. R.
Palmer, E. A.
Peirce, W. B.
Purcell, E. J.
Purchard, Paul
Posteraro, S. F.
Rankin, B. B.
Rauschart, E. A.

Record, J. F.
Renshaw, W. B.
Robertson, A. S.
Rowan, John R.
Rushneck, G. L.
Ryan, D. W.
Schadt, A. D.
Schiller, John
Schrecongost, C. P.
Searles, E. J.
Severn, A. B.
Sheridan, T. F.
Shingledecker, John C.
Simons, Philip
Smith, Robert B.
Snyder, F. I.
Steiner, P. E.
Stemen, E. M.
Stevens, L. V.
Sutherland, Lloyd
Taylor, J. M.
Terkelsen, Bernhard
Ternent, H. J.
Teskey, Dr. Walter J.
Thomas, George P.
Tracey, J. B. A.
Trautman, H. J.
Unger, Dr. J. S.
Van Blarcom, G. C.
Van Vranken, S. E.
Vollmer, Karl L.
Vowinkel, Fred F.
Welton, Alvin A.
West, Troy
White, H. A.
Wikander, O. R.
Wilson, W. F.
Yarnall, Jesse
Yohe, J. K., Jr.

VISITORS:

Adams, W. C.
Ball, J. B.
Barnum, H. M.
Carey, G. W.
Carter, E. D.
Dankmyer, F. C.
Devlin, Robert
Dickinson, F. H.
Edsall, S. D.
Gow, J. Steel

Gyekis, J. R.
Harsch, C. H.
Henon, Hamilton
Hilgert, T. J.
Hope, R. A.
Huber, C. G.
Hughes, Shelly
Jackovic, J. O.
Jones, Edward
Lanahan, James K., II

Laughlin, R. B.
Lewis, S. B.
Lind, B. C.
Long, R. D.
Malenoch, William
Mambourg, Frank
Miller, Earl
McIlvaine, C. L.
Oaks, L. H.
O'Hagan, J. E.
Pigott, William J.
Rau, William R., Jr.

Reagan, P. H.
Redman, H. W.
Renton, S. H.
Robinson, H. J.
Severn, Harry A.
Smith, J. W.
Smith, Sion B.
Vollmer, Paul F.
Walker, W. S.
Weyman, Frank
Young, James L.
Zell, Harry A.

Zwordel, Martin L.

PRESIDENT: As all present signed registration cards upon entering the room, we will dispense with the call of the roll.

The minutes of the last meeting have been printed and distributed to the members, therefore, unless there is objection, we will dispense with the reading of the minutes of the last meeting.

I will ask the Secretary to read the list of proposals for membership.

Blair, H. A., Supervisor, Federal Safety Appliances, B. & O. R. R., B. & O. Road Building, Baltimore, Md. Recommended by T. E. Britt.

Stemen, E. M., Chief Clerk of Accounting, Edgewater Steel Company. Box 364, Verona. Pa. Recommended by T. E. Britt.

Wilson, W. F., Manager Pittsburgh Works, American Steel Foundries, 36th Street and AVRR., Pittsburgh, Pa. Recommended by William F. Lowry.

Young, J. E., Agent, Pennsylvania Railroad, Federal Street Station, 411 Center Avenue, Verona, Pa. Recommended by D. K. Chase.

PRESIDENT: These names having been approved by the Executive Committee, in accordance with our By-laws, the gentlemen are duly admitted to membership. I am glad there are four, but I see a large field for increased activity in this line, and we look for large returns next month.

. Are there any announcements, Mr. Secretary?

SECRETARY: Since our last meeting we have received information of the death of a member Edward M. Sexton, Railroad Sales Manager, Air Reduction Sales Company, New York, N. Y., which occurred on February 15, 1937, and Timothy E. Doyle, Foreman Painter, Montour Railroad, Coraopolis, Pa., died February 16, 1937.

PRESIDENT: An appropriate memorial minute will appear in the next issue of the Proceedings.

Is there any further business to be taken up at this

time? If not, I will ask Mr. D. W. McGeorge, of the Subjects Committee, to introduce the speaker of the evening.

MR. D. W. McGEORGE: The speaker of the evening is no stranger to this Club. He is the Director of the Maurice and Laura Falk Foundation, and gave us a wonderfully interesting and informative talk on a somewhat similar subject one year ago. The Foundation of which he is Director sponsored a special study by the Brookings Institution, the outstanding non-partisan, non-political and strictly scientific investigating organization of our day, on the depression and subsequent recovery movement, and it is the meat of this study that Mr. Gow will present to us this evening. I am greatly pleased to present to you Mr. J. Steele Gow, Director of the Maurice and Laura Falk Foundation.

MR. J. STEELE GOW: It was very gracious in you to invite me to address you this evening, and I appreciate your courtesy. I am not so sure that I can say the same for your judgment!

After the introduction of Mr. McGeorge, I am not quite sure what it is I am to talk about.

THE RECOVERY PROBLEM IN THE UNITED STATES

By J. STEELE GOW, Director, The Maurice and Laura Falk Foundation, Pittsburgh, Pa.

The crucial economic problem in the United States today is not so much to defeat depression as it is to minister to recovery. If we can judge from current signs, the depression has been pretty well defeated. But in the minds of many intelligent people there remains a question of whether or not the current recovery is of a sort that will be substantial and enduring. Some economists believe it will be substantial and enduring. Others are doubtful. The latter groups fears that the present upward movement of business rests on supports which will make for trouble in the years ahead.

Under a grant from the Falk Foundation, the Brookings Institution of Washington, D. C., a private and independent research organization, has, for two years, been studying the depression period and the subsequent recovery movement. The central purpose of the investigation has been to consider whether a more complete and enduring recovery might be promoted by modifications in public and private policies. The investigation is perhaps the most extensive that has been made of the depression and of the recovery period; though the study focuses its attention on the United States, it, of necessity, has given consideration to the world forces which converged to create the depression. It traces the development of these world forces, analyzes the world impact of the depression, reviews the efforts which various governments have made to defeat the depression, and, finally, proposes for the United States an integrated program of action which, it is believed, will aid in achieving a more complete and lasting recovery.

At the outset, may I make clear that my role is merely to interpret this study to you. I am making no attempt to appraise it, pro or con; I am trying to take the role of a newspaper reporter who is charged with giving you a brief and simple synopsis of the study and its conclusions.

The study begins with a review of the sweep of world events during the last fifteen years, in order to give the setting in which the American depression and recovery may be properly investigated. The review focuses its attention on the world situation in 1929, and points out that the economic mechanism was then out of adjustment in a number of important respects. Briefly, there were in 1929 the following sources of maladjustment:

1. International trade and financial relations were fundamentally unbalanced, and the so-called "stabilized international exchanges" were, in many instances, dependent solely upon a continuous stream of credits from creditor to debtor nations.

> For example, international trade in agriculture was unbalanced as a result of the great increase of agricultural production in Europe in the post-War period for which no corresponding readjustment was made in the United States or in other countries. The result was a precipitate price decline in agriculture and a persistent piling up of unsold stocks.

> Similar maladjustments in international trade existed also in industry. The granting of huge international credits led to a great expansion in the volume of production in the post-War period, but the

process did not restore the pre-War state of economic equilibrium. On the contrary, it served to increase some of the pre-War maladjustments.

2. Intensive industrial competition was stimulating the growth of barriers to international trade.

Tariff increases, quota restrictions, and similar impedimenta to international trade resulted from the frantic efforts of countries throughout the world to build their economies on a basis of self-sufficient nationalism.

3. The governments of many countries were burdened with domestic indebtedness and in only a few cases were budgets safely in balance.

4. In many countries private credit, for both productive and consumptive purposes, had proceeded at a pace that could not be indefinitely maintained.

5. In the United States the increasing concentration of income in the higher income groups was serving to retard the growth of consumptive demand.

The incomes of people in the middle and lower income groups were not advancing rapidly enough to supply the amount of purchasing power which was needed to take off the market the consumptive goods which we had the capacity to produce. Therefore, our national economy developed a condition of disequilibrium which, during the 1920's, was increasing in magnitude.

6. The excessive flow of savings and of bank credit into investment channels was producing an inflation of security prices and consequent financial instability.

The tendency of a larger and larger proportion of the national income to concentrate itself in the higher income groups created this excessive flow of savings. In other words, the concentration of income in the higher income groups did not increase the demand of these groups for consumptive goods but served merely to provide them with surplus funds to put into investment channels. These investments were not needed to increase our productive capacity. The result was an inflation of security prices by bidding up the prices of existing securities. With the world economic system vulnerable in these important respects, it was only a question of time until a break would occur somewhere. And it was inevitable that, once the break had occurred, the repercussions upon the economic system would be world-wide in scope and devastating in effect.

Let us look now at some of the impacts of the depression upon the economic life of the world, as it is revealed by this study.

1. World production of raw materials declined about one-third between 1929 and 1932.

The decline was greatest in North America (about 40 per cent), and North America remains relatively depressed.

2. World manufacturing activity suffered a similar decline, with North America suffering more severely than Europe.

The degree of recovery in North America has been substantially less than in Europe.

3. The volume of world trade declined 25 per cent between 1929 and 1932.

4. The downswing of business throughout the world reached its bottom in the mid-summer of 1932, although the upswing did not start until the spring of 1933.

In the United States the decline was not only severe and protracted, but the recovery movement is marked by wider variations than in most other countries.

5. The degree of recovery as of June, 1936, shows wide variations in the different countries.

The greatest recovery occurred in Japan, Chile, Hungary, Great Britain, Sweden, and Germany. The United States and Canada stand in an intermediate position, while France, Belgium, Poland, and Czecho-Slovakia lag noticeably.

So much for an outline of the impact of the depression on the world at large.

Let us now turn attention to what the study reveals as the characteristics of the current recovery in its world setting. The present recovery movement differs from previous revivals in a number of important respects, some of which may have an important bearing on future trends.

1. In general, the rate of recovery has been slower and more halting than is normally the case.

2. The recovery movement has, however, continued for an unusually long period—four years as compared with an average of 25 months.

3. The recovery in **international** trade has lagged materially behind domestic trade.

4. International monetary relations have remained relatively unstable.

5. Commodity prices, particularly manufacturing prices, have remained comparatively stable since the end of 1933.

6. There has been a lag in the production of durable goods.

7. An extraordinary volume of unemployment has persisted in most countries throughout the recovery movement.

8. In many countries the public debt has increased enormously even during the course of the recovery. This phenomenon is particularly true in the United States.

Up to this point I have been discussing the study's findings with respect to the world situation. The task now is to look at the picture within the United States. Here there are five effects to note:

1. The truest gauge of the effects of the depression in the United States is found in the trends of production. This study reveals that if the pre-depression production trends had been continued until 1936, production in this latter year would have been about 20 per cent higher than in 1929. The actual condition in 1936 was that production in that year was only 90 per cent of the 1929 level.

2. The percentage of the total national income which was distributed as wages and salaries declined some between 1929 and 1933, and then recovered to a point where the net change was not material. "Other payments"—including dividends, interest, and so forth—would have shown a much greater decline than they did, had it not been for the use of surplus funds by corporations for these payments.

3. Hourly earnings in relation to commodity prices increased. While those unemployed or partially employed have suffered severely during the depression, the position of the regularly employed has been an improving one.

4. The farmer found that on the downswing the prices he received fell much more rapidly than the prices he had

to pay for the products he purchased, but during the upswing there has been a marked return to former relationships.

5. The Federal debt of the United States has shown an enormous increase throughout the entire course of the depression and particularly since the recovery movement began.

> The effect of this situation on taxation will be interesting to watch. If the Federal budget were to be balanced at a level of approximately $6,000,-000 of expenditures, with state and local expenditures remaining at their present level, then 20 per cent of the present national income would be absorbed in taxation for governmental purposes. If the national income were to rise to $70,000,000,000 and the Federal budget were to be balanced at the level of $7,000,000,000, about 19 per cent of the national income would be required for tax purposes.

I have now given you a very hasty and, therefore, inadequate review of the maladjustments which converged to create the depression and of the extent of the depression's impact on the world at large and on the United States in particular. This review has not at all done justice to many parts of the study's findings, but for a more adequate treatment I shall have to refer you to the study.

I must now make an effort to clarify the recovery problem in the United States, as it presents itself today. This I can best do through a recapitulation of significant trends and developments of the past four years. Many of the changes that have occurred may be regarded as constituting favorable factors in the present situation, while others may be set down as unfavorable.

Among the favorable factors in the present situation—factors which indicate that our present recovery may continue on a sound basis—are these:

1. There is available an abundance of loanable funds at low rates of interest.

> This condition is an important essential for possible business expansion. The danger against which we must guard is the use of these abundant funds, available at low rates, in such a way that would stimulate speculative activity.

2. In the course of the last three years, the burden of private indebtedness has been materially reduced.

As a result of the substantially higher level of prices, refunding at lower rates of interest, the replacement of bonds by stocks, financial reorganization and scaling down of mortgages, the shifting of debt from private to governmental hands, and a reduction in interest rate by government lending agencies, the burden of private debt has been appreciably lightened in the past few years. This is a factor that is favorable to sustained recovery.

3. The trend with respect to wage and price relationships has been unusually satisfactory.

Since the end of 1933 wage rates have gradually increased, while the prices of manufactured goods have remained at a practically stationary level. The purchasing power of the labor population has thus been steadily expanded. Increasing efficiency of production and a fuller utilization of capacity has made it possible for wage rates to advance relatively to prices and at the same time for profits to increase satisfactorily.

4. The balance between agriculture and industry has been materially improved.

Normal recovery from the extreme depths of depression, dollar devaluation, and weather conditions have combined with the government program to restrict agricultural production and thus raise prices which have put the farmer in a more advantageous position than he was prior to the depression.

5. Uncertainty with respect to monetary and banking policies has, in large part, disappeared.

The fear of depositors and investors with reference to the security of their savings has been largely alleviated, and the advances of recovery have short-circuited the political importance of pressure groups which advocated money panaceas. For three years the Administration itself has followed a policy of monetary stabilization and has taken a definite stand in favor of international stabilization, to be achieved as soon as conditions in general are propitious.

6. In the field of commercial policy, developments have been laying foundations for the expansion of foreign trade.

The trade agreements being consummated under the leadership of the United States Government are eliminating economic restrictions and barriers and are thus clearing the way for a renewed expansion of international trade.

7. The enormous accumulated deficiency of production should serve as a powerful stimulus to further expansion.

The backlog of requirements in the field of durable goods is so great that we do not need to wait on the development of any new industries to lead the way forward. The mere process of making good deferred maintenance and expanding production sufficiently to provide an increased population with the usual types of consumption goods would tax the nation's productive energies for some years. The opportunity for a great expansion along clearly defined and established lines has never been greater than it is today. Indeed, the impetus from this direction is largely responsible for the substantial increase of business activity during the past year.

8. The confusion with respect to government policies has been, in a measure, reduced.

The early part of the New Deal program was heavily charged with inconsistencies within itself— as, for example, between the objectives of the N.R.A. and the A.A.A. Lately many of these inconsistencies have been eliminated.

It will be agreed, I think, that the foregoing is rather a substantial list of favorable factors, but before optimism mounts too high, we must look with equal frankness at the factors in the present situation which are unfavorable. On this darker side of the picture, interest centers not so much on the number of the unfavorable factors as upon the vast potential significance of some of them. Indeed, any one of several possible trends or developments might completely change the whole economic outlook. The unfavorable factors are these:

1. It remains a problem of major difficulty to maintain fiscal stability.

The study's analysis shows that while the early balancing of the Federal budget is possible, such a consummation will require resolute action in curtailing wasteful and unnecessary Federal expenditures. If fiscal stability is not achieved, the resulting financial and monetary disorganization and price inflation would, in due course, completely disturb the process of constructive economic expansion now under way.

2. There is some danger of an inflationary movement generating in the forces operating in the field of private enterprise.

We have a superabundance of bank reserves and investment funds which, unless we are careful, will make for speculative activity and create price inflation. Thus far, this danger has been held in check. The most direct pressure in the direction of higher prices is that exerted by factors relating to industrial costs and market conditions. Rapidly rising costs in a time of expanding and buoyant business activity lead to a rising spiral of prices, costs, and again prices. The abundance of credit which lenders are desirous of putting to work makes possible, facilitates, and encourages such a price inflation. At the present moment, the possibility of such an inflationary movement — which would have a temporarily stimulating effect but which would promote longer-run instability—is very real.

3. The recovery process may be endangered by emerging labor policies.

The most important of these policies is that pertaining to the reduction of working hours on the mistaken theory that we can thus raise standards of living. The sharp rise in costs unrelated to efficiency would be certain to result either in rapid rises in industrial prices, with profoundly disturbing effects on the operation of the economic system as a whole, or the immediate halting of business activity with a consequent increase in unemployment. Further, the struggle now going on within the ranks of labor over the conflicting theories of labor organization and the intensive efforts being made to strengthen the power of labor over industry constitute a possible serious menace to the continuance of business prosperity.

4. The recovery movement could be checked by ill-conceived industrial legislation.

Premature and inadequately considered legislation with respect to industrial practices, price policies, wages, hours of work, output, capital expansion, and so forth, may well cause endless confusion and give rise to a new period of uncertainty.

5. The international situation remains highly unstable.

In many foreign countries prosperity is being attained largely by expenditures on military programs. Such conditions do not directly raise standards of living or increase wealth-producing capacity. On the other hand, they increase the burdens of taxation and threaten financial stability. The threat of new wars not only forecasts the possibility of wealth destruction but also constitutes a barrier to the re-establishment of constructive international economic policies.

So much for the bright and dark sides of the present picture. Under these conditions, what can the United States do in the way of an integrated program to promote further recovery in this country and put it on as sound a basis as possible?

The underlying necessity to which every policy must be related is, of course, the reabsorption of the unemployed into productive activities. It is only through increased production that improved standards of living can be realized. Whatever merit production restriction programs may have possessed as a means of correcting any special cases of serious maladjustment in the depths of the depression and of stimulating the beginning of recovery, they have no regular place in the continuous process of economic progress. The expansion of real incomes depends upon the increase of productive activity; it cannot be derived from an artificial expansion of money incomes unaccompanied by increases in the output of goods and services.

The study, then, lists the following essential requirements for a program of further recovery:

1. The re-establishment of a balanced federal budget as a foundation on which to build enduring progress.

2. The continuance of the present policy of maintaining a fixed price of gold and the establishment, through international cooperation, of a system of stable foreign exchanges

3. The extension of the program of reciprocal trade agreements as the most practical means of reducing artificial barriers to commerce and reopening the channels of international trade.

4. The preservation of the generally favorable ratio of prices and wage rates, in the interest of progressively expanding the real purchasing power of workers and creating a demand for added production and employment—placing emphasis upon price reductions as a means of carrying the benefits of technological progress to all groups within the nation.

5. The maintenance, in general, of prevailing hours of labor as the only means of meeting the production requirements involved in restoring during the next few years the standards of living of the laboring masses and promoting the economic advancement of the nation as a whole.

6. The elimination of industrial practices and policies —private and public—which tend to restrict output or to prevent the increase of productive efficiency.

7. Shifting the emphasis in agricultural policy from restricted output and rising prices to the abundant furnishing of the supplies of raw material and foodstuffs required by gradually expanding markets.

It can be seen, therefore, that the economic situation today is one of delicate balance. That balance may be easily upset. We may move gradually forward along a broad front, achieving progressively higher levels of wellbeing; or we may suffer a reversal of current trends and enter upon a new period of recession.

One thing is sun-clear. The welfare of all groups is indissolubly linked in a common enterprise. The mutual welfare of all depends on our pulling together in a common program of increased production.

So much for an outline of the entire study in general terms. Several items in this study are worthy of special and more extended development. These items deal with fundamental issues which are of high importance to the American people today.

SOME FUNDAMENTAL ISSUES

There is universal agreement that the goal is progressively higher standards of living for the masses of the people. But there exists wide differences of view as to what is involved economically in raising the income of the nation. In order to provide a definite gauge of the production requirements involved, the Brookings Institution has made a detailed analysis of the extent to which production has been curtailed during the depression in major lines of activity and the expansion that would be required to restore former levels of output.

The production task now before the country may be stated as follows: First, to make good the actual deterioration of plant and equipment sustained during the depression; second, to increase productive capital in line with the growth of population; and, third, to expand the output of consumption goods in accordance with this growth of population. The Brookings Institution set it as its problem to determine how great an increase would be required to restore by 1941 a per capita level of production and consumption equal to that of 1929. The Brookings economists believed that if they could establish the magnitude of such requirements with a reasonable degree of accuracy they would have a factual foundation for gauging both employment requirements and the standards of working hours which should prevail.

Inasmuch as the curtailment of production has been greatest in the field of the durable goods the detailed analysis of the Brookings staff was concentrated on the production requirements there. The staff studied in turn the situation in the fields of housing; passenger automobiles; "other" consumers' durable goods; steam railroads; public utilities; industrial enterprises; agricultural plant and equipment; and public and semi-public construction. Each of these studies involved taking account of the restricted rate of production during the last seven years, the extent of deferred replacement and maintenance, and the requirements resulting from the growth of population. In other words, the study's approach was essentially of an engineering character. In endeavored to take an inventory of the existing situation in the durable goods industries and on this basis to project the production rquirements over the next five years if the population in 1941 is to be as well supplied with goods and services as

76

it was in the late twenties. In these various analyses a con-scious effort was made to avoid possible exaggeration by stressing minimum requirements. It is the firm belief of the Brookings Institution economists that whatever shortcom-ings may exist in the estimates for the separate categories of goods the aggregate figures may be taken as reasonable and conservative approximations.

The study's estimates indicate that it would be necessary to produce in the field of the durable goods at the rate of approximately 33 billion dollars annually from 1937 to 1941. This annual average may be compared with an actual produc-tion of about 21 billions in 1936 and an average production between 1925 and 1929 of about 25 billion dollars. In other words, to make good accumulated deficiencies and provide for needs of an expanding population we should have to produce in the field of durable goods during the next five years at a rate 60 per cent higher than the present rate, and one-third higher than the level attained in the boom period, 1925-29.

What would such an expansion of production over pres-ent levels mean in terms of employment? The answer is that it would require the full-time work of from 8 to 9 million additional laborers in the field of the durable goods alone. At the same time a considerable increase of output would also be necessary in the field of non-durable goods if we are to restore the 1929 per capita level of consumption. Hence the production requirements on the basis of present working hours are more than sufficient to absorb the entire volume of existing unemployment, which we estimate as the equiv-alent on a full-time basis of computation of about 9.5 mil-lion workers. The outright full-time unemployment of avail-able workers is materially less than this.

LIVING STANDARDS AND WORKING HOURS

This analysis furnishes the answer to one of the most important issues now before the American people, namely the necessary and desirable length of working hours. The large volume of unemployment which has persisted even during the recovery period has not unnaturally suggested to many peo-ple that a remedy must be sought in the form of shorter working hours. Indeed, as an outgrowth of the unemploy-ment situation there has recently been evolved a policy re-garded by its exponents as of vital significance to labor. It has been enunciated as a definite principle that working hours should be reduced at the present juncture sufficiently to absorb all the existing unemployment, and that henceforth they should be systematically reduced in proportion to further increases in productive efficiency. What would be the economic results of such a policy upon living standards, and what would be its bearing upon recovery?

The advocates of this principle are apparently quite unconscious of its implications from the standpoint of production. The confusion of mind arises from concentration of attention upon money income to the exclusion of everything else. What is seen is that if the working week is shortened sufficiently to absorb unemployment, but without any reduction in weekly wages per person, the total volume of money flowing to the laboring population would be increased. What is not seen is that the expenditure of this increased money income in the markets would not bring forth any larger volume of goods and services—since the very process by which the increased volume of money income is made available prevents any increase in production. We would have on the one side an increasing flow of money into trade channels; but on the other side a flow of goods and services of unchanging magnitude. The certain outcome would be rising prices. By the very nature of the plan real income—in terms of goods and services—would have to remain stationary. Labor would merely obtain increased leisure.

It is also assumed that this plan assures, in any event, a more "equitable participation in the output of industry". Even the most "equitable" distribution of a fixed and limited national income of 60 billion dollars would not enable labor to obtain any significant increase in real wages. If the profits of 1936 had been completely diverted to employees the increase accruing to each working-class family would be less than $150. It is, moreover, by no means certain that the plan would lead to an increase in wages at the expense of profits. The rise in prices might leave profits much the same as before.

The adoption of this plan as a means of absorbing present unemployment would, however, undoubtedly lead to a different distribution of real income among the laboring groups themselves. Those who would secure employment as a result of the scheme would, of course, receive an increase in money income and in real purchasing power. On the other hand, those who now have jobs would find their real purchasing power reduced as a result of rising prices. Putting the matter more directly, since a larger number of workers would have claims against an unchanging volume of production, the share going to labor now employed would inevitably be reduced. The salaried and fixed income groups, together with the 30 million people constituting the agricultural population, would likewise be adversely affected.

Because of the sharp increases in costs that would be entailed, legislation requiring a universal shortening of the working week would be certain to halt the present recovery movement and precipitate a new period of reaction. The interests of labor, quite as much as those of the employer demand that hours of labor be adjusted in the light of production and consumption requirements rather than for the purpose of absorbing unemployment.

It is sometimes alleged that the real objective of the short work week is not so much to reduce actual working hours as to place labor in a position to exact extra pay for overtime, computed on a shorter standard week. Hence, it is argued that the shorter work week would not necessarily mean a smaller volume of work performed, though it would mean larger money wages. It is obviously true that a 30-hour regular week plus ten hours of overtime would actually be the equivalent of 40 hours of work. But it does not follow that this would increase the standard of living of labor in general. This is because no increase in efficiency would result from the process. The increase in wage costs would promptly lead to an effort to recoup the added outlays through advancing prices. It may be recalled that this is precisely what occurred under the NRA program of forcing shorter hours with a view to increasing wage rates. Here and there, in highly profitable enterprises, the increased costs might be absorbed without proportionate increases in prices; but in the great majority of cases this would result either in advancing prices or crippled operations and the discharge of labor. In short, the further reduction of working hours would prevent the rise in standards of living which are so essential to the welfare of our people.

If the principle of reducing hours in proportion to increases in productive efficiency had been in operation between 1900 and 1929 it would have meant that all of the gains resulting from the increase in productive efficiency would have had to be realized in the form of greater leisure—none in the form of higher standards of living. If such a plan were to be put into operation now with a view to absorbing existing unemployment, it would mean that the volume of national production would be frozen at its present low level—concretely, at about $470 per capita. If the principle of reducing working hours in the future in direct proportion to increasing efficiency were adopted and enforced there could henceforth be no increase in production per worker or in living standards.

WAGES AND PRICES IN RELATION TO RE-EMPLOYMENT

The study turns now from production requirements to a consideration of private business policies in relation to further recovery. The expansion of production programs depends primarily upon the growth of demand for the products of industry, and this in turn roots back in the purchasing power of the masses. Thus attention must be centered upon wage and price relationships.

It should be noted first that during a period of business recovery there are two ways in which the buying power of industrial workers may be increased. The first and most obvious is through the mere expansion of employment that has occurred.

The second means of enlarging the purchasing power of the workers is through increasing wage rates relatively to prices, or decreasing prices relatively to wage rates. This process differs from the former in that it may operate both during a period of recovery and permanently. Indeed, once the slack in employment has been completely taken up, the increase in the ratio of wage rates to prices is the only means by which standards of living may be further increased. This conception is so important to an understanding of the requirements for sustained prosperity and progress that it must be given emphasis before we continue the analysis of its relation to the recovery movement.

In a pecuniary society—in which incomes are received in the form of money and disbursed for goods selling on a money price basis—the process of raising the standard of living of wage earners necessarily involves increasing the spread between wage rates and prices. That is, a wage earner can increase the volume of his purchases from year to year only if wage rates are increased relatively to the prices of the commodities which he buys. If he gets more dollars and prices remain unchanged, his purchasing power is expanded. If he gets the same number of dollars and prices decline, his purchasing power is expanded. It cannot be expanded, however, unless the spread between wages and prices is increased.

A second principle—too often forgotten—must also be emphasized. It is that an increasing spread between wage rates and prices depends fundamentally upon increasing the efficiency of production. Only inconsequential increases in wages can, as we have seen, be achieved by trenching upon profits. The primary requirement for an improvement in the wage-price ratio is increased productive output through the acceleration of technical advances, improved management, increased labor efficiency, and so forth. Any practices or policies that tend to work in this direction are economically sound; and any that work in the opposite direction are economically unsound.

Attention has been called earlier in this discussion to the fact that the spread between wage rates and prices during the course of the present recovery movement has increased. During the early months of the recovery period, wage rates were sharply increased as a result of the code agreements. These advances were made with a view to increasing purchasing power and were not directly related to efficiency. Although prices of manufactured goods advanced even more quickly than wage rates, they did not on the whole rise to quite the same extent. Since the end of 1933 wage rates have continued to increase at a moderate pace; but the prices of manufactured goods have meanwhile remained practically stationary. Indeed, the trend was slightly downward until the last quarter of 1936.

The theory has often been advanced that recovery requires an increase of prices relatively to wage rates—rather than the reverse. Underlying this line of reasoning is the assumption that an increase in prices is essential to the establishment of profit margins. The facts with reference to the present recovery movement conclusively refute the theory that the only means of re-establishing a profit margin is to increase prices faster than wage rates.

Two factors have made it possible to have higher wage rates relatively to prices and at the same time much larger profits. The first is the increase in productive efficiency that has been occurring in many lines of manufacturing activity, and a consequent decline in other costs than wage rates. The second is the reduction in unit costs which has accompanied increasing output; as the percentage of utilization of plant capacity arises, the overhead charges are distributed over an expanding volume of business.

In the present recovery period, especially since the end of 1933, we have thus had a double force operating to increase purchasing power among the masses. The absorption of additional workers has automatically increased the flow of funds to the working population; and at the same time those regularly employed have had an expanding purchasing power resulting from the increasing spread between wage rates and prices. Had prices risen faster than wage rates, the decreased real purchasing power of those already employed would have tended to offset the gains resulting from the reabsorption of those who had been out of work. Moreover, had prices been rising, other groups of consumers, with stationary money incomes, would have had declining purchasing power.

Profits which result from increasing efficiency and an expansion in the total volume of production are soundly based, while those arising out of price advances are not. Profits derived from rising prices tend to be offset by the shrinking purchasing power of those whose incomes from wages, salaries, or investments are not expanding proportionally. Rising prices may indeed stimulate an increase in production and bring on an industrial boom. But since the buoyant activity that results merely from rising prices is not accompanied by corresponding increases in the purchasing power of the masses, it is not self-sustaining.

The encouraging feature of the present recovery movement has been its failure—thus far—to generate a period of rapidly advancing prices. The purchasing power of the industrial working population has been expanding in proportion to the recovery of production. Similarly the stability of the prices of manufactured goods has contributed in a vital way to the rise in the real purchasing power of the farm population. It is not surprising, therefore, that we have witnessed no piling up of speculative inventories or other evidence of a growing disequilibrium between production and consumption.

Whether it will be possible to preserve this generally favorable ratio between wages and the prices of finished goods no one can foretell. Rising prices of important raw materials, increasing taxes, pressure for shorter hours, and higher wages—regardless of efficiency—are exerting a powerful influence in the direction of price advances. These are very real forces—perhaps irresistible. Moreover, the recent expansion of business activity has been creating a situation in which it appears more readily possible to advance prices without checking demand.

In any case, once an advance in prices is well under way the process tends to become cumulative—since the selling prices of commodities in the intermediate stages of production promptly appear as costs in succeeding stages. The customary spiral of rising prices, wages, costs, and again prices is the sure road to an inflationary boom. An increase in the volume of production would for a time no doubt be stimulated, and in any event large speculative gains would be realized. But on the other hand there would be a great increase in industrial unrest, resulting from the rising cost of living. Not the least significant result would be the changing ratio of industrial to agricultural prices and consequent renewed efforts to use the machinery of government to protect the relative position of the farmer.

The primary necessity at this particular juncture is to resist the pressures toward higher prices, just as far as possible, with a view to preserving and improving the existing favorable ratio of wage rates to prices. To the extent that the spread can be increased we shall be laying foundations for further solid growth; to the extent that it is narrowed, we shall be undermining the basis of sustained recovery.

As output continues to expand and efficiency to increase, prices should be reduced. Even under present conditions, it may be desirable in many instances to lower prices as a means of increasing demand and promoting a fuller utilization of productive capacity. The basic principle remains that price reductions, as a general policy, constitute the surest means of promoting continuous economic progress.

PRESIDENT: I feel, after hearing this very interesting paper, that there are a number of our members who would like to ask Mr. Gow some questions, and he has kindly consented to answer such questions as you may wish to ask. To open the discussion I would like to call on Professor Endsley.

PROF. L. E. ENDSLEY: I followed the talk very carefully and with a great deal of interest, and it was so well put that I do not know of any question I could ask that would bring it out any clearer.

I have thought for a good many months, from things that I read and from the evidence of my own experience, that the thirty-hour week will not produce all we want. I would think I was loafing very much if I only worked thirty hours a week. But I do think we have had a very fine description of what can be done by a thorough study of the problem. I think that any attempt to have a thirty-hour week is going to retard the living conditions of the middle and lower wage classes very materially in our growing population. I would not be surprised if in 1941—unless we have another depression—it would be impossible to increase your force from the labor supply of the United States.

PRESIDENT: May we hear from Mr. F. I. Snyder?

MR. F. I. SNYDER: It is generally recognized, I think, that the Brookings Institution is the foremost economic research authority in the country. When they have anything to say we all listen with a great deal of interest. I have done that tonight.

PRESIDENT: Mr. Lanahan, have you anything to add?

MR. FRANK J. LANAHAN: Mr. Chairman, Fellow Members, surely, we have enjoyed an economic treat. It is apparent our guest speaker tonight has given thorough study and careful analysis to the subject, for its presentation has been most scholarly. Vital in the lives of all of us are the facts reviewed by the speaker, as they involve pressing questions of the hour. Surely what we have heard is worthy of careful consideration by all who have been fortunate enough to be within hearing of Mr. Gow's intellectual discourse. All of us can look forward to the publication of the "Official Proceedings" with the expectancy of seeing there transcribed on its pages, everything that the speaker has covered this evening. Then can we all devote time to a more thorough absorbing of the points Mr. Gow so ably presented.

The rapt attention with which the address was received is a well deserved compliment to our guest. Deep thought so clearly expressed is a stimulus to each of us in turn to get a better understanding of these economic problems, for no matter what may be our position in life, that of employer or employee, enjoying affluence or on the verge of poverty, what has been covered tonight touches each of us vitally. It is well to bear in mind, as we weigh the pros and cons of Mr. Gow's discourse, that in America it is clearly demonstrated that it is only one generation from shirt-sleeves to shirt-sleeves; those who today may be enjoying luxury, may be found in the next generation working for those who but a few years ago were identified as "horny handed sons of toil". There is no limit or restrictions to the ambition and energy of any individual, that's one of the splendid things that's the product of our unique American development.

Mr. President, we have had an important economic subject understandingly presented and I believe we are indebted, unusually so, to Mr. Gow for his splendid paper tonight and if the rest of the audience feels that way about it, let an expression of thanks to the speaker of the evening be given by a rising vote—he certainly deserves this compliment.

PRESIDENT: Now, through the courtesy of Mr. F. I. Snyder, Vice President and General Manager of the Bessemer and Lake Erie Railroad Company, a voca-film, "All Aboard—We Are Going Places," will be presented. I suppose every person here, employee or friend of the railroads, is aware by this time that the American railways, under the leadership of the Association of American Railroads, have embarked on an intensive campaign to make America again "rail conscious".

Briefly, this campaign contemplates telling, through all appropriate means, the great story of railroad achievement, progress and enterprise. The ultimate goal is, of course, to secure a better public understanding and appreciation of what the railroads are, what they do and what they mean to the daily life on this Continent.

Those in charge of this work for the Association recognize that the Association, by itself, can accomplish very little; that the individual railroads, with their widespread local contacts, can accomplish vastly more; and that the individual railroad employees, in all lines of work, can accomplish most of all.

To provide railroad employees with interesting facts about the railroad industry, which they can transmit to their friends, neighbors and those with whom they do business, the Association has produced—for showing to railway employees—a "slide-film-talkee" which dramatizes the history, romance, and the amazing progress of the American Railways. It also highlights important features of the new public relations campaign, and shows how railway employees can assist in making this campaign a success.

As the story of the railways is of vital importance to all of us, I believe you will enjoy seeing this film.

(Here a most interesting presentation, both vocal and visual, was given of the history and development of the American railroads.)

PRESIDENT: I think you will all agree with me that what we have just seen provides much food for thought. The facts presented are just a few of the thousands which could be cited as concrete evidence of the railways' amazing efficiency and progressiveness.

Our job, the jobs of all of us who are interested in the railroads, is to become familiar with these facts; to realize that the things which perhaps are an old story to us may be news to others; and to take advantage of every proper opportunity to supply an interested public with the information that will give it a better understanding and appreciation of the day-by-day achievements of the railroads.

It is not expected, of course, that all of the facts presented in this film will be remembered indefinitely. With that in mind, there has been prepared a little booklet which contains essentially the same story and pictures. Copies will be available after the meeting for those who care to have them.

MR. HENRY F. GILG: Mr. President, I have lived through the era of development of railroads from the time railroad cars had rubber balls on the bolsters for cushions, and the appearance about 1870 or 1871 of steel springs to supplant them. The growth has been so great in my lifetime that I marvel at the progress which has been made in spite of all opposition towards railroads, and their being prevented from making money.

When I was night yard clerk on a railroad in my youth, the standard of capacity of the freight car was 24,000 lbs. During my engagement, the capacity was increased to 30,000 lbs. and eventually to 40,000 lbs. Since then I have seen cars with capacities up to 75,000 lbs.

The locomotives I had to handle had a capacity of 200 tons, while today on the same road there are trains of 6,000 to 7,000 tons.

Even railroad men think that the all-metal car came within the past generation. I saw all-metal passenger cars as early as 1869. They were made of wrought iron plates. While working as night yard clerk, I forwarded frequently all-metal powder cars which belonged to the Lake Shore & Michigan Southern Railroad.

The steel springs which were introduced about 1870 were made by Aaron French in a blacksmith shop opposite the Union (now Pennsylvania) Station on Liberty Avenue between Eleventh and Twelfth Streets. Later he built a large plant at Twenty-first and Liberty and then one at Twentieth and Liberty. I worked in the general office of the company, A. French Spring Company, Limited, for six years from January 26th, 1885. This kept me in touch with the railroads and gave me many opportunities of witnessing the progress of the railroads all over the country.

PRESIDENT: Is there anything further before we adjourn? If not we will stand adjourned. The usual lunch will be served at either end of the room.

J. D. CONWAY, Secretary.

In Memoriam

EDWARD M. SEXTON
Joined Club May 24, 1934
Died February 15, 1937

TIMOTHY E. DOYLE
Joined Club December 19, 1929
Died February 16, 1937

DON'T BE "CRANKY"

Be Wise!

for Quick Starts use Pennzip and Pennzoil

Ole Man Winter holds all the trumps against you when you neglect to keep you car in shape for cold weather driving. You can tell he's won a trick when your battery hardly turns the motor over—or when you have to push or tug on the gear shift lever. But his most costly toll of all is the wear that takes place in your motor—**the wear** you can't see or feel.

Wise motorists play two cards that win trouble-free motoring all winter long. They fill their crankcases with Pennzoil motor oil and their tanks with Pennzip gasoline. These perfect partners for winter driving start motors quickly—keep down wear and repairs—and give you better mileage. Get both at your nearest Pennzip dealer.

THE PENNZOIL COMPANY

Chamber of Commerce Bldg. . . . . Pittsburgh, Pa.

OFFICIAL PROCEEDINGS
RAILWAY CLUB OF PITTSBURGH

$1.00 Per Year   25¢ Per Copy

Vol. XXXVI.   MARCH 25, 1937.   No. 5.

STEEL CASTINGS IN HIGH SPEED RAILROADING
By WILLIAM M. SHEEHAN, Manager, Eastern District Sales,
General Steel Castings Corporation, Eddystone, Pa.

The proof of your interest

in the Club can be

enhanced

by securing a

NEW MEMBER.

Application form is available

in this magazine. Look

it up and

"ACT NOW."

OFFICIAL PROCEEDINGS

OF

The Railway Club of Pittsburgh

Organized October 18, 1901

Published monthly, except June, July and August, by the Railway Club of
Pittsburgh, J. D. Conway, Secretary, 515 Grandview Ave., Pittsburgh, Pa..

Entered as Second Class Matter February 6, 1915, at the Postoffice at Pittsburgh,
under the Act of March 3, 1879.

No 5
Vol. XXXVI.   **Pittsburgh, Pa., Mar. 25, 1937** $1.00 Per Year
25c Per Copy

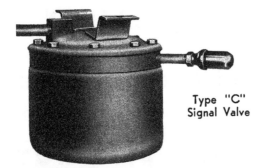

KOPPERS SERVES the RAILROADS

KOPPERS PRODUCTS AND WHERE THEY APPLY IN THE RAILROAD FIELD	TREATED TIMBER, TIES, POSTS, ETC.	ROOFING MATERIALS	PISTON RINGS	COAL	WATER-PROOFING MATERIALS	BITUMINOUS PAINTS	TARMAC ROAD MATERIALS	FAST'S COUPLINGS	CREOSOTE	CYLINDER AND VALVE PACKING	WEED KILLERS	INSECTI-CIDES AND DISINFEC-TANTS	PLATE WORK	CAR FERRIES, RAILROAD BARGES, ETC.
ROADBEDS	A								D		F			
LOCOMOTIVES			C	B		D				C				
STATIONS	A	D	C	B	D	D			D			F		
SHOPS	A	D		B	D	D		E	D			F	E&G	
BRIDGES	A				D	D	D		D				E&G	
TUNNELS	A				D	D	D						E&G	
DRIVEWAYS	A				D	D	D				F			
POWER HOUSES	A	D	C	B	D	D		E	D	C			E&G	
STRUCTURAL	A	D			D	D			D				E&G	
GRADE CROSSINGS	A						D							
CATTLE PENS	A	D			D	D			D			F		
RAILROAD MARINE OPERATIONS	A	D	C	B	D	D			D	C		F	E&G	H

A—The Wood Preserving Corporation, Pittsburgh, Pa.   B—The Koppers Coal Company, Pittsburgh, Pa.   C—American Hammered Piston Ring Division, Baltimore, Md.   D—Tar and Chemical Division, Pittsburgh, Pa.   E—Bartlett Hayward Division, Baltimore, Md.   F—The White Tar Company of New Jersey, Inc.   G—Western Gas Division, Fort Wayne, Ind.   H—The Maryland Drydock Company, Baltimore, Md.

INDEX—ADVERTISERS.

NOTE—This form to be filled out in full by typewriter or printed and mailed to J. D. Conway, Secretary, 1941 Oliver Building, Pittsburgh, Pa. Membership fee, including dues, is $3.00 for each fiscal year or part thereof, except those proposed in September or October. Those proposed in these months will be credited upon payment for the following fiscal year. Dues are payable in advance.

The fiscal year ends with the month of October.

The Railway Club of Pittsburgh:

....19........

Gentlemen:

Will you kindly consider my Application for Membership in your Club at the next meeting:

Name..

Title..

Company..

My Address..

....

Recommended by..

OFFICIAL PROCEEDINGS

OF

The Railway Club of Pittsburgh

Organized October 18, 1901

| Vol.   I.
No. XXXVI | Pittsburgh, Pa., Mar. 25, 1937 | $1.00 Per Year
25c Per Copy |

OFFICERS FOR 1936-1937

President

E. A. RAUSCHART,

Mechanical Superintendent, Montour Railroad Co., Coraopolis, Pa.

First Vice President	Secretary
G. M. SIXSMITH,	J. D. CONWAY,
Supt., Pennsylvania Railroad,	Railway Supply Manufacturers' Association,
Pittsburgh, Pa.	Pittsburgh, Pa.

Second Vice President	Treasurer
J. D. BELTZ,	E. J. SEARLES,
Supt., B. & O. R. R. Co.,	Manager, Schaefer Equipment Co.,
Pittsburgh, Pa.	Pittsburgh, Pa.

EXECUTIVE COMMITTEE:

FRANK J. LANAHAN, Chairman, President, Fort Pitt Malleable Iron Co., Pittsburgh, Pa
A. STUCKI, Engineer, A. Stucki Company, Pittsburgh, Pa
G W. WILDIN, Consulting Engineer, Westinghouse Air Brake Company, Pittsburgh, Pa
W. S. McABEE, Vice Pres. & General Supt., Union Railroad Co., East Pittsburgh, Pa
E. W. SMITH, Vice President, Pennsylvania Railroad, Pittsburgh, Pa.
LOUIS E. ENDSLEY, Consulting Engineer, 516 East End Avenue, Pittsburgh, Pa.
F. I. SNYDER, Vice President & General Manager, B. & L. E. R. R. Co., Pittsburgh, Pa
C. O. DAMBACH, General Manager, P. & W. Va. Ry. Co., Pittsburgh, Pa.
R. H. FLINN, General Superintendent, Pennsylvania Railroad, Pittsburgh, Pa.
R. P. FORSBERG, Chief Engineer, P. & L. E. R. R. Co., Pittsburgh, Pa.

SUBJECT COMMITTEE:

D. W. McGEORGE, Chairman, Secretary, Edgewater Steel Company, Pittsburgh, Pa
G. H. BURNETTE, Asst Chief Engineer, P. & L. E. R. R. Co, Pittsburgh, Pa

RECEPTION AND ATTENDANCE COMMITTEE:

J. W. JOHNSON, Chairman, Superintendent, Railway Express Agency, Pittsburgh, Pa.
W. C. BUREL, Vice Chairman, Master Mechanic, Western Allegheny Railroad, Kaylor, Pa
J. W. BOYD, Superintendent, Monongahela Railway Company, Brownsville, Pa.
THOMAS E. CANNON, General Supt. Equipment, P. & W. Va. Ry. Co., Pittsburgh, Pa
T. W. CARR, Superintendent Rolling Stock, P. & L. E. R. R. Co., McKees Rocks, Pa.
D. C. CARROLL, Assistant Agent, Pennsylvania Railroad, Pittsburgh, Pa.
S. G. DOWN, Vice-President, Westinghouse Air Brake Company, Wilmerding, Pa.
HARRY C. GRAHAM, Pittsburgh Screw & Bolt Corporation, Pittsburgh, Pa.
J. W. SCHAD, Division Master Mechanic, B. & O. R. R. Co., Pittsburgh, Pa.
GEORGE S. WEST, Division Superintendent, Pennsylvania Railroad, Pittsburgh, Pa.
J. W. HOOVER, Asst. Chief of Transpn., Subsidiary Cos. U. S. Steel Corp., Pittsburgh, Pa
A. A. READ, Duquesne Slag Products Company, Pittsburgh, Pa.
C. P. SCHRECONGOST, Traffic Manager, Hillman Coal & Coke Company, Pittsburgh, Pa.
J. A. WARFEL, Special Representative, Air Reduction Sales Company, Pittsburgh, Pa.
J. C. SHINGLEDECKER, Supervisor of Service Stations, The Pennzoil Co., Pittsburgh, Pa.
J. C. DILWORTH, Manager Railroad Sales, Carnegie-Illinois Steel Corp., Pittsburgh, Pa

ENTERTAINMENT COMMITTEE:

J. PORTER GILLESPIE, Chairman, Asst. Gen. Supt., Lockhart Iron & Steel Co., Pgh., Pa.
FRANK E. WEIS, Vice Chairman, Transportation Clerk, Penna. R. R., Pittsburgh, Pa.
JAMES NAGEL, Superintendent Transportation, Montour Railroad, Coraopolis, Pa.
E. H. HOLMES, Sales Department, Fort Pitt Malleable Iron Co., Pittsburgh, Pa.
C. C. CLARK, Sales Manager, Central District, Pressed Steel Car Co., Pittsburgh, Pa.
A. I. KESSLER, Clearance Clerk, Pennsylvania Railroad, Pittsburgh, Pa.
T. F. SHERIDAN, Asst. to S.M.P. and S.R.S., P. & L. E. R. R. Co., McKees Rocks, Pa.

FINANCE COMMITTEE:

M. A. SMITH, Chairman, General Manager, P. & L. E. R. R. Co., Pittsburgh, Pa.
J. B. DIVEN, Superintendent Motive Power, Pennsylvania Railroad, Pittsburgh, Pa.
F. J. RYAN, District Representative, Detroit, Toledo & Ironton Railroad, Pittsburgh, Pa.
C. E. CATT, Division Accountant, B. & O. R. R. Co., Pittsburgh, Pa.
G. W. HONSBERGER, Transpn. Mgr., Westinghouse Electric & Mfg. Co., Pittsburgh, Pa.

ADVERTISING COMMITTEE:

H. H. HAUPT, Chairman, Gen. Supt., Motive Power, Pennsylvania Railroad, Pittsburgh, Pa.
KARL BERG, Superintendent Motive Power, P. & L. E. R. R. Co., McKees Rocks, Pa.
H. E. PASSMORE, Representative, The American Hammered Piston Ring Co., Pgh., Pa.

MEMBERSHIP COMMITTEE:

T. E. BRITT, Chairman, Div. Storekeeper, B. & O. R. R. Co., Glenwood Shops, Pgh., Pa.
C. M. WHEELER, Vice Chairman, Sales Engr., Union Switch & Signal Co., Swissvale, Pa.
F. H. EATON, Sales Engineer, American Car & Foundry Co., Pittsburgh, Pa.
C. W. GOTTSCHALK, Asst. Traffic Manager, Jones & Laughlin Steel Corp., Pgh., Pa.
LLOYD SUTHERLAND, General Storekeeper, P. & L. E. R. R. Co., McKees Rocks, Pa.
THOMAS R. FITZPATRICK, Freight Traffic Mgr., P. & L. E. R. R. Co., Pittsburgh, Pa.
P. W. HEPBURN, Sales Engineer, Gulf Refining Company, Pittsburgh, Pa.
W. B. MOIR, Chief Car Inspector, Pennsylvania Railroad, Pittsburgh, Pa.
C. W. TRUST, Assistant Traffic Manager, Carnegie-Illinois Steel Corp., Pittsburgh, Pa
WILLIAM R. GELLATLY, President, Superior Railway Products Corp., Pittsburgh, Pa.
R. S. BULL, Supt. Power & Inclines, Pittsburgh Railways Co., N. S., Pittsburgh, Pa.
A. F. COULTER, Master Car Builder, Union Railroad Co., East Pittsburgh, Pa.
T. R. DICKINSON, Purchasing Agent, B. & L. E. R. R. Co., Pittsburgh, Pa.
D. K. ORR, Road Master, Monongahela Railway Co., Brownsville, Pa.
W. F. AMBROSE, Master Mechanic, Aliquippa & Southern Railroad, Aliquippa, Pa
JOHN I. MULVEY, Traffic Manager, Hubbard & Company, Pittsburgh, Pa.

PAST PRESIDENTS:

*J. H. McCONNELL	October, 1901, to October, 1903
*L. H. TURNER	November, 1903, to October, 1905
*F. H. STARK	November, 1905, to October, 1907
*H. W. WATTS	November, 1907, to April, 1908
*D. J. REDDING	November, 1908, to October, 1910
*F. R. McFEATTERS	November, 1910, to October, 1912
*A. G. MITCHELL	November, 1912, to October, 1914
*F. M. McNULTY	November, 1914, to October, 1916
*J. G. CODE	November, 1916, to October, 1917
*D. M. HOWE	November, 1917, to October, 1918
*J. A. SPIELMAN	November, 1918, to October, 1919
H. H. MAXFIELD	November, 1919, to October, 1920
FRANK J. LANAHAN	November, 1920, to October, 1921
*SAMUEL LYNN	November, 1921, to October, 1922
*D. F. CRAWFORD	November, 1922, to October, 1923
*GEO. D. OGDEN	November, 1923, to October, 1924
A. STUCKI	November, 1924, to October, 1925
F. G. MINNICK	November, 1925, to October, 1926
G. W. WILDIN	November, 1926, to October, 1927
E. J. DEVANS	November, 1927, to October, 1928
W. S. McABEE	November, 1928, to October, 1929
E. W. SMITH	November, 1929, to October, 1930
LOUIS E. ENDSLEY	November, 1930, to October, 1931
*JOHN E. HUGHES	November, 1931, to October, 1932
F. I. SNYDER	November, 1932, to October, 1933
C. O. DAMBACH	November, 1933, to October, 1934
R. H. FLINN	November, 1934, to October, 1935
R. P. FORSBERG	November, 1935, to October, 1936

*—Deceased.

Meetings held fourth Thursday of each month except June, July and August.

PROCEEDINGS OF MEETING
MARCH 25, 1937

The meeting was called to order at eight o'clock, P. M., at the Fort Pitt Hotel, with President E. A. Rauschart in the chair.

Registered attendance, 185, as follows:

MEMBERS:

Ainsworth, John R.	Fair, J. M.
Ambrose, W. F.	Flinn, R. H.
Anderson, Burt T.	Frauenheim, Pierce H.
Babcock, F. H.	Furch, George J.
Baer, H. L.	Galbraith, James R.
Balph, M. Z.	Gelston, George A.
Balzer, C. E.	Gilg, Henry F.
Beltz, J. D.	Gillespie, J. Porter
Berg, Karl	Glaser, J. P.
Beswick, R. M.	Goda, P. H.
Black, C. R.	Goldstrom, G. E.
Bone, H. L.	Goodwin, A. E.
Burel, W. C.	Griest, E. E.
Campbell, J. A.	Groves, W. C.
Carey, C. D.	Haller, Nelson M.
Cavanaugh, T. J.	Hamilton, W. H.
Chalker, A. R.	Hansen, William C.
Chilcoat, H. E.	Haupt, H. H.
Christy, F. X.	Hayward, Carlton
Clark, C. C.	Hemma, Charles H.
Connelly, J. T.	Herpst, R. C.
Conway, J. D.	Hilstrom, A. V.
Courtney, Harry	Hodges, R. C.
Crawford, A. B.	Hoopes, R. E.
Cree, W. M.	Huston, F. T.
Crenner, J. A.	Hutchinson, G. C., Jr.
Cruikshank, J. C.	James, J. H.
Cudworth, H. D.	Johnson, Ira S.
Dalzell, W. E.	Kearfott, W. E.
Dambach, C. O.	Keck, L. M.
Davis, Charles S.	Keller, P. R.
Dean, E. E.	Kelly, L. J.
Dean, Robert W.	Kentlein, John
Dickson, K. B.	Koenig, Walter A.
Diven, J. B.	Lanahan, Frank J.
Downing, N. H.	Lincoln, R. B.
Eaton, Frederick H.	Loder, C. C.
Edwards, Walter	Loeffler, George O.
Emery, E.	Logan, J. W., Jr.
Endsley, Prof. Louis E.	Lowry, William F., Jr.

Lundeen, Carl J.
Maliphant, C. W.
Mann, Henry S.
Matchneer, W. W.
Maxwell, R. E.
Menk, C. W.
Misner, George W.
Mitchell, W. S.
Morgan, A. L.
Morgan, Homer C.
McCully, D. L.
McKinley, John
McNamee, W.
Nagel, James
Nash, R. L.
Nichols, Samuel A.
Noonan, Daniel
Paisley, F. R.
Palmer, E. A.
Pickard, S. B.
Purchard, Paul A.
Rauschart, E. A.
Redding, R. D.
Renshaw, W. B.
Roberts, E. L.
Robertson, A. S.
Rushneck, G. L.
Rutter, H. E.
Searles, E. J.
Severn, A. B.
Schadt, A. D.

Schako, E. J.
Sheehan, W. M.
Shellenbarger, H. M.
Sheridan, T. F.
Shuster, W. W.
Sixsmith, G. M.
Smith, Robert B.
Steiner, P. E.
Stoffregen, Louis E.
Stucki, A.
Sudell, D. W.
Sutherland, L.
Terkelsen, B.
Ternent, H. J.
Teskey, Dr. Walter J.
Thomas, Theo.
Trax, L. R.
Tryon, I. D.
Van Blarcom, W. C.
Van Woert, F. E.
Welton, Alvin A.
Wheeler, C. M.
Whitehead, C. P.
Wikander, O. R.
Williams, David L.
Wilson, James R.
Wilson, W. F.
Woodings, Robert T.
Yarnall, Jesse
Yohe, J. K., Jr.
Young, Paul S.

VISITORS:

Bell, Z. E.
Benner, Charles A.
Cawthorn, J. F., Jr.
Dankmyer, F. C.
Davis, William B.
Edsall, S. D.
Elliott, L. M.
Ford, J.
Gebhart, Otto
Gumz, Fred
Heaslett, R. C.
Herman, J. L.
Hicks, E. S., Jr.
Hoopes, Ralph
Howat, C. W.
Hutchinson, E. M.
Kemble, Thomas J.
Kennedy, Harry

Koch, C. S.
Lewis, S. B.
Lippert, Henry E.
Lockard, C. P.
Long, R. D.
Morin, Francis X., Sr.
Murphy, D. L.
McConnell, F. B.
McCormick, J. A.
Rabold, W. E.
Rau, William R., Jr.
Reagan, P. H.
Robinson, H. J.
Sheldon, Fred B.
Sixsmith, W. L.
Smith, Sion B.
Thripp, C. W.
Tomb, Howard L., Jr.

Trautman, W. E.   Wehner, A. J.
Wallace, W. S.   Wickerham, F. A.
Walther, George W.   Williams, S. L.
                    Winton, C. A.

Before the regular session was opened a fine program of instrumental music was presented by the Westinghouse Airbrake Band.

PRESIDENT RAUSCHART: You have just been listening to the Westinghouse Airbrake Company band, boys between the ages of fourteen and eighteen and all sons of employees of the Westinghouse Airbrake Company. They are not strangers to you for you have heard them over the radio frequently.

MR. G. M. SIXSMITH: As Mr. Rauschart has announced we have been delightfully entertained by the Westinghouse Band, furnished for our entertainment, through the courtesy of Mr. John B. Wright, Vice President of the Westinghouse Airbrake Company, and in order that we may show proper appreciation of that courtesy and the talent the band has displayed, I move a rising vote of thanks to Mr. Wright and the Westinghouse Airbrake Company, together with a generous round of applause.

The motion prevailed by unanimous rising vote and enthusiastic applause.

PRESIDENT: The meeting will come to order.

As all of us have signed the registration cards, we will dispense with the call of the roll.

The printed Proceedings of the last meeting have been in your hands for some days, and therefore unless there is objection, we will dispense with the reading of the minutes of the last meeting.

I will ask the Secretary to read the list of proposals for membership.

SECRETARY: Mr. President and Gentlemen: We have the following proposals for membership:

Bishop, D. B , Salesman, Dearborn Chemical Company, 3538 California Avenue, N. S , Pittsburgh, Pa. Recommended by J. A. Crenner.

Ewing, George S., Salesman. Sirger, Deane & Scribner, Inc., Royal York Apartments, Pittsburgh, Pa. Recommended by Harry Barney.

Gelston, George A., Yard Brakeman, Pennsylvania Railroad, 512 James Street, Turtle Creek, Pa. Recommended by J. G. McCrea.

Helsel, W. G., Manager of Works, Pullman-Standard Car Manufacturing Company, P. O. Box 627, Butler, Pa. Recommended by E. A. Rauschart.

Huber, C. G., Timekeeper, Bessemer & Lake Erie Railroad Company, 351 Main Street, Greenville, Pa. Recommended by W. M. Johnson.

Hunzeker, H. J., Salesman, James B Sipe & Company, 2500 Middletown Road, Pittsburgh, Pa. Recommended by E. A. Rauschart

Keiser, C. E., Purchasing Department, Pullman-Standard Car Manufacturing Company, Butler, Pa. Recommended by E. A. Rauschart.

Keller, P. R., Sales Representative, General Steel Castings Corporation, Eddystone, Pa Recommended by H. H. Haupt.

Koenig, Walter A., Yard Brakeman, Pennsylvania Railroad, 519 Second Street, Pitcairn, Pa. Recommended by Jesse Yarnall.

Little, W. R., Local Purchasing Agent, Pullman-Standard Car Manufacturing Company, Butler, Pa. Recommended by E. A. Rauschart.

Martin, George A., Jr., President, W. W. Lawrence & Company, Pittsburgh, Pa. Recommended by E. A. Rauschart.

Miller, L. P., Brakeman, Pennsylvania Railroad, 1140 Morrell Avenue, East McKeesport, Pa. Recommended by Jesse Yarnall.

Morneweck, W. L., Train Master, Bessemer & Lake Erie Railroad Company, Brown Apartments, Unity, Pa. Recommended by W. M. Johnson.

Reed, Earl W., Superintendent of Production, Pullman-Standard Car Manufacturing Company, Butler, Pa. Recommended by E. A. Rauschart.

Sheehan, William M., Manager Eastern District Sales, General Steel Castings Corporation, Eddystone, Pa. Recommended by W. B. Moir.

Swenk, Raymond, Chief Engineer Maintenance of Way, Pennsylvania Railroad, Pennsylvania Station, Pittsburgh, Pa. Recommended by J. M. Fair.

Van Krogh, F. F., Mechanical Engineer, Pullman-Standard Car Manufacturing Company, 405 Elm Street, Butler, Pa. Recommended by E. A. Rauschart.

Whitehead, Charles P., Manager of Sales, General Steel Castings Corporation, Eddystone, Pa. Recommended by J. D. Conway.

Young, Paul S., Investigator, Bessemer & Lake Erie Railroad Company, Downtown Y. M. C. A., Pittsburgh, Pa. Recommended by A. D. Schadt.

PRESIDENT: These names, having been approved by the Executive Committee in accordance with our By-Laws, the gentlemen are now Members of the Club.

Are there any announcements, Mr. Secretary?

SECRETARY: Since our last meeting we have received information of the death of two of our members, Leo Finegan, Eastern Sales Manager, Flannery Bolt Company, Pittsburgh, Pa., which occurred March 8, 1937, and D. F. Crawford, Consulting Engineer, Pittsburgh, Pa., who passed away on March 16, 1937.

PRESIDENT: An appropriate memorial minute will appear in the next issue of the Proceedings.

As Mr. Crawford was one of the charter members of the Club, and a Past President, it is appropriate that some special note should be made of his passing, and I will call upon Mr. Flinn for remarks.

MR. R. H. FLINN: As Mr. Conway has said, Mr. Crawford was one of the founders of this Club, on October 18, 1901, together with Mr. L. H. Turner, of the Pittsburgh and Lake Erie Railroad, and a number of others.

In 1917, if I recall correctly, he was made General Manager of the Pennsylvania Lines West, at Pittsburgh, and in 1919 he resigned to go into the manufacturing business, at that time taking charge of the Locomotive Stoker Company over on the North Side. ·

Until very recently he was actively interested and a regular attendant at the meetings of this Club, and its President in 1922 and 1923.

It was my privilege in my early days on the Pennsylvania Railroad to be associated with Mr. Crawford and I worked in his office when he was General Superintendent, Motive Power of the Pennsylvania Lines West. I can only say that no word of mine could add to Mr. Crawford's character and reputation as a leader and a railroad officer of efficiency and ability. He gained recognition and won a great many honors in the mechanical field. At one time he was President of the American Railway Master Mechanics Association, and the Master Carbuilders Association, now the Mechanical Division of the Association of American Railroads. He was a distinguished engineer.

I am very proud that this Club included in its membership a man like that. He was a man with many friends and I value most highly my association with him.

PRESIDENT: Thank you, Mr. Flinn.

Is there any other business to be presented at this time? If not we will proceed to the paper of the evening. It affords me great pleasure to present to you the speaker of th evening, Mr. William M. Sheehan, Manager, Eastern District Sales, General Steel Castings Corporation, Eddystone, Pa., who will address the Club upon the subject "Steel Castings in High Speed Railroading."

STEEL CASTINGS IN HIGH SPEED RAILROADING

By WILLIAM M. SHEEHAN, Manager, Eastern District Sales, General Steel Castings Corporation, Eddystone, Pa.

It is an honor to be invited to meet tonight with you here in the heart of the great steel industry. That branch to which I belong has no real differences with the manufacturers and fabricators of rolled steel. Each most decidedly has its place and, for at least 95% of steel uses, that place is clearly defined. Of course, in a narrow overlapping fringe comprising probably the other 5%, the products of the mill and the foundry could be substituted and adapted one for the other.

During periods of decreased business activity, when we are each hungry for work for our plants, there is an inclination to invade the others' business in this fringe, but with a return of normal conditions, real economy dictates the selection of material.

Periods, such as we have recently passed through, bring out the resourcefulness of all who deserve to survive. We have seen this exemplified in the development of special alloy high tensile rolled steels, the wide variety of uses for which have been of so much value in hastening general recovery.

The steel foundry-man too has been active. His product has been, through research and engineering effort, brought to a much higher degree of perfection. Though the surface has as yet hardly been scratched, I will attempt to touch on a few high spots in this activity.

Though time will allow no extensive resume, I would be happy to endeavor to answer any questions asked and to develop such discussion as the space of one evening would permit.

The subject chosen, "Steel Castings in High Speed Railroading," is a timely one.

The railroads are just emerging from a terrific depression with large accumulations of under-maintenance to be made up. They need many new locomotives and freight and passenger cars not only to accommodate increasing business but to meet the demands of the public for modern equipment and better service. Interstate Commerce Commissioner Eastman made a statement in Boston several weeks ago with which we will all agree, he said: " 'Old Man Railroad' is being rejuvenated. He has shaken off the signs of incipient senility and is proving that an industry, unlike an individual, can be born again."

You men who have been a part of this rejuvenation know that this job of railroading is a problem for all of us, whether we are railroad men or engaged in the manufacture of railroad equipment. To do effectively the best job, it is essential to consider as foremost always the interest of the passenger and shipper, for the railroad must continue to form the backbone of transportation.

For years the railroads enjoyed a practical monopoly of transportation, but this is no longer so. Automotive and aerial carriers have provided active competition made possible by highway and airway development. This was largely financed by public funds, without which aid, neither competitive service could be provided at anywhere near the present charges.

Despite the unfairness of this subsidized competition, we must realize that in some degree it will continue. The way to meet it, is by providing better service and equipment. Although railroad men have grown up with a monopoly, they have made wonderful strides in adapting themselves to this competitive situation. During the past four years the art of railroading has been truly reborn, and this has been a major factor in the return of general prosperity.

Regardless of our individual views on the present passenger fares, we will agree that they have nevertheless contributed to a greater volume of business, and this, coupled with shorter schedules, finer equipment, easier riding, noise reduction, air conditioning, etc., has brought back to the railroads a portion of the business previously taken by the automotive vehicles, both private and commercial. And for the shorter distances, the trains such as the "Mercury" of the New York Central have regained traffic from the Airways because of the greater comfort such trains provide. Coupled with this, is the fact that there is very little difference in time when measured between downtown points in such cities as Cleveland and Detroit. The railroads, too, have given much thought to making their accommodations exceedingly attractive so that the more modern trains are really clubs on wheels.

The evolution of high speeds in passenger service has been quite marked. The schedule of the fastest trains between New York and Chicago was set at twenty hours in 1902, later being reduced in 1905 to eighteen hours, from which, except for the interruption during Federal Control, it has been gradually brought down to sixteen and a half hours. It is fairly safe to predict that the schedule between these two major cities will be further shortened in the not too distant future.

The most striking recent changes in railroading and certainly the most highly publicized were the advent in 1934 of the Diesel powered articulated streamlined trains of the Union Pacific and the Burlington, the first built by Pullman and the second by the Budd Co. Other roads quickly followed suit, some with steam propulsion, others with Diesel, each with the objective of better, faster service, and with these shorter schedules have gone lower fares, more comfortable riding and travel luxuries enjoyed on no other land transport agency in the world.

Railroading is a highly fascinating vocation, and during the years of "empire building" the developments taking place stirred the imagination of the public. But for a period we seemed to be "resting on our oars" and an entire generation grew up in this country to whom the railroad was something entirely apart from their daily lives. And it was found that when people travelled by highway, they shipped their goods by truck. Since passenger travel has been made more attractive, there has been a noticeable increase in freight traffic which can undoubtedly be directly credited to this psychological factor. The public's present interest may be gauged by the fact that more free advertising has been recently given the improved railroad passenger facilities than probably in the entire previous railroad history.

Among the older common criticisms of railroad passenger travel was that it was dirty and noisy, that in summer with the windows open, one was covered with cinders and dust, and that it was difficult to converse or read in comfort because of the outside noise. Air conditioning by sealing the windows and keeping the doors closed, got rid of the dirt and also of much of the noise for it was found that closed car prevented most of the outside reverberations.

Much of the noise noticeable around the ends of passenger cars and which is usually attributed by the lay passenger to the truck and associated parts is really caused by couplers, buffers, draft gear, foot plate and diaphragms. A great deal of this has been eliminated by improvements in these various parts, in fact sound deadening and removal of noise creating conditions are very live subjects to the mechanical man.

In the study of noise elimination it was found that insulating sheets or other sound deadening elements could be applied between various parts of the truck and car body, and thus greatly cut down the sounds passing into the car, and many modern passenger trucks now embody these features. One improvement which has been made in recent high speed trucks is the application of brake cylinders directly to the truck frame. By thus attaching all of the brake foundation parts to the frame, one source of noise is entirely eliminated and a much smoother truck and brake action is assured.

A better track including heavier rails, more substantial ballast, closer track alignment and more perfect rail joints are factors which have an important effect on noise elimination. But track maintenance represents a considerable part of the operating budget, and it is therefore essential to design equipment to conserve this more expensive track from which heavier loads, higher speeds and greater traffic density already are exacting a high toll.

Damaged lading, in express, refrigerator, baggage and box cars as well as rough riding of all types of cars and tenders, comes as much from transverse shocks as from longitudinal and vertical forces. The attention given to draft gears, longitudinal cushioning devices and truck spring combinations, the latter to break up spring harmonics, evidences the recognized importance of neutralizing these two latter forces.

A railroad train in motion might be likened to a string or a chain being pulled along. It tends to remain in a straight line unless forcibly deflected therefrom. When passing through a curve or crossover, this deflection occurs when the contact of wheel flanges with rails adjusts the path of the train to the curve. Each car must be thus transversely moved by the effect of the force developed by the wheel flange and rail contact and through an arm equal in height to the vertical distance from this contact point to center of gravity of the car. The force required is multiplied and greatly augmented by the speed at which the train is moving, and high speeds during this operation impose most severe strains on rail and track as well as on truck and car body. The punishment the track receives becomes very great at certain times of the year due to the effect of weather and climatic conditions. The observations of many railroads are that there is a very definite relation between high speeds and heavy maintenance of way and equipment.

This punishment of rail and track, and truck and car body is much more severe if there is no transverse resiliency between the truck wheels and car body, i. e. if the truck bolster is restrained against lateral movement such as exists in the ordinary freight car. In a way, it would be similar to substituting solid blocks for the friction draft gears. The use of swing hangers, rollers, rockers or other such means for allowing controlled transverse movement, eases this lateral pressure on the rail and wheel flange, and greatly lengthens their lives and at the same time reduces the frictional resistance of the train. This controlled transverse movement need not be very great in extent anymore than the movement at each draft gear need be, but if some cushion transversely is not provided, the truck, car body and track will suffer.

It is estimated by a prominent Maintenance of Way engineer as a result of research and field determination that rail under traffic has both an outward and an inward movement. The inward movement amounts to between 40% and 45% of the outward movement. This study brought out the importance of relieving the forces produced by these movements.

In additional to the advantage cited, the effect of swing hanger action on a curve is to aid the elevated rail to overcome the outward movement of the car body produced by centrifugal force. It is impracticable to secure a rail elevation sufficient to overcome the effect of this force for generally current high speeds. In curving, the outer swing hanger moves outwardly and upwardly, the inner one outwardly and downwardly, causing the car body to incline toward the inside of curve until the car returns to tangent track.

Wheels too have to take a lot of punishment; they not only carry the vertical load and are subjected to cold rolling as a result, but also have to take all the effects of braking with resultant heating, shelling and such. To increase flange pressures and transverse rail thrusts seems a step in the wrong direction and contrary to the established trend for taking care of longitudinal and vertical forces. Rather should we reduce these transverse forces, for our so-called freight trains now operate at passenger-train speeds and the trend is continually toward still higher speeds.

A great deal of thought, time and money during the past four years has gone into the subject of design of trucks for very high speed passenger trains. The feeling that weight would not permit the use of a six-wheel truck, has confined the studies largely to a four-wheel type. Many different schemes have been tried and with varying success. But one point stands out through all of these tests, and that is the importance of getting sufficient spring movement. This has been emphasized in connection with a review of results obtained on the car of the "Mercury" on the New York Central. It was the desire of this railroad to utilize existing light weight car bodies and trucks, and to prove the adequacy of these trucks for the required service, some very extensive tests were conducted. As a result, specially alloy steel springs were developed with greater movement but same overall dimensions.

It is agreed that the riding of these "Mercury" cars is very good. The same satisfactory comments are made about the riding of the cars of the "Hiawatha" on the Milwaukee, the later Burlington's "Zephyrs" and the light weight cars recently built for the Santa Fe. It is interesting to observe that all of these cars are equipped with an orthodox type of cast steel one-piece 4-wheel truck, but with spring movement considerably greater in extent than was previously the practice.

It is generally conceded that a 6-wheel truck gives better riding results than a 4-wheel. This advantage is associated with the longer wheelbase and the fact that it gives a more perfect equalization between each of its six wheels than does the 4-wheel truck.

To secure perfect equalization longitudinally on a 4-wheel truck, the equalizer fulcrum should be placed central of the wheels. This, however, would not provide vertical stability as there would be a tendency due to weak equalizer springs for the truck frame to lean downward at one end or the other. To prevent this unstable effect, two sets of equalizer springs are provided on each side and spaced apart to insure stability and at the same time equalize the loads between the wheels.

On the 6-wheel truck, two equalizers are used on each side and the fulcrum correctly spaced one-third of the distance between outer and center wheels. This more perfect equalization thus removes from the 6-wheel truck considerable friction which cannot be gotten out of the 4-wheel truck without impairing its stability.

Transversely of the truck the bolsters on both wheel arrangements rest on bolster springs, which are in turn suspended from the truck frame by swing hangers. This provides not only a cushioned transverse equalization of the center plate load, but through the swing hangers a controlled lateral movement, which eases the travel of the car through a curve.

98

One of the most important factors in providing easier riding on a 6-wheel truck is the spring support at each of the four corners of the bolster. This allows not only the transverse equalization through the bolster, but due to spring resiliency also permits equalization between diagonally opposite corners of the truck. This combination of substantially perfect longitudinal equalization, cushioned transverse equalization, diagonal equalization and controlled transverse movement, coupled with ample spring range, offers the best mechanical riding arrangement so far developed.

The so-called triple bolster 4-wheel truck as used on the Union Pacific and Southern Pacific stream lined trains built by Pullman secures this diagonal equalization by providing coil springs at the four points of application of center plate load to the truck frame.

Another method of securing the same result is used in the so-called double bolster 4-wheel truck. This provides substantially the same bolster suspension as on the 6-wheel truck, giving the same transverse and diagonal equalization, coupled with the usual 4-wheel type of longitudinal equalization.

Some of you who attended the Century of Progress at Chicago may have noticed under the car "George M. Pullman," a special type of cast aluminum truck, which had this double bolster construction. The Monon have used trucks of this general type for many years and some coaches recently built by the South Australian Railways also followed the same general principles.

The reason for the general movement toward a 4-wheel truck in the last several years has been principally to save weight. But it may well be that we should consider a light weight 6-wheel truck, designed to obtain all of the advantages set forth, and which will also provide better braking at high speeds and less heating of the wheel tread from the brakes, all of great advantage on high speed trains.

Such a truck properly designed and utilizing the knowledge developed on 4-wheel trucks, would not weight a great deal more than the later 4-wheel types.

As there are so many of these various new designs of high speed passenger trucks in service, all of which are being followed closely by the railroads, there is as yet insufficient data on which to reach a conclusion as to the ultimate type which will prevail. It seems safe, however, to predict that when a type is determined upon, it will have a one-piece cast steel frame and bolster, and thus keep truck maintenance to the same low state that the cast steel trucks have provided during the past thirty years.

Nearly thirty years ago the railroads in various sections were experiencing an epidemic of tender derailments. The tender trucks then used were mostly of the four-wheel freight car type with truck restrained against lateral movement. Some few were equalized but the majority were not. No difficulties were being experienced with derailments of passenger cars, so a number of these roads naturally turned for a solution to the principles embodied in their passenger car trucks as a basis for new tender truck design.

At that time the eight thousand gallon tender was considered large so it was comparatively easy to develop a four-wheel tender truck to meet the conditions. This provided longitudinal equalization and controlled transverse movement by means of swing hangers of the same general type as on passenger car trucks. This new 4-wheel tender truck stopped the derailments and its use was rapidly extended.

But locomotives grew and tenders with them. Several years before the World War began, the Santa Fe, which ran through a bad water territory in the Southwest, decided to develop a twelve thousand gallon tender in order to permit longer runs without so often taking water. The management determined on a 6-wheel truck, and as the only type then in existence was the long wheel base bottom equalized passenger truck, this was utilized. The results obtained were very pleasing to the railroad, but as the overhang at each end was considerable and the clearances were restricted, it was decided to design a special short wheel base truck for this tender service.

The result was substantially in principle the 6-wheel tender truck so generally used today. The Santa Fe found that in addition to avoiding bad water stops, the larger tenders gave them important operating economies. This knowledge they shared with other roads which, while having good water conditions, were able to profit by the economies the larger tenders offered. Sizes of these larger tenders grew as road after road adopted them. These 6-wheel tender trucks which started with 5½x10" axles, now have 6½x12" and many 7"x14". The two pin equalizer arrangement orginally used for stability has given way to a roller top equalizer which, while sufficiently stable, is more sensitive and easier on the springs. The tops of wheel pieces have been opened to permit easier application, removal and inspection of truck springs. Truck center plates may now be cast integral and made of sufficient depth so that shims of proper thickness can be applied in the bowl when necessary to vary the tender heights. This truck also puts the brake shoes in the clear so that they can be easily inspected and renewed.

These tender trucks above journal boxes are spring supported, thus reducing unsprung weight to a minimum with resulting reduction in track stresses. The carrying of tender tank on controlled transversely movable elements reduces the tendency of tender to heel over, thus permitting higher train speeds on curves.

These very large capacity tenders operating at high speeds with swing motion trucks, have been singularly free from derailments and easy on track and rail. But though they save track maintenance, it is necessary to replace swing hanger pins and bushings regularly at shoppings. Although the fact that these parts wear is clear evidence that the trucks swing as was intended, it has been advocated by some that as swing hanger parts wear and require replacement, this feature should be omitted. Six-wheel tender trucks have been recently built without controlled transverse motion, and while they are lighter than the swing motion trucks and cost somewhat less, experience is proving that track and tender structure will have to take a more severe punishment and this will involve not only a much greater expense in track maintenance because of the absence of controlled transverse movement, but will eventually produce leads and cracks in the tank structure.

This controlled transverse motion is equally as important on tangent track as on curves, as this lateral freedom adjusts the truck wheels to the rails in passing through frogs and switches. The hazard of the split switch and the tendency of wheel flanges to climb frog points at turnouts and crossovers with their resulting derailments, is avoided. Nearly every accident of this kind is caused by trucks restricted against lateral movement and could be prevented by providing such movement.

As the "tail pull" on the tender is greater than that on any other car in the train, due to its position next to the locomotive, the lateral component at rail when curving is correspondingly increased. The center plate load is also much greater and the center of gravity higher. Therefore the importance of controlled transverse movement on tender trucks must be recognized. High track and rail maintenance are penalties for failing to consider this principle. On this account, the record has been examined and the reasons for using swing motion tender trucks reviewed.

There is at present in experimental operation on a high speed tender a new type of transverse motion control. It was recently examined at 50,000 miles and was in excellent condition. It utilizes the principle of a roller on an inclined plane and provides the same characteristics as the present swing hangers. It will be necessary to get more experience with it before extending its use, but as it promises to simplify greatly the maintenance of the truck parts, while at the same time protecting the track, reference is made to it as a probable further truck improvement.

Cast steel tender frames are so familiar to railway mechanical men as to need no introduction here. Since 1907 they have helped cut upkeep and are standard almost everywhere. They have assured the availability of tenders for the past thirty years despite the fact that water and coal capacities have nearly tripled.

The later cast steel one-piece water bottom tender frames with their rigidity and freedom from corrosion, and the strong non-weaving tank foundation which they provide have permitted lighter tank superstructure additional water capacity and rendered the tank almost maintenance free.

Water bottom tenders of same outer dimensions but with further increased capacity are now obtainable as result of using in combination a cast steel water bottom stoker trough furnished by the stoker manufacturer, which is permanently welded to the top of tender frame. This is a most decided improvement in stoker as well as tender construction and will greatly reduce the maintenance of the stoker equipment on tender. The former stoker trough compartment is eliminated and the capacity of the tender can, with the water bottom stoker trough, be increased about six hundred gallons as the space under the trough is used for water storage. A great many tenders on the New York Central, Lehigh Valley and Nickel Plate are equipped with this improvement.

All water bottom tender frames may now be made with integral center plates except in special cases where separate center plates are required. The weight of the water bottom tender has been steadily reduced as experience has shown the way to simplify and improve the design and still retain the high safety factor and low maintenance feature.

No discussion of high speed railroading would be complete without reference to electrified portions of steam roads. Practically every major electric locomotive project of the past twenty years has utilized cast steel foundations. The most recent, that of the Pennsylvania Railroad from New York to Washington uses for passenger work the G. G. 1 locomotive which has cut the running time between New York and Washington on the fastest train to three and one-half hours for the 225-mile run. This locomotive has one-piece cast steel driving and guiding trucks.

It is recognized by those familiar with the problem that the present day steam locomotive to meet existing and prospectively still higher speed requirements, must take advantage of every factor that will increase its speed, efficiency and availability. To secure this result, recourse is being made to high boiler pressures which permit smaller cylinders and lighter reciprocating parts, the latter contributing to lower dynamic augment at rail. And as it has been proven that locomotives equipped with one-piece cast steel beds, tender frames and guiding, trailer and tender trucks can make longer continuous runs without attention and secure a much higher monthly mileage, these also are being incorporated.

The use of the one-piece steam locomotive bed which now embodies integrally the component parts of the frame and cylinder structure, has since its introduction on the New York Central in 1924 been so extended that with very few exceptions it is now being applied on nearly all modern locomotives built not only in the United States and Canada, but also in Australia. The almost impossible task of permanently holding together with bolts the parts of the built-up locomotive frame, has been responsible for this transition.

The principal sort of maintenance on built-up locomotive frames is that caused by loose bolts between the two rail frames and the connecting and attaching parts, especially the front deck, air pump brackets, cylinders, engine truck center pin, guide bearer cross tie and motion work cross tie. Some of these bolts work so fast that the frame and cylinder, and the frame and cross tie bolts often have to be renewed one or more times between shoppings. It is a common thing to find that these bolts, which are usually about 1½″ diameter when new, grow in size in five to seven years through successive reamings and renewals to as much as 2¼″ diameter. As the initial spacing between bolts, especially at the various cylinder connections is usually made as small as possible in order to provide the greatest number of bolts in each connection, this reduction of approximately ¾″ in the bridge between bolt holes, is a serious matter and invites and eventually causes a crack across the bridge. In addition, it has been found that although the bolt body diameter may be increased with successive reamings, the room required for wrench clearance for turning the nuts necessitates adhering to the original thread and nut size, thus resulting in a bolt with two diameters. This aggravates the difficulty of keeping bolts tight as the larger bolt in combination with smaller nut has proved to be inadequate as the renewed bolts loosen in a progressively shorter period of time after each replacement.

Bolts stretch in service at the root of the thread and require constant inspection and tightening, which in turn reduces the availability of the equipment.

A recent survey of the comparative frame and cylinder maintenance costs, by a road having several lots of the same class of locomotive, showed that the first lot of fifty with built-up frames and two-piece cylinders had a great deal less availability than the latest type equipped with beds. The miles per month decreased with the age of the built-up framed locomotives, while the monthly mileage of the compared bed equipped power remained fairly constant. The first lot was about eight years old and the latest lot about six years, so the compared results were considered as reasonably representative. All of the bolt conditions previously mentioned were found to be present in these built-up frames and in addition a great many cross ties had been replaced and nearly all of them had been welded in one or more places. The point had also been reached on this lot of locomotives where cylinder replacements were necessary so it was deemed advisable and economically justifiable to begin a program of replacing these built-up frames and cylinders with one-piece beds, and this replacement has already begun. The decision was hastened by main frame failures which had followed the welding of cross ties and cylinders to the frames. The frames had broken adjacent to some of the welds from thermal

104

strains set up in the high carbon steel due to application of melting temperatures at points where it was impracticable to normalize.

The development of the one-piece steam locomotive bed was along no "royal road," for it must be recognized that it represented a long step forward in locomotive design and foundry practice, and much had to be learned, for the manufacturers traveled an hitherto unblazed trail. The rules governing frame and cylinder design heretofore used were largely empirical, and it was early found that they could not be applied to the one-piece bed. A new technique had to be developed not only in the art of molding and machining, but all previous ideas on locomotive casting design had to be either discarded or entirely revamped. It was inevitable that difficulties would be experienced and it is to the everlasting credit of the railroad mechanical officer that he wholeheartedly co-operated with the manufacturer in working out what he regarded as their joint problem.

Experience on several roads with the earlier designs of beds showed that weaknesses developed where calculated stresses seemed to be very low. Extensive tests and research brought about knowledge which resulted in the elimination of most of these earlier weaknesses. It was found during these tests that thermal strains produced by expansion and contraction of the steam in the cylinders and passages were responsible for most of the difficulties that had been experienced with these beds. These studies also demonstrated conclusively that the loose bolts and failures of the cylinders and other parts of the built-up frame construction could be directly traceable to the same source.

As a result of this research, ways and means were found by changes in design to relieve these stresses in the one-piece bed, and now even a slight service defect in the vicinity of the integral cylinders is a rare occurrence. The performance of these beds in service is closely followed as it is recognized that there is still much to be learned about locomotive design and operation in which the bed plays a fundamental part, all of which knowledge will be of inestimable value in increasing the reliability of the locomotive and its continuous availability for service.

Attempts have been made from time to time to improve the construction of the so-called bar or two-rail type main frame. The cast steel frame of this type has been brought to a high degree of efficiency, so much so that a frame failure now rarely occurs from direct stress; in fact the difficulties encountered with the built-up construction are those caused by loose bolts and inadequate sections at bolted connections. Exeprience clearly proves that only through co-ordination of all the members of the entire frame such as is obtained by a one-piece bed can the best results be secured.

No steam locomotive frame structure is subjected to harder usage than that of an articulated locomotive operating at high speeds. Especially is this true of the front unit which, unlike other steam locomotive frames, receives no supporting assistance from the boiler. This unit is really a driving truck. These front unit built-up frames have been a source of much higher maintenance expense than non-articulated boiler connected built-up frames. The Southern Pacific have had a number of locomotives built which incorporate the one-piece beds on front and back units. The Norfolk and Western have also utilized the same construction on several lots of articulated locomotives, as have several other roads.

The day of the slow drag locomotive is past. The present day requirement for speedy deliveries of goods and merchandise makes necessary sustained high speeds in freight service, these movements being in very many instances much faster than the same roads used for passenger trains only a few years ago. There are really no modern steam locomotives which are not high speed machines.

Many passenger locomotives built during the past couple of years have been streamlined, notably the "Hiawatha" type of the Milwaukee, built by American Locomotive Company, the "Daylight" locomotive of the Southern Pacific, built by Lima Locomotive Works, and the Hudson type of the New Haven, built by the Baldwin Locomotive Works. The freedom from bolts afforded by the one-piece cast steel beds and trucks. which were incorporated in each lot, permitted streamlining with a greater degree of assurance as the problem of foundation maintenance was thereby reduced to a minimum.

Much is being done to reduce the dynamic augment of the driving wheels at the rail. Lighter reciprocating and revolving parts have been introduced as well as cross balancing. While it was realized that this would reduce wear and tear on the machinery, the lower dynamic augment was considered of far greater importance to protect the rails and track and reduce the cost of maintenance of way. The necessity of having a higher degree of track perfection is going to get increasing attention from all railroad men in the future.

It may be of interest to observe that one mile of the main line four track railroad of either the New York Central or Pennsylvania costs approximately as much as one of the very latest types of modern steam locomotives.

Much attention has also been paid to the design of the driving wheel center. Almost from the inception of the steam locomotive, driving wheel centers have been of the solid individual spoke type, in general design an outgrowth of the old stage coach wheel. Originally they were made of cast iron but of later years of cast steel. The tendency of the spoked wheel center to flatten at the rim and to crown transversely, both of which contributed to low tire mileage, provided the incentive to obtain a better construction.

The increasing weights at rail and the higher speeds being demanded of modern locomotives, coupled the desire for a stronger wheel with the recognized importance of securing a lighter wheel. The Boxpok wheel center secures these required factors in combination. It presents a pleasing appearance, will hold its cylindrical contour, and due to its double plate construction, will prevent transverse crowning of the rim. This will permit a tighter tire and will give not only more tire mileage but a greater freedom from flat rim spots.

The box section principle of design is not only followed through the spokes but is also carried out at the rim and hub sections. The large openings between the box spokes permit access for inspection and lubrication. The transverse strength is also much greater than would be obtained with plain solid spokes, and the cross walls of the box section members give a higher degree of homogeneity that can be obtained with any other arrangement.

The Boxpok wheel center can be made much lighter than the ordinary solid spoked centers and it will allow, especially in the smaller diameters, a more perfect counter and cross balancing, thus greatly reducing the dynamic augment and the resultant wear and tear on track structure.

Locomotive speeds and tractive power are limited by the weights which can be placed on the rails by the driving wheels. Better balancing by contributing to lower dynamic augment at rail tends to raise these weight limits and correspondingly the speed and power of the locomotive.

There are now in service over 25,000 cast steel tender frames and more than 3,000 cast steel underframes for freight cars, these latter covering almost every type of car. The largest single order was for a lot of 1,500 flat cars built in 1934 by the Pennsylvania Railroad. The cast steel underframe makes the freight car embodying it a much stronger unit and almost indestructible even in a wreck. Many of these underframes are veterans of quite severe accidents in which other cars of conventional construction in the same wreck were badly damaged or destroyed.

For service involving high corrosive lading such as sulphur cars, their use is generally agreed to be essential as it is the only type of underframe which has been able to survive this severe punishment.

The use of steel castings in railroad service today is so general that no historical reference seems necessary. They have in nearly all railway vehicles superseded gray and malleable iron castings, and for almost all but uses requiring resistance to high dynamic stresses, such as main and side rods and axles, they have taken the place of forgings.

There has been considerable discussion as to the physical and chemical characteristics of various cast steels for different railway needs. It would seem logical to determine this question largely on the basis of the use to which the particular casting is to be put. It must always be borne in mind that every railway vehicle is subject to the hazards of wreck or other emergency conditions. It is important therefore that structures of the size of beds, tender frames, etc., be made of a material that will withstand much shock and at the same time be readily welded without the necessity of subsequent heat treatment if damaged in accidents. It is equally important that the casting be made of a material that will withstand deformation with the least amount of fracture, for often in wrecks portions are likely to be bent out of shape. And when this occurs it is essential that it can be readily straightened.

For this reason a low carbon steel similar to the A.S.T.M. specifications, Grade "A" was selected, and the results over long periods have been most satisfactory. As there are many machined surfaces on these large integral castings, heat treatment subsequent to their machining would warp them and impair their usefulness. On the other hand, by proper selection of welding rod and using accepted welding technique, damaged portions of these large low carbon steel castings can be repaired with the expectation of permanently successful results.

Conditions encountered in service with these large castings clearly indicate that it is wise both with lower carbon steels as well as alloys to sacrifice some degree of tensile strength in order to obtain toughness and weldability.

Experience over a great many years evidences that a properly designed steel casting of the minimum thickness which may be satisfactorily cast, will give excellent results if made of this low carbon shock resisting steel. There are of course uses such as driving wheel centers where, on account of special requirements such as withstanding axle and crank pin pressure fits, which require a harder steel. There are also cases where alloys can be economically introduced at a higher cost in order to obtain minimum weight and maximum strength, but these must be treated and considered as special individual cases.

PRESIDENT: After listening to this very instructive and informative paper I feel sure there are a number in the audience who will have some questions to ask or comments to make. And you will recall that in the early part of the paper Mr. Sheehan said that he would be glad to answer any questions you might wish to ask. I am therefore going to ask for volunteers.

MR. F. R. PAISLEY: I have enjoyed the paper very much from a Maintenance of Way standpoint, especially the part dealing with devices such as swing hangers, rockers and rollers, designed to reduce the vertical and horizontal forces acting on the rails. Our job is to provide as good riding track as possible, with the funds and forces at our command, and anything the mechanical men can do to provide such devices makes our job much easier. Reference was made to the relationship between swing hangers and lateral pressure on the rail on curves, and I would like to ask Mr. Sheehan to what extent, if any, the swing hangers are applied to freight cars?

MR. SHEEHAN: Up to the present time there have been no swing hanger trucks applied to freight cars. There has been some degree of transverse motion control by means of rollers, such as the Barber truck. Outside of freight cars the great majority of railroad high speed goods cars, such as refrigerators, milk cars, baggage cars, postal cars, and nearly all tenders—I would say probably 90 per cent of all tenders built in the past eighteen years have been equipped with swing motion trucks.

MR. J. B. DIVEN: Mr. Sheehan made a very interesting presentation of a very interesting subject. I believe it may be said that the development of the modern large locomotives has been the development of the large steel castings, and this I think Mr. Sheehan has shown. With the use of what we call large steel castings and steel tender bottoms, the largest tenders of that kind now have 21,000 gallons capacity and carry 63,000 lbs. of coal. They are about seventy feet long and they run in both freight and passenger service. That tender has gone 189 miles with one load.

I do not know that there is anything I can add. Seeing in the picture the box type wheel, I am reminded that that runs back a good while. That was used on some of the cast iron wheels, so we are getting back to first principles there.

Speaking of dynamic loading, the largest Atlantic type engines used in the Pennsylvania Railroad service showed some of the first radical reductions on that kind.

MR. R. H. FLINN: After the very excellent remarks that have been made in the discussion, I am not going to discuss the mechanical field that this paper has covered so completely. But he did speak in the early part of the paper of the rejuvenation of the railroads and of the industry being reborn. Well that is true. Among other things this has been brought about by meeting the public demand for speed. But that speed is a combination of two things, not only higher maximum speed but a higher average speed, which is a great deal harder to accomplish. There has been a larger percentage of increase in the average speed than in the maximum. That is because of the development of better track and better equipment, equipment being largely improved along the lines Mr. Sheehan has indicated, things that permit a better operation, an operation with less delays.

I had a conversation with one of our shippers the other day and we were discussing among other things the cast steel truck frames that we have to have on our freight car equipment by January 1, 1938. That has been brought about by the very poor results and high maintenance costs and dangerous conditions brought about by the higher speed of heavy equipment on the arch bar truck. If there is any further increase in the maximum speed of freight trains, one of the first things I would want is a cast steel side frame. And that has already been provided for by the Association of American Railroads.

With the development of high speed passenger service came these streamline trains and electrification. There may or may not be more effort devoted to the attainment of higher maximum speeds, but due to geographical or other limiting conditions, there will be more effort devoted to increasing the average speed. There is no doubt about the demand and the determination of the railroads to produce what is wanted.

MR. KARL BERG: Some remarks were made in the paper just read concerning improvement of locomotive equipment on the New York Central System. The Pittsburgh & Lake Erie being a part of this System, I believe it would be proper for me to say something with reference thereto. I firmly believe that all railroad men in this country, as well as a good many other countries, fully realize the great assistance they have been rendered in this respect through the General Steel Castings Corporation or as it was formerly called, the Commonwealth Steel Company. They have for a good many years patiently and effectively pointed the way to a better construction, also made great efforts in developing better means and methods for manufacturing.

Speaking of the locomotive tender, which is primarily a fuel-carrying unit, but must also be considered a link between the propelling locomotive and the train, and as such has to withstand a great many extraordinary strains, I can still recall that this unit caused us a great deal of trouble in the earlier days before the present tender construction was adopted. We then had the experience of a good many tender derailments, due, no doubt, to improper equalization, and we were sometimes at a loss to know how to overcome the trouble.

The General Steel Castings Corporation came to the rescue, the construction of tenders was changed, and in spite of the fact that these tenders are today much heavier, derailments due to the causes mentioned before are practically unknown.

We should also remember that a train in running over a water track-pan at a speed that not so many years ago was an ordinary passenger train speed, has the tender refilled in a few minutes in that manner, causing it to withstand great strains at that time without any serious results.

I have enjoyed the paper read, and as a railroad man, greatly appreciate the effects of the advancement that has been made in locomotive and car construction.

MR. A. STUCKI: Referring to tender trucks especially, I wish to mention two essential features, flexibility and lateral motion.

When years ago I was connected with an eastern railroad, I designed several tender trucks myself. In one case we employed gusset braces to keep the transoms and truck sides in position. They broke, and kept on breaking in spite of increasing them in size and strength several times. Finally we removed them altogether and found the trucks working nicely from then on, because they had the necessary freedom to adjust themselves diagonally.

Most of you remember the Fox truck. It was a beautiful piece of work, simple in design, but rigid. Tens of thousands of those trucks were put in service, but the rivets holding the transoms and wheel pieces together became loose always, because the whole structure was too stiff and the arch bar and the cast steel side frame truck survived.

On a southern road five hundred cars of a very heavy capacity were equipped with a cast steel design of truck, but on account of its rigidity it caused too many wrecks and had to be abandoned. Another more flexible design took its place.

I am confident that the various trucks mentioned by Mr. Sheehan are free from similar shortcomings.

Regarding the lateral motion device, be it swing link or other construction, patented or novel, accomplishing the same thing, it is claimed that by its use the track and truck upkeep was greatly reduced. However, considering the fact that the locomotive and the train were the same, it would seem that a single vehicle could not alone produce this noticeable improvement, unless other unmentioned influences would help in this.

Not any of these lateral motion devices reduces the centrifugal force, but simply delays its taking hold. When a tender strikes a curve the load swings outward, and being away up in the air with the resistance at the rail, the outer truck springs have to yield until this force is absorbed, hence there will be no shocks with or without any of these devices.

It is not the centrifugal force, anyhow, which derails a tender. At sharp curves, where it is small, the rail wear is a maximum, neither have I ever seen a tender tilted. What causes the derailments, in most of the cases, is a faulty working condition of the trucks. They should swivel freely and always carry some load on the leading wheel.

The first requirement is easily obtained, but the second is not. Since the body is rigid, not yielding as the passenger and most of the freight cars, it requires a good deal of spring motion and vertical clearance between truck and body to offset the elevation of the rail, as far as the distribution of the load is concerned.

An eastern road once had a regular epidemic of tender derailments on this account, and after analyzing the case I found six contributing conditions which invariably would result in derailments. This was published in the Railway Age Gazette of January 17, 1913.

I met Mr. Sheehan two days ago in New York, at which time he told me that he was to read a paper before our Club and give us something to think about. He certainly did, and great credit is due him.

MR. J. M. FAIR: I enjoyed very much the reading of this paper. Mr. Sheehan not only knows everything about trucks, but also appreciates the problem of the man who maintains the tracks over which they run. I have been particularly interested in his remarks on the lateral transverse thrust and his efforts to control it. As he states, this is even more important on straight track than on a curve since on a curve the flange of the outside wheel will hug the rail with some degree of uniformity.

We, in the Track Department, are attempting to take care of this transverse thrust by improvements along a number of lines. We have redesigned our joints and have been much interested in experiments conducted near Pittsburgh, on the Bessemer, where continuous rails have been laid welded, thus eliminating the action of the joint. While we are not sure what the solution will be of the problem of expansion and contraction, nevertheless it is a most interesting experiment. We are using a double shoulder tie plate to keep the rail in better line; the fastening of the rail to the tie has been improved; we are also getting better drainage and using a fuller ballast section. We are improving joints by welding and grinding.

We are removing 130 lb. rail and replacing with 131 lb. which, while approximately the same weight, has a moment of inertia of 89 against 72. In high speed tracks we are laying 152 lb. rail which has a moment of inertia of 130 lbs.

In this way we are working hand in hand with Mr. Sheehan toward better riding track at higher speeds and we realize that efficient design of trucks pays big dividends in track maintenance.

PRESIDENT: Mr. Sheehan, have you any comment to make or reply to anything that may have been brought out?

MR. SHEEHAN: I want to thank you very much for the splendid discussion. I hoped that we would get some discussion and I have been especially pleased that it took the form that it did, because it was constructive. It will help us all to do a better job of railroading, which after all is the thing to which we have dedicated our lives. And I want to thank you again for the privilege of being with you this evening.

PROF. L. E. ENDSLEY: Mr. President, I had the pleasure last week of spending several hours with Mr. Sheehan and he told me he was coming here. I have known him a great many years, and I want to say to you that he has been very modest, in that a great deal of this development of which he has explained to us tonight has been his own work. So I want to propose that a rising vote of thanks be extended to the speaker for his very excellent description and explanation of what is being done and can be done for our high speed trains in truck and frame design.

The motion was duly seconded and prevailed by unanimous vote.

PRESIDENT: Mr. Sheehan, we extend to you the thanks of the Club.

MR. SHEEHAN: I thank you.

PRESIDENT: If there is no further business, we will adjourn to the refreshment tables in the rear of the room.

J. D. CONWAY, Secretary.

In Memoriam

LEO FINEGAN
Joined Club April 29, 1921
Died March 8, 1937

D. F. CRAWFORD
Joined Club October 18, 1901
(Charter Member)
Died March 16, 1937

IT'S TIME TO CHANGE!

Be Wise . . . Use PENNZIP and PENNZOIL

Motoring in the spring has all the thrills but none of the spills or dangers of winter. It's zippy, zestful, healthy motoring, and it's safe and economical, too—that is—if you're driving with the perfect partners, Pennzip gasoline and Pennzoil motor oil.

Pennzip gives you full power because it burns cleanly and completely. It saves you money because added mileage, pep and pick-up are packed into every gallon. Pennzoil, with sludge-forming elements removed, cuts oil and gasoline consumption, and saves you on repair bills.

Get these perfect driving partners *today*—at your nearest Pennzip dealer.

THE PENNZOIL COMPANY

Chamber of Commerce Bldg.　　Pittsburgh, Penna.

OFFICIAL PROCEEDINGS
RAILWAY CLUB OF PITTSBURG
$1.00 Per Year   25¢ Per Copy

| Vol. XXXVI. | APRIL 22, 1937. | No. 6. |

RAILROAD ELECTRIFICATION

By MR. CHARLES KERR, JR., Railway Engineer, Westinghouse Electric & Manufacturing Company, East Pittsburgh, Pa.

The proof of your interest

in the Club can be

enhanced

by securing a

NEW MEMBER.

Application form is available

in this magazine. Look

it up and

"ACT NOW."

OFFICIAL PROCEEDINGS

OF

The Railway Club of Pittsburgh

Organized October 18, 1901

Published monthly, except June, July and August, by the Railway Club of
Pittsburgh, J. D. Conway, Secretary, 515 Grandview Ave., Pittsburgh, Pa..

Entered as Second Class Matter February 6, 1915, at the Postoffice at Pittsburgh,
under the Act of March 3, 1879.

No. 6. Vol. XXXVI.	Pittsburgh, Pa., Apr. 22, 1937	$1.00 Per Year 25c Per Copy

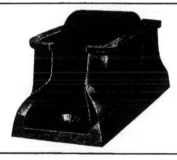

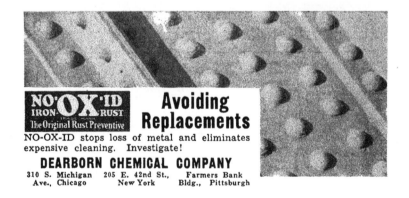

KOPPERS SERVES the RAILROADS

KOPPERS PRODUCTS AND WHERE THEY APPLY IN THE RAILROAD FIELD	TREATED TIMBER, TIES, POSTS, ETC.	ROOFING MATERIALS	PISTON RINGS	COAL	WATER-PROOFING MATERIALS	BITUMINOUS PAINTS	TARMAC ROAD MATERIALS	FAST'S COUPLINGS	CREOSOTE	CYLINDER AND VALVE PACKING	WEED KILLERS	INSECTICIDES AND DISINFECTANTS	PLATE WORK	CAR FERRIES, RAILROAD BARGES, ETC.
ROADBEDS	A								D		F			
LOCOMOTIVES			C	B		D			D	C				
STATIONS	A	D	C	B	D	D			D			F		
SHOPS	A	D	C	B	D	D		E	D			F	E&G	
BRIDGES	A	D			D	D	D		D				E&G	
TUNNELS	A	D			D	D	D		D				E&G	
DRIVEWAYS	A				D		D				F			
POWER HOUSES	A	D	C	B	D	D		E	D	C			E&G	
STRUCTURAL	A	D			D	D			D				E&G	
GRADE CROSSINGS	A						D							
CATTLE PENS	A	D			D	D			D			F		
RAILROAD MARINE OPERATIONS	A	D	C	B	D	D			D	C		F	E&G	H

A—The Wood Preserving Corporation, Pittsburgh, Pa. B—The Koppers Coal Company, Pittsburgh, Pa. C—American Hammered Piston Ring Division, Baltimore, Md. D—Tar and Chemical Division, Pittsburgh, Pa. E—Bartlett Hayward Division, Baltimore, Md. F—The White Tar Company of New Jersey, Inc. G—Western Gas Division, Fort Wayne, Ind. H—The Maryland Drydock Company, Baltimore, Md.

INDEX—ADVERTISERS.

NOTE—This form to be filled out in full by typewriter or printed and mailed to J. D. Conway, Secretary, 1941 Oliver Building, Pittsburgh, Pa. Membership fee, including dues, is $3.00 for each fiscal year or part thereof, except those proposed in September or October. Those proposed in these months will be credited upon payment for the following fiscal year. Dues are payable in advance.

The fiscal year ends with the month of October.

The Railway Club of Pittsburgh:

_____19____

Gentlemen:

Will you kindly consider my Application for Membership in your Club at the next meeting:

Name_____

Title_____

Company_____

My Address_____

_____

Recommended by_____ . _____ _____

OFFICIAL PROCEEDINGS

OF

The Railway Club of Pittsburgh

Organized October 18, 1901

No. 6.
Vol. XXXVI.
Pittsburgh, Pa., Apr. 22, 1937
$1.00 Per Year
25c Per Copy

OFFICERS FOR 1936-1937

President
E. A. RAUSCHART,
Mechanical Superintendent, Montour Railroad Co., Coraopolis, Pa.

First Vice President
G. M. SIXSMITH,
Supt., Pennsylvania Railroad,
Pittsburgh, Pa.

Secretary
J. D. CONWAY,
Railway Supply Manufacturers' Association,
Pittsburgh, Pa.

Second Vice President
J. D. BELTZ,
Supt., B. & O. R. R. Co.,
Pittsburgh, Pa.

Treasurer
E. J. SEARLES,
Manager, Schaefer Equipment Co.,
Pittsburgh, Pa.

EXECUTIVE COMMITTEE:

FRANK J. LANAHAN, Chairman, President, Fort Pitt Malleable Iron Co., Pittsburgh, Pa.
A. STUCKI, Engineer, A. Stucki Company, Pittsburgh, Pa.
G W. WILDIN, Consulting Engineer, Westinghouse Air Brake Company, Pittsburgh, Pa.
W. S. McABEE, Vice Pres. & General Supt., Union Railroad Co., East Pittsburgh, Pa
E. W. SMITH, Vice President, Pennsylvania Railroad, Pittsburgh, Pa.
LOUIS E. ENDSLEY, Consulting Engineer, 516 East End Avenue, Pittsburgh, Pa.
F. I. SNYDER, Vice President & General Manager, B. & L. E. R. R. Co., Pittsburgh, Pa.
C. O. DAMBACH, General Manager, P. & W. Va. Ry. Co., Pittsburgh, Pa.
R. H. FLINN, General Superintendent, Pennsylvania Railroad, Pittsburgh, Pa.
R. P. FORSBERG, Chief Engineer, P. & L. E. R. R. Co., Pittsburgh, Pa.

SUBJECT COMMITTEE:

D. W. McGEORGE, Chairman, Secretary, Edgewater Steel Company, Pittsburgh, Pa.
G. H. BURNETTE, Asst. Chief Engineer, P. & L. E. R. R. Co., Pittsburgh, Pa.

RECEPTION AND ATTENDANCE COMMITTEE:

J. W. JOHNSON, Chairman, Superintendent, Railway Express Agency, Pittsburgh, Pa.
W. C. BUREL, Vice Chairman, Master Mechanic, Western Allegheny Railroad, Kaylor, Pa
J. W. BOYD, Superintendent, Monongahela Railway Company, Brownsville, Pa.
THOMAS E. CANNON, General Supt. Equipment, P. & W. Va. Ry. Co., Pittsburgh, Pa.
T. W. CARR, Superintendent Rolling Stock, P. & L. E. R. R. Co., McKees Rocks, Pa.
D. C. CARROLL, Assistant Agent, Pennsylvania Railroad, Pittsburgh, Pa.
S. G. DOWN, Vice President, Westinghouse Air Brake Company, Wilmerding, Pa.
HARRY C. GRAHAM, Pittsburgh Screw & Bolt Corporation, Pittsburgh, Pa.
J. W. SCHAD, Division Master Mechanic, B. & O. R. R. Co., Pittsburgh, Pa.
GEORGE S. WEST, Division Superintendent, Pennsylvania Railroad, Pittsburgh, Pa.
J. W. HOOVER, Asst. Chief of Transpn., Subsidiary Cos. U. S. Steel Corp., Pittsburgh, Pa.
A. A. READ, Duquesne Slag Products Company, Pittsburgh, Pa.
C. P. SCHRECONGOST, Traffic Manager, Hillman Coal & Coke Company, Pittsburgh, Pa
J. A. WARFEL, Special Representative, Air Reduction Sales Company, Pittsburgh, Pa.
J. C. SHINGLEDECKER, Supervisor of Service Stations, The Pennzoil Co., Pittsburgh, Pa.
J. C. DILWORTH, Manager Railroad Sales, Carnegie-Illinois Steel Corp., Pittsburgh, Pa.

ENTERTAINMENT COMMITTEE:

J. PORTER GILLESPIE, Chairman, Asst. Gen. Supt., Lockhart Iron & Steel Co., Pgh., Pa
FRANK E. WEIS, Vice Chairman, Transportation Clerk, Penna. R. R., Pittsburgh, Pa.
JAMES NAGEL, Superintendent Transportation, Montour Railroad, Coraopolis, Pa.
E. H. HOLMES, Sales Department, Fort Pitt Malleable Iron Co., Pittsburgh, Pa.
C. C. CLARK, Sales Manager, Central District, Pressed Steel Car Co., Pittsburgh, Pa.
A. I. KESSLER, Clearance Clerk, Pennsylvania Railroad, Pittsburgh, Pa.
T. F. SHERIDAN, Asst. to S.M.P. and S.R.S., P. & L. E. R. R. Co., McKees Rocks, Pa.

FINANCE COMMITTEE:

M. A. SMITH, Chairman, General Manager, P. & L. E. R. R. Co., Pittsburgh, Pa.
J. B. DIVEN, Superintendent Motive Power, Pennsylvania Railroad, Pittsburgh, Pa.
F. J. RYAN, District Representative, Detroit, Toledo & Ironton Railroad, Pittsburgh, Pa.
C. E. CATT, Division Accountant, B. & O. R. R. Co., Pittsburgh, Pa.
G. W. HONSBERGER, Transpn. Mgr., Westinghouse Electric & Mfg. Co., Pittsburgh, Pa.

ADVERTISING COMMITTEE:

H H. HAUPT, Chairman, Gen. Supt., Motive Power, Pennsylvania Railroad, Pittsburgh, Pa.
KARL BERG, Superintendent Motive Power, P. & L. E. R. R. Co., McKees Rocks, Pa.
H. E. PASSMORE, Representative, The American Hammered Piston Ring Co., Pgh., Pa.

MEMBERSHIP COMMITTEE:

T. E. BRITT, Chairman, Div. Storekeeper, B. & O. R. R. Co., Glenwood Shops, Pgh., Pa.
C. M. WHEELER, Vice Chairman, Sales Engr., Union Switch & Signal Co., Swissvale, Pa.
F. H. EATON, Sales Engineer, American Car & Foundry Co., Pittsburgh, Pa.
C. W. GOTTSCHALK, Asst. Traffic Manager, Jones & Laughlin Steel Corp., Pgh., Pa.
LLOYD SUTHERLAND, General Storekeeper, P. & L. E. R R. Co., McKees Rocks, Pa.
THOMAS R. FITZPATRICK, Freight Traffic Mgr., P. & L. E. R. R. Co., Pittsburgh, Pa.
P. W. HEPBURN, Sales Engineer, Gulf Refining Company, Pittsburgh, Pa.
W. B. MOIR, Chief Car Inspector, Pennsylvania Railroad, Pittsburgh, Pa.
C. W. TRUST, Assistant Traffic Manager, Carnegie-Illinois Steel Corp., Pittsburgh, Pa.
R. S. BULL, Supt. Power & Inclines, Pittsburgh Railways Co., N. S., Pittsburgh, Pa.
A. F. COULTER, Master Car Builder, Union Railroad Co., East Pittsburgh, Pa.
T. R. DICKINSON, Purchasing Agent, B. & L. E. R. R. Co., Pittsburgh, Pa.
D. K. ORR, Road Master, Monongahela Railway Co., Brownsville, Pa.
W. F. AMBROSE, Master Mechanic, Aliquippa & Southern Railroad, Aliquippa, Pa.
JOHN I. MULVEY, Traffic Manager, Hubbard & Company, Pittsburgh, Pa.

PAST PRESIDENTS:

*J. H. McCONNELL	October, 1901, to October, 1903
*L. H. TURNER	November, 1903, to October, 1905
*F. H. STARK	November, 1905, to October, 1907
*H. W. WATTS	November, 1907, to April, 1908
*D. J. REDDING	November, 1908, to October, 1910
*F. R. McFEATTERS	November, 1910, to October, 1912
*A. G. MITCHELL	November, 1912, to October, 1914
*F. M. McNULTY	November, 1914, to October, 1916
*J. G. CODE	November, 1916, to October, 1917
*D. M. HOWE	November, 1917, to October, 1918
*J. A. SPIELMAN	November, 1918, to October, 1919
H. H. MAXFIELD	November, 1919, to October, 1920
FRANK J. LANAHAN	November, 1920, to October, 1921
*SAMUEL LYNN	November, 1921, to October, 1922
*D. F. CRAWFORD	November, 1922, to October, 1923
*GEO. D. OGDEN	November, 1923, to October, 1924
A. STUCKI	November, 1924, to October, 1925
F. G. MINNICK	November, 1925, to October, 1926
G. W. WILDIN	November, 1926, to October, 1927
E. J. DEVANS	November, 1927, to October, 1928
W. S. McABEE	November, 1928, to October, 1929
E. W. SMITH	November, 1929, to October, 1930
LOUIS E. ENDSLEY	November, 1930, to October, 1931
*JOHN E. HUGHES	November, 1931, to October, 1932
F. I. SNYDER	November, 1932, to October, 1933
C. O. DAMBACH	November, 1933, to October, 1934
R. H. FLINN	November, 1934, to October, 1935
R. P. FORSBERG	November, 1935, to October, 1936

*—Deceased.

Meetings held fourth Thursday of each month except June, July and August.

PROCEEDINGS OF MEETING
APRIL 22nd, 1937

The meeting was called to order at 8 o'clock, P. M., at the Fort Pitt Hotel by the Secretary in the unavoidable absence from the City of the President.

Registered attendance, 212, as follows:

MEMBERS

Adams, Frank W.
Allen, Earl M.
Ambrose, W. F.
Aulbach, A. J.
Babcock, F. H.
Balla, J. A.
Balph, M. Z.
Beeson, H. L.
Beltz, J. D.
Bender, H. P.
Bergman, C. R.
Best, D. A.
Black, C. R.
Blyth, F. G.
Boyd, John R.
Britt, T. E.
Brown, E. F.
Bull, R. S.
Carey, C. D.
Campbell, F. R.
Campbell, J. A.
Carr, T. W.
Chilcoat, H. E.
Clausen, Harold C.
Conway, J. D.
Cree, W. M.
Crenner, Joseph A.
Cruikshank, J. C.
Cudworth, H. D.
Cunningham, J. D.
Dalzell, W. E.
Davis, Charles S.
Deakins, H. H.
Dean, E. E.
Dean, W. A.
Dickson, K. B.
Durnell, W. E.
Emery, E.
Endsley, Prof. Louis E.
Failor, Charles W.

Farlow, G. B.
Ferguson, J. H.
Flinn, R. H.
Frauenheim, A. M.
Fralic, C. F.
Galbraith, James R.
Gelston, George A.
George, W. J.
Gilbert, William J.
Gilg, Henry F.
Goda, P. H.
Goodwin, A. E.
Griest, E. E.
Gross, John
Groves, W. C.
Hamilton, R. F.
Harper, John T.
Heed, H. L.
Hemma, Charles H.
Hilstrom, A. V.
Holland, S. E.
Honsberger, G. W.
Hovey, O. W.
Huston, F. T.
Irvin, R. K.
Jennings, A. S.
Johnson, J. W.
Kearfott, W. E.
Keck, L. M.
Keeney, A. R.
Kelly, L. J.
Kemmerer, R. R.
Kentlein, John E.
Kerr, Charles, Jr.
Koenig, W. A.
Kromer, William F.
Kroske, J. F.
Lanahan, Frank J.
Lanahan, J. S.
Larson, W. E.

Lincoln, R. B.
Long, R. M.
Longstreth, W. L.
Lundeen, C. J.
Lytle, L. J.
Maliphant, C. W.
Masterman, T. W.
Metzger, C. L.
Miller, John
Miller, L. P.
Misner, George W.
Mitchell, W. S.
Molyneaux, Dawes S.
Moore, D. O.
Morgan, H. C.
McCandless, William A.
McIntyre, R. C.
McKee, F. C.
McKinley, John T.
McLaughlin, H. B.
McLean, J. L.
Nash, R. L.
Nathan, W. P.
Nichols, Samuel A.
Nies, E. L.
Orchard, Charles
Osborne, Raymond S.
O'Sullivan, J. J.
Paisley, F. R.
Palmer, E. A.
Phillips, T. H.
Pickard, S. B.
Posteraro, S. F.
Provost, S. W.
Purchard, Paul
Rensch, R. H.
Renshaw, W. B.
Rupp, E. S.
Rutter, H. E.

Ryan, D. W.
Ryan, Frank J.
Schrecongost, C. P.
Sekera, C. J.
Severn, A. B.
Shellenbarger, H. M.
Sheridan, T. F.
Shingledecker, John C.
Shuster, W. W.
Simpson, E. W.
Sixsmith, G. M.
Sarchet, Roger
Searles, E. J.
Smith, Folger M.
Smith, R. B.
Stamm, Bruce B.
Steiner, P. E.
Stevens, L. V
Stevens, R. K.
Stoffregen, Louis E.
Stucki, A.
Sutherland, Lloyd
Tate, M. K.
Terkelsen, B.
Ternent, H. J.
Teskey, Dr. Walter J.
Thomas, George P.
Thompson, H. C.
Tracey, J. B. A.
Van Blarcom, W. C.
Van Horne, C. F.
Van Vranken, S. E.
Vollmer, Karl L.
Welton, Alvin A.
Wikander, O. R.
Winton, C. A.
Woodward, R.
Wright, John B.
Young, Paul S.

VISITORS

Bennett, J. B.
Brungess, F. N.
Caldwell, C. B.
Candee, A. H.
Colliflower, J. E.
Craick, George
Cruikshank, M. T.
Davis, William B.
Day, Calvin L.
Edsall, S. D.

Farbacher, John B.
Fugate, H. W.
Gray, A. F.
Hensley, D. E
Hilgert, T. J.
Jefferson, Harvey F.
Jenkins, William
Johnson, Carl E.
Jones, W. F.
Kemble, T. J.

Kemmler, Edward C.	Plaick, A. C.
Kromer, Walter W.	Provost, Dr. Charles
Lanahan, James K.	Provost, W. J.
Lewis, S. B.	Ralston, James
Loughner, L. J.	Reagan, P. H.
MacNamara, R. J.	Robinson, H. J.
Miller, Earl	Smith, Sion B.
Molyneaux, L.	Taylor, John M.
Morgan, J. P.	Thomas, Edgar C.
Moses, G. L.	Thompson, F. R.
Mulligan, H. J.	Tracey, B. A.
McCandless, William Q.	Turner, E. H.
McConnel, F. B.	Wallace, O. F.
McKinley, L. C.	Walsh, J. R.
McNeal, Donald L.	Walther, George W.
Newhouse, S. E.	Yeager, H. M.
Parvin, C. F.	Zell, Harry A.

SECRETARY CONWAY: Our President, Mr. Rauschart, told me that he would probably not be able to get back in time for the meeting, and in his absence I am going to call on our First Vice-President, Mr. G. M. Sixsmith, to preside. He has been practicing at it all afternoon so he ought to get along fairly well, with your indulgence.

MR. SIXSMITH: Mr. Secretary and Gentlemen: I have no apology to offer for the position in which you and I find ourselves at this moment. It seems to be not unusual to be called upon to preside at one of these meetings in the unavoidable absence of the President, without prior knowledge of that contingency and my unpreparedness in this instance will, I hope, be overlooked by the membership. Therefore, Gentlemen, once again you will have to accept me in an emergency and with your usual fine co-operation I have no doubt we will have a fine meeting, for, regardless of absentees, the progress of the Club must continue. I think it is needless for me to say that I am always glad to serve the Club in any capacity and under any circumstances and I am sure that Mr. Rauschart regrets as much as we do, his unavoidable absence tonight.

Now, as I understand from the Secretary, there is entertainment provided for your enjoyment this evening. Mr. Wright, a ventriloquist of some considerable accomplishment, has been engaged to present an act of that nature and if the Gentleman is present and the dummy is in proper working order, we will now be favored with that part of the program.

(The entertainment by Mr. Wright was interesting in its technical perfection, and replete with many local allusions to prominent members of the Club.)

CHAIRMAN: The meeting will now come to order and we will proceed with the business session.

The record of attendance is covered by the registration cards signed at the door and we will, therefore, dispense with the roll call of those present.

The printed proceedings of the last meeting are, I believe, already in your hands and, unless there is some objection, we will dispense with the reading of the minutes of that meeting.

I will now ask the Secretary to read the list of proposals for membership.

SECRETARY: We have the following proposals for membership:

Blanchard, Henry, Sales Representative, The Baldwin Locomotive Works, Paschall Station, Philadelphia, Pa. Recommended by E. A. Rauschart.

Blyth, F. G., General Agent, Railway Express Agency, 926 Penn Avenue, Pittsburgh, Pa. Recommended by E. L. Nies.

Fleming, Harry W., Salesman, J. Frank Lanning & Company, 327 First Avenue, Pittsburgh, Pa. Recommended by E. A. Rauschart.

Grove, C. G., Superintendent, Pennsylvania Railroad, Pennsylvania Station, Pittsburgh, Pa. Recommended by C. M. Wheeler.

Klorer, C P., Stationary Engineer, Lowrie Street, Troy Hill, Pittsburgh, Pa. Recommended by H. M. Shellenbarger.

League, W. D., Chief Clerk, The Monongahela Railway Company, 16 Elm Street, S. S., Brownsville, Pa. Recommended by H. L. Beeson.

Lytle, L. J., Barco Manufacturing Company, 239 Fourth Avenue, Pittsburgh, Pa. Recommended by R. H. Flinn.

Riley, S. B., General Superintendent & Superintendent Motive Power, P. & W. Va. Ry. Co., Wabash Building, Pittsburgh, Pa. Recommended by J. D. Conway.

Simpson, E. W., Superintendent Traffic & Transportation, Westinghouse Electric & Manufacturing Company, East Pittsburgh, Pa. Recomemnded by Frank J. Ryan.

Snyder, Joseph C., Vice President, Pullman-Standard Car Manufacturing Company, Midland Building, Cleveland, Ohio. Recommended by E. A. Rauschart.

Winton, Charles A., Research Engineer, U. S. Steel Corporation Subsidiaries, Frick Building, Pittsburgh, Pa. Recommended by A. B. Severn.

CHAIRMAN: The persons whose names you have just heard read have been approved for membership by the Executive Committee in accordance with the By-Laws of the Club and it is, therefore, my pleasure on behalf of the President, to extend to them a hearty welcome and to express the hope that their participation in the future in the activities of this organization will be as beneficial to them as to ourselves.

At this time I would like to say a word of welcome to any guests that may be with us tonight. As you know, it is the practice for members to bring guests to these meetings and I have sometimes wondered if these guests have been made to feel as welcome as they should be. Therefore, I want to say that any guests that may be with us on these occasions are entirely welcome and we hope they will enjoy themselves, coming back again if they so desire and in that connection I would like to suggest that the membership of this Club develop further the policy of bringing guests to the meetings and a hearty welcome will be accorded them. If any of them should desire to become a member of the Club, so much the better, but we want them to feel that they are welcome and we deem it a privilege to have them present.

Mr. Secretary, are there any announcements?

SECRETARY: As many of you know, a man who worked actively in the interests of the Club for many years, and was a member of one of our important Committees for the current year, Mr. William R. Gellatly, died on April 8th. He became a member of the Club on October 23, 1924.

CHAIRMAN: An appropriate memorial minute will appear in the next issue of the Proceedings. However, I believe that practically all of the membership of this Club were well acquainted with Mr. Gellatly and I feel that in view of his efforts in behalf of this Club we should take further note of his passing, and I wonder if Mr. Lanahan would not make a few remarks at this time in his memory.

MR. FRANK J. LANAHAN: Mr. President and Fellow Members: Mr. William R. Gellatly was one of the younger members of the Railway Club of Pittsburgh, but in proportion to his term of membership as determined by the services rendered, he deserved well earned recognition. During his tenure of office both as Chairman and just identified with the Membership Committee, he was a prodigious worker and a factor in the enlargement of the Club's roster.

In the midst of his energetic efforts he was seized with a heart affliction and reluctantly relinquished his activities but with a confident expectancy when he recovered he would come back into harness. But, "the best laid plans of mice and men aft ganglee," for this unusually good looking active young man quietly saw the shadows lengthen, the evening came and his busy world was ended. During a sojourn in the delightful climate of Florida, on April 8th with little warning, the Grim Reaper took his toll and our fellow member joined that caravan that now contains, oh, so many of our former Railway Club good fellows.

Beautiful were the impressive funeral services in the Chapel at the Homewood Cemetery, where surrounded by his devoted family and many friends who crowed the edifice with just myriads of choicest flowers, good-natured, likeable Bill participated in the last contact with those whose affections were sincere and deep. His memory will linger long with us who grieve his all-too-soon departure.

CHAIRMAN: Thank you very much, Mr. Lanahan.

We will now proceed with the address of the evening. Once again it is my privilege to compliment the members of the Subject Committee for their selection and their ability to induce such a speaker as we are to hear tonight to come here and talk to us on the very important subject that is proposed.

Mr. Charles Kerr, Jr., the speaker, is of the Railway Engineering Department of the Westinghouse Electric and Manufacturing Company, East Pittsburgh, one of our own industries. Mr. Kerr was active in the engineering development associated with the Pennsylvania Railroad electrification between New York City and Washington, also the same classification of work for the Illinois Central Railroad. His talk, I understand, will be along the line of electric operation of the past forty years, with description of modern electric motive power, etc. I am sure that all of us, whether we be connected with the transportation industry or whether it be with industrial activities, are interested in electrical development, and I am sure we can anticipate with considerable interest and pleasure Mr. Kerr's talk on this important subject. Without further explanation I present to you Mr. Charles Kerr, Jr., who will address you upon the subject, Railroad Electrification.

RAILROAD ELECTRIFICATION
By MR. CHARLES KERR, JR., Railway Engineer,
Westinghouse Electric & Manufacturing Company, East Pittsburgh, Pa.

Railroad electrification is an exceedingly extensive subject, and naturally, all of its ramifications cannot be covered during the course of a single paper. Therefore, certain phases of the subject which may be of greater interest have been selected for discussion.

First—The development of electric operation in the

United States, which has extended over a period of forty years.

Second—The modern electric locomotive and its place in rail transportation.

Third—The future outlook for electrification and its economic field of application.

Before dealing specifically with the general subject of railroad electrification, I wish to state emphatically that most of the electrical manufacturers, and particularly the Company with which I am associated, do not consider electrification as a cure-all for the railroad problem in America.

At various times, most of us have heard various statements made about electrification, extending anywhere from complete electrification as proposed by extreme optimists, to the claims of the pessimists who say that there should be none. Careful and exhaustive studies made by us indicate that under present conditions the economic field of electrification in this country is confined to the lines of densest traffic, comprising about 5% of the country's mileage and handling about 25% of the nation's traffic. The remaining 75% of the traffic is not considered sufficiently dense to be economically handled electrically, and should be moved by either steam or diesel electric power. Thus, we start the discussion of electrification on the premise that all three types of power —steam, diesel-electric and electric—have their field.

Development of Electric Operation:

The first railroad electrification in the United States was in 1895 in the Baltimore tunnels of the B. & O. Railroad. Since that time, some 28 railroads have installed electric operation to some extent, the most comprehensive of all installations being that of the Pennsylvania Railroad between New York and Washington, which is now being extended to Harrisburg.

A few pertinent statistics of 1936 operation may be of value to indicate the extent to which electrification has been carried in this country. There are 2,768 route miles and 6,441 track miles of electric operation, over which are operated 960 locomotives and 3,400 multiple unit cars. About 10% of the passenger car miles of all Class I roads are electrically operated, and in the Eastern District about 17½%. The power consumption in 1936 was:

Switching Service	57,000,000 K.W. Hrs.
Freight Service	441,000,000 " "
Passenger Service	1,072,000,000 " "
Total	1,570,000,000 K.W. Hrs.

The annual electric locomotive miles average between 30 and 35 million, and the multiple unit car miles over 96 million.

In general, these electrifications were installed principally for one of two reasons, either to meet an operating condition which could not be met otherwise, or for improved service and operating economies.

Two principal systems of electrification have been used, the direct current system with trolley voltages ranging from 600 to 3000 volts, and the alternating current system, in every case except one, with an 11,000 volt trolley. Each system has had its advocates and each system has its place. In general, the 600 and 1500 volt D.C. electrifications have been confined to suburban electrification, while the 3000 volt D.C. and the 11,000 volt A.C. installations have been for both suburban and main line operation. To date, the system most universally used has been the 11,000 volt A.C., having been installed among others on the Reading, Pennsylvania, Norfolk and Western, Virginian, Great Northern and New Haven Railroads.

Pennsylvania Electrification:

Of all electrifications, the most outstanding in practically every respect is that of the Pennsylvania Railroad between New York and Washington. This electrification handles the railroads service, both passenger and freight, between these cities, one of the busiest sections of rail line in the world. Daily about 700 passenger and freight trains are operated some 30,000 train miles over 1,343 miles of track. To move this traffic requires 191 electric passenger, freight and switching locomotives and 431 multiple unit cars.

It can truthfully be said that by electrification, the Pennsylvania Railroad is providing this territory with a standard of rail service not approached on any other line. Passenger trains, running 12 to 14 cars or more, are handled between New York and Washington, 225 miles, with 6 intermediate stops, in 215 minutes. Such high schedules through congested territory have never been approached before. It is probably not generally realized that in this territory the Pennsylvania is providing schedule speeds higher than most of the Streamline trains of the west, and doing so with standard cars on runs averaging about 30 miles between stops, while the Streamline trains average well over 100 miles between stops. To make these fast schedules in this congested territory takes motive power of unusual capacity, especially with high sustained accelerating capacity. The passenger locomotives used in this service are by far the most powerful in this country, being capable of outputs at the rail of 8,000 H.P. up to 70 m.p.h., and in excess of 5,000 H.P. up to 90 m.p.h.

Similarly, in freight service, maximum tonnage trains are being moved between terminals at average road speeds in excess of 40 m.p.h., corresponding to normal passenger schedules on many railroads. In freight service, the maximum outputs per train are in the neighborhood of 13,000 H.P. with a two-cab locomotive.

The power to supply this electrification is partly generated by the railroads and the balance is purchased from central station companies which have installed a total of 306,320 KVA. of frequency changer and generator capacity. From the point of purchase, the railroad distributes power over its own 132,000 volt transmission lines to 40 substations where the voltage is reduced to 11,000 volts for the overhead trolley.

The results of this electrification have been so successful, that recently the railroad has announced that it would extend its electrified service for both freight and passenger operation to Harrisburg.

Modern Electric Motive Power:

While much has been said about the development of the steam locomotive, probably many do not realize that the electric locomotive has also undergone a very rapid development. The first A.C. passenger locomotives built for main line service were those for the New Haven in 1907. These locomotives, many of which are still operated, had a continuous rating of 1,012 H.P. and weighed 217,000 lbs., or a locomotive weight of 214 lbs. per horsepower. At that time, these locomotives were considered the last word. The most recent A.C. locomotive weighs 380,000 lbs. with a continuous rating of 5,000 H.P., or only 76 lbs. per horsepower. This specific weight of the entire locomotive is less than that of the motors alone on the first New Haven locomotives. This weight of 76 lbs. per horsepower furthermore compares with 160 lbs. per horsepower for the diesel electric and about 170 lbs. per horsepower for engine and tender of the modern steam locomotive.

The principal reason back of the rapid development in locomotive design is the outstanding tendency in rail transportation today towards higher speeds. The best rail minds apparently consider that future operation will embrace passenger speeds of 90-100 m.p.h. and freight speeds of 60-70 m.p.h. When these speeds are reached, the horsepower capacities of the motive power will be far in excess of anything which most railroads now operate. Fig. 1 shows graphically the requirements of operation at these speeds. It should be noted that to operate a freight train at 60 m.p.h. requires, on level track, 3½ times the capacity that it requires at 30 m.p.h., and similarly passenger operation at 100 m.p.h. requires 3½ times the capacity needed for 50 m.p.h. operation.

With these increased demands for high speeds, carrying with them a demand for locomtives of increased capacities, the economic field for electrification is materially expanded. The electric locomotive differs from other locomotives in that it does not carry with it its own source of power, and is thus not restricted by boiler capacity, etc. Today the electric locomotive has reached the point where the only restriction to its output at any speed from zero to 100 m.p.h. is adhesion, not the equipment. In other words, the output curve of the electric locomotive for any axle loading can be the tractive effort permitted by adhesion. At all speeds, no other type of locomotive has yet reached this development.

The modern electric locomotive has tended to follow, in wheel arrangement, the same arrangement as the steam locomotive. With few exceptions, the latest engines have been of the following types, 4-6-4, 2-8-2, 4-8-4, 4-6-6-4. As an example of the principal characteristics of modern electric locomotives, there are listed below a few pertinent items pertaining to locomotives now built or building, or locomotives which could be built with electrical equipment now in service:

	Freight Service		Passenger Service	
Wheel Arrangement	2-8-2	2-6-6-2	4-8-4	4-6-6-4
Weight per Driver	70000 lbs.	70000 lbs.	60000 lbs.	60000 lbs.
Total Wt. of Loco.	190 tons	260 tons	200 tons	260 tons
Starting T.E. lbs	70000	105000	60000	90000
Continuous H.P.	5000	7500	5000	7500
Maximum H.P.	8000-10000	12000-15000	8000-10000	12000-15000
Max. Speed m.p.h.	70	70	100	100

These units can be operated in multiple by one crew, so that even greater capacities can be supplied by two or three cab locomotives. To date, the maximum tractive effort used is on the three cab Virginian locomotives which provide 236,-000 lbs at starting.

Fig. II shows the typical performance curves of two electric locomotives compared to that of a modern steam locomtive. Several features of the electric curves should be particularly noted. First, the maximum tractive effort can be sustained to about half of the top speed, while that of the steam locomotive begins to fall off very rapidly as the speed increases. Secondly, the maximum horsepower output of the electric is carried to very high speeds. This ability to sustain high outputs permits rapid acceleration—particularly advantageous in congested territory—or in automobile parlance, quick pick-up.

As can be seen, the electric locomotive still represents the type of motive power whereby the maximum output can be realized from the motive power for rail service. With the present tendency for accelerated schedules, it seems evident that future locomotive requirements will no longer be of the order of 2500-4000 horsepower for freight operations, but increased to the point where 10,000-15,000 horsepower per train must be provided. Similarly, 6000-8000 horsepower as a maximum requirement, will exist for heavy passenger service. These estimates of motive power capacities do not represent idle dreams, for five railroads, already, have motive power of this order; and this is merely a forerunner of a more widespread super-standard of railroad performance.

Economic Field for Electrification:

For a number of years, the Engineering Department of the Westinghouse Company has been engaged in a study to determine the economic field of electrification. Unfortunately, we have never been able to arrive at a simple formula which would give the answer, and there is serious doubt if one can be derived. However, we have succeeded in compiling a series of charts which indicate quite closely the field of electrification and which merit consideration.

In considering the economies of electric motive power, several variable factors influence the conclusion, principally among which are:

(a) Density of traffic, both freight and passenger,
(b) Speed of operation,
(c) Profile conditions,
(d) Relative Costs of fuel and power,
(e) Number of tracks.

For simplification in presenting the charts referred to above, the economic comparison shown by them has been confined to electric and steam operation. In its present state of development, the diesel-electric locomotive is a competitor of the steam locomotive but wherever the traffic concentration is sufficient to justify electrification, we do not believe that, in general, the diesel-electric locomotive is economically justified. However, this statement is in no way intended to minimize the importance of the diesel-electric locomotive, which has a tremendous field in switching service alone, supplemented by other applications for it, where the traffic is too light to justify electrification.

Many remarks have been made about the first costs of electrification. Fig. III shows the relative first costs of new steam motive power and of electrification for various densities of traffic, speeds, grades and number of tracks. The steam costs include only new locomotives; the electric costs include motive power and roadway equipment (trolley, transmission, sub-station and signal changes).

These curves show that the relative first cost of electrification rapidly decreases and approaches that of new steam power as the density of traffic increases, the speed increases, and the grades become more severe. Thus, dense traffic, high speed and severe grades make for economical electrification. Irrespective of the speeds operated or the grades encountered, a certain density of traffic is necessary to reduce the ratio of first costs to the point where electrification can become economical. If high speeds are involved, the first cost of electrification more rapidly approaches that of steam power and reaches a reasonable ratio to that of steam at a much lower traffic density. Thus, the popular conception that electrification, in all cases, is excessive in first cost, is erroneous. For future high-speed operation over the heavy traffic routes of the country, the first cost of electrification will be comparable with the first cost of new steam power.

Fig. IV shows for various sustained speeds, ruling grades and number of tracks, the density of traffic as which electrification becomes economical with present average coal and power costs.

This chart is worthy of considerable study.

The curves represent the minimum density at which the annual expenses of steam power and electrification, including all fixed charges on each, are equal. For densities lower than those shown by the curves, electrification is not economical. As densities become higher than those shown by the curves, electrification becomes increasingly economical. The curves take into account speed, density, grade and number of tracks and, furthermore, cover the extreme variations in these factors encountered on Class I railroads. Thus, in general, they are applicable to the entire rail system of America.

The basis for the curves in Fig. IV are the best operating figures that we have been able to collect. We believe the figures shown represent the dividing line between the fields of steam and electric operation, as closely as it is possible to carry a general analysis of this kind. The charts have been compared with detailed application studies, made over a period of years on particular projects, and in each case the general charts shown agree quite closely with the detail studies.

Conclusions:

In this paper, a brief resume of the development of electric traction has been presented. In each instance where electrification has been installed, it has been more than able to fulfill the expectations. While its growth has not been as rapid as many of us had hoped, it has experienced a steady expansion and during the past few years the manufacturers have had some of their biggest years in electrification business.

Electrification is primarily a form of motive power for handling the traffic over those roads which demand a heavy concentration of motive power capacity. On such lines, it can perform this service more economically than any other form of power. As such, it is confined to the heavy density lines which handle roughly one-fourth of the nation's traffic. We believe that with the future demands which will be placed on these lines, demanding service never before offered, electrification will prove to be the economical answer. The remaining three-fourths of the nation's traffic, we believe, should continue to be steam or diesel-electric hauled.

CHAIRMAN: Thank you very much Mr. Kerr for that fine presentation on Electrical Development. It is a very interesting subject and I am sure we have all been very much benefitted by it.

In case I might not have the opportunity later, or in case some of the other speakers may not mention it, I would like to have you take back to the Officers of your Company a word of greeting from this Club and an expression of our thanks and appreciation for their having made it possible for you to be with us tonight.

Now, Mr. Kerr, I have no doubt you would like to think that you are through, but no doubt you have been warned that it is the policy of this Club after the paper of the evening has been presented to give such of our members as may desire to do so an opportunity to ask questions. So, if any of you Gentlemen present would like to ask Mr. Kerr any questions, I have no doubt he will be very glad to entertain them and to make such answer as he may see fit.

QUESTION: I would like to ask what was the dominating factor in the selection of the type of electrical equipment used over the Rocky Mountains?

MR. KERR: Most of the electrifications were installed to save money. The Great Northern I think was primarily due to the fact that they had a condition they could not operate with steam. And after they electrified they found they were saving money. They were largely interested in operating conditions they could not operate otherwise.

QUESTION: I would like to ask what was the primary reason for the use of direct current for some electrifications rather than alternating current?

MR. KERR: That is a question on which there are two schools of thought. Certain people prefer direct current and certain others alternating current. I think—and this is only my own idea—that when the traffic is relatively light you can do the job cheaper without direct current. Where you have a very dense traffic, you can do it cheaper with alternating current. For heavy traffic, alternating current is better as higher voltages can be used. Where low voltage is used, the investment in overhead structures is very much higher. It is primarily a question of economy.

QUESTION: What is the advantage of electric locomotives over units using the electric power right on the car itself?

MR. KERR: There are two or three factors involved in that. In the first place with suburban traffic necessitating very frequent stops and a short distance between stops you can distribute the motors on each car and get faster acceleration than by putting it all in one locomotive. You can make better schedules with the individually motored car than by pulling them with a locomotive. Another feature is the rush hour problem. Multiple car trains can be run during the rush hours and during the day only single cars. With locomotive operation you would have a big locomotive to haul all the time, though you would have to handle big trains only in the rush hours. When it comes to through service where the run extends out of electrified territory and that same train is picked up and carried on by steam you have a different problem.

QUESTION: What is the difference between the side rod drive and the geared wheel drive and why the change?

MR. KERR: The tendency is to individual axle drive. In low speed work the motor is direct connected but in high speed the motor is carred on the locomotive frame.

The use of side rods was primarily a question of applying motors of sufficient capacity. In the early days we had to get a motor between the axle and the wheels and side rods constituted the only means of doing so. Now we can do it with individual axle drives.

QUESTION: What is the economic reason for the choice of direct current motors on the long mountain runs on the transcontinental lines, the Great Northern especially?

MR. KERR: The thing there is the question of regeneration. The motor acts as a generator going down hill and feeds current back into the line. The alternating current series motor has never been used for regenerating in this country. It is possible to do so but it has not been done and at the time of the Great Northern electrification it had not been done. That is the primary reason. Where you do not require regeneration it is the most satisfactory locomotive motor.

The motor generator looks like a complication. The cost and weight of a motor generator locomotive compares favorably with the other types.

QUESTION: What are the economic reasons governing electrification?

MR. KERR: As I pointed out, the higher the traffic, etc., the more electrification. The cost of the locomotives is about the same as steam. In electrification the locomotive cost is about half the total cost. The cost of the overhead and sub-stations is about the same irrespective of the density of the traffic.

QUESTION: How about third rail operation and 11,000 volt operation with the same locomotive on the New Haven?

MR. KERR: On the New York Central the motors operate direct from the third rail, on the New Haven from an 11,000 volt trolley where the voltage is reduced on the locomotive by a transformer. The motors run on either A.C. or D.C.

QUESTION: You mentioned earlier about the Illinois Central electrification. I believe that is one of the densest suburban traffic lines in the country. Have you any figures as to how that was worked out?

MR. KERR: No specific figures.

CHAIRMAN: Thank you very much, Mr. Kerr. I am going to ask our past President, Mr. Flinn, to close the discussion.

MR. R. H. FLINN: We have listened here tonight to a very intelligent and interesting discussion. Mr. Kerr remarked to me that he did not like to talk very much. I told him at least since he knew his subject he should not mind telling us something about what he knows. And he has done it in a very delightful and friendly way. I think we always prefer in this Club an educational rather than an oratorical effort and a sincere explanation of what the speaker knows. That is what we have had tonight, and we have all of us found it very interesting and instructive. There is nothing I can think of to add to the discussion, but I think we as a Club owe the speaker a very enthusiastic rising vote of thanks for his admirable address, and I move you that we so express ourselves.

The motion was duly seconded and carried by unanimous rising vote.

CHAIRMAN: If there is no further business to come before the meeting, before I ask for a motion to adjourn I would like to express my personal satisfaction for your co-operation in making this meeting a success under the emergency conditions that existed. We will now entertain a motion to adjourn.

ON MOTION Adjourned.

J. D. CONWAY, Secretary.

In Memoriam

WILLIAM R. GELLATLY
Joined Club October 23, 1924
Died April 8, 1937

'AYE MON, 'TIS A GOOD BUY!'

PENNZIP AND PENNZOIL ARE PERFECT PARTNERS

Be Wise
Use
PENNZIP

Here's the moneysaving gasoline that you've been looking for. It's Pennzip, the gasoline that motorists are talking about . . . and they're talking about it because it gives them EXTRA MILES in every gallon!

There are other things you get when you use Pennzip. More power under the hood . . . better pep and pickup . . . quicker starting . . . and real no-knock action.

Treat yourself and your car to a pleasant surprise. Drive in to your nearest Pennzip station today for a tankful of Pennzip, the perfect partner of Pennzoil motor oil.

THE PENNZOIL COMPANY

Chamber of Commerce Building   Pittsburgh, Pa.

OFFICIAL PROCEEDINGS

IWAY CLUB OF PITTSBUR

$1.00 Per Year   25¢ Per Copy

Vol. XXXVI.   MAY 27, 1937.   No. 7.

RAILROAD COMMUNICATION SYSTEMS AND PRACTICES
By MR. W. R. TRIEM, General Superintendent of Telegraph, The Pennsylvania Railroad, Philadelphia, Pa.

The proof of your interest

in the Club can be

enhanced

by securing a

NEW MEMBER.

Application form is available

in this magazine. Look

it up and

"ACT NOW."

OFFICIAL PROCEEDINGS

OF

The Railway Club of Pittsburgh

Organized October 18, 1901

Published monthly, except June, July and August, by the Railway Club of
Pittsburgh, J. D. Conway, Secretary, 515 Grandview Ave., Pittsburgh, Pa..

Entered as Second Class Matter February 6, 1915, at the Postoffice at Pittsburgh,
under the Act of March 3, 1879.

| Vol. XXXVI.
No. 7 | Pittsburgh, Pa., May 27, 1937 | $1.00 Per Year
25c Per Copy |

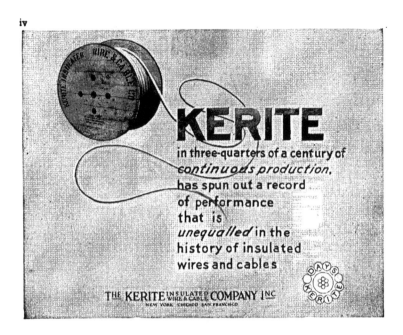

KOPPERS SERVES the RAILROADS

KOPPERS PRODUCTS AND WHERE THEY APPLY IN THE RAILROAD FIELD	TREATED TIMBER, TIES, POSTS, ETC.	ROOFING MATERIALS	PISTON RINGS	COAL	WATER-PROOFING MATERIALS	BITUMINOUS PAINTS	TARMAC ROAD MATERIALS	FAST'S COUPLINGS	CREOSOTE	CYLINDER AND VALVE PACKING	WEED KILLERS	INSECTICIDES AND DISINFECTANTS	PLATE WORK	CAR FERRIES, RAILROAD BARGES, ETC.
ROADBEDS	A								D		F			
LOCOMOTIVES			C	B		D				C				
STATIONS	A	D		B	D	D			D			F		
SHOPS	A	D	C	B	D	D		E	D			F	E&G	
BRIDGES	A				D	D	D		D				E&G	
TUNNELS	A				D	D	D						E&G	
DRIVEWAYS	A				D		D				F			
POWER HOUSES	A	D	C	B	D	D		E	D	C			E&G	
STRUCTURAL	A	D			D	D			D				E&G	
GRADE CROSSINGS	A						D							
CATTLE PENS	A	D			D	D			D			F		
RAILROAD-MARINE OPERATIONS	A	D	C	B	D	D			D	C		F	E&G	H

A—The Wood Preserving Corporation, Pittsburgh, Pa.   B—The Koppers Coal Company, Pittsburgh, Pa.   C—American Hammered Piston Ring Division, Baltimore, Md.   D—Tar and Chemical Division, Pittsburgh, Pa.   E—Bartlett Hayward Division, Baltimore, Md.   F—The White Tar Company of New Jersey, Inc.   G—Western Gas Division, Fort Wayne, Ind.   H—The Maryland Drydock Company, Baltimore, Md.

INDEX—ADVERTISERS.

NOTE—This form to be filled out in full by typewriter or printed and mailed to J. D. Conway, Secretary, 1941 Oliver Building, Pittsburgh, Pa. Membership fee, including dues, is $3.00 for each fiscal year or part thereof, except those propsed in September or October. Those proposed in these months will be credited upon payment for the following fiscal year. Dues are payable in advance.

The fiscal year ends with the month of October.

The Railway Club of Pittsburgh:

———————————————19———

Gentlemen:

Will you kindly consider my Application for Membership in your Club at the next meeting:

Name————————————————

Title————————————————

Company————————————————

My Address————————————————

————————————————

Recommended by———— . ——————————

OFFICIAL PROCEEDINGS

OF

The Railway Club of Pittsburgh

Organized October 18, 1901

Vol. XXXVI. No. 7	Pittsburgh, Pa., May 27, 1937	$1.00 Per Year 25c Per Copy

OFFICERS FOR 1936-1937

President
E. A. RAUSCHART,
Mechanical Superintendent, Montour Railroad Co., Coraopolis, Pa.

First Vice President
G. M. SIXSMITH,
Supt., Pennsylvania Railroad,
Pittsburgh, Pa.

Secretary
J. D. CONWAY,
Railway Supply Manufacturers' Association,
Pittsburgh, Pa.

Second Vice President
J. D. BELTZ,
Supt., B. & O. R. R. Co.,
Pittsburgh, Pa.

Treasurer
E. J. SEARLES,
Manager, Schaefer Equipment Co.,
Pittsburgh, Pa.

EXECUTIVE COMMITTEE:

FRANK J. LANAHAN, Chairman, President, Fort Pitt Malleable Iron Co., Pittsburgh, Pa.
A. STUCKI, Engineer, A. Stucki Company, Pittsburgh, Pa.
G W. WILDIN, Consulting Engineer, Westinghouse Air Brake Company, Pittsburgh, Pa.
W. S. McABEE, Vice Pres. & General Supt., Union Railroad Co., East Pittsburgh, Pa.
E. W. SMITH, Vice President, Pennsylvania Railroad, Pittsburgh, Pa.
LOUIS E. ENDSLEY, Consulting Engineer, 516 East End Avenue, Pittsburgh, Pa.
F. I. SNYDER, Vice President & General Manager, B. & L. E. R. R. Co., Pittsburgh, Pa
C. O. DAMBACH, General Manager, P. & W. Va. Ry. Co., Pittsburgh, Pa.
R. H. FLINN, General Superintendent, Pennsylvania Railroad, Pittsburgh, Pa.
R. P. FORSBERG, Chief Engineer, P. & L. E. R. R. Co., Pittsburgh, Pa.

SUBJECT COMMITTEE:

D. W. McGEORGE, Chairman, Secretary, Edgewater Steel Company, Pittsburgh, Pa.
G. H. BURNETTE, Asst. Chief Engineer, P. & L. E. R. R. Co., Pittsburgh, Pa.

RECEPTION AND ATTENDANCE COMMITTEE:

J. W. JOHNSON, Chairman, Superintendent, Railway Express Agency, Pittsburgh, Pa.
W. C. BUREL, Vice Chairman, Master Mechanic, Western Allegheny Railroad, Kaylor, Pa.
J. W. BOYD, Superintendent, Monongahela Railway Company, Brownsville, Pa.
THOMAS E. CANNON, General Supt. Equipment, P. & W. Va. Ry. Co., Pittsburgh, Pa.
T. W. CARR, Superintendent Rolling Stock, P. & L. E. R. R. Co., McKees Rocks, Pa.
D. C. CARROLL, Assistant Agent, Pennsylvania Railroad, Pittsburgh, Pa.
S. G. DOWN, Vice President, Westinghouse Air Brake Company, Wilmerding, Pa.
HARRY C. GRAHAM, Pittsburgh Screw & Bolt Corporation, Pittsburgh, Pa.
J. W. SCHAD, Division Master Mechanic, B. & O. R. R. Co., Pittsburgh, Pa.
GEORGE S. WEST, Division Superintendent, Pennsylvania Railroad, Pittsburgh, Pa.
J. W. HOOVER, Asst. Chief of Transpn., Subsidiary Cos. U. S. Steel Corp., Pittsburgh, Pa.
A. A. READ, Duquesne Slag Products Company, Pittsburgh, Pa.
C. P. SCHRECONGOST, Traffic Manager, Hillman Coal & Coke Company, Pittsburgh, Pa.
J. A. WARFEL, Special Representative, Air Reduction Sales Company, Pittsburgh, Pa.
J. C. SHINGLEDECKER, Supervisor of Service Stations, The Pennzoil Co., Pittsburgh, Pa.
J. C. DILWORTH, Manager Railroad Sales, Carnegie-Illinois Steel Corp., Pittsburgh, Pa.

ENTERTAINMENT COMMITTEE:

J. PORTER GILLESPIE, Chairman, Asst. Gen. Supt., Lockhart Iron & Steel Co., Pgh., Pa.
FRANK E. WEIS, Vice Chairman, Transportation Clerk, Penna. R. R., Pittsburgh, Pa.
JAMES NAGEL, Superintendent Transportation, Montour Railroad, Coraopolis, Pa.
E. H. HOLMES, Sales Department, Fort Pitt Malleable Iron Co., Pittsburgh, Pa.
C. C. CLARK, Sales Manager, Central District, Pressed Steel Car Co., Pittsburgh, Pa.
A. I. KESSLER, Clearance Clerk, Pennsylvania Railroad, Pittsburgh, Pa.
T. F. SHERIDAN, Asst. to S.M.P. and S.R.S., P. & L. E. R. R. Co., McKees Rocks, Pa.

FINANCE COMMITTEE:

M. A. SMITH, Chairman, General Manager, P. & L. E. R. R. Co., Pittsburgh, Pa.
J. B. DIVEN, Superintendent Motive Power, Pennsylvania Railroad, Pittsburgh, Pa.
F. J. RYAN, District Representative, Detroit, Toledo & Ironton Railroad, Pittsburgh, Pa.
C. E. CATT, Division Accountant, B. & O. R. R. Co., Pittsburgh, Pa.
G. W. HONSBERGER, Transpn. Mgr., Westinghouse Electric & Mfg. Co., Pittsburgh, Pa.

ADVERTISING COMMITTEE:

H. H. HAUPT, Chairman, Gen. Supt., Motive Power, Pennsylvania Railroad, Pittsburgh, Pa.
KARL BERG, Superintendent Motive Power, P. & L. E. R. R. Co., McKees Rocks, Pa.
H. E. PASSMORE, Representative, The American Hammered Piston Ring Co., Pgh., Pa.

MEMBERSHIP COMMITTEE:

T. E. BRITT, Chairman, Div. Storekeeper, B. & O. R. R. Co., Glenwood Shops, Pgh., Pa.
C. M. WHEELER, Vice Chairman, Sales Engr., Union Switch & Signal Co., Swissvale, Pa.
F. H. EATON, Sales Engineer, American Car & Foundry Co., Pittsburgh, Pa.
C. W. GOTTSCHALK, Asst. Traffic Manager, Jones & Laughlin Steel Corp., Pgh., Pa.
LLOYD SUTHERLAND, General Storekeeper, P. & L. E. R. R. Co., McKees Rocks, Pa.
THOMAS R. FITZPATRICK, Freight Traffic Mgr., P. & L. E. R. R. Co., Pittsburgh, Pa.
P. W. HEPBURN, Sales Engineer, Gulf Refining Company, Pittsburgh, Pa.
W. B. MOIR, Chief Car Inspector, Pennsylvania Railroad, Pittsburgh, Pa.
C. W. TRUST, Assistant Traffic Manager, Carnegie-Illinois Steel Corp., Pittsburgh, Pa.
R. S. BULL, Supt. Power & Inclines, Pittsburgh Railways Co., N. S., Pittsburgh, Pa.
A. F. COULTER, Master Car Builder, Union Railroad Co., East Pittsburgh, Pa.
T. R. DICKINSON, Purchasing Agent, B. & L. E. R. R. Co., Pittsburgh, Pa.
D. K. ORR, Road Master, Monongahela Railway Co., Brownsville, Pa.
W. F. AMBROSE, Master Mechanic, Aliquippa & Southern Railroad, Aliquippa, Pa.
JOHN I. MULVEY, Traffic Manager, Hubbard & Company, Pittsburgh, Pa.

PAST PRESIDENTS:

*J. H. McCONNELL	October, 1901, to October, 1903
*L. H. TURNER	November, 1903, to October, 1905
*F. H. STARK	November, 1905, to October, 1907
*H. W. WATTS	November, 1907, to April, 1908
*D. J. REDDING	November, 1908, to October, 1910
*F. R. McFEATTERS	November, 1910, to October, 1912
*A. G. MITCHELL	November, 1912, to October, 1914
*F. M. McNULTY	November, 1914, to October, 1916
*J. G. CODE	November, 1916, to October, 1917
*D. M. HOWE	November, 1917, to October, 1918
*J. A. SPIELMAN	November, 1918, to October, 1919
H. H. MAXFIELD	November, 1919, to October, 1920
FRANK J. LANAHAN	November, 1920, to October, 1921
*SAMUEL LYNN	November, 1921, to October, 1922
*D. F. CRAWFORD	November, 1922, to October, 1923
*GEO. D. OGDEN	November, 1923, to October, 1924
A. STUCKI	November, 1924, to October, 1925
F. G. MINNICK	November, 1925, to October, 1926
G. W. WILDIN	November, 1926, to October, 1927
E. J. DEVANS	November, 1927, to October, 1928
W. S. McABEE	November, 1928, to October, 1929
E. W. SMITH	November, 1929, to October, 1930
LOUIS E. ENDSLEY	November, 1930, to October, 1931
*JOHN E. HUGHES	November, 1931, to October, 1932
F. I. SNYDER	November, 1932, to October, 1933
C. O. DAMBACH	November, 1933, to October, 1934
R. H. FLINN	November, 1934, to October, 1935
R. P. FORSBERG	November, 1935, to October, 1936

*—Deceased.

Meetings held fourth Thursday of each month except June, July and August.

PROCEEDINGS OF MEETING
MAY 27th, 1937

The meeting was called to order at the Fort Pitt Hotel at eight o'clock, P. M., with President E. A. Rauschart in the Chair.

Registered attendance, 265, as follows:

MEMBERS:

Adams, C. E.
Allen, Earl M.
Ambrose, W. F.
Anderson, Burt T.
Aulbach, Albert J.
Babcock, F. H.
Baer, Harry L.
Baker, W. E.
Balla, J. A.
Balzer, C. E.
Barnhart, B. F.
Barr, H. C.
Baughman, G. W.
Baumann, E. G.
Beam, E. J.
Beeson, H. L.
Beitsch, George F.
Beltz, J. D.
Bender, H. P.
Binyon, T. E.
Black, C. R.
Blyth, F. G.
Brown, E. F.
Buffington, W. P.
Burel, W. C.
Burnette, G. H.
Campbell, F. R.
Cannon, T. E.
Carey, C. D.
Carmody, J. J.
Catt, Clyde E.
Chase, D. K.
Chilcoat, H. E.
Cipro, Thomas
Clausen, H. C.
Conway, J. D.
Courtney, Harry
Crawford, B. H.
Cree, W. M.
Crenner, Joseph

Cudworth, H. D.
Cunningham, J. D.
Dambach, C. O.
Davis, Charles S.
Deakins, H. H.
Dean, E. E.
Dean, W. A.
Dickinson, B. F.
Diven, J. B.
Dunham, C. W.
Durell, W. A.
Durnell, W. E.
Emery, E.
Endsley, Louis E., Prof.
Failor, Charles W.
Fair, J. M.
Fike, J. W.
Fleming, Harry W.
Flinn, R. H.
Fugate, H. W. B.
Furch, G. J.
Galbraith, James R.
Gardner, George R.
Gaston, Charles
Geertz, Allan O.
Gelston, George A.
George, W. J.
Gilg, Henry F.
Gillespie, J. Porter
Gillum, J. S.
Goda, P. H.
Goodwin, A. E.
Gray, H. H.
Griest, E. E.
Grove, C. G.
Groves, W. C.
Haggerty, J. F.
Haller, Nelson M.
Hamilton, R. F.
Heed, H. L.

Hemma, Charles H.
Hess, Charles A.
Hill, John A.
Hilstrom, A. V.
Holland, S. E.
Honsberger, G. W.
Huber, C. G.
Huber, H. G.
Huston, F. T.
Jados, W. T.
Johnson, J. W.
Johnson, W. M.
Kane, H. S.
Kearfott, W. A.
Keck, L. M.
Keeney, A. R.
Kellenberger, K. E.
Keller, R. Bruce
Kemmerer, R. R.
Kentlein, John
Kessler, A. L.
King, E. C.
Koenig, W. A.
Krahmer, E. F.
Kulp, J. G.
Lanahan, Frank J.
Lanahan, J. S.
Larson, W. E.
Lee, L. A.
Longstreth, W. L.
Lunz, G. J.
Lytle, L. J.
May, John D.
Miller, Lloyd P.
Miller, R. C.
Mitchell, F. K.
Mitchell, W. S.
Morgan, Homer C.
Morris, J. M.
Morris, W. F., Jr.
Morse, J. W.
Moulis, F. J.
Mulvey, J. I.
McCarthy, F. W.
McCormick, E. S.
McElravy, J. W.
McGeary, E. J.
McHail, J. L.
McKim, Hollis
McKinley, John T.
McNamee, W.
McTighe, B. J.

Nathan, W. S.
Nestor, T. E.
Nichols, Samuel A.
Nies, E. L.
Noonan, Daniel
Norris, J. L.
O'Reilly, G. Arthur
Overholt, B. C.
Paisley, F. R.
Passmore, H. E.
Pevler, H. H.
Pickard, S. B.
Posteraro, S. F.
Pry, E. B.
Purchard, Paul
Rauschart, E. A.
Rebstock, J. B.
Rensch, R. H.
Renshaw, W. B.
Roberts, E. L.
Robertson, A. S.
Roney, H. E.
Rowles, H. N.
Rudd, W. B.
Rumbarger, F. A.
Rupp, E. S.
Rushneck, G. L.
Rutter, H. E.
Sarchet, Roger
Schoonover, W. H.
Schrecongost, C. P.
Searles, E. J.
Servais, F. W.
Sixsmith, G. M.
Shellenbarger, H. M.
Sheridan, T. F.
Sladden, F. T.
Smith, R. B.
Spencer, A. C.
Steiner, P. E.
Stucki, A.
Sutherland, Lloyd
Swope, B. M.
Taylor, H. D.
Terkelsen, B.
Teskey, Dr. Walter J.
Thompson, H. A.
Trautman, J. A.
Triem, W. R.
Tucker, John L.
Van Blarcom, W. C.
Van Horne, C. F.

Walton, W. K.　　　　　Williams, J.
Weis, F. E.　　　　　　Wilson, James R.
Welton, Alvin A.　　　　Wright, O. L.
Wheeler, C. M.　　　　　Yarnall, Jessee

VISITORS:

Alexander, T. W.　　　　Jackson, W. A.
Angel, A. J.　　　　　　Jakovac, V.
Angerman, J. C.　　　　Jeno, Hamilton
Anson, J. M.　　　　　　Johnson, A. H.
Arden, M. E.　　　　　　Jones, J. A.
Armstrong, E. W.　　　　Kacy, Ralph A.
Beilsmith, R. J.　　　　Kemble, T. J.
Bevan, George H.　　　　Leitzsimmons, D. P.
Bewen, J. N.　　　　　　Lewis, S. B.
Biddle, H. C.　　　　　MacMurdo, James G.
Brinskey, A. A.　　　　MacNamara, R. J.
Burke, D. J.　　　　　　Maxfield, Arthur
Burkitt, E. A.　　　　　Meixner, J. E.
Carrow, T. H.　　　　　Melton, W. S.
Carver, William　　　　Metz, R. A.
Chellman, H. R. L.　　　Mitchell, John
Correy, C. L.　　　　　Moore, N. K.
Dankmyer, F. C.　　　　McConnell, F. B.
Davis, William B.　　　Nauman, C. E.
Desmond, John　　　　　Reeser, H. J.
Eisenhart, R. A.　　　　Robinson, H. J.
Elliott, C. A.　　　　　Rogers, J. D.
Engel, Frank, Jr.　　　Ronsen, J. R.
Evans, W. H.　　　　　　Schaffer, E. F.
Fairbanks, W. A.　　　　Shroads, Paul E.
Field, W. E.　　　　　　Smith, H. H.
Flynn, F. E.　　　　　　Smith, Sion B.
Forster, Walter　　　　Souders, J. W.
Goodwin, H. L.　　　　　Speed, C. M.
Graham, S. B.　　　　　Stephens, I. F.
Gray, A. E.　　　　　　Triem, John S.
Grissol, J. M.　　　　　Wallace, O. T.
Grondahl, L. O.　　　　Walther, George W.
Hare, J. E.　　　　　　Watson, W. H.
Hilgert, T. J.　　　　　Wheeler, H. H.
Hough, Alvin L., Jr.　　Zell, Harry A.
　　　　　　Zoog, J. H.

PRESIDENT: As you all signed registration cards at your entrance this evening, we have a full record of attendance and therefore the call of the roll will be dispensed with.

As the printed Proceedings are already in your hands,

unless there is objection we will dispense with the reading of the minutes.

A very splendid program of entertainment has been prepared for you, which will be presented after the paper of the evening.

I will now ask the Secretary to read to you the list of proposals for membership.

SECRETARY: We have the following proposals for membership:

Condon, William H., President, Condon Brothers Company, Inc., 5242 Perrysville Road, N. S., Pittsburgh, Pa. Recommended by A. B. Coombe.

Armstrong, Edward W., Supervisor—Tracing Service, Pennsylvania Railroad, Pennsylvania Station, Pittsburgh, Pa. Recommended by J. D. Conway.

Dunkelberger, Harry E., Master Mechanic, Weirton Steel Company, Weirton, W. Va. Recommended by E. A. Rauschart.

Fugate, Henry W. B., Agent, Pennsylvania Railroad, 512 State Street, Clairton, Pa. Recommended by E. F. Krahmer.

Gaston, Charles, Salesman, Ashton Valve Company, 21 Albany Street, New York, N. Y. Recommended by E. A. Rauschart.

Geertz, A. O., Assistant Engineer Motive Power, Pennsylvania Railroad, 3955 Bigelow Boulevard, Pittsburgh, Pa. Recommended by C. M. Wheeler.

Gillespie, S. E., Director, Bureau of Railway Signaling Economics, 347 Madison Avenue, New York, N. Y. Recommended by C. M. Wheeler.

O'Reilly, G. Arthur, Salesman, Williams & Company, Inc., 1719 Crafton Boulevard, Pittsburgh, Pa. Recommended by E. A. Rauschart.

Smith, H. H., Superintendent Transportation, U. S. Steel Corporation Subsidiaries, Frick Annex, Pittsburgh, Pa. Recommended by J. D. Conway.

Thompson, F. L., Locomotive Inspector, Monongahela Railway Company, R. D. No. 1, Brownsville, Pa. Recommended by H. L. Beeson.

White, Frank F., General Master Mechanic, Weirton Steel Company, P. O. Box 521, Weirton, W. Va. Recommended by E. A. Rauschart.

PRESIDENT: These proposals having been submitted to the Executive Committee and approved by them, in accordance with our By-laws, the gentlemen whose names have been read are now members of the Club. I will ask those of the number who are present to rise, that we may welcome you into the fellowship of our Club. We hope that our association will be as pleasant for you as we expect it to be for ourselves.

Mr. Secretary, are there any announcements?

SECRETARY: Since our last meeting we have received information of the death of two of our members, B. H. Rodeniser. Superintendent Transportation, Meadow Gold Dairies, Inc., Pittsburgh, Pa., died April 24, 1937, and E. A. Forbriger, District M. of W. Storekeeper, B. & O. R. R. Co., Pittsburgh, Pa., died May 6, 1937.

PRESIDENT: An appropriate memorial minute will appear in the next issue of the Proceedings.

Committee No. 1 of the Telegraph and Telephone Section of the Association of American Railroads is meeting in

Pittsburgh today and are the guests of this Club this evening. I understand there are fifteen members of that Committee present, and we extend to you a most cordial welcome.

It is now my very great pleasure to introduce to you Mr. W. R. Triem, General Superintendent of Telegraph, Pennsylvania Railroad, Philadelphia, Pa., who will address you upon the subject of Railroad Communication Systems and Practices.

RAILROAD COMMUNICATION SYSTEMS
AND PRACTICES

**By MR. W. R. TRIEM, General Superintendent of Telegraph,
The Pennsylvania Railroad, Philadelphia, Pa.**

MR. W. R. TRIEM: I need not say to you that it is a great pleasure for me to be here for everybody likes to get back home. And it seems to me to be quite fitting that, coming from our headquarters I convey the greetings and best wishes of the Management of the Pennsylvania Railroad to the Club and to all of you who have so many friends in that organization in Philadelphia.

Believing you to know about as much about Telephone and Telegraph matters, on the average, as I did before I became associated with the T. & T. Department of the Pennsylvania Railroad, it is possible that you may be entertained by a brief recital of some of the things I have learned since I left here a year ago.

We all have a more or less hazy idea that railroads use various kinds of communication systems and generally agree that without them we would be in a rather sorry state. But, as a matter of fact, the communication plant is the nerve system of the railroad. Affect any part of it, and the reaction is almost instantaneously and automatically registered by this nerve system upon the headquarters or brain. The length of time that elapses between an accident and its reaction is that which is required for an employe to reach the nearest telephone. The rule "Proceed to the nearest point of communication and report to the Superintendent" is one that never requires supervision, and when fulfilled, the voice on the telephone acts as the stimulus for the entire nerve system. Whatever is to be done to restore normal conditions is likewise arranged for or directed through this same communication system. Our efficiency as railroad men, and the personal and financial interest of patrons is materially affected by this ability of practically all railroads to react instantly to any disturbance, affecting in · the slightest, the normal operation of the railroad.

During the recent· Ohio River floods it was my good fortune to ·spend considerable time at headquarters of the Pennsylvania Railroad at Philadelphia. It was an awe inspiring experience to note the advance of that flood from Pittsburgh down that valley. One town after another was submerged, and the railroads one by one sent out their embargoes, backed up their freight and equipment, and—no, they didn't stop at that and wait for the flood to subside. Instead, by telephone and telegraph, and yes—sometimes by amateur radio, freight was rerouted through open gateways, passenger service was detoured, lines were cleared for movement of emergency trains carrying relief units and supplies and the most stupendous mass rescue work was performed by the railroads that has probably ever been undertaken, and this was all most successfully consummated. Weaving in and out of all communities during this period throughout the entire flooded area by boat, wading boots, airplane, light engine and automobile, was a vast army of telephone and telegraph men, —railroad, Western Union, Bell Telephone System, Postal Telegraph and Cable, local telephone companies, all working together to restore the means of communication and to maintain in service by guts and brains, the systems not completely demolished. Heroes were everywhere, strong determined men and women in stations, block offices, telephone exchanges, often completely surrounded by water, but carrying on, making connections maintaining communication, keeping the outside world advised of conditions and giving invaluable aid to relief and rescue work. An Agent, whom I know personally, put in a bed and supplies in his freight office, and calmly watched the water surround him, and for five days he "held the fort". For a good part of that time through his ingenuity he was able to patch telephone connections so that conditions in that locality were accurately described to the outside world, and so that the needs of his town were made known and relief and rescue work materially advanced, not to mention the aid furnished to the quick reconstruction of his railroad.

During that period many a railroad officer put in unbelievable hours at the telephone. A type of left-arm paralysis was not uncommon as a result of holding a telephone receiver for long periods. To describe what they talked about is out of the question, but I can safely leave it to your imagination, after giving one personal experience. Drinking water was needed in these submerged towns. A State officer asks for help—of course by telephone; a railroad suggests tank cars, and the offer is gladly accepted. Now note the speed of communication: From the site of the submerged town where a railroad officer has a telephone in a business car on the edge of the river to Chicago is one transaction; railroad office to tank car office, another telephone call; tank car office, Chicago, to tank car shops at Philadelphia, another telephone call; railroad office, Chicago, to railroad office Philadelphia, another telephone call; Philadelphia railroad office to tank car shop foreman's home three telephone calls. (It took 3 calls to get him—he happened to be at the movies and was finally called out by telephone. From railroad General Office to Division office, to yard office, to Crew Dispatcher, to engine-house, to individual members of two crews (ten men in all) and when the train of fifty new, clean, empty, tank cars pulled out of Philadelphia four hours and thirty minutes from the time the idea was broached on the banks of the flooded Ohio, the telephone call that advised Chicago that the train was on its way was the 22nd telephone conversation required in the transaction!

Similar emergencies were being met in this same manner by all of the railroads at this time. Life-boats and crews; hospital and medical units; fire engines; police groups; all the forces and paraphernalia of relief—were loaded, moved and unloaded, all by telephone and telegraph arrangements.

Now, how was all this possible? What kind of a system is it, and how does it happen that intercommunication between railroads, parts of railroads, and the public can function so successfully?

Perhaps we should first trace the history of railroad communication systems briefly—

First the TELEGRAPH—Morse, the Philadelphia artist— "What has God wrought"—the story is known to all. The system seems of the utmost simplicity to us, but how difficult it was for Morse to sell his idea. A long time before Morse adapted the idea to the operation of the telegraph in-

138

strument, the principle of the solenoid, in which a piece of iron wrapped in a coil of wire became magnetized by current flow, was well understood. The magnetizing of this iron by flow of current caused a small armature or lever to oscillate as the bar was magnetized and demagnetized, resulting in a succession of sounds that was indicated in Morse's code by dots and dashes. This system was quickly adopted by the railroads for transacting business of all kinds that could not be handled by mail, but its real importance was found in train dispatching. Without the telegraph, it is safe to say that the early expansion of the railroads would not have occurred. The effect of the use of telegraph for directing train movements, prior to the development of the telephone and modern signaling methods, is visible in many of the rules and customs of our railroads today. It has been but a short time since an Operating Officer could not be appointed unless he were a Morse Operator. Much of the credit for the development of the science of safe railroad train operation can be given to the key-pounding Morse Operators of the past two or three generations. As an interesting side-light, I am the first General Superintendent of Telegraph on our railroad that could not work a key.

But the historical significance of telegraph in the development of modern railroads is a subject that we had better drop while we can, in spite of the interest many of us here might have in it.

Next came the TELEPHONE. From time to time, before the telephone was developed, tales were told by telegraph operators located at lonely outlying offices of faint voices sometimes heard for a few moments in the quiet of the night, and seeming to come from the group of telegraph instruments on the table so dimly illuminated by the oil lamp that the blue sparks could be seen sometimes as the instruments clicked away their messages. Just old wives' tales, perhaps a dream, many a man never told that he thought he heard these things, some were afraid to tell, others weren't sure, perhaps, and then, too, many a boomer liked his "likker" and didn't want to create suspicion. We believe now that some vibrations, with, of course, only a hint of voice frequency range, must have been carried from point to point when the conditions happened to be just right, and that some of these mysterious voices were heard by many an operator long before Bell invented his telephone.

But there was the magnet, the solenoid and the electric current; it was only a question of time until the vibrations produced by voice sounds would be transmitted by wire, and so came Mr. Alexander Graham Bell and the telephone, and in its turn all the sound-transmitting and reproducing apparatus that is so familiar to us today.

The first sentence transmitted by a telephone was in the test of his new apparatus by Mr. Bell on March 10, 1876— "Watson, come here, I want you." There are men here in this audience who were youngsters at that time; they were not much older when the first telephone used by a railroad was installed on the Pennsylvania Railroad at Altoona on May 21, 1877.

From that modest beginning the telephone plant grew; at first just a few telephones, one in the yard office, one in the block station, one in the agent's office, another at the enginehouse, and so on, until finally, all departments found them practically indispensable. Concurrently, the commercial telephone was being put in many of these offices, and rentals charged for each one. Then things got complicated and the economy and efficiency of simplification was apparent. A switchboard with an operator to break down the long multi-party lines into several units usable simultaneously, instead of one conversation at a time, was the first step, followed by the discovery that one man could not answer and use two telephones at once, and that the commercial phone was usually idle any way a great part of the time. Why have two telephone instruments when one would do? This was a problem that was solved by the mutual agreement of the commercial companies and the railroads, whereby trunk lines between the switchboard of the telephone company were carried into switchboards rented from the telephone company and placed on the property of the railroad, into which all the lines of the railroad were then connected. Finally, we find all railroads fully equipped with standard telephone apparatus connected into a complete system of switchboards from each of which trunk lines were extended into local telephone company exchanges. Thus, in emergency, an employe of most any railroad at the most remote location—say a branch up in the mountains, or a water tank in the desert,—no matter where, can reach through his railroad telephone a telephone exchange and then the whole world.

But that isn't by any means all of the story, for, the

clicking of the telegraph is absent these days in many dispatchers' offices. Quiet now reigns, where formerly, to the uninitiated, was noise and confusion. In an acoustically treated office a clear modulated voice, reproduced in a loud speaker, is heard followed by a quiet unhurried response of the dispatcher into a transmitter or microphone, or the click of a button pushed to call an operator many miles away—that is a modern dispatcher's office.

On many railroad Divisions today telephones are used as the sole means of dispatching and block system communication. It is not extravagant to claim that the one single factor having the greatest beneficial effect upon train operations is probably the use of the telephone for directing train movements. By the judicious location of telephones where they can be used by train employes, direct contact is possible between the engineman or the conductor and block operators and dispatchers, as well as trainmasters, road foremen of engines, engine-house foremen, and any other officer whose advice or authority is required in emergency. By contrast, many of you railroad and ex-railroad men can recall the time not so many years ago when a train had no means of communication with the dispatcher except at block stations where the telegraph operator acted as interpreter and trains on sidings between stations stayed there for many long unproductive hours because they were out of touch with headquarters.

Telephone lines of the best, reaching from the dispatcher's desk to each block office, replace the old telegraph lines. The dispatcher's receiver, the amplifying loud speaker in fact, is always on the line so that any operator can talk to him without signaling in any way. Each operator's telephone is automatically cut out of the circuit when not in use, but his selector is always across the line so that he may be called by the dispatcher. It is necessary for the dispatcher to signal the operator to have him come in on the line. This is done by the mere pressing of a button or turning a key for each office, and through code impulses sent over the telephone circuit the signal is transmitted to the one office wanted, or by the use of a master key every office on the line is signaled simultaneously.

The telegraph key is also becoming a museum piece in many railroad telegraph offices, particularly in the larger offices where messages are relayed. A relay office has the same relation to message traffic that an assembly yard has to freight traffic. All stations have a routing set-up for their guidance so that, no matter how small and remote the sending and receiving stations may be, the message will receive prompt handling through one or more relay offices to which the receiving and sending stations are connected. Of course, where there is a sufficient volume of business, direct wires are established.

The electrically operated typewriter printer, often referred to by the name of the product of the principal manufacturer, the "Teletype," is rapidly supplanting the telegraph key. These printers operate on electrical circuits using electrical impulses on the same general principle as underlies the Morse telegraph. Each letter of the alphabet, figures and many other characters are represented by code impulses produced by the sending machine and picked up by one or more receiving machines which operate synchronously with the sending machine. Any number of receiving printers can be operated by the impulses sent by the sending printer. By the use of a selector system, one sending printer can be connected in turn to any one or more printers to which circuits extend from the sending unit just as one telephone is connected through the telephone exchange with any other telephone.

Ordinarily, where two printers are connected together by a circuit, the typewriter apparatus on each prints the message on ordinary paper, but printed forms, carbon copies and in fact any product of a typewriter can be secured just as would be the case if the receiving machine were being manually operated.

When the volume of traffic is heavy, and messages are to be sent to many different printers from the larger offices, it has been found desirable to store up work for the sending printer by the use of perforated tape for transmission. Instead of sending electrical impulses by the use of key board connected directly to the sending apparatus, the key board is connected to a perforator by means of which a narrow continuous tape is punched with holes in sequence, each set of holes representing a letter or other character. The receiving printer can also be arranged to perforate tape or print messages on paper, or both, as desired. In this way the receiving office can make copies of the messages, reports, etc., and at the same time reperforate a tape which can be run through other sending machines, thus transmitting the information to any number of offices, and of course, exactly as it was transcribed originally on the first tape that was punched.

It is possible to transmit waybills, bills of lading, consists, in fact almost any conceivable kind of a report by printer. A number of railroads are using printers for these purposes. No doubt you have seen descriptions in advertisements and in articles in magazines of some of these developments, the most important to date being the transmission of waybills, the transmission of shipping instructions between a manufacturing plant's shipping office and the railroad's billing office, and the transmission of train consists giving information as to the movement of cars in trains as they are dispatched from the yards.

The printer will send from 40 to 60 words per minute, depending upon the circuit characteristics and other factors. This speed, coupled with the ability to reproduce at the receiving office the exact form of message as sent, makes the use of the printer one of the most important factors in providing the railroads with advance information upon which efficient operations depends, but also permits the railroad to furnish information to the public that is both authentic and practically up-to-the-minute.

The line circuits and the apparatus used in them are of course of equal importance with the telephone, the printer telegraph and all the other operating facilities we have just described. The so-called "outside plant" of our communication system embodies some of the most outstanding results of scientific and engineering study and development. Its story would fill volumes, and requires the pen of an accomplished writer to do it justice. A brief synopsis only can be sketched here.

TELEPHONE CIRCUITS — A pair of wires, insulated from each other and the ground, connecting two telephones, constitutes a telephone circuit. They will provide satisfactory service for about 50 to 100 or more miles for telephone transmission, and for much greater distances for telegraph transmission, depending upon the character of the wire, its size, the degree of insulation, amount of inductive interference from electric currents in other circuits, and so on. By using copper wires of large gage, carefully insulating them, keeping them free from inductive interference, satisfactory telephone transmission has been possible over great distances. However, the cost of such circuits is very great, and a method of boosting the telephone message along the wires of smaller gage was sought, and the apparatus known as the Telephone Repeater was designed.

A TELEPHONE REPEATER is an amplifier using vacuum tubes that look like the tubes of your radio set. Current from a local source, either battery or from rectifiers and transformers connected to a lighting circuit is supplied to the repeater in such a manner that the voice currents in the telephone circuits are amplified or boosted, so that, leaving the repeater apparatus, the voice current is just as strong as it was leaving the original transmitter.

For satisfactory telephone transmission, a complete two-wire metallic circuit was found necessary, and in the early development of the telephone the open wire lines became loaded with wires to the limit. Ten crossarms of ten wires each was not uncommon. But 100 wires only provided 50 circuits, until a method was devised by which the number of separate circuits that could be carried by the wires was increased 50 per cent. Four wires, called a quad, provides two metallic circuits and a phantom, or 3 telephone circuits from 4 wires. In addition, each quad group can be used for 4 two-way channels of telegraph or printer. 8 telegraph or printer messages can be sent on 4 wires at the same time that 3 telephone conversations are being carried on.

But that isn't all, for by using higher frequencies, such as employed in some radio transmission, a pair of wires can provide a number of separate channels through the use of the so-called "carrier" systems. This is being done on some railroad lines today. A twelve-channel carrier system may be employed to give twelve two-way telegraph or printer circuits on two pairs of wires.

In many locations, for various reasons, open wire lines are uneconomical, or practically impossible to construct, or subject to so much inductive interference that the circuits cannot be used.

On our line between Washington and New York, which is completely electrified, all communications and signal circuits are carried in cables. These cables are in underground ducts, free from storm prostration and less subject to interference except the ground currents which must be reckoned with, else electrolysis would soon put the cables out of business. Sufficient to say, in that regard, that communication and electrical engineers have quite successfully solved the electrolysis problem as they have a habit of doing with respect to these many difficult ones that are constantly presenting themselves to the telephone and telegraph men.

Insulated wire, closely wrapped together in a protective sheath is known as cable. There are many kinds of cable, but the one type generally used in telephone and telegraph work consists of small gage copper wires wrapped in paper, associated in pairs and quads. The wires can be so twisted and arranged in the cable that phantom circuits are satisfactorily used just as in the open lines. The wires, arranged in various combinations as required for the particular use to which they are to be put, are wrapped individually, and all put together in paper, which in turn is encased in a lead sheath. This is the minimum protection afforded. Many different kinds of additional sheath materials are used around the lead depending upon the location where the cable will be used. For instance, the communication cable being installed in connection with the new electrification of the lines of the Pennsylvania Railroad west of Trenton, Philadelphia and Baltimore to Harrisburg will be of aerial type supported on poles along the edge of the right-of-way. Around the lead sheath is a layer of impregnated jute, which in turn is protected by two bands of galvanized steel wrapped around it. This is the type of cable known as tape armored, and it is just as substantial as the name implies. This cable, as is the case with all of the cables used in the electrified territory of our railroad and as is also the practice of many railroads and commercial companies in many locations, is kept under dry nitrogen gas pressure constantly. A drop in the pressure which is kept at about 9 pounds, is indicated by alarms in the various block offices, or at Wire Chief's desk at Division headquarters, so that immediate attention can be given to the section of cable that is giving signs of leaking. Pressure is at once increased, thereby preventing the entrance of moist air or water; the insulation is therefore preserved, and no interruption of service occurs while the repairs are in progress.

Circuits in cables have, of course, a greater loss of volume or attenuation than open wire circuits. Repeaters are required to amplify the voice currents in the same manner as in open wire lines. There is, however, a distortion of the quality of the reception caused by "electro-static capacitance" that is the result of the close association of the wires together in the cable and which is scarcely noticeable in open wire lines. Under these conditions the conversation is unintelligible even though the sounds coming from the receiver may be quite loud. It was finally found that the introduction of coils at intervals producing so-called lumped inductance successfully overcame the difficulty, and the apparatus was named a loading coil. The illustration usually given to explain the action of these coils is that of a thin light string in which one attempts without success to cause a wave to traverse its length because the wave quickly disappears or rapidly becomes attenuated. Now fasten at short intervals small beads of lead on this same string and see how successfully a wave can be made to traverse the length of the string. So, when these inductance coils are placed in a circuit at intervals of 6,000 feet, the circuit is said to be LOADED with loading coils.

No discussion of communication systems would be complete without some reference to radio. On the railroads, however, the transmission of telephone conversations and messages by radio is not important. The use of radio in connection with "front-to-rear" communication on trains has been found entirely practicable. In cases of extreme emergency there have been some temporary uses made of amateur stations. Many of our blue-ribbon trains, as you know, are equipped with standard radio receiving sets which are used for entertainment of our patrons. Experiments have proven that telephone conversations can be carried on between patrons on moving trains and telephone subscribers through commercial telephone company exchanges, by means of radio, but the scheme is not considered of sufficient value to justify the cost.

I will now exhibit a few pictures that may give you a better idea of what goes on behind the scenes on many railroads, than I can describe. We will show these now please.

(SLIDE 1.) As previously mentioned, the first telephone on any railroad was installed at Altoona in 1877. Excerpt from letter of Gardener D. Hubbard, associate of Alexander Graham Bell, to his mechanical expert Mr. T. A. Watson, with reference to tests just concluded at Altoona, is shown in this picture.

(SLIDE 2.) Map or diagram of the telephone system of the Pennsylvania Railroad showing the principal telephone exchanges and the lines radiating from them and connecting with other exchanges. Quite a large communication system—in fact, representing a valuation of about 22 million dollars, and consisting of 98,700 miles of open wire, 956 miles of cable, and serving 20,210 telephones. When you remember that this is but one of many such systems, for every railroad, large or small, has one of some kind, you can realize what an enormous industry this separate department of all the railroads really is.

(SLIDE 3.) This slide illustrates the size and complexity of the equipment required to terminate the radiating lines of the communication system.

On the right is the terminating frame into which all lines, both local and trunk of our railroad at Philadelphia, are terminated. Practically every piece of telephone and telegraph apparatus used on the Pennsylvania Railroad at Philadelphia is reached by wires leading from this frame.

On the left is the composite equipment which makes it possible to secure telegraph channels over the telephone trunk circuits as previously described.

(SLIDE 4.) These are metallic terminal repeaters used in telegraph service in electrified territory where grounded circuits are unsatisfactory.

(SLIDE 5.) Here is the solar plexis of the whole system—the Wire Chief's test panels. Here are instruments for measuring the electrical characteristics of the various circuits terminating on the terminal frame you saw in the preceding picture, and by means of jacks and cords any wire can be connected to any other wire. Here is the place that trouble with circuits is first reported, and here is where temporary circuits are set up to get through or around trouble. Each of the many wire chiefs at Division headquarters works with other wire chiefs in such manner that the interruptions to service are traced quickly to a cause, the location is calculated quite accurately and repair crews are able to restore service in minimum of time.

(SLIDE 6.) Next is shown the New York City telephone exchange of our Company. This is the manual board taking care only of long distance trunks and incoming calls from the commercial telephone exchanges. All local telephones in the New York area on the P. R. R. PBX are handled by the automatic switchboard, or as commonly described, by "machine switching".

(SLIDES 7 and 8.) Next we will step into a dispatcher's office. These men are running the Philadelphia Terminal Division—average of about 800 trains per day. You will recall the description of a quiet office—well, here is one.

(SLIDE 9.) In the same building in the Pennsylvania Station at Philadelphia is "PO" Telegraph Office. Here you can see the teletype writers, telephone selectors, and if you are observant you will note that all the telegraph instruments have not been removed from this office.

(SLIDE 10.) Now the service to the public—this picture is a typical "Information Office" layout. When you are again in New York, and desire train information by telephone, your conversation will be carried on with one of these employes in all likelihood.

(SLIDE 11.) This picture is of the Pullman Reservation room. This is the office the ticket clerk calls when you get a reservation on a train from New York. Not shown here, but a part of this installation is the separate manual telephone switchboard by which the patron is routed to the employe in charge of the Pullman space with which you are concerned.

(SLIDE 12.) This is the last picture. It indicates more forcibly than anything I can say, the complexity, the magnitude and the large investment in, the communication system. This is a unique picture, taken by an amateur in a dark hole in the ground, with an exposure of about five minutes. I won't keep you in suspense any longer—this is the interior of a manhole called a "CABLE VAULT", into which all the signal and communication cables of the Pennsylvania Railroad entering Philadelphia are carried. It is deeply buried under the Pennsylvania Station, the entrance being from the lower track level. It is 300 feet long, by 12 feet wide, by 12 feet high; the bottom being 10 feet below the mean surface of the Schuylkill River.

And that's all of the pictures. They were not much considered as "art", and not so exciting either, but I wanted to show the inside of some of the offices that most people never see, and illustrate some of the things I'm afraid my descriptions did not make very clear.

In closing this brief and quite inadequate description of our railroad communication system, you may be wondering if it is of much personal concern after all. You may be right so far as the railroad business is concerned, but is it not possible that a system found so valuable by the railroads may have possibilities of value in your own line of work?

Speaking as a member of the craft of telephone and telegraph men who are most anxious to serve you, it seems to me that you railroad and industrial supervisors and executives may find, upon investigation, that there may be undeveloped profit in an adequate and efficient communication system in your line of work. By taking advantage of the experiences of the railroad and commercial communications departments, the new telephones, microphones, loud speakers, and teletype apparatus may well be adapted to your use with advantage.

The railroad T&T Departments and commercial companies will be found sympathetic and helpful if you consult them with your problems. So far as my department's relations with the other departments of my railroad and with its patrons are concerned we have but one objective—adequate and efficient communication, suitable to the needs of the railroad in its operations and in furnishing accurate and up-to-date information to its patrons.

PRESIDENT: Before going into a discussion of the paper, we have with us Mr. W. A. Jackson, Superintendent of Telegraph of the New York Central Lines, who is Chairman of the whole Telegraph and Telephone Section of the Association of American Railroads. This Section is one of the most active and influential Sections of the Association, and much of the credit for the uniformly high standard or maintenance and operation of Railroad Communication plants can be given to the members of this group. It is a privilege to have Mr. Jackson with us, and we would be honored to have a word from him.

MR. W. A. JACKSON: Mr. President and Gentlemen: If you listened to the paper you will have noticed that there has not been a single advance and improvement in connection with Telephone and Telegraph equipment that the railroads have not taken advantage of. It is often said that the railroads are not progressive. Not only the Telegraph Department, but all other departments are taking advantage of everything that can be used to help the service.

One thing in the paper that aroused my interest as much as anything else was the little historical sketch. I do not know how many men in this room can remember back to the time when the only telephone service we had was a so-called party line. You rang four or five, or maybe two long and two short rings, finally getting someone, but if he did not know just how to talk into the transmitter, you couldn't understand a word he said. This was a Blake transmitter. That instrument has been changed and developed until today it is almost perfect.

Speaking of hearing conversations over telegraph wires, I remember when I was a kid operator back in 1893 we had what was called a pony wire with a battery on one end and grounded on the other and two sounders on it doing a local business between two points close together. This pony wire was carried in the same cable with the telephone wires and every once in a while conversations could be heard coming from the sounder. If any of you ever heard the conversations they use to carry on over those so-called yard lines, you will agree with me that it was not only unusual, but picturesque.

I am very glad to have had the opportunity of meeting with you. You have listened to a splendid discussion of the Telephone and Telegraph on the railroads by one who is a leader in that branch of service. I would like to emphasize what he has said that the Telegraph Department is only there to serve the other departments, and that unless the other departments open up and make suggestions, frequently they will not get the full advantage of the service which we might furnish. I thank you Gentlemen.

MR. R. H. FLINN: The speaker referred to the work of "pounding the keys" as passing out of the picture. There are still quite a few men around the railroads who can still operate the telegraph. I know a number of them in this room and I think it would be quite interesting if you would ask those capable of sending by a telegraph key to stand up.

(More than a score of men stood up and were received with great applause).

MR. HENRY F. GILG: There was mention of a little

telephone box with the crank which was turned for a telephone call. I talked over the first telephone that came to Pittsburgh in 1876 at the Exposition on the North Side. A couple of years later I was working as night yard clerk at Outer Depot of the Pittsburgh, Ft. Wayne & Chicago R. R. There were no telephones there, so I had to walk to Strawberry Lane for leaving time of freight sections and to the roundhouse to order power, and any other messages which had to be conveyed.

Had there been the convenience of the telephone, I would have had time to get in a little sleep instead of having to work all night.

PRESIDENT: We have with us Mr. W. R. Fairbanks, and we would like to hear a word from him.

MR. W. R. FAIRBANKS: I am very glad to have had the opportunity of attending this meeting and listening to the paper. I have enjoyed it very much. I do not know that I can add anything to the discussion. I thank you.

PRESIDENT: Mr. Dambach, have you anything to add?

MR. C. O. DAMBACH: I enjoyed Mr. Triem's talk very much. And I also enjoyed the pictures. But I am sorry that he did not deal a little more in detail with the telephone-radio feature, for I believe that the possibilities in the telephone-radio development are of the greatest value to the railroads. If the engineer can talk to the rear end of the train, and if the train despatcher will be able to telephone directly to the conductor on the train, that will save a lot of time and money.

I was very much interested in what he had to say about telephone train despatching, because I was responsible for the first installation of selective ringing in connection with train despatching in the East and the third in the United States. I am glad to be here and have learned a lot from the paper. Thank you.

PRESIDENT: The hour is getting late and we have the male chorus here to sing for us, and I will ask Mr. Lanahan to close the discussion.

MR. FRANK J. LANAHAN: Mr. President and Fellow Members: It is quite proper that the Railway Club of Pittsburgh should be the first to hear this interesting and instructive paper on "Railroad Communication Systems and Practices" which has been presented to us tonight by the author, Mr. Triem. We are but maintaining the best traditions of the Club in giving approval to this story, in non-technical terms, of telegraphing and telephoning as now developed.

From the very inception of the Railway Club of Pittsburgh, it has sponsored new transportation ideas, encouraged pioneering and given both recognition and commendation to accomplishments in all the ramifications of railroading, and so it is with exceptional pleasure that we welcome as our speaker, tonight, a gentleman who for many years has been a full-fledged member of our Club and participated regularly in the monthly meetings while belonging to the official family of the Pennsylvania Railroad in Pittsburgh.

Impressed were we all by the story that Mr. Triem so well related and depicted on the screen. Well does he bring forth the truth of the saying that "Perfection is made up of trifles, but perfection itself is no trifle." No better way is there to designate the paper of the evening than appropriate the superlatives on the Atlantic City Convention advertisement in front of us, "fascinating, scientific and educational." To this we can all subscribe.

The very large attendance of members here tonight are much indebted to Mr. Triem and his co-workers for this paper, as outstanding in its importance is it as a historical document, while our "Proceedings" will be enhanced in value by this contribution to its pages for reference. The genial manner of the speaker, his affableness and modesty were factors that added to the general ensemble. On behalf of the organization of which you, Mr. Triem, are an important member, permit me to express our sincere thanks and appreciation for your contribution and it is our hope you will often come back to give us the benefit of both your wisdom and genial companionship.

PRESIDENT: Thank you, Mr. Lanahan. And to you, Mr. Triem, we extend our sincere thanks and appreciation.

The Weirton Steel Company Male Chorus of forty voices is here ready to entertain us, and I will ask Mr. Morris, Vice President of the Company, to introduce the Chorus to you.

MR. J. M. MORRIS: Mr. President and Gentlemen: As I stand here tonight and look around this room and see so many friends of years gone by, I am fully rewarded for my first attendance at any function of the Railway Club.

The address of our honored guest, my friend, Bill Triem, was most instructive and clearly indicates the progress he has made in another form of transportation. In his remarks he made the statement that he had never pounded a key; however, I know of no one who ever came to Pittsburgh who pounded out more sincere friends than he, through which friends his company materially benefited.

In the rear of this room is a group of men who will entertain us tonight, all of whom are employees of the company with which I am associated, and I am sure you will all enjoy the splendid entertainment they will provide. I am proud to have them here, proud of their appearance, and, above all, proud of their loyalty to the interests they represent.

The Weirton Chorus will open their entertainment and will close by singing "Moonlight and Roses," which was the favorite song of the late Mr. David M. Weir. I can't refrain from making reference to two boys—brothers—who organized and managed the Weirton Steel Company. Two finer characters never lived than Mr. E. T. and Mr. D. M. Weir, and it is unfortunate that God chose to call one of them home early in life. His memory lingers with me, and always will, because it was by reason of him that I became associated with the company.

I am sure you will all now enjoy hearing from the Weirton Chorus, and I am certainly happy to be here with you.

The Male Chorus presented a program unusual in the character of the music, the quality of the voices and the balance and training of the chorus, which was received with close attention and unbounded enthusiasm.

J. D. CONWAY, Secretary.

In Memoriam

B. H. RODENISER
Joined Club December 20, 1934
Died April 24, 1937

E. A. FORBRIGER
Joined Club December 20, 1934
Died May 6, 1937

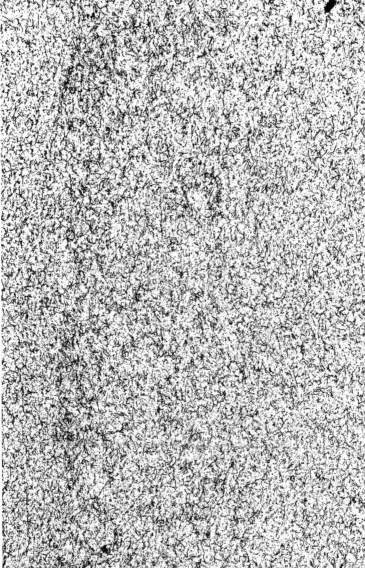

OFFICIAL PROCEEDINGS

LWAY CLUB OF PITTSBURG

$1.00 Per Year   25¢ Per Copy

Vol. XXXVI.   SEPT. 23, 1937.   No. 8.

Progress In Track Maintenance To Meet The Requirements Of Present Day Traffic

By ROBERT FARIES, Asst. Chief Engineer of the Maintenance
of Way Department, Pennsylvania Railroad, Philadelphia, Pa.

The proof of your interest

in the Club can be

enhanced

by securing a

NEW MEMBER.

Application form is available

in this magazine. Look

it up and

"ACT NOW."

OFFICIAL PROCEEDINGS

OF

The Railway Club of Pittsburgh

Organized October 18, 1901

Published monthly, except June, July and August, by the Railway Club of
Pittsburgh, J. D. Conway, Secretary, 515 Grandview Ave., Pittsburgh, Pa..

Entered as Second Class Matter February 6, 1915, at the Postoffice at Pittsburgh,
under the Act of March 3, 1879.

| Vol. XXXVI. No. 8 | Pittsburgh, Pa., Sept. 23, 1937 | $1.00 Per Year 25c Per Copy |

RAILROAD DIESELS FOR RAILROAD MEN

Reliability in service with low cost and ease of maintenance are the factors of prime importance to a buyer of Diesel locomotives.

These factors predominated all others at all times in the minds of the designers of the Alco unit.

KOPPERS SERVES the RAILROADS

KOPPERS PRODUCTS AND WHERE THEY APPLY IN THE RAILROAD FIELD	TREATED TIMBER, TIES, POSTS, ETC.	ROOFING MATERIALS	PISTON RINGS	COAL	WATER-PROOFING MATERIALS	BITUMINOUS PAINTS	TARMAC ROAD MATERIALS	FAST'S COUPLINGS	CREOSOTE	CYLINDER AND VALVE PACKING	WEED KILLERS	INSECTICIDES AND DISINFECTANTS	PLATE WORK	CAR FERRIES, RAILROAD BARGES, ETC.
ROADBEDS	A								D		F			
LOCOMOTIVES			C	B		D				C				
STATIONS	A	D		B	D	D			D			F		
SHOPS	A	D	C	B	D	D		E	D			F	E&G	
BRIDGES	A				D	D	D		D				E&G	
TUNNELS	A				D	D	D						E&G	
DRIVEWAYS	A				D		D				F			
POWER HOUSES	A	D	C	B	D	D		E	D	C			E&G	
STRUCTURAL	A	D			D	D			D				E&G	
GRADE CROSSINGS	A						D							
CATTLE PENS	A	D			D	D			D			F		
RAILROAD MARINE OPERATIONS	A	D	C	B	D	D			D	C		F	E&G	H

A—The Wood Preserving Corporation, Pittsburgh, Pa. B—The Koppers Coal Company, Pittsburgh, Pa. C—American Hammered Piston Ring Division, Baltimore, Md. D—Tar and Chemical Division, Pittsburgh, Pa. E—Bartlett Hayward Division, Baltimore, Md. F—The White Tar Company of New Jersey, Inc. G—Western Gas Division, Fort Wayne, Ind. H—The Maryland Drydock Company, Baltimore, Md.

INDEX—ADVERTISERS.

NOTE—This form to be filled out in full by typewriter or printed and mailed to J. D. Conway, Secretary, $1 Oliver Building, Pittsburgh, Pa. Membership fee, including dues, is $3.00 for each fiscal year or part thereof, except those proposed in September or October. Those proposed in these months will be credited upon payment for the following fiscal year. Dues are payable in advance.

The fiscal year ends with the month of October.

The Railway Club of Pittsburgh:

_____19____

Gentlemen:

   Will you kindly consider my Application for Membership in your Club at the next meeting:

Name_____

Title_____

Company_____

My Address_____

_____

Recommended by_____ . _____

OFFICIAL PROCEEDINGS

OF

The Railway Club of Pittsburgh

Organized October 18, 1901

Vol. XXXVI.
No. 8

Pittsburgh, Pa., Sept. 23, 1937

$1.00 Per Year
25c Per Copy

OFFICERS FOR 1936-1937

President
E. A. RAUSCHART,
Mechanical Superintendent, Montour Railroad Co., Coraopolis, Pa.

First Vice President
G. M. SIXSMITH,
Supt., Pennsylvania Railroad,
Pittsburgh, Pa.

Secretary
J. D. CONWAY,
Railway Supply Manufacturers' Association,
Pittsburgh, Pa.

Second Vice President
J. D. BELTZ,
Supt., B. & O. R. R. Co.,
Pittsburgh, Pa.

Treasurer
E. J. SEARLES,
Manager, Schaefer Equipment Co.,
Pittsburgh, Pa.

EXECUTIVE COMMITTEE:

FRANK J. LANAHAN, Chairman, President, Fort Pitt Malleable Iron Co., Pittsburgh, Pa.
A. STUCKI, Engineer, A. Stucki Company, Pittsburgh, Pa.
G W. WILDIN, Consulting Engineer, Westinghouse Air Brake Company, Pittsburgh, Pa.
W. S. McABEE, Vice Pres. & General Supt., Union Railroad Co., East Pittsburgh, Pa.
E. W. SMITH, Vice President, Pennsylvania Railroad, Pittsburgh, Pa.
LOUIS E. ENDSLEY, Consulting Engineer, 516 East End Avenue, Pittsburgh, Pa.
F. I. SNYDER, Vice President & General Manager, B. & L. E. R. R. Co., Pittsburgh, Pa.
C. O. DAMBACH, General Manager, P. & W. Va. Ry. Co., Pittsburgh, Pa.
R. H. FLINN, General Superintendent, Pennsylvania Railroad, Pittsburgh, Pa.
R. P. FORSBERG, Chief Engineer, P. & L. E. R. R. Co., Pittsburgh, Pa.

SUBJECT COMMITTEE:

D. W. McGEORGE, Chairman, Secretary, Edgewater Steel Company, Pittsburgh, Pa.
G. H. BURNETTE, Asst. Chief Engineer, P. & L. E. R. R. Co., Pittsburgh, Pa.

RECEPTION AND ATTENDANCE COMMITTEE:

J. W. JOHNSON, Chairman, Superintendent, Railway Express Agency, Pittsburgh, Pa.
W. C. BUREL, Vice Chairman, Master Mechanic, Western Allegheny Railroad, Kaylor, Pa.
J. W. BOYD, Superintendent, Monongahela Railway Company, Brownsville, Pa.
THOMAS E. CANNON, General Supt. Equipment, P. & W. Va. Ry. Co., Pittsburgh, Pa.
T. W. CARR, Superintendent Rolling Stock, P. & L. E. R. R. Co., McKees Rocks, Pa.
D. C. CARROLL, Assistant Agent, Pennsylvania Railroad, Pittsburgh, Pa.
S. G. DOWN, Vice President, Westinghouse Air Brake Company, Wilmerding, Pa.
HARRY C. GRAHAM, Pittsburgh Screw & Bolt Corporation, Pittsburgh, Pa.
J. W. SCHAD, Division Master Mechanic, B. & O. R. R. Co., Pittsburgh, Pa.
GEORGE S. WEST, Division Superintendent, Pennsylvania Railroad, Pittsburgh, Pa.
J. W. HOOVER, Asst. Chief of Transpn., Subsidiary Cos. U. S. Steel Corp., Pittsburgh, Pa.
A. A. READ, Duquesne Slag Products Company, Pittsburgh, Pa.
C. P. SCHRECONGOST, Traffic Manager, Hillman Coal & Coke Company, Pittsburgh, Pa.
J. A. WARFEL, Special Representative, Air Reduction Sales Company, Pittsburgh, Pa.
J. C. SHINGLEDECKER, Supervisor of Service Stations, The Pennzoil Co., Pittsburgh, Pa.
J. C. DILWORTH, Manager Railroad Sales, Carnegie-Illinois Steel Corp., Pittsburgh, Pa.

ENTERTAINMENT COMMITTEE:

J. PORTER GILLESPIE, Chairman, Asst. Gen. Supt., Lockhart Iron & Steel Co., Pgh., Pa.
FRANK E. WEIS, Vice Chairman, Transportation Clerk, Penna. R. R., Pittsburgh, Pa.
JAMES NAGEL, Superintendent Transportation, Montour Railroad, Coraopolis, Pa.
E. H. HOLMES, Sales Department, Fort Pitt Malleable Iron Co., Pittsburgh, Pa.
C. C. CLARK, Sales Manager, Central District, Pressed Steel Car Co., Pittsburgh, Pa.
A. I. KESSLER, Clearance Clerk, Pennsylvania Railroad, Pittsburgh, Pa.
T. F. SHERIDAN, Asst. to S.M.P. and S.R.S., P. & L. E. R. R. Co., McKees Rocks, Pa.

FINANCE COMMITTEE:

M. A. SMITH, Chairman, General Manager, P. & L. E. R. R. Co., Pittsburgh, Pa.
J. B. DIVEN, Superintendent Motive Power, Pennsylvania Railroad, Pittsburgh, Pa.
F. J. RYAN, District Representative, Detroit, Toledo & Ironton Railroad, Pittsburgh, Pa.
C. E. CATT, Division Accountant, B. & O. R. R. Co., Pittsburgh, Pa.
G. W. HONSBERGER, Transpn. Mgr., Westinghouse Electric & Mfg. Co., Pittsburgh, Pa.

ADVERTISING COMMITTEE:

H. H. HAUPT, Chairman, Gen. Supt., Motive Power, Pennsylvania Railroad, Pittsburgh, Pa.
KARL BERG, Superintendent Motive Power, P. & L. E. R. R. Co., McKees Rocks, Pa.
H. E. PASSMORE, Representative, The American Hammered Piston Ring Co., Pgh., Pa.

MEMBERSHIP COMMITTEE:

T. E. BRITT, Chairman, Div. Storekeeper, B. & O. R. R. Co., Glenwood Shops, Pgh., Pa.
C. M. WHEELER, Vice Chairman, Sales Engr., Union Switch & Signal Co., Swissvale, Pa.
F. H. EATON, Sales Engineer, American Car & Foundry Co., Pittsburgh, Pa.
C. W. GOTTSCHALK, Asst. Traffic Manager, Jones & Laughlin Steel Corp., Pgh., Pa.
LLOYD SUTHERLAND, General Storekeeper, P. & L. E. R R. Co., McKees Rocks, Pa.
THOMAS R. FITZPATRICK, Freight Traffic Mgr., P. & L. E. R. R. Co., Pittsburgh, Pa.
P. W. HEPBURN, Sales Engineer, Gulf Refining Company, Pittsburgh, Pa.
W. B. MOIR, Chief Car Inspector, Pennsylvania Railroad, Pittsburgh, Pa.
C. W. TRUST, Assistant Traffic Manager, Carnegie-Illinois Steel Corp., Pittsburgh, Pa.
R. S. BULL, Supt. Power & Inclines, Pittsburgh Railways Co., N. S., Pittsburgh, Pa.
A. F. COULTER, Master Car Builder, Union Railroad Co., East Pittsburgh, Pa.
T. R. DICKINSON, Purchasing Agent, B. & L. E. R. R. Co., Pittsburgh, Pa.
D. K. ORR, Road Master, Monongahela Railway Co., Brownsville, Pa.
W. F. AMBROSE, Master Mechanic, Aliquippa & Southern Railroad, Aliquippa, Pa.
JOHN I. MULVEY, Traffic Manager, Hubbard & Company, Pittsburgh, Pa.

PAST PRESIDENTS:

*J. H. McCONNELL	October,	1901, to October, 1903
*L. H. TURNER	November,	1903, to October, 1905
*F. H. STARK	November,	1905, to October, 1907
*H. W. WATTS	November,	1907, to April, 1908
*D. J. REDDING	November,	1908, to October, 1910
*F. R. McFEATTERS	November,	1910, to October, 1912
*A. G. MITCHELL	November,	1912, to October, 1914
*F. M. McNULTY	November,	1914, to October, 1916
*J. G. CODE	November,	1916, to October, 1917
*D. M. HOWE	November,	1917, to October, 1918
*J. A. SPIELMAN	November,	1918, to October, 1919
H. H. MAXFIELD	November,	1919, to October, 1920
FRANK J. LANAHAN	November,	1920, to October, 1921
*SAMUEL LYNN	November,	1921, to October, 1922
*D. F. CRAWFORD	November,	1922, to October, 1923
*GEO. D. OGDEN	November,	1923, to October, 1924
A. STUCKI	November,	1924, to October, 1925
F. G. MINNICK	November,	1925, to October, 1926
G. W. WILDIN	November,	1926, to October, 1927
E. J. DEVANS	November,	1927, to October, 1928
W. S. McABEE	November,	1928, to October, 1929
E. W. SMITH	November,	1929, to October, 1930
LOUIS E. ENDSLEY	November,	1930, to October, 1931
*JOHN E. HUGHES	November,	1931, to October, 1932
F. I. SNYDER	November,	1932, to October, 1933
C. O. DAMBACH	November,	1933, to October, 1934
R. H. FLINN	November,	1934, to October, 1935
R. P. FORSBERG	November,	1935, to October, 1936

*—Deceased.

Meetings held fourth Thursday of each month except June, July and August.

PROCEEDINGS OF MEETING
SEPTEMBER 23, 1937

The meeting was called to order at the Fort Pitt Hotel at 8 o'clock P. M., with President E. A. Rauschart in the chair.

Registered attendance, 263, as follows

MEMBERS

Adams, F. W.
Allen, Earl M.
Ambrose, W. F.
Anderegg, George W.
Angel, A. J.
Aulbach, Albert J.
Babcock, F. H.
Baer, H. L.
Baker, W. E.
Balla, J. A.
Balph, M. Z.
Balzer, C. E.
Barr, H. C.
Baumann, E. G.
Beeson, H. L.
Beitsch, George F.
Beltz, J. D.
Bender, H. P.
Berg, Karl
Bishop, D. B.
Black, C. R.
Britt, T. E.
Brown, Earl F.
Button, L. R.
Buzzerd, J. P.
Callahan, D. E.
Campbell, F. R.
Cannon, T. E.
Carr, T. W.
Carroll, D. C.
Chilcoat, H. E.
Chipley, G. R.
Cipro, Thomas
Clausen, Harold
Clowes, W. K.
Code, C. J.
Colbert, J. T.
Conway, J. D.
Courtney, Harry
Crawford, Burt H.
Crede, W. A.

Creighton, D. M.
Crenner, J. A.
Critchfield, W. P.
Cruikshank, J. C.
Cunningham, J. D.
Dambach, C. O.
Davis, Charles S.
Dean, E. E.
Dickinson, B. F.
Dunham, C. W.
Durnell, W. E.
Edwards, Walter
Endsley, Prof. Louis E.
Evans, David F.
Fair, J. M.
Farlow, G. B.
Ferguson, George
Ferguson, J. H.
Flinn, R. H.
Forsberg, R. P.
Forsythe, George B.
Freshwater, F. H.
Fry, L. H.
Furch, George J.
Galbraith, James R.
Geiser, W. P.
Gelston, George A.
George, R. H.
George, W. J.
Gilbert, William J.
Gilg, Henry F.
Gillespie, J. Porter
Gleeson, H. L.
Glenn, J. H.
Goldstrom, G. E.
Grieve, Robert E.
Groves, W. C.
Haller, Nelson M.
Hamilton, W. H.
Hansen, William C.
Harper, G. C.

Harper, J. T.
Hayward, Carlton
Hellriegel, W. H.
Hemma, Charles H.
Henry, C. J.
Hepburn, P. W.
Hess, Charles A.
Holland, S. E.
Holmes, E. H.
Hoopes, R. E.
Hoover, J. W.
Jados, W. T.
Jarres, F. A.
Johnson, Ira S.
Johnson, J. W.
Johnson, Le Vere H.
Kearfott, W. E.
Keeney, John H.
Kemmerer, R. R.
Kentlein, John
King, George A. H.
Kirby, D. D.
Kiskadden, H. L.
Koenig, Walter A.
Kuhn, S. H.
Lanahan, Frank J.
Lanahan, J. S.
Lee, L. A.
Leonard, P. J.
Logan, J. W., Jr.
Longsteeth, W. L.
Lutz, Harry
Maliphant, C. W.
Masterman, T. W.
Masters, W. C.
Megee, C. R.
Miller, John
Miller, L. P.
Miller, R. C.
Miller, W. J.
Mitchell, W. S.
Moir, W. B.
Moulis, F. J.
Mulligan, Michael
McLaughlin, H. B.
Nagel, James
Nash, R. L.
Nathan, W. S.
Nelson, W. S.
Nichols, Samuel A.
Nieman, Charles J.

Nies, E. L.
Noble, J. A.
Noonan, Daniel
Paisley, F. R.
Peirce, W. B.
Pollack, Joseph W.
Rauschart, E. A.
Reymer, Charles H.
Rief, Joseph
Riley, S. B.
Roberts, E. L.
Rushneck, G. L.
Rutter, H. E.
Ryan, D. W.
Sanders, C. R.
Sayre, H. A.
Schako, E. J.
Schaller, A. J.
Schmitt, Andrew
Schrecongost, C. P.
Searles, E. J.
Sekera, C. J.
Severn, A. B.
Sheffer, R. W.
Shellenbarger, H. M.
Shepherd, R. M.
Sheridan, T. F.
Sipe, C. P.
Sipe, D. A.
Sixsmith, G. M.
Smith, G. M.
Smith, Robert B.
Snyder, F. I.
Stamm, B. B.
Steding, H. L.
Steigerwalt, R. W.
Steiner, P. E.
Stephen, James
Stevens, L. V.
Stewart, J. C.
Stoffregen, Louis E.
Strople, G. H.
Stucki, A.
Swenk, Raymond
Taylor, Joseph M.
Teskey, Dr. Walter J.
Thomas, Teodore
Thompson, H. A.
Thornton, A. W.
Tipton, G. M.
Tomasic, N. M., Jr.

Tracey, J. B. A.
Tryon, Ira D.
Tyler, B. W., Jr.
Uhar, John J.
Van Woert, F. E.
Von Pein, A. N.
Vowinkel, Fred F.
Wallace, C. M.

West, Troy
Williams, D. L.
Williamson, J. A.
Wilson, James R.
Woodings, R. T.
Woodward, R.
Yarnall, Jesse
Young, J. E.

VISITORS

Angerman, John C.
Barr, Albert S., Jr.
Buckley, William
Bugbee, W. E.
Cashdollar, Roy G.
Conrad, S. L.
Corbett, W. A.
Cramer, F. F.
Davis, William B.
Dunn, G. L.
Earnest, W. F.
Eberlein, George
Eisele, H. G.
Faries, Robert
Flynn, F. E.
Fulkerson, A.
Geist, Eugene
Gipe, C. E.
Glovin, Edward
Grove, L. T.
Henning, C. F.
Henry, W. C.
Herman, J. L.
Hilgert, T. J.
Johnson, H. C.
Kendall, W. H.
Ketler, C. P.
Knipe, Arthur H.
Laessig, A. C.
Lanahan, J. K.
Lewis, S. B.

Maguire, J. Frank, Jr.
Mason, E. R.
Mosford, R. T.
McCartney, Howard
McGregor, S. S.
Newburn, S. H.
Niggl, F. E.
Palmros, A.
Parvin, Charles F.
Potter, Charles
Radtke, J. E.
Raus, William R.
Ramsey, Hugh A.
Riddle, F. L.
Schwab, John A.
Sennstrom, Harold
Shelkey, L. D.
Smith, Sion B.
Stell, M. A.
Stirrett, D. N.
Stype, W. G.
Thomas, Martin F.
Unangst, H. S.
Vandivort, R. E.
Villella, C. A.
Wallace, D. T.
Walther, G. C.
Wassel, P.
Wattles, H. Starr
Wilcox, Walter
Woodings, C. L.

Woozley, D. E.

PRESIDENT: As all of you signed the registry cards as you entered the room, we will dispense with the calling of the roll.

Also the minutes of the last meeting having been printed in the Proceedings and distributed some time ago, unless there is objection the reading of the minutes of the last meeting will be dispensed with.

I will ask the Secretary to read the list of proposals for membership.

SECRETARY: We have the following proposals for membership:

Angel, A. J., Purchasing Agent, P. & W. Va. Ry. Co., Wabash Building, Pittsburgh, Pa. Recommended by C. O. Dambach.

Berg, Max, Locomotive Engineer, Montour Railroad Company, R. D. No. 6, Mt. Oliver Station, Pittsburgh, Pa. Recommended by E. A. Rauschart.

Boyer, W. W., Assistant Division Engineer, Pennsylvania Railroad, 35 Dinsmore Avenue, Crafton, Pittsburgh, Pa. Recommended by C. M. Wheeler.

Button, L. R., General Freight and Passenger Agent, The Pittsburgh & Shawmut Railroad Company, 129 N. McKean St., Kittanning, Pa. Recommended by J. T. Colbert.

Edsall, S. D., Manager, Air Reduction Sales Company, 1116 Ridge Avenue, North Side, Pittsburgh, Pa. Recommended by Lloyd Sutherland.

Forquer, Edwin A., Stationary Engineer, Montour Railroad Company, 1109 Chartiers Avenue, McKees Rocks, Pa. Recommended by E. A. Rauschart.

Hansen, F. Karl, Metallurgical Contact Representative, Carnegie-Illinois Steel Corporation, Frick Annex Building, Pittsburgh, Pa. Recommended by K. B. Dickson.

Jackovac, Victor P., Sales Department, Edgewater Steel Company, 337 Penn street, Verona, Pa. Recommended by Charles A. Hess.

Kenny, Mark P., Coal Freight Agent, Pennsylvania Railroad, Pennsylvania Station, Pittsburgh, Pa. Recommended by W. P. Buffington.

King, George A. H., Clerk, Monongahela Connecting Railroad Company, 311 Ross Street, Pittsburgh, Pa. Recommended by George W. Anderegg.

Mowery, John F., Painter Foreman, Montour Railroad Company, 780 Greenfield Avenue, Pittsburgh, Pa. Recommended by E. A. Rauschart.

McKirdy, C. W., District Manager, Iron & Steel Products, Inc., Investment Building, Pittsburgh, Pa. Recommended by Henry F. Gilg.

Schane, Frank A., Contact Representative, Carnegie-Illinois Steel Corporation, 3446 Beechwood Boulevard, Pittsburgh, Pa. Recommended by K. B. Dickson.

Sheffer, R. W., Division Engineer, Pennsylvania Railroad, Pennsylvania Station, Pittsburgh, Pa. Recommended by C. M. Wheeler.

Shepherd, R. M., President, Pittsburgh & Shawmut Railroad, Kittanning, Pa. Recommended by Charles J. Nieman.

Smith, Lewis H., Sales Manager, Downflow Syphon Company, 3029 Prospect Avenue, Cleveland, Ohio. Recommended by E. A. Rauschart.

Snyder, Paul H., Assistant General Car Foreman, Montour Railroad Company, 1115 Main Street, Coraopolis, Pa. Recommended by E. A. Rauschart.

Steigerwalt, R. W., Manager, Railroad Material and Commercial Forgings Bureau, Metallurgical Division, Carnegie-Illinois Steel Corporation, Frick Annex Building, Pittsburgh, Pa. Recommended by K. B. Dickson.

Wallace, C. M., Supervisor, Pennsylvania Railroad, Pennsylvania Station, Pittsburgh, Pa. Recommended by C. M. Wheeler.

Wickerham, F. A., Manager, Bureau of Information and Service Tests, Metallurgical Division, Carnegie-Illinois Steel Corporation, Frick Annex Building, Pittsburgh, Pa. Recommended by K. B. Dickson.

PRESIDENT: According to our By-laws proposals for membership must be approved by the Executive Committee, whereupon the gentlemen become members without further action. This approval having been given, I will ask any who may be present to rise, that we may recognize you and extend to you a welcome.

Mr. Secretary, are there any announcements?

SECRETARY: Since our last meeting we have received information of the death of the following members: F. G.

Minnick, who served as President of the Club from November, 1925, to October, 1926, died May 31, 1937; S. T. Barr, Air Brake Instructor, Pennsylvania Railroad, died May 24, 1937; Charles A. Teerkes, Freight Agent, P. & L. E. R. R., died June 28, 1937, and J. H. Weygandt, Assistant Yard Master, Pennsylvania Railroad, died May 11, 1937.

PRESIDENT: An appropriate memorial minute will appear in the next issue of the Proceedings.

Is there any further business to come before the meeting? If not, we come to the paper of the evening. We will be addressed by Mr. Robert Faries, Assistant Chief Engineer of the Maintenance of Way Department of the Pennsylvania Railroad, Philadelphia, Pa., on the subject, Progress in Track Maintenance to Meet the Requirements of Present Day Traffic. I take pleasure in presenting Mr. Faries.

Progress In Track Maintenance To Meet The Requirements Of Present Day Traffic

By ROBERT FARIES, Assistant Chief Engineer of the Maintenance of Way Department, Pennsylvania Railroad, Philadelphia, Pa.

Mr. President and Members of The Railway Club of Pittsburgh:

I appreciate the opportunity you have given me to speak here. A good many years ago a country boy came to this city to work. The hoarse whistles of the river steamers and the night glare of countless furnaces were new to him. The energy and movement of the great city were wonderful to contemplate. A land of enchantment was pictured for him on every side. The thrills of those days will never be lost from my memory. My associations here have been most pleasant. During the activities in the latter part of the World War I was Division Engineer of our Pittsburgh Division; and in contemplating that period, when a great deal of work had to be done, I always feel grateful to my associates and the maintenance men on the division for their assistance and remarkable ability to do more than was expected of them. I remember one night we had a stock train wrecked near the Horseshoe Curve and a number of hogs got away in the mountains. After carefully checking up the Claim Department said there were exactly 292 hogs missing which had to be rounded up and driven into the Altoona stock pens. The trackmen went at the job early in the morning. They scoured the hills and rounded up the 292 hogs and 37 more.

Railroading has been changing rapidly in the past few years, and with these changes the demands upon the track have been increased. Higher speeds; or, more properly speaking, sustained high speeds with elimination of stops and restrictions have been attained. Increased size of power with increased tractive effort have provided greater acceleration and greater speed on ascending grades. The close schedules of freight trains require quickened operation in yards and make freedom from yard derailments imperative. Restrictions put on tracks in order to carry out repairs are increasingly detrimental and must be minimized.

In order to gain knowledge of the effect of weight and speed upon track, we conducted prolonged and extensive tests in developing a Heavy Powerful High Speed Electric Locomotive. In these tests we used novel instruments to determine stress, acceleration and lateral forces—stress with magnetic strain gauges, acceleration with special types of accelerometers, and lateral forces with magnetic strain gauges, and Brinell type steel tie track. Stress measurements have been taken on rails, joint bars, bridges and on equipment. The speeds used in tests have been generally up to 100 to 105 miles per hour. We are arranging now to conduct one of the tests at a speed of 120 miles per hour. A number of interesting facts have been developed. For instance, considering lateral forces exerted upon the rail:

A 4-6-6-4 electric articulated locomotive at 100 MPH delivered 23,300 lbs. and the intensity of the blow was increasing at the rate of 130 lbs. per mile per hour.

A 4-6-4 electric locomotive at 100 MPH delivered 40,000 lbs., and the intensity of the blow was increasing at the rate of 1,111 lbs. per miles per hour.

A 4-6-2 steam locomotive at 100 MPH delivered 25,000 lbs., and the intensity of the blow was increasing at the rate of 250 lbs. per mile per hour.

A 4-8-2 steam locomotive at 80 MPH delivered 52,000 lbs., and the intensity of the blow was increasing at the rate of 1,250 lbs. per mile per hour.

This latter engine, when provided with additional lateral resistance in the trailer truck, delivered 26,500 lbs. at 80

MPH. In general it was found that at the high speeds, which were of course made where the alignment was good, increased resistance in truck and trailer to lateral movement, something of the effect of a longer wheel base reduced the lateral trust. This increased resistance on truck and trailer is not so good when the locomotive is using short turnouts and negotiating sharp curves in terminals. To overcome this our electric locomotives are so arranged that the increased resistance applies only when the locomotive is on tangent or moderate curve. When trucks are shifted considerably from the normal position, as when on a sharp curve, the resistance to further shifting is lessened. I am citing these cases to show how definitely the design of equipment affects the track structure. The substantial increases in speeds have brought out the necessity for giving more attention to distribution of weight, cross-counterbalance and truck and trailer resistance. "The relation of the rolling stock to the track" is a subject now being handled by Dr. Talbot's A. R. E. A. Committee on Stresses in Railroad Track.

The effect of poor track on the lateral forces is indicated by a test in which the cross level was made about ½ inch low on one side, then reversed and ½ inch low on the other. At the same speed and with the same equipment lateral forces were increased from 7,000 lbs. on the good track to 35,000 lbs. on the irregular track.

We are making a study of the effect of depressions in the rail and flat spots on wheels to check the mathematical theory that where there are depressions in the rail there is a critical speed to produce the maximum effect, which speed increases with the length of the defect and if operating at this critical speed the force of the impact will vary directly with the depth of defect. We are continuing these tests in collaboration with Dr. Talbot's Committee on Stresses in Railroad Track. There is a large amount of data not yet analyzed which should give considerable additional information on the subject. We are also studying the effect of harmonic and non-harmonic types of springs on cars and the effect of different weights of unbalanced counterweight in relation to reciprocating parts to determine their effect upon track stresses.

The effect of a 30 MPH speed restriction ½ mile long has been studied. It takes from two to three times the distance from start of retardation to restoration of full speed when running 90 MPH compared with 75 MPH. In a 100-mile run, the elimination of from five to six such speed restrictions will accomplish the same result as an increase of speed from 75 MPH to 90 MPH. As the speed increases the effect of speed restrictions rapidly increases. This is particularly true with respect to freight train speed since the restoration of the higher freight train speed after observing a restriction may take many miles of otherwise unrestricted territory. The elimination of several speed restrictions on a Division will, in many cases, result in the elimination of double heading both passenger and freight in order to make the tight schedules with heavy trains. The elimination of speed restrictions in dense traffic territory adds to the capacity of the railroad.

Field Tests.

In order that proper materials be provided for our maintenance, we carry out both field and laboratory tests covering a great number of the items of materials and tools that we purchase. We have a total of approximately 200 field tests under way continuously. This work is under the direction of our Assistant Engineer of Standards, who is located at the Test Plant in Altoona, Penna., and he examines and measures the materials frequently and observes the performance throughout the entire cycle of life. The most valuable information is received towards the termination of the life of the material. Thus, we are enabled to know with reasonable certainty just how these materials are going to perform before purchases are made in any quantity. The facts developed in these tests are made available to manufacturers upon request and should be beneficial to them. Unless field tests are directly under an organization established for the sole purpose of following these tests and observing the performance during the entire life, the tests are of little value. To scatter test material over a number of locations and expect the local man, whose time is taken up by what he considers more important matters, to give definite information is very unsatisfactory, particularly since the local personnel changes frequently. You may get as many different answers as there are locations, that is, provided they can all find the test material.

As a result of the knowledge gained from these tests, such as I have described, we have been able to improve our conditions, and it is to some of these improvements I would like to direct your attention.

Roadbed.

In starting to stabilize track, the natural approach is, first, consideration of the roadbed. There is a vast difference in the materials which make up roadbeds of railroad track and differences in the methods of construction which affect the stability of the track. Fills made of clay, or fills on soft material, are rarely satisfactory. Cuts through clay always give trouble unless careful study is made of the contours of the clay surface under the roadbed and the low points drained in a permanent manner. In an area of particularly poor subgrade on our line between Philadelphia and Washington it was necessary to make such surveys as I have indicated, and to preserve the drainage of the low spots by placing mats of treated wood on a layer of cinders. The clay surfaces in these trenches were covered with a bituminous mixture to prevent capillary water from reaching the surface. At other points the general water level has been lowered from 4 ft. to 8 ft. by open ditches, by drains of treated wood and by the use of iron pipes laid in trenches and back filled with a porous material such as pit run gravel.

Ballast.

Samples of all the ballast used on our line are subjected to a laboratory test. Certain standards are set up and the different products graded so that the best ballast available will be provided. Our standards now provide for an additional foot of ballast on the shoulders to add to the stability of the track. A great deal of ballast cleaning and track surfacing can be avoided by the use of good hard ballast that will not break up under tamping.

Ties.

Our people assure me that they can treat ties to last as long as the mechanical wear and splitting will let them last. Mechanical wear has been reduced by larger plates and better fastenings of the plate to the tie and the spliting of ties, which rsults in quite a large item of expense, has been controlled by a better method of using anti-splitting irons. Ties usually fail from vertical splits which start at both top and bottom of tie. We now place two irons in each end, locating one near the top and one near the bottom instead of using one iron near the center. The center iron did not come into use until quite a large split had formed, and then it was inadequate to resist the strain caused by the wedging action of dirt and stones in the crack and the freezing action of the wet material in the cracks. Treated ties make a stronger track because nearly all of the ties in a rail panel are sound all of the time. With untreated ties a number in the panel were always near to renewal time.

Rail.

During the past few years, the quality of rail steel has been greatly improved both by methods employed prior to rolling, and by slow cooling and normalizing of the rail after it leaves the rolls. These improvements give every indication of completely eliminating the shatter cracks which result in the transverse fissure. The Rail Committee of the American Railway Engineering Association, working jointly with the manufacturers, has been very active in these studies for the past few years. The stresses in 152-lbs. rail under our heaviest locomotives are just about one-half of what they were in the rail used twenty-five years ago. About this same relation exists with respect to the amount of depression under load; and it is thus apparent that the wave motion in the track, which is one of the principal causes of track deterioration, has been to a great extent eliminated. Both the 131-lb. RE rail section and the 152-lb. PS rail section, which have the same contour of the top of the head, show after six years in a test track under heavy traffic only 50% to 70% the amount of abrasion there is on the former 130-lb. section in the same test. This applies both to tangent and curve. The advantages of the new rail sections are very apparent in this test. I attribute this resistance to abrasion to the fact that the rail head contour of the new sections are flatter and the initial cold rolling extends entirely across the head of the rail, consolidating and improving the metal in this area quickly so that it is more resistant to subsequent wear.

We have had end hardened rail in a test track which has now carried approximately 300,000,000 tons of traffic and the ends of the rail are slightly higher, about .015", than the general surface of the rest of the rail. With very little grinding the rail can be restored to its top condition when new.

Joints.

We have found a number of advantages in a long joint flexible enough to insure a tight fit at the rail ends and at the bar ends, and have gone to this type exclusively. We carry out a substantial program of welding and grinding at the joints, approximately 500 miles of track, annually. The several experienments involving welded rail on the Delaware & Hudson Railroad and the test location near Pittsburgh on the Bessemer & Lake Erie Railroad are being followed with a great deal of interest. This is, indeed, revolutionary and there is naturally a great deal of caution in the minds of the majority of Railroad men in an approach to the subject. However, I believe that it is entirely with an open mind. The gradual improvement in the quality of the welds and performance of the track in service so far are very interesting.

Frogs and Switches.

Frogs and switches have been redesigned to give additional strength and longer service life. This has been accomplished by the elimination of short bends and fillets, and by reinforcing parts where weakness has developed in the past. Bolt shrouds have been eliminated in the manganese body casting, and cross ribs to reinforce the manganese casting have been substituted, and we thereby obtain a more uniform thickness and reduce the shrinkage cracks and strains set up by cooling. Wing wheel risers have been provided to relieve the thin portion of the frog point of wheel loads, thereby reducing batter and spalling at the point of the frog. On the spring type of frogs the individual tie plates have been replaced with continuous base plates held rigidly to base of frog with clips and bolts. The toe of the spring rail has been shortened so that there is less movable rail about the frog. Heavy toe blocks have been provided and the planing of the base of the rail changed to eliminate the short fillet which formerly caused numberous breaks. Hydraulic snubbers have been applied to spring rail frogs where there is frequent movement through the turnout runs. This prevents excessive pounding by the spring rail, which tends to loosen all parts of the frog. Heel blocks have been provided to insure the position and fit of switch with respect to the stock rail, and to give increased strength about the heel of the switch. Most switches are protected by providing a machined housing in the stock rail approximately ⅛ inch deep. We are now installing a number of 45-ft. switches. Switches of this length eliminate the abrupt angle at the switch point, which always resulted in considerable thrust at this point and added to the cost of maintaining the turnouts.

Bridges.

By the use of magnetic strain gauges, knowledge of the actual stress in certain types of bridges has been obtained, which types of bridges are incapable of accurate calculation. From a better knowledge of impact stresses we have been able to permit higher speeds than were thought justified by former inadequate knowledge of this subject. This has resulted in saving us a great amount of money for the renewal of bridges which were formerly thought questionable. Low impact values 17 bridges were found where the electric locomotives were tested, as had been anticipated. This is an important advantage in the use of electric locomotives.

With steam locomotives particularly maximum dynamic stresses are produced at a certain critical speed. This being the case, arbitrary reduction of speed as a safety measure may not actually help the situation, which is different for each different type of locomotive and each different bridge.

Derailments.

The speeding up of the movement of cars through yards is a very important factor in meeting fast freight schedules. There are many things that can be done to prevent yard derailments, among which I would mention elimination of short turnouts, protection of switch points by guard rails or other devices, grinding of switch points and stock rails to preserve the proper fit, providing heel blocks for switches, and preserving proper flangeways in frogs by grinding.

Mechanization of Maintenance Work.

For a number of years there has been a constant trend toward doing Maintenance of Way work mechanically wherever it was found possible to do it. This was not only from reasons of economy, but for safety reasons and to provide better and more lasting work. The mechanical cleaning of ballast originated on our Pittsburgh Division a number of years ago. Now we have machines to tap track, adze ties, bolt and unbolt joints, drive and pull spikes, burn weeds, mow the right-of-way, saw and frame bridge timbers, grade banks and bore holes in almost anything. A recent development is a grinder to smooth the surface of the rail where corrugations and burns exist. This is a car carrying two Diesel engines which generate electricity. The grinders, six on each side, are driven by motors and are arranged to float with the irregularities in the rail surface but to hold a definite pressure. This is controlled hydraulically. The 10-inch high speed surface grinding wheels are arranged in planes which very closely approximate the rail contour.

In fact, nearly all Maintenance of Way operations are mechanized. Several notable exceptions are lining track, except as provided by special forms of jacks, and renewing ties. Many of these machines are highly developed, but there are a great number which are in a transition and development state and there is yet a great field for advancement along these lines.

The tendencies are toward machines which operate without blocking the track, and there is also a tendency toward doing many small jobs formerly done by hand by use of very small and very portable power plants.

Training of Men.

All of these technical problems are interesting and important, but I would like to say a few words about the greatest problem we have—the training of men. The development of officers to carry on the management of our property is one of the primary duties of those now in charge of the property. The study involves such factors as the rate at which vacancies in the various classes occur, adequate apprenticeship periods, age limits for employment, age limits beyond which the attainment of certain intermediate positions result in inadequate time for subsequent and necessary training, and many such related problems. While most of our apprentices are college trained men, the opportunity for advancement is not confined to this class. In fact we make special effort to search out and assist any employe who shows exceptional initiative, energy and administrative ability. It is the duty of the officers to know the capacities of all of these young men and by adding to their responsibilities at the proper time to give them the opportunity to fully develop themselves by proper contacts to the limits of their natural ability, tending always toward the ultimate result—proper management of men and affairs through ability to analyze problems, primarily from an economical standpoint and at the same time conforming to sound engineering practice, and the ability through energy and resourcefulness to put into effect the result of such analysis. As the development of these men advances, it is the duty of their superiors to decide for each one the lines of endeavor in which they are best suited and to provide future development accordingly. In this way provision is made for the higher positions in engineering, research, and operating management.

Collective Bargaining.

A description of the progress in maintenance matters, to be complete, should include progress in employe relationship.

Collective bargaining, as this term is generally used, is not new in the sense of its practical application on the Pennsylvania Railroad, this relationship having been practiced with our employes for many years. In our conception, it is a partnership between the employes and the Management. We charge the supervisory groups of our railroad family with the responsibility of carrying into effect the policies of the Company as determined by the Directors and Executive Officers. We point out to our supervisors that no collective bargaining plan, however complete on paper, is a panacea unless every man in a supervisory position has a sympathetic grasp of its spirit, and deals with those he directs in a sympathetic and humane manner. We also point out to our supervision that human emotions are inevitably influenced by great upheavals in our economic life and that it is their responsibility to treat an employe as a human being gifted with individuality, personality, initiative and a reserve capacity to draw upon in the future, which makes each and every employe very different than a cog in a machine, and infinitely more valuable.

We believe, on the Pennsylvania Railroad, in our collective bargaining relationship with our employes, that it is not the known that causes trouble and fear, but rather the unknown. Ghosts never appear in the daylight, they appear at night because daylight discloses their non-existence.

Today, if there exists between our supervision and those supervised a close and friendly relationship so that there are no hidden corners and dark places for suspicion to lurk, a proper industrial companionship can be maintained.

At the present time, the Pennsylvania Railroad has agreements covering rates, rules and working conditions with practically all of its classified forces, and practically all of these agreements are made with employes through their chosen representatives under the Railway Labor Act, and generally, the agencies of representation are national labor organizations.

We have, on the Pennsylvania Railroad, System Boards of Adjustment to settle disputes growing out of interpretations and application of working agreements. These boards are composed of an equal number of Management and Employe representatives who meet on stated dates for the purpose of considering and disposing of all controversies growing out of the application of working agreements. These boards have successfully operated for more than sixteen years.

The agreements and manner of adjustment that I have just mentioned form, what we believe on the Pennsylvania Railroad, to be a complete collective bargaining relationship between the Company and its employes.

The success which has attended the handling of our employe problems, through the medium of adjustment by the methods just described, is well established by continued agreement on the part of our employes to pursue the adjustment of controversies through this medium, and it may be proper to, at this time, state that, of the many hundreds of cases handled by our Boards of Adjustment, very few have required more than thirty to sixty days for amicable settlement.

The success of collective bargaining, in labor relations on the railroads generally, has been brought to public notice on several occasions, the most notable examples being the following:

   (1)   Protection to employes affected by consolidations of railroad facilities, commonly known as the Coordination agreement.

   (2)   Retirement annuities.

We are happy to say we look upon the present high morale on the railroads, in general, as an outstanding example of what men and management can accomplish in a great enterprise by an intelligent effort to understand each other and, with honesty, attempt to be just in all matters in which there is mutual concern.

In the foregoing I have attempted to present to you some of the problems of maintenance and to indicate our methods of attacking these problems. Our testing work, undertaken to develop facts to aid us, has seemed extensive, and yet it has only served to show how large is the field for future reseach in railroad work. There is every indication that such research will be carried forward with greater energy and with increasing co-ordination between the various railroads under the guidance of the Engineering Division of the Association of American Railroads.

It is unfortunate that the primary transportation agency of the Nation, the agency which carries 70% of freight and 60% of passenger business of the country—the only agency capable of mass transportation on land—is faced with so many artificial uncertainties which restrict the freedom to advance commensurate with the advance in knowledge gained from these studies. The progress made in recent years in all departments of the Railroad has been in the face of these uncertainties and is, therefore, all the more outstanding. Let us hope that with future advance in knowledge there will be nothing to prevent the Railroad industry in promptly and freely providing for advantages so developed. If such be the case the future efficiency and usefulness of the Railroad plant in National transportation will be gratifying to all concerned.

PRESIDENT: Mr. Faries, we thank you for your very interesting and instructive paper. As Mr. Faries has consented to answer any questions that may be asked, the subject of the paper is now before you for discussion.

And I would like to call on Mr. R. P. Forsberg for some remarks.

MR. R. P. FROSBERG: Mr. President, you should have forewarned me that I was to be a victim tonight and not subjected me to a sudden increase in blood pressure or an attack of "buck fever." However, as the oustanding paper Mr. Faries has just presented to us is right down my alley, I will have little difficulty in saying something relative to it, in fact my trouble will be to not talk too long, which I am sure I will do, if I attempt to review, in any detail, the wealth of information contained in his paper.

In my opinion, the present day traffic (referred to in the title of his paper) that necessitates a change in our former standards of track maintenance in order that we may properly meet it, is in reality present day and future day higher speeds. Mr. Faries has advised us in a masterly manner what is being done and what remains to be done in order that we may solve the problem that has been thrust upon us.

If there was one part of his address that impressed me more than another it was the statement he made towards the close relative to the plight of the steam railroads of our country today. The facts are as he stated them, namely, that our railroads find it difficult today to advance along proven lines of economical transportation while our competitors are being favored. May I attempt to very briefly further develop that thought.

Gentlemen, the United States today has no unified transportation policy. Instead of being welded into a co-ordinated system, our various transportation agencies are working more or less at cross purposes. Instead of a unified program of regulation designed to promote a common objective, we have a series of unrelated and often antagonistic policies carried out by a variety of government agencies.

Every form of transportation—be it by Airplane, Motor Coach, Motor Truck, Steam Railroad or Inland Waterway, should stand on its own feet, with competition in a free field deciding the survival of the fittest. That condition, unhappily for our steam railroads, does not obtain today.

I believe that I voice the sentiment of the steam railroads of this country when I say they do not complain of or fear competition if it is on a just and equitable basis. The railroads are not requesting the elimination of competition by highways, the elimination of competition by inland waterways, they are only asking that these agencies using such facilities, pay a proper proportion of the costs and be subjected to the same regulations that confront the railroads at every turn. If and when such measures are taken and the Railroads are then unable to retain their traffic, there will be little left to say in their defense. But if they are expected to continue to compete with other transportation agencies, subsidized to a greater or less extent by the Federal Government, then they may well read, as privately owned corporations, their ultimate end in the setting sun.

PRESIDENT: I would like to call on Mr. G. B. Farlow, Division Engineer, Baltimore and Ohio Railroad.

MR. G. B. FARLOW: Mr. Chairman, I would like first to add my word of appreciation of what the speaker has brought out. May I ask him one question? and that is whether in his experimental work he has come to any conclusion as to the merits of some of the recent improvements in the rail fastening to the tie. I have in mind particularly the various clips, springs and bolts fastenings designed to replace the time honored track spike.

MR. FARIES: I would say that something can be done along that line. There are other forms of fastenings, and some of them show improvement in holding the plate to the tie. However, they are more expensive and the question becomes an economical one—is the added advantage worth the additional cost?

PRESIDENT: Would any one else like to ask Mr. Faries a question?

MR. HENRY F. GILG: I do not know anything about roadbed, but I do know that the ties were not spaced properly for me to walk on them when I was working for a railroad.

I was interested when Mr. Faries referred to the properties of rails. Some of the older members will remember the 129 rails reported as having failed, and then a change was made from the Bessemer to the open-hearth rails.

Shortly after the Interstate Commerce Commission's report, I saw an old friend who was a rail-mill roller, and asked his opinion as to the cause of the failures. He said that the broken rails had been rolled at too high a temperature, and that it was his practice to let the rail cool off before putting through the last pass. The time allowed was five minutes.

My friend showed me a fracture of one of the failures and of his rail which had been allowed to cool. They were quite different.

Another point in Mr. Faries' address attracted my interest, and that was the difficulty of getting good men. In my own experience and in those of many boys whom I knew, the fond mothers wanted their sons to be above the common laborer, the molder, the boilermaker and other "coarse" trades. This has been the wrong education, so we have college graduates who look for the positions they were told to expect when they graduated, and many of them are disappointed. They have become mere hacks.

My advice to the graduate is to get a job in a boiler shop or in the track gang and learn the rudiments of engineering for which they had only a preparation in college. Promotion comes quickly in the railroad service in these two branches and the pay is regular. A writer of erotic novels said he could make a railroad executive from a college boy in three weeks. Some people believe that, for they don't know he gets paid so much a word for saying things whether they are true or not. It sounds smart to say what he did, but it is not true. Any boy who is interested in his work will find the problems of track and boiler work to be intensely absorbing.

MR. C. R. MEGEE, District Manager, Car Service Division, Association of American Railroads, Pittsburgh, Pa: I have had the pleasure of being acquainted with Mr. Faries for a period of years, and I have been immensely interested in his paper tonight. I would like to ask if he would care to make any remarks on the experiments that have been made in the use of the concrete tie.

MR. FARIES: Some 25,000 concrete ties have been used at some fifteen or twenty different locations, in quarter mile or half mile sections, under varying conditions. They were put in about ten years ago. Some of those stretches remain in fair shape. Of those that were in heavy traffic territory, a great many of them failed by crushing and breaking off at the ends and, also, they rotated under the rail. I do not say that would be true if properly designed, but you have to make a concrete tie pretty cheap to compete with the treated wooden tie.

PRESIDENT: Mr. Berg, may we hear from you?

MR. KARL BERG: Mr. President: As has already been stated by several of the members, certain studies, experiments and work described in the paper just read, touch upon very important points in railroading with reference to economy and efficiency, as well as safety. The paper indicates that a great deal of persistent engineering work, as well as co-operation, have been necessary in order to bring about these improvements. Personally, I want to add my word of appreciation.

As a locomotive man, I fully realize that I know very little, if anything, about the details of maintenance of tracks, but I shall enjoy reading the paper when it appears in print in the journal.

In view of the treat we have just had, and as an expression of our appreciation, I move a rising vote of thanks to Mr. Faries for his most excellent paper.

The motion prevailed by unanimous rising vote.

PRESIDENT: In accordance with Section ?, Article VI, of our Constitution, providing that the President appoint a Nominating Committee consisting of five members, three of whom must be regularly elected members of the Executive Committee, who shall at the September meeting recommend nominations for all offices to be filled at the annual meeting in October, the following Committee has been selected: Frank J. Lanahan, Chairman; Louis E. Endsley, C. O. Dambach, R. H. Flinn, T. E. Britt, and at this time we shall be pleased to have the report of the Nominating Committee:

MR. FRANK J. LANAHAN: Mr. President, your Nominating Committee makes its report as follows, but please bear in mind under our By-laws, commitees are elected for three-year terms, one-third of which is filled each year, so nominations now are made of those who will succeed the members who have served their allotted time and are **not** eligible for re-election. Two-thirds of the membership of these committees are not involved in the nomination tonight. It is due to the limitations of our By-laws that these splendid members who have served so faithfully in the past three years are not again proposed by your Nominating Committee. With this explanation, your Committee recommends the following nominations:

REPORT OF NOMINATING COMMITTEE

FOR PRESIDENT: G. M. Sixsmith, Superintendent, The Pennsylvania Railroad, Pittsburgh, Pa.

FOR FIRST VICE PRESIDENT: J. D. Beltz, Superintendent, B. & O. R. R. Co., Pittsburgh, Pa.

FOR SECOND VICE PRESIDENT: Karl Berg, Superintendent Motive Power, P. & L. E. R. R. Co., McKees Rocks, Pa.

FOR SECRETARY: J. D. Conway.

FOR TREASURER: E. J. Searles.

EXECUTIVE COMMITTEE: (Eleven to Mominate)
Frank J. Lanahan, Chairman,
A. Stucki,
G. W. Wildin,
W. S. McAbee,
E. W. Smith,
Louis E. Endsley,
F. I. Snyder,
C. O. Dambach,
R. H. Flinn,
R. P. Forsberg,
E. A. Rauschart.

SUBJECT COMMITTEE: (One to Nominate)
(3 Yrs.) H. H. Haupt, General Superintendent Motive Power, The Pennsylvania Railroad, Pittsburgh, Pa.

RECEPTION AND ATTENDANCE COMMITTEE: (Six to Nominate)
(3 Yrs.) C. E. Adams, Division Superintendent, The Pennsylvania Railroad, Pittsburgh, Pa.
(3 Yrs.) T. E. Britt, Division Storekeeper, B. & O. R. R. Co., Pittsburgh, Pa.
(3 Yrs.) W. P. Buffington, Traffic Manager, Pittsburgh Coal Company, Pittsburgh, Pa.
(3 Yrs.) William C. Hansen, Sales Engineer, A. Stucki Company, Pittsburgh, Pa.
(3 Yrs.) C. H. Reymer, Sales Representative, Oliver Iron & Steel Corporation, Pittsburgh, Pa.
(3 Yrs.) T. F. Sheridan, Assistant to Superintendents, Motive Power and Rolling Stock, P. & L. E. R. R. Co., McKees Rocks, Pa.

ENTERTAINMENT COMMITTEE: (Five to Nominate)
(3 Yrs.) Vincent Kroen, Vice Chairman—Supervisor Express Service, The P. R. R., Pittsburgh, Pa.
(3 Yrs.) W. C. Burel, Master Mechanic, Western Allegheny Railroad, Kaylor, Pa.

(3 Yrs.) H. E. Chilcoat, General Manager of Sales, Koppel Industrial Car & Equipment Company, Pittsburgh, Pa.

(3 Yrs.) F. L. Foster, Superintendent Freight Transportation, P. & L. E. R. R. Co., Pittsburgh, Pa.

(3 Yrs.) J. S. Lanahan, Vice President, Fort Pitt Malleable Iron Company, Pittsburgh, Pa.

ADVERTISING COMMITTEE: (Three to Nominate)

(3 Yrs.) J. H. James, Chairman—Purchasing Agent, P & L. E. R. R. Co., Pittsburgh, Pa.

(3 Yrs.) John C. Shingledecker, Supervisor of Service Stations, The Pennzoil Co., Pittsburgh, Pa.

(3 Yrs.) Charles M. Wheeler, Sales Engineer, Union Switch & Signal Company, Swissvale, Pa.

MEMBERSHIP COMMITTEE: (Nine to Nominate)

(3 Yrs.) T. Fitzgerald, Vice President and General Manager, Pittsburgh Railways Co., Pittsburgh, Pa.

(3 Yrs.) G. C. Harper, General Superintendent, Montour Railroad Company, Coraopolis, Pa.

(3 Yrs.) Frank A. Jarres, Assistant Storekeeper, B. & O. R. R. Co., 213 Second Street, Aspinwall, Pa.

(3 Yrs.) C. S. Leet, Assistant General Manager, B. & L. E. R. R. Co., Pittsburgh, Pa.

(3 Yrs.) Caleb R. Megee, Dist. Mgr. Car Service Div., Association of American Railroads, Pittsburgh, Pa.

(3 Yrs.) R. C. McIntyre, Superintendent Motive Power, Union Railroad Company, East Pittsburgh, Pa.

(3 Yrs.) H. C. Pringle. Vice Pres. and Supt., Monongahela Connecting Railroad Co., Pittsburgh, Pa.

(3 Yrs.) S. B. Riley, General Supt. and Supt. Motive Power, P. & W. Va., Ry. Co., Pittsburgh, Pa.

(3 Yrs.) John B. Wright, Assitant Vice President, Westinghouse Air Brake Co., Wilmerding, Pa.

NOMINATING COMMITTEE:

Frank J. Lanahan, Chairman,
Louis E. Endsley,
C. O. Dambach,
R. H. Flinn,
T. E. Britt.

PRESIDENT: You will understand that these nominations are not exclusive. Under our By-laws any member has the privilege of making other nominations from the floor, and if there are any such additional nominations to be made we will be glad to receive them.

Printed ballots will be mailed to the members and the results of the election will be announced at the next meeting, which will be the Annual Meeting of the Club, October 28, 1937.

Is there any further business? If not, the meeting will stand adjourned, and you are all invited to the luncheon tables at either end of the room, and we hope you will spend a pleasant social hour.

J. D. CONWAY, Secretary.

In Memoriam

F. G. MINNICK
Joined Club February 24, 1921
Died May 31, 1937

S. T. BARR
Joined Club December 20, 1934
Died May 24, 1937

CHARLES A. TEERKES
Joined Club January 23, 1936
Died June 28, 1937

J. H. WEYGANDT
Joined Club November 22, 1934
Died May 11, 1937

HERE'S HOW TO GET "NEW CAR" MILEAGE!

Be Wise

Use

PENNZIP

and

PENNZOIL

PENNZIP AND PENNZOIL ARE PERFECT PARTNERS

• You can have a motor that runs like new for thousands of extra miles. The secret is in using a gasoline and an oil that are equally as modern . . . Pennzip and Pennzoil, the perfect partners!

Pennzip is the gasoline that's actually matched to your motor. With carbon-forming impurities removed by a special process Pennzip gives you a smooth-running, carbon-free motor. And Pennzip's perfect partner, Pennzoil, is the oil that gives you more miles of safe lubrication per quart or per gallon!

Switch to Pennzip and Pennzoil, the perfect partners!

THE PENNZOIL COMPANY
CHAMBER OF COMMERCE BLDG.

PITTSBURGH   PENNA.

OFFICIAL PROCEEDINGS
LWAY CLUB OF PITTSBURG

$1.00 Per Year   25¢ Per Copy

Vol. XXXVI   OCTOBER 28, 1937.   No. 9.

ANNUAL MEETING—ELECTION OF OFFICERS
LIST OF MEMBERS

The proof of your interest

in the Club can be

enhanced

by securing a

NEW MEMBER.

Application form is available

in this magazine. Look

it up and

"ACT NOW."

OFFICIAL PROCEEDINGS

OF

The Railway Club of Pittsburgh

Organized October 18, 1901

Published monthly, except June, July and August, by the Railway Club of
Pittsburgh, J. D. Conway, Secretary, 515 Grandview Ave., Pittsburgh, Pa..

Entered as Second Class Matter February 6, 1915, at the Postoffice at Pittsburgh,
under the Act of March 3, 1879.

| Vol. XXXVI. No. 9 | Pittsburgh, Pa., Oct. 28, 1937 | $1.00 Per Year 25c Per Copy |

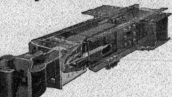

KOPPERS SERVES the RAILROADS

KOPPERS PRODUCTS AND WHERE THEY APPLY IN THE RAILROAD FIELD	TREATED TIMBER, TIES, POSTS, ETC.	ROOFING MATERIALS	PISTON RINGS	COAL	WATER-PROOFING MATERIALS	BITUMINOUS PAINTS	TARMAC ROAD MATERIALS	FAST'S COUPLINGS	CREOSOTE	CYLINDER AND VALVE PACKING	WEED KILLERS	INSECTICIDES AND DISINFECTANTS	PLATE WORK	CAR FERRIES, RAILROAD BARGES, ETC.
ROADBEDS	A								D		F			
LOCOMOTIVES			C	B						C		F		
STATIONS	A	D		B	D	D			D			F		
SHOPS	A	D	C	B	D	D		E	D			F	E&G	
BRIDGES	A				D	D	D		D				E&G	
TUNNELS	A				D	D	D						E&G	
DRIVEWAYS	A				D		D				F			
POWER HOUSES	A	D	C	B	D	D		E	D	C			E&G	
STRUCTURAL	A	D			D	D			D				E&G	
GRADE CROSSINGS	A						D							
CATTLE PENS	A	D			D	D			D			F		
RAILROAD MARINE OPERATIONS	A	D	C.	B	D	D			D	C		F	E&G	H

A—The Wood Preserving Corporation, Pittsburgh, Pa.   B—The Koppers Coal Company, Pittsburgh, Pa.   C—American Hammered Piston Ring Division, Baltimore, Md.   D—Tar and Chemical Division, Pittsburgh, Pa.   E—Bartlett Hayward Division, Baltimore, Md.   F—The White Tar Company of New Jersey, Inc.   G—Western Gas Division, Fort Wayne, Ind.   H—The Maryland Drydock Company, Baltimore, Md.

INDEX—ADVERTISERS.

The Railway Club of Pittsburgh:

_____ 19____

Gentlemen:

Will you kindly consider my Application for Membership in your Club at the next meeting:

Name_____

Title_____

Company_____

My Address_____

_____

Recommended by_____. _____

OFFICIAL PROCEEDINGS

OF

The Railway Club of Pittsburgh

Organized October 18, 1901

Vol. XXXVI. No. 9	Pittsburgh, Pa., Oct. 28, 1937	$1.00 Per Year 25c Per Copy

OFFICERS FOR 1936-1937

President

E. A. RAUSCHART,

Mechanical Superintendent, Montour Railroad Co., Coraopolis, Pa.

First Vice President

G. M. SIXSMITH,

Supt., Pennsylvania Railroad,
Pittsburgh, Pa.

Secretary

J. D. CONWAY,

Railway Supply Manufacturers' Association,
Pittsburgh, Pa.

Second Vice President

J. D. BELTZ,

Supt., B. & O. R. R. Co.,
Pittsburgh, Pa.

Treasurer

E. J. SEARLES,

Manager, Schaefer Equipment Co.,
Pittsburgh, Pa.

EXECUTIVE COMMITTEE:

FRANK J. LANAHAN, Chairman, President, Fort Pitt Malleable Iron Co., Pittsburgh, Pa
A. STUCKI, Engineer, A. Stucki Company, Pittsburgh, Pa.
G W. WILDIN, Consulting Engineer, Westinghouse Air Brake Company, Pittsburgh, Pa.
W. S. McABEE, Vice Pres. & General Supt., Union Railroad Co., East Pittsburgh, Pa.
E. W. SMITH, Vice President, Pennsylvania Railroad, Pittsburgh, Pa.
LOUIS E. ENDSLEY, Consulting Engineer, 516 East End Avenue, Pittsburgh, Pa.
F. I. SNYDER, Vice President & General Manager, B. & L. E. R. R. Co., Pittsburgh, Pa.
C. O. DAMBACH, Superintendent, P. & W. Va. Ry. Co., Pittsburgh, Pa.
R. H. FLINN, General Superintendent, Pennsylvania Railroad, Pittsburgh, Pa.
R. P. FORSBERG, Chief Engineer, P. & L. E. R. R. Co., Pittsburgh, Pa.

SUBJECT COMMITTEE:

D. W. McGEORGE, Chairman, Secretary, Edgewater Steel Company, Pittsburgh, Pa.
G. H. BURNETTE, Asst. Chief Engineer, P. & L. E. R. R. Co., Pittsburgh, Pa.

RECEPTION AND ATTENDANCE COMMITTEE:

J. W. JOHNSON, Chairman, Superintendent, Railway Express Agency, Pittsburgh, Pa.
W. C. BUREL, Vice Chairman, Master Mechanic, Western Allegheny Railroad, Kaylor, Pa.
J. W. BOYD, Superintendent, Monongahela Railway Company, Brownsville, Pa.
THOMAS E. CANNON, P. & W. Va. Ry. Co., Pittsburgh, Pa.
T. W. CARR, Superintendent Rolling Stock, P. & L. E. R. R. Co., McKees Rocks, Pa.
D. C. CARROLL, Assistant Agent, Pennsylvania Railroad, Pittsburgh, Pa.
S. G. DOWN, Vice President, Westinghouse Air Brake Company, Wilmerding, Pa.
HARRY C. GRAHAM, Pittsburgh Screw & Bolt Corporation, Pittsburgh, Pa.
J. W. SCHAD, Division Master Mechanic, B. & O. R. R. Co., Pittsburgh, Pa.
GEORGE S. WEST, Division Superintendent, Pennsylvania Railroad, Pittsburgh, Pa.
J. W. HOOVER, Asst. Chief of Transpn., Subsidiary Cos. U. S. Steel Corp., Pittsburgh, Pa.
A. A. READ, Duquesne Slag Products Company, Pittsburgh, Pa.
C. P. SCHRECONGOST, Traffic Manager, Hillman Coal & Coke Company, Pittsburgh, Pa.
J. A. WARFEL, Special Representative, Air Reduction Sales Company, Pittsburgh, Pa.
J. C. SHINGLEDECKER, Supervisor of Service Stations, The Pennzoil Co., Pittsburgh, Pa.
J. C. DILWORTH, Manager Railroad Sales, Carnegie-Illinois Steel Corp., Pittsburgh, Pa.

ENTERTAINMENT COMMITTEE:

J. PORTER GILLESPIE, Chairman, Asst. Gen. Supt., Lockhart Iron & Steel Co., Pgh., Pa.
FRANK E. WEIS, Vice Chairman, Transportation Clerk, Penna. R. R., Pittsburgh, Pa.
JAMES NAGEL, Superintendent Transportation, Montour Railroad, Coraopolis, Pa.
E. H. HOLMES, Sales Department, Fort Pitt Malleable Iron Co., Pittsburgh, Pa.
C. C. CLARK, Sales Manager, Central District, Pressed Steel Car Co., Pittsburgh, Pa.
A. I. KESSLER, Clearance Clerk, Pennsylvania Railroad, Pittsburgh, Pa.
T. F. SHERIDAN, Asst. to S.M.P. and S.R.S., P. & L. E. R. R. Co., McKees Rocks, Pa.

FINANCE COMMITTEE:

M. A. SMITH, Chairman, General Manager, P. & L. E. R. R. Co., Pittsburgh, Pa.
J. B. DIVEN, Superintendent Motive Power, Pennsylvania Railroad, Pittsburgh, Pa.
F. J. RYAN, District Representative, Detroit, Toledo & Ironton Railroad, Pittsburgh, Pa.
C. E. CATT, Division Accountant, B. & O. R. R. Co., Pittsburgh, Pa.
G. W. HONSBERGER, Transpn. Mgr., Westinghouse Electric & Mfg. Co., Pittsburgh, Pa.

ADVERTISING COMMITTEE:

H. H. HAUPT, Chairman, Gen. Supt., Motive Power, Pennsylvania Railroad, Pittsburgh, Pa.
KARL BERG, Superintendent Motive Power, P. & L. E. R. R. Co., McKees Rocks, Pa.
H. E. PASSMORE, Representative, The American Hammered Piston Ring Co., Pgh., Pa.

MEMBERSHIP COMMITTEE:

T. E. BRITT, Chairman, Div. Storekeeper, B. & O. R. R. Co., Glenwood Shops, Pgh., Pa.
C. M. WHEELER, Vice Chairman, Sales Engr., Union Switch & Signal Co., Swissvale, Pa.
F. H. EATON, Sales Engineer, American Car & Foundry Co., Pittsburgh, Pa.
C. W. GOTTSCHALK, Asst. Traffic Manager, Jones & Laughlin Steel Corp., Pgh., Pa.
LLOYD SUTHERLAND, General Storekeeper, P. & L. E. R R. Co., McKees Rocks, Pa.
THOMAS R. FITZPATRICK, Freight Traffic Mgr., P. & L. E. R. R. Co., Pittsburgh, Pa.
P. W. HEPBURN, Sales Engineer, Gulf Refining Company, Pittsburgh, Pa.
W. B. MOIR, Chief Car Inspector, Pennsylvania Railroad, Pittsburgh, Pa.
C. W. TRUST, Assistant Traffic Manager, Carnegie-Illinois Steel Corp., Pittsburgh, Pa.
R. S. BULL, Supt. Power & Inclines, Pittsburgh Railways Co., N. S., Pittsburgh, Pa.
A. F. COULTER, Master Car Builder, Union Railroad Co., East Pittsburgh, Pa.
T. R. DICKINSON, Purchasing Agent, B. & L. E. R. R. Co., Pittsburgh, Pa.
D. K. ORR, Road Master, Monongahela Railway Co., Brownsville, Pa.
W. F. AMBROSE, Master Mechanic, Aliquippa & Southern Railroad, Aliquippa, Pa
JOHN I. MULVEY, Traffic Manager, Hubbard & Company, Pittsburgh, Pa.

PAST PRESIDENTS:

*J. H. McCONNELL	October, 1901, to October, 1903
*L. H. TURNER	November, 1903, to October, 1905
*F. H. STARK	November, 1905, to October, 1907
*H. W. WATTS	November, 1907, to April, 1908
*D. J. REDDING	November, 1908, to October, 1910
*F. R. McFEATTERS	November, 1910, to October, 1912
*A. G. MITCHELL	November, 1912, to October, 1914
*F. M. McNULTY	November, 1914, to October, 1916
*J. G. CODE	November, 1916, to October, 1917
*D. M. HOWE	November, 1917, to October, 1918
*J. A. SPIELMAN	November, 1918, to October, 1919
H. H. MAXFIELD	November, 1919, to October, 1920
FRANK J. LANAHAN	November, 1920, to October, 1921
*SAMUEL LYNN	November, 1921, to October, 1922
*D. F. CRAWFORD	November, 1922, to October, 1923
*GEO. D. OGDEN	November, 1923, to October, 1924
A. STUCKI	November, 1924, to October, 1925
F. G. MINNICK	November, 1925, to October, 1926
G. W. WILDIN	November, 1926, to October, 1927
E. J. DEVANS	November, 1927, to October, 1928
W. S. McABEE	November, 1928, to October, 1929
E. W. SMITH	November, 1929, to October, 1930
LOUIS E. ENDSLEY	November, 1930, to October, 1931
*JOHN E. HUGHES	November, 1931, to October, 1932
F. I. SNYDER	November, 1932, to October, 1933
C. O. DAMBACH	November, 1933, to October, 1934
R. H. FLINN	November, 1934, to October, 1935
R. P. FORSBERG	November, 1935, to October, 1936

*—Deceased.

Meetings held fourth Thursday of each month except June, July and August.

PROCEEDINGS OF MEETING
OCTOBER 28, 1937

The Annual Meeting was called to order at the Fort Pitt Hotel at eight o'clock P. M., with President E. A. Rauschart in the chair.

Registered attendance, 563, as follows:

MEMBERS

Adams, C. E.
Adams, Frank W.
Adams, W. A.
Ainsworth, John R.
Allison, John
Ambrose, W. F.
Ament, F. Chalmer
Angel, A. J.
Arnold, J. J.
Aulbach, A. J.
Bacon, John L.
Baer, Harry L.
Baker, W. E.
Balla, J. A.
Balsley, J. I.
Balzer, C. E.
Barr, H. C.
Barrie, J. S.
Baumann, E. G.
Berg, Karl
Black, C. R.
Blest, M. C.
Blyth, F. G.
Beam, E. J.
Beatty, Raymond N.
Beeson, H. L.
Beitsch, George F.
Beltz, J. D.
Bender, H. P.
Beswick, R. M.
Bishop, D. B.
Bishop, M. L.
Boyd, John R.
Boyer, W. W.
Braun, O. F.
Brennan, J. T.
Britt, T. E.
Brown, C. C.

Bryant, L. J.
Buckley, William
Buffington, W. P.
Burk, Clyde
Burnette, G. H.
Burriss, Walter C.
Byrne, W. L.
Callahan, F. J.
Campbell, F. R.
Campbell, J. Alan
Campbell, W. T.
Cannon, T. E.
Carr, T. W.
Carroll, D. C.
Carson, John
Carter, E. D.
Case, H. D.
Chaffin, H. B.
Chase, D. K.
Chilcoat, H. E.
Christy, F. X.
Cipro, Thomas
Clardy, W. J.
Clark, C. C.
Code, C. J.
Conway, J. D.
Coombe, A. B.
Cotter, G. L.
Courtney, Harry
Crawford, A. B.
Crawford, Burt H.
Cree, Walter M.
Crenner, J. A.
Cruikshank, J. C.
Cunningham, J. D.
Cunningham, R. I.
Dalzell, W. E.
Dambach, C. O.

Daugherty, W. A.
Davis, John W.
Davis, William B.
Day, T. R.
Deakins, H. H.
Dean, E. E.
Dean, R. W.
Dean, W. A.
Dehne, George C.
Dempsey, Alex
Dickinson, B. F.
Dickson, K. B.
Diven, J. B.
Dixon, C. P.
Dixon, J. M.
Donovan, L. T.
Dunham, C. W.
Dunkuly, E. R.
Eaton, Fred'k. H.
Eckels, W.
Edsall, S. D.
Emery, E.
Endsley, Louis E.
Evans, Charles S.
Evans, David F.
Farlow, G. B.
Farmer, C. C.
Ferguson, George
Fieldson, P. H.
Fike, J. W.
Fischer, G, E.
Flinn, R. H.
Forquer, Edwin A.
Forsberg, R. P.
Forsythe, George B.
Fox, George W.
Frauenheim, Pierce H.
Freshwater, F. H.
Friend, E. F.
Fulton, K. H.
Galbraith, James R.
Ganz, C. A.
Gardner, George R.
Gardner, K. C.
Geertz, Allan O.
Geiser, W. P.
Gelston, George A.
George, W. J.
Gilg, Henry F.
Gillespie, J. Porter
Gillum, J. S.

Glaser, C. J.
Glaser, J. P.
Goldstrom, G. E.
Gorman, A. T.
Goron, F. W.
Griest, E. E.
Gross, John
Grove, C. G.
Groves, W. C.
Guinnip, M. S.
Gunnison, W. L.
Hackett, C. M.
Haller, Nelson M.
Hamilton, R. F.
Hamilton, W. H.
Hance, R. H.
Hancock, Milton L.
Hansen, William C.
Harper, G. C.
Harper, J. T.
Haupt, Harold H.
Hayward, Carlton
Heinz, W. J.
Hemma, Charles H.
Hengst, G. E.
Hepburn, P. W.
Herpst, R. C.
Herrold, A. E.
Hess, Charles A.
Hill, J. A.
Hilstrom, A. V.
Holbrook, E. L.
Holland, S. E.
Holmes, E. H.
Honsberger, G. W.
Huggans, A. V.
Huston, F. T.
Irwin, R. D.
Jakovac, V. P.
Jarres, F. A.
Jeffrey, John
Johnson, Ira S.
Johnson, J. W.
Kaup, H. E.
Kearfott, W. E.
Keeney, J. H.
Kellenberger, K. E.
Keller, R. B.
Kemmerer, R. R.
Kentlein, John
Keppelman, H. S.

Kirby, D. D.
Klassen, F. G.
Koenig, W. A.
Krahmer, E. F.
Kroske, J. F.
Kuhn, S. H.
Kuhnert, P. C.
Kusick, Harry F.
Lanahan, Frank J.
Lanahan, J. S.
Lanning, E. H.
Larson, W. E.
Laurent, Joseph A.
Leet, C. S.
Leonard, C. W.
Lewis, Benjamin
Lewis, N. F.
Livingston, W. C.
Loder, C. C.
Long, R. M.
Longstreth, W. L.
Loucks, W. V.
Lowry, William F., Jr.
Maliphant, C. W.
Malone, Frank B.
Matchett, H. K.
Matchneer, W. W.
Matuzeski, Robert R.
Maxwell, Thomas
Mayer, L. I.
Megee, Caleb R.
Meinert, Henry J.
Menk, C. W.
Metzger, C. L.
Millar, C. W.
Miller, John
Miller, L. P.
Mills, C. C.
Mitchell, W. S.
Moir, W. B.
Morgan, Homer C.
Morrison, R. A. J.
Mowery, J. F.
Muir, R. Y.
Mulvey, J. I.
Murphy, C. E. Ted
Murray, C. C.
Musgrove, W. W.
Myers, Arnold
McAbee, W. S.
McCormack, E. S.

McCully, D. L.
McHugh, C. A.
McIntyre, R. C.
McKinley, John T.
McKinstry, C. H.
McKinzie, E.
McLaughlin, H. B.
McMillan, A. P.
McNamee, William
McPherson, A. R.
McQuiston, C. A.
Nagel, James
Nathan, W. S.
Nieman, Charles J.
Nieman, H. L.
Nies, E. L.
Noonan, Daniel
O'Leary, J. J.
O'Sullivan, J. J.
Overholt, B. C.
Paisley, F. R.
Palmer, E. A.
Park, C. L.
Passmore, H. E.
Patterson, C. L.
Peirce, W. B.
Pillar, Michael
Pollock, Joseph H.
Posteraro, S. F.
Pringle, Paul V.
Purcell, E. J.
Purchard, Paul
Rau, W. R., Jr.
Rauschart, E. A.
Redding, R. D.
Reeve, George
Renshaw, W. B.
Reymer, Charles H.
Riley, S. B.
Roberts, E. L.
Robertson, A. S.
Robinson, Lester L., Jr.
Rumbarger, F. A.
Rushneck, G. L.
Rutter, Harley E.
Ryan, D. W.
Sarchet, Roger
Schadt, A. D.
Schaffer, W. E.
Schiller, John
Schmitt, Raymond F.

Schrecongost, C. P.
Searles, E. J.
Sekera, C. J.
Seltman, O. W.
Severn, A. B.
Sheehan, W. M.
Sheffer, R. W.
Shellenbarger, H. M.
Sheridan, T. F.
Showalter, Joseph
Shull, C. O.
Seibert, W. L.
Sixsmith, G. M.
Slater, A. H.
Smith, Charles F.
Smith, L. H.
Snyder, F. I.
Snyder, J. C.
Snyder, J. J.
Sperry, C. E.
Stack, J. E.
Stebler, W. J.
Steding, H. L.
Steiner, P. E.
Stephen, James
Sterling, C. C.
Stevens, L. V.
Stevenson, R. F.
Stillwagon, C. K.
Stocker, H. I.
Stoffregen, Louis E.
Stucki, A.
Stype, William G.
Sullivan, A. W.
Sullivan, R. J.
Sutherland, Lloyd
Sutton, R. C.
Sykes, A. H.
Taylor, H. D.
Taylor, Joseph M.

Terkelsen, Bernhard
Teskey, Dr. Walter J.
Thompson, Frederick H.
Thompson, G. C.
Thompson, H. A.
Thunell, F. G.
Tracey, J. B. A.
Trautman, H. J.
Trump, Perry
Tyler, B. W.
Uhar, John J.
Unger, Dr. J. S.
Urtel, E. J.
Vanderbosch, C. J.
Van Horne, C. F.
Van Woert, F. E.
Von Pein, A. N.
Vowinkel, Fred F.
Wallace, C. M.
Walther, G. C.
Ward, M. H.
Weis, Frank E.
West, Troy
White, H. A.
Wheeler, C. M.
Wickerham, F. A.
Widmyer, Robert G.
Wilson, James R.
Wilson, W. H.
Wilson, W. S.
Winning, Robert W.
Winslow, G. W.
Winton, C. A.
Woodings, Robert T.
Woods, G. M.
Woodward, R.
Wright, John B.
Wynne, F. E.
Yohe, J. K., Jr.
Young, Paul S.

Zoog, H. J.

VISITORS

Abbott, L. J.
Acton, J. C.
Acton, Oliver C.
Acloquer, C. C.
Alberts, J. F.
Alexander, R. P.
Allshouse. Frank

Alpern, Myer
Ames, Louis
Anderson, C. A.
Anderson, J. P.
Angerman, John C.
Arnold, J. G.
Bagaley, W. W.

Baker, George N.
Barnett, J. B.
Barton, Raymond E.
Bell, C. W.
Bell, R. P.
Berger, John S.
Bierman, William
Birkay, J. W.
Bitzel, Harry
Bochert, C. G.
Boynes, John D.
Brose, J. A.
Brown, R. J.
Bruce, B. L.
Buczek, Paul
Bugbee, W. E.
Burgess, W. C.
Burkhardt, A. J.
Burriss, H. E.
Clark, John M.
Cohen, Alfred J.
Cohen, Leonard M.
Colclaser, L. A.
Collins, J. J.
Cooper, J. P.
Core, Daniel H.
Cravener, J. H.
Cunningham, J. B.
Cupp, C. J.
Dalzell, William E., Jr.
Dambach, J. C.
Dankmyer, F. C.
Davern, Fred C.
Davin, T. W.
Davis, R. E.
Dawe, Gilbert E.
De Balt, R. S.
Divens, Kenneth E.
Durkin, James E.
Earnest, W. F.
Eberlein, George
Egerstener, A. R.
Eisele, H. G.
Enders, E. G.
Ervine, William
Flaherty, Thomas J.
Feeny, Lyman C.
Fletcher, A.
Freedman, Arnold H.
Friend, R. A.
Fritz, A. A.

Fulkerson, A.
Germak, George A.
Gilbert, Gerard
Gillespie, William A.
Gillen, J. B.
Gilliland, J. O.
Gilson, S. D.
Gleeson, H. R.
Goodwill, Don G.
Gower, Robert
Greenawald, M. G.
Greenwood, J. A.
Grimm, W. R.
Gross, Michael A.
Gumz, Fred A.
Gwyn, W. H.
Hahn, H. A.
Haney, J. T.
Harbourt, C. W.
Harrison, A. M.
Hawthorne, V. R.
Hayford, B. H.
Helly, Charles R.
Henderson, Gene
Henkel, William L.
Herman, J. L.
Hewlett, H. D.
Hicks, E. S., Jr.
Hildenbrand, L. B.
Holt, C.
Hughes, William W.
Jarres, Leo
Jacobs, Arthur
Johnson, C.
Johnson, M. P.
Jones, Lloyd B.
Jones, T. J.
King, J. E.
King, K. F.
Kittelberger, H. C.
Kouche, N. J.
Kustetter, Arthur W.
Latshaw, T. R.
Lamborn, S. W.
Laughlin, R. B.
Lauth, Frank D.
Lauth, H. J.
Leay, John G., Jr.
Lemley, J. S.
Lewis, S. B.
Lewis, Stephen B.

Lindner, John G.
Lovett, Samuel C.
Lucas, C. W.
Malenock, W. M.
Marp, C. P.
Mateer, William M.
Meinert, William J.
Messimer, W. N.
Miles, R. E.
Miles, R. E., Jr.
Miller, Bernard
Miller, Theodore P.
Mitchell, John
Moeller, Frank J.
Monk, J. Thomas
Muir, J.
Myers, R. C.
McConn, G. E.
McGinnis, P. B.
McKinstry, Clair M.
McPhee, R. W.
McPherson, K. W.
Nagel, James, Jr.
Nelson, C. J.
Nieseman, F.
Niggl, Frank E.
Oldham, R. W.
Parvin, C. F.
Peirce, John
Penn, William
Petrie, William J.
Ranck, J. F.
Rauschart, R. E.
Reagan, Henry V.
Reagan, P. H.
Rehrer, Roland C.
Reuter, Paul C.
Reynolds, D. E.
Roberts, William E.
Robertson, E. J.
Robertson, M. R.
Robinson, H. H.

Robinson, Lester L., III
Rodgers, J. W.
Ross, B. J.
Rushton, H. J.
Ryan, J. C.
Sands, Joseph G.
Septer, J. C.
Sexton, E. P.
Schertzinger, L. G.
Schomberg, F. L.
Shannon, David E.
Sheldon, Fred B.
Shepherd, George B.
Smith, C. R.
Smith, Sion B.
Sneid, J. R.
Snyder, H. C.
Stewart, E. P.
Stewart, Kenneth D.
Stewart, William
Stohner, W. A.
Stremmel, F. H.
Summers, James F.
Super, E. E.
Thomas, M. F.
Thomson, C. F.
Todd, Thomas S.
Tovey, L. A.
Turner, E. H.
Vandivort, R. E.
Vogel, E. E.
Walton, H. R.
Warrensford, Fred S.
Whitehouse, William B.
Wiechels, W. L.
Wilborn, A. G.
Wiland, O. M.
Williamson, J. A.
Willoughby, F. R.
Wolf, Joseph
Wynne, B. E.
Zell, H. A.

Card Unsigned

After a community sing, led by Mr. Frank E. Weis, the regular business of the Annual Meeting was taken up.

PRESIDENT: As you all signed registration cards upon entering the room, we will dispense with the call of the roll.

The minutes of the last meeting having been printed in

the Proceedings and distributed through the mails, with your consent we will dispense with the reading of the minutes.

I will ask the Secretary to read the list of proposals for membership.

SECRETARY: We have the following proposals for membership:

Behm, Harry, Gang Leader, Monongahela Railway Company, Box 138, Hiller, Pa. Recommended by H. L Beeson.

Bevan, James Ira, Special Apprentice, Westinghouse Air Brake Company, 787 Third Street, East McKeesport, Pa. Recommended by N F. Lewis.

Brown, Harold A., Advertising Manager, Railway Equipment & Publication Company, 424 West 33rd Street, New York, N. Y. Recommended by J. D. Conway.

Buckley, William, Air Brake Instructor, Pennsylvania Railroad, Pennsylvania Station, Pittsburgh, Pa. Recommended by W. B. Moir.

Bryant, Lewis J., Westinghouse Air Brake Company, 1231 Greensburg Avenue, East McKeesport, Pa. Recommended by N. F. Lewis.

Cherry, Dale C., Assistant Master Mechanic, Pennsylvania Railroad. 203 Franklin Avenue, Wilkinsburg, Pa. Recommended by W. B. Moir.

Duff, William G, Secretary and Auditor, The Lake Terminal Railroad Co., Frick Building. Pittsburgh, Pa. Recommended by J. M. Morris.

Dunkuly, E. R., Superintendent, Monessen Southwestern Railway Company, Monessen. Pa. Recommended by F. E Van Woert.

Ganz, C. A., Gang Foreman, Pennsylvania Railroad, 617 Second Street, Pitcairn, Pa Recommended by W. B. Moir.

Good, W. G., Secretary, Pittsburgh Smelting & Refining Company, 3524 Brighton Road, Pittsburgh, Pa. Recommended by E. A. Rauschart.

Gorman, Andrew T., Tester, Westinghouse Air Brake Company, 574 Fifth Street, Pitcairn, Pa. Recommended by N. F. Lewis.

Hastings, David T., Vice President, The Lake Terminal Railroad Company, Frick Building, Pittsburgh, Pa. Recommended by J. M. Morris.

Hengst, Guy E., Tester, Westinghouse Air Brake Company, 664 Air Brake Avenue, Wilmerding, Pa. Recommended by N. F. Lewis.

Hill, Lloyd C., Engine Inspector, Monongahela Railway Company, Box 334, Brownsville, Pa. Recommended by H. L. Beeson.

Holbrook, Edward L., Tester, Westinghouse Air Brake Company, 2028 Bridge Street, McKeesport, Pa. Recommended by N. F. Lewis.

Hughes, Oscar W., Sales Engineer, Signode Steel Strapping Company, 3957 Howard Street, Youngstown, Ohio. Recommended by W. B. Moir

Jeffrey, John, Patent Engineer, Westinghouse Air Brake Company, 312 Arlington Avenue, East McKeesport, Pa. Recommended by N. F. Lewis.

Keppelman, H. S, Superintendent Car Department, Reading Company, Sixth and Perry Streets, Reading, Pa. Recommended by W. B. Moir.

Kuhnert, P. C, Westinghouse Air Brake Company, 145 La Crosse Street, Edgewood, Pittsburgh, Pa. Recommended by N. F. Lewis.

Logsdon, Fred H., Tester, Westinghouse Air Brake Company, 658 Middle Avenue, Wilmerding, Pa Recommended by N. F. Lewis.

Malone, Frank B., Engineer, Conemaugh Division, Pennsylvania Railroad, 235 45th Street, Pittsburgh, Pa. Recommended by R N. Beatty.

Matchett, H. K., "Retired", Pennsylvania Railroad, 5517½ Broad Street, East End, Pittsburgh, Pa. Recommended by Carlton Hayward.

Miller, James B., Tester, Westinghouse Air Brake Company, 905 Punta Gorda Street, East McKeesport, Pa. Recommended by N. F. Lewis.

Morrison, R. A. J,, Train Master, B. & O R. R. Co., Smithfield and Water Streets, Pittsburgh, Pa. Recommended by T. E. Britt.

Murphy, C E., President, The Acme Railway Supply Company, 415 Midland Building. Cleveland, Ohio Recommended by Lloyd Sutherland.

Nicklas, Chester J., Salesman, Union Asbestos & Rubber Company, Equipment Specialties Division, Commonwealth Building, Pittsburgh, Pa. Recommended by E. A. Rauschart.

Nields, Benjamin, Assistant Vice President, National Malleable & Steel Castings Company, Cleveland, Ohio. Recommended by J. D. Conway.

Ord, George H., Eastern Sales Manager, Ewald Iron Company, 501 Fifth Avenue, New York, N Y. Recommended by T. F. Sheridan.

Patterson, Charles L., Assistant Master Mechanic, Pennsylvania Railroad, 215 Pine Road. Edgeworth, Pa. Recommended by W. B. Moir

Rau, William R., Jr., President, National Model Railroad Association, 1430 Elm Street, Wilkinsburg, Pa. Recommended by Dr. Walter J. Teskey.

Servard, Arthur M., Superintendent Passenger Transportation, Pennsylvania Railroad, 5237 Ellsworth Avenue, Pittsburgh, Pa. Recommended by W. B. Moir.

Sennstrom, Harold R., Special Apprentice, Westinghouse Air Brake Company, 809½ Franklin Avenue, Wilkinsburg, Pa. Recommended by R. L. Nash.

Sharp, James, Superintendent Motive Power, McKeesport Connecting Railroad Company, P. O. Box 404, McKeesport, Pa. Recommended by J. M. Morris.

Shull, C. O., Master Mechanic, Pennsylvania Railroad, Pitcairn Shop, Pitcairn, Pa. Recommended by W. B. Moir.

Salomon, S. N., Pittsburgh Manager, Signode Steel Strapping Company, Grant Building, Pittsburgh, Pa. Recommended by W. B. Moir.

Stype, William G., Chief Dispatcher, Montour Railroad Company, 1436 Ridge Avenue, Coraopolis, Pa. Recommended by E. A. Rauschart.

Vanderbosch, C. J., District Storekeeper, B. & O. R. R. Co., B&O Station, Pittsburgh, Pa. Recommended by T. E. Britt.

Walther, G. C., Gang Foreman, Pennsylvania Railroad, 877 Second Street, Verona, Pa Recommended by G. M. Sixsmith.

Widmyer, Robert G., Foreman, Westinghouse Air Brake Company, 604 Warden Street, Irwin, Pa. Recommended by N. F. Lewis.

Wilson, Walter Herr, Tester, Westinghouse Air Brake Company, 505 Larimer Avenue, Pittsburgh, Pa. Recommended by N. F. Lewis.

Woodings, Wilbert H., Salesman, Woodings-Verona Tool Company, 1020 Hulton Road, Oakmont, Pa. Recommended by T. E. Britt.

Yarhouse, Walter T., Representative, The Sherwin-Williams Company, 228 Castle Shanon Boulevard, Mt. Lebanon, Pittsburgh, Pa. Recommended by E. A. Rauschart

Zoog, H. J., Serviceman, Air Reduction Sales Company, N. Central Avenue, Canonsburg, Pa. Recommended by H. C. Thompson

PRESIDENT: Under our By-laws proposals for membership are referred to the Executive Committee, and upon approval by them the gentlemen become members without further action. These names have been referred to the Executive Committee and have been duly approved by them, and I therefore declare the gentlemen members in full standing and I will ask those who are present to stand that we may recognize you and welcome you into our fellowship.

Are there any communications, Mr. Secretary?

SECRETARY: Since our last meeting we have received information of the death of Club member Harry A. Krause, Gang Foreman, Pennsylvania Railroad, Pittsburgh, Pa., which occurred September 7, 1937.

PRESIDENT: An appropriate memorial minute will appear in the next issue of the Proceedings.

If there is no further preliminary business, we will proceed at once to the Annual Reports of Officers. First, the Report of the Treasurer, Mr. E. J. Searles.

TREASURER'S REPORT

Pittsburgh, Pa., October 26, 1937.

To the Officers and Members of

The Railway Club of Pittsburgh.

Gentlemen:

I herewith submit my report for the year ended October 28, 1937:

ON HAND AND RECEIPTS

Cash on hand, October 22, 1936................$1,198.35
Moneys received from J. D. Conway, Secre-
    tary, from October 23, 1936, to Octo-
    ber 28, 1937, both inclusive................ 5,279.90
Interest on bonds 73.12
Proceeds of sale of one $1,000.00 U. S.
    Treasury Bond, interest $3\frac{1}{8}\%$............. 1,042.71

    Total Receipts $7,594.08

DISBURSEMENTS

Paid on Vouchers No. 891 to 922, inclusive................ 5,627.12

    Cash Balance $1,966.96

RESOURCES

Two U. S. Treasury Bonds, $1,000.00 each,
    bearing interest at $2\frac{7}{8}\%$................$2,000.00
Cash balance 1,966.96

    Total Resources $3,966.96

E. J. SEARLES, Treasurer.

APPROVED:

EXECUTIVE COMMITTEE,
FRANK J. LANAHAN, Chairman.

Next we will hear the report of the Secretary.

SECRETARY'S REPORT

Pittsburgh, Pa., October 28, 1937.

To the Officers and Members of
    The Railway Club of Pittsburgh.
Gentlemen:

    The following is a summary of membership and financial statement for the fiscal year ended October 28, 1937:

Membership reported last year................ 1,381
Received into membership during year.............. 157
    ———— 1,538

Suspended 73
Resigned 74
Loss of address 6
Deaths reported during year................ 14
    ———— 167

Present membership 1,371

Of the above membership three are honorary. They are:
D. C. Buell, Samuel O. Dunn and John A. Pentón.

DECEASED MEMBERS

Name	Died
S. T. Barr	May 24, 1937
D. F. Crawford	March 16, 1937
Timothy E. Doyle	February 16, 1937
Leo Finegan	March 8, 1937
E. A. Forbriger	May 6, 1937
Charles L. Fortescue	December 4, 1936
William R. Gellatly	April 8, 1937
Harry A. Krause	September 7, 1937
F. G. Minnick	May 31, 1937
B. H. Rodeniser	April 24, 1937
W. A. Skellie	March 23, 1935
E. M. Sexton	February 15, 1937
Charles A. Teerkes	June 28, 1937
J. H. Weygandt	May 11, 1937

RECEIPTS

In hands of Treasurer at close of last year	$4,147.74
From advertisements	1,062.50
From dues	3,780.00
From sale of Proceedings	3.50
Smoker tickets and dinner October 22, 1936	424.75
Miscellaneous sources	9.15
Interest on bonds	73.12
Profit from sale one $1,000.00 U .S. Treasury Bond, 3⅛%, cost $949.39, selling price $1,042.71	93.32
	————$9,594.08

DISBURSEMENTS

Printing Proceedings, notices, mailing, etc.	$2,506.12
Luncheons, cigars, postage, etc.	998.95
Reporting meetings	180.00

Dinner, entertainment, smoker, etc.,
        October 22, 1936 .... 643.50
Salaries and advertising expense 1,106.25
Moving pictures 24.00
Messenger service, affidavits, etc.—............ 18.00
Premium on bonds—Treasurer and
        Secretary 14.00
Floral pieces 35.40
Various entertainment at meetings 83.25
Incidentals 17.65
                                            —————$5,627.12

Net Balance at close of year $3,966.96

NOTE:—Balance is made up of $1,966.96 cash and two U. S. Treasury Bonds, $1,000.00 each—2⅞% interest.

                                        J. D. CONWAY, Secretary.

APPROVED:

                    EXECUTIVE COMMITTEE,
                    FRANK J. LANAHAN, Chairman.

PRESIDENT: You have heard these reports. What is your pleasure? On Motion the reports are accepted and filed.

We have audited the accounts of the Secretary and Treasurer, for the year ended October 28, 1937, and find them correct as reported.

                    FINANCE COMMITTEE,
                            M. A. SMITH, Chairman,
                            J. B. DIVEN,
                            F. J. RYAN,
                            C. E. CATT,
                            G. W. HONSBERGER.

PRESIDENT: The next order of business is the report of the Tellers of Election. I will ask the Secretary to read the report.

SECRETARY: The report of the Tellers of Election shows a total of 288 votes cast, and the vote in each case unanimous for the candidates listed on the ballot, as follows:

PRESIDENT—G. M. Sixsmith, Superintendent, The Pennsylvania Railroad, Pittsburgh, Pa.

FIRST VICE PRESIDENT—J. D. Beltz, Superintendent, B. & O. R. R. Co., Pittsburgh, Pa.

SECOND VICE PRESIDENT—Karl Berg, Superintendent Motive Power, P. & L. E. R. R. Co., McKees Rocks, Pa.

SECRETARY—J. D. Conway, Secretary-Treasurer, The Railway Supply Manufacturers' Association, Pittsburgh, Pa.

TREASURER—E. J. Searles, Manager, Schaefer Equipment Company, Pittsburgh, Pa.

EXECUTIVE COMMITTEE

Frank J. Lanahan (Chairman), Fort Pitt Malleable Iron Company, Pittsburgh, Pa.

A. Stucki, Engineer, A. Stucki Company, Pittsburgh, Pa.

G. W. Wildin, Consulting Engineer, Westinghouse Air Brake Company, Pittsburgh, Pa.

W. S. McAbee, Vice President and General Superintendent, Union Railroad Co., East Pittsburgh, Pa.

E. W. Smith, Vice President, The Pennsylvania Railroad, Pittsburgh, Pa.

Louis E. Endsley, Consulting Engineer, 516 East End Avenue, Pittsburgh, Pa.

F. I. Snyder, Vice President and General Manager, B. & L. E. R. R. Co., Pittsburgh, Pa.

C. O. Dambach, Superintendent, P. & W. Va. Ry. Co., Pittsburgh, Pa.

R. H. Flinn, General Superintendent, The Pennsylvania Railroad, Pittsburgh, Pa.

R. P. Forsberg, Chief Engineer, P. & L. E. R. R., Pittsburgh, Pa.

E. A. Rauschart, Mechanical Superintendent, Montour Railroad Company, Coraopolis, Pa.

SUBJECT COMMITTEE*

H. H. Haupt (Chairman), General Superintendent Motive Power, The Pennsylvania Railroad, Pittsburgh, Pa.

G. H. Burnette, Assistant Chief Engineer, P. & L. E. R. R. Co., Pittsburgh, Pa.

D. W. McGeorge, Secretary, Edgewater Steel Company, Pittsburgh, Pa.

RECEPTION AND ATTENDANCE COMMITTEE*

J. W. Johnson (Chairman), Superintendent, Railway Express Agency, Pittsburgh, Pa.

J. W. Hoover (Vice Chairman), Assistant Chief of Transportation, Subsidiary Companies, U. S. Steel Corporation, Pittsburgh, Pa.

C. E. Adams, Division Superintendent, The Pennsylvania Railroad, Pittsburgh, Pa.

T. E. Britt, Division Storekeeper, B. & O. R. R. Co., Pittsburgh, Pa.

W. P. Buffington, Traffic Manager, Pittsburgh Coal Company, Pittsburgh, Pa.

William C. Hansen, Sales Engineer, A. Stucki Company, Pittsburgh, Pa.

C. H. Reymer, Sales Representative, Oliver Iron & Steel Corporation, Pittsburgh, Pa.

T. F. Sheridan, Asst. to Supts. Motive Power and Rolling Stock, P. & L. E. R. R. Co., McKees Rocks, Pa.

J. W. Boyd, Superintendent, Monongahela Railway Company, Brownsville, Pa.

Thomas E. Cannon, P. & W. Va. Ry. Co., Pittsburgh, Pa.

T. W. Carr, Supt. Rolling Stock, P. & L. E. R. R. Co., McKees Rocks, Pa.

D. C. Carroll, Asst. Agent, The Pennsylvania Railroad, Pittsburgh, Pa.

S. G. Down, Vice President, Westinghouse Air Brake Company, Wilmerding, Pa.

Harry C. Graham, Pittsburgh Screw & Bolt Corporation, Pittsburgh, Pa.

J. W. Schad, Division Master Mechanic, B. & O. R. R. Co., Pittsburgh, Pa.

A. A. Read, Duquesne Slag Products Company, Pittsburgh, Pa.

C. P. Schrecongost, Traffic Manager, Hillman Coal & Coke Co., Pittsburgh, Pa.

ENTERTAINMENT COMMITTEE*

J. Porter Gillespie (Chairman), Asst. Gen. Supt., Lockhart Iron & Steel Co., Pittsburgh, Pa.

Vincent Kroen (Vice Chairman), Supervisor Express Service, The Pennsylvania Railroad, Pittsburgh, Pa.

W. C. Burel, Master Mechanic, Western Allegheny Railroad, Kaylor, Pa.

H. E. Chilcoat, Gen. Mgr. of Sales, Koppel Div., Pressed Steel Car Company, Inc., Pittsburgh, Pa.

F. L. Foster, Supt. Freight Transportation, P. & L. E. R. R Co., Pittsburgh, Pa.

J. S. Lanahan, Vice President, Fort Pitt Malleable Iron Co., Pittsburgh, Pa.

James Nagel, Asst. Gen. Supt., Montour Railroad Company, Coraopolis, Pa.

FINANCE COMMITTEE*

M. A. Smith (Chairman), General Manager, P. & L. E. R. R. Co., Pittsburgh, Pa.

J. B. Diven, Supt. Motive Power, The Pennsylvania Railroad, Pittsburgh, Pa.

F. J. Ryan, District Rep., Detroit, Toledo & Ironton Railroad, Pittsburgh, Pa.

C. E. Catt, Division Accountant, B. & O. R. R. Co., Pittsburgh, Pa.

G. W. Honsberger, Transportation Manager, Westinghouse Electric & Manufacturing Company, Pittsburgh, Pa.

ADVERTISING COMMITTEE*

J. H. James (Chairman), Purchasing Agent, P. & L. E. R. R. Co., Pittsburgh, Pa.

John C. Shingledecker, Supervisor of Service Stations, The Pennzoil Company, Pittsburgh, Pa.

Charles M. Wheeler, Sales Engineer, Union Switch & Signal Company, Swissvale, Pa.

MEMBERSHIP COMMITTEE*

W. B. Moir (Chairman), Chief Car Inspector, The Pennsylvania Railroad, Pittsburgh, Pa.

Lloyd Sutherland (Vice Chairman), General Storekeeper, P. & L. E. R. R. Co., McKees Rocks, Pa.

T. Fitzgerald, Vice Pres. & Gen. Mgr., Pittsburgh Railways Co., Pittsburgh, Pa.

G. C. Harper, Gen. Supt., Montour Railroad Company, Coraopolis, Pa.

Frank A. Jarres, Asst. Storekeeper, B. & O. R. R. Co., Pittsburgh, Pa.

C. S. Leet, Asst. General Manager, B. & L. E. R. R. Co., Pittsburgh, Pa.

Caleb R. Megee, Dist. Mgr. Car Service Div., Association of American Railroads, Pittsburgh, Pa.

R. C. McIntyre, Supt. Motive Power, Union Railroad Company, East Pittsburgh, Pa.

H. C. Pringle, Vice Pres. & Supt., Monongahela Connecting Railroad Co., Pittsburgh, Pa.

S. B. Riley, General Superintendent, P. & W. Va. Ry. Co., Pittsburgh, Pa.

John B. Wright, Asst. Vice President, Westinghouse Air Brake Company, Wilmerding, Pa.

F. H. Eaton, Sales Engineer, American Car & Foundry Company, Pittsburgh, Pa.

C. W. Gottschalk, Asst. Traffic Manager, Jones & Laughlin Steel Corporation, Pittsburgh, Pa.

Thomas R. Fitzpatrick, Freight Traffic Manager, P. & L. E. R. R. Co., Pittsburgh, Pa.

P. W. Hepburn, Sales Engineer, Gulf Oil Corporation, Pittsburgh. Pa.

C. W. Trust, Asst. Traffic Manager, U. S. Steel Corporation Subsidiaries, Pittsburgh, Pa.

PRESIDENT: Mr. Sixsmith, I am happy to inform you that by the unanimous choice of the members of the Club you have been elected as its President for the ensuing year. I therefore ask you to assume the chair and enter at once upon the performance of your duties as President.

PRESIDENT G. M. SIXSMITH in the Chair: Mr. Rauschart, Gentlemen of the Railway Club of Pittsburgh and Guests: I take it, and I think properly, that this large and enthusiastic attendance tonight during such inclement weather as we have been experiencing recently, is a glowing and personal tribute to your retiring President, Mr. Rauschart. And I think it can be taken as an indication that we are completing in this Club a very successful year under his leadership.

Now, gentlemen, as for myself, what can I say that will more adequately express my feelings at this moment than to

*In addition to the newly elected members, the complete committees are shown above, including those previously elected whose terms of office have not expired.

thank you from the bottom of my heart for extending to me the privilege and honor of serving you in the capacity of President. It is an honor and responsibility that is not to be taken lightly, and I promise you that during the coming year, and with the assistance of the membership, everything possible that can be done will be done to carry this Club on to even better and greater things.

And in making this pledge, I am not unmindful of the fact that I am following a long line of capable men who have served this Club as President successfully and with credit, and during my term I probably should be satisfied if I could complete my tenure of office with a record of successful achievement such as they accomplished during their terms of office. But, with this attendance and the interest displayed here tonight, I have no misgivings about the future, and when we participate in a similar affair a year hence—and I hope we will all be here on that occasion—we will be able to look back over the year that will then have passed, and feel that it has been one of even greater success than those that have gone before.

Now just a word with respect to the men you have selected to carry on with me in the capacity of Vice Presidents. I am indeed fortunate in having men of their interest in Club affairs and of their caliber, nominated and elected as First and Second Vice Presidents, and with them as teammates, the prediction I have just made, I feel sure, will come true. And notwithstanding the fact that we are now a little behind schedule, the proper seating of such a large attendance having occasioned some delay in starting these proceedings, I think it is only fitting that they be asked to acknowledge their election to office and be presented to you now, although I feel sure that they are already well-known to the membership. Therefore, I would like to ask Mr. John D. Beltz, Superintendent, Baltimore & Ohio Railroad Company, your new First Vice President, to stand and take a bow. It is unnecessary for me to tell you that John is a real asset to this Club, he is well-known not only here but elsewhere, is a regular attendant at our meetings, and I hope you all feel as I do that his elevation to this important office is well deserved. I could not ask for a better team-mate.

I would also like to present, although your acquaintanceship with him might seem to make this unnecessary, Mr. Karl

Berg, Superintendent Motive Power, Pittsburgh & Lake Erie Railroad, your newly elected Second Vice President. Mr. Berg is also a regular attendant at our meetings, is highly regarded by all who know him, and his assistance in directing the affairs of this Club during the coming year can be confidently expected and well worth while.

With these introductions and in the light of your hearty approval of these men, I only want to give further assurance to you and to them that it is going to be a pleasure for me to work with them in close relationship for the benefit of our affairs during the coming year. With respect to the committees and committee chairmen, I will have more to say at a later meeting. The relationship and importance of the personnel of these committees with the success of this Club is well-known and I feel sure we will receive from them the same support and assistance as that supplied in the past, and everything possible will be done to encourage that result.

Now, gentlemen, this is your Club, the officers are your servants, and their success in office is measured largely by the general assistance rendered from time to time by the membership. I have no suggestions for changes in general procedure or policy to offer, and as you know, anything of that nature must first have the approval of the Executive Committee. However, as you know, aside from meeting details, the most important feature of our sessions is the speaker secured for the occasion and the subject that he is to present. Sometimes I wonder whether the selection, more particularly with respect to the discussion of technical matters, always has the approval of all of the members of this Club. What I have in mind more particularly is to encourage the membership to assist the Subject Committee in suggesting and securing speakers, as I feel sure that the Committee would welcome suggestions from members for consideration; in fact, we want our membership to feel free to make any suggestion that might be considered for the future good of the Club. I do not know that they will all be adopted, or even that they could be adopted, but I think it would be a very fine thing if any of our members know of a speaker that they would like to have address the Club, that the suggestion be passed on to the Subject Committee for consideration.

And now, gentlemen, I am not going to try your patience any longer by discussing matters that can very well be deferred until some future meeting. I realize that in addition to the election of officers and other necessary business, this is your annual Smoker and Entertainment, and no doubt, you are anxious to get along with that end of the program. However, in concluding, I want to again thank you, on behalf of myself and the other officers elected here tonight, for the confidence you have placed in us and to again promise you that we will do everything we know how to advance the progress of this Club during the coming year, but first we must hear from Mr. Lanahan, as I understand he has a message that he would like to convey before the entertainment is started.

MR. FRANK J. LANAHAN: At these annual meetings, the Executive Committee always like to advertise the organization just a bit. Tonight, we have every reason to do a little boasting, for it is our birthday. This organization is thirty-six years old. Proud are we of what has been accomplished in that period.

As you are all aware, this is a Railway Club interested in transportation and its affiliated activities. Especially are we addicted to the mechanical field, but there is no barrier to all other activities. Our membership roll contains the highest executives and the humblest laborers, and there is no distinction on the social side, we all meet on a common ground. A genial spirit predominates our meetings and acrimonious debates are prohibited. The annual dues are but Three Dollars, and for that modest expenditure, you are privileged to attend nine meetings, at which splendid papers are presented by men who are authorities in their respective lines. A liberal education is received by reason of these addresses and ensuing discussions. In addition, there is sent to each member the printed "Proceedings" containing in full the papers and discussions that have been presented, and the membership can, if so inclined, pursue the various subjects with gratifying results. Further, when the intellectual side of the evening has been taken care of, a delicious collation is served for the pleasure of those who desire to partake of food before they go home.

May attention be called to a broad feature of this organization? No doubt as you heard tonight the names of the members elected to the different positions, you marveled at the diversity of the membership as typified in the gentlemen who have been selected to carry on the official duties of the organization. There is no body of this character that I have known that is so completely diverse. If you will check the large number of men named tonight with your Official Proceedings, you will observe that the different railroads in this section are represented in these offices and on committees. That policy is what maintains the high standard of the Club.

In the thirty-six years of our history, we have had as presiding officers, gentlemen enjoying the exalted rank of President, Vice President, General Manager, or dominating men in their respective railroad systems, mechanical men, track men, operating men, and those from every department of railroading, with a straggling from the railway supply fraternity.

Last year when we were looking for the proper type of man for the Presidency, we turned to the mechanical department of what might be designated as a minor railroad for this exalted office. How well he has functioned you all are aware. We here tonight and who have been present during the past year, can well testify as to the quiet, dignified and unpretentious manner in which the duties of the office have been discharged. It has long been the custom of the Club to tender some visible token of appreciation to those who, after a full year of arduous administration, retire from the Presidency, and this year is no exception. Following the custom, the Committee selected have functioned exceptionally well and are presenting to the retiring President as a token of esteem and regard, a set of silver that is beautiful to behold, practical in application and will last during generations yet unborn.

Mr. Retiring President, on behalf of not alone those members of the Railway Club of Pittsburgh who are here tonight on this most delightful occasion, as well as in the name of those who could not be here in person but with us in spirit, I present to you, as their representative, this chest of silver.

I am going to ask all those assembled before they leave to come up to the rostrum and see what has been deemed fitting to convey to our retiring president the respect and affection in which he is held by each of us. Sure I am Mr. Rauschart you will prize this gift for its beautiful workman- ship and artistic design while it is substantial and serviceable and I can not think of anything to make you happier than to go home tonight and display this present to your wife as concrete evidence of our high regard. On behalf of all the members, I wish you every happiness and joy in the future.

MR. RAUSCHART: I wish right at this moment that I was either a Frank Lanahan or a Rufus Flinn, when I could hold you here for several hours to give adequate expression to my feelings. I am sure it would take at least that long to tell you how deeply I appreciate not only the gift but the sentiment of regard and affection with which you have accompanied it. But I am not much good at expressing my feelings in words that are fitting, and I can only assure you that I feel proud at this evidence of your kindly feeling toward me, that I shall always remember the Railway Club of Pittsburgh as the source of the happiest friendships and experiences of my life, and that I shall always be eager to do the best I can for this splendid Club.

PRESIDENT SIXSMITH: Gentlemen, is there any further business that should come before the Club at this time? If not, the necessary business under the requirements of our By-laws has been completed and I want to thank you for your patience and interest in the proceedings up to now, which necessarily had to precede the entertainment that has been provided. I recognize that this is primarily a fun-making night and without further delay I am going to turn the affairs of the evening over to your very capable Chairman of the Entertainment Committee, Mr. Gillespie. It is a privilege and pleasure for me to ask Mr. J. Porter Gillespie to assume charge of this gathering for the balance of the evening.

Under the auspices of the Entertainment Committee, a very delightful program was presented by the Liberty Vaudeville Contracting Company, Pittsburgh, Pa., as follows:

The Three Fish Brothers—Colored Singing, Dancing and Comedy Artists.

The Lawson Sisters—Harmony Song Presentations.

The Apollo Brothers — Sensational Gymnasts and Hand Balancers.

Miss Margia Dwora—Character and Blues Singing Artist.

Miss Honey Thomas—Novelty and Acrobatic Dancer.

Miss Catherine Rice—Oriental, Hawaiian and Wing Dancer.

Miss Rae Russell—Mistress of Ceremonies.

Mrs. Joe Shaffer—Pianist and Accompanist.

J. D. CONWAY, Secretary.

CONSTITUTION

ARTICLE I

The name of this organization shall be "THE RAILWAY CLUB OF PITTSBURGH."

ARTICLE II

OBJECTS

The objects of this Club shall be mutual intercourse for the acquirement of knowledge by reports and discussion, for the improvement of railway operation, construction, maintenance and equipment, and to bring into closer relationship men employed in railway work and kindred interests.

ARTICLE III

MEMBERSHIP

SECTION 1. The membership of this Club shall consist of persons interested in any department of railway service or kindred interests, or persons recommended by the Executive Committee upon the payment of the annual dues for the current year.

SEC. 2. Persons recommended by the Executive Committee and by unanimous vote of all members present at any regular meeting of the Club may be made an Honorary Member and shall be entitled to all the privileges of membership and not be subject to the payment of dues or assessments.

ARTICLE IV

OFFICERS

The officers of this Club shall consist of a President, First Vice President, Second Vice President, Secretary, Treasurer and an Executive Committee of seven or more members, elected at the Annual Meeting of the Club, for a term of one year. There shall be a Finance Committee of five or more members; a Membership Committee of twelve or more members; an Entertainment Committee of seven or more members; a Reception and Attendance Committee of twelve or more members; a Subject Committee of three or more members; and an Advertising Committee of three or more members; all elected at the Annual Meeting, the term of office to be specified, but in no case to exceed three years. Chairmen and Vice Chairmen of these committees where not named on the ballot will be elected from among the elected members by the Executive Committee.

ARTICLE V

DUTIES OF OFFICERS

SECTION 1. The President shall preside at all regular or special meetings of the Club and perform all duties pertaining to a presiding officer; also serve as a member of the Executive Committee.

SEC. 2. The First Vice President, in the absence of the President, will perform all the duties of that officer; the Second Vice President, in the absence of the President and First Vice President, will perform the duties of the presiding officer. The First and Second Vice Presidents shall also serve as members of the Executive Committee.

SEC. 3. The Executive Committee will exercise a general supervision over the affairs of the Club and authorize all expenditures of its funds.

SEC. 4. The Secretary will attend all meetings of the Club or Executive Committee, keep full minutes of their proceedings; preserve the records and documents of the Club, accept and turn over all moneys received to the Treasurer at least once a month, draw cheques for all bills, when approved by a majority of the Executive Committee present at any meeting of the Club or Executive Committee meeting. He shall have charge of the publication of the Club Proceedings and perform other routine work pertaining to the business affairs of the Club under direction of the Executive Committee.

SEC. 5. The Treasurer shall receipt for all moneys received from the Secretary, and deposit the same in the name of the Club within thirty days in a bank approved by the Executive Committee. All disbursements of the funds of the Club shall be by check signed by the Secretary and Treasurer.

SEC. 6. The Subject Committee will arrange programs and select speakers for the regular meetings of the Club and perform such other duties as may be assigned them by the President or First and Second Vice Presidents, working in conjunction with the Entertainment Committee as may be required. The Chairman of the Subject Committee will serve as an advisory member of the Executive Committee.

SEC. 7. The Membership Committee will actively engage in building up and maintaining the list of active members of the Club and perform such other duties as may be assigned them by the President or First and Second Vice Presidents. The Chairman of this Committee will serve as an advisory member of the Executive Committee.

SEC. 8. The Advertising Committee will solicit advertisements for the Official Proceedings and perform such other duties as may be assigned them by the President or First and Second Vice Presidents. The Chairman of this Committee will serve as an advisory member of the Executive Committee.

SEC. 9. The Reception and Attendance Committee will receive members, guests and visitors at the meetings and generally assist in promoting social intercourse and good fellowship, securing attendance of the members, and performing such other duties as may be assigned them by the President or First and Second Vice Presidents. The Chairman of this Committee will serve as an advisory member of the Executive Committee.

SEC. 10. The Entertainment Committee will perform such duties as may be assigned them by the President or First and Second Vice Presidents, and such other duties as may be proper for such a committee.

SEC. 11. The Finance Committee will perform the duties of an auditing committee to audit the accounts of the Club at the close of a term or at any time necessary to do so and perform such other duties as may be assigned them by the President or First and Second Vice Presidents.

ARTICLE VI

ELECTION OF OFFICERS

SECTION 1. The officers shall be elected at the regular annual meeting as follows, except as otherwise provided for:

SEC. 2. The President will appoint a Nominating Committee of five members, three of whom must be regularly elected members of the Executive Committee, who shall at the September meeting recommend nominations for all offices to be filled at the annual meeting and these, together with any other nominations which may be made from the floor under proper procedure, will be printed and mailed as a letter-ballot to all of the members of the Club, not less than twenty days previous to the Annual Meeting, by the elective members of the Executive Committee. Each member may express his choice for the several offices to be filled by properly marking the letter-ballot and returning it to the Chairman of the Executive Committee.

SEC. 3. The elective members of the Executive Committee will present to the President the names of the members receiving the highest number of votes for each office, together with the number of votes received.

SEC. 4. The President will announce the result of the ballot and declare the election.

SEC. 5. Should two or more members receive the same number of votes, it shall be decided by a vote of the members present, by ballot.

ARTICLE VII

AMENDMENTS

Amendments may be made to this Constitution by written request of ten members, presented at a regular meeting and decided by a two-thirds vote of the members present at the next regular meeting.

BY-LAWS

ARTICLE I

MEETINGS

SECTION 1. The regular meetings of the Club shall be held at Pittsburgh, Pa., on the fourth Thursday of each month, except June, July and August, at 8 o'clock P. M.

SEC. 2. The annual meeting shall be held on the fourth Thursday of October each year.

SEC. 3. The President may, at such times as he deems expedient, or upon request of a quorum, call special meetings.

ARTICLE II

QUORUM

At any regular or special meeting twenty-five members shall constitute a quorum.

ARTICLE III

DUES

SECTION 1. The annual dues of members shall be Two Dollars, payable in advance on or before the fourth Thursday of September each year.

SEC. 2. The annual subscription to the printed Proceedings of the Club shall be at the published price of One Dollar. Each member of the Club shall pay for both dues and subscription. Dues and subscription paid by members proposed at the meetings in September or October shall be credited for the following fiscal year.

SEC. 3. At the annual meeting members whose dues and subscription are unpaid shall be dropped from the roll after due notice mailed them at least thirty days previous.

SEC. 4. Members suspended for non-payment of dues shall not be reinstated until all arrearages have been paid.

ARTICLE IV

ORDER OF BUSINESS

1. Roll call.
2. Reading of the minutes of preceding meeting.
3. Reception of new members.
4. Announcements and communications.
5. Appointment of committees.
6. Reports of officers or committees.
7. Unfinished business.
8. New business.
9. Election of officers.
10. Presentation of program and discussion.
11. Adjournment.

ARTICLE V

PUBLICATIONS

SECTION 1. The Proceedings or such portion as the Executive Committee may approve shall be published (standard size, 6x9 inches) and mailed to the members of the Club or other similar clubs with which exchange is made.

ARTICLE VI

The stenographic report of the meetings will be confined to resolutions, motions and discussions of papers unless otherwise directed by the presiding officer.

ARTICLE VII

AMENDMENTS

These By-Laws may be amended by written request of ten members, presented at a regular meeting, and a two-thirds vote of the members present at the next meeting.

In Memoriam

HARRY A. KRAUSE

Joined Club December 23, 1920

Died September 7, 1937

MEMBERS

Adams, Charles E.,
Superintendent,
Pennsylvania Railroad,
Pennsylvania Station,
Pittsburgh, Pa

Adams, Frank W.,
Local Storekeeper,
B. & O. R. R.,
137 Minooka St.,
Mt. Oliver Station,
Pittsourgh, Pa

Adams, Walter A.,
Chief Clerk,
P. & L. E. R. R.,
230 Ohio Ave.,
Glassport, Pa

Adrian, J. H.,
Clerk,
Pennsylvania Railroad,
1931 Noblestown Road,
Pittsburgh, Pa.

Ainsworth, J. H.,
Sales Engineer,
Carnegie-Illinois Steel Corp.,
Carnegie Bldg.,
Pittsburgh, Pa.

Ainsworth, John R.,
Special Apprentice,
Westinghouse Air Brake Co.,
353 Marguerite Ave.,
Wilmerding, Pa.

Aivalotis, John,
Assistant Car Foreman,
B. & O. R. R. Co.,
Midway, Pa.

Allderdice, Norman,
Sales Representative,
General American Transp.
Corp.,
P. O. Box 46,
Sewickley, Pa

Allen, Earl M.,
Engineer (Signal),
Union Switch & Signal Co,
1318 Lancaster Ave.,
Pittsburgh (18), Pa.

Allison, John,
Sales Engineer,
Pgh. Steel Foundry Corp.,
Glassport, Pa.

Ambrose, W. F.,
M. M. & M. C. B., Aliquippa
& So. R. R.,
1301 Meadow St.
Aliquippa, Pa.

Ament, F. Chalmer,
Retired Traveling Engineman,
Pennsylvania Railroad,
6940 Bishop St.,
Pittsburgh (6) Pa.

Anderegg, G. W.,
Electrician,
P. & L. E. R. R. Co.,
814 Freeland St.,
Pittsburgh, Pa.

Anderson, Burt T.,
General Sales Manager,
Union Switch & Signal Co.,
Swissvale, Pa.

Anderson, G. S.,
Foreman,
Pennsylvania System,
Box 19, Penna. Station,
Pittsburgh, Pa.

Anderson, H. N.,
Division Engineer,
B. & O. R. R.,
2 Victory Blvd.,
Tompkinsville, S. I., N. Y.

Angel, A. J.,
Purchasing Agent,
P. & W. Va. Ry. Co.,
Wabash Building,
Pittsburgh, Pa.

Anne, George E.,
Representative,
American Brake Shoe &
Foundry Co.,
R. D. 2,
Hollidaysburg, Pa.

Arensberg, F. L.,
President,
Vesuvius Crucible Co.,
Box 29,
Swissvale, Pa.

Armstrong, C. B.,
Railway Sales Manager,
Central Division,
Air Reduction Sales Co.,
332 South Michigan Ave.,
Chicago, Ill.

Armstrong, Edward W.,
Supervisor-Tracing Service,
Pennsylvania Railroad,
Pennsylvania Station,
Pittsburgh, Pa

Armstrong, J. L.,
Foreman P. P. & Elec.,
Pennsylvania Railroad,
2 Grandview Avenue,
Crafton, Pittsburgh, Pa.

Arnold, C. C.,
Water Service Inspector,
P. & L. E. R. R. Co.,
Room 506 Terminal Bldg.,
Pittsburgh, Pa.

Arnold, J. J.,
Sales Dept.,
Pressed Steel Car Co.,
McKees Rocks, Pa

Ashley, F. B.,
Vice President,
Pruett Schaffer Chemical Co,
Tabor St.,
Corliss Station,
Pittsburgh, Pa.

Ater, Byron F.,
Assistant Secretary,
Y. M. C. A.,
P. & L. E. R. R. Co.,
Newell, Pa.

Atkins, T. Earl,
Branch Manager,
The Pennzoil Company,
Chamber of Commerce
Building,
Pittsburgh, Pa

Aulbach, A. J.,
Yardmaster, P. & L. E. R. R.,
318 Quincy Ave.,
Mt. Oliver Station,
Pittsburgh, Pa.

Babcock, F. H.,
Safety Agent,
P. & L. E. R. R.,
221 Magnolia Ave.,
Mt. Lebanon,
Pittsburgh, Pa.

Bacon, J. L.,
Manager of Sales,
Valve Pilot Corporation,
230 Park Avenue,
New York, N. Y.

Baer, Harry L.,
Pres., Water Treatment Co
of America,
1536 Madison Ave.,
N. S., Pittsburgh, Pa.

Bailey, F. G.,
Mech. Engr., Truck Dept.,
Standard Steel Car Corp'n,
P. O. Box 839,
Butler, Pa

Bailey, J. C.,
Car Service Agent,
B. & L. E. R. R.,
350 Main St.,
Greenville, Pa.

Baily, J. H.,
Vice President,
Edgewater Steel Co.,
P. O. Box 478,
Pittsburgh, Pa.

Bain, Clarence R.,
Triple Valve Repairer,
P. & L. E. R. R. Co.,
532 Russellwood Ave.,
McKees Rocks, Pa.

Bair, J. K.,
Locomotive Engineer,
Union Railroad,
415 Osborne St.,
Turtle Creek, Pa.

Baker, Dale,
Car Foreman,
B. & O. R. R. Co.,
Cor. State and Murry St.,
East Salamanca, N. Y.

Baker, J. B.,
Chief Engineer,
Pennsylvania Railroad,
Harrisburg, Pa.

Baker, W. E.,
Supervisor,
Pennsylvania Railroad,
51 McMunn Avenue,
Crafton, Pittsburgh, Pa.

Bakewell, Donald C.,
Vice President,
Blaw Knox Co.,
Farmers Bank Bldg.,
Pittsburgh, Pa.

Ball, Fred M.,
District Manager,
Franklin Ry. Sup. Co., Inc.,
Broad St. Station Bldg.,
Philadelphia, Pa.

Ball, George L.,
Secretary and Treasurer,
Ball Chemical Co.,
230 S. Fairmont Ave.,
Pittsburgh, Pa.

Balla, J. A.,
Asst. Supervisor T. & S.,
Pennsylvania Railroad,
5825 Elgin Ave.,
E. E., Pittsburgh, Pa.

Balph, M. Z.,
Assistant Engineer,
P. & L. E. R. R.,
3308 Sixth Ave.,
Beaver Falls, Pa.

Balsley, J. I.,
Asst. General Foreman,
B. & O. R. R. Co.,
406 Zara Street,
Knoxville,
Pittsburgh, Pa.

Balzer, C. E.,
Inspector of Tests,
P. & L. E. R. R.,
3432 Allendale St.,
Pittsburgh, Pa.

Barclay, J. R.,
Cost Engineer,
P. & L. E. R. R.,
4 Oakwood Road,
Crafton, Pittsburgh, Pa.

Barkley, Sherwood W.
Triple Valve A.B. Tester,
P. & L. E. R. R. Co.,
Box 126, R. D. No. 1,
McKees Rocks, Pa.

Barnett, George,
Salesman,
W. W. Lawrence & Co.,
West Carson St.,
Pittsburgh, Pa.

Barney, Harry,
President-Treasurer,
Barney Machinery Co., Inc.,
2410 Koppers Bldg.,
Pittsburgh, Pa.

Barnhart, B. F.,
Road Foreman of Engines,
B. & L. E. R. R.,
9 Shady Ave.,
Greenville, Pa.

Barr, H. C.,
Agent, P. & L. E. R. R.,
131 Sycamore St.,
Pittsburgh (11), Pa.

Barrie, James S.,
Material Inspector,
New York Central Lines,
130 Elmcnt St.,
Crafton, Pittsburgh, Pa.

Barth, E. H.,
Triple Valve Repairer,
P. & L. E. R. R. Co.,
1119 Faust Street,
Pittsburgh (4), Pa.

Barton, E. E.,
Asst. Local Treasurer,
P. & L. E. R. R. Co.,
1718 Ridge Avenue,
Coraopolis, Pa

Bash, J. E.,
District Inspector,
R. R. Perishable Inspection
Agency,
P.R.R. Produce Terminal,
Pittsburgh, Pa.

Batchelar, E. C.,
Manager, The Motch &
Merryweather Mach'y Co.,
1315 Clark Bldg.,
Pittsburgh, Pa.

Batson, J. F.,
Asst. Master Mechanic,
Pennsylvania Railroad,
Pitcairn, Pa.

Bauer, F. C.,
Assistant Agent,
Railway Express Agency,
2223 Lucina Ave.,
Overbrook,
Pittsburgh (10), Pa.

Bauer, Lawrence M.,
Car Repairer,
Pennsylvania Railroad,
7217 Kedron St.,
Pittsburgh, Pa.

Bauer, R. B.,
General Yard Master,
P. & L. E. R. R. Co.,
Dickerson Run, Pa.

Baughman, G. W.,
Union Switch & Signal Co.,
103 Biddle St.,
Wilkinsburg, Pa.

Baumann, Edward G.,
Supervisor Tel. & Signals,
Pennsylvania Railroad,
East Waldheim Road,
Aspinwall, Pa

Beall, C. R.,
Chief Engineer,
Union Switch & Signal Co ,
Braddock Avenue,
Swissvale, Pa

Beam, E. J.,
Car Builder, Penna. System,
577 Fourth St.,
Pitcairn, Pa

Beattie, J. A.,
1090 Shady Ave.,
Pittsburgh, Pa

Beatty, Raymond N.,
Conductor,
Pennsylvania Railroad,
1207 Allegheny Ave.,
N. S. Pittsburgh, Pa

Beaver, J. D.,
General Supt.,
P. S. & N. R. R.,
St. Marys, Pa.

Beaver, R. C.,
Asst. Mechanical Engineer,
B. & L. E. R. R.,
122 West Main St.,
Greenville, Pa

Beeson, H. L.,
General Foreman,
Monongahela Ry. Co.,
207 Riverview Terrace, ·
West Brownsville, Pa

Behm, Harry,
·Gang Leader,
Monongahela Railway Co.,
Box 138,
Hiller, Pa

Beitsch, George F.,
Gang Foreman,
Pennsylvania Railroad,
1110 Allegheny Street,
New Brighton, Pa.

Bell, R. A.,
Clerk,
P. & L. E. R. R. Co.,
325 Mathews Ave.,
Carrick, Pittsburgh, Pa.

Bell, W. T.,
Inspector Train Service,
Pennsylvania Railroad,
Pennsylvania Station,
Pittsburgh, Pa

Beltz, J. D.,
Superintendent,
B. & O. R. R.,
2915 Belrose Ave.,
South Hills,
Pittsburgh, Pa

Bender, H. P.,
Mechanical Engineer,
P. & L. E. R. R. Co ,
400 Island Ave.,
McKees Rocks, Pa.

Berg, Karl,
Supt. Motive Power,
P. & L. E. R. R.,
6319 Morrowfield Ave.,
Pittsburgh, Pa

Berg, Max,
Locomotive Engineer,
Montour Railroad Co.,
R. D. 6, Mt. Oliver Station,
Pittsburgh, Pa.

Berghane, A. L.,
Mechanical Expert,
Westinghouse Air Brake Co.,
Wilmerding, Pa

Bergman, Carl R.,
Supervisor—Track,
Pennsylvania Railroad,
270 Center Way,
Beaver, Pa.

Bessolo, A. J.,
Asst. Gen. Traf. Mgr.,
Gulf Refining Co.,
Gulf Building,
Pittsburgh, Pa

Best, C. Thomas,
President,
American Shim Steel Co.,
1304 Fifth Ave.,
New Kensington, Pa.

Best, D. A.,
Test Engineer,
Westinghouse Air Brake Co.,
Wilmerding, Pa.

Best, Rankin M.,
Clerk,
P. & L. E. R. R. Co.,
Aliquippa, Pa.

Beswick, Richard M.,
Tester,
Westinghouse Air Brake Co
514 Chicora Street,
East McKeesport, Pa

Bevan, James Ira,
Special Apprentice,
Westinghouse Air Brake Co.,
787 Third Street,
East McKeesport, Pa

Bickett, M. A.,
Freight Agent,
P. & L. E. R. R. Co..
303 Boyles Ave.,
New Castle, Pa

Biggerstaff, James M.,
Electrical Foreman,
P. & L. E. R. R. Co..
P. O. Box 48,
Wireton, Pa

Bingham, W. C.,
Proprietor,
Bingham Metal Co.,
Law & Finance Bldg.,
Pittsburgh, Pa

Binyon, Thomas E.,
Telegraph & Telephone Engr.
Pennsylvania Railroad,
Pennsylvania Station,
Pittsburgh, Pa

Bishop, D. B.,
Salesman,
Dearborn Chemical Co,
Farmers Bank Bldg.,
Pittsburgh, Pa.

Bishop, H. G.,
Asst. Road Fore. of Engines
Pennsylvania Railroad,
422 North Highland Ave.,
Pittsburgh, Pa

Bishop, M. L.,
Chief Clerk,
P. & W. Va. Ry. Co.,
126 Sanford St.,
20th Ward,
Pittsburgh, Pa

Bittner, George,
Asst. Engine House Foreman
Pennsylvania Railroad,
247 Ivory Ave.,
N. S. Pittsburgh, Pa.

Bixler, Warren,
Secretary-Treasurer,
Foster Bixler Fuel Co,
Grant Building,
Pittsburgh, Pa.

Black, C. R.,
Salesman,
Westinghouse Electric and
Manufacturing Co.,
306 Fourth Ave.,
Pittsburgh, Pa

Blackmore, G. A.,
President,
Union Switch & Signal Co..
Swissvale, Pa.

Blair, H. A., Supervisor,
Federal Safety Appliances,
B. & O. R. R. Co.,
B. & O. Road Bldg.,
Baltimore, Md.

Blair, John R.,
Asst. Mgr. of Sales,
Pittsburgh Steel Co.,
P. O. Box 118,
Pittsburgh, Pa.

Blanchard, Henry,
Sales Representative,
The Baldwin Locomotive
Works,
Paschall Station,
Philadelphia, Pa.

Blest, Minot C.,
Ass't. to Vice Pres't.,
Pressed Steel Car Co.,
McKees Rocks, Pa

Blyth, F. G.,
General Agent,
Railway Express Agency,
926 Penn Avenue,
Pittsburgh, Pa.

Boden, A. S.,
Traffic Manager,
Coal Control Assn.,
Western Pennsylvania,
Oliver Bldg.,
Pittsburgh, Pa

Boggs, L. S.,
825 N. Negley Ave.,
Pittsburgh, Pa

Bone, H. L.,
General Mechanical Engr.,
Union Switch & Signal Co..
Swissvale, Pa

Bonhoff, E. L.,
Engine House Foreman,
Pennsylvania Railroad,
718 Blackburn Road,
Sewickley, Pa.

Booth, W. F.,
Asst. Superintendent,
B. & O. R. R. Co.,
B. & O. Station,
Pittsburgh, Pa.

Borg, John Edw.,
Chief Draftsman,
Julian Kennedy,
232 Martsolf Ave.,
West View, Pa.

Bottomly, E. S.,
Chief Joint Inspector,
P. R. R., B. & O.,
Rdg. and W. M.,
P. O. Box 646,
Martinsburg, W. Va.

Bovard, William R.,
Clerk, Office G. S. M. P,
Pennsylvania Railroad,
1210 Fairdale Street,
Pittsburgh, Pa.

Bowden, Foster S.,
Supervisor—Track,
Pennsylvania Railroad,
136 Como Ave.,
Buffalo, N. Y.

Bowden, T. C.,
Coal Inspector,
B. & L. E. R. R.,
97 S. Mercer St.,
Greenville, Pa.

Bowen, C. R.,
Pennsylvania Railroad,
3265 Raleigh Ave.,
Dormont,
Pittsburgh, Pa.

Bowery, Frank J.,
Chief Estimator, F. C. D.,
P. S. C. Co.,
214 Birmingham Ave.,
Avalon, Pa.

Boyd, John,
Clerk,
J. T. & A. Hamilton Co,
1432 Arnold St.,
Pittsburgh (20), Pa.

Boyd, John R.,
Designing Engineer,
P. & L. E. R. R. Co.,
P&LE Terminal Bldg.,
Pittsburgh, Pa.

Boyd, J. W.,
Superintendent,
Monongahela Railway Co.,
Brownsville, Pa.

Boyer, W. W.,
Asst. Division Engineer,
Pennsylvania Railroad.
35 Dinsmore Ave.,
Crafton, Pittsburgh, Pa.

Boyland, William E.,
Train Master,
B. & O. R. R. Co.,
109 Green Street,
Connellsville, Pa.

Bradley, J. P.,
(Retired),
Railway Express Agency,
Inc.,
550 Dawson Ave.,
Pittsburgh (2), Pa.

Bradley, W. C.,
C. C. to Gen'l. Supt.,
Union R. R.,
260 Cascade Road,
Wilkinsburg, Pa.

Brady, T. Jos.,
President,
Powell Coal Co.,
303 Kearsage St.,
Mt. Washington Sta.,
Pittsburgh, Pa.

Brandt, George F.,
Triple Valve Repairer,
P. & L. E. R. R. Co.,
925 Woodward Ave.,
McKees Rocks, Pa.

Brant, Wm. J.,
709 East Ohio St.,
N. S., Pittsburgh, Pa.

Braun, Otto F.,
Gen. Mach. Shop Foreman,
P. & L. E. R. R.,
R. D. 1—Herbst Road,
Coraopolis, Pa.

Brennan, John T.,
Assistant Vice President,
Greenville Steel Car Co.,
Greenville, Pa.

Brewer, H. W.,
Supt. of Shops,
B. & O. R. R. Co.,
N. Jared Street,
Du Bois, Pa

Brice, A. E.,
Special Representative.
Gulf Refining Co.,
Gulf Building,
Pittsburgh. Pa

Bricker, O. F.,
Mgr., Transp'n. Advertising,
Westinghouse Electric &
Mfg. Co.,
East Pittsburgh. Pa.

Britt, T. E.,
Division Storekeeper,
B. & O. R. R.,
2818 Clermont Ave.,
Pittsburgh, (10), Pa.

Brown, C. C.,
Rep., Dearborn Chemical Co..
Farmers Bank Bldg.,
Pittsburgh. Pa.

Brown, Earl F.,
Electrical Supervisor,
P. & L. E. R. R. Co.,
Terminal Station,
Pittsburgh, Pa.

Brown, F. M.,
Supt., P. & L. E. R. R.,
Pittsburgh. Pa.

Brown,, H. C.,
Salesman,
Independent Pneumatic
Tool Co.,
Wabash Building,
Pittsburgh. Pa.

Brown, Harold A.,
Advertising Manager,
Railway Equipment &
Publication Co..
424 West 33rd St.,
New York. N. Y.

Browne, Bard,
Asst. to Vice President,
The Superheater Co.,
60 East 42nd St.,
New York. N. Y.

Bruce, S. S.,
General Traffic Manager,
The Koppers Co.,
Koppers Bldg.,
Pittsburgh. Pa.

Brunnings, George H.,
District Manager,
American-Hawaiian
Steamship Co.,
Gulf Building,
Pittsburgh. Pa.

Bryant, Jess H.,
Station Agent,
Pennsylvania Railroad,
Vandergrift, Pa.

Bryant, Lewis J.,
Westinghouse Air Brake Co.,
1231 Greensburg Ave.,
East McKeesport, Pa.

Buchanan, Charles C.,
Engineer,
Union Switch & Signal Co.,
Swissvale, Pa.

Bucher, Fred J.,
Electrical Engineer,
Hillman Coal & Coke Co.,
First National Bank
Bldg.,
Pittsburgh, Pa.

Buck, L. L.,
Engineer,
Union Switch & Signal Co.,
441 Olymuia Road,
Mt. Washington,
Pittsburgh, Pa.

Buckbee, W. A.,
The Superheater Co.,
Nyack, N. Y.

Buckley, William,
Air Brake Instructor,
Pennsylvania Railroad,
Pennsylvania Station,
Pittsburgh, Pa.

Buckwalter, T. V.,
Vice President,
Timken Roller Bearing Co.,
Canton, Ohio.

Buell, D. C.,
Director, The Railway Educational Bureau,
1809 Capitol Ave.,
Omaha, Neb.

Buffington, W. P.,
Traffic Manager,
Pittsburgh Coal Co.,
Oliver Bldg.,
Pittsburgh, Pa.

Buhrmester, H. C.,
Chief Clerk, Eastern Div.,
Pennsylvania Railroad,
3418 Clearfield St.,
Pittsburgh, Pa.

Bull, R. S.,
Supt. Power & Inclines,
Pittsburgh Railways Co.,
600 Sandusky St.,
N. S., Pittsburgh, Pa.

Burchell, R. W.,
Wreck Master,
B. & O. R. R. Co.,
232 Glencaladh Street
Hazelwood, Pittsburgh, Pa.

Burel, W. C.,
Master Mechanic,
Western Allegheny R. R.,
Kaylor, Pa.

Burk, G. C.,
Engine House Foreman,
Pennsylvania Railroad,
Blairsville, Pa.

Burkhart, A. E.,
Foreman, Car Department,
Pennsylvania Railroad,
260 Woodlawn Road,
Steubenville, Ohio

Burkhart, G. A.,
Engine House Foreman,
Monongahela Railway Co.,
P. O. Box 97,
Hiller, Pa.

Burnett, C. E.,
Engineer,
Anchor Sanitary Co.,
213 Water Street,
Pittsburgh, Pa.

Burnette, G. H.,
Asst. Chief Engineer,
P. & L. E. R. R.,
Terminal Building,
Pittsburgh, Pa

Burnside, G. M.,
Boiler Inspector,
Monongahela Railway Co.,
1025 Second Street,
South Brownsville, Pa.

Burriss, W. C.,
Inspector,
Westinghouse Air Brake Co.,
Wilmerding, Pa.

Button, L. R.,
Gen. Freight & Pass. Agt.,
Pittsburgh & Shawmut R.R.,
129 N. McKean Street,
Kittanning, Pa.

Buzzerd, J. P.,
Signal Supervisor,
B. & O. R. R. Co.,
318 Rochelle Street,
Pittsburgh (10), Pa.

Byers, Thomas,
General Agent,
Delaware & Hudson R. R.,
Koppers Bldg.,
Pittsburgh, Pa.

Byrne, William L.,
W. L. Byrne Co.,
4 Smithfield St.,
Pittsburgh, Pa.

Byron, Robert J.,
Asst. Foreman,
Pennsylvania Railroad,
4050 Cambronne St.,
Pittsburgh, Pa.

Cable, H. E.,
District Engineer,
National Aluminate Corp.,
150 South Euclid Ave.,
Bellevue, Pittsburgh, Pa.

Cadwallader, W. H.,
Vice Pres. & Gen. Mgr.,
Union Switch & Signal Co.,
Swissvale, Pa.

Cage, Charles A.,
Gen. Fore., Mech. Dept.,
B. & O. R. R. Co.,
213 Kimberly Avenue,
Somerset, Pa.

Callahan, D. E.,
Asst. Div. Engineer,
Pennsylvania Railroad,
210 Grant Ave.,   .
Bellevue, Pa.

Callahan, F. J.,
Foreman,
Montour Railroad,
1109 Chartiers Ave.,
McKees Rocks, Pa.

Callahan, Lawrence H.,
Yardmaster, P. & L. E. R. R.,
600 Monongahela Ave.,
McKeesport, Pa.

Campbell, Edward D.,
Traffic Manager,
B. & L. E. R. R.,
P. O. Box 536,
Pittsburgh, Pa.

Campbell, F. R.,
Shop Foreman,
Donora Southern Railroad
Co.,
664 Thompson Ave.,
Donora, Pa.

Campbell, J. Alan,
Special Apprentice,
Westinghouse Air Brake Co.,
353 Marguerite Ave.,
Wilmerding, Pa.

Campbell, W. T.,
Secretary & Treasurer,
Montour Railroad,
Oliver Building,
Pittsburgh, Pa.

Cannon, T. E.,
Gen. Supt. Equipment,
P. & W. Va. Ry.,
Wabash Bldg.,
Pittsburgh, Pa.

Capps, W. P.,
Stoker Supervisor,
B. & O. R. R. Co.,
c/o Mechanical Engin'r.,
Mt. Clare Shops,
Baltimore, Md.

Cardwell, J. R.,
President,
Cardwell Westinghouse Co.,
332 S. Michigan Ave.,
Chicago, Ill

Carey, Charles D.,
Railway Sales,
Gulf Refining Company,
Gulf Bldg.,
Pittsburgh, Pa.

Carlson, Lawrence E.,
Westinghouse Air Brake Co.,
904 Munsey Bldg.,
Washington, D. C.

Carmody, J. J.,
Agent,
Pennsylvania Railroad,
228 Chestnut St.,
Kittanning, Pa.

Carothers, J. A.,
President,
Pittsburgh Tool-Knife
& Mfg. Co.,
75 Sycamore St.,
Etna, P. O., Pgh. Pa.

Carpenter, J. F.,
Agent,
P. & L. E. R. R. Co.,
Monaca, Pa.

Carr, T. W.,
Supt. Rolling Stock,
P. & L. E. R. R.,
400 Island Ave.,
McKees Rocks, Pa.

Carrick, J. E.,
Asst. Yard Master,
Pennsylvania Railroad,
Elrama Ave.,
Elrama, Pa.

Carroll, D. C.,
Asst. Agent,
Pennsylvania Railroad,
Eleventh & Etna Sts.,
Pittsburgh, Pa.

Carson, John,
Foreman Pattern Shop,
Ft. Pitt Malleable Iron Co.,
1705 Morningside Ave.,
Pittsburgh, Pa.

Carter, E. D.,
Lineman,
Union Railroad Co.,
1305 Meadow Street
McKeesport, Pa.

Carter, John D.,
General Agent,
Union Pacific System,
Oliver Building,
Pittsburgh, Pa.

Cartwright, Wm. E.,
Vice President,
National Bearing Metals
Corp.,
928 Shore Ave.,
N. S., Pittsburgh, Pa.

Case, H. D.,
Live Stock Agent,
Pennsylvania Railroad,
34 Fourth St.,
Aspinwall, Pa.

Casey, John F.,
Chairman of the Board,
John F. Casey Co.,
P. O. Box 1888,
Pittsburgh, Pa.

Cashdollar, C. J.,
Foreman, Pgh. 11th St.,
Pennsylvania Railroad,
40 North Harrison Ave.,
Bellevue, Pa

Catt, C. E.,
Division Accountant,
B. & O. R. R..
1032 Chelton Ave.,
Pittsburgh, Pa.

Cavanaugh, T. J.,
Chief Special Agent,
P. & W. Va. Ry. Co.,
100 Beltzhoover Ave.,
Pittsburgh, Pa

Chaffin, H. B.,
M. M.,
Pennsylvania Railroad,
1523 Fulton Road, N.W.,
Canton, Ohio

Chalker, A. R.,
Mechanical Engineer,
William K. Stamets,
473 Dawson Ave.,
Bellevue, Pittsburgh, Pa.

Chase, Daniel K.,
Superintendent,
Pennsylvania Railroad,
Pennsylvania Station,
Pittsburgh, Pa.

Cherry, Dale C.,
Asst. Master Mechanic,
Pennsylvania Railroad,
203 Franklin Ave.,
Wilkinsburg, Pa.

Chesley, J. O.,
Mgr., Development Division,
Aluminum Co. of America,
Gulf Building,
Pittsburgh, Pa.

Chilcoat, H. E.,
General Manager of Sales,
Koppel Div.,
Pressed Steel Car Co., Inc.,
Grant Building,
Pittsburgh, Pa.

Chipley, G. R.,
Traveling Freight Agent,
Pennsylvania Railroad,
Pennsylvania Station,
Pittsburgh, Pa.

Chittenden, A. D.,
Supt. Transportation,
B. & L. E. R. R.,
P. O. Box 536,
Pittsburgh, Pa.

Christfield, J. G.,
Mechanical Engineer,
American Rolling Mill Co.,
Butler, Pa.

Christner, L.,
Electrician,
B. & O. R. R. Co.,
2709 Queensboro Ave.,
Brookline, Pittsburgh, Pa.

Christy, F. X.,
Inspector,
Pennsylvania Railroad,
1628 Duffield St.,
Pittsburgh, Pa.

Christy, P. J.,
Asst. District Manager,
Chicago Pneumatic Tool Co.,
237 North 12th St.,
Philadelphia, Pa.

Cipro, Thomas,
Gang Foreman,
Union Railroad Co.,
Box 204,
Unity, Pa.

Clapper, H. L.,
Supt. Freight Transpn.,
Pennsylvania Railroad,
Pennsylvania Station,
Pittsburgh, Pa.

Clardy, W. J.,
Transportation Engineer,
Westinghouse Elec. &
Mfg. Co.,
East Pittsburgh, Pa.

Clark, C. C.,
  Sales Manager, Central Dist.,
  Pressed Steel Car Co.,
  Grant Building,
                Pittsburgh, Pa.

Clark, E. C.,
  Clerk,
  Pennsylvania Railroad,
  77 Kendall Ave.,
    Bellevue. Pittsburgh, Pa.

Clark, H. C.,
  Freight Agent,
  Pennsylvania Railroad,
  30th & Race Sts.,
                Philadelphia, Pa.

Clark, R. A.,
  Vice President,
  Mellon-Stuart Company,
  Oliver Building,
                Pittsburgh, Pa

Clarke, A. C.,
  Asst. Chief Engineer,
  B. & O. R. R. Co.,
  Maloney Building,
                Pittsburgh, Pa.

Clausen, Harold C.,
  Mechanical Engineer,
  Althea Road, R. D. No. 1,
    Wilkinsburg, Pgh., Pa.

Clements, B. A.,
  President,
  American Arch Co., Inc.,
  60 E. 42nd Street,
    New York City, N. Y

Clements, Frank C.,
  Foreman,
  P. & L. E. R. R.,
  844 Island Ave.,
                McKees Rocks, Pa.

Clokey, John,
  Assistant Trainmaster,
  Pennsylvania Railroad,
  Sixteenth Street,
                Pittsburgh, Pa

Clowes, W. K.,
  Freight Agent,
  Pennsylvania Railroad,
  P.R.R. Produce Terminal,
                Pittsburgh, Pa.

Coakley, J. A.,
  Gen. Traffic Manager,
  Subsidiary Companies of
  U. S. Steel Corp.,
  Carnegie Building,
                Pittsburgh, Pa.

Coakley, John A., Jr.,
  Vice President and Secretary,
  Lincoln Electric Railway
  Sales Co.,
  Marshall Bldg.,
                Cleveland, Ohio.

Cochran, Harry A.,
  Traffic Manager,
  A. M. Byers Company,
  Clark Building,
                Pittsburgh, Pa

Code, C. J.,
  Asst. to Chief Engr. M. of W.,
  Pennsylvania Railroad,
  42 East Steuben St.,
  Crafton,
                Pittsburgh, Pa.

Coffin, C. W. Floyd,
  Vice President,
  Franklin Railway Supply
  Co., Inc.,
  60 E. 42nd St.,
                New York, N. Y.

Colbert, J. T.,
  General Superintendent,
  Pittsburgh & Shawmut R. R.,
  500 N. McKean Street,
                Kittanning, Pa.

Condon, William H.,
  President,
  Condon Brothers Co., Inc.,
  5242 Perrysville Road,
    N. S., Pittsburgh, Pa.

Conneely, E. K.,
  Manager of Railroad Sales,
  Republic Steel Corporation,
  3 Linden Place,
                Sewickley, Pa.

Connelly, John T.,
  General Foreman,
  B. & O. R. R. Co.,
  1705 Hays Street,
                Swissvale, Pa.

Connolly, R. D.,
  Metallurgical Dept.,
  Carnegie-Illinois Steel Corp.,
  317 N. Dallas Ave.,
                Pittsburgh, Pa.

214

Connors, John M.,
Asst. to Car Foreman,
Montour Railroad Co.,
87 Aztec Way,
Mt. Washington,
Pittsburgh, Pa

Conway, J. D.,
Sec'y-Treas., Railway Supply
Manufacturers' Association,
1941 Oliver Bldg.,
Pittsburgh, Pa

Coombe, A. B ,
Superintendent,
Pressed Steel Car Co , Inc ,
1515 Quail Ave.,
Bellevue, Pa

Cooper, A. H.,
Manager,
Savarins, Inc.,
220 Jefferson Drive,
Mt. Lebanon,
Pittsburgh, Pa

Cotter, George L.,
District Engineer,
Westinghouse Air Brake Co.,
Wilmerding, Pa.

Coulter, A. F.,
Supt. of Rolling Stock,
Union R. R. Company,
East Pittsburgh, Pa

Courtney, Harry,
Shop Supt., P. & L. E.,
520 Giffin Ave.,
Mt. Oliver Sta.,
Pittsburgh, Pa

Cowen, Harry E.,
Triple Valve Tester,
P. & L. E. R. R. Co ,
1115 Adon Street,
Pittsburgh (4), Pa.

Cox, George P.,
Division Engineer,
Monongahela - Railway Co.,
Union Street,
Brownsville, Pa.

Cox, W. E.,
Asst. Superintendent,
Monongahela Connecting
R. R.,
2535 Brownsville Road,
Pittsburgh, Pa

Craig, W. J.,
District Boiler Inspector,
B. & O. R. R.,
3507 Powhattan St.,
Baltimore, Md

Crawford, Alvin B.,
Manager Railway Sales,
Continental Roll & Steel
Foundry Co.,
Grant Bldg.,
Pittsburgh, Pa.

Crawford, A. M.,
Asst Supt. Telegragh &
Signals,
Pennsylvania Railroad,
Broad Street Station,
Philadelphia, Pa.

Crawford, Burt H.,
Clerk,
Pennsylvania Railroad,
316 Fisk Avenue,
Bellevue, Pittsburgh, Pa.

Crede, Wm. A.,
Asst. Pass. Train Master,
Pittsburgh Division,
Pennsylvania Railroad,
1605 Clark St.,
Wilkinsburg, Pa.

Cree, W. M.,
Salesman,
Edgewater Steel Co ,
P O. Box 478,
Pittsburgh, Pa.

Creighton, D. M.,
Engineers' Field Man,
P. & L. E. R. R. Co.,
Kennedy Place,
New Brighton, Pa.

Creighton, W. R.,
Captain of Police,
Pennsylvania Railroad,
83 Valeview Drive,
Kennywood Park, Pa.

Crenner, Jos. A.,
District Manager,
Dearborn Chemical Co.,
Farmers Bank Building,
Pittsburgh, Pa.

Crissman, L. N.,
Sales Engineer,
Electric Storage Battery Co.,
1015 Cochran Road,
Mt. Lebanon,
Pittsburgh, Pa.

215

Critchfield, W. P.,
Supervisor—Track,
Pennsylvania Railroad.
287 North Walnut St.,
Blairsville, Pa.

Critchlow, J. N.,
Sales Department,
Union Steel Casting Co..
62nd & Butler Sts.,
Pittsburgh. Pa.

Cromwell, H. T..
Asst. Supt. Shops,
B. & O. R. R.,
Glenwood Shops.
Pittsburgh, Pa.

Cross. J. H.,
Coal & Ore Agent,
Pennsylvania Railroad.
Union Trust Bldg.,
Cleveland. Ohio.

Crow, C. C.,
Freight Agent.
Pennsylvania Railroad,
1477 Davenport Ave.,
Cleveland, Ohio

Crowell. F. C.,
Foreman. Car Dept.,
Pennsylvania Railroad,
1120 Piedmont Ave.,
Canton. Ohio.

Cruikshank. J. C..
Div. Engr., P. & W. Va. Ry.,
439 Wabash Bldg.,
Pittsburgh, Pa.

Cudworth. H. D.,
Apprentice,
Westinghouse Air Brake Co..
430 East End Ave.,
Pittsburgh. Pa.

Cunningham. J. Donald.
Sales Engineer.
Southern Wheel Co.,
1510 Grace Ave.,
Lakewood, Ohio.

Cunningham. J. L.,
Asst. to Gen. Supt. Mo. Power.
Pennsylvania Railroad,
1009 Penna. Station.
Pittsburgh. Pa.

Cunningham. R. L.
Mech. Expert, W. A. B. Co.,
606 Hampton Ave..
Wilkinsburg. Pa.

Cunningham, W. P.,
Shop Inspector,
P. & L. E. R. R. Co.,
McKees Rocks. Pa.

Curley, Walter J.,
President,
Penna.-Conley Tank Car Co..
Koppers Building,
Pittsburgh, Pa.

Cushman, P. J.,
Foreman. Car Department,
Pennsylvania Railroad,
91 Union Ave.,
Crafton, Pittsburgh, Pa.

Dalzell. J. C.,
Chief Clerk, Auditor Freight
Accounts,
P. & L. E. R. R. Co.,
307 Natchez St..
Pittsburgh, Pa.

Dalzell, W. E.,
Asst. Planner,
Pressed Steel Car Co.,
1014 Milton St.,
Coraopolis, Pa.

Dambach, C. O..
Superintendent,
P. & W. Va. Ry.,
Wabash Bldg..
Pittsburgh, Pa.

Damrau, Edward A..
District Manager,
The Okonite Co..
Gulf Bldg.,
Pittsburgh, Pa.

Danforth. G. H.,
Schenley Apartments,
Pittsburgh, Pa.

Danielson, W. D.,
Supervisor of Track,
P. & L. E. R. R. Co..
113 Duquesne Ave.,
Dravosburg, Pa.

Darr, Elsworth E..
Yard Master,
P. & L. E. R. R.,
235 Meridan St.,
Mt. Washington,
Pittsburgh, Pa.

Darrah. C. B..
Supvr. Telegraph & Signals,
Pennsylvania Railroad,
612 Pennsylvania Stattion,
Pittsburgh, Pa.

Daugherty, W. A.,
Gang Fore., Car Dept.,
Union Railroad,
Box 237,
North Bessemer, Pa.

Davidson, John C.,
Branch Manager,
General Cable Corp,
Koppers Building,
Pittsburgh, Pa.

Davies, Benjamin S.,
General Secretary,
Y. M. C. A.,
2685 Wilson Ave.,
Campbell, Ohio

Davin, W. E.,
Road Master,
P. & L. E. R. R.,
P. & L. E. Terminal Bldg.,
Pittsburgh, Pa.

Davis, Chas. S.,
Traffic Manager
Standard Tin Plate Co.
Canonsburg Pa

Davis, John W.,
General Manager,
Penn Iron & Steel Co.,
Creighton, Pa

Day, Tom R.,
Chief Draftsman,
Pennsylvania Railroad,
179 Steuben Street,
Crafton, Pittsburgh, Pa

Day, U. G.,
Asst. Yard Master,
Pennsylvania Railroad,
4200 Noble St.,
Bellaire, Ohio.

Deakins, H. H.,
Chief Clerk,
Pennsylvania Railroad,
Pennsylvania Station,
Pittsburgh, Pa.

Dean, E. E.,
Car Foreman,
B. & O. R. R. Co.,
6040 Stanton Ave.,
E. E., Pittsburgh, Pa.

Dean, Robert W.,
Asst. Car Foreman,
B. & O. R. R. Co.,
4124 Stanley Street,
Pittsburgh, Pa.

Dean, William A.,
Signal Supervisor,
P. & L. E. R. R. Co.,
1515 Grandin Avenue,
Dormont, Pittsburgh, Pa.

Dean, W. H.,
Division Storekeeper,
B. & O. R. R. Co.,
1224 Sycamore St.,
Connellsville, Pa.

Dehne, G. C.,
Asst. to Vice President,
W. A. B. Co.,
Wilmerding, Pa.

Dempsey, Alex.,
A. R. A. Clerk,
P. & W. Va. Ry. Co.,
1104 Bidwell St.,
N. S., Pittsburgh, Pa.

Denehey, Robert H.,
Publicity Representative,
Pennsylvania Railroad,
Pennsylvania Station,
Pittsburgh, Pa.

Dennis, J. G.,
Freight Train Master,
Pennsylvania Railroad,
324 Pennsylvania Sta.,
Pittsburgh, Pa.

Derr, A. I.,
Asst. to President,
P. & W. Va. Ry.,
Wabash Bldg.,
Pittsburgh, Pa.

Devine, John C.,
Asst. Yard Master,
Pennsylvania Railroad
243 South Pacific Ave.,
Pittsburgh, Pa.

Dickinson, B. F.,
Engineer Tel. & Signals,
Pennsylvania Railroad,
Pennsylvania Station,
Pittsburgh, Pa.

Dickinson, T. R.,
Purchasing Agent,
B. & L. E. R. R.,
Union Trust Bldg.,
Pittsburgh, Pa.

Dickson, K. B.,
Carnegie-Illinois Steel Corp.,
227 Oakview Ave.,
Edgewood, Pa

Dierker, R. H.,
Agent,
B. & O. R. R. Co.,
R. D. 2.
Allison Park, Pa.

Dietrich, W. S.,
Vice-President,
Greenville Steel Car Co.,
Greenville, Pa.

Diettrich, John J.,
President,
J. J. Diettrich & Son,
417 Chartiers Ave.,
McKees Rocks, Pa.

Dihle, James E.,
Locomotive Engineer,
P. & L. E. R. R.,
Fourth Ave.,
Beaver Falls, Pa.

Dillon, Arthur L.,
Engineer Computer,
P. & L. E. R. R. Co.,
77 Hawthorne Ave.,
Crafton, Pittsburgh, Pa.

Dillon, H. W.,
Sales Engineer,
Paxton-Mitchell Company,
312 Main Street,
South Amboy, N. J.

Dindinger, Charles C.,
Agent,
P. & L. E. R. R. Co.,
487 Duquesne Drive.
Mt. Lebanon, Pa.

Dipper, F. W.,
Cashier,
P. & L. E. R. R. Co.,
Churchview Avenue,
Carrick, Pittsburgh, Pa.

Dittman, George
General Foreman,
P. & L. E. R. R. Co.,
100 Roycraft Ave.,
Mt. Lebanon, Pittsburgh, Pa.

Dilworth, John C.,
Mgr. of Railroad Sales,
Carnegie-Illinois Steel Corp.,
Carnegie Bldg.,
Pittsburgh, Pa.

Diven, J. B.,
Supt. Motive Power,
Pennsylvania Railroad,
Pennsylvania Station,
Pittsburgh, Pa.

Dixon, Charles P.,
Asst. Train Master,
Pennsylvania Railroad,
156 North Spring St.,
Blairsville, Pa.

Dixon, C. R.,
District Sales Manager,
N. Americ'n Refractories Co.
Oliver Building,
Pittsburgh, Pa.

Dixon, Joseph M.,
Asst. Yard Master,
Pennsylvania Railroad,
110 California Ave.,
Oakmont, Pa.

Dobson, F. L.,
General Fuel Manager,
Pennsylvania Railroad,
Philadelphia, Pa.

Donovan, J. J.,
Gen. Fore., P. & L. E. R. R.,
426 Jones St.,
Belle Vernon, Pa.

Donovan, Lawrence T.,
Acting Gang Foreman,
Pennsylvania Railroad,
146 Noble Ave.,
Crafton, Pittsburgh, Pa.

Down, S. G.,
First Vice President,
Westinghouse Air Brake Co.,
Wilmerding, Pa.

Downing, J. A.,
District Freight Claim Agent,
Pennsylvania Railroad,
1013 Penn Avenue,
Pittsburgh, Pa.

Downing, N. H.,
Engine House Foreman,
B. & O. R. R. Co.,
1617 Monongahela Ave.,
Swissvale, Pa.

Draper, Thos.,
President, Draper Mfg. Co.,
Port Huron, Mich.

Duff, William G.,
Secretary & Auditor,
The Lake Terminal Railroad
Company,
Frick Bldg.,
Pittsburgh, Pa

Duffley, F. M.,
Machinery Inspector,
P. & L. E. R. R. Co.,
902 Liberty Street,
McKees Rocks, Pa.

Dugan, G. R.,
City Passenger Agent,
B. & O. R. R. Co.,
Union Trust Bldg.,
Pittsburgh, Pa.

Dunbar, Harold F.,
Sales Manager, McConway
& Torley Corp.,
48th St. & A. V. R. R.,
Pittsburgh, Pa

Dunham, C. W.,
Union Switch & Signal Co.,
1219 Braddock Ave.,
Edgewood, Pittsburgh, Pa.

Dunkelberger, Harry E.,
Master Mechanic,
Wierton Steel Co.,
Wierton, W. Va

Dunkuly, E. R.,
Superintendent,
Monessen Southwestern
Railway Co.,
Monessen, Pa.

Dunlop, Robert J., Jr.,
Terminal Foreman,
Montour Railroad Co.,
R. D. 1,
Willock, Pa

Dunn, J. W.,
Foreman, Mechanical Dept.,
B. & O. R. R. Co.,
244 Trowbridge St.,
Hazelwood, Pittsburgh, Pa

Dunn, Samuel O.,
Editor, Railway Age Gazette,
105 W. Adams St.,
Chicago, Ill

Durell, W. A.,
Movement Director,
Pennsylvania Railroad,
Pennsylvania Station,
Pittsburgh, Pa

Durnell, W. E.,
T. & S. Signals,
Pennsylvania Railroad,
218 Buffalo Street,
Freeport, Pa.

Duryea, O. C.,
President,
O. C. Duryea Corp.,
30 East 42nd St.,
New York, N. Y.

Dusenberry, S. H.,
Engine House Foreman,
P. & L. E. R. R. Co.,
P. O. Box 532,
Newell, Pa.

Eagan, Daniel F.,
Train Rules Examiner,
Pennsylvania Railroad,
252 Humbolt Blvd.,
Buffalo, N. Y.

Easler, E. H.,
Chief Clerk to Superintendent,
Monongahela Railway Co.,
11 Third Avenue,
Brownsville, Pa.

East, Louis P.,
Live Stock Supervisor,
Pittsburgh Joint Stock
Yards Co.,
21 N. W. Fifth St.,
Richmond, Ind.

Eaton, Fred'k. H.,
Sales Engineer,
American Car &
Foundry Co.,
Farmers Bank Bldg.,
Pittsburgh, Pa.

Eberle, E. J.,
Air Brake Foreman,
B. & O. R. R. Co.,
3014 Vernon Avenue,
Brentwood, Pgh. (10), Pa.

Eckels, Wilber,
Representative,
Cardwell Westinghouse Co.,
332 So. Michigan Ave.,
Chicago, Ill.

Edgett, Joseph W.,
Sales Engineer,
Walworth Company,
703 Gulf Bldg.,
Pittsburgh, Pa.

Edmiston, R. J.,
Special Representative,
U. S. Graphite Co.,
Fulton Bldg.,
Pittsburgh, Pa.

Edmonston, George F.,
Supervisor Labor & Wage,
Pennsylvania Railroad,
Pennsylvania Station,
Pittsburgh, Pa.

Edsall, S. D..
Manager,
Air Reduction Sales Co.,
1116 Ridge Ave.,
N. S. Pittsburgh, Pa.

Edwards, H. F.,
Road Foreman of Engines,
Monongahela Railway Co.,
South Brownsville, Pa.

Edwards, W.,
Section Stockman,
Stores Dept.,
B. & O. R. R. Co.,
4714 Sylvan Avenue,
Hazelwood, Pittsburgh. Pa.

Egbert, J. A.,
President,
Railway Products Co..
Gulf Building,
Pittsburgh, Pa.

Egly, M. J.,
Chief Clerk to Gen. Mgr..
Pennsylvania Railroad,
Pennsylvania Station,
Pittsburgh, Pa.

Eichenlaub, W. C.,
Sales Manager,
Pittsburgh Steel Foundry
Corp.,
Glassport, Pa.

Ekey, J. S.,
Engineer of Bridges,
B. & L. E. R. R.,
4 College Ave.,
Greenville, Pa

Ely, J. L.,
Supervising Agent,
Pittsburgh Division,
Pennsylvania Railroad,
Pennsylvania Station,
Pittsburgh, Pa.

Emerick, J. B,
Sales Representative,
Garlock Packing Co..
256 Beverly Road,
Pittsburgh, Pa.

Emery, E.,
Railway Supplies,
6511 Darlington Road,
Pittsburgh, Pa.

Emery, L. F.,
General Foreman,
P. & L. E. R. R. Co.,
180 Marion Avenue,
Struthers, Ohio.

Enders, I. O.,
Superintendent Labor &
Wage,
Pennsylvania Railroad,
Pennsylvania Station,
Pittsburgh, Pa.

Endsley, Louis E., Prof.,
Consulting Engineer,
516 East End Ave.,
Pittsburgh, Pa.

Evans, Charles S.,
Chief Car Service Clerk,
Donora Southern Railroad
Company,
Box 133,
Fayette City, Pa.

Evans, David F.,
District Manager,
The Duff-Norton Mfg. Co.,
N. S. Pittsburgh, Pa.

Evans, Robert E.,
Yardmaster,
Pennsylvania Railroad,
814 Norwich St.,
South Hills Station,
Pittsburgh, Pa.

Ewing, George S,
Salesman,
Singer, Deane & Scribner,
Royal York Apartments,
Pittsburgh, Pa.

Failor, Charles W.,
General Engineer,
Union Switch & Signal Co.,
107 Elmore Road,
Forest Hills, Pa.

Fair, J. M.,
Engineer M. & W.,
Pennsylvania Railroad,
Pennsylvania Station,
Pittsburgh, Pa.

Falkner, Andrew J.,
Clerk,
B. & O. R. R.,
4014 Coleman St.,
Pittsburgh, Pa.

Farlow, George B.,
Division Engineer,
B. & O. R. R.,
Smithfield & Water Sts.,
Pittsburgh, Pa.

Farmer, C. C.,
Director of Engineering,
W. A. B. Co.,
Wilmerding, Pa

Farrell, G. R.,
Sales Agent,
Nat'l Mall. & Steel Cstgs. Co.,
10600 Quincey Ave.,
Cleveland, Ohio.

Fay, Frank L., Hon.,
Chairman of the Board,
Greenville Steel Car Co.,
Greenville, Pa.

Feidt, J. J.,
Chief Clerk—Operating Dept.,
P. & L. E. R. R. Co.,
863 Marshall Avenue,
N. S., Pittsburgh, Pa.

Ferguson, George,
Air Brake Instructor,
Pennsylvania Railroad,
3719 Mahoning Road, N.E.,
Canton, Ohio.

Ferguson, R. G.,
Electrician,
Pennsylvania Railroad,
1938 East St.,
N. S., Pittsburgh, Pa.

Fieldson, P. H.,
Master Car Builder,
P. & L. E. R. R.,
220 Greydon Ave.,
McKees Rocks, Pa.

Fike, James W.,
Division Operator,
Pennsylvania Railroad,
2236 Valera Ave.,
Mt. Oliver, Pittsburgh, Pa.

Finegan, Thomas A.,
Wreck Foreman,
Eastern Division,
Pennsylvania Railroad,
P. O. Box 702,
Conway, Pa.

Fischer, G. E.,
Clerk, Union Railroad,
2202 Hampton St.,
Swissvale, Pa.

Fischer, John G.,
Chief Rate Clerk,
B. & O. R. R. Co.,
109 Shady Drive, West,
Mt. Lebanon, Pittsburgh, Pa.

Fisher, E. M.,
Asst. R. F. of E.,
Penna. Railroad System,
909 E. Washington St.,
New Castle, Pa.

Fisher, Earl H.,
Sales Engineer,
Unitcast Corporation,
Box C—Station E,
Toledo, Ohio.

Fitzgerald, T.,
Vice President & Gen. Mgr.,
Pittsburgh Railways Co.,
435 Sixth Ave.,
Pittsburgh, Pa.

Fitzpatrick, T. R.,
Freight Traffic Manager,
P. & L. E. R. R.,
Terminal Bldg.,
Pittsburgh, Pa.

Fitzsimmons, Edward J.,
City Manager,
City Ice & Fuel Co.,
5550 Claybourne St.,
Pittsburgh, Pa.

Fitz Simmons, E. S.,
Vice President,
Flannery Bolt Co.,
Bridgeville, Pa

Flaherty, Michael,
Yard Master,
Pennsylvania Railroad,
145 Wildon Ave.,
Steubenville, Ohio.

Flaherty, P. J.,
Pres. and General Mgr.,
Johnson Bronze Co.,
So. Mill Street,
New Castle, Pa.

Flanigan, A. C.,
Freight Agent,
P. & L. E. R. R. Co.,
McKees Rocks, Pa.

Flannery, J. Rogers,
Flannery Bolt Co.,
Flannery Bldg.,
Pittsburgh, Pa

Fleckenstein, August,
P. W. Insp'r., P. & L. E. R. R.,
1108 Crucible St., 20th Wd.,
Pittsburgh, Pa.

Fleming, Harry W.,
Salesman,
J. Frank Lanning & Co.,
327 First Avenue,
Pittsburgh, Pa.

Flick, Samuel H.,
Asst. Yard Master,
Pennsylvania Railroad,
509 Hay St.,
Wilkinsburg, Pa.

Flinn, R. H.,
General Superintendent,
Pennsylvania Railroad,
Pennsylvania Station,
Pittsburgh, Pa.

Flocker, R. M.,
General Passenger Agent,
Pennsylvania Railroad,
Pennsylvania Station,
Pittsburgh, Pa.

Foard, Edwin A.,
Supt. Stations & Transfers,
Pennsylvania Railroad,
Pennsylvania Station,
Pittsburgh, Pa.

Folan, J. V.,
Clerk,
Pennsylvania Railroad,
7720 St. Lawrence Ave.,
Swissvale, Pa.

Follett, W. F.,
Asst. Superintendent,
Aliquippa & Southern
R. R. Co.,
652 Highland Ave.,
Aliquippa, Pa.

Forquer, Edwin A.,
Stationary Engineer,
Montour Railroad Co.,
1109 Chartiers Ave.,
McKees Rocks, Pa.

Forsberg, R. P.,
Chief Engineer,
P. & L. E. R. R.,
P. & L. E. Terminal Bldg.,
Pittsburgh, Pa.

Forst, J. F.,
Supervisor of Truck,
P. & L. E. R. R. Co.,
3103 Fourth Avenue,
Beaver Falls, Pa.

Forsythe, G. B.,
Foreman, Car Dept.,
Pennsylvania Railroad,
Baden, Pa.

Foster, F. L.,
Supt. Frt. Transportation,
P. & L. E. R. R.,
Pittsburgh, Pa.

Foulk, R. S.,
Asst. Train Master,
Division Operator,
Pennsylvania Railroad,
653 Sherwood Ave.,
Corliss Station, Pittsburgh, Pa.

Fowler, W. E.,
President,
Pgh., Lisbon & Western
R. R.,
P. O. Box 688,
Youngstown, Ohio.

Fox, George W.,
Secretary,
Davis Brake Beam Co.,
146 Second Ave.,
Westmont,
Johnstown, Pa.

Fox, M. C.,
Supervisor—Track,
Pennsylvania Railroad,
Wheeling, W. Va.

Fralic, C. F.,
Section Stockman,
B. & O. R. R. Co.,
3470 Beechview Blvd.,
Pittsburgh, Pa.

Frauenheim, A. M.,
Vice President,
Auto-Tite Joints Co.,
7501 Thomas Blvd.,
Pittsburgh, Pa.

Frauenheim, Pierce H.,
 Purchasing Agent,
 Auto-Tite Joints Co.,
 7501 Thomas Blvd.,
  Pittsburgh, Pa.

Freshwater, F. H.,
 Sales Engineer,
 Koppel Division,
 Pressed Steel Car Co., Inc,
 Grant Bldg.,
  Pittsburgh, Pa.

Friend, Edward F.,●
 Asst. Chief Clerk,
 Traffic Department,
 Pittsburgh Coal Co.,
 Oliver Bldg.,
  Pittsburgh, Pa.

Fry, Lawford H.,
 Railway Engineer,
 Edgewater Steel Co.,
 P. O. Box 478,
  Pittsburgh, Pa

Fugate, Henry W. B.,
 Agent,
 Pennsylvania Railroad,
 512 State Street,
  Clairton, Pa

Fulks, B. M.,
 Movement Director,
 Pennsylvania Railroad,
 428 Center Ave.,
  Carnegie, Pa.

Fulton, K. H.,
 Salesman,
 Ball Chemcial Co.,
 Fulton Building,
  Pittsburgh, Pa.

Funk, E. J.,
 General Foreman,
 P. & L. E. R. R. Co.,
 42 Laclede Street,
  Pittsburgh, Pa.

Furch, George J.,
 Gang Fore., Penna. R. R. Co.,
 319 Fifth St.,
  Freeport, Pa.

Gainer, Alva,
 Supply Car Storekeeper,
 B. & O. R. R. Co.,
 5115 Blair Street,
 Hazelwood, Pittsburgh, Pa.

Galbraith, James R.,
 Fire Marshal,
 P. & L. E. R. R. Co.,
 500 Rossmore Ave.,
 Brookline, Pittsburgh, Pa.

Galinis, J. W.,
 Draftsman,
 Pennsylvania R. R. Co.,
 709 Broadway,
  East McKeesport, Pa.

Galloway, W. R.,
 Division Trainmaster,
 B. & O. R. R. Co.,
 B & O. Station,
  Pittsburgh, Pa.

Gallowich, Louis J.,
 Car Inspector,
 Pennsylvania Railroad,
 3 Matson St.,
  N. S., Pittsburgh, Pa.

Gandy, R. H.,
 Mechanical Draftsman,
 B. & O. R. R. Co.,
 Baptist Rd., R. D. 1,
  Library, Pa.

Ganz, C. A.,
 Gang Foreman,
 Pennsylvania Railroad,
 617 Second St.,
  Pitcairn, Pa. '

Gardiner, Jas. E.,
 Spl. Rep. Schaefer Equipt. Co.,
 Koppers Bldg.,
  Pittsburgh, Pa.

Gardner, George R.,
 Chief Clerk—Traffic Dept.,
 Pittsburgh Coal Co.,
 1024 Oliver Bldg.,
  Pittsburgh, Pa.

Gardner, K. C.,
 Vice President,
 Greenville Steel Car Co.,
  Greenville, Pa

Gariepy, L. H.,
 Gang Foreman,
 Pennsylvania Railroad,
  Freeport, Pa.

Gaston, Charles,
 Salesman,
 Ashton Valve Co.,
 21 Albany Street,
  New York, N. Y.

Gatens, A. J.,
Asst. Chief Clerk,
P. & L. E. R. R. Co.,
302 South Pacific Ave.,
E. E., Pittsburgh, Pa

Gates, C. F.,
Asst. Chief Clerk,
P. & L. E. R. R.,
Pittsburgh, Pa.

Gatfield, Philip I.,
Mechanic,
Keystone Sand & Supply Co..
219 Zara St.,
Knoxville,
Pittsburgh, Pa.

Gauvey, Fred J.,
Captain of Police,
Pennsylvania Railroad,
Pennsylvania Station,
Pittsburgh, Pa.

Geertz, A. O.,
Asst. Engr. Motive Power,
Pennsylvania Railroad,
3955 Bigelow Blvd.,
Pittsburgh, Pa.

Geiser, W. P.,
Supervisor Track,
Pennsylvania Railroad,
610 Dick Street,
Carnegie, Pa

Gelston, George A.,
Yard Brakeman,
Pennsylvania Railroad,
512 James Street,
Turtle Creek, Pa

Gemmell, R. W.,
Transportation Engineer,
Westinghouse Electric &
Mfg. Co.,
East Pittsburgh, Pa

George, R. H.,
Assistant Engineer,
P. & L. E. R. R.,
Terminal Building,
Pittsburgh, Pa

George, W. J.,
Asst. Sales Manager,
Edgewater Steel Co.,
P. O. Box 478,
Pittsburgh, Pa.

Germerodt, Oscar C.,
Chief Clerk to Mech Supt.,
Montour Railroad Co.,
1412 Ridge Avenue,
Coraopolis, Pa.

Gibson, B. G.,
Asst. Master Mechanic,
Pennsylvania Railroad,
2947 Morris Road,
Ardmore, Philadelphia, Pa.

Gibson, Sam D.,
Salesman,
Ingersoll-Rand Company,
Chamber of Commerce
Bldg.,
Pittsburgh, Pa.

Gilbert, William J.,
Supervisor—Track,
Pennsylvania Railroad,
New Kensington, Pa.

Gilg, Henry F,.
Railway Supplies,
1424 Orchlee St.,
N. S., Pittsburgh, Pa.

Gillespie, J. Porter,
Asst. General Supt.,
Lockhart Iron & Steel Co.,
P. O. Box 1165,
Pittsburgh, Pa.

Gillespie, John M.,
Vice President,
Lockhart Iron & Steel Co.,
P. O. Box 1243,
Pittsburgh, Pa.

Gillespie, S. E,
Director,
Bureau cf Railway Signai-
ing Economics,
347 Madison Avenue,
New York, N. Y.

Gillie, H. C.,
Electric Welder,
Monongahela Railway Co.,
Pearl Street,
Brownsville, Pa.

Gillum, J. S.,
Supt., Mon. Div.,
Pennsylvania Railroad,
Pennsylvania Station,
Pittsburgh, Pa

Glaser, C. J.,
Statistical Clerk,
B. & O. R. R. Co.,
302 Winston Street,
Pittsburgh, Pa.

Glaser, J. P.,
Auditor Disbursements,
P. & L. E. R. R.,
909 Bellaire Ave.,
Pittsburgh, Pa

Gleeson, Harry L.,
Sp'l. Sales Agent,
The Lorain Division,
Carnegie-Illinois Steel
Corporation,
Frick Bldg.,
Pittsburgh, Pa

Glenn, J. H.,
Master Mechanic,
P. & W. Va. Ry. Co.,
20 Obey St.,
Pittsburgh, Pa.

Goble, A. S.,
Baldwin Locomotive Works,
Paschall Station,
Philadelphia, Pa.

Goda, P. H.,
Foreman, P. R. R.,
311 South Ave.,
Wilkinsburg, Pa.

Goff, J. P.,
T. M., P. & L. E. R. R.,
615 Montour St.,
Coraopolis, Pa.

Goldstrom, G. E.,
Draftsman,
P. & W. Va. Ry.,
1305 Highman St.,
Pittsburgh, Pa.

Good, W. G.,
Secretary,
Pittsburgh Smelting &
Refining Co.,
3524 Brighton Road,
N. S., Pittsburgh, Pa.

Goodwin, A. E.,
Tool Designer,
Westinghouse Electric &
Mfg. Co.,
602 Marion Ave.,
Forest Hills, Wilkinsburg, Pa.

Gordon, C. M.,
Asst. to General Auditor,
P. & L. E. R. R. Co.,
995 Second Street,
Beaver, Pa.

Gorman, Andrew T.,
Tester,
Westinghouse Air Brake Co.,
574 Fifth Street,
Pitcairn, Pa.

Gorman, Charles,
1301 Adams St.,
N. S., Pittsburgh, Pa.

Goron, F. W.,
General Foreman,
P. & L. E. R. R.,
Dickerson Run, Pa.

Goss, Richard C.,
District Sales Manager,
Ohio Brass Company,
Oliver Building,
Pittsburgh, Pa.

Gottschalk, C. W.,
Asst. Traffic Manager,
Jones & Laughlin Steel Corp.,
J. & L. Building,
Pittsburgh, Pa.

Graf, Benjamin,
Foreman, M. E. Dept.,
Pennsylvania Railroad,
1425 Straka St.,
Pittsburgh, Pa.

Graham, A. C.,
Traffic Manager,
Youngstown Sheet and
Tube Company,
Stambaugh Bldg.,
Youngstown, Ohio.

Graham, Chas. J.,
Vice President,
Pressed Steel Car Co., Inc.,
Grant Bldg.,
Pittsburgh, Pa.

Graham, Harry C.,
Pittsburgh Screw & Bolt Corp.
P. O. Box 72,
Pittsburgh, Pa.

Graham, H. E.,
Asst. to Pres. & Gen. Traf. Mgr.
Jones & Laughlin Steel Corp.,
3rd Ave. & Ross St.,
Pittsburgh, Pa.

Graham, Herbert W.,
General Metallurgist,
Jones & Laughlin Steel Corp.,
J. & L. Building,
Pittsburgh, Pa.

Gray, C. C.,
General Freight Agent,
Western Maryland Railway
Company,
Koppers Bldg.,
Pittsburgh, Pa.

Gray, Guy M.,
S. M. P.,
B. & L. E. R. R. Co.,
Greenville, Pa.

Gray, M. L.,
Vice President,
Union Switch & Signal Co.,
Swissvale, Pa.

Gray, T. H.,
Master Carpenter,
Pennsylvania Railroad,
Pennsylvania Station,
Pittsburgh, Pa.

Greek, Joseph,
Section Foreman,
P. & W. Va. Ry. Co.,
812 Logan St.,
Carnegie, Pa.

Green, M. E.,
Asst. Chief Clerk to
Vice President,
P. & L. E. R. R. Co.,
P&LE Terminal Bldg.,
Pittsburgh, Pa.

Griest, E. E.,
Vice Pres. & Gen. Mgr.,
Fort Pitt Malleable
Iron Co.,
P. O. Box 505,
Pittsburgh, Pa.

Grieve, Robert E.,
Passenger Train Master,
Pennsylvania Railroad,
740 East End Ave.,
Pittsburgh, Pa.

Grimshaw, F. G.,
Works Mgr., P. R. R.,
Altoona, Pa.

Gross, John,
Captain of Police,
B. & O. R. R. Co.,
625 Churchview Avenue
Extension,
Pittsburgh (10), Pa.

Grove, C. G.,
Superintendent,
Pennsylvania Railroad,
85 Bradford Ave.,
Pittsburgh, Pa.

Groves, Walter C.,
Chief Engineer,
Donora Southern R. R. Co.,
Donora, Pa.

Grunden, B. C.,
Commercial Agent,
Railway Express Agency,
Inc.,
926 Penn Avenue,
Pittsburgh, Pa.

Guinnip, M. S.,
Sales Engineer,
Ingersoll-Rand Co.,
706 Chamber of Commerce
Building,
Pittsburgh, Pa.

Gunnison, Walter L.,
Assistant General Manager,
Enterprise Railway
Equipment Co.,
59 E. Van Buren St.,
Chicago, Ill.

Guy, W. S.,
Traffic Manager,
U. S. Steel Corp.,
Subsidiaries, E. D.,
614 Carnegie Bldg.,
Pittsburgh, Pa.

Haase, L. R.,
District Boiler Inspector,
B. & O. R. R. Co.,
7358 Whiple pSt.,
Swissvale Branch,
Pittsburgh, Pa.

Hackett, C. M.,
Division Boiler Maker Fore.,
Pennsylvania Railroad,
618 Pennsylvania Ave.,
Oakmont, Pa.

Hackett, S. E.,
  President,
    Jones & Laughlin Steel Corp.,
    J. & L. Building,
        Pittsburgh, Pa

Haggerty, J. F.,
  General Foreman,
    B. & O. R. R. Co.,
    1602 Chelton Ave.,
    Brookline, Pittsburgh, Pa

Hague, James R.,
  Clerk,
    P. & L. E. R. R. Co.,
    5120 Second Avenue,
        Pittsburgh, Pa.

Haller, C. T.,
  President,
    Colonial Supply Co.,
    217 Water St.,
        Pittsburgh, Pa.

Haller, Nelson M.,
  Sup'r. Scrap and Reclamation.
    P. & L. E. R. R.,
    3678 Middletown Road,
    Corliss Station,
        Pittsburgh, Pa

Hamilton, Joseph K.,
  Examiner, Labor & Wage
  Bureau,
    Pennsylvania Railroad,
    Pennsylvania Station,
        Pittsburgh, Pa

Hamilton, R. F.,
  Practice & Methods Man.,
    Monongahela Connecting
    Railroad Co.,
    2357 Brownsville Road,
        Pittsburgh, Pa

Hamilton, W. H.,
  Supt., of Roadway &
  Structures,
    Montour Railroad Co.,
    1711 State Ave.,
        Coraopolis, Pa

Hamsher, W. E.,
  Mechanical Representative,
    Hennessy Lubricator Co.,
    245 East King St.,
        Chambersburg, Pa

Hance, R. H.,
  Supervising Agent.-
  Div. Operator,
    Pennsylvania Railroad,
    Pennsylvania Station,
        Pittsburgh, Pa.

Hancock, Milton L.,
  Office Engineer,
    Westinghouse Air Brake Co.,
    557 Broadway Extension,
        East McKeesport, Pa.

Handloser, Bertram F.,
  General Superintendent,
    Dilworth Porter Division,
    Republic Steel Corp.,
    4th & Bingham Sts.,
        Pittsburgh, Pa

Hankey, E. B.,
  Asst. Gen. Freight Agent,
    Pennsylvania Railroad,
    Pennsylvania Station,
        Pittsburgh, Pa.

Hankins, F. W.,
  Asst. Vice President—
  Chief of Motive Power,
    Pennsylvania Railroad,
    Broad St. Station Bldg.,
        Philadelphia, Pa.

Hansen, F. Karl,
  Metallurgical Contact Rep.,
    Carnegie-Illinois Steel Corp.,
    Frick Annex Bldg.,
        Pittsburgh, Pa.

Hansen, Wm. C.,
  Sales Engr., A. Stucki Co.,
    419 Oliver Bldg.,
        Pittsburgh, Pa.

Hardy, James E.,
  Agent,
    P. & L. E. R. R. Co.,
    303 Monongahela Ave.,
        Otto, McKeesport, Pa.

Harig, George J.,
  District Freight Agent,
    Nelson Steamship Co.,
    2647 Smallman St.,
        Pittsburgh, Pa.

Harman, H. H.,
  Engineer—Track,
    B. & L. E. R. R.,
        Greenville, Pa

Harper, A. M.,
  Manager of Sales,
    Carnegie-Illinois Steel Corp.,
    Carnegie Bldg.,
        Pittsburgh, Pa.

Harper, G. C.,
General Supt.,
Montour Railroad,
1711 State Ave.,
Coraopolis, Pa.

Harper, J. S.,
Locomotive Engineer,
Montour Railroad Co.,
1341 Fourth Ave.,
Coraopolis, Pa.

Harper, J. T.,
Asst. to Mech. Supt.,
Montour Railroad,
R. F. D. No. 1,
McKees Rocks, Pa.

Harper, James W.,
Medical Examiner,
Pennsylvania Railroad,
4263 Andover Terrace,
Pittsburgh, Pa.

Harper, James W., Jr.,
Locomotive Engineer,
Montour Railroad Co.,
1610 Vance Ave.,
Coraopolis, Pa.

Harris, Edward W.,
Air Brake Foreman,
Montour Railroad Co.,
Coraopolis, Pa.

Harris, J. P.,
Chief Clerk to Div. Engr.,
B. & O. R. R. Co.,
3429 Meadowcroft Ave.,
South Hills Branch,
Pittsburgh, Pa.

Harter, Arnold,
Asst. Fore., W. A. B. Co.,
353 Marguerite Ave.,
Wilmerding, Pa

Hartnett, C. J.,
Supervisor of Tracks,
P. & L. E. R. R. Co.,
610 Arlington Ave.,
McKeesport, Pa.

Harwig, C. G.,
Engineer,
Union Switch & Signal Co.,
1023 Mifflin Avenue,
Wilkinsburg, Pa.

Haser, A. J.,
Funeral Director,
512 Chartiers Ave.,
McKees Rocks, Pa.

Hassler, E. S.,
Car Foreman,
Pennsylvania Railroad,
5526 Beverly Place,
Pittsburgh, Pa.

Hastings, David T.,
Vice President,
The Lake Terminal
Railroad Co.,
Frick Building,
Pittsburgh, Pa.

Haupt, H. H.,
Gen. Supt. Motive Power,
Pennsylvania Railroad,
Pennsylvania Station,
Pittsburgh, Pa

Hawkes, T. L.,
Pennsylvania Railroad,
625 West 169th St.,
New York, N. Y.

Hawkins, J. M.,
District Sales Manager,
Elwell-Parker Electric Co.,
Investment Bldg.,
Pittsburgh, Pa

Hawkins, Paul R.,
Pullman-Standard Car
Mfg. Co.,
P. O. Box 928,
Pittsburgh, Pa

Hays, Harry E.,
R. F. of E.,
Pennsylvania Railroad,
3148 Huxley St.,
Corliss Station,
Pittsburgh, Pa.

Hayward, Carlton,
C. C. to Gen. Supt. Motive
Power,
Pennsylvania Railroad,
7412 Penfield Place,
Pittsburgh, Pa

Hayward, C. R.,
Insurance,
419 Highland Ave.,
Aliquippa, Pa.

Heed, H. L.,
Agent, 26th St. Terminal,
Railway Express Agency,
Inc.,
5742 Howe Street,
Pittsburgh, Pa.

Heimbach, A. E.,
Principal Assistant Engineer,
P. & L. E. R. R.,
Terminal Annex Bldg.,
Pittsburgh, Pa.

Heinz, W. J.,
Mgr. Central R. R. Dept.,
Ingersoll-Rand Company,
Williamson Building,
Cleveland, Ohio.

Heinzenberger, Arthur E.,
Assistant Car Foreman,
B. & O. R. R. Co.,
435 Knarr St.,
DuBois, Pa.

Hektner, Joel,
Asst. Engr., Ry. Division,
Timken Roller Bearing Co.,
Canton, Ohio

Helfrich, F. A.,
Chief Electrician,
B. & O. R. R. Co.,
404 Olympia Road,
Pittsburgh, Pa.

Hellriegel, W. H.,
Traffic Representative,
P. & W. Va. Ry.,
Wabash Bldg.,
Pittsburgh, Pa

Helsel, W. G.,
Manager of Works,
Pullman-Standard Car Mfg.
Company,
P. O. Box 627,
Butler, Pa.

Hemma, Charles H.,
Draftsman,
P. & L. E. R. R. Co.,
1210 Valley Street,
McKees Rocks, Pa.

Henderson, Geo. L.,
Engr., P. & L. E. R. R.,
228 Sheridan Ave.,
New Castle, Pa.

Hengst, Guy E.,
Tester,
Westinghouse Air Brake Co.,
664 Air Brake Ave.,
Wilmerding, Pa.

Henry, C. J.,
Division Engineer,
Pennsylvania Railroad,
89 Bradford Ave.,
Crafton, Pittsburgh, Pa.

Hepburn, P. W.,
Sales Engineer,
Gulf Oil Corporation,
6963 Frankstown Ave.,
Pittsburgh, Pa.

Herpst, R. C.,
Sales Agent,
American Steel Foundries,
29 De Foe Street,
N. S., Pittsburgh, Pa.

Herring, John R.,
Conductor,
P. & L. E. R. R. Co.,
Moredale St.,
South Hills Branch,
Pittsburgh, Pa.

Herrold, A. E.,
M. M. & M. C. B.,
Mon. Conn. R. R.,
3915 Winterburn Ave.,
Pittsburgh, Pa.

Hervey, R. S.,
Auditor, Freight Accounts,
P. & L. E. R. R.,
722 Main St.,
Coraopolis, Pa.

Hess, Charles A.,
Sales Department,
Edgewater Steel Co.,
P. O. Box 478,
Pittsburgh, Pa.

Hewes, John, Jr.,
Transportation Assistant,
B. & O. R. R.,
B. & O. Passenger Station,
Pittsburgh, Pa.

Hicks, W. A.
Vice President,
Penn Iron & Steel Co.,
Creighton, Pa

Higginbottom, S. B.,
Engineer Tel. & Sigs.,
Western Region,
Pennsylvania Railroad,
Chicago, Ill.

Higgins, George A.,
Asst. Manager of Sales,
Carnegie Steel Co.,
Carnegie Bldg.,
Pittsburgh, Pa.

Hill, George W.,
Blacksmith Foreman,
B. & O. R. R. Co.,
310 Twenty-sixth Street,
McKeesport, Pa.

Hill, John A.,
Manager,
Independent Pneumatic Tool
Co.,
Wabash Bldg.,
Pittsburgh, Pa.

Hill, Lloyd C.,
Engine Inspector,
Monongahela Railway Co.,
Box 334,
Brownsville, Pa

Hilstrom, Anton V.,
Foreman,
P. & L. E. R. R.,
R. D. 3, Box 226-B,
Coraopolis, Pa.

Hocking, Harry A.,
Representative,
Air Reduction Sales Co.,
60 East 42nd St.,
New York, N. Y.

Hodge, Edwin, Jr.,
President,
Pittsburgh Forgings Co.,
Gulf Bldg.,
Pittsburgh, Pa.

Hodges, A. H.,
District Master Mechanic,
B. & O. R. R. Co.,
3100 Gaylord Ave.,
Dormont. Pittsburgh, Pa.

Hodges, R. C.,
Assistant Car Foreman,
B. & O. R. R. Co.,
3100 Gaylord Ave.,
Dormont, Pittsburgh, Pa.

Hofmann, Eugene L.,
Asst. Passenger Train Master,
Pennsylvania R. R.,
Pennsylvania Station,
Pittsburgh, Pa.

Hohn, George W.,
Track Supervisor,
B. & L. E. R. R.,
538 East Pearl St.,
Butler, Pa.

Holbrook, Edward L.,
Tester,
Westinghouse Air Brake Co.,
2028 Bridge St.,
McKeesport, Pa.

Holiday, Harry,
Works Manager,
The American Rolling
Mill Company,
Butler, Pa.

Holland, S. E.,
Asst. Div. Engr., Pgh. Div.,
Pennsylvania Railroad.
318 West St.,
Wilkinsburg, Pa.

Holmes, E. H.,
Sales Department,
Ft. Pitt Malleable Iron Co.,
3662 Middletown Road,
Corliss Station,
Pittsburgh, Pa.

Holmes, J. R.,
Movement Director,
Pennsylvania Railroad,
35 Schley Ave.,
Ingram, Pa.

Honsberger, G. W.,
Transportation Manager,
Westinghouse E. & M. Co.,
Union Bank Bldg.,
Pittsburgh, Pa.

Hood, A. N.,
Freight Agent,
P. & L. E. R. R. Co.,
831 Neely Heights Ave.,
Coraopolis, Pa.

Hook, Charles H.,
Asst. on Engineering Corps,
Pennsylvania Railroad,
621 Brownsville Road,
Pittsburgh (10), Pa.

Hoon, F. R.,
Supervising Agent,
Pennsylvania Railroad,
7225 McCurdy Place,
Ben Avon, Pa.

Hoop, J. H.,
  Freight Agent,
    P. & L. E. R. R. Co.,
      413 Eleventh Street,
        Beaver Falls, Pa.

Hoopes, R. E.,
  Agent,
    Pennsylvania Railroad,
      Donora, Pa

Hoover, Jacob W.,
  Asst. Chief of Transportation,
    Subsidiary Co.'s, U. S. Steel
      Corp.,
        816 Carnegie Bldg.,
          Pittsburgh, Pa.

Hopper, George,
  Chief Clerk to Terminal Agent
    B. & O. R. R. Co.,
      Grant & Water Sts.,
        Pittsburgh, Pa.

Horne, John S.,
  Gang Foreman,
    Pass. Car Insprs.,
      Pennsylvania Railroad,
        427 So. Pacific Ave.,
          Pittsburgh, Pa

Hornefius, S. Reed,
  Movement Director,
    Pennsylvania Railroad,
      Pennsylvania Station,
        Pittsburgh, Pa

Hovey, Otis W.,
  Engineer, Railway Research
    Bureau,
      U. S. Steel Corporation,
        Frick Building,
          Pittsburgh, Pa.

Howe, Harry,
  Engr. of Ry. Equipment,
    Manganese Steel Forge Co.,
      Richmond & Castor Ave.,
        Philadelphia, Pa

Huber, C. G.,
  Timekeeper,
    B. & L. E. R. R. Co,
      351 Main Street,
        Greenville, Pa

Huber, H. G.,
  Assistant Foreman,
    Pennsylvania Railroad,
      Pennsylvania Station,
        Pittsburgh, Pa

Huff, A. B.,
  Foreman,
    Pennsylvania Railroad,
      819 North Second St.,
        Dennison, Ohio

Huggans, A. V.,
  Agent,
    P. & L. E. R. R. Co.,
      1211 Berkshire Ave.,
        Pittsburgh, Pa.

Hughes, I. Lamont,
  Woodland Road,
        Pittsburgh, Pa.

Hughes, L. H.,
  Supervisor, Eastern Demur-
    rage & Storage Bureau,
      Pennsylvania Railroad,
        427 Vermont Ave.,
          Rochester, Pa.

Hughes, Oscar W.,
  Sales Engineer,
    Signode Steel Strapping Co,
      3957 Howard St.,
        Youngstown, Ohio

Humphrey, A. L.,
  Chairman of Executive Com.,
    Westinghouse Air Brake Co.,
      Wilmerding, Pa.

Hunker, G. F,
  Asst. Division Sales Manager,
    Gulf Oil Corporation,
      Gross St. & P. R. R.
        Pittsburgh, Pa.

Hunt, C. T.,
  Asst. Engineer, M P.,
    Pennsylvania Railroad,
      709 W. 26th St.,
        Wilmington, Del.

Hunt, Lawrence,
  General Foreman,
    Tank Car Department,
      Pressed Steel Car Co.,
        McKees Rocks, Pa.

Hunt, Roy A.,
  President,
    Aluminum Co. of America,
      Gulf Building,
        Pittsburgh, Pa.

Hunzeker, H. J.,
  Salesman,
    James B. Sipe and Co.,
      2500 Middletown Road,
        Pittsburgh, Pa.

Hursh, Samuel R.,
Division Superintendent,
Penna. Railroad Co.,
Wilmington, Del

Huston, Frederick T.,
Master Mechanic,
Pennsylvania Railroad,
611 Pennsylvania Station,
Pittsburgh, Pa.

Hutchinson, George, Jr.,
District Sales Manager,
The Duff-Norton
Manufacturing Co.,
P. O. Box 1889,
Pittsburgh, Pa.

Hykes, W. H.,
Assistant Trainmaster,
Penna. R. R. Co.,
526 Sixth St.,
Oakmont, Pa

Ingman, E. B.,
Patrolman,
B. & O. R. R. Co.,
131 Tipton St.,
Pittsburgh, Pa.

Inks, S. W.,
Master Mechanic,
Monongahela Railway Co.,
P. O. Box 653,
Dawson, Pa.

Irvin, Robert K.,
Conductor,
P. & L. E. R. R. Co.,
427 South Main St.,
Pittsburgh, Pa.

Irwin, Robert D.,
Foreman,
Westinghouse Air Brake Co.,
521 Holmes St.,
Wilkinsburg, Pa.

Israel, E. J., Jr.,
Industrial Agent,
Pennsylvania Railroad,
Pennsylvania Station,
Pittsburgh, Pa

Jackovac, Victor P.,
Sales Department,
Edgewater Steel Co.,
337 Penn Street,
Verona, Pa.

Jados, Walter T.,
Westinghouse Air Brake Co.,
104 Clara St.,
Wilmerding, Pa.

Jahnke, Karl W.,
Piece Work Inspector
P. & L. E. R. R. Co.,
238 Singer Avenue,
McKees Rocks, Pa.

James, J. H.,
Purchasing Agent,
P. & L. E. R. R.,
Pittsburgh, Pa.

Jarden, Carroll,
Railway Sales Engineer,
Sherwin-Williams Co.,
401 No. Broad St.,
Philadelphia, Pa.

Jarres, Frank A.,
Asst. Storekeeper,
B. & O. R. R. Co.,
213 Second Street,
Aspinwall, Pa.

Jeffrey, John,
Patent Engineer,
Westinghouse Air Brake Co.,
312 Arlington Ave.,
East McKeesport, Pa.

Jenkins, G. A.,
Patrolman,
B. & O. R. R. Co.,
362 Flowers Avenue,
Pittsburgh, Pa.

Jenness, D. H.,
R. F. of E., Penna. R. R,.
620 Sheridan Ave.,
Pittsburgh, Pa

Jennings, A. S.,
Gen. Coal Freight Agent,
Pennsylvania Railroad,
Pennsylvania Station,
Pittsburgh, Pa.

John, William,
Freight Claim Agent,
P. & L. E. R. R. Co.,
202 Dewey St.,
Edgewood, Swissvale P. O., Pa.

Johnson. George T.,
First Vice President, The
Buckeye Steel Castings Co.,
South Parsons Ave.,
Columbus, Ohio

Johnson, I. S.,
Resident Material Inspector,
The Pennsylvania Railroad,
Room 402, 1013 Penn Ave.,
Pittsburgh, Pa.

Johnson, J. W.,
Superintendent,
Railway Express Agency,
926 Penn Ave.,
Pittsburgh, Pa.

Johnson, Le Vere H.,
Executive Secretary,
Penna. Railroad Y. M. C. A.,
28th St. & Liberty Ave.,
Pittsburgh, Pa

Johnson, Nelson E.,
Gang Leader,
P. & L. E. R. R. Co ,
1429 Summit St.,
McKees Rocks, Pa

Johnson, Stephen, Jr.,
Chief Engineer,
Bendix Westinghouse
Automotive Air Brake Co.,
5001 Center Avenue,
Pittsburgh, Pa.

Johnson, Wm. M.,
Gen. Superintendent,
B. & L. E. R. R.,
Greenville, Pa.

Johnston, J. T.,
Asst. to Supy'r of Wage
Schedules,
P. & L. E. R. R. Co.,
1418 Fourth Ave.,
Beaver Falls, Pa.

Jones, George, Sr.,
General Boiler Foreman,
B. & O. R. R. Co.,
605 Hazelwood Avenue,
Pittsburgh, Pa.

Jones, H. W.,
General Superintendent,
Pennsylvania Railroad,
2518 North Second St.,
Harrisburg, Pa.

Jones, L. E.,
Engr. to Vice President,
Carnegie-Illinois Steel Corp.,
Carnegie Bldg.,
Pittsburgh, Pa.

Jones, Louis E.,
Department Manager,
American Steel Foundries,
North Wrigley Bldg.,
Chicago, Ill.

Joyce, P. H.,
President,
C. G. W. R. R.,
309 West Jackson Blvd.,
Chicago, Ill.

Kamerer, R. W.,
General Agent,
P. & L. E. R. R. Co.,
Terminal Bldg.,
Pittsburgh, Pa.

Kane, Henry S.,
Freight Agent,
Pennsylvania Railroad,
433 Library Ave.,
Carnegie, Pa.

Kapp, A. C.,
General Foreman,
B. & L. E. R. R.,
R. F. D. No. 1,
Verona, Pa.

Karnes, W. T.,
General Foreman,
P. & L. E. R. R.,
330 Ohio Ave.,
Glassport, Pa.

Kaup, Harry E.,
General Superintendent,
Pressed Steel Car Co.,
McKees Rocks, Pa.

Kavanagh, D.,
Storekeeper,
Union Railroad,
East Pittsburgh, Pa.

Kearfott, W. E.,
Asst. Engineer M. of W.,
B. & O. R. R. Co.,
231 Martin Avenue,
Mt. Lebanon, Pittsburgh, Pa.

Keck, L. M.,
Agent, Junction Transfer,
B. & O. R. R. Co.,
Liberty & 32nd Sts.,
Pittsburgh, Pa.

Keeney, A. R.,
Foreman Foundry,
Union Switch & Signal Co.,
4803 Cypress Street,
Pittsburgh, Pa.

Keeney, John H.,
Salesman,
Air Reduction Sales Co.,
1116 Ridge Ave.,
N. S., Pittsburgh, Pa.

Keiser, C. E.,
Purchasing Department,
Pullman-Standard Car
Mfg. Company,
Butler, Pa.

Kellenberger, K. E.,
Advertising Manager,
Union Switch & Signal Co.,
Swissvale, Pa.

Keller, P. R.,
Sales Representative,
General Steel Casting Corp.,
Eddystone, Pa

Keller, R. B.,
Supervisor,
Air Reduction Sales Co,
942 California Ave.,
Avalon, Pittsburgh, Pa

Keller, R. E.,
Lead Car Inspector,
P. & L. E. R. R.,
560 Stokes Ave.,
Braddock, Pa

Kellerman, Dewey W.,
Clerk,
Pennsylvania Railroad,
1430 Nixon St.,
N. S., Pittsburgh, Pa.

Kelly, Eugene V.,
Yard Master,
P. & L. E. R. R. Co.,
313 Oneida Street,
Duquesne Heights,
Pittsburgh, Pa

Kelly, H. B.,
Gen. R. F. of E.,
P. & L. E. R. R.,
3115 Ashlyn St.,
Corliss Station,
Pittsburgh, Pa.

Kelly, J. P.,
Asst. Superintendent,
P. & L. E. R. R.,
922 School St.,
Coraopolis, Pa

Kelly, Leo J.,
Superintendent,
Fort Pitt Mall. Iron Co.,
3036 Bergman St.,
Pittsburgh, Pa

Kemmerer, R. R.,
General Engineer,
Union Switch & Signal Co.,
8012 St. Lawrence Ave.,
Swissvale, Pa.

Kemp, Archie,
Engineer,
Pennsylvania Railroad,
P. O. Box 262,
Altoona, Pa.

Kennedy, A. R.,
6689 Woodwell St.,
Pittsburgh, Pa.

Kennedy, F. J.,
Auditor Pass. Accounts,
P. & L. E. R. R.,
Box 206,
New Brighton, Pa.

Kennedy, G. N.,
Foreman,
Pennsylvania Railroad,
575 So. Negley Ave.,
House No. 14,
Pittsburgh, Pa.

Kenny, Mark P.,
Coal Freight Agent,
Pennsylvania Railroad,
Pennsylvania Station,
Pittsburgh, Pa.

Kentlein, John,
Chief Draftsman,
H. K. Porter Co.,
49th & Harrison Sts.,
Pittsburgh, Pa

Keppelman, H. S.,
Superintendent Car Dept.,
ReRading Company,
Sixth & Perry Sts.,
Reading, Pa.

Kern, Roy S.,
Chairman,
Coal, Coke & Iron Ore Com.,
Wabash Building,
Pittsburgh, Pa

Kerr, Alexander D.,
Asst. Supervisor,
Pennsylvania Railroad,
Mansfield, Ohio.

Kerr, Charles, Jr.,
Railway Engineer,
Westinghouse Electric &
Mfg. Co.,
231 Elm St.,
Edgewood, Swissvale P. O., Pa.

Kerr, James P., M. D.,
Chief Surgeon,
P. & W. Va. Ry. Co.,
Wabash Building,
Pittsburgh, Pa.

Kessler, A. L.,
Clearance Clerk,
Pennsylvania Railroad,
402 Knox Avenue,
Pittsburgh, Pa.

Kessler, Bernard J.,
Clerk, Accounting Dept.,
B. & O. R. R. Co.,
901 Third St.,
Versailles, McKeesport, Pa.

Keys, A. H.,
Dist. Master Car Builder,
B. & O. R. R. Co.,
1651 Potomac Ave.,
Dormont,
Pittsburgh, Pa

Kilborn, W. T.,
President,
Flannery Bolt Co.,
Bridgeville, Pa.

Kim, J. B.,
Gang Foreman,
Pennsylvania Railroad,
193½ Meade St.,
Wilkinsburg, Pittsburgh, Pa

Kimling, Carl,
Chief Clerk,
Central Warehouse,
P. & L. E. R. R.,
85 Harwood St.,
Pittsburgh, Pa.

King, E. C.,
Route Agent,
Railway Express Agency,
Inc.,
5801 Rippey Street,
Pittsburgh, Pa

King, George A. H.,
Clerk, ·
Monongahela Connecting
R. R.,
311 Ross Street,
Pittsburgh, Pa.

King, J. C.,
Yard Master,
Pennsylvania Railroad,
2200 Nance Ave.,
Wheeling, W. Va

Kinter, John B.,
Salesman,
Union Steel Casting Co.,
1220 S. Negley Ave.,
Pittsburgh, Pa.

Kirby, D. D.,
President,
Kirby Trans. & Storage Co.,
2536 Smallman St.,
Pittsburgh, Pa.

Kirk, Charles C.,
Supervisor Reg. Express,
Pennsylvania Railroad,
Pennsylvania Station,
Pittsburgh, Pa.

Kirkland, Norman L.,
Partner,
Acme Printing & Stationery
Company,
1475 Greenmont Ave.,
Dormont, Pittsburgh,
Pa.

Kiskadden, H. L.,
Clerk,
Pennsylvania Railroad,
115 Stewart Ave.,
Freeport, Pa.

Klassen, Fred G.,
Traveling Engineer,
P. & W. Va. Ry.,
Carnegie, Pa.

Kleber, P. C.,
Gang Leader,
P. & L. E. R. R. Co.,
803 Eighth St.,
McKees Rocks, Pa.

Klein, J. W.,
President & General Manager,
Pittsburgh Refrigeration Co.,
1115 Penn Ave.,
Pittsburgh, Pa.

Klein, Nicholas P.,
Foreman Car Repairs,
Pennsylvania Railroad,
50 South 33rd St.,
Pittsburgh, Pa

Klein, S. J.,
Asst. Traffic Manager,
P. & W. Va. Ry. Co.,
Wabash Building,
Pittsburgh, Pa.

Kleinhans, Harry,
President,
H. Kleinhans Co.,
419 Union Trust Bldg.,
Pittsburgh, Pa.

Klorer, C. P.,
Stationary Engineer,
Lowrie Street,
Troy Hill,
Pittsburgh, Pa.

Knable, G. Elkins,
Manager Structural and
Plate Division,
Carnegie-Illinois Steel
Corp.,
Carnegie Bldg.,
Pittsburgh, Pa.

Knoff, R. A.,
National Railroad Adjustment
Board, First Div.,
220 South State St.,
Chicago, Ill.

Knoke, H. C.,
Secretary to District
Master Mechanic,
B. & O. R. R. Co.,
Cumberland, Md.

Knox, Wm. J.,
112 Second Ave.,
DuBois, Pa.

Koch, C. W.,
Clerk,
P. & L. E. R. R. Co.,
1257 Clairhaven St.,
Pittsburgh, Pa.

Koenig, Walter A.,
Yard Brakeman,
Pennsylvania Railroad,
519 Second Street,
Pitcairn, Pa.

Kohl, H. J.,
Gen. Car Foreman,
P. & L. E. R. R.,
1106 Tweed St.,
Pittsburgh, Pa.

Kohl, Leo H.,
S. W. District Secretary,
State R. R., Y. M. C. A.,
241 Whipple St.,
Swissvale, Pittsburgh, Pa

Kondej, Henry,
Test Engineer,
Westinghouse Air Brake Co.,
577½ East End Ave.,
Pittsburgh, Pa.

Krahmer, Edward F.,
Supvr. Agt.—Div. Opr.,
Pennsylvania Railroad,
Pennsylvania Station,
Pittsburgh, Pa.

Kramer, F. E.,
P. & W. Va. Ry. Co.,
3260 Beaconhill Ave.,
Dormont,
Pittsburgh, Pa.

Kramer, W. H.,
Train Rider,
B. & O. R. R. Co.,
203 Maytide Street,
Carrick, Pittsburgh, Pa.

Kramer, William E.,
Representative,
Acme Steel Co.,
3674 Middletown Road,
Corliss Station,
Pittsburgh, Pa

Kraus, Raymond E.,
Mechanical Draftsman,
P. & L. E. R. R.,
241 Dickson Ave.,
Ben Avon,
Pittsburgh, Pa.

Kroen, Vincent,
Supervisor Express Service,
Pennsylvania Railroad,
Pennsylvania Station,
Pittsburgh, Pa.

Kromer, Wm. F.,
Chief Mechanical Engineer,
H. K. Porter Co.,
49th & Harrison Sts.,
Pittsburgh, Pa.

Kroske, J. F.,
Mgr., P. T. Sales,
Ingersoll-Rand Co.,
706 Chamber of Commerce
Building,
Pittsburgh, Pa.

Kruse, J. F. W.,
Superintendent,
Hubbard & Co.,
528 Washington Ave.,
Oakmont, Pa.

Kuhn, Samuel H.,
Office Engineer,
Pennsylvania Railroad,
51 Division St.,
Crafton, Pittsburgh, Pa.

Kuhnert, P. C.,
Westinghouse Air Brake Co.,
145 La Crosse St.,
Edgewood, Pittsburgh, Pa.

Kulp, J. G.,
Train Master,
Pennsylvania Railroad,
810 Rebecca Ave.,
Wilkinsburg, Pa

Kusick, Harry F.,
Engineer,
Union Switch & Signal Co.,
Swissvale. Pa.

Lackner, Ray A.,
District Sales Manager,
Penna. Forge Corp.,
5724 Bartlett St.,
Pittsburgh, Pa.

Lanahan, Frank J.,
President, Fort Pitt Malleable
Iron Co,
P. O. Box 492,
Pittsburgh, Pa

Lanahan, J. S.,
Vice President, Fort Pitt
Malleable Iron Co.,
127 Elysian Ave.,
Pittsburgh, Pa.

Landis, W. C.,
Asst. Works Manager,
Westinghouse Air Brake Co.,
Wilmerding, Pa.

Langhurst, R. O.,
Gang Leader,
P. & L. E. R. R. Co.,
1502 Orchlee St.,
N. S., Pittsburgh, Pa

Lanken, C. C.
President-Treasurer,
Lincoln Electric Railway
Sales Company,
Marshall Building,
Cleveland, Ohio.

Lanning, Edward H.,
Acting Gang Foreman,
Pennsylvania Railroad,
7341 Fluery Way,
Homewood, Pittsburgh, Pa.

Lanning, J. Frank,
President,
J. Frank Lanning & Co.,
327 First Ave.,
Pittsburgh, Pa.

Largent, J. R,
Ticket Agent,
P. & L. E. R. R. Co.,
P&LE Station,
Pittsburgh, Pa.

Larson, W. E.,
Vice President, Superior
Railway Products Corp.,
7501 Thomas Blvd.,
Pittsburgh, Pa.

Lauderbaugh, Moss,
Freight Agent,
P. & L. E. R. R. Co.,
16 Fifth Street,
Ellwood City, Pa.

Laurent, Jos. A.,
Foreman,
Fort Pitt Mall. Iron Co.,
206 Bruce St.,
McKees Rocks, Pa.

Lavine, Ralph D.,
Chief Rate & Div. Clerk,
P. & L. E. R. R. Co.,
324 Ophelia St.,
Pittsburgh, Pa.

Lawler, Joseph A.,
Sup't Trans.,
Carnegie Steel Co.,
Edgar Thomson Works,
Braddock, Pa.

Lawrence, Norman M.,
Superintendent E. & A.
Division,
Pennsylvania Railroad,
322 E Lincoln Ave.,
New Castle, Pa.

Layng, Frank R.,
Chief Engineer,
B. & L. E. R. R.,
Greenville, Pa.

League, W. D.,
Chief Clerk,
Monongahela Railway Co.,
16 Elm Street,
S. S., Brownsville, Pa.

Lear, E. J.,
Hostler,
B. & O. R. R. Co.,
409 Allen Ave.,
Pittsburgh (10), Pa.

Leban, J. L.,
Asst. District Supt.,
Pullman Co.,
1434 Gulf Bldg.,
Pittsburgh, Pa.

Lee, L. A.,
Secretary, General
Safety Committee,
P. & L. E. R. R.,
645 Bigelow Street,
Pittsburgh, Pa

Lees, Thomas,
Reymer & Brothers, Inc.,
123 Bascom St.,
Pittsburgh, (14) Pa.

Leet, C. S.,
Asst. Gen. Mgr.,
B. & L. E. R. R.,
P. O. Box 536,
Pittsburgh, Pa.

Leiper, C. I.,
Gen. Mgr., Central Region,
Pennsylvania Railroad,
Pennsylvania Station,
Pittsburgh, Pa.

Leonard, C. W.,
Salesman,
Independent Pneumatic Tool
Co.,
Wabash Building,
Pittsburgh, Pa.

Leonard, J. F.,
Engineer, Bridges & Bldgs.,
Pennsylvania Railroad,
Pennsylvania Station,
Pittsburgh, Pa.

Leonard, P. J.,
General Foreman,
B. & O. R. R. Co.,
5220 Holmes Street,
Pittsburgh, Pa.

Lewis, Benjamin,
961 Main St.,
Aliquippa, Pa.

Lewis, Herbert,
Vice President & Secretary,
The Durametallic Corp.,
24 Commerce St.,
Newark, N. J.

Lewis, N. F.,
Test Engineer,
Westinghouse Air Brake Co.,
503 Hill Ave.,
Wilkinsburg, Pa.

Lincoln, John J.,
District Manager,
Air Reduction Sales Co.,
1116 Ridge Ave.,
N. S., Pittsburgh, Pa

Lincoln, R. B.,
Director of Weld Testing,
Pittsburgh Testing
Laboratory,
Locust & Stevenson Sts.,
Pittsburgh, Pa.

Little, John G.,
Asst. to Vice President,
Simmons-Boardman Pub-
lishing Co.,
Terminal Tower,
Cleveland, O.

Little, W. R.,
Local Purchasing Agent,
Pullman-Standard Car
Mfg. Company,
Butler, Pa.

Livingston, W. C.,
Regional Storekeeper,
Pennsylvania Railroad,
1125 Savannah Ave.,
Edgewood, Pittsburgh, Pa.

Lloyd, John,
Asst. General Superintendent
Edgar Thomson Works,
Carnegie-Illinois Steel
Corp.,
Braddock, Pa

Loder, C. C.,
Representative,
Plibrico Jointless Fire-
brick Co.,
298 Duquesne Way,
Pittsburgh, Pa.

Loeffler, George O.,
District Representative,
Climax Molybdenum Co.,
905 Union Trust Bldg.,
Pittsburgh, Pa.

Logan, J. W., Jr.,
Engineer,
Union Switch & Signal Co.,
Swissvale, Pa.

Logsdon, Fred H.,
Tester,
Westinghouse Air Brake Co.,
658 Middle Ave.,
Wilmerding, Pa.

Long, Alfred J.,
Movement Director,
Pennsylvania Railroad,
1828 Pioneer Ave.,
Pittsburgh, Pa

Long, R. M.,
"Retired" Air Brake
Inspector and Instructor,
P. & L. E. R. R.,
3118 Pioneer Ave.,
South Hills Branch,
Pittsburgh, Pa

Long, Walter,
President,
Walter Long Mfg. Co.,
1315 Bingham St.,
S. S., Pittsburgh, Pa.

Longdon, Clyde V.,
Asst. Engineer,
T. & E. D. Dept.,
Westinghouse Air Brake
Company,
R. D. 1, Box 260,
Turtle Creek, Pa.

Longstreth, W. L.,
Road Foreman of Engines,
Conemaugh Div.,
Pennsylvania Railroad,
301 Delaware Ave.,
Oakmont, Pa.

Looman, F. W.,
Freight Agent,
Pennsylvania Railroad,
Canton, Ohio

Lortz, Elmer A.,
Safety Engineer,
Pressed Steel Car Co.,
3924 Winshire St.,
N. S., Pittsburgh, Pa.

Loucks, William V.,
Yard Master,
Pennsylvania Railroad,
207 North Walnut St.,
Blairsville, Pa.

Lowe, William T.,
Traffic Manager,
American Window Glass Co.,
Farmers Bank Bldg.,
Pittsburgh, Pa.

Lowery, J. V.,
Passenger Train Master,
Pennsylvania Railroad,
707 Nevin Ave.,
Sewickley, Pa.

Lowry, Wm. F., Jr,
Sales Agent,
American Car &
Foundry Co.,
Farmers Bank Bldg.,
Pittsburgh, Pa.

Lundeen, Carl J.,
Asst. Mechanical Engr.,
P. & L. E. R. R.,
400 Island Ave.,
McKees Rocks, Pa

Lunz, G. J.,
Chief Clerk, Freight Traffic
Department,
P. & L. E. R. R. Co.,
Terminal Bldg.,
Pittsburgh, Pa.

Lupton, E. J.,
Salesman,
The Sherwin-Williams Co.,
601 Canal Road,
Cleveland, Ohio

Lustenberger, L. C.,
Asst. to Vice Pres. & Gen.
Mgr. of Sales,
Carnegie Steel Co.,
Subsidiaries,
R. F. D. No. 4,
Millvale Branch,
Pittsburgh, Pa

Lutz, Harry,
Supvr. Tel. & Signals,
Pennsylvania Railroad,
499 Roosevelt Ave.,
Bellevue, Pa.

Lynn, William,
Foreman Car Repairs,
P. & L. E. R. R.,
1521 Ridge Ave.,
Coraopolis, Pa.

Lytle, L. J.,
Barco Manufacturing Co.,
19 Alfred St.,
Mt. Lebanon,
Pittsburgh, Pa

MacDonald, George F.,
Chief Clerk to Chief Engineer,
P. & L. E. R. R. Co.,
Pittsburgh, Pa.

MacDonald, William C.,
Special Agent, Contracts,
Penna. R. R. Co.,
254 Allison Ave.,
Emsworth, Pa.

MacElveny, A. W.,
General Traffic Manager,
Schenley Products Co.,
20 West 40th St.,
New York, N. Y.

Machin, Norman H.,
Gang Foreman,
Pennsylvania Railroad,
359 Reno Street,
Rochester, Pa.

Magner, John H.,
Clerk,
B. & L. E. R. R. Co.,
R. D. 6—Box 172,
Mt. Oliver Station,
Pittsburgh (10), Pa.

Mahaney, A. R.,
Transportation Apprentice,
Pennsylvania Railroad,
Amber Club, Wellesley Ave.,
E. E., Pittsburgh, Pa.

Maliphant, C. W.,
Test Dept.,
W. A. B. Co.,
Westinghouse Apartments,
Wilmerding, Pa.

Malone, Creed,
General Yard Master,
Monongahela Railway Co.,
Morgantown, W. Va.

Malone, Frank B.,
Engineer, Conemaugh Div.,
Pennsylvania Railroad,
285 45th St.,
Pittsburgh, Pa.

Mann, Henry S.,
District Sales Manager,
Standard Stoker Co., Inc.,
1801 McCormick Bldg.,
Chicago, Ill.

Mannion, M. F.,
Office Asst. to Chief Engr.,
B. & L. E. R. R.,
96 North High St.,
Greenville, Pa.

Manson, Arthur J.,
Asst. Sales Manager,
Westinghouse Electric &
Mfg. Co.,
700 Braddock Ave.,
East Pittsburgh, Pa.

Marble, A. E.,
Metallurgical Dept.,
Jones & Laughlin Steel
Corp.,
Third Ave. & Ross St.,
Pittsburgh, Pa.

Marble, Robert A.,
Structural Engineer,
Carnegie Steel Co.,
Carnegie Bldg.,
Pittsburgh, Pa.

Marquis, G. E.,
Asst. Superintendent,
P. & L. E. R. R. Co.,
702 Sixth Avenue,
New Brighton, Pa.

Marsh, E. A.,
Car Foreman,
B. & O. R. R. Co.,
2830 Louisiana St.,
Dormont, Pgh., Pa.

Martin, George A , Jr.,
President,
W. W. Lawrence & Co.,
West Carson Street,
Pittsburgh, Pa.

Mason, W. N.,
General Yard Master,
P. & L. E. R. R. Co.,
936 Atlantic Ave.,
Monaca, Pa.

Masterman, T. W.,
Asst. to Chief Design Engr.,
Westinghouse Air Brake Co.,
1249 McClure Ave.,
East McKeesport, Pa.

Masters, W. C.,
Eastern Sales Manager,
Flannery Bolt Co.,
Bridgeville, Pa

Matchett, H. K.,
"Retired",
Pennsylvania Railroad,
5517½ Broad Street,
E. E., Pittsburgh, Pa.

Matchneer, Wm. W.,
Sales Engineer,
Buckeye Steel Castings Co.,
Columbus, Ohio

Matuseski, Robert R.,
Gang Foreman,
Pennsylvania Railroad,
Pittsburgh, Pa.

Maxfield, Col. H. H.,
S. M. P., Southern Div.,
Pennsylvania Railroad,
402 Pennsylvania Bldg.,
Wilmington, Del.

Maxwell, R. E.,
Special Representative,
Carnegie-Illinois Steel Corp.,
Carnegie Bldg.,
Pittsburgh, Pa.

Maxwell, Thomas,
Foreman Tool & Equipment
Design Department,
Westinghouse Air Brake
Co.,
933 Milton Street,
Pittsburgh, Pa.

May, Herbert A.,
Vice President,
Union Switch & Signal Co.,
Swissvale, Pa.

May, J. D.,
Yard Master,
Pennsylvania Railroad,
1410 Penn Ave.,
Steubenville, Ohio

Mayer, George E.,
Photographer,
P. & L. E. R. R. Co.,
Terminal Annex Bldg.,
Pittsburgh, Pa.

Mayer, Luke I.,
Westinghouse Air Brake Co.,
412 Arlington Ave.,
East McKeesport, Pa.

Meagher, Maurice E.,
Railway Equip. Rep.,
Peter E. Meagher,
Lyceum Building,
Duluth, Minn.

Megee, Caleb R.,
District Manager,
Car Service Division,
Association of American
Railroads,
1103 Penna. Station,
Pittsburgh, Pa.

Meinert, Henry, J.,
Locomotive Inspector,
Montour Railroad,
11 Geneva St.,
Etna, Pa.

Mekeel, David L.,
Consulting Engineer,
Jones & Laughlin Steel Corp.
J. & L. Building,
Pittsburgh, Pa.

Mellon, Curtis B.,
Asst. Foreman,
Pennsylvania Railroad,
Sixth Street,
Pitcairn, Pa.

Mellor, C. L.,
Vice President,
Barco Manufacturing Co.,
1801 Winnemac Ave.,
Chicago, Ill.

Menaglia, Victor A.,
District Sales Manager,
S K F Industries,
Grant Bldg.,
Pittsburgh, Pa

Menk, C. W.,
Agent,
Pennsylvania Railroad,
New Kensington, Pa.

Meredith, A. R.,
Real Estate Agent,
Pennsylvania Railroad,
Pennsylvania Station,
Pittsburgh, Pa

Merz, G. L.,
Asst. Fore., Pgh. 11th St.,
Pennsylvania Railroad,
500 Curtin Ave.,
Pittsburgh, Pa

Metcalf, George E.,
Locomotive Engineer,
Montour Railroad Co.,
717 School St.,
Coraopolis, Pa.

Metzgar, Herbert T.,
Storehouse Foreman,
B. & O. R. R. Co.,
5301 Gertrude St.,
Hazelwood, Pittsburgh, Pa.

Metzgar, C. L.,
Secretary,
Auto-Tite Joints Co.,
RD. 1, Box 103,
Turtle Creek, Pa.

Micheals, John H.,
Yard Master,
Pennsylvania Railroad,
1550 Marlborro Ave.,
Wilkinsburg, Pa.

Miller, Carl A.,
Salesman,
Ingersoll-Rand Company,
Chamber of Commerce
Building,
Pittsburgh, Pa.

Millar, Clarence W.,
Mgr. Order Dept.,
Pressed Steel Car Co.,
McKees Rocks, Pa.

Miller, Henry,
General Manager,
Fort Pitt Spring Company,
Box 1377,
Pittsburgh, Pa.

Miller, J. F.,
Sales Engineer,
Carnegie Steel Co.,
Carnegie Bldg.,
Pittsburgh, Pa.

Miller, James B.,
Tester,
Westinghouse Air Brake Co.,
905 Punta Gorda St.,
East McKeesport, Pa.

Miller, John,
General Car Foreman,
Montour Railroad,
5127 Blair St.,
Hazelwood, Pa.

Miller, L. F.,
Brakeman,
Pennsylvania Railroad,
1140 Morrell Ave.,
East McKeesport, Pa

Miller, R. C.,
General Superintendent,
Pennsylvania Railroad,
Pennsylvania Station,
Pittsburgh, Pa.

Miller, R. E.,
General Engineer,
Westinghouse Air Brake Co.,
Wilmerding, Pa.

Miller, S. H.,
President,
Fort Pitt Chemical Co.,
26th & Smallman Sts.,
Pittsburgh, Pa.

Miller, W. J.,
Storekeeper,
Pennsylvania Railroad,
349 Moyhend St.,
Springdale, Pa.

Milliken, Roy C.,
Asst. Yard Master,
Pennsylvania Railroad,
Box 125,
Allegheny River Bldg.,
Verona, Pa.

Mills, C. C.,
President & General Manager,
Unity Railways Co.,
Union Trust Bldg.,
Pittsburgh, Pa

Misner, George W.,
Westinghouse Air Brake Co.,
304 Arlington Ave.,
East McKeesport, Pa

Mitchell, A. T.,
Chief Smoke Inspector,
Pennsylvania Railroad,
413 McNair St.,
Wilkinsburg, Pa.

Mitchell, Frank K.,
Signal Inspector,
P. & L. E. R. R.,
240 East End Ave.,
Beaver, Pa

Mitchell, W. S.,
Signal Inspector,
P. & L. E. R. R.,
540 River Road,
Beaver, Pa.

Mittelstadter, Howard,
Foreman,
P. & L. E. R. R. Co.,
1139 Wisconsin Ave.,
Dormont,
Pittsburgh, Pa.

Mohn, Louis,
District Manager,
Garlock Packing Co.,
339 Blvd. of Allies,
Pittsburgh, Pa.

Moir, W. B.,
Chief Car Inspector,
Pennsylvania Railroad,
1009 Penna. Station,
Pittsburgh, Pa.

Montague, C. F.,
Master Carpenter,
Monongahela Division,
Pennsylvania Railroad,
Pennsylvania Station,
Pittsburgh, Pa

Montgomery, J. L.,
Assistant Auditor,
Union Railroad,
Frick Building,
Pittsburgh, Pa

Moore, Donald O.,
Mgr. of Traffic Div.,
Chamber of Commerce,
Chamber of Com. Bldg.,
Pittsburgh, Pa

Morgan, A. L.,
Supt. on Special Duty,
Penna. R. R. Co.,
24 Maple Ave.,
Woodlawn,
Wheeling, W. Va.

Morgan, Homer C.,
613 Frederick St.,
McKees Rocks, Pa

Morneweck, W. L.,
Trainmaster,
B. & L. E. R. R. Co.,
Brown Apartments,
Unity, Pa.

Morris, J. M.,
President & Gen. Mgr.,
The Lake Terminal R. R. Co.
McKeesport Connecting
R. R.,
Frick Bldg.,
Pittsburgh, Pa.

Morris, W. F., Jr.,
Vice President,
Weirton Steel Co.,
Grant Bldg.,
Pittsburgh, Pa.

Morrison, R. A. J.,
Train Master,
B. & O. R. R. Co.,
Smithfield & Water Sts.,
Pittsburgh, Pa.

Morse, J. W.,
Asst. T. M.-Asst. R. F. of E.,
Pennsylvania Railroad,
303 North 4th St.,
Youngwood, Pa

Morton, R. A.,
Machine Shop Foreman,
B. & O. R. R. Co.,
236 Johnstone Ave.,
Hazelwood, Pittsburgh, Pa

Moser, G. B.,
Clerk,
Pittsburgh, Chartiers &
Youghiogheny Ry.,
P&LE Terminal Annex
Bldg.,
Pittsburgh, Pa.

Moulis, F. J.,
Cash Clerk,
B. & O. R. R. Co.,
1412 Alton St.,
Beechview,
Pittsburgh, Pa.

Mowery, George B.,
Gen. Fore., Allegheny Shops,
B. & O. R. R. Co.,
101 Hazelwood Ave.,
Pittsburgh, Pa

Mowery, John F.,
Painter Foreman,
Montour Railroad Co.,
780 Greenfield Avenue,
Pittsburgh, Pa.

Mowry, James G.,
Railway Representative,
Pittsburgh Plate Glass Co.,
30 Rockefeller Plaza,
New York, N. Y.

Mowry, John W.,
Salesman,
Scully Steel Products Co.,
1281 Reedsdale St.,
Pittsburgh, Pa.

Muir, Robert Y.,
Master Car Builder,
P. & W. Va. Ry. Co.,
1237 Hillsdale Ave.,
Dormont,
Pittsburgh, Pa.

Mulligan, Michael,
Engine House Foreman,
Monongahela Railway Co.,
315 Water Street,
South Brownsville, Pa.

Mulvey, John I.,
Traffic Manager,
Hubbard & Co.,
6301 Butler St.,
Pittsburgh, Pa.

Munn, Alex D.,
First Aid Inspector,
P. & L. E. R. R.,
Box 307,
Glenwillard, Pa.

Murphy, C. E.,
President,
The Acme Railway Supply
Co.,
415 Midland Bldg.,
Cleveland, Ohio

Murphy, Martin,
General Yard Master,
P. & L. E. R. R. Co.,
316 Jucunda St.,
Knoxville, Pittsburgh, Pa.

Murray, Charles C.,
Asst. C. C. to Storekeeper,
B. & O. R. R. Co.,
5312 Gertrude St.,
Pittsburgh, Pa.

Murray, Stewart,
Salesman,
Joseph Dixon Crucible Co.,
6615 Northumberland St.,
Pittsburgh, Pa.

Murray, Thomas A.,
Stenographer,
P. & L. E. R. R. Co.,
Terminal Bldg.,
Pittsburgh, Pa.

Muse, Thos. Charles,
Traveling Car Agent,
P. & L. E. R. R.,
253 Fourth St.,
Beaver, Pa

Musgrove, W. W.,
Piece Work Inspector,
P. & L. E. R. R.,
Box 301,
Glenwillard, Pa

Myer, Charles R.,
Engine House Foreman,
Pennsylvania Railroad,
529 Hill Avenue,
Wilkinsburg, Pa.

Myers, Arnold,
Equipment Inspector,
B. & L. E. R. R. Co.,
217 Woodlawn Ave.,
Munhall, Pa.

Myers, Robert H.,
Sales Manager,
American Shim Steel Co.,
1304 Fifth Avenue,
New Kensington, Pa

McAbee, W. S.,
Vice Pres. & Gen. Supt.,
Union Railroad,
664 Linden Avenue,
East Pittsburgh, Pa

McAndrew, R. E.,
General Storekeeper,
B. & L. E. R. R.,
Greenville, Pa.

McBride, Gordon P.,
Supervisors' Field Man,
P. & L. E. R. R. Co.,
Terminal Bldg.,
Pittsburgh, Pa

McCandless, William A.,
Passenger Trainman,
Pennsylvania Railroad,
206 Alwine Ave.,
Greensburg, Pa.

McCarthy, F. W.,
Supt. Road Operation,
Pittsburgh Railways Co.,
435 Sixth Ave.,
Pittsburgh, Pa.

McCarthy, Frank C.,
Fitter,
Mesta Machine Company,
207 Woolslayer road,
Pittsburgh, (24) Pa.

McCartney, John H.,
Gustin-Bacon Mfg. Co.,
230 Park Ave.,
New York, N. Y.

McCauley, William,
Road Foreman of Engines,
Pennsylvania Railroad,
1013 Savannah Ave.,
Wilkinsburg, Pa.

McClintock, John D.,
Manager, Injector Dept.,
Wm. Sellers & Co., Inc.,
1600 Hamilton St.,
Philadelphia, Pa.

McComb, R. J.,
Sales Manager,
Woodings-Verona Tool
Works,
648 Peoples Gas Bldg.,
Chicago, Ill.

McConnell, Frank P.,
Yard Master,
P. & L. E. R. R.,
2101 Arlington Ave.,
Pittsburgh, Pa.

McCorkle, J. B.,
General Freight Agent,
Pennsylvania Railroad,
Pennsylvania Station,
Pittsburgh, Pa.

McCormick, E. S.,
Train Master,
Pennsylvania Railroad,
511 Sixth St.,
Oakmont, Pa.

McCrea, James G.,
Brakeman,
Pennsylvania Railroad,
811 Franklin Ave.,
Wilkinsburg, Pa.

McCready, R. E.,
General Foreman,
Water Supply,
P. & L. E. R. R. Co.,
296 Park Street,
Beaver, Pa.

McCrossin, C. D.,
Tel. & Sig. Foreman,
Pennsylvania Railroad,
204 Emerson Ave.,
Aspinwall, Pa

McCuen, J. T.,
Salesman,
Motch & Merryweather
Machinery Co.,
Clark Building,
Pittsburgh, Pa.

McCully, D. L.,
Safety Supervisor,
Westinghouse Air Brake Co.,
8001 Westmoreland Ave.,
Edgewood, Pa.

McCune, J. C.,
Asst. Director Engineering,
Westinghouse Air Brake Co.,
Wilmerding, Pa.

McElravy, J. W.,
Terminal Agent,
P. & L. E. R. R.,
Terminal Annex Bldg.,
S. S., Pittsburgh, Pa.

McFetridge, W. S.,
Principal Asst. Engineer,
B. & L. E. R. R. Co.,
Greenville, Pa.

McGaughey, J. V.,
Asst. Road Fore. of Engines,
Pennsylvania Railroad,
313 South Avenue,
Wilkinsburg, Pa.

McGeary, E. J.,
Superintendent,
B. & L. E. R. R.,
P. O. Box 471,
Greenville, Pa.

McGeorge, D. W.,
Secretary & Sales Manager,
Edgewater Steel Co.,
P. O. Box 478,
Pittsburgh, Pa.

McGuirk, John J.,
Div. Car Foreman,
B. & O. R. R. Co.,
414 Moore Ave.,
Knoxville,
Pittsburgh, Pa.

McHail, J. L.,
Agent,
Pennsylvania Railroad,
P. O. Box 254,
Homestead, Pa.

McHugh, C. A.,
Train Master,
P. & W. Va. Ry.,
21 Cannon St.,
Crafton, Pa.

McIntyre, R. C.,
Supt. Motive Power,
Union Railroad,
East Pittsburgh, Pa.

McKalip, W. B.,
Agent,
Pennsylvania Railroad,
Tarentum, Pa.

McKay, N. H.,
President,
U. S. Chromium Corp.,
1100 Pitt St.,
Wilkinsburg, Pa.

McKedy, H. V.,
Rep., Railway Dept.,
The Patterson, Sargent Co.,
135 East 42nd St.,
New York, N. Y.

McKee, Frederick C.,
Pres., Winfield R. R.,
2215 Oliver Bldg.,
Pittsburgh, Pa.

McKibbin, J. S.,
Local Treasurer,
P. & L. E. R. R. Co.,
3111 Wainbell Avenue,
Dormont, Pgh. (16), Pa.

McKim, Hollis,
Office Manager,
Edgewater Steel Company,
P. O. Box 478,
Pittsburgh, Pa.

McKinley, Archie J.,
Chief Motive Power Inspector
P. & L. E. R. R.,
613 Broadway Ave.,
McKees Rocks, Pa.

McKinley, John T.,
Stenographer,
P. & L. E. R. R.,
200 Gregg St.,
Carnegie, Pa.

McKinstry, C. H.,
Asst. Research Engineer,
W. A. B. Co.,
46 Sprague St.,
Wilmerding, Pa.

McKinzie, Edward,
General Yard Master,
P. & W. Va. Ry.,
1524 Alabama Ave.,
Dormont,
Pittsburgh, Pa.

McKirdy, C. W.,
District Manager,
Iron & Steel Products, Inc.,
Investment Bldg.,
Pittsburgh, Pa.

McKisson, R. W.,
Sales Agent,
American Steel Foundries,
410 N. Michigan Ave.,
Chicago, Ill.

McLain, J. E.,
Special Representative,
Bethlehem Steel Co.,
1214 Oliver Bldg.,
Pittsburgh, Pa.

McLaughlin, Howard B.,
R. F. of E.,
P. & L. E. R. R.,
2401 Alwyn St.,
Pittsburgh, (16) Pa.

McMillan, A. P.,
Boiler Foreman,
P. & W. Va. Ry.,
520 Washington Ave.,
Carnegie, Pa.

McMillan, J. G.,
Secretary,
The M. N. Landay Co.,
Clark Building,
Pittsburgh, Pa

McMillen, Harry,
Car Inspector,
P. & L. E. R. R.,
P. O. Box 378,
Braddock, Pa.

246

McMullen, Clark E.,
Inspector Transportation,
P. & L. E. R. R. Co.,
P. & L. E. Terminal Bldg.,
Pittsburgh, Pa.

McNamee, William
District Manager,
Briggs & Turivas Co.,
41 Marion St.,
Crafton, Pa.

McNary, Frank R.,
Movement Supervisor,
Pennsylvania Railroad,
Pennsylvania Station,
Pittsburgh, Pa.

McNeal, A. R.,
Asst. Fore., Pgh. 11th St.,
Pennsylvania Railroad,
828 Walnut St.,
Heidelberg, Pa.

McPherson, A. R.,
Train Master,
Montour Railroad,
1711 State Avenue,
Coraopolis, Pa.

McQuillen, J. J.,
President,
The Durametallic Corp.,
24 Commerce St.,
Newark, N. J.

McQuiston, C. A.,
Commercial Agent,
Railway Express Agency,
Inc.,
926 Penn Avenue,
Pittsburgh, Pa.

McTighe, B. J.,
Hubbard & Co.,
5253 Carnegie Ave.,
Pittsburgh, Pa.

McVicker, Allen,
Agent,
P. & L. E. R. R. Co.,
P. O. Box 36,
West Pittsburgh, Pa.

McWilliams, J. B.,
President,
Railway Maintenance
Corporation,
Box 1888,
Pittsburgh, Pa

Nabors, W. F.,
Scale Inspector,
P. & L. E. R. R. Co.,
7122 Schoyer Avenue,
Swissvale, Pa.

Nagel, James,
Asst. General Superintendent,
Montour Railroad,
. 1711 State St.,
Coraopolis, Pa.

Nash, R. L.,
Test Engr., Test Division,
Westinghouse Air Brake Co.,
Wilmerding, Pa.

Nathan, W. S.,
General Manager,
Construction Specialties Co.
Oliver Building
Pittsburgh, Pa.

Neff, Charles,
Yard Master,
Pennsylvania Railroad,
7439 Pennfield Court,
Homewood, Pgh. Pa.

Neff, John P.,
Vice President,
American Arch Co.,
60 E. 42nd St.,
New York, N. Y.

Nelson, King R. H.,
Asst. Director of Exhibits,
American Sheet & Tin
Plate Co.,
Morrowfield Apartments,
Pittsburgh, Pa.

Nestor, T. E.,
Division Engineer,
Pennsylvania Railroad,
Pennsylvania Station,
Pittsburgh, Pa

Nethken, H. W.,
Vice President—Traffic,
Pgh. & West Va. R. R.,
405 Wabash Bldg.,
Pittsburgh, Pa.

Newell, J. P., Jr.,
Asst. Div. Engineer,
Pennsylvania Railroad,
1662 Broad Street
Station Bldg.,
Philadelphia, Pa.

Newman, S. A.,
Asst. Dist. Sales Mgr.,
Gulf Refining Co.,
Gross St. & P. R. R.,
Pittsburgh, Pa.

Nichols, Samuel A.,
129 East Kennedy Ave.,
N. S., Pittsburgh, Pa

Nicklas, Chester J.,
Salesman,
Equipment Specialties Div.,
Union Asbestos & Rubber
Co.,
Commonwealth Bldg.,
Pittsburgh, Pa

Nields, Benjamin,
Asst. Vice President,
National Malleable & Steel
Castings Co.,
Cleveland, Ohio

Nieman, Charles J.,
Secretary-Treasurer,
Penn Iron & Steel Co.,
Creighton, Pa.

Nieman, H. L.,
Gang Foreman,
P. & L. E. R. R.,
208 Copeland St.,
McKees Rocks, Pa.

Nies, E. L.,
Chief Clerk,
Railway Express Agency,
926 Penn Avenue,
Pittsburgh, Pa.

Noble, Jesse A.,
Supv'r Bridges & Bldgs.,
P. & L. E. R. R.,
1643 Broadway,
McKees Rocks, Pa.

Noonan, Daniel,
Sales Representative,
Air Reduction Sales Co.,
1116 Ridge Ave.,
N. S., Pittsburgh, Pa

Noonan, W. C.
Supt. Car Service
P. & W. Va. Ry. Co.,
Wabash Building,
Pittsburgh, Pa.

Norris, J. L.,
R. F. of E., B. & O. R. R.,
4818 Chatsworth St.,
Pittsburgh, Pa

Oberlin, A. C.,
Auditor,
Schaefer Equipment Co.,
Koppers Building,
Pittsburgh, Pa.

O'Connor, Edward L.,
Manager,
Savon Sales Co.,
4746 Mossfield St.,
Pittsburgh, Pa.

O'Connor, M. J.,
Rep., Dearborn Chemical Co.,
Farmers Bank Bldg.,
Pittsburgh, Pa.

Oehlschlager, W. A.,
Engineer,
Union Switch & Signal Co.,
Swissvale, Pa.

O'Leary, Jeremiah J.,
Machinist, Penna. System,
132 Fourth St.,
Oakmont, Pa.

Olson, A. O.,
General Agent,
C. & N. W. Ry. Co.,
Oliver Building,
Pittsburgh, Pa.

Orbin, George N.,
Retired,
Engineman, B. & O. R. R.,
Box 7953,
Dormont, Pittsburgh, Pa.

Orbin, Joseph N.,
District Sales Manager,
Oliver Iron & Steel Corp.,
South 10th & Muriel Sts.,
Pittsburgh, Pa

Orchard, Charles,
President,
Lubrication Products Co.,
5849 Hobart St.,
Pittsburgh, Pa.

Ord, George H,
Eastern Sales Manager,
Ewald Iron Company,
501 Fifth Avenue,
New York, N. Y.

O'Reilly, G. Arthur,
Salesman,
Williams & Company, Inc.,
1719 Crafton Blvd.,
Pittsburgh, Pa.

Orr, D. K.,
Road Master,
The Monongahela Ry. Co.,
Brownsville, Pa.

Osborne, Raymond S.,
Mechanical Engineer,
Sewickley, Pa.

O'Sullivan, John J.,
Pipe Fitter, P. & L. E. R R,
1130 Wayne Ave.,
McKees Rocks, Pa.

O'Toole, J. L.,
Asst. to Gen. Manager,
P. & L. E. R. R.,
Pittsburgh, Pa.

Overholt, Bruce C.,
Tel. & Sig. Foreman,
Pennsylvania Railroad,
205 Buffalo St.,
Freeport, Pa.

Paisley, F. R.,
Engineer Maintenance of Way
P. & L. E. R. R. Co.,
Pittsburgh, Pa.

Palmer, E. A.,
Manager,
Light Traction Section,
Transportation Dept.,
Westinghouse Elec. &
Mfg. Company,
East Pittsburgh, Pa.

Park, Charles L.,
Salesman,
Goodall Rubber Co.,
522 Second Ave.,
Pittsburgh, Pa.

Passmore, H. E.,
Representative,
The American Hammered
Piston Ring Co.,
5668 Darlington Road,
Pittsburgh, Pa.

Patterson, Charles L.,
Asst. Master Mechanic,
Pennsylvania Railroad,
215 Pine Road,
Edgeworth, Pa.

Paul, William C.,
Plant Manager,
American Chain & Cable
Co., Inc.,
First St. & P.&L.E.R.R.,
Braddock, Pa

Peabody, Reuben T.,
Railroad Sales Assistant,
Air Reduction Sales Co.,
60 East 42nd St.,
New York, N. Y.

Pearl, W. W.,
Section Stockman, Stores
Dept., B. & O. R. R. Co.,
R. D. 2, Box 411,
Connellsville, Pa

Peebles, A. T.,
Chief Clerk,
P. R. R. Produce Terminal,
Pennsylvania Railroad,
Twenty-first Street,
Pittsburgh, Pa.

Peel, Joseph E., Jr.,
Movement Director,
Pennsylvania Railroad,
81 Evans Ave.,
Ingram, Pa

Pehrson, A. K.,
Mechanical Engineer,
Pressed Steel Car Co.,
McKees Rocks, Pa

Peirce, W. B.,
Works Manager,
Flannery Bolt Co.,
Bridgeville, Pa.

Penton, John A.,
Pres., The Penton Pub. Co.,
Cleveland, Ohio

Perreas, S. J.,
Carman,
B. & O. R. R. Co.,
2224 Starkamp Street,
Brookline, Pittsburgh, Pa.

Peters, L. A.,
Train Rider,
B. &. O. R. R. Co.,
4829 Liberty Ave.,
Pittsburgh, Pa.

Peters, R. F.,
Car Foreman,
B. & O. R.R. Co.,
6821 Thomas Blvd.,
Pittsburgh, Pa

Peterson, E. J.,
Foreman Carpenters,
P. & L. E. R. R. Co.,
2004 Bailey Avenue,
McKeesport, Pa.

Pevler, H. H.,
Division Engineer,
Pennsylvania Railroad,
1444 N. Euclid Ave.,
Pittsburgh, Pa.

Phillips, Robert A.,
Purchasing Agent,
Safety First Supply Co.,
Glenfield, Pa.

Phillips, T. H.,
Boiler Maker,
P. & L. E. R. R. Co.,
3200 Sacramento St.,
Corliss Sta., Pittsburgh, Pa.

Phillips, W. A.,
Asst. Gen. Pass. Agent,
Pennsylvania Railroad,
Pennsylvania Station,
Pittsburgh, Pa.

Pickard, S. B.,
Chief Electrician,
P. & L. E. R. R.,
R. D. No. 3,
Coraopolis, Pa.

Pillar, Michael,
Piece Work Inspector,
P. & L. E. R. R.,
206 Jane St.,
McKees Rocks, Pa.

Pitcher, C. C.,
Assistant Superintendent,
B. & O. R. R. Co.,
B. & O. Station,
Pittsburgh, Pa.

Plunkett, James, Jr.,
Car Foreman,
B. & O. R. R. Co.,
4714 Monongahela St.,
Pittsburgh, Pa.

Poe, C. F.,
Timekeeper,
B. & O. R. R. Co.,
1309 Brookline Blvd.,
Pittsburgh, Pa.

Pollock, J. H.,
Boiler Foreman,
Montour Railroad,
1431 Ridge Ave.,
Coraopolis, Pa.

Porter, H. N.,
Box 5,
Glenwillard, Pa.

Porter, J. V.,
Locomotive Air Brake Inspt.,
Montour Railroad Co.,
1528 Hiland Avenue,
Coraopolis, Pa.

Posteraro, S. F.,
Frt. Cashier,
B. & O. R. R.,
Grant and Water Sts.,
Pittsburgh, Pa

Powell, H. C.,
Asst. Foreman Car Dept.,
Pennsylvania Railroad,
362 Ohio Ave.,
Rochester, Pa

Prinkey, Clyde M.,
Clerk,
B. & O. R. R. Co.,
Room 407,
B. & O. Passenger Sta.,
Pittsburgh, Pa.

Pringle, H. C.,
Vice Pres. and Supt.,
Mon. Con. R. R.,
25 Lakemont Drive,
Pittsburgh (16), Pa

Pringle, J. L.,
Freight Train Master,
Pennsylvania Railroad.
1011 California Ave.,
Avalon, Pgh. Pa.

Pringle, P. V.,
Commercial Engineer,
Westinghouse Air Brake Co.,
1236 McClure Ave.,
East McKeesport, Pa.

Pringle, W. D.,
Sales Engineer,
W. S. Tyler Co.,
6648 Wilkins Avenue,
Pittsburgh, Pa.

Provost, S. W.,
Representative,
American Locomotive Co.,
Terminal Tower Bldg.,
Cleveland, Ohio

Pry, E. B.,
Supt. Tel. & Signals,
Pennsylvania Railroad,
Pennsylvania Station,
Pittsburgh, Pa.

Purcell, Edward J.,
Westinghouse Air Brake Co.,
353 Marguerite Ave.,
Wilmerding, Pa.

Purchard, Paul,
Registered Professional
Engineer,
Park Bldg.,
Pittsburgh, Pa

Pye, David W.,
President,
Tuco Products Corp.,
30 Church St.,
New York, N. Y.

Queer, Thomas H.,
Sales Engineer,
Pittsburgh Coal Company.,
Oliver Building,
Pittsburgh, Pa

Quinn, W.,
Section Stockman,
Stores Dept.,
B. & O. R. R. Co.,
2208 Lynnbrook Ave.,
Brookline, Pittsburgh, Pa

Ralston, John A.,
Manager,
Railroad Research Bureau,
Subsidiary Mfg. Co.'s of
U. S. Steel Corp.,
Frick Bldg. Annex,
Pittsburgh, Pa.

Rambo, Jay B.,
Asst. Road Foreman of
Engines,
Pennsylvania Railroad,
1402 Oak Hill Ave.,
Hagerstown, Md

Rambo, M. H.,
Station Inspector.
Pennsylvania Railroad,
Pennsylvania Station,
Pittsburgh, Pa

Rankin, B. B.,
Gen. Auditor,
P. & L. E. R. R.,
1502 Park Blvd.,
Dormont, Pittsburgh, Pa

Rankin, R. E.,
Manager,
Pgh. Repair & Supply Dept.,
Goodman Mfg. Co.,
1011 California Ave.,
Avalon, Pittsburgh, Pa

Raser, George B.,
R. D. No. 2,
Millville,
Columbia Co., Pa.

Rau, William R., Jr.,
President,
National Model Railroad
Association,
1430 Elm St.,
Wilkinsburg, Pa.

Rauschart, E. A.,
Mechanical Supt.,
Montour Railroad,
948 Greenfield Ave.,
Pittsburgh, Pa.

Raymer, I. S.,
Signal-Telegraph Engineer,
P. & L. E. R. R.,
959 Fourth Street,
Beaver, Pa

Read, A. A.,
Duquesne Slag Products Co.,
Diamond Bank Bldg.,
Pittsburgh, Pa.

Ream, A. H.,
S. M. P. & E.,
P. & S. R. R.,
Brookville, Pa

Reardon, M. J.,
General Yard Master,
P. & L. E. R. R. Co.,
904 Kable Way,
Coraopolis, Pa.

Rebstock, J. B.,
Chief Clerk, Div.,
P. R. R. Co.,
Penna. Station,
Pittsburgh, Pa

Record, J. Fred,
Supt. of Production,
Westinghouse Air Brake Co.
Wilmerding, Pa.

Redding, R. D.,
General Foreman,
P. & L. E. R. R. Co.,
Campbell, Ohio

Reed, E. S.,
Superintendent,
P. R. R. Co.,
Louisiana & Seneca Sts.,
Buffalo, N. Y.

Reed, Earl W.,
Supt. of Production,
Pullman-Standard Car
Mfg. Company,
Butler, Pa.

Reeder, N. S.,
Pressed Steel Car Co.,
80 Broad St.,
New York, N. Y.

Reese, R. H.,
General Agent,
Green Bay & Western R. R.,
Gulf Building,
Pittsburgh, Pa.

Reeve, George,
Foreman Electrical Dept.,
Ft. Pitt Malleable Iron Co.,
330 Woodward Ave.,
McKees Rocks, Pa.

Regan, W. J.,
Mechanical Engineer,
McConway & Torley Corp.,
48th St. & A. V. Ry.,
Pittsburgh, Pa.

Reifsnyder, J. W.,
Engineer of Tests,
Pgh. Testing Laboratory,
P. O. Box 1115,
Pittsburgh, Pa.

Reno, D. A.,
Yard Master,
P. R. R. Co.,
3011 Zephyr Ave.,
Corliss Station,
Pittsburgh, Pa.

Renshaw, W. B.,
Representative,
Westinghouse Air Brake Co.,
Wilmerding, Pa.

Reymer, C. H.,
Special Representative,
Oliver Iron & Steel Corp'n.,
So. 10th & Muriel Sts.,
Pittsburgh, Pa.

Richardson, E. F.,
Asst. Engr. Motive Power,
B. & L. E. R. R.,
57 Chambers Ave.,
Greenville, Pa.

Richardson, H. R.,
Suprv. of Wage Schedules,
P. & L. E. R. R.,
Pittsburgh, Pa

Rider, C. E,
Timekeeper,
B. & O. R. R Co.,
25 Craighead Street,
Mt. Washington,
Pittsburgh, Pa

Rief, Joseph,
O. S. & D. Clerk,
B. & O. R. R. Co.,
328 Mathews Ave.,
Station 10, Pittsburgh, Pa

Riley, O. W.,
Chief Clerk to Storekeeper,
B. & O. R. R. Co.,
2606 Belmar Place,
Swissvale, Pa

Riley, S. B.,
Gen. Supt. & Supt. Mo. Power,
P. & W. Va. Ry. Co.,
Wabash Building,
Pittsburgh, Pa.

Rizzo, C. M.,
Agent, P. & W. Va. Ry.,
Box 331,
Castle Shannon, Pa

Roberts, E. L.,
Chief Clerk,
Donora Southern R. R. Co.,
567 McKean Ave.,
Donora, Pa

Robertson, A. S.,
Traffic Manager,
Montour Railroad,
8 Market St.,
Pittsburgh, Pa

Robinson, John M.,
Engineer,
Westinghouse Elec. &
Mfg. Co.,
Nuttall Works,
200 McCandless Ave.,
Pittsburgh, Pa.

Robinson, Lester L.,
Dist. Mo. Power Inspector,
B. & O. R. R.,
1521 Orangewood Ave.,
Pittsburgh, Pa

Rode, Harry,
Platform Foreman,
P. & L. E. - P. R. R. Cos.,
21 Elton Avenue,
Pittsburgh, Pa.

Rodkey, C. C.,
 Cap't. of Police,
 P. R. R. Co.,
 3001 Graham Blv'd.
  Wilkinsburg, Pa.

Rogers, Robert E.,
 Coal Freight Representative,
 P. & L. E. R. R. Co.,
 Terminal Bldg.,
  Pittsburgh, Pa.

Roney, H. E.,
 Circuit Supervisor,
 P. & L. E. R. R.,
 3111 College Ave.,
  Beaver Falls, Pa.

Root, E. E.,
 Master Mechanic,
 D. L. & W. R. R. Co.,
 458 N. Arlington Ave.,
  East Orange, N. J.

Rose, A. J.,
 Salesman,
 Greenville Steel Car Co.,
  Greenville, Pa.

Ross, C. R.,
 Asst. Supervisor Operating,
 Expenditures,
 P. R. R. Co.,
 Broad St. Suburban
  Station,
   Philadelphia, Pa

Rossell, R. T.,
 President, B. & L. E. R. R.,
 Union Trust Building,
  Pittsburgh, Pa.

Rowan, J. R.,
 Salesman,
 J. B. Ford Sales Company,
 P. & L. E. Annex Bldg.,
  Pittsburgh, Pa.

Rowles, H. N.,
 Asst. Train Master,
 Pennsylvania Railroad,
 1466 Greenmont Ave.,
 South Hills,
  Pittsburgh, Pa.

Roy, L. E.,
 Gang Foreman,
 Pennsylvania Railroad,
 117 Peebles Street,
  Wilkinsburg, Pa.

Rudd, W. B.,
 General Engineer,
 Union Switch & Signal Co.,
  Swissvale, Pa.

Rumbarger, F. A.,
 Sales Manager,
 The Browning Crane &
  Shovel Co.,
 1639 Oliver Bldg.,
  Pittsburgh, Pa.

Rupp, Edwin S.,
 Asst. Div. Accountant,
 B. & O. R. R. Co.,
 228 Lelia St.,
  Pittsburgh (11), Pa.

Rushneck, George L.,
 Draftsman,
 P. & L. E. R. R.,
  McKees Rocks, Pa.

Rutter, Harley E.,
 Electrician,
 Duquesne Light Co.,
 101 Grandview Ave.,
 Mt. Washington Sta.,
  Pittsburgh, Pa.

Ryan, D. W.,
 Sales Representative,
 Fort Pitt Malleable Iron Co.,
 3138 Landis St.,
  Pittsburgh, Pa.

Ryan, Frank J.,
 District Representative,
 Detroit, Toledo & Ironton
  R. R.,
 Wabash Bldg.,
  Pittsburgh, Pa.

Ryan, John F.,
 Special Representative,
 The Ramtite Company,
 511 Overbrook Blvd.,
  Pittsburgh (10), Pa.

Rys, C. F. W.,
 Chief Metallurgical Engr.,
 Carnegie-Illinois Steel Corp.,
 Carnegie Bldg.,
  Pittsburgh, Pa.

Salomon, S. N.,
 Pittsburgh Manager,
 Signode Steel Strapping Co.,
 Grant Bldg.,
  Pittsburgh, Pa.

Saltic, Thomas,
Foreman,
Ft. Pitt Malleable Iron Co.,
321 Russellwood Ave.,
McKees Rocks, Pa.

Sample, W. E.,
Supervisor Loco. Operation,
B. & O. R. R.,
5 Holmhurst Ave.,
Eatonville, Maryland

Sanders, C. R.,
Supervisor,
Pennsylvania Railroad,
411 Duquesne Avenue,
Trafford, Pa

Sanders, Colonel Walter C.,
Gen. Mgr., Ry. Div.,
Timken Roller Bearing Co.,
Canton, Ohio

Sarchet,. Roger,
Chief Clerk,
Labor & Wage Bureau,
Pennsylvania Railroad,
Pennsylvania Station,
Pittsburgh, Pa.

Satterfield, A. T.,
Section Stockman-Stores
Dept.,
B. & O. R. R. Co.,
2918 Claremont Ave.,
Brentwood,
Pittsburgh, Pa.

Sayre, Herschel A.,
Principal Asst. Engineer,
Union Railroad Co.,
103 Sumner Avenue,
Forest Hills Boro.,
Wilkinsburg, Pa.

Schad, J. W.,
Division Master Mechanic,
B. & O. R. R. Co.,
Glenwood. Pittsburgh, Pa.

Schadt, Alton D.,
Clerk-Office V. P. & G. M.,
B. & L. E. R. R.,
7338 Whipple St.,
Pittsburgh (18), Pa.

Schaefer, Frederic,
Schaefer Equipment Co.,
Koppers Bldg.,
Pittsburgh, Pa.

Schaeffer, F. E.,
Secretary,
Union Spring & Mfg. Co.,
New Kensington, Pa.

Schaffer, W. E.,
Back Shop Foreman.
P. & W. Va. Ry.,
242 Boden Ave.,
Carnegie, Pa.

Schako, E. J.,
Superintendent,
Superior Railway Products
Corp.,
7501 Thomas Blvd.,
Pittsburgh, Pa

Schaller, Andrew J.,
Supervisor,
Pennsylvania Railroad,
219 Laurel Ave.,
Cresson, Pa.

Schane, Frank A.,
Contact Represetative,
Carnegie-Illinois Steel Corp.,
3446 Beechwood Blvd.,
Pittsburgh, Pa.

Schauers, Robert W.,
Gen. Fore., Stores Dept.,
B. & O. R. R. Co.,
495 Muldowney Ave.,
Lincoln Place, Pa.

Scheline, William A.,
Gang Foreman,
Pennsylvania Railroad,
125 Maywood St.,
Pittsburgh (14), Pa.

Schenck, S. B.,
Special Engineer,
B. & L. E. R. R. Co,,
18 Rosedale Ave.,
Greenville, Pa.

Schiller, John,
Cond'r., P. & W. Va. Ry.,
337 Seventh Ave.,
Carnegie, Pa.

Schiller, Joseph, Jr.,
Rate Clerk,
B. & O. R. R. Co.,
Grant & Water Streets,
Pittsburgh, Pa.

Schmied, Fred J.,
Foreman,
Railway Service & Supply
Corporation,
210 Jane Street,
McKees Rocks, Pa.

Schmitt, Andrew,
Car Inspector,
B. & O. R. R. Co.,
2650 Veteran Street,
N. S. Pittsburgh, Pa.

Schmitt, Raymond F.,
Clerk,
Mon. Con. R. R. Co.,
1531 Hoff St.,
N. S., Pittsburgh, Pa.

Schoch, A. J.,
Application Engineer,
Westinghouse Elec. &
Mfg. Co.,
5863 Hobart St.,
Pittsburgh, Pa

Schoen, W. H., Jr.,
Vice President,
Pgh. Knife & Forge Co.,
Park Building,
Pittsburgh, Pa.

Schonover, W. H.,
Asst. Supt. Freight Transpn.,
Pennsylvania Railroad,
Pennsylvania Station,
Pittsburgh, Pa

Schrecongost, C. P.,
Traffic Manager,
Hillman Coal & Coke Co.,
First Nat. Bank Bldg.,
Pittsburgh, Pa

Schultz, H P.,
General Yard Master,
P. & L. E. R. R. Co.,
2714 Fifth Avenue,
Beaver Falls, Pa

Schweinsberg, C. E.,
Joint Chief Clerk,
P&LE-PRR Warehouse
& Transfer Station,
213 West Canal St.,
N. S., Pittsburgh, Pa.

Scott, J. M.,
General Superintendent,
B. & O. R. R. Co.,
Pittsburgh, Pa.

Scudder, D. F.,
District Superintendent,
The Pullman Company,
Gulf Bldg.,
Pittsburgh, Pa.

Searles, E. J.,
Manager,
Schafer Equipment Co.,
Koppers Bldg.,
Pittsburgh, Pa.

Seibert, Wm. L.,
Engine House Foreman,
P. & L. E. R. R.,
327 Russellwood Ave.,
McKees Rocks, Pa.

Seidel, John, Jr.,
Chief Clerk to Asst. Chief Engr.,
P. & L. E. R. R. Co.,
Terminal Bldg.,
Pittsburgh, Pa.

Seitz, Warren W.,
Circuit Engr., T.&S. Dept.,
Pennsylvania Railroad,
1559 Montier St.,
Wilkinsburg, Pa.

Seivard, Arthur M.,
Supt. Passenger Transpn.,
Pennsylvania Railroad,
5237 Ellsworth Ave.,
Pittsburgh, Pa.

Sekera, Charles J.,
Westinghouse Air Brake Co.,
1108 Oak Ave.,
Turtle Creek, Pa.

Seltman, O. W.,
Cashier
P. R. R. Co.,
11th & Etna Sts.,
Pittsburgh, Pa

Semmer, M. R.,
Salesman,
Air Reduction Sales Co.,
281 Dixon Ave.,
Mt. Lebanon,
Pittsburgh, Pa

Sennstrom, Harold R.,
Special Apprentice,
Westinghouse Air Brake Co.,
809½ Franklin Ave.,
Wilkinsburg, Pa.

Sersch, J. G.,
Supt. of Police,
P. R. R. Co.,
3 Eastern Ave.,
Aspinwall, Pa.

Servais, F. W.,
Signal Stockman-Stores
Dept.,
B. & O. R. R. Co.,
400 Johnston Avenue,
Hazelwood,
Pittsburgh, Pa.

Severn, A. B.,
General Manager,
A. Stucki Co.,
419 Oliver Bldg.,
Pittsburgh, Pa.

Shackelford, L. P.,
Asst. Yard Master,
P. R. R. Co.,
2001 West St.
Homestead, Pa.

Shafer, J. S.,
Safety Inspector,
Union Railroad,
Linden Ave.,
East Pittsburgh, Pa

Shaffer, R. G.,
Agent,
Pennsylvania Railroad,
Box 97,
Emlenton, Pa.

Sharp, James,
Supt. Motive Power,
McKeesport Connecting
R. R. Co.,
P. O. Box 403,
McKeesport, Pa.

Sharpless, G. G.,
Mgr. Pgh. Joint Stock Yards
Co.,
Herrs Island,
Pittsburgh, Pa

Shaw, George M.,
Sales Representative,
Pullman-Standard Car
Mfg. Co.,
Box 266,
Baltimore, Md.

Sheehan, William M.,
Mgr. Eastern District Sales,
General Steel Castings Corp.
Eddystone, Pa

Sheffer, R. W.,
Division Engineer,
Pennsylvania Railroad,
Pennsylvania Station,
Pittsburgh, Pa

Shellenbarger, Herbert M.,
Com. Engr., W. A. B. Co.,
1624 Dellrose Ave.,
Carrick, Pittsburgh, Pa

Shepherd, R. M.,
President,
Pittsburgh & Shawmut
R. R.,
Kittanning, Pa.

Shepherd, W. B.,
Asst. General Traffic Manager
Aluminum Co. of America,
Gulf Building,
Pittsburgh, Pa

Sheridan, Thomas F.,
Asst. to S. M. P. & S. R. S.,
P. & L. E. R. R.,
McKees Rocks, Pa

Sherlock, D. V.,
President,
Union Steel Casting Co.,
62nd & Butler Sts.,
Pittsburgh, Pa

Sherrard, H. M.,
Dist. Motive Power Inspector,
B. & O. R. R. Co.,
c/o Master Mech. Office,
Newark, Ohio.

Shield, Arthur,
Asst. Auditor Freight Acct's.
P. & L. E. R. R.,
1230 Penn Ave.,
New Brighton, Pa

Shields, J. C.,
Office Manager,
Carnegie-Illinois Steel Corp.,
Carnegie Bldg.,
Pittsburgh, Pa

Shingledecker, John C.,
Superv'r of Service Stations,
The Pennzoil Co.,
C. of C. Bldg.,
Pittsburgh, Pa

Shippert, Frank,
Yard Foreman,
P. & L. E. R. R. Co.,
1738 Edgebrook Ave.,
Pittsburgh, Pa.

Shira, William A.,
Yard Master,
P. & L. E. R. R. Co.,
134 Euclid Avenue,
New Castle, Pa.

Showalter, Joseph,
Boiler Maker Foreman,
Aliquippa & Southern
R. R. Co.,
116 Carrol St.,
Aliquippa, Pa.

Shuck, Wm. C.,
Salesman,
Lockhart Iron & Steel Co.,
P. O. Box 1165,
Pittsburgh, Pa.

Shull, C. O.,
Master Mechanic,
Pennsylvania Railroad,
Pitcairn Shop,
Pitcairn, Pa.

Shull, George S.,
President,
Safety First Supply Co.,
Brady Bldg.,
Pittsburgh, Pa.

Shumaker, John W.,
Capt. of Police,
P. R. R. Co.,
1401 Jeffers St.,
Pittsburgh, Pa.

Shuman, Forrest R.,
Movement Director,
P. R. R. Co.,
405 Franklin St.,
Wilkinsburg Station,
Pittsburgh, Pa.

Shuster, C. A.,
Agent,
Pennsylvania Railroad,
Box 46,
Red Bank, Pa.

Shuster, William W.,
Division Engineer,
P. & W. Va. Ry. Co.,
Wabash Bldg.,
Pittsburgh, Pa.

Simpkins, Fred E.,
Freight Movement Director,
P. R. R. Co.,
915 Ross Ave.,
Wilkinsburg, Pa.

Simpson, Clifford E.,
Asst. General Freight Agent,
P. & L. E. R. R. Co.,
329 Stratford Avenue,
Pittsburgh (6), Pa.

Simpson, E. W.,
Supt. Traffic & Transpn.,
Westinghouse Electric &
Manufacturing Co.,
East Pittsburgh, Pa.

Simpson, Walter B.,
Salesman,
A. M. Byers Company,
Clark Building,
Pittsburgh, Pa.

Sipe, C. P.,
Supervisor,
Pennsylvania Railroad,
Federal Street Station,
N. S., Pittsburgh, Pa.

Sipe, D. A.,
Supervisor Track,
Pennsylvania Railroad,
6373 Stanton Avenue,
Pittsburgh, Pa.

Sixsmith, G. M.,
Superintendent,
Pennsylvania Railroad,
Room 211, Penna. Station,
Pittsburgh, Pa.

Sladden, F. T.,
G. F. A., P. & L. E. R. R.,
Terminal Building,
Pittsburgh, Pa

Slagle, Charles E.,
Fore. Produce Yard,
P. R. R. Co.,
114 View St.,
Oakmont, Pa

Slater, A. H.,
Chief Clerk to Gen. Supt.,
Pennsylvania Railroad,
Pennsylvania Station,
Pittsburgh, Pa.

Slick, Frank F.,
General Superintendent,
Edgar Thomson Works,
Carnegie-Illinois Steel
Corp.,
Braddock, Pa.

257

Small, Walter J.,
Sales Engineer,
Dodge Steel Co.,
6501 Tacony Street,
Philadelphia. Pa.

Smith, A. H.,
Sales Engineer,
Kerite Insulated Wire &
Cable Co.,
30 Church Street,
New York, N. Y.

Smith, Charles F.,
103 Sixth St.,
Pittsburgh. Pa.

Smith, Daniel J.,
Executive Assistant,
U. S. Steel Corporation,
Room 1517,
71 Broadway,
New York, N. Y.

Smith, E. E.,
General Passenger Agent,
P. & L. E. R. R. Co.,
Terminal Bldg.,
Pittsburgh. Pa.

Smith, E. W.,
Vice President,
Pennsylvania Railroad,
Pennsylvania Station,
Pittsburgh. Pa.

Smith, G. C.,
Assist. Yard Master,
P. R. R. Co.,
8 Center Avenue,
Aspinwall. Pa.

Smith, Gilbert M.,
Gang Foreman,
Pennsylvania Railroad,
376 Pennsylvania Ave.,
Rochester, Pa.

Smith, H. H.,
Supervisor, Transportation,
U. S. Steel Corp. Subsidiaries
Frick Annex,
Pittsburgh. Pa.

Smith, J. Frank,
Gang Foreman,
Union Railroad,
141 Brown Ave.,
Turtle Creek, Pa.

Smith, Lewis H.,
Sales Manager,
Downflow Syphon Co.,
3029 Prospect Ave.,
Cleveland, Ohio.

Smith, M. A.,
General Manager,
P. & L. E. R. R.,
Pittsburgh. Pa.

Smith, M. S.,
Storekeeper,
Monongahela Railway Co.,
South Brownsville, Pa.

Smith, Robert B.,
Transportation Sales,
Westinghouse E. & M. Co.,
East Pittsburgh, Pa.

Smith, T. R.,
Sales Representative,
Oakite Products, Inc.,
6854 Meade St.,
Pittsburgh, Pa.

Smith, Theodore F.,
Vice President,
Oliver Iron & Steel Corp.,
S. 10th and Muriel Streets,
Pittsburgh, Pa.

Sneckenberger, E. R.,
Yard Master.
P. & L. E. R. R.,
803 Emerson Ave.,
New Castle, Pa.

Snitehurst, James G.,
Engine House Foreman,
Pennsylvania Railroad,
109 N. Sprague Ave.,
Bellevue,
Pittsburgh, Pa.

Snyder, F. I.,
Vice Pres. & General Mgr.,
B. & L. E. R. R. Co.,
Box 536,
Pittsburgh, Pa.

Snyder, J. J.,
Coal Freight Agent,
P. & L. E. R. R.,
Pittsburgh, Pa.

Snyder, Jesse L.,
Yard Master,
P. R. R. Co.,
216 N. Linden Ave.,
Pittsburgh, Pa.

Snyder, Joseph C.,
Vice President,
Pullman-Standard Car
Mfg. Co.,
Midland Building,
Cleveland, Ohio.

Snyder, Paul H.,
Asst. Gen. Car Foreman,
Montour Railroad Co.,
1115 Main Street,
Coraopolis, Pa.

Sommers, William C.,
Asst. Gen. Freight Agent,
Pennsylvania Railroad,
Pennsylvania Station,
Pittsburgh, Pa.

Sparks, Hynes,
Manager Eastern Sales,
The Symington-Gould Corp.,
230 Park Ave.,
New York, N. Y.

Spencer, Albert C.,
Supervisor Train Service,
P. R. R. Co.,
Penna. Station,
Pittsburgh, Pa.

Sperry, C. E.,
Engineer,
Detroit Lubricator Co.,
40 West 40th St.,
New York, N. Y.

Squibb, L.,
Auditor Station Accounts,
P. & L. E. R. R. Co.,
Terminal Building,
Pittsburgh, Pa.

Stack, J. E.,
Superintendent,
Pittsburgh Coal Co.,
210½ Olympia St.
Mt. Washington, Pgh., Pa.

Stackhouse, R. K.,
Gen. Supt. Stations, Transfers,
Penna. R. R.,
1636 Broad St. Station
Building,
Philadelphia, Pa.

Stamets, William K.,
4026 Jenkins Arcade,
Pittsburgh, Pa.

Stamm, B. B.,
Inspector,
Pullman-Standard Car Mfg.
Co.,
Butler, Pa.

Stapleton, H. B.,
General Agent.
P. & L. E. R. R. Co.,
Brownsville, Pa.

Starke, H. F.,
General Agent,
Southern Pacific Lines,
Gulf Building,
Pittsburgh, Pa.

Stayman, Ralph J.,
Gen. Mgr. of Warehouses,
Jones & Laughlin Steel
Corp.,
J. & L. Building,
Pittsburgh, Pa.

Stebler, W. J.,
Vice President,
Pennsylvania Conley Tank
Car Co.,
Koppers Building,
Pittsburgh, Pa.

Steding, Henry L.,
Special Duty Engineman,
P. R. R. Co.,
3470 Ligonier Street,
Pittsburgh, Pa.

Steigerwalt, R. W.,
Mgr. R. R. Matl. & Coml.
Forgings Bureau,
Metllurgical Div.,
Carnegie-Illinois Steel
Corp.,
Frick Annex Bldg.,
Pittsburgh, Pa.

Steiner, P. E.,
Maintainer T. & S.,
Pennsylvania Railroad.
P. O. Bldg., Market St.,
Freeport, Pa.

Stemen, E. M.,
Chief Clerk of Accounting,
Edgewater Steel Company,
Box 364,
Verona, Pa

Stephen, James
    Foreman, Carpenter Shop,
    Montour Railroad,
        620 Vine St.,
                Coraopolis, Pa.

Stephens, E. C.,
    Conductor,
    Pennsylvania Railroad,
    1613 Alverado Avenue,
                Pittsburgh, Pa.

Sterling, C. C.,
    Engine House Foreman,
    Union R. R.,
    339 Albert St.,
                Turtle Creek, Pa.

Stevens, L. V.,
    President,
    Stoker Parts Co.,
    P. O. Box 207,
                Rochester, Pa.

Stevens, R. R.,
    Asst. Design Engineer,
    Westinghouse Air Brake
    Co.,
        Elmore Road,
                Wilkinsburg, Pa.

Stevenson, H. G.,
    Engineering Department,
    Hillman Coal & Coke Co.,
    First National Bank
    Bldg.,
                Pittsburgh, Pa.

Stevenson, R. F.,
    C. C., Pgh. Eleventh St.,
    P. R. R. Co.,
    365 College Ave.,
                Oakmont, Pa.

Stevenson, W. M.,
    Dist. Rep., Railway Dept.,
    Crucible Steel Co. of
    America,
    1258 East 55th St.,
                Cleveland, Ohio.

Stewart, C. D.,
    Chief Engineer,
    Westinghouse Air Brake
    Co.,
                Wilmerding, Pa.

Stewart, C. G.,
    Leading Draftsman,
    P. & L. E. R. R. Co.,
                Wildwood, Pa.

Stewart, J. C.,
    Freight Agent,
    Pennsylvania Railroad,
    Eleventh St. Station,
                Pittsburgh, Pa.

Stewart, J. D.,
    Supt. Rolling Mills,
    Jones & Laughlin Steel Corp.,
    27th & Carson Sts.,
                Pittsburgh, Pa.

Stiles, Lawson A.,
    Baggage Agent,
    P. & L. E. R. R.,
        P. & L. E. Terminal,
                Pittsburgh, Pa.

Stillwagon, Charles K.,
    Superintendent,
    Davis Brake Beam Co.,
    R. D. 5, Box 80,
                Johnstown, Pa.

Stiver, Joseph R.,
    Conductor,
    B. & O. R. R.,
    116 Cypress St.,
                Punxsutawney, Pa.

Stocker, H. F.,
    President,
    H. F. Stocker & Co.,
    Clark Building,
                Pittsburgh, Pa.

Stoecker, J. P.,
    Transportation Assistant,
    Pittsburgh Steel Co.,
    Grant Bldg.,
                Pittsburgh, Pa.

Stoffregen, Louis E.,
    Draftsman,
    P. & L. E. R. R.,
    804 Southern Ave.,
    Mt. Washington,
                Pittsburgh, Pa.

Stone, E. C.,
    Assistant to President,
    Philadelphia Company,
    435 Sixth Avenue,
                Pittsburgh, Pa.

Strahl, Herman,
    Chief Clerk, Auditor Freight
    Accts.,
        P. & L. E. R. R. Co.,
                Pittsburgh, Pa.

Streamer, A. C.,
Manager, Switchgear Div.,
West. Elec. & Mfg. Co.,
East Pittsburgh, Pa.

Strople, George H.,
Track Supervisor,
B. & O. R. R. Co.,
Callery, Pa

Stucki, A.,
Engineer,
419 Oliver Bldg.,
Pittsburgh, Pa.

Stuebing, A. F.,
Railroad Mechanical
Engineer,
United States Steel
Corpn.,
71 Broadway,
New York, N. Y

Stype, William G.,
Chief Dispatcher,
Montour Railroad Co.,
1436 Ridge Avenue,
Coraopolis, Pa.

Suckfield, G. A.,
Mechanical Engineer,
Pressed Steel Car Co., Inc.,
McKees Rocks, Pa

Sudell, Donald W.,
Lubrication Engineer,
Cities Service Oil Co.,
738 Brookline Boulevard,
Pittsburgh, Pa.

Suffern, R. J.,
Asst. R. F. of E.,
P. R. R. Co.,
3500 Allendale St.,
Corliss Station.
Pittsburgh, Pa.

Sullivan, Ambrose, W.,
Sales Agent,
American Locomotive Co.,
Plaza Bldg.,
Pittsburgh, Pa

Sullivan, P. W.,
Asst. to Gen. Mgr.,
Pennsylvania Railroad,
Pennsylvania Sta.,
Pittsburgh, Pa

Sullivan, Robert J.,
Examiner,
Pennsylvaina Railroad,
Pennsylvania Station,
Pittsburgh, Pa.

Sutherland, Lloyd,
Gen. Storekeeper,
P. & L. E. R. R.,
Club Road, Rosslyn Farms
Carnegie, Pa.

Sutton, K. B.,
Chemist,
P. & L. E. R. R. Co.,
1056 Hiland Ave.,
Coraopolis, Pa.

Suydam, R. S.,
President,
M. B. Suydam Co.,
Island & Preble Aves.,
N. S., Pittsburgh, Pa.

Swank, W. E.,
Chief Clerk to Freight Agent,
B. & O. R. R. Co.,
38 Cowan Street,
Pittsburgh, Pa.

Swanson, Carl A.,
C. C. to Gen. Mgr.,
P. & L. E. R. R.,
468 Irvin Ave.,
Rochester, Pa.

Swenk, Raymond,
Chief Engineer M. of W.,
Pennsylvania Railroad,
Pennsylvania Station,
Pittsburgh, Pa.

Swope, Bruce M.,
Supt. Motive Power,
Pennsylvania Railroad,
3955 Bigelow Blvd.,
Pittsburgh, Pa.

Sykes, Arthur H.,
Asst. Baggage Agent,
P. & L. E. R. R.,
707 Florida Ave.,
Mt. Lebanon,
Pittsburgh, Pa.

Sylvester, H. G.,
Freight Agent,
P. & L. E. R. R. Co.,
Aliquippa, Pa.

Taggart, J. G.,
Transitman,
P. & L. E. R. R. Co.,
719 Thirty-fifth St.,
Beaver Falls, Pa.

Taggart, Ross E.,
Field Engineer,
P. & L. E. R. R.,
2733 Amman Street,
South Hills Branch,
Pittsburgh, Pa.

Taplin, Frank E.,
Chairman of Board,
P. & W. Va. Ry. Co.,
Union Trust Bldg.,
Cleveland, Ohio.

Tate, James B.,
Representative,
Industrial Supply Co.,
Oliver Building,
Pittsburgh, Pa.

Tate, M. K.,
Manager Railway Division,
Lima Locomotive Works,
Inc.,
Lima Trust Bldg.,
Lima, Ohio

Taylor, H. G.,
Pres., Ball Chemical Co.,
Fulton Bldg.,
Pittsburgh, Pa.

Taylor, Harry D.,
Captain of Police,
P. R. R. Co.,
448 Trenton Ave.,
Wilkinsburg, Pa.

Taylor, John T.,
District Manager,
E. F. Houghton & Co.,
215 Beverly Road,
Mt. Lebanon, Pgh., Pa.

Taylor, Joseph M.,
Asst. To President,
Ball Chemical Co.,
1201 Fulton Bldg.,
Pittsburgh, Pa.

Terkelsen, B.,
R. D. 3—Box 226-B,
Coraopolis, Pa.

Ternent, Harry J.,
Clerk,
B. & O. R. R. Co.,
816 Jones Ave.,
Braddock, Pa.

Terry, Edward,
Salesman,
Safety First Supply Co.,
Brady Building,
Pittsburgh, Pa.

Teskey, Dr. Walter J.,
Superintendent,
Dream City Lines,
(Miniature B. & O. R. R.)
Empire Bldg.,
Pittsburgh, Pa.

Teufel, W. O.,
Master Mechanic,
P. R. R. Co.,
663 Berkley Road,
Columbus, Ohio.

Thiele, Fred,
Asst. General Yardmaster,
P. & L. E. R. R. Co.,
543 Woodward Avenue,
McKees Rocks, Pa.

Thomas, Frank B.,
General Engineer,
W. A. B. Co.,
606 Walnut St.,
Irwin, Pa.

Thomas, George P.,
President,
Thomas Spacing Machine
Co.,
Etna Branch P. O.,
Pittsburgh, Pa.

Thomas, Harold N.,
Auto-Tite Joints Co.,
4733 Centre Ave.,
Pittsburgh, Pa.

Thomas, T. T.,
Foreman,
Union Railroad Co.,
422 Albert St.,
Turtle Creek, Pa.

Thompson, Frederick H.,
Vice President,
Railway Age,
Terminal Tower,
Cleveland, Ohio.

Thompson, F. L.,
Locomotive Inspector,
Monongahela Railway Co.,
R. D. 1,
Brownsville, Pa

Thompson, H. C.,
Salesman,
Air Reduction Sales Co.,
Grandview Ave.,
Glenshaw, Pa

Thompson, Harry T.,
District Manager,
Thermit Department,
Metal & Thermit Corp.,
1514 North Ave., West,
N. S., Pittsburgh, Pa.

Thompson, Howard A.,
General Engineer,
Union Switch & Signal Co.,
311 W. Swissvale Ave.,
Edgewood,
Swissvale P. O., Pa

Thornton, A. W.,
Resident Engineer,
P. & L. E. R. R.,
Terminal Bldg.,
Pittsburgh, Pa.

Thunell, Frederick G.,
Rate Clerk,
B. & O. R. R. Co.,
301 Marie Ave.,
Avalon, Pittsburgh, Pa.

Tibbals, D. B.,
Locomotive Engineer,
Montour Railroad Co.,
617 School Street,
Coraopolis, Pa.

Timmis, A. F.,
Foreman of Carpenters,
P. & L. E. R. R. Co.,
1195 Island Avenue,
McKees Rocks, Pa.

Tipton, George M.,
Terminal Agent,
B. & O. R. R.,
Grant and Water Sts.,
Pittsburgh, Pa.

Tobasco, P.,
Section Stockman,
B. & O. R. R. Co,.
295 Baldwin Road,
Hays, Pittsburgh, Pa.

Todd, Wm. B.,
Vice President,
J. & L. Steel Corp'n.,
J. & L. Bldg.,
Pittsburgh, Pa.

Tomasic, Nicholas M., Jr.,
Locomotive Mechanic,
Pennsylvania Railroad,
412 Tintsman St.,
Turtle Creek, Pa.

Touceda, Prof. Enrique,
Consulting Engineer,
Malleable Foundries Ass'n.,
943 Broadway,
Albany, N, Y.

Toussaint, R.,
Chief of Police,
P. & L. E. R. R.,
Pittsburgh, Pa.

Tovey, G. F.,
Asst. Train Master,
Aliquippa & Southern R. R,.
1213 Boundry St.,
Aliquippa, Pa.

Tracey, J. B. A.,
Chief Clerk Div.,
P. R. R. Co.,
Penna. Station,
Pittsburgh, Pa.

Trainer, M. N.,
Vice President,
American Brake Shoe &
Foundry Co.,
230 Park Ave.,
New York N. Y.

Trautman, Harry J.,
Superintendent,
Briggs & Turivas,
R. D. No. 2,
Coraopolis, Pa

Trax,, Louis R.,
Inspector,
Union Railroad,
321 George St.,
Turtle Creek, Pa.

Triem, W. R.,
Gen. Supt. of Telegraph,
Pennsylvania Railroad,
Philadelphia, Pa.

Troxell, Henry K.,
Railroad Sales Dept.,
Carnegie-Illinois Steel
Corp.,
Carnegie Bldg.,
Pittsburgh, Pa

Trump, Perry,
Chief Clerk, Car Dept.,
B. & O. R. R. Co.,
229 Winston Street,
Pittsburgh, Pa.

Trumpeter, W. C.,
Chief Clerk,
P. & L. E. R. R. Co.,
917 Indiana Ave.,
Monaca, Pa.

Trust, C. W.,
Asst. Traffic Mgr.,
U. S. Steel Corp.
Subsidiaries,
Carnegie Bldg.,
Pittsburgh, Pa.

Tryon, I. D.,
Freight Agent,
P. &. W. Va. Ry. Co.,
Fourth & Liberty,
Pittsburgh, Pa

Tucker, Jas. W.,
Division Storekeeper,
B. & O. R. R.,
Box 156,
Chillicothe, Ohio.

Tucker, John L.,
"Retired" Trainmaster,
Pennsylvania Railroad,
5514 Center Ave.,
Pittsburgh, Pa.

Turner, A. L.,
Extra Agent,
P. R. R. Co.,
334 School St.,
Springdale, Pa.

Turner, C. B.,
Vice-President,
South Penn Oil Company,
Chamber of Commerce
Building,
Pittsburgh, Pa.

Turner, F. M.,
General Superintendent,
A. & S. S. R. R. Co.,
Cor. 10th and Muriel Sts.,
S. S., Pittsburgh, Pa.

Tuttle, C. L.,
Mech. Engr., B. & L. E. R. R.,
15 Shady Ave.,
Greenville, Pa.

Tyler, Buford W., Jr.,
Div. Engr., Pittsburgh Div.,
Pennsylvania R. R.,
Pennsylvania Station,
Pittsburgh, Pa.

Tyrie, Robert M.,
Road Foreman of Engines,
Montour Railroad,
815 Ferree St.,
Coraopolis, Pa.

Uhar, John J.,
Auditor,
Penn Iron & Steel Co.,
Creighton, Pa.

Unger, Dr. J. S.,
5538 Aylesboro Avenue,
Pittsburgh, Pa.

Urtel, E. J.,
District M. of W.
Storekeeper,
B. & O. R. R.,
3908 Brownsville Rd.,
Brentwood,
Pittsburgh, Pa.

Van Blarcom, Warren C.,
Vice President, Aliquippa &
Southern R. R.,
Aliquippa, Pa.

Vanderbosch, C. J.,
District Storekeeper,
B. & O. R. R. Co.,
B. & O. Station,
Pittsburgh, Pa.

Van Horne, C. F.,
Applied Engineering Dept.,
Air Reduction Sales Co.,
92 Sheridan Ave.,
Bellevue, Pa.

Van Krogh, F. F.,
Mechanical Engineer,
Pullman-Standard Car
Mfg. Company,
405 Elm Street,
Butler, Pa.

Van Nort, C. W.,
Supt., Wilkes-Barre Div.,
Pennsylvania Railroad,
Sunbury, Pa.

Van Vranken, S. E.,
  Vice President,
    Soap & Chemical Inc.,
    319 Federal St.,
      N. S., Pittsburgh, Pa.

Van Woert, F. E.,
  Vice Pres. & Gen. Supt.,
    Donora Southern R. R
    Co.,
    137 Ida Avenue,
      Donora, Pa

Villee, R. E.,
  Chief Clerk,
    P. & L. E. R. R. Co.,
    88 La Clede Street,
    Mt. Washington,
      Pittsburgh, Pa

Volkert, E. L.,
  Supervisor Transportation,
    Railway Express Agency,
    Inc.,
    26th & Liberty Ave.,
      Pittsburgh, Pa

Vollmer, Karl L.,
  Steam Engineer,
    Spang-Chalfant Co.,
    106 W. Undercliff St.,
      Etna, Pa.

Von Pein, A. N.,
  Traffic Manager,
    Oliver Iron & Steel Corp.,
    1001 Muriel St.,
      S. S., Pittsburgh, Pa.

Vowinkel, Fred F.,
  Salesman,
    J. & L. Steel Corp'n.,
    J. & L. Bldg.,
      Pittsburgh, Pa

Wagoner, Karl J.,
  Asst. Engineer, Engineering
  Dept.
    B. & O. R. R. Co.,
    Maloney Bldg.,
      Pittsburgh, Pa.

Wait, William Bell,
  President,
    Valve Pilot Corporation,
    230 Park Ave.,
      New York, N. Y.

Wallace, C. M.,
  Supervisor,
    Pennsylvania Railroad,
    Pennsylvania Station,
      Pittsburgh, Pa

Wallace, W. E.,
  Section Foreman,
    P. & L. E. R. R.,
    452 Motheral Ave.,
      Monessen, Pa.

Walter, E. R.,
  Movement Director,
    P. R. R. Co.,
    1504 Foliage St.,
      Wilkinsburg, Pa.

Walter, H. L.,
  Freight Representative,
    Pennsylvania Railroad,
    Pennsylvania Station,
      Pittsburgh, Pa.

Walther, G. C.,
  Gang Foreman,
    Pennsylvania Railroad,
    877 Second Street,
      Verona, Pa.

Walton, W. K.,
  C. C. Coal Freight Traffic
  Dept.,
    P. R. R. Co.,
    Penna. Station,
      Pittsburgh, Pa.

Warfel, John A.,
  Special Representative,
    Air Reduction Sales Co.,
    1116 Ridge Ave.,
      N. S., Pittsburgh, Pa.

Wark, J. M.,
  Foreman,
    Pennsylvania Railroad,
    202 Lincoln Ave.,
    Swissvale Branch,
      Pittsburgh, Pa.

Warner, E. O.,
  District Sales Manager,
    National Malleable &
    Steel Casting Co.,
    1617 Pennsylvania Blvd.,
      Philadelphia, Pa.

Watson, W. R.,
  Locomotive Engineer.
    P. & L. E. R. R. Co.,
    408 Monongahela Ave.,
      McKeesport, Pa.

Watt, Herbert J.,
District Sales Manager,
Jones & Laughlin Steel
Corporation,
500 Fifth Avenue,
New York, N. Y.

Waxler, Brice,
Clerk, Pay Roll Dept.,
Pennsylvania Railroad,
37 Haldane Street,
Crafton, Pittsburgh, Pa.

Webb, William W.,
Manager,
National Carloading Corpn.,
1013 Penn Ave.,
Pittsburgh, Pa.

Weber, Robert J.,
Central Station Manager,
Westinghouse Electric
& Mfg. Co.,
Union Bank Bldg.,
Pittsburgh, Pa.

Webster, H. D.,
392 S. Main St.,
Greenville, Pa.

Webster, R. L.,
Agent,
Fruit Growers Express Co.,
21st & Pike St.,
Pittsburgh, Pa.

Weis, Frank E.,
Transportation Clerk,
Pennsylvania Railroad,
26 East Crafton Blvd.,
Pittsburgh, Pa

Welch, E. M.,
Service Engineer,
Dearborn Chemical Co.,
2615 Mackinaw Ave.,
Pittsburgh, Pa

Weldon, Dewey,
Asst. Train Master,
P. R. R. Co.,
255 Brighton Road,
Bellevue, Pittsburgh, Pa.

Welton, Alvin A.,
Special Apprentice,
Westinghouse Air Brake Co.,
353 Marguerite Ave.,
Wilmerding, Pa.

Weltz, E. E.,
Asst. Agt., 23rd St. Station,
P. & L. E. R. R. Co.,
2218 Lutz Street,
Pittsburgh, Pa.

Wendt, Edwin F.,
Consulting Engr.,
Union Trust Bldg.,
Washington, D. C.

Weniger, Oscar S.,
Sales Engineer,
Electric Storage Battery Co.
Union Trust Bldg.,
Pittsburgh, Pa.

Wenzel, J. Louis,
Asst. Manager, Tool Dept.,
Hubbard & Company,
6301 Butler Street,
Pittsburgh, Pa.

Werner, L. A.,
Chief Clerk,
P. & L. E. R. R. Co.,
3608 Mayfair St.,
McKeesport, Pa.

West, George S.,
General Superintendent,
Pennsylvania Railroad,
Indianapolis, Ind.

West, Troy,
Draftsman,
Union Railroad Co.,
1713 Tonette St.,
Swissvale, Pa.

Westerman, F. R.,
Asst. Treasurer,
P. & W. Va. Ry. Co.,
Wabash Bldg.,
Pittsburgh, Pa.

Westerman, M. A.,
Sales Department,
Edgewater Steel Co.,
P. O. Box 478,
Pittsburgh, Pa.

Wheeler, Charles M.,
Asst. District Manager,
Union Switch & Signal Co.,
Swissvale, Pa.

Whipple, A. L.,
District Sales Manager,
Standard Stoker Co., Inc.,
350 Madison Ave.,
New York City

White, A. F.,
Time Clerk,
P. & L. E. R. R. Co.,
47 Haberman Ave.,
Pittsburgh, Pa

White, Frank F.,
General Master Mechanic,
Wierton Steel Company,
Box 521,
Wierton, W. Va.

White, Herbert A.,
Sales Mgr., Pgh. Dist.,
National Bearing
Metals Corp.,
928 Shore Ave.,
N. S., Pittsburgh, Pa.

Whitehead, Charles P.,
Manager of Sales,
General Steel Castings Corp..
Eddystone, Pa

Whitehouse, E. L.,
Station Agent,
P. R. R. Co.,
Ford City, Pa

Wickerham, F. A ,
Mgr. Bureau of Information
and Tests,
Metallurgical Div.,
Carnegie-Illinois Steel
Corp.,
Frick Annex Bldg.,
Pittsburgh, Pa.

Widmyer, Robert G.,
Foreman,
Westinghouse Air Brake Co.,
604 Warden Street,
Irwin, Pa

Wiesen, E. S.,
Joint Agent,
B. & L. E. R. R.-
P. & W. Va. Ry.,
R. D. 6—Box 138-C,
Mt. Oliver Station,
Pittsburgh (10), Pa

Wikander, Oscar R.,
Mechanical Engineer,
Ring Spring Dept.,
Edgewater Steel Co.,
900 South Negley Ave.,
Pittsburgh, Pa.

Wildin, G. W.,
Consulting Engineer,
Westinghouse Air Brake
Company,
Westinghouse Bldg.,
Pittsburgh, Pa.

Wilkins, Harry,
203 Allegheny Ave.,
Emsworth,
Pittsburgh, Pa.

Wilkinson, F. C.,
Superintendent,
Penna. Railroad,
621 South Bowman Ave.,
Merion,
Montgomery Co., Pa

Wilkinson, William E.,
Assistant Foreman,
The Pullman Company,
4819 Broad Street,
Pittsburgh, Pa.

Wilkoff, Louis C.
Vice President,
Youngstown Steel Car Corp.
Box 268,
Niles, Ohio.

Williams, David L.,
Salesman,
G. W. Griffin Co.,
P. O. Box 1322,
Pittsburgh, Pa.

Williams, I. R.,
Agent,
B. & O. R. R. Co.,
Dasher & Robinson Sts.,
N. S., Pittsburgh, Pa.

Williams, J.,
Yardmaster,
P. R. R. Co.,
Fifth St.,
West Elizabeth, Pa.

Williams, O. J.,
Movement Supervisor,
P. R. R. Co.,
816 Ivy St.,
E. E., Pittsburgh, Pa

Williamson, A. G.,
Engineer,
Union Switch & Signal Co.,
721 Washington Ave.,
Carnegie, Pa.

Williamson, E. F.,
Movement Director, Supt.
Passenger Transportation,
Pennsylvania Railroad,
609 Dick Street,
Carnegie, Pa.

Willis, Paul,
Vice President,
J. S. Coffin, Jr., Co.,
2304 West 119th Place,
Blue Island, Ill.

Wilson, J. N.,
President,
Aliquippa & Southern
R. R. Co.,
311 Ross Street,
Pittsburgh, Pa.

Wilson, James M.,
Sales Engineer,
Metal & Thermit Corp'n.,
2961 Stafford St.,
Corliss Station,
Pittsburgh, Pa.

Wilson, James R.,
Draftsman,
P. R. R. Co.,
Penna. Station,
Pittsburgh, Pa.

Wilson, W. F.,
Manager, Pittsburgh Works,
American Steel Foundries,
36th St. & A. V. R. R.,
Pittsburgh, Pa.

Wilson, W. S.,
M. of W. Inspector,
P. R. R. Co.
911 California Ave.,
Avalon, Pittsburgh, Pa.

Wilson, Walter Herr,
Tester,
Westinghouse Air Brake Co,
505 Larimer Avenue,
Pittsburgh, Pa.

Wilt, Howard H.,
Sales Representative,
Carnegie Steel Co.,
Carnegie Bldg.,
Pittsburgh, Pa.

Winning, Robert W.,
Yard Master,
Montour Railroad Co.,
823 Wood Street,
Coraopolis, Pa.

Winslow, George W.,
Manager,
Ingersoll-Rand Co.,
Chamber of Commerce
Building,
Pittsburgh, Pa.

Winslow, Sidney H.,
Service Engineer,
Franklin Rwy. Supply Co.,
1105 Biltmore Ave.,
S. H. B., Pittsburgh, Pa.

Winter, P. S.,
Master Car Builder,
B. & L. E. R. R.,
42 First Ave.,
Greenville, Pa.

Winton, Charles A.,
Research Engineer,
U. S. Steel Corporation
Subsidiaries,
Frick Building,
Pittsburgh, Pa

Wisegarver, F. H.,
Train Master,
P. R. R. Co.,
63 Bradford Ave.,
Crafton, Pittsburgh, Pa.

Withrow, R. C.,
Sales Engineer,
Freedom Oil Works Co.,
Brighton Heights,
New Brighton, Pa.

Wittmann, Edward A.,
Loco. Boiler Inspector,
Montour Railroad.
627 Kerr Avenue,
Pittsburgh, (20) Pa.

Wolf, William M.,
Chief Clerk, A. F. A. Dept.,
P. & L. E. R. R. Co.,
358 La Marido St.,
Pittsburgh, Pa.

Wood, John H.,
Operator & Wire Chief,
P. & L. E. R. R.,
1613 Chelton Avenue,
Pittsburgh (16), Pa.

Woodings, R. T.,
Vice President,
Woodings-Verona Tool
Works.
Verona, Pa.

Woodings, Wilbert H.,
Salesman,
Woodings-Verona Tool Co.,
1020 Hulton Road,
Oakmont, Pa.

Woods, G. M.,
Ry. Engineer,
W. Elec. & Mfg. Co.,
East Pittsburgh, Pa.

Woodward, Robert,
Machinist, P. R. R. Co.,
314 George St.,
Turtle Creek, Pa.

Woollen, A. H.,
Engineer,
Development Division,
Aluminum Company of
America,
New Kensington, Pa.

Wright, C. W.,
Vice President,
Pullman-Standard Car Mfg.,
Co.,
Gulf Bldg.,
Pittsburgh, Pa.

Wright, E. W.,
Asst. to President,
Ft. Pitt Malleable Iron Co.,
5442 Baywood St.,
Pittsburgh, Pa.

Wright, John B.,
Assistant Vice President,
W. A. B. Co.,
Wilmerding, Pa.

Wright, O. L.,
District Manager,
The Joyce-Cridland Co.,
421 Chestnut St.
Philadelphia, Pa.

Wright, Roy V.,
Secretary,
Simmons-Boardman
Publishing Co.,
30 Church St.,
New York, N. Y

Wuerthele, Howard A,
Clerk,
B. & O. R. R. Co.,
1239 McNeilly Ave.,
Dormont, Pittsburgh, Pa.

Wurts, T. C.,
Heavy Traction Section Head,
Westinghouse Elec. &
Mfg. Co.,
East Pittsburgh, Pa.

Wyke, John W.,
Road Foreman of Engines,
Union Railroad,
East Pittsburgh, Pa.

Wynne, F. E.,
Section Engr.,
Ry Engr'g. Dept.,
Westinghouse Elec.,
& Mfg. Co.,
East Pittsburgh, Pa.

Yarhouse, Walter T.,
Representative,
The Sherwin-Williams Co.,
228 Castle Shannon Blvd.,
Mt. Lebanon, Pittsburgh, Pa.

Yarnall, Jesse,
Asst. Yard Master,
Pennsylvania Railroad,
123 Race St.,
Edgewood, Pa.

Yeardley, H.,
Gang Fore., Car Dept.,
Pennsylvania Railroad,
2662 Center St.,
Ingram,
Pittsburgh (5), Pa.

Yochem, Joseph P.,
Boiler Tube Expert,
National Tube Company,
4213 N. High Street,
Columbus, Ohio.

Yohe, C. M.,
Vice President,
P. & L. E. R. R.,
Pittsburgh, Pa.

Yohe, J. K.,
Train Master,
Monongahela Railway Co.,
Brownsville, Pa.

Yohe, J. K., Jr.,
Supervisor's Field Man,
P. & L. E. R. R. Co.,
2215 Hawthorne St.,
Pittsburgh (18), Pa.

Yorke, P. H.,
General Agent,
Great Northern Railway,
Oliver Building,
Pittsburgh, Pa.

Young, F. C.,
    Credit Manager,
        Westinghouse Air Brake Co.,
            Wilmerding, Pa

Young, J., Jr.,
    Engine House Foreman,
        P. R. R. Co.,
            4073 Cambronne St.,
                N. S., Pittsburgh, Pa.

Young, J. E., Agent,
    Federal Street Station,
        Pennsylvania Railroad,
            411 Center Avenue,
                Verona, Pa.

Young, Paul S.,
    Investigator,
        B. & L. E. R. R. Co.,
            Union Trust Bldg.,
                Pittsburgh, Pa.

Zearley, J. P.,
    Asst. Supervisor-Track,
        Pennsylvania Railroad,
            637 North Ninth St.,
                Cambridge, Ohio.

Ziegler, S. L.,
    Gang Foreman,
        Pennsylvania Railroad,
            8 Salter St.,
                N. S., Pittsburgh, Pa.

Zitzman, N. E.,
    Chief Clerk to S. F. T.,
        P. & L. E. R. R.,
            Terminal Bldg.,
                Pittsburgh, Pa.

Zoog, H. J.,
    Serviceman,
        Air Reduction Sales Co.,
            N. Central Avenue,
                Canonsburg, Pa.

STATEMENT OF THE OWNERSHIP, MANAGEMENT, CIRCULATION, ETC., REQUIRED BY THE ACT OF CONGRESS OF MARCH 3, 1933

Of Official Proceedings of The Railway Club of Pittsburgh, published Monthly, except June, July and August, at Pittsburgh, Pa., for October 1, 1937.

STATE OF PENNSYLVANIA
COUNTY OF ALLEGHENY } SS:

Before me, a Notary Public, in and for the State and county aforesaid, personally appeared, J. D. Conway, Secretary, who, having been duly sworn according to law, deposes and says that he is the Editor of the Official Proceedings—Railway Club of Pittsburgh.

Publisher, Official Proceedings—The Railway Club of Pittsburgh.

Editor, J. D. Conway, 515 Grandview Avenue, Pittsburgh, Pa., (19th Ward.)

Managing Editor, J. D. Conway, 515 Grandview Avenue, Pittsburgh, Pa., (19th Ward.)

Business Manager, J. D. Conway, 515 Grandview Avenue, Pittsburgh, Pa., (19th Ward.)

Official Proceedings—The Railway Club of Pittsburgh.

President, E. A. Rauschart, Coraopolis, Pa.

Vice President, G. M. Sixsmith, Pittsburgh, Pa.

Secretary, J. D. Conway, Pittsburgh, Pa.

Treasurer, E. J. Searles, Pittsburgh, Pa.

Known Bondholders—None.

Sworn to and subscribed before me this 27th day of September, 1937.

J. D. CONWAY, Secretary.

[Seal]   EMMA LEA MONTGOMERY, Notary Public.
(My commission expires February 21, 1939)